ASSISTANTS IN INTERNATIONAL DISPUTE SETTLEMENT

This book examines the role of actors who support adjudicators at various stages of the dispute resolution process, comparing their functions across some 20 international dispute systems. Referred to as 'Dispute Assistants', they include legal officers, référendaires, jurisconsults, and other registry or secretariat staff. Their functions are studied through doctrinal research, supplemented by discussions with relevant actors, so as to capture their actual influence on the adjudication process. The book highlights the widespread nature of their contribution. It also addresses legitimacy concerns about their potential undue influence on the mandate of adjudicators, drawing on case law, critiques from states, scholars, practitioners, and informal interviews with insiders. The last part of the book focuses on the WTO; inspired by various practices in other systems, it offers suggestions to address concerns over the quality and credibility of dispute actors, and to enhance the legitimacy of the WTO DSS and other systems.

Assistants in International Dispute Settlement

Navigating Legitimacy

Gabrielle Marceau and Maria George

•HART•
OXFORD • LONDON • NEW YORK • NEW DELHI • SYDNEY

HART PUBLISHING
Bloomsbury Publishing Plc
Kemp House, Chawley Park, Cumnor Hill, Oxford, OX2 9PH, UK
1385 Broadway, New York, NY 10018, USA
Bloomsbury Publishing Ireland Limited, 29 Earlsfort Terrace, Dublin 2, D02 AY28, Ireland

First published in Great Britain 2026

1

A catalogue record for this book is available from the British Library.

A catalogue record for this book is available from the Library of Congress.

ISBN: HB: 978-1-50999-221-8
ePDF: 978-1-50999-220-1
ePub: 978-1-50999-219-5

Typeset by Amnet

For product safety related questions contact productsafety@bloomsbury.com

PREFACE

This book is about an issue that goes to the heart of international dispute settlement. International dispute settlement ultimately involves humans whose actions can affect the legitimacy of the system they work for. This book looks closely at one such set of actors: 'Dispute Assistants'.

Since I left university in 1993, I have worked in dispute settlement. I will always remain grateful to University of Geneva for giving me the privilege to teach, research and publish, inter alia, in dispute settlement. For over 30 years at the WTO, I participated in dispute settlement as a legal officer. This explains, in part, the context of this book which reviews the functioning of 20 dispute settlement systems with respect to dispute assistants, the ethical concerns invoked about them, and safeguard mechanisms that have been developed.

This book has benefitted from the work of several research assistants, and the intellectual generosity of many international experts, most of whom have insisted to remain anonymous. First, Scott Falls and Pravarshini Palanivel compiled information on staff assistance to adjudicators based on the existing literature, rules and practices of select international dispute settlement mechanisms. The limitations of this methodology revealed that insights from relevant actors from within these institutions would be necessary to fully appreciate the unique rules and practices of different mechanisms.

With another team of researchers, we reached out to different actors across a range of dispute resolution mechanisms. This includes present and previous judges, arbitrators, and panellists; heads of registries, secretariats and other relevant departments; staff assisting adjudicators like référendaires, legal officers, legal advisers, legal clerks, judicial fellows, jurisconsults, assistants and other relevant staff from institutions; as well as counsel appearing before these dispute settlement mechanisms. Thanks to comments from the team at Hart Publishing, we also expanded the list of tribunals under review. Almost all the experts we reached out to, for help to understand better what we had read in books, requested anonymity in discussing our questions. Some of them accepted to comment on some of our written work on the institutional structure and practice of each mechanism in Part I. Those discussions shed light on some common concerns and useful practices, improving our understanding of the ethical and legitimacy implications thereof. It also gave us insights into the tools and mechanisms developed to deal with those concerns. These issues were not fully addressed in the existing literature. After so many years working with Roberta Bassi, Publisher at Hart Publishing, and my long-term respect for Richard Hart, who when he was Chief Editor of Oxford University Press published my 1993 PhD (London), I am very pleased, 45 years later, to publish with Hart again.

We want to thank again all those whom we consulted and who graciously agreed to respond to our multiple questions. Thank you again to Akshaya Venkataraman, Leon Seidl and Maria George for all their excellent work in research, preparation, note taking and drafting of memos and texts during the research period of this project.

We are indebted to the international experts who were kind enough to provide extensive comments and feedback on various chapters of this book. Their reviews triggered important revisions and refined core aspects our work. In alphabetical order, we thank Mateo Diego-Fernández Andrade, Carlos M. Cantore, Kathleen Claussen, William Davey, Lothar Ehring, Valerie Hughes, Pieter Jan Kuijper, Vladyslav Lanovoy, Clément Marquet, Petros Mavroidis, Donald McRae, Joost Pauwelyn, Debra Steger and Akshaya Venkataraman. We are most grateful to have benefited from their respective unique expertise, wisdom and frank suggestions. I owe to them profound gratitude, for helping me both professionally and personally in different circumstances and at different times.

Finally, we also thank Akshaya Venkataraman, Rebecca Walker, Saniya Khanna and Sean Rappa for their tedious editorial work.

Of course, any mistakes made in this book are only our misunderstandings and is under our exclusive responsibility.

This book comes from a place of immense appreciation for the work undertaken by all actors involved in international dispute resolution processes, and my conviction on the benefits of continuous work to refine the WTO dispute settlement system.

Gabrielle Marceau
Honorary Professor, University of Geneva
Visiting Professor, University of Ottawa
Associate Professor, University Laval Québec

FOREWORD

If, as some claim, faith in multilateralism is fading and if, as some fear, geopolitical tensions will continue to increase apace, efforts to enhance and strengthen international dispute settlement mechanisms – vital tools for upholding international law and maintaining stability – are sorely needed. This is why *Assistants in International Dispute Settlement: Navigating Legitimacy* could not be a timelier publication.

Never has it been more important to bolster confidence in international dispute settlement mechanisms than it is today. Deep global economic integration and acute supply chain interconnection have increased commercial and state actors' exposure to international disputes over legal rights and obligations, be they set forth in international treaties and agreements, private arrangements, domestic laws, or otherwise. While a number of multilateral institutions struggle to maintain relevance, and as the ability of the rules based international order to constrain particularly harmful breaches of international trade law is increasingly tested, bolstering the ability of international mechanisms to resolve international trade law disputes fairly and efficiently is of paramount importance. Such mechanisms provide legal certainty and foster economic predictability, both of which are much in need in the current economic environment.

Dispute settlement mechanisms addressing international law fields other than trade law are also front of mind given current geopolitical realities. The International Court of Justice considered relatively few cases in its first 50 years due, perhaps, to some states' lack of confidence in the Court's ability to fairly resolve inter-state disputes. Currently, the Court is dealing with an unprecedented level of activity, suggesting an enhanced level of trust. Nevertheless, the Court has its detractors, with some major powers viewing it as more of a political tool than a valuable legal recourse. The International Criminal Court, charged with prosecuting individuals accused of war crimes, crimes against humanity, and genocide, experienced a surge in its workload in 2022 and record levels of work continue. It, too, has faced challenges to its legitimacy from African leaders as well as Western powers. Similarly, international human rights courts are experiencing historically high workloads; they sometimes face backlash from governments that see them as interfering with domestic political agendas.

In *Assistants in International Dispute Settlement: Navigating Legitimacy*, co-authors Professor Gabrielle Marceau, one of the world's leading experts in international trade law with over 30 years' experience in WTO dispute settlement, and Maria George, a PhD candidate at the Graduate Institute of International Studies in Geneva with expertise in international dispute settlement, explore the role of dispute settlement assistants in 20 different international dispute settlement mechanisms that serve the various fields of international law. Marceau and George catalogue the role played by dispute assistants in each of these mechanisms and then compare how dispute assistants support the work of the respective adjudicators through functions ranging from providing administrative and logistical support to conducting research to drafting and reviewing draft rulings. The result is a novel and thought-provoking study about a critical, rarely studied and often opaque aspect of international dispute settlement mechanisms: whether and how the role of dispute settlement assistants impact the work *and even the outcome* of an international dispute.

A logical assumption is that relying on dispute assistants likely enhances procedural efficiency. One might also expect that it would improve the overall quality of the result in terms of its legal foundation. But questions about the degree of influence assistants have – or are perceived to have – over decision-making by adjudicators also arise. Do specific roles they exercise, or excessive delegation by adjudicators, permit assistants to overstep their mandate and encroach improperly upon the decision-making function of adjudicators? Could the advice of a seasoned and well-respected dispute assistant carry undue weight in the approach eventually adopted by the adjudicator? It is these types of concerns that lie at the heart of unspoken – and even spoken – concerns about a particular mechanism's legitimacy as a fair and impartial decision-making body.

Marceau and George shine a light on these and other aspects of dispute assistants' work across 20 institutions and probe whether and how these factors affect the performance as well as the reputation of the various dispute settlement mechanisms. The authors also identify and evaluate a variety of practices and procedures adopted by one or more of the examined institutions with a view to guarding against situations that could give rise to outsized roles for dispute assistants and, in turn, to concerns about the legitimacy and fairness of the institutions' decision-making.

Part III of *Assistants in International Dispute Settlement: Navigating Legitimacy* transitions from a general overview and comparative study of several dispute settlement mechanisms to focus on the World Trade Organization (WTO) dispute settlement mechanism, once described as "an extraordinary achievement that comes close to a miracle"[1], but that now operates under the cloud of a hobbled appellate mechanism and calls from WTO Members for reform. Marceau and George's more detailed inquiry into the WTO dispute settlement system benefits from Marceau's extensive hands-on experience working within that system. In addition, the rich inventory of WTO practice – as compared to the relatively limited dispute settlement practice under some of the other mechanisms discussed in the book – provides valuable material to inform their expert analysis. Indeed, no other state-to-state dispute settlement mechanism has such an extensive record of practice.

The original drafters of the WTO Dispute Settlement Understanding (DSU) – the agreement setting forth rules and procedures governing WTO dispute settlement – must be commended for crafting a set of rules and procedures that has successfully assisted WTO Members – developed and developing countries alike – to resolve hundreds of disputes during the past 30 years. High confidence in the mechanism was demonstrated through its frequent and broad-based use to address all manner of trade rights, obligations, and permissible exceptions. The high compliance rate with legal rulings is also a sign of the system's strengths. At the same time, WTO Members believe the system

[1] C-D Ehlermann, 'Some Personal Experiences as Member of the Appellate Body of the WTO', Policy Paper RSC No. 02/9, The Robert Schuman Centre for Advanced Studies, European University Institute, 44.

has fallen short in several ways, including in respect of its design as it relates to the role of Secretariat staff who assist adjudicators with disputes. Accusations about WTO Secretariat staff having too much influence over the work of WTO dispute settlement adjudicators have been levelled from time to time during the 30-year history of WTO dispute settlement activities.

As Marceau and George point out, perceived weaknesses in dispute settlement results under the GATT (the WTO's predecessor) led WTO negotiators to design a system with a prominent role for dispute assistants. This approach seems no less expedient today given that: (1) complex, technical, and fact-laden cases involving multiple legal claims and a number of WTO agreements, as well as numerous participants and thousands of pages of legal argument and evidentiary material, are typical in WTO disputes; and (2) first-instance WTO adjudicators must be selected on an *ad hoc* basis for each dispute and they carry out their duties on a part-time basis, often while continuing to perform duties associated with their full time positions as diplomats, government employes, legal practitioners, or academics. Under the circumstances, it should be expected that part-time adjudicators – even those who are expert in the specialized trade questions at issue in a particular dispute – would rely on experienced trade law or policy-savvy dispute assistants to support their time-sensitive work. Although there is nothing inherently improper in this type of arrangement, it has led to concerns that some adjudicators may not be in a position, given their full-time occupations and the part-time nature of the WTO panelist appointment, to retain sufficient control over the result. Criticism has also been levied that WTO panelists who do not have deep WTO law or policy expertise, or who have little or no experience sitting as an adjudicator, could be inclined to turn for advice and guidance to dispute assistants who have years of experience working within the system, its procedures, and its rules. Naturally, any such disquiet undermines the legitimacy of the WTO system and its results, no matter its other successes.

The risks and pitfalls associated with the prominent role of WTO dispute assistants and the concerns that have been raised about that role are expertly presented and considered in Chapters 23 and 24 of this book. The skillful analysis benefits from Marceau and George's unique and deep experience working in and studying the WTO dispute settlement system. The authors review the various steps and phases of a WTO dispute and the role the dispute assistant plays at each step, from assisting disputing parties or the WTO Director-General to select adjudicators, to conducting analysis of written argument and evidence submitted by disputants, to attending oral hearings and sitting in on deliberations, and finally to drafting and translating awards and decisions. The authors also identify WTO provisions and other rules (such as the Rules of Conduct applicable to adjudicators as well as WTO Secretariat staff, the Staff Regulations addressing staff neutrality, and the procedures governing adjudicator remuneration) that are relevant for evaluating the nature of the dispute assistants' contribution throughout the dispute settlement process.

Perhaps the true gem of these two Chapters is the rich discussion and thoughtful analysis of the many proposals, suggestions and ideas that have been put forward with a view to addressing concerns about the role dispute assistants play in the WTO. Marceau and George maintain that dispute assistants play a critical and positive role in WTO dispute settlement, but at the same time they acknowledge the need to develop mechanisms to safeguard against situations that could give rise to assistants playing inappropriate or outsized roles. Some of the proposals examined in these two Chapters were put forward by WTO Members in the context of negotiations to improve the WTO dispute settlement process more generally and were not necessarily motivated by a concern about dispute assistants. For example, Marceau and George discuss one Member's proposal to establish a permanent roster of adjudicators to hear disputes, which would replace the need to make *ad hoc* adjudicator appointments for every case. The primary intention of the proposal was to enhance adjudicator expertise. However, Marceau and George explain that eliminating the *ad hoc* appointment system would also eliminate the role of dispute assistants in adjudicator selection, a role the authors report as raising potential concerns about panelist-assistant relationships. In addition, they point out that appointing seasoned panelists from a set roster could go some way to addressing concerns about dispute assistants having more expertise than the adjudicators they are assigned to assist. Marceau and George also assess other proposals specifically directed at the dispute assistant role, including one stipulating that WTO Secretariat staff providing assistance in drafting rulings must do so only on the basis of written instructions provided by the adjudicators deciding the case. Finally, the authors offer a number of their own inspired suggestions for addressing concerns about the role played by dispute assistants. Some of the ideas were developed in the light of their extensive hands-on work in and study of the system, while others were gleaned from their review of relevant practices and procedures in the other dispute settlement institutions examined in this book.

Over 70 percent of global merchandise trade is conducted under Most-Favoured-Nation (MFN) terms – a cornerstone of the WTO disciplines. (The percentage was higher but decreased following tariff and trade restrictions imposed by the United States in early 2025.) Hence the economic and policy implications of effective and impartial WTO dispute settlement cannot be overstated. A review of WTO litigation history underscores this point. Many WTO disputes concerned discriminatory market access issues with underlying financial implications that ran into the millions or billions of dollars. Other disputes addressed critical policy issues such as food safety claims related to genetically-modified crops or hormone-treated beef. Some cases examined the WTO consistency of labelling requirements in respect of dolphin-safe tuna fishing methods or product origin of meat cuts. Legal challenges have been brought contesting alleged government subsidies in numerous sectors including aircraft manufacturing, automobile manufacturing, cotton production, lumber harvesting, dairy products, the sugar sector, renewable energy, biodiesel production, and shipbuilding, to name a few. Services trade measures governing telecommunications, electronic payment systems, audiovisual entertainment products, and cross-border gambling have also been challenged, as have patent and trademark issues in respect of pharmaceuticals and tobacco product packaging. WTO rulings also addressed permissible exceptions for WTO-inconsistent measures such as measures necessary to protect human, animal and plant life or health, measures necessary to protect public morals, measures relating to the conservation of exhaustible natural resources, and measures necessary for the protection of essential security interests taken in time of war or other emergency in international relations.

Although it is true that questions about the utility of the WTO as a forum for trade negotiations arise from time to time and that doubts about WTO rules being sufficiently robust to meet today's economic challenges are prevalent today, it is also true that more disputes were filed in 2025 than in each of the past several years. This attests to the continued value that WTO Members place in the WTO dispute settlement mechanism. It is in this light that Marceau and George's closer look at one highly critical aspect of that system is very timely and welcome.

Assistants in International Dispute Settlement: Navigating Legitimacy is a well-researched, thorough and highly instructive overview of the structure and procedures of 20 different international dispute settlement mechanisms, with a special focus on the little-known role of the dispute assistant in each system. Leading experts Marceau and George have crafted a first-ever, thought-provoking analysis of the contribution dispute assistants make at different steps in the dispute settlement process including, in some instances, at the decision-making stage itself. They expertly assess the criticisms that have been levied about dispute assistants overstepping their roles and the impact this may have on the legitimacy of the dispute settlement institution itself. Marceau and George also include an extremely helpful comparative review of various guardrails that have been put in place or that have been proposed to mitigate against assistants acting beyond their mandate.

Marceau and George's *Assistants in International Dispute Settlement: Navigating Legitimacy* is a 'must have' for any student of or practitioner in international dispute settlement. The analysis will certainly prove invaluable to administrators of existing international dispute settlement institutions, to those seeking to establish such an institution, to those seeking to improve such systems, to those who appear before such institutions, and to those hoping to work within an international dispute settlement mechanism. In one sense, this is a 'how to' book, or perhaps a 'how not to' book. But it is much more than that, for it also examines critical questions about practices and procedures that affect – or that could affect – the legitimacy of international dispute settlement systems across the board. Put simply, this book is essential reading for scholars across the spectrum of international law disciplines.

Valerie Hughes
April 2026

CONTENTS

PART II: COMPARATIVE STUDY ON DISPUTE ASSISTANTS

ABBREVIATIONS

ACtHPR	African Court of Human and Peoples' Rights
AB	Appellate Body
AB Report	Appellate Body Report
CIETAC	China International Economic and Trade Arbitration Commission
CJEU	Court of Justice of the European Union
COMESA Court	Court of Justice of the Common Market for Eastern and Southern Africa
DIS	German Arbitration Institute
DG	WTO Director-General
DSB	WTO Dispute Settlement Body
DSU	Understanding on Rules and Procedures Governing the Settlement of Disputes
EACJ	East African Court of Justice
ECJ	European Court of Justice
ECtHR	European Court of Human Rights
ECOWAS Court	Court of Justice of the Economic Community of West African States Court of Justice
EFTA Court	Court of Justice of the European Free Trade Area
HKIAC	Hong Kong International Arbitration Centre
IACtHR	Inter-American Court of Human Rights
IBA	International Bar Association
ICC	International Criminal Court
ICJ	International Court of Justice
ICSID	International Centre for Settlement of Investment Disputes
ICTY	International Criminal Tribunal for Former Yugoslavia
ITLOS	International Tribunal for the Law of the Sea

IUSCT	Iran-US Claims Tribunal
LCIA	London Court of International Arbitration
MERCOSUR	Mercado Común del Sur
MPIA	Multi-Party Interim Appeal Arbitration Arrangement
PCA	Permanent Court of Arbitration
SCAI	Swiss Chambers' Arbitration Institution
SCC	Stockholm Chamber of Commerce
SIAC	Singapore International Arbitration Centre
STL	Special Tribunal for Lebanon
USMCA	United States–Mexico–Canada Agreement
UNCLOS	United Nations Convention on the Law of the Sea
WTO	World Trade Organization

TABLE OF CASES

WTO Law

International Dispute Settlement

Domestic Law

TABLE OF LEGISLATION

International Treaties, Conventions and Protocols

Rules and Regulations

1

Introduction

I. The Aim of the Book and Methodology

It is a misconception to characterise dispute resolution as an exclusive exchange between disputing parties and adjudicators. The term 'adjudicator' is used broadly to mean relevant actors designated to authoritatively determinate the outcome of a dispute.[1] The specific terminology varies across forums, they may be called 'Judges', 'Arbitrators', 'Members' of the Tribunal, 'Panel members' etc. Several actors provide critical assistance to adjudicators at various stages of the dispute resolution process. Just as the material scope and procedural rules of each forum differ, the roles and functions of each of these actors vary. This book is dedicated to the study of actors that *assist* adjudicators and parties in the dispute resolution process. Based on these discursive ties, we have termed them 'Dispute Assistants', broadly capturing the essential characteristics of their functions. Across institutions, Dispute Assistants may be referred to by different names such as 'Administrative Assistants', 'Tribunal Secretary/Registrar', 'Tribunal Assistant', 'Legal Officer' and 'référendaires'.

The role of Dispute Assistants has raised some controversy, specifically on the subject of substantive assistance to adjudicators. These concerns question the legitimacy of the dispute resolution process. The core challenge relates to the alleged influence of Dispute Assistants over the decision-making process, encroaching upon the domain of the adjudicator. This challenge has taken different forms across institutions. Let us briefly examine an example at this juncture. We hope to impress upon those of you who have picked up this book the significance of our research and findings to legitimacy in international dispute resolution. The most publicised example of legitimacy concerns relating to Dispute Assistants is in commercial arbitration institutions. This can largely be attributed to the mechanisms available to disputing parties to challenge arbitral awards on various grounds, including those relating to excessive delegation of functions to Dispute Assistants beyond what was consented to by the parties. Similar concerns have also been raised in other dispute settlement mechanisms, specifically on excessive delegation to Dispute Assistants. Given the centrality of consent to arbitration and international adjudication in general, such challenges affect the very legitimacy of the decision-making process, and the award or judgment so produced. International dispute resolution mechanisms are based on consent of States, whether in the form of a special agreement, a treaty or a comprimissory clause in a treaty. When such mechanisms are confronted with

[1] See generally JE Alvarez, 'What are International Judges for? The Main Functions of International Adjudication' in CPR Romano, KJ Alter and Y Shany (eds), *The Oxford Handbook of International Adjudication* (Oxford University Press, 2013).

issues relating to the role of Dispute Assistants, what they are actually being confronted with are questions of whether the consent of their parties have been disregarded. These concerns warrant and require closer attention from lawyers, policy-makers and anyone interested in the continuity of peaceful settlement of international disputes. However, the solution is not as simple as eliminating the role of Dispute Assistants. These actors are critical in ensuring continuity and stability to the international dispute resolution process. As international law itself enters an age of increasing uncertainty, the functions discharged by Dispute Assistants in international dispute settlement mechanisms can contribute towards strengthening and safeguarding the rule of law. Therefore, responding to these concerns that weaken their positions is critical.

One of the key reasons driving these concerns is the level of opacity surrounding the various actors considered to be 'Dispute Assistants'. The information gap on the precise role and nature of their functions feeds into legitimacy concerns on lack of transparency and procedural fairness of the dispute resolution process. Therefore, one of the main aims of this book is to present a descriptive account, situating Dispute Assistants within institutional frameworks and through the dispute resolution process. We undertake this study in 20 identified dispute settlement mechanisms (DSMs or collectively referred to as 'identified DSMs'), detailing their specific institutional structures and rules, unique dispute resolution processes and procedures, and breadth of functions discharged by them. While important studies have been undertaken on Dispute Assistants within some DSMs, they are often limited to select institutions which have documented practice. Further, these studies have not attempted to shine a comparative lens on procedures and practices of Dispute Assistants across DSMs. This book aims to fill this gap. There is also a difference between the formal rules and procedures governing Dispute Assistants and the practical on ground realities of their functions. This understandably raises legitimacy concerns on the mandate of such assistants. Accordingly, we supplemented our research through a long list of informal meetings with adjudicators, practitioners, Dispute Assistants and disputing parties across all 20 DSMs. We have aimed to move beyond the specific written rules and instead comprehensively capture the institutional frameworks governing Dispute Assistants and their functions through the life of a dispute. Drawing inspiration from this comparative exercise, we turn our attention to these concerns in the context of the WTO Dispute Settlement System, and make suggestions for reform.

Before detailing the structure of this book, we explain the scope of the term 'Dispute Assistant' and the actors captured by it.

II. The Scope of the Term 'Dispute Assistant'

We were careful in how we defined the term 'Dispute Assistants' to include the relevant actors, while also avoiding overinclusion. We have adopted a broad functional definition to comprehensively identify all the relevant actors that play a role in the dispute resolution process. The functional scope includes any person, or group of persons, discharging the following functions in the service of the DSM or its adjudicator(s):

a) *Administrative functions* in the regular day-to-day course of general dispute settlement procedures, without going into the substantive aspects of a case. These may be functions of a supportive or logistical nature, aiming to expedite and facilitate the dispute resolution process. Examples include arranging travel and accommodation for adjudicators, logistical arrangements for conducting hearings, and communication with the disputing parties.

b) *Assistance in adjudicative functions* relating to specific dispute settlement proceedings or cases. These include the following functions: pre-screening of cases; assistance in the pre-hearing stage through the drafting of notes and/or research; attendance of and participation in hearings; preparation, attendance and participation in deliberations; research and assistance for drafting; drafting of the judgment and/or individual or dissenting opinions; and substantive or formalistic review of the judgments, including translations.

c) *Assistance to parties in selection of adjudicators* in some institutions. The same actors who assist adjudicators may also assist disputing parties with the selection of adjudicators (for example, for appointment of ad hoc panellists in the World Trade Organization Dispute Settlement System (WTO DSS)). While this is not purely an adjudicative function, it is nevertheless a crucial step in starting the adjudicative process.

At the same time, we have excluded many administrative and professional actors who perform important work for the DSM, but are not specifically related to the dispute settlement proceeding – for example, the ushers in the WTO, those working on the budget, in the cafeteria and on the maintenance.

We will return to these functions, especially assistance in adjudicative functions (b) and selection of adjudicators (c), in detail throughout the course of our book.

The first category of actors that emerged from our study are part of institutional frameworks within DSMs or form an organ of the DSM itself. They are formally employed by the mechanism, providing assistance to the parties or the adjudicators of the DSM more generally. The Dispute Assistants in this category go by different names and work in different organisational and operational structures within their DSMs. For example, in the International Court of Justice (ICJ), such assistants are found in the Registry of the Court. The Registry staff are international civil servants (rather than representatives of the state parties to the ICJ) and work for the court as a whole. In the WTO DSS, such Dispute Assistants are a part of the WTO Secretariat (and, earlier, the Appellate Body (AB) Secretariat) and are also international civil servants. We term them 'Institutional Assistants', based on similarities in their formal institutional status and who they report to. At the same time, just as there are key differences between the functions discharged by the Registry staff of the ICJ and the Secretariat staff of the WTO DSS, there is a wealth of diversity amongst these actors in the 20 identified DSMs in this book. The Institutional Assistants generally enjoy the most visibility amongst Dispute Assistants, often officially acknowledged in the founding documents granting jurisdiction to the DSMs. Our definition of Dispute Assistants includes, but ventures beyond, Institutional Assistants. From our research and discussions, two other categories of Dispute Assistants emerged: 'Assigned Assistants' are formally part of the mechanism, but, unlike Institutional Assistants, are assigned to individual adjudicators/bench of adjudicators; and 'External Assistants' are not formally part of the mechanism (unlike Institutional Assistants and Assigned Assistants) and work for individual adjudicators.

In performing these functions, the Dispute Assistants are not tasked with replacing, or stepping into the shoes of, the adjudicators. The mandate of the adjudicator is to *decide* the dispute, while the mandate of the Dispute Assistants is to *assist* the adjudicator(s) collectively or individually or the DSM. The functions discharged by the Dispute Assistants remain critical in enabling a successful dispute resolution process. However, their functions necessarily exclude (independent or autonomous) decision-making power. This is the heart of the concerns that have been raised across DSMs on whether Dispute Assistants exceed their mandate by encroaching upon the decision-making authority of the adjudicator.

III. The Structure of the Book

This book is divided into three parts, after this first introduction chapter. *Part I* consists of 18 descriptive chapters dedicated to the identified DSMs. These smaller chapters detail the organisational structure and dispute resolution procedure of each DSM, identify the relevant adjudicators and Dispute Assistants, and recount the functions discharged by them through the course of a dispute/case. Building on this descriptive framework, *Part II* employs a *comparative lens* to the study of Dispute Assistants. We begin by comparing the functions discharged by Dispute Assistants in seven identified stages of the dispute resolution process, and the formal and de facto frameworks of control over their functions. This comparative lens reveals certain vulnerabilities in their roles, as well as potential safeguards employed by DSMs. With this in mind, we turn to the concerns that have been raised regarding Dispute Assistants and match them with potential solutions that emerge. We also examine how these concerns uniquely impact three facets of the legitimacy of the dispute resolution process: consent, independence and diligence of adjudicators, and procedural fairness. The need to address these concerns by operationalising the potential solutions leads us to *Part III*, which zooms in on one DSM: the *WTO DSS*. Two chapters are dedicated to understanding the different functions discharged by the WTO Secretariat in dispute settlement, at the stage of selection of adjudicators, and in assisting adjudicators. After elaborating the concerns that have been raised regarding these actors, the specific provisions, and existing proposals for reform addressing them, we suggest further avenues of reform that may be introduced. Recognising the institutional deadlock on various aspects of WTO reform, the last chapter examines how to operationalise these suggestions in a principled and pragmatic manner. We detail each of these below.

A. Part I: Overview of the DSMs

To capture the complexity of each DSM and ensure that diversity and depth of the functions discharged by Dispute Assistants are sufficiently detailed, this part is devoted to each of these mechanisms. There are 20 DSMs that form the basis of this study, the following chapters are devoted to two aspects of each DSM: the institutional frameworks and structure governing adjudicators and Dispute Assistants, and their role throughout the dispute resolution process. We briefly capture the relevant DSMs and actors below.

Chapter 2 examines the African Court of Human and Peoples' Rights (ACtHPR), which is part of the African Union judicial structure. It was established to complement the protective mandate of the African Commission on Human and Peoples' Rights, extending to all cases and disputes concerning the interpretation and application of the Charter,[2] the Protocol[3] and any other relevant human rights instrument ratified by the states concerned. The ACtHPR consists of 11 judges who perform their functions on a part-time basis during four ordinary sessions annually. However, the President[4] works on a full-time basis. The Dispute Assistants are the staff of the Registry, who assist in the dispute resolution process of the ACtHPR.

Chapter 3 examines the Court of Justice of the European Union (CJEU), which is the judicial institution of the European Union (EU) in charge of ensuring that the law is observed in the application and interpretation of the treaties. The CJEU consists of two institutions: the General Court and the European Court of Justice (ECJ). The General Court comprises 54 judges, two from each Member State of the EU, and the ECJ comprises 27 judges, one for each Member State. The judges all work on a full-time basis. The Dispute Assistants include the staff of the Registries of the General Court and the ECJ, the Directorate-General of Multilingualism, Research and Documentation Directorate, the référendaires and other Assistants in the cabinets of the Judges. This chapter also details the functions of another important set of actors in the CJEU, the Advocates-General, as well as their respective assistants.

Chapter 4 examines the Court of Justice of the Common Market for Eastern and Southern Africa (hereinafter 'COMESA Court'). The COMESA Court was established to ensure adherence to law in interpretation and application of the Treaty Establishing the Common Market for Eastern and Southern Africa. It consists of 12 judges appointed by the COMESA Authority,[5] seven of whom are appointed to the first division and five of whom are appointed to the Appellate Division.[6] The Dispute Assistants include the staff of the Registry, as well as external researchers hired for specific disputes.

Chapter 5 refers to the practice of commercial arbitration institutions. We consider these institutions as a single group or DSM, while highlighting the distinctions between each institution when relevant to our analysis. We examine the rules and practice of the China International Economic and Trade Arbitration Commission (CIETAC), the German Arbitration Institute (DIS), the International Chamber of Commerce Arbitration, the Hong Kong International Arbitration Centre (HKIAC), the London Court of International Arbitration (LCIA), the Singapore International Arbitration

[2] African Charter on Human and Peoples' Rights on the Establishment of an African Court on Human and Peoples' Rights (adopted 27 June 1981, entered into force 21 October 1986) OAU Doc CAB/LEG/67/3 rev 5, 21 ILM 58 (1982).

[3] Protocol to the African Charter on Human and Peoples' Rights on the Establishment of an African Court on Human and Peoples' Rights (adopted 9 June 1998, entered into force 25 January 2004) OAU Doc OAU/LEG/EXP/AFCHPR/PROT, arts 2–3.

[4] ibid art 15(4).

[5] Treaty Establishing the Common Market for Eastern and Southern Africa (signed 5 November 1993, entered into force 8 December 1994) 33 ILM 1067 (COMESA Treaty), art 8. The COMESA Authority consists of the heads of states or governments of the Member States of COMESA.

[6] ibid art 20(1).

Centre (SIAC), the Stockholm Chamber of Commerce (SCC) and the Swiss Chambers' Arbitration Institution (SCAI). The Dispute Assistants in these institutions include the staff of the institutional offices (with different names across institutions), as well as external assistants to arbitrators in a particular dispute.

Chapter 6 examines the dispute settlement mechanism of the United States–Mexico–Canada Agreement (USMCA), also known as the Canada–United States–Mexico Agreement (CUSMA) or the Tratado entre México, Estados Unidos y Canadá (T-MEC). The USMCA includes several modes of dispute settlement concerning different subject matters. However, we focus on the state-to-state dispute settlement mechanism under Chapter 31 USMCA. Such disputes are adjudicated by a panel. Parties may appoint panellists from a pre-established roster they maintain.[7] Appointment from the pre-established roster is not mandatory, and parties have appointed panellists outside of it.[8] The Dispute Assistants include the staff of the Secretariat (divided into three Sections, each maintained by one of the parties), and external assistants appointed to support panellists in a particular dispute.

Chapter 7 examines the East African Court of Justice (EACJ), which is tasked with ensuring consistency and compliance in the application of the Treaty Establishing the East African Community. It consists of a first instance division with seven judges, one from each Partner State,[9] and an Appellate Division with five judges. The Dispute Assistants include the staff of the central Registry, and the clerks of the sub-registries.

Chapter 8 examines the Court of Justice of the Economic Community of West African States (hereinafter 'ECOWAS Court'). It was established to ensure observance of law and justice in the interpretation and application of the Treaty Establishing the Economic Community of West African States, as well as other matters identified in the treaty, including adjudicating alleged violations of human rights in any Member State.[10] The ECOWAS Court is composed of five full-time judges. The Dispute Assistants include the staff of the Registry, the Research and Documentation Department, and the Executive Assistants of the Judges.

Chapter 9 examines the European Court of Human Rights (ECtHR). This is a regional court which adjudicates alleged violations of rights under the European Convention on Human Rights. The ECtHR comprises a number of judges equal to the number of contracting parties (presently stands at 46 judges) of the European Convention on Human Rights, and sits in any of the following formations: in a single-judge formation, in committees of three judges, in Chambers of seven judges and in a Grand Chamber of 17 judges.[11] The judges of the ECtHR are organised into five sections, and within these sections, the Committees and Chambers are composed.[12] The judges of the ECtHR work full-time. The Dispute Assistants include the staff of the Registry and the Grand Chamber Registry, the Filtering Section and the Directorate of the Jurisconsult.

[7] Agreement between the United States of America, the United Mexican States, and Canada (signed at Buenos Aires 30 November 2018, entered into force 1 July 2020) (USMCA) art 31.8.

[8] If Panellists are appointed outside the roster, the conditions in art 31.9 USMCA must be followed.

[9] This refers to the states granted membership to the East African Community.

[10] Protocol on the Community Court of Justice, as amended by the Supplementary Protocol on the Court of Justice of the Economic Community of West African States (adopted 19 January 2005) art 9.

[11] Convention for the Protection of Human Rights and Fundamental Freedoms (Rome, 4 November 1950) 213 UNTS 221 (ECHR) art 26(1).

[12] Rules of Court of the European Court of Human Rights (as amended 30 October 2023) r 27(2).

Chapter 10 examines the Court of Justice of the European Free Trade Area (hereinafter 'EFTA Court'), which is the court of the EFTA pillar of the European Economic Area (EEA) (which comprises Norway, Iceland and Liechtenstein, but not the fourth Member State of EFTA, Switzerland).[13] It is responsible for interpreting the EEA Agreement and settling disputes between the three states and the EFTA Surveillance Authority, which fulfils a role similar to the European Commission. The EFTA Court consists of three judges, one from each Member State, who work on a full-time basis. The Dispute Assistants include the staff of the Registry, and the référendaires and other assistants in the cabinets of the Judges.

Chapter 11 examines the Inter-American Court of Human Rights (IACtHR), which is the regional court responsible for ensuring that states abide by the American Convention on Human Rights. The IACtHR comprises seven judges who are not employed full-time – the judges spend several weeks per year at the Court's seat in San José, Costa Rica.[14] The Dispute Assistants include the staff of the Secretariat and may include external researchers hired by individual judges (informally).

Chapter 12 examines the International Court of Justice (ICJ), which is the principal judicial organ of the United Nations. The ICJ consists of 15 judges and in cases where one or both parties do not have a national on the bench, an ad hoc judge to complement the bench for the case in question.[15] The judges of the ICJ work full time. The Dispute Assistants include the staff of the Registry, specifically the Department of Legal Matters and the Associate Legal Officers, the Special Assistant to the President and the judicial fellows.

Chapter 13 examines the arbitration undertaken by the International Centre for Settlement of Investment Disputes (ICSID). The ICSID is not a court in the traditional sense, but rather an institution that facilitates the work of tribunals in investor-state arbitration cases. The ICSID was established by the contracting states to the International Convention on Settlement of Investment Disputes, and initially undertook only arbitration and conciliation functions. Now, it also undertakes mediation and fact-finding functions, which are not covered by this chapter. The Dispute Assistants include the staff of the Secretariat, particularly staff in case management teams, and the supplementary case assistants hired by arbitrators in a specific dispute.

Chapter 14 examines three international criminal law DSMs: the International Criminal Court (ICC), the International Criminal Tribunal for Former Yugoslavia (ICTY) and the Special Tribunal for Lebanon (STL). We have collectively referred to them as 'International Criminal Tribunals'. They have been examined together owing to the similarity in the stages of their proceedings; however, the authors are mindful of the differences in their institutional structures. The International Criminal Court was established by the Rome Statute,[16] with jurisdiction over the most serious crimes of concern

[13] HH Fredriksen, 'EFTA Court' in *Max Planck Encyclopedia of International Procedural Law* (Oxford University Press, online edn, June 2018).

[14] 14PG Domínguez, 'The Role of the Secretariat in the Inter-American Court of Human Rights: A Comparative Analysis' in *Symposium on Joost Pauwelyn and Krzysztof Pelc, 'Who Guards the "Guardians of the System"? The Role of the Secretariat in WTO Dispute Settlement'*, 393.

[15] Statute of the International Court of Justice (adopted 26 June 1945, entered into force 24 October 1945) 33 UNTS 993 (ICJ Statute) art 31(2)–(3).

[16] Rome Statute of the International Criminal Court (adopted 17 July 1998, entered into force 1 July 2002) 2187 UNTS 90 (Rome Statute) art 1.

to the international community as a whole. It consists of four organs: the Presidency, the Chambers, the office of the Prosecutor, and the Registry. The Chambers (or the Judicial Division) in turn consists of the Appeals Division (consisting of the President and four other judges),[17] a Trial Division (presently consisting of seven judges)[18] and a Pre-Trial Division (presently consisting of five judges).[19] The STL was established in 2005 as an international tribunal for the prosecution of the terrorist attack that took place in Lebanon and related crimes. Since July 2022, the STL has entered a residual phase to, inter alia, preserve its records and archives, and safeguard residual obligations to victims and witnesses. Much like the ICC, the STL had four independent organs: the Chambers, the office of the Prosecutor, the Defence office and the Registry. The Chambers in turn comprise one pre-trial judge, a Trial Chamber (consisting of three judges, two of whom are international and one Lebanese), an Appeals Chamber (consisting of five judges, three of whom are international and two Lebanese) and two alternate judges (one of whom is international and the other Lebanese). The ICTY was a tribunal established through UN Security Council Resolution 827 to deal with war crimes that took place during the conflicts in the Balkans in the 1990s as a temporary institution. It consisted of three organs: the Chambers, the Prosecutor and the Registry. The Chambers in turn comprises three Trial Chambers (a total maximum of 16 permanent judges and 12 *ad litem* judges,[20] with each Trial Chamber consisting of three permanent judges and a maximum of six *ad litem* judges at any given time)[21] and an Appeals Chamber (comprising seven permanent judges and two judges appointed from the International Criminal Tribunal for Rwanda (ICTR)).[22] They also served as the Appeals Chamber for the ICTR, and accordingly we have examined the practice from the ICTR to the extent that it is relevant in understanding the role of Dispute Assistants. The Dispute Assistants across these three DSMs include the staff of the Registry and the Legal Officers in Chambers of Judges.

Chapter 15 examines the International Tribunal for the Law of the Sea (ITLOS), which was established by the 1982 United Nations Convention on the Law of the Sea (UNCLOS) to have jurisdiction over any dispute concerning the interpretation or application of UNCLOS and all matters specifically provided for in any other agreement which confers jurisdiction on ITLOS. The Tribunal consists of 21 judges, elected by the state parties of UNCLOS. The ITLOS functions as a full court. The judges of ITLOS do not work full-time at the tribunal. The Dispute Assistants, who work full-time, include the staff of the Registry, notably its Legal Office.

Chapter 16 examines the Iran-US Claims Tribunal (IUSCT), which was established as an international arbitral tribunal for the purpose of deciding claims as specified in

[17] International Criminal Court, *Appeals Division* (comprising five judges, as at 28 July 2024) www.icc-cpi.int/judges/judicial-division?f[0]=division:580.

[18] International Criminal Court, *Trial Division* (comprising seven judges, as at 28 July 2024) www.icc-cpi.int/judges/judicial-division?f[0]=division:582.

[19] International Criminal Court, *Pre-Trial Division* (comprising five judges, as at 28 July 2024) www.icc-cpi.int/judges/judicial-division?f[0]=division:581.

[20] Statute of the International Criminal Tribunal for the Former Yugoslavia, annexed to UNSC Res 827 (1993), UN Doc S/RES/827(1993) (adopted 25 May 1993) (ICTY Statute) art 12(1).

[21] ibid art 12(2).

[22] ibid art 14(4).

the US-Iran Claims Settlement Declaration[23] as well as any disputes between the US and Iran concerning the interpretation or performance of provisions of the Algeria General Declaration of 1981.[24] The IUSCT consists of nine 'Members' (the term used for adjudicators in IUSCT), with the US and Iran appointing three Members each, while the remaining Members are appointed either by the mutual agreement of the party-appointed Members, or by an 'Appointing Authority' in the absence of such agreement. Thereafter, the party-appointed Members appoint one of the third-country Members as President by mutual agreement; in the absence of agreement, the Appointing Authority appoints the President.[25] Today, the IUSCT only sits as a full tribunal as it has resolved all private claims; only disputes involving the two states remain pending.[26] The Dispute Assistants include the staff of the Registry and the Legal Advisers of Members of the IUSCT.

Chapter 17 examines the dispute settlement system of the Mercado Común del Sur Dispute Settlement System (MERCOSUR), which was established by the Protocol of Olivos for the Southern Common Market (referred to as the Mercado Común del Sur). It is a two-tiered dispute settlement system. The first stage is an ad hoc tribunal, and the review stage is the Tribunal Permanente de Revisión (TPR), which consists of five arbitrators.[27] Besides appellate review, the TPR is also responsible for emergency measures[28] and examining compliance with its own rulings.[29] It can be called upon as a tribunal of first instance if both parties agree.[30] The Dispute Assistants include the staff of the Secretaría del TPR.

Chapter 18 examines arbitration proceedings taking place under the Permanent Court of Arbitration (PCA), established by the 1899 Hague Convention for the Pacific Settlement of International Disputes.[31] Despite its name, it is not an actual court but an institution that supports tribunals in resolving disputes through various dispute settlement procedures. The PCA administers disputes under many different arbitration rules, and the cases before it involve various combinations of states, state entities, international organisations and private parties.[32] The Dispute Assistants include the staff of the International Bureau, and the external assistants hired by arbitrators for a particular dispute.

[23] Declaration of the Government of the Democratic and Popular Republic of Algeria concerning the Settlement of Claims by the Government of the United States of America and the Government of the Islamic Republic of Iran (19 January 1981) (Claims Settlement Declaration) 20 ILM 223 (1981) art II.

[24] Declaration of the Government of the Democratic and Popular Republic of Algeria (19 January 1981) 20 ILM 224 (1981).

[25] ibid art III; Rules of Procedure of the Iran–United States Claims Tribunal (adopted 3 May 1983, as amended), arts 6–8. The Appointing Authority is to be agreed upon by the parties. If the parties fail to agree on an Appointing Authority or if the Appointing Authority fails to appoint an arbitrator within the prescribed time, the Secretary-General of the PCA is the default Designating Authority to designate an Appointing Authority.

[26] C Pinto and B McAsey, 'Iran–United States Claims Tribunal' in *Max Planck Encyclopaedia of Public International Law* (Oxford University Press, online edn, June 2018) para 46.

[27] Protocol of Olivos for the Settlement of Disputes in MERCOSUR (adopted 18 February 2002, entered into force 1 January 2004) (Protocol of Olivos) arts 17–18.

[28] ibid art 24.

[29] ibid art 30.1.

[30] ibid art 23.

[31] Convention for the Pacific Settlement of International Disputes (signed 29 July 1899) 187 CTS 410; see also K Claussen, 'Old and New Dispute Secretariats' (2022) 116 *American Journal of International Law: Unbound* 400, 401.

[32] Permanent Court of Arbitration, 'Services', www.pca-cpa.org/en/services.

Chapter 19 examines the disputes settlement system of the WTO (referred to as the 'WTO DSS'). The WTO DSS covers all disputes arising under agreements listed in Appendix 1 of the Understanding on Rules and Procedures Governing the Settlement of Disputes (DSU), between Members of the WTO. It consists of several detailed and distinct processes (specifically, 15[33] processes) with specific adjudicators. For the purposes of the comparative study, we focus on original panel stage, arbitrations and the appeal stage. The ad hoc panels are normally constituted of three panellists, unless the parties specifically agree to constitute a panel of five panellists.[34] The second tier, which became non-operational in 2019, was the AB. It was a standing body of seven members, acting as the appellate and final stage of the adjudicatory mechanism.[35] Although it was a standing body, the AB members only worked part-time. In responding to this vacuum, since the AB is not operational, some WTO Members created an arbitration appeal mechanism under Article 25 of the DSU – the Multi-Party Interim Appeal Arbitration Arrangement (MPIA). The appeals under the MPIA are heard by three appeal arbitrators selected from the standing pool of 10 appeal arbitrators. The Dispute Assistants include the staff of the WTO Secretariat, specifically the Legal Affairs Division who assist panellists together with staff from other operations divisions, and staff from the Rules Division. The AB members were assisted by the AB Secretariat. The MPIA appeal arbitrators are assisted by Secretariat staff assigned by the WTO Director-General (DG) on an *ad hoc* basis for a specific appeal arbitration. These staff are not part of the LAD/Rules Division in order to avoid any conflict with staff that may have assisted in the prior panel proceedings stage. They are from other operations divisions, whose responsibilities are not necessarily related to dispute settlement.

B. Part II: Comparative Study on Dispute Assistants

The two chapters in this part are aimed at collating the information across the DSMs and bringing them together to address legitimacy concerns on the role of Dispute Assistants.

Chapter 20 lays the foundation for a comparative study on the role of various Dispute Assistants in the DSMs, and the institutional framework for their appointment,

[33] The 15 processes are: (1) selection of ad hoc panellists by parties in original panel; (2) selection of ad hoc panellists by parties in implementation panels; (3) selection of ad hoc arbitrators by parties in arbitration for the determination of the reasonable period of time for implementation of a ruling; (4) selection of ad hoc arbitrators by parties in arbitration for determination of the level of retaliation; (5) selection of arbitrators (Art 25 of the DSU (non-MPIA)); (6) selection of ad hoc panellists by DG in original panel; (7) selection of ad hoc panellists by DG in implementation panels; (8) selection of ad hoc arbitrators by DG in arbitration for the determination of the reasonable period of time for implementation of a ruling; (9) selection of ad hoc arbitrators by DG in arbitration for determination of the level of retaliation; (10) original Panel proceedings; (11) implementation panel proceedings or compliance panel; (12) arbitration for the determination of the reasonable period of time for implementation of a ruling; (13) arbitration for the determination of level of suspension of concessions; (14) Appellate Body proceedings (not operational); and (15) arbitration under MPIA and Understanding on Rules and Procedures Governing the Settlement of Disputes, Marrakesh Agreement Establishing the World Trade Organization, Annex 2 (adopted 15 April 1994) art 25.

[34] *Rules of Conduct for the Understanding on Rules and Procedures Governing the Settlement of Disputes*, WTO Doc WT/DSB/RC/1 (11 December 1996), art 8.5. To date, only three-member panels have been created.

[35] World Trade Organization, *Dispute Settlement Handbook* (Cambridge University Press, 2017) 31–32. See also *Decision Establishing the Appellate Body*, Recommendations by the Preparatory Committee for the WTO approved by the Dispute Settlement Body on 10 February 1995, WTO Doc WT/DSB/1 (19 June 1995).

supervision and control. We recount the three categories of Dispute Assistants mentioned above – Institutional, Assigned and External Assistants – and we fill these categories with relevant actors from the 20 identified DSMs. Thereafter, to chart a comparative view of the functions discharged by these actors, we identify seven stages of the dispute resolution process where they assist the DSMs and/or its adjudicators: *first*, assistance relating to the appointment of adjudicators; *second*, the acceptance of submissions and the screening of cases; *third*, undertaking preparatory work in the form of research or preparatory notes; *fourth*, assisting during hearings; *fifth*, assisting during deliberations; *sixth*, assisting with drafting; and *seventh*, reviewing draft decisions. In analysing these functions, we map both the degree of assistance allowed under institutional rules as well as the actual extent of their involvement in practice. While the specific functions themselves are important, equally important is the level of institutional and functional control exerted over these functions. Accordingly, we discuss the formal and de facto forms of supervision and control on Dispute Assistants, and the impact of such control on their contribution to the dispute resolution process. These two aspects of the comparative study (ie, the functions and control) set the necessary context for the analytical exercise in the next chapter: on concerns and their impact on legitimacy.

Chapter 21 plunges into the controversy surrounding the role of Dispute Assistants. We identify the concerns on the role and functions of Dispute Assistants, based on examples that have been raised across the identified DSMs. These concerns impact three facets of the actual and perceived legitimacy of the dispute resolution process: the consent to be bound-by dispute resolution process; the independence and diligence expected of adjudicators; and the expected transparency and procedural fairness of the dispute resolution process. At the same time, the comparative study also reveals several potential solutions to relevant concerns within the procedures and practices of DSMs. This chapter untangles these concerns and attempts to weave together solutions from the common threads identified in the comparative study.

First, we consider examples of concerns on asymmetry between the adjudicator and Dispute Assistants owing to institutional frameworks that have been raised in the ACtHPR, IACtHPR and the WTO DSS. The potential solutions examined relate to enhancing the expertise/capacity of adjudicators through the qualifications of adjudicators, strengthened selection procedures for adjudicators, mechanisms for training of adjudicators, development of expertise through training and working practices and some useful procedures and practices on strengthening the relative institutional capacity and subject-matter expertise of the adjudicators. *Second*, we look at examples of concerns relating to the asymmetry in expertise over the language of the proceedings, raised in the CJEU, the ECOWAS Court and the WTO DSS. The useful practices on strengthening capacity of adjudicators through language requirements at the time of selection, dedicated department for translations and interpretation, and Assigned Assistants specifically for language procedures provide avenues to address this concern. *Third*, we turn to concerns over the lack of direct supervision and control over Dispute Assistants that have been raised in the WTO DSS. The practices and procedures on checks on the functions of Dispute Assistants and diversification of sources of assistance can re-balance control over the Dispute Assistants in favour of adjudicators. *Fourth*, the concerns relating to the risk of adjudicators delegating functions to the

Dispute Assistants, or allowing Dispute Assistants to participate in certain stages of the dispute resolution process, have been raised in the PCA, the ICSID, commercial arbitration institutions, the IUSCT, as well as the WTO DSS. Procedures on transparency and disclosures, and practices to strengthen party consent, can mitigate against such concerns. *Fifth*, a specific form of delegation relating to drafting the judgment/order/award has raised concerns in international arbitration institutions and the WTO DSS. Practices to ensure more participation and engagement by the adjudicators in the decision-making process, and procedures monitoring the role of the Dispute Assistants in substantive drafting, can address these concerns. *Sixth*, concerns have been raised in the International Criminal Tribunals and arbitration institutions on the conduct of the Dispute Assistant affecting the impartiality and independence of the adjudicator. Specific rules of conduct on Dispute Assistants and mechanisms to raise challenges against adjudicators and Dispute Assistants can potentially mitigate against these concerns enhancing the legitimacy of the DSM.

C. Part III: Dispute Assistants and the WTO DSS

In this part III, in Chapters 22, 23 and 24, we zoom in on the complex and multifaceted framework of the WTO DSS. The historical background, established practice and explicit treaty provisions create a unique role for Dispute Assistants in the WTO DSS. At the same time, concerns have been raised about the role of adjudicators and the functions discharged by Dispute Assistants. Even if they have not been demonstrated, these claims adversely impact the legitimacy of the WTO DSS. The Secretariat staff are critical to the institutional stability, memory and continuity of the WTO DSS. Therefore, these concerns deserve closer attention, examination and discussions in relation to possible ways of addressing them.

The 15 different adjudicative processes in the WTO DSS are grouped into two broad categories: *Chapter 22*, on the role of Dispute Assistants in assisting parties/DG in selection of ad hoc adjudicators; and *Chapter 23*, on the role of Dispute Assistants in assisting the adjudicators with the dispute settlement work. Each of these chapters details the concerns over legitimacy arising from the functions discharged by Dispute Assistants, the relevant provisions and practices, and possible suggestions to address them, inspired by and drawing from the useful practices of the identified DSMs as well as existing proposals for reform. The suggestions are built around five principled themes: strengthening the capacity and expertise of adjudicators, diversification of sources of staff assistance, clarity on the functions of Dispute Assistants as well as adjudicators, enhancement of transparency, and accountability.

Chapter 24 turns to the practical question relating to the operationalisation and implementation of these suggestions for reform. We examine various routes available in the WTO, for example, DSB/General council decisions; *softer* forms of law-making like Guidelines, DSB practices or chairman's statements; decisions and practices by a sub-group of WTO Members, open to the entire membership; and decisions by the DG and Secretariat practices. The aim is to show possibilities existing in the WTO that does not necessarily rely on the formal amendment procedure.

Every international dispute settlement mechanism must take legitimacy concerns seriously, particularly when they go to the very root of the process. Dispute Assistants play a key role in maintaining the quality of legal analysis and reasoning and accordingly promote the rule of law in the DSMs. Therefore, resolving the concerns relating to the role of Dispute Assistants has immense purpose for any dispute settlement mechanism, and can contribute to the legitimacy of the decision-making process. We conclude by offering comparative lessons and guidance on avenues to legitimise and make transparent the role of Dispute Assistants in the WTO DSS.

PART I

Overview of the DSMs: Structure, Procedure and Observations on the Role of Dispute Assistants

2

The African Court of Human and Peoples' Rights

I. Institutional Overview and Structure

The African Court of Human and Peoples' Rights (hereinafter ACtHPR or 'Court') was established under the Protocol on the African Charter on Human and Peoples' Rights on the Establishment of an African Court on Human and Peoples' Rights.[1] The Protocol was adopted in 1998 and entered into force in 2004, with the ACtHPR operationalised in 2006.[2] Despite the adoption of Protocols for establishing the African Court of Justice[3] and, later, one combined African Court of Justice and Human Rights,[4] the African Union (previously the 'Organisation of the African Unity' (OAU)) has not operationalised either of these Courts. Only the ACtHPR is presently functional.[5] The ACtHPR is part of the African Union judicial structure, which has a complex history of interconnected institutions.[6] The Court was established to complement the protective mandate of the African Commission on Human and Peoples' Rights (hereinafter 'African Commission'), extending to all cases and disputes concerning the interpretation and application of the Charter, the Protocol and any other relevant human rights instrument ratified by the states concerned.[7]

A. Adjudicators

The Court consists of 11 judges who are nationals of the Member States of the African Union. No two judges shall be nationals of the same state and no judge shall hear a

[1] Protocol to the African Charter on Human and Peoples' Rights on the Establishment of an African Court on Human and Peoples' Rights (adopted 10 June 1998, entered into force 25 January 2004) OAU Doc OAU /LEG/AFCHPR/PROT (III) (hereinafter 'African Charter').

[2] ibid.

[3] Protocol of the Court of Justice of the African Union (adopted 1 July 2003, entered into force on 11 February 2009) (hereinafter 'Protocol AU').

[4] Protocol on the Statute of the African Court of Justice and Human Rights (adopted 1 July 2008) (2009) 48 ILM 334 (hereinafter 'Protocol African Court').

[5] For an overview of the historical development of these judicial institutions, see KM Clarke, CC Jalloh and VO Nmehielle, 'Introduction: Origins and Issues of the African Court of Justice and Human Peoples' Rights' in CC Jalloh, KM Clarke and VO Nmehielle (eds), *The African Court of Justice and Human Peoples' Rights in Context: Development and Challenges* (Cambridge University Press, 2019) 1–54.

[6] See M Wiebusch, 'African Court on Human and Peoples' Rights' (iCourts Working Paper Series No 253, 2021) in C Binder et al (eds), *Elgar Encyclopedia of Human Rights* (Edward Elgar, 2022) 81–82.

[7] African Charter, arts 2–3.

case against their Member State.[8] State parties[9] nominate candidates for the role, giving due consideration to gender representation.[10] Candidates are to be individuals of 'high moral character and of recognized practical, judicial or academic competence and experience in human and peoples' rights'.[11] The Assembly of Heads of State and Government of the African Union (hereinafter the 'Assembly')[12] elects the judges from a list of nominees prepared by the Secretary-General of the OAU (and now, the African Union).[13] In practice, state parties elect two judges from each of the five regions of the African Continent (North, South, East, West and Central), with one additional judge from any of the regions. Judges are elected for a six-year term and can only be re-elected once.[14] The Court itself elects a President and Vice-President for a two-year term, which can be renewed once.[15] The judges of the Court perform their functions on a part-time basis during four ordinary sessions annually, each of which lasts at least four weeks. However, the President[16] works on a full-time basis.

The Dispute Assistants do not play any role in the appointment of the judges of the Court.

B. Dispute Assistants

The Court is supported by its Registry, led by a Registrar, assisted by a Deputy Registrar and such other staff from among the nationals of the Member States of the African Union. The Registrar must be of the highest moral standing and possess the necessary legal, managerial, administrative and linguistic knowledge and experience.[17] The Registrar assists the Court in the exercise of its judicial function and is in charge of the general administration of the Court's Registry.[18] The Office of the Registrar also includes the Communication Department, the Language Department and administrative Clerks who receive and send communications and case documentation.

There are two main divisions under the Registrar: the Legal Division and the Finance Division.[19] Both divisions are headed by a Head of Division holding a P5 position in the African Union grade scale.[20] The Legal Division is further divided into three Legal Units: the Legal Aid Unit; the Documentation Unit; and the Library Unit. The Legal

[8] ibid art 11.
[9] 'State parties' refers to states that are parties to the ACtHPR Protocol; African Charter, arts 12, 14–15.
[10] African Charter, arts 12, 14–15
[11] ibid art 11.
[12] ibid art 14.
[13] ibid art 13.
[14] ibid art 15.
[15] ibid art 21.
[16] ibid art 15(4).
[17] African Court on Human and Peoples' Rights, Rules of Court (September 2020) (hereinafter 'Rules of Court') r 17.2.
[18] ibid r 21.
[19] The Finance and Administration Division consists of the Finance Unit, the Human Resources Unit, the Procurement, Travel and Stores Unit, and the Information Technology Unit. As these units do not assist the judges in the exercise of judicial functions, they are not examined further here.
[20] The African Union Grade scale is equivalent to the Professional and Higher categories as per the International Civil Servant Commission, United Nations Common System of Salaries, Allowances and Benefits (UN Grade scale).

Officers assist the judges of the Court in their judicial functions. Presently, out of the Registry's total of over 70 staff, 13 are Legal Officers.

The Registrar, the Deputy Registrar and staff members of the Registry are appointed by the Court.[21] In the composition of the Registry, gender parity and representation of different regions and legal traditions are observed.[22] The Rules of the Court state that the Court shall prescribe the organisation of the Registry. Further, the Court, the Bureau (the President and Vice-President) or the President of the Court can issue instructions to the Registry.[23]

The Legal Officers assist the court as a whole; they are not assigned to individual judges. Therefore, they are Institutional Assistants. However, the President of the Court is assigned a Special Assistant, typically a lawyer, who assists the President with his or her judicial and other functions such as speech writing.[24] The Special Assistant to the President is an Assigned Assistant. The role of these Dispute Assistants in the dispute resolution process of the ACtHPR is discussed below.

II. The Dispute Resolution Process

The ACtHPR has the mandate to protect human rights in two types of proceedings: contentious proceedings relating to human rights violations, and advisory proceedings to provide guidance on legal questions.[25] We will briefly touch upon the difference between the two types of proceedings, as it affects the work of Dispute Assistants.

For contentious proceedings, cases can be submitted to the Court by the African Commission on Human and Peoples' Rights, a state party to the Protocol, an African intergovernmental organisation, a state party whose citizen is a victim of a human rights violation, or an African Commission on Human and Peoples' Rights observer.[26] Individuals and non-governmental organisations can only institute contentious proceedings against a state before the Court if the state submits a declaration under Article 34(6) of the Protocol.[27] Although a limited number of states have submitted such declarations, the overwhelming majority of the cases before the Court are of this nature.[28] In advisory proceedings, a request for an advisory opinion may be filed before the Court by a Member State, the African Union, any organ of the African Union or an African organisation recognized by the African Union.[29] As will be explained below, the procedure in contentious proceedings also applies to advisory proceedings,[30] unless otherwise specified.

[21] Rules of Court, rr 17.1, 18.1 and 20.
[22] ibid r 16.2.
[23] ibid r 16.
[24] The President also has other personal staff (for example, a secretary) for assisting him or her in administrative capacities.
[25] African Charter, art 4.
[26] Rules of Court, r 39.
[27] African Charter, art 5(3).
[28] About 99 per cent of the cases; see www.african-court.org/cpmt/statistic.
[29] Rules of Court, r 82.
[30] ibid r 87.

An application must be submitted to the Court in one of its official languages.[31] The requirements that an application must fulfil differ in contentious and advisory proceedings. In the case of contentious proceedings, the application must specify, inter alia, the alleged violation, evidence of exhaustion of local remedies, and the order sought.[32] In advisory proceedings, the request must specify the provisions of the Charter or other international human rights instrument in respect of which the opinion is being sought, the context or background giving rise to the request, and the names and addresses of the representatives of the entities making the request.[33]

At this stage, the administrative clerks of the Registry detailed above receive the application and documents and then send these documents to the Head of the Legal Division. The Head of the Legal Division thereafter summarily reviews the application primarily on personal jurisdiction. In contentious cases, this includes questions like whether the application is made against a state party, whether that state is party to the Protocol accepting the jurisdiction of the Court, and, in the case of individual applicants, whether the state has made a declaration under Article 34(6) (accepting personal jurisdiction).[34] In a request for advisory opinion, the Head of the Legal Division examines if the applicant is one of the entities capable of requesting the opinion and if the opinion concerns a legal matter relating to human rights.[35] If the application fails to satisfy the personal jurisdiction criteria, the Head of the Legal Division instructs the clerks to send a letter explaining to the applicant why the case cannot proceed.

If the criteria for personal jurisdiction are satisfied,[36] the case is allocated to one (or, exceptionally, two) Legal Officer(s) for further examination. Cases are assigned to Legal Officers primarily based on language. However, Legal Officers do not work on cases against the state of their nationality. The Legal Officer undertakes a prima facie examination of the jurisdiction and admissibility of the application, based on the criteria applicable to contentious cases and requests for advisory opinions. In contentious cases, various cumulative criteria determine the admissibility of the application. Such criteria may include an assessment of whether the evidence used in the complaint is based exclusively on news disseminated through the mass media, whether the applicants exhausted local remedies etc.[37] In a request for advisory opinion, the Legal Officer examines admissibility based on whether the African Commission is already examining the subject matter of the opinion.[38]

The Legal Officer examines the case documents substantively and drafts a case note detailing, inter alia, the prima facie recommendations on jurisdiction and admissibility,[39]

[31] The Court's official languages are 'Arabic, English, French, Portuguese, Spanish, Kiswahili and any other African language'.

[32] Rules of Court, r 41.

[33] ibid r 82.

[34] For an overview of the criteria for determining material, temporal and territorial jurisdiction, see M Wiebusch, 'African Court on Human and Peoples' Rights' in Binder et al (n 6) 83.

[35] Rules of Court, r 82.1–82.2.Arguably, this assessment goes beyond the criteria for personal jurisdiction alone and also examines whether material jurisdiction criteria as per r 81.2 of the Rules of Court is also satisfied.

[36] In contentious cases, as per rr 49–50 of the Rules of Court, and in request for advisory opinions, as per r 82 of the Rules of Court.

[37] For a list of criteria for admissibility, see Wiebusch (n 34) 83.

[38] ibid 85.

[39] In some cases, the registration is done on the instruction of the Head of the Legal Division.

and how to proceed with the case. Based on this case note, the Head of the Legal Division recommends to the Bureau of the Court which cases should be registered on the docket.[40] In requests for advisory opinions, the Head of the Legal Division forwards copies of the case note to the members of the Court and, subject to the permission of the President, publishes the request online. The Head of the Legal Division also invites observations from all the African Union Member States and any other entity that may be interested in the matter.[41]

The President[42] thereafter assigns the case to a Judge Rapporteur.[43] In practice, the President allocates cases primarily on the basis of the language. The Legal Officer assigned to the case works under the instruction of the Judge Rapporteur on all substantive and procedural aspects of the case, including drafting communications/letters to the parties and receiving responses. The Legal Officer offers recommendations on the course of action to the Judge Rapporteur, and the Judge Rapporteur makes the final call on whether to follow these recommendations. The decision-making function remains well within the purview of the Judges; however, the Legal Officers do provide substantive input and support to help the Judges arrive at their decision. While in most cases, the Judge Rapporteur follows the Legal Officer's recommendations, these recommendations are purely internal and do not bind the Judge in any way. The procedure offers an interesting insight into the changing nature of organisational supervision of the Legal Officer. While the Legal Officer is an Institutional Assistant under the supervision of the Head of Legal Division, they are also assigned to work under the supervision and control of the Judge Rapporteur as the case progresses.

Although the Court may hold oral hearings, it usually reserves them for exceptional cases. Presently, the majority of cases are decided on the basis of written pleadings. If the Court does hold oral hearings, the Legal Aid Unit suggests the schedule of public hearings. The Registrar, Deputy Registrar and Legal Officer assigned to the case attend the hearings.

In most cases, the Legal Officer drafts the judgment based on the written pleadings and the instructions from the Judge Rapporteur. If there are oral hearings, the Legal Officer notes the discussions and answers to questions posed by the judges.

Thereafter, an internal review is undertaken within the Legal Aid Unit. The draft is subsequently reviewed by the Judge Rapporteur and finalised by the Legal Officer. Through the Deputy Registrar, the Judge Rapporteur shares this draft with the other judges of the Court for deliberations. The deliberation on a draft judgment includes all the judges of the Court,[44] except where the matter concerns their national state.[45] All the Legal Officers, including those who have not worked on the case, are permitted (and,

[40] Although the Bureau, or President of the Court, is formally free to disagree with the recommendation of the Head of Legal Division on registration of the case, it is unclear whether, and how often, this power is exercised in practice.

[41] Rules of Court, r 83.2; Wiebusch (n 34) 85.

[42] Unless the case is against the state which is the nationality of the President; in such cases, the President is required to recuse himself or herself, and the Vice President shall discharge his or her functions.

[43] Earlier there was a practice of assigning the case to a Judicial Committee of three judges, but this is not the case at present.

[44] Rules of Court, r 67.

[45] O Akingube, 'The Role of the Registry and Legal Division of the African Court on Human and Peoples' Rights in Dispute Settlement' (2022) 116 *American Journal of International Law*: Unbound 385, 387.

at times, even encouraged) to attend the deliberations. The Legal Officer assigned to the case is required to attend the deliberations. One other Legal Officer from another language group is always assigned to assist with translation and language issues in the translated draft judgment during the deliberations.

The deliberations begin with the Judge Rapporteur's presentation of the draft judgment. The deliberation on the judgment is undertaken section by section. During the deliberations, the level of participation of the Legal Officer depends on the individual approach of each Judge Rapporteur. On the one end, the Legal Officer may take over from the Judge Rapporteur entirely after the presentation of the draft judgment. Conversely, the Legal Officer's role may be limited to providing input on specific questions posed by the other judges. Most often, the Legal Officers directly respond to questions posed by the judges. In cases where an important or broader jurisprudential question is raised, the Head of the Legal Division, the Registrar or Deputy Registrar may be requested to provide input.

The Court's decisions are made by a majority of the Members of the Bench present,[46] with a minimum quorum of seven judges.[47] Judges may draft separate or dissenting opinions, or declarations disagreeing with the majority's decision without providing reasons.[48] Although there have been requests for Legal Officers to assist in drafting these opinions, in practice they are almost always done by the judges themselves.

The Court renders the judgment within ninety days of having completed its deliberations, and there is no mechanism for appeal.[49] However, the Court may review its decision in light of new evidence or interpret its decision upon request.[50] The Legal Officer may also assist in this process.

The official languages of the Court are the same as the official languages of the African Union.[51] The Language Unit, employing non-lawyers who may specialise in legal translations, translates the judgments into all the official languages. As per the rules of the Court, Arabic, English, French and Portuguese are the working languages of the Court.[52] In practice, owing to the composition of the judges, the working languages of the Court are English and French. Arabic judges are provided with interpreters and make their interventions in French. As stated earlier, the allocation of cases to Legal Officers and Judge Rapporteurs is, in practice, done on the basis of language. This is to enable ease of procedure. Bilingual Legal Officers check the translated drafts of the cases they are assigned. In other cases, another Legal Officer who is fluent in the language of the translation reviews the translated draft and assists in taking notes on the translated draft judgment during the deliberations.

[46] Rules of Court, r 69.2.

[47] African Charter, art 23. Given that this is part of the Protocol, the Court is prevented from sitting in smaller formations of Chambers or single-judge benches to hear cases and expedite disposal.

[48] Rules of Court, r 70.

[49] African Charter, Art 28.

[50] ibid.

[51] Arabic, English, French, Portuguese, Spanish, Kiswahili and any other African language.

[52] Rules of Court, r 27. It is worth noting that Kiswahili and Spanish also became African Union working languages recently, but the Court's rules have not yet been updated to reflect that. The current ongoing Session of the Court has Swahili interpretation and various (not all) documents are translated into Swahili. Spanish has been used occasionally for big meetings, in terms of interpretation and some meeting documents.

III. Observations on the Role of Dispute Assistants

The ACtHPR has Dispute Assistants that are Institutional Assistants in its Registry, specifically the Legal Division of the Registry. These Institutional Assistants work under the supervision of the Head of Legal Division in some stages of the dispute, and then under the supervision of both the Head of Legal Division and their assigned Judge Rapporteur in later stages of the dispute. They do not have Assigned Assistants or External Assistants for judges.

The Legal Division and the Legal Officer assigned to a particular case play a significant role throughout all stages of the proceedings of the case, starting from receipt of the applications, preliminary review of the application, suggesting the course of action to be endorsed by the Judge Rapporteur, actively participating in the organisation of hearings and the deliberations, and drafting of the judgment. In all such functions, the Legal Officers are not undertaking the decision-making role, but rather are aiding the judges in reaching a decision. However, it is important not to diminish the role played by the Legal Officers and the Legal Division merely because they are not the decision-makers; their role is critical in assisting the judicial and legal functions exercised by the judges of the ACtHPR.

3

The Court of Justice of the European Union

I. Institutional Overview and Structure

The Court of Justice of the European Union (CJEU) is the judicial institution of the EU in charge of ensuring that the law is observed in the application and interpretation of the treaties. The CJEU consists of the General Court and the European Court of Justice (ECJ).[1] The General Court is responsible, inter alia, for handling direct actions by individuals (natural and legal persons) against the acts adopted by the institutions of the EU,[2] including disputes between the Union and its staff,[3] some direct actions brought by Member States, mostly against the Commission, and claims for compensation of damages against the EU.[4] The ECJ, on the other hand, has jurisdiction over appeals against decisions of the General Court,[5] actions brought by the Commission or a Member State against another Member State for failure to fulfil its obligations under EU law,[6] actions brought by a Member State or an institution of the EU against another institution of the EU for acting unlawfully that do not fall within the jurisdiction of the General Court,[7] and requests for a preliminary ruling on the interpretation or validity of EU law by a court in a Member State (70 per cent of its caseload consists of these preliminary ruling proceedings).[8]

[1] Called the Tribunal and the Cour de justice or simply Cour in French. Consolidated Version of the Treaty on European Union [2016] OJ C202/13 (TEU), art 19(1).

[2] Treaty on the Functioning of the European Union [2016] OJ C202/47 (TFEU), arts 256(1) (first subpara) and 260(4). This includes, for example, challenges against determinations made by the Commission on competition law.

[3] ibid arts 256(1), subpara 1 and 270.

[4] ibid arts 256(1), subpara 1 and 268.

[5] ibid art 256(1), subpara 2.

[6] ibid arts 258(2) and 259(1).

[7] ibid art 263, read with Statute of the Court of Justice of the European Union [2012] OJ C326/210, art 51. Actions can also be brought for failure to act if there was an obligation to (TEU, art 265).

[8] TFEU, art 267. A proposed amendment made in December 2022 of the TFEU (proposed art 50b) seeks to give the General Court the jurisdiction to hear and determine requests for a preliminary ruling exclusively relating to VAT, excise duties, customs etc. The request submitted by the Court of Justice pursuant to the second paragraph of art 281 TFEU, with a view to amending Protocol No 3 on the Statute of the Court of Justice of the European Union is available at: https://curia.europa.eu/jcms/upload/docs/application/pdf/2022-12/demande_transfert_ddp_tribunal_en.pdf.

A. Adjudicators

The ECJ comprises 27 judges, one for each Member State. Member States appoint judges of the ECJ for a term of six years.[9] In addition to the judges, there are 11 Advocates General in the ECJ, whose function is to present to the Court their view on a case in the form of a so-called Opinion.[10] They are not representatives of either party; instead, they assist the Court with their expert opinion in the case (though they do not present an Opinion in every case). Member States appoint the Advocates General for a term of six years.[11] Five of the 11 Advocates General have mandates that are, in principle, renewable.[12] Candidates for judges and Advocates General of the ECJ are expected to be persons whose independence is beyond doubt and who possess the qualifications required for appointment to the highest judicial offices in their respective countries or who are jurisconsults of recognised competence.[13]

The General Court comprises 54 judges, two from each Member State. Member States appoint judges of the General Court for a renewable term of six years.[14] Candidates for members of the General Court are expected to be persons whose independence is beyond doubt and who possess the ability required for appointment to high judicial office.[15] There are currently no permanent Advocates General in the General Court. The President of the General Court may appoint a judge of the General Court as an Advocate General for a particular case on an ad hoc basis.[16] The plenum takes the decision to designate an Advocate General at the request of the chamber to which the case is assigned.[17] In practice, such appointments have been rare.[18]

The judges and Advocates General are appointed by common accord of the governments of the Member States based on the nomination made by a Member State and the recommendations of a panel of experts who examines the qualifications of candidates. The panel of experts 'give[s] an opinion on candidates' suitability to perform the duties of Judge [of the CJEU]'.[19] It comprises seven persons chosen from among former members of the CJEU, members of national supreme courts and lawyers of recognised competence.[20] The panel uses six criteria to evaluate the suitability of candidates: the candidates' legal capabilities; their professional experience; their ability to perform the

[9] TEU, art 253(1).

[10] ibid art 252(2).

[11] ibid art 253(1). Of the 11 Advocates General, five come from the most populated Member States (France, Germany, Italy, Poland and Spain), while the rest are appointed from the remaining Member States on a rotational basis. See R Manko, *Role of Advocates General at the CJEU* (European Parliament Research Service, October 2019).

[12] These five countries are France, Germany, Italy, Poland and Spain (and previously the UK before Brexit).

[13] TEU, art 253(1).

[14] ibid art 254(2).

[15] ibid.

[16] Rules of Procedure of the General Court [2015] OJ L105/1, art 31(2).

[17] ibid art 31(1).

[18] However, this could change considering the Request submitted by the Court of Justice pursuant to the second paragraph of art 281 TFEU, with a view to amending Protocol No 3 on the Statute of the Court of Justice of the European Union, December 2022; see also European Parliament Research Service, *Reform of the EU Judicial System* (2023), www.europarl.europa.eu/RegData/etudes/BRIE/2023/754559/EPRS_BRI(2023)754559_EN.pdf.

[19] TEU, art 255.

[20] ibid.

duties of a judge; their language skills; their ability to work as part of a team in an international environment in which several legal systems are represented; and whether their independence, impartiality, probity and integrity are beyond doubt.[21] Between 2010 and 2022, the panel issued 243 opinions, 27 of which were objections to the selection and nomination of candidates.[22] The panel's opinions were always followed by the governments of Member States.[23]

The Dispute Assistants do not play any role in the appointment of the judges of the General Court or the ECJ.

B. Dispute Assistants to the Adjudicators and the Advocates General

A considerable number of supporting staff assist the judges and Advocates General in their work, as Institutional Assistants or Assigned Assistants. Such assistance include the following functions:

a) *The Registry*: The ECJ and the General Court have separate dedicated registries, each headed by their Registrar, appointed by their respective court[24] and assisted by a Deputy Registrar.[25] The Registrar of the ECJ acts as the Secretary General of the CJEU as an institution and is responsible for the global administration of the CJEU. The Deputy Registrar of the ECJ, and the Registrar and Deputy Registrar of the General Court are responsible for the day-to-day functioning of their respective courts, including tracking the cases before their respective courts. The Deputy Registrar of the ECJ has around 50 people working under them, who are from different Member States and are fluent in one or more official languages. The Registrar and Deputy Registrar of the General Court have a larger team of over 70 people assisting them in their functions. These staff members (over 120 in number) are Institutional Assistants respectively of the ECJ and the General Court, who aid the CJEU as a whole.

b) *The Directorate-General of Multilingualism*: The language service of the CJEU comprises the Directorate for Interpretation and Directorates A and B for Legal Translation.[26] While the working language of the CJEU is French, cases before the CJEU may come in any of the 24 languages of the EU and will be interpreted/translated at multiple points. The

[21] *Seventh Activity Report of the Panel provided for by Art 255 of the Treaty on the Functioning of the European Union (2022)* (Curia, July 2022) 17, www.curia.europa.eu/jcms/upload/docs/application/pdf/2022-07/2022.2597-qcar22002enn_002.pdf.

[22] ibid 9.

[23] ibid.

[24] Rules of Procedure of the General Court, art 32; Rules of Procedure of the Court of Justice [2012] OJ L265/1, art 18.

[25] F Heeren, 'The Court of Justice of the European Union' in F Baetens (ed), *Legitimacy of Unseen Actors* (Cambridge University Press, 2019) 126.

[26] Directorates A and B for Legal Translations are shared between the ECJ and the General Court, and the language units are apportioned between them. For more on this, see Court of Justice of the European Union, *Décision du 17 février 2009 portant adoption des règles de bonne conduite des Référendaires* [2009] OJ C 64/1, https://curia.europa.eu/site/jcms/qua1_6645.

language of proceedings will be the 'language of the case',[27] which can be any of the 24 languages of the EU. Given the importance of language before the CJEU, the Directorate-General of Multilingualism is the institution's largest service, employing over 1,000 people. It is staffed by experts with adequate legal training and a thorough knowledge of several official languages of the EU.[28] The translation service in particular only hires persons who have completed their education in law and possess the necessary language qualifications, as the texts translated by the translation service are highly technical.[29]

A Director General supervises the Directorate's day-to-day work, with overall supervision and authority lying with the Registrar of the ECJ. The Directorate's role is examined further below in the discussion of specific stages of cases before the ECJ and the General Court. These are Institutional Assistants are Institutional Assistants respectively of the ECJ and the General Court, who aid the CJEU as a whole.

c) *The Research and Documentation Directorate*: This team consists of around 35 lawyers covering, in principle, all Member States.[30] There are two main functions of this Directorate: the first is the filtering function, where the Directorate conducts a review of the preliminary ruling applications and of some categories of appeals brought before the ECJ. This function is further elaborated in section II below. The second, less frequently employed function of the Directorate is conducting comparative research on a question of law and collating the jurisprudence across Member States and even other jurisdictions. The Directorate usually initiates comparative research after the written phase of the case is closed if the Advocate General and/or the Judge Rapporteur finds that it is useful to know the practice of Member States on a particular question of law or procedure.

Given the resources and expertise of the Directorate's lawyers, the Directorate is well equipped to perform both functions, which requires competence in Members States' national laws. In both these functions, the Directorate does not work for individual judges, but for the Court as a whole. The Research and Documentation Directorate is under the direct control of the Registrar of the ECJ. These are Institutional Assistants respectively of the ECJ and the General Court, who aid the CJEU as a whole.

d) *Référendaires*: The référendaires are legal secretaries to the judges and Advocates General that form their cabinets. The respective judges and Advocates General effectively have complete discretion in the selection of their référendaires, who are formally appointed by the general meeting of the Court.[31] The référendaires are bound by a code

[27] Rules of Procedure of the Court of Justice, arts 36–38; Rules of Procedure of the General Court, arts 44–46.

[28] Rules of Procedure of the Court of Justice, art 42.

[29] Court of Justice of the European Union, 'Annual Reports', www.curia.europa.eu/jcms/jcms/Jo2_10744.

[30] Court of Justice of the European Union, 'Research and Documentation Directorate', www.curia.europa.eu/jcms/jcms/Jo2_7024.

[31] D Sarmiento, 'Référendaires, CJEU' in MPP Durbán (ed), *Max Planck Encyclopedia of European Private Law* (Oxford University Press 2018) 22. The official appointment is purely a formality, as the general meeting seems to have never rejected a référendaire. However, this does not imply that every single référendaire proposed by a Judge/Advocate General are accepted. The 'rejection' will normally occur informally through the President/Vice-President/President of Chamber warning the proposing judge/Advocate General before the general meeting/plenary conference that the candidate they intend to propose may not be acceptable.

of conduct, in addition to that generally applicable to the staff of the EU.[32] These provisions impose various duties on référendaires, including duties to abstain in cases when in the past they have been involved or have supported or advised one of the parties.[33] Further, with respect to instances where the référendaires wish to publicly express their opinions in academic writings and/or public speaking events, they must obtain prior authorisation to do so.[34] Once they have ceased their work, they are precluded from participating in any way in cases pending if they have participated in them before.[35] However, these rules do not include specific procedure or remedy in case of breach of the duties by référendaires. Commentators have noted that this is probably due to the fact that the référendaires' position depends on a relationship based on trust with their supervisor, the judge or Advocate General. Therefore, any breach of these rules is tantamount to a breach of the relation of trust that serves as the basis of the référendaires' position,[36] and obliges their supervisor to take action.

The référendaires are paid from the part of the EU's General Budget, which is assigned to the CJEU as an institution.

In practice, there is a significant representation of French and Belgian nationals amongst the référendaires due to the importance of the French language in the Court and the need to address complex questions of law and fact[37] in French.[38] This is particularly relevant before the General Court, where the référendaires distil large documents of complex facts in the preparation of a draft.

Owing to the formalised structure of appointment and remuneration of référendaires, there are fixed numbers of référendaire positions that each judge or Advocate General is allowed to have:

- At present, each judge of the ECJ has four référendaires. Previously, the judges had three référendaires and an additional Legal Assistant position. The Legal Assistant position was generally offered to young law graduates to allow them to gain experience. A few years ago, this position was transformed into a 'real' référendaire position if requested by the judge and if the candidate met certain conditions (mostly relating to experience). The reason for this change was the increasing workload and the need to be able to hire more experienced personnel. Presently, all such Legal Assistant positions in the ECJ have been converted into référendaire positions.
- Each Advocate General at the ECJ has four référendaires. As noted above, in the past, judges of the ECJ had three référendaires, which gave Advocate Generals one more référendaire than the judges (although now the judges of the ECJ also have four référendaires). Such allotment of an additional référendaire position

[32] Court of Justice of the European Union, *Décision du 17 février 2009 portant adoption des règles de bonne conduite des Référendaires* [2009] OJ C64/1.

[33] Sarmiento (n 31) 11.

[34] ibid.

[35] ibid.

[36] ibid .

[37] Especially in the General Court, where référendaires need to engage closely with applications which may not always be as well structured as preliminary requests before the ECJ. These applications require an in-depth understanding of French, which is the working language of the Court.

[38] In very exceptional circumstances, individuals without a nationality of an EU Member State have also been appointed, although this is rare.

in the past could be due to the increased workload, which is divided between 11 Advocates General of the ECJ. Even in cases where the Court does not seek the Advocate General's Opinion, the Advocate General and their référendaires have to devote time and effort to examine the case documents and form a view on the necessity of their opinion to discuss with the Judge Rapporteur, as well as before the weekly meetings of the Court.

- In the General Court, since the doubling of the number of judges, each judge is assigned only two référendaires.[39] However, the President of each Chamber (consisting of five judges) has an additional référendaire to assist them with their functions. Further, each Chamber of five judges is assigned two additional référendaires. Each of the additional référendaires is shared between two judges in the Chamber (other than the President of the Chamber). The allocation of work to these référendaires depends on the practice of the specific Chamber. Between the two judges, the allocation could be decided, for example, based on the needs or complexity of their caseload or by taking turns. In practice, it is often the case that the référendaires allocated to the Chamber assist the Judge who has been assigned as a Judge Rapporteur to a case. Separately, a team of référendaires is attached to the cabinet of the President of the General Court. This team of référendaires has been described as a 'fire brigade' or 'task force' available to individual judges for additional assistance when working on a large or complicated case.

The référendaires who form the cabinet of the judges and Advocate Generals are Assigned Assistants.

e) Other members of the Cabinet: Each judge may also have Assistants, who do not work on the substantive aspects of the case, and a Trainee. In the General Court, the judges may choose to have a Legal Assistant who assists them with the substantive aspects of a case in a smaller role compared to the référendaire. However, the practice may vary from judge to judge. Some judges can also have a 'magistrat national détaché', a national judge who is seconded to the Court for six months in the context of a cooperation programme with the national courts.[40] They are also Assigned Assistants.

f) Lecteurs d'arrêts: The Lecteurs d'arrêts are a team of lawyers providing input on the language and consistency of drafts per the formal requirements of a judgment. They are senior lawyers fluent in French and, because of their experience, may also go beyond merely formalistic edits in their role. However, in practice, this is rare. They are attached to the office of the President of the ECJ and the office of the President of the General Court. The stage at which the Lecteurs intervene differs between the ECJ and the General Court.

The next section details the procedure of a case before the General Court and the ECJ, and identifies the roles that the Dispute Assistants play at each stage.

[39] Sarmiento (n 31) 9. Given that there were twice the number of judges at the General Court as had been the case previously, the number of référendaires assigned to each cabinet was reduced. Additionally, there is now a pool of unassigned référendaires that judges can draw from if their cabinets are at capacity.

[40] However, numbers are limited so it is not for every cabinet, every year.

II. The Dispute Resolution Process

A. Receiving Applications and Procedural Aspects

A case before the General Court and the ECJ begins with a written filing, followed by an exchange of written pleadings or filings of different submissions by interested parties, depending on the type of case. These documents are received and processed by the Registry.[41] At this point, the Registry undertakes a preliminary review of the application to ensure compliance with procedural rules – for example, applications brought by individuals fall within the jurisdiction of the General Court. If an individual mistakenly files an application before the ECJ, the Registry of the ECJ transfers the case to the General Court.[42]

The Registry also examines if the file is complete. The Registry's Administrators and case lawyers, who work under the supervision of the Deputy Registrar (in the case of the ECJ) or the Registrar and Deputy Registrar (in the case of the General Court), handle these procedural aspects. Their work involves contacting and liaising with the agents and lawyers representing the parties, and with the national courts in requests for preliminary rulings, depending on the type of case.

Once the documents are received, they are sent to the Directorate-General of Multilingualism for translation, which may take up to a month, depending on the number of languages (see below).

During this time, the Administrators of the Registry analyse issues such as whether there should be a joinder; whether the Court should stay the case where there is a similar, currently pending, case before the Court; and whether to make a recommendation to the President that an urgent preliminary ruling or expedited procedure is appropriate. However, these are still strictly issues of procedure. Final and substantive decisions are taken by the judges of the Court. For example, even if the Registry finds that a case is manifestly inadmissible, the Registry must still propose the dismissal of the case to the President. If the President agrees, they assign the case to a Judge Rapporteur. The Judge Rapporteur, in turn, proposes the adoption of an order for dismissal to be issued by a three-judge chamber.

B. Preliminary Reviews

The Research and Documentation Directorate of the Registry conducts a preliminary review of (i) all preliminary ruling applications and (ii) appeals brought before the Court of Justice against decisions of the General Court. The Directorate analyses preliminary ruling applications to identify problems at an early stage (for example, regarding admissibility), while it examines appeals to identify those that can be dealt with by reasoned order. As mentioned earlier, the Directorate consists of lawyers from Member States with expertise in national law. Therefore, they can competently assess the applications based on relevant national law and the rules of the Court. The Research

[41] Rules of Procedure of the Court of Justice, art 20(1); Rules of Procedure of the General Court, art 35(1).

[42] Even in situations where the application is in the form of a letter, the Registry is obliged to answer these stating why it cannot be registered as a case before the Court.

and Documentation Directorate prepares a short note on the case, including the relevant facts and cases. This note is obviously not binding on the judges' final judgment.

C. Translations

At this stage, the Directorate-General for Multilingualism translates all documents relevant to the case. The documents are then sent to all interested parties. As mentioned earlier, while the Court drafts and deliberates exclusively in French, the language of the case depends on various factors[43] and can be any one of the 24 official languages of the Union. The Directorate-General for Multilingualism puts in significant work to ensure that all documents are available in both French and the language of the case.[44] In ECJ preliminary ruling applications, the request for a preliminary ruling from the national court is translated into all the official languages of the EU in order to allow any Member State to participate in the proceedings.[45] In direct actions, the file is only translated into French.

After the first round of translations, the Registry sends the translated preliminary ruling applications to all the member states and institutions of the EU. They may send their written observations, in their respective languages, on the questions posed by the preliminary application. The written observations are further translated into French and the language of the case; thereafter, these are the two languages of translation during the proceedings.

D. Assignment of Cases

In the assignment of cases, the practice of the ECJ and the General Court are different.

In the case of the *ECJ*, as soon as possible after the applicant has lodged the document initiating proceedings,[46] but always before the written part of the procedure is closed, the President of the Court assigns a judge as a Judge Rapporteur, and the First Advocate General assigns an Advocate General to the case. In consultation with the Advocate General, the Judge Rapporteur will draft a *preliminary report*[47] that recommends, inter alia:

1) the size of the chamber to which the case should be assigned;
2) if there should be an opinion of the Advocate General;
3) if there should be an oral hearing in the case; and
4) if there are questions to be clarified before the oral hearing – for example, relating to the relevant national law in the case.

[43] For example, in the General Court, the language of the case is determined as per art 43 of the Rules of Procedure of the General Court, which states that in direct actions, the language of the case is chosen by the applicant unless it falls within the scope of art 43(1)(a)–(c). In the Court of Justice, r 37(3) of the Rules of Procedure of the Court of Justice provides that in preliminary rulings, the language of the case shall be the language of the referring court or tribunal.

[44] A Sennekamp and IV Damme, 'A Practical Perspective on Treaty Interpretation: The Court of Justice of the European Union and the WTO Dispute Settlement System' (2014) 3(2) *Cambridge Journal of International and Comparative Law* 13.

[45] Rules of Procedure of the Court of Justice, rr 96–98.

[46] ibid art 15,

[47] ibid art 59.

At this stage, the Judge Rapporteur will also assign one of their référendaires to the case, who will draft the preliminary report under the Judge Rapporteur's instruction and direction.[48] Sometimes, the référendaires draft these recommendations in coordination with the Registry and the assigned Advocate General in a process that is, due to practicalities, handled by the respective référendaires.

A lot of communication occurs between the Advocates General and Judges Rapporteurs once the preliminary report is drafted. The main point of discussions may revolve around the need for an Opinion from the Advocate General[49] and, consequently, whether the case raises jurisprudential questions that warrant a hearing by a larger bench[50] (previously, the practice was that the Court would request the opinion of the Advocate General in cases before a Chamber of five (or more) judges). This results in a lot of communication and, sometimes, negotiation between the respective référendaires. However, they act strictly under the direction of their supervisor and do not exceed the discretion granted to them in communications.

The Judge Rapporteur presents the preliminary report to the general meeting, which is referred to as the 'Réunion Générale',[51] comprising the judges and Advocate General (the Registrar is also present unless the Court decides to the contrary). If the Judge Rapporteur and the Advocate General agree on the recommendations in the preliminary report, the recommendations of the Judge Rapporteur are presented as accepted in agreement with the Advocate General. If the Advocate General disagrees with the Judge Rapporteur, they submit a note explaining their disagreement. In most cases, there is consensus between the Judge Rapporteur and the Advocate General. In the rare instances of disagreement, the recommendations are put to the vote and decided by the majority.[52] No référendaires attend this Réunion Générale.

After the general meeting decides on the procedural aspects of the case, the référendaires in charge of the file in the cabinets of the Judge Rapporteur and the Advocate General (if the Court seeks the opinion of the Advocate General) will prepare for the hearing, if any, by conducting further analysis and in-depth research on the case.[53] Before the hearing, the Judge Rapporteur and the Advocate General may discuss the case amongst themselves, involving their référendaires in the exchanges as well.

During the hearing, the Judges and the Advocate General actively engage with the parties. The Advocate General will also announce when their opinion will be issued. In the courtroom, the référendaires are seated at a desk in front of the judges, at the level where the representatives of the parties are seated. The Registry staff assigned to the case are seated next to the judges. During the hearings, there may be communication between the référendaires and their Judge/Advocate General. In practice, this is done by notes passed along by a dedicated staff member or through direct messaging on their court laptops.

After the hearing, if the Court has requested the opinion of the Advocate General, the judges will wait until the Advocate General submits their Opinion. Only then will

[48] Sarmiento (n 31) 14. The référendaire will also liaise with their counterpart in the Advocate General's office.

[49] This essentially revolves around the question whether the case raises a new point of law, as per art 20 of the Statute of the Court of the European Union.

[50] This depends on the difficulty or importance of the case or on the particular circumstances of the case.

[51] Rules of Procedure of the Court of Justice, arts 25, 59–60.

[52] ibid art 25.

[53] The hearing is attended by the référendaires and also the Registrar.

the judges begin their deliberations on the case.[54] There is a strict Chinese wall between the Judge Rapporteur and the Advocate General after the hearings and the same applies to the respective Dispute Assistants. The référendaire of the Advocate General will draft the Opinion, under the instruction and direction of their Advocate General.[55] There may be a practice in very complex cases that the draft prepared by a référendaire is reviewed and discussed with other référendaires in the cabinet of the Advocate General. However, owing to the large caseload, this is rare.

Once the Advocate General publishes his/her Opinion, the Judge Rapporteur will draft a memo taking a position on the proposals made in the Opinion. If the Judge Rapporteur disagrees with the Opinion, the President of the Chamber may conduct a 'round table' with the other Judges in the Chamber to understand their positions on the issues. In this meeting, no référendaires or other Dispute Assistants are present. Thereafter, the Judge Rapporteur will charge their référendaire with drafting a *projet de motifs* or a first draft of the judgment.

In the case of the *General Court*, cases are heard in chambers of three or five judges.[56] The President of the General Court assigns the cases to a particular Chamber according to criteria laid down by the General Court. The General Court publishes these criteria in the Official Journal of the European Union.[57] The President of the General Court usually assigns cases following two separate rotas: one for cases concerning the application of competition rules applicable to undertakings, the rules on state aid, trade protection measures, foreign subsidies distorting the internal market, and digital market and services; and one for all other cases.[58] However, the President may deviate from this to take account of connections between cases or to spread caseload evenly. Additionally, some Chambers specialise in two specific subject matters: intellectual property cases (six Chambers) and cases relating to civil service law (four Chambers). The General Court may also sit as a Grand Chamber (15 judges) when required to do so due to the legal complexity or importance of a case,[59] and as the 'intermediate chamber' of nine judges. The judges of each Chamber also elect Presidents of Chambers sitting with three (for a defined term) or five judges (for a once-renewable term of three years).[60] In practice, the Presidents of Chambers of five judges also act as the Presidents of the Chambers of three judges (in this case, the Chambers of three judges are composed of the same judges sitting in the Chamber of five judges).

After the President of the General Court assigns the case to a Chamber, the President of the Chamber proposes the appointment of a judge as Judge Rapporteur. The President of the General Court appoints the Judge Rapporteur based on this proposal in every case.[61] As in the ECJ, the Judge Rapporteur is responsible for producing the Preliminary

[54] Deliberations do not start before that as, according to art 82(2) of the Rules of Procedure of the Court of Justice, the oral part of the procedure is closed only after the Advocate General has delivered their Opinion. In practice, in very exceptional circumstances, such as some urgent preliminary ruling procedures, the judges could start an informal discussion before the Opinion of the Advocate General is officially published.

[55] Sarmiento (n 31) 15.

[56] In some cases, it may also be heard by a single judge: Rules of Procedure of the General Court, art 14.

[57] ibid art 25.

[58] European Union General Court, *Criteria for the Assignment of Cases to Chambers* [2023] OJ C286/2, www.eur-lex.europa.eu/legal-content/EN/TXT/PDF/?uri=CELEX:C2023/286/02.

[59] Rules of Procedure of the General Court, art 15.

[60] ibid art 18.

[61] ibid art 26.

Report and the first draft of the judgment, and similarly assigns the case to a référendaire in their cabinet who assists with the drafting. As mentioned earlier, there are no permanent Advocates General in the General Court. The President of the General Court may appoint a judge of the General Court as an Advocate General for a particular case on an ad hoc basis.[62] Nevertheless, this has rarely occurred in the Court's history, and the rule is being considered for reform.

When the written part of the procedure is closed, the President fixes a date on which the Judge Rapporteur is to present the Preliminary Report to the General Court stating: analysis of the relevant issues of fact and law raised by the action; proposals as to whether the Court should undertake measures of organisation of procedure or measures of inquiry; whether there should be an oral part of the procedure; and whether the case should be referred to the Grand Chamber or a Chamber sitting with a different number of judges; and whether the case should be delegated to a single judge.[63] The general practice is that the Preliminary Report is not sent to all the judges of the General Court; instead, it is only shared with the Chamber to which the case is assigned, as well as the President and Vice-President of the Court. There are exceptions to this practice. For example, the Preliminary Report is sent to all the judges for information in intellectual property cases. Further, every judge receives a summary of every report and there are mechanisms in place for them to obtain the full report if needed.

In the General Court, the Chamber to which the case is assigned decides how to proceed with the case and discusses the preliminary report. This is different from the situation in the ECJ, where the decision is taken at a general meeting of the entire Court. However, if the Chamber proposes that the case be attributed to a bigger Chamber, then this decision is taken by the general meeting of the entire Court.[64] The depth and substance of the discussion in the general meeting varies from case to case and can sometimes involve detailed discussions on the merits of the case.

If there is a hearing, the President of the Chamber is responsible for its proper conduct, and there is active engagement between the members of the Chamber and the parties in the form of questions.[65] The référendaires of the Judges are also present during the hearings, in the same manner as the ECJ. Thereafter, the Judge Rapporteur drafts the judgment in the same manner as the ECJ.

E. First Round of Review by Lecteurs d'arrêts at the ECJ

Before being circulated to the judges, the *projet de motifs* will be passed to the Lecteurs d'arrêts, who will review it for language, terminology and alignment with the particular style the Court adopts in judgments. In rare cases, the Lecteurs also ensure that there have been no obvious legal errors.[66] However, there is limited scope for legal corrections

[62] ibid ch 5.
[63] ibid art 87.
[64] ibid art 28.
[65] ibid art 110(M3).
[66] Droit Européen, 'Découvrez la fonction de lecteurs d'arrêt à la CJUE, interview Anne Schneider part 1' (20 January 2017) 3:00–7:04, www.https://blogdroiteuropeen.com/2017/01/20/decouvrez-la-fonction-de-lecteur-darret-a-la-cjue-interview-anne-schneider-part-1.

as the Judge Rapporteur drafts the *projet*, taking into account all relevant aspects of the jurisprudence. Some corrections recommended by the Lecteurs – for example, on sentence construction – can impact the substantive aspects of the case. Unlike the ECJ, in the General Court, the Lecteurs only intervene after the judges have finalised the draft, after the deliberations.

F. Circulation of Draft and Comments

In the ECJ, the *projet* is circulated to the other judges in the Chamber after the Judge Rapporteur finalises the *projet*. The other judges, with the assistance of their référendaire, will send their comments and notes on the *projet* to the Judge Rapporteur a few days before the deliberations.[67] In the General Court, the *projet* is shared with the other judges of the Chamber without any intervention or review by the Lecteurs.

In both the ECJ and the General Court, the référendaire of the Judge Rapporteur coordinates closely with the référendaires of the judges who raise comments on the draft, but always on the instruction and under the direction of their judges. In case of minor corrections or comments, the other judges on the Chamber may share them with the Judge Rapporteur through their référendaire instead of making a short note on the *projet*, which is reserved for when there are more significant comments. Thereafter, the Judge Rapporteur will instruct their référendaire to revise the draft into a *projet de motifs modifié*, based on the comments and notes received from the other Judges. In the ECJ, the Judge Rapporteur circulates the *projet de motifs modifié* at least two full days before the deliberations. In the General Court, the time for which the Judge Rapporteur circulates the *projet de motifs modifié* depends on the practice of the Chamber.

G. Deliberations

The Court holds deliberations in absolute secrecy. Only the judges are allowed to attend them. The procedure leading up to the deliberations is designed to develop and promote consensus: judges are allowed to provide their views on the *projet* before deliberations, and the Judge Rapporteur is allowed to incorporate these views into the final judgment. Even the structure of the deliberation process between the judges is intended to reach a consensus. The face-to-face deliberations conducted by the judges also ensure they retain sufficient control over the final draft. In turn, this procedural set up ensures that no other actor can exert unwarranted influence over the draft. In the French-inspired practice of the Court, there are no known dissenting opinions, partly owing to the secrecy of deliberations. After the deliberations, the Judge Rapporteur will instruct their référendaire to prepare, based on the *projet de motifs modifié*, a *projet d'arrêt*, incorporating all the final changes decided during the deliberations.

[67] Sarminento (n 31) 15; Rules of Procedure of the Court of Justice, art 32(1)–(2).

H. Second Round of Review by Lecteurs d'arrêts

Once the Judge Rapporteur finalises the draft, at the ECJ there is a second – and purely linguistic – intervention by the Lecteurs d'arrêts, after which the judges officially finalise the decision.[68]

In the General Court, as mentioned earlier, this post-finalisation review by the Lecteurs d'arrêts is their first and only intervention in reviewing the draft. Thereafter, the Judge Rapporteur reviews the suggestions made by the Lecteurs and shares them with the Chamber for finalisation as per the changes made. If the Lecteurs' recommendations are substantial, the deliberations may be unofficially re-opened to get the approval of all the judges in the Chamber.

Once the judgment is finalised, it is translated into the language of the case or, depending on the type of case or the importance of the legal issues it raises, into all 24 languages, and is delivered. This process can be very lengthy, depending on the length of the judgment and the number of languages, and may take six months or more.

III. Observations on the Role of Dispute Assistants

The procedure of the CJEU is one of the most elaborate and sophisticated mechanisms, with multiple Institutional Assistants and Assigned Assistants aiding the Judges or Advocates General with their judicial and legal functions. Throughout the dispute settlement process, the CJEU system maintains a unique check and balance. The judge-led judicial process is very much at the centre of the institutional structure; however, the Institutional Assistants of the Registry, the Directorate-General for Multilingualism, the Directorate of Research and Documentation, and the Assigned Assistants of the judges, notably the référendaires (Assigned Assistants) provide crucial support to the judges. All those legal actors are of very high competence as their selection follows very competitive processes with attractive work conditions. The balance is reflected in three complementary ways: first, in terms of the level of control exercised and direction given by the judges and Advocates General over the work of their référendaires; second, in the amount of trust reposed by the judges and Advocates General in the work of their référendaires; and, third, owing to the multiplicity of actors with specified roles, the system ensures that no single actor can exert influence over the final judgment, and the judge directs the whole operation.

Regarding the référendaires of the judges of the ECJ and the General Court, the nature and consequences of their functions are affected by the jurisdiction of the Court in which they sit. Owing to the nature of direct-action cases before the General Court, référendaires in the General Court are required to sift through voluminous documents with complex questions of fact. This requires référendaires of the General Court to have an excellent command of French and be closely involved with the factual aspects of the case. In contrast, the ECJ's work involves grappling with complex legal issues. The consequences of the decisions of the ECJ also impact the nature of the work undertaken

[68] Sarmiento (n 31) 18.

by the référendaires. For example, in preliminary ruling cases, the decision of the ECJ is binding on all national courts *erga omnes*, and not merely on the national court requesting the ruling. This binding effect creates an additional texture of responsibility on the tasks performed by référendaires of the ECJ. Therefore, although the tasks undertaken by the référendaires in the ECJ and the General Court are conceptually similar, the nature and implications of these tasks are influenced by differences in the cases heard by the two courts.

Furthermore, fluency in the French language is essential when drafting judgments. Although concerns have been raised about the quality of judges at the CJEU and their ability to work in French,[69] the strict quality control in the selection process through the panel under Article 255 of the Treaty on the Functioning of the European Union ensures that all judges are outstanding jurists. Working exclusively in French drives judges to learn the language rather quickly, even if they are not proficient when they first arrive at the Court.[70] Thus, control over the process always lies with the judges. At the same time, the extremely demanding caseload makes the delegation of drafting to the référendaires the only practically viable option. This highlights the importance of trust in the working relationships within a cabinet.

One area where the référendaires may develop a dynamic of their own is in their communication with each other, either between two référendaires in the cabinets of the Judge Rapporteur and Advocate General, or between the judges' référendaires. However, a clear understanding that référendaires only act in the name of their judges, paired with the check that any final draft needs to be signed off by the Judge Rapporteur, limits even this potential. In sum, while the référendaires are crucial for the functioning of the Court, the judges ultimately hold decision-making power and control the direction of any case.

[69] AH Zhang, 'The Faceless Court' (2016) 38(1) *University of Pennsylvania Journal of International Law* 71.
[70] Sarmiento (n 31) 31.

4

The COMESA Court of Justice

I. Institutional Overview and Structure

The Treaty Establishing the Common Market for Eastern and Southern Africa (hereinafter 'COMESA Treaty') provided for the setting up of the Common Market for Eastern and Southern Africa Court of Justice (hereinafter 'COMESA Court of Justice')[1] as an organ of the Common Market. The COMESA Court of Justice was established in 1998[2] to ensure the adherence to law in the interpretation and application of the COMESA Treaty,[3] and adjudicate upon all matters referred to it pursuant to the Treaty.[4] The Court may receive references from a Member State against the conduct another Member State or the COMESA Council, or regarding the legality of any act, regulation, directive or decision of the COMESA Council.[5] The Secretary-General of COMESA also has the power to bring certain issues before the Court,[6] and individual residents of Member States may also refer certain matters for the determination of the Court.[7] In addition, the Court has jurisdiction to hear certain disputes between the Common Market and its employees, or certain claims by any person against the Common Market or its institutions.[8] Lastly, the Court also has jurisdiction to hear certain disputes arising out of arbitration clauses or special agreements.[9]

The COMESA Court of Justice consists of the First Instance Division, which functions as a trial court, and an Appeal Division, which serves as an appellate court from the decisions of the First Instance Division.[10]

[1] Treaty Establishing the Common Market for Eastern and Southern Africa (hereinafter 'COMESA Treaty') (signed 5 November 1993, entered into force 8 December 1994) 2314 UNTS 1, art 7.

[2] COMESA Council of Ministers, 'Seventeenth Meeting Report' (4–5 June 2004, Nile International Conference Centre, Kampala, Uganda).

[3] For a more detailed overview of the COMESA Court of Justice, see JT Gathii, 'The COMESA Court of Justice' in R Howse, HR Fabri, G Ulfstein and M Zang (eds), *The Legitimacy of International Trade Courts and Tribunals* (Cambridge University Press, 2018).

[4] COMESA Treaty, art 23.

[5] ibid art 24.

[6] ibid art 25.

[7] ibid art 26.

[8] ibid art 27.

[9] ibid art 28.

[10] Gathii (n 3) 317.

A. Adjudicators

The COMESA Court of Justice consists of 12 judges appointed by the COMESA Authority,[11] with seven judges appointed to the First Division, and five judges appointed to the Appellate Division.[12] The COMESA Treaty specifies that the judges of the Court must be 'persons of impartiality and independence who fulfil the conditions required for the holding of high judicial office in their respective countries of domicile' or 'who are jurists of recognised competence'.[13] The Authority designates one of the judges of the Appellate Division as the President of the Court,[14] and one of the judges of the First Instance Division as the Principal Judge.[15] The Appellate Division of the COMESA Court of Justice sits either in plenary session or with a quorum of three judges, as the President determines. The First Instance Division sits either in plenary session or with a quorum of five or three judges, as the Principal Judge determines.[16]

The Dispute Assistants do not play any role in the appointment of the judges of the COMESA Court of Justice.

B. Dispute Assistants

The COMESA Council appoints a Registrar from among the nationals of the Member States, who is qualified to hold high judicial office in their respective state.[17] The Registrar is subject to the overall supervision of the President of the Court and is responsible for the day-to-day administration of the business of the Court.[18] The staff in the Registry presently includes the Registrar, Deputy Registrar, Assistant Registrar and Legal Officer/clerk, along with administrative and finance staff, an internal auditor, IT staff, and staff from the general service category.[19] Although separate registries are maintained,[20] the staff service both the judges of the First Division and the Appellate Division. The Registry and its staff are Institutional Assistants.

The Registry also recruits researchers from institutions like the Trade Policy Training Centre in Africa. They may be lecturers or students and are recruited for specific cases, according to the needs of each case. There are no official criteria for their selection. The scope of their research depends on the complexity of the case, including substantive aspects. The researchers are assigned to a particular bench and not individual judges. These are External Assistants, working for a specific dispute and paid by the Court.

We examine the role of these Dispute Assistants in the dispute resolution process below.

[11] The COMESA Authority consists of the heads of state or government of the Member States of COMESA. See COMESA Treaty, art 8.

[12] ibid art 20(1).

[13] ibid art 20(2).

[14] ibid art 20(4).

[15] ibid art 20(5).

[16] KK Mwenda, 'Court of Justice of the Common Market for Eastern and Southern Africa (COMESA)' in *Max Planck Encyclopedias of International Law* (Oxford University Press online edition) para 30.

[17] COMESA Treaty, art 41.

[18] ibid.

[19] COMESA Court of Justice, 'Staff Members', www.comesacourt.org/comesa-court-of-justice-staff-members.

[20] COMESA Court of Justice Rules of Procedure (adopted 2016), r 14.

II. The Dispute Resolution Process

The powers and functions of the Registrar are listed in Rule 11 of the COMESA Court of Justice Rules of Procedure, 2016. The scope of the functions discharged by the Institutional Assistants is therefore clearly detailed and limited. In terms of the dispute resolution process, the Registrar is responsible for acceptance, transmission and custody of the documents for cases, preparation of the cause list, attending all the sittings of the Court, implementing the instructions issued by the President and Principal Judge, keeping records of the Court, and arranging for the publication of reports of cases decided by the Court.[21] Further, the general functions of the Registrar include maintaining custody of the seals of the Court and assisting the Court, the President, the Principal Judge and the judges in all their official functions.[22] In practice, the Registrar and the staff of the Registry do not assist the judges further in the dispute resolution process. Occasionally, the clerk of the Registry may be requested to provide limited research assistance to the Judges.

The external researchers recruited by the Registry provide the substantive research assistance. The functions discharged by such External Assistants vary on a case-by-case basis, depending on the complexity and volume of the case in question.

Although the Registrar and some registry staff attend Court hearings, the judge's deliberations are closed-door and is not open to the Registry staff or the External Assistants.

In terms of drafting, the judges undertake the drafting themselves, with research assistance from their researchers, who are External Assistants. The Registry does not assist in the drafting stage; however, in practice, the Registrar may be unofficially tasked with checking or verifying specific research points. Additionally, once the judgment is drafted, the Registrar is tasked with checking for inconsistencies, not in terms of substance, but in the flow of the arguments, language and formatting.

Once the judges finalise the draft, the Registry gets the draft translated externally. The Registry does not have internal translators. Neither the Registry staff nor the Registrar plays a substantive role in the translations. The three official languages of COMESA are Arabic, English and French. In cases where the bench is bilingual or multilingual, the Court also uses external interpreters during court sessions. Interpreters may also be present during closed-door deliberations if judges so request.

The judgment is taken by majority and at present, there are no dissenting opinions in the COMESA Court of Justice.

III. Observations on the Role of Dispute Assistants

The Institutional Assistants of the Registry of the COMESA Court play a limited role in assisting judges with their decision-making functions. However, the Registrar's expertise and experience remain available to the judges with respect to substantive questions. External researchers, who are under the supervision and control of the judges, and

[21] ibid r 11.
[22] ibid.

assigned to a bench as a whole, assist the judges of the COMESA Court. The role of these External Researchers is presently determined on a case-by-case basis depending on the needs of the Court. Although they are hired by the Registry, they are under the supervision and control of the bench of judges. This suggests that the decision-making function is firmly within the control of the judges.

5

Commercial Arbitration Institutions

I. Institutional Overview and Structure

In this chapter, we aim to distil the practice of commercial arbitration institutions, while being mindful that they are certainly not all identical, and nor are the Dispute Assistants aiding their arbitrators. We have decided to cover this wealth of practice in one chapter owing to the significant commonalities in their organisational structure and procedures, including that none of the dispute settlement processes are state to state. In this chapter we examine the China International Economic and Trade Arbitration Commission (CIETAC), the German Arbitration Institute (DIS), International Chamber of Commerce Arbitration (ICC Arbitration), the Hong Kong International Arbitration Centre (HKIAC), the London Court of International Arbitration (LCIA), the Singapore International Arbitration Centre (SIAC), the Stockholm Chamber of Commerce (SCC) and the Swiss Chambers' Arbitration Institution (SCAI). We hope to highlight unique or differing characteristics of certain institutions wherever appropriate and aim to focus on the roles of Dispute Assistants in these institutions.

A. Adjudicators

A defining characteristic of international arbitration is that there is no standing court or tribunal which hears disputes, much unlike many international tribunals, which have a standing and pre-established roster of judges.[1] Individual arbitral tribunals are set up for each case, with the tribunal's exact composition varying according to the parties' agreement and the applicable arbitral rules. The Dispute Assistants of the institutions play a role in the appointment of arbitrators, to differing degrees, depending on the specific rules of the institution as well as the arbitration agreement. As this forms an essential step in the dispute resolution process of arbitration, we will cover this arbitrator selection process in more detail below in section II.

B. Dispute Assistants

Each arbitral institution examined has an Institutional Office or Secretariat, which is generally presided over by a single head, although the nomenclature differs. They are referred to

[1] G Born, 'Selection, Challenge and Replacement of Arbitrators in International Arbitration' in *International Commercial Arbitration*, 3rd edn (Wolters Kluwer, 2021) 1764.

as the Registrar in the LCIA[2] and SIAC,[3] the Secretary-General in the HKIAC,[4] the SCC,[5] the ICC Arbitration,[6] the DIS[7] and the CIETAC,[8] and the Executive Director in the SCAI.[9] They oversee a team of legal officers and administrators that varies in size between the institutions and are often subdivided into smaller case management teams.[10] In many of the institutions examined, the administration of the arbitration is undertaken by a 'court' that is assisted by the Institutional Office. The CIETAC has an organ called the Arbitration Court that oversees case administration. The CIETAC Secretariat is responsible only for the ordinary administrative duties of the Commission.[11] Similarly, the ICC International Court of Arbitration is responsible for the administration of the dispute resolution undertaken by the arbitral tribunals as per the ICC Rules.[12] The ICC Court is assisted by the Secretariat of the Court under the direction of its Secretary-General.[13] The LCIA Court is assisted by the Registrar of the LCIA,[14] and the SIAC Court is assisted by the SIAC Secretariat. The Board of the SCC also discharges similar functions, with the assistance of the SCC Secretariat.[15] Arbitrations under the Swiss Rules are administered by the Arbitration Court of the Swiss Arbitration Centre of the SCAI Secretariat. In DIS, there is an Arbitration Council and an Appointing Committee distinct from the Secretariat.[16]

In terms of assistants, tribunals may choose to be assisted by a tribunal secretary from the institution or a tribunal assistant (externally appointed),[17] usually with the consent of the parties to the dispute. However, the specific appointment of these assistants varies between institutions, as will be discussed below. The tribunal secretary/assistant acts under the supervision and control of the tribunal or, in some cases, the President of the tribunal. For example, in CIETAC, the role of tribunal secretary is filled by the Secretariat-appointed case manager (Institutional Assistant), leaving no room for an additional personal assistant.[18] HKIAC, on the other hand, encourages the use of its

[2] London Court of International Arbitration, 'Organisation', www.lcia.org/lcia/organisation.aspx.

[3] Singapore International Arbitration Centre, 'Our Team', www.siac.org.sg/about-us/our-team.

[4] Hong Kong International Arbitration Centre, 'Secretariat', www.hkiac.org/about-us/secretariat.

[5] Stockholm Chamber of Commerce Arbitration Institute, 'Contact Us', www.sccarbitrationinstitute.se/en/about-scc/contact-us.

[6] International Chamber of Commerce, 'Chairmanship and Secretary General', www.iccwbo.org/governance/chairmanship-and-secretary-general.

[7] German Arbitration Institute, 'Team', www.disarb.org/en/about-us/team.

[8] Although note that CIETAC actually maintains several Secretariats – one for each seat. See China International Economic and Trade Arbitration Commission, 'Secretariats', www.cietac.org/index.php?m=Page&a=index&id=35&l=en.

[9] Swiss Arbitration Centre, 'Leadership', www.swissarbitration.org/centre/leadership.

[10] See, eg, International Chamber of Commerce, 'Counsel Swiss Italian Team, ICC Dispute Resolution Services, Paris', www.iccwbo.org/careers/job-opportunities/counsel-swiss-italian-teamicc-dispute-resolution-services-paris/.

[11] China International Economic and Trade Arbitration Commission, CIETAC Arbitration Rules (2024), art 2(6).

[12] International Chamber of Commerce, ICC Arbitration Rules (2021) art 1(2).

[13] ibid art 1.5.

[14] See generally London Court of International Arbitration, LCIA Arbitration Rules (2020).

[15] Arbitration Institute of the Stockholm Chamber of Commerce, SCC Arbitration Rules (2023), art 11.

[16] German Arbitration Institute (DIS), DIS Arbitration Rules 2016, Annex I, r 14.

[17] Note that while 'tribunal secretary' is the term commonly used in academic writing, the designation of these assistants may vary. The HKIAC and the LCIA refer to them as 'tribunal secretaries', while the ICC, the SIAC, the SCAI and the SCC call them 'Administrative Secretaries'.

[18] D Wen and L Bergmann, 'Comparison between SCC Arbitration and CIETAC Arbitration' (15 April 2011) www.transnational-dispute-management.com/article.asp?key=1753; see also A Eernisse, 'Interviews

tribunal secretary service but does not otherwise assign one to the tribunal. The tribunal secretary service consists of members of the Secretariat (Institutional Assistant).[19] However, once they are assigned as a tribunal secretary, they are under the supervision and control of the tribunal. In SIAC, the rules allow the tribunal to appoint a member of the SIAC Secretariat as the Tribunal Secretary, after consulting the parties and with the approval of the Registrar.[20] In the ICC, staff members are not permitted to serve as 'administrative secretaries'.[21]

II. The Dispute Resolution Process

An arbitral proceeding always begins with a request for arbitration. Some, but not all, arbitral institutions conduct a basic pre-screening of the submissions received from the parties to ensure that it is not obviously inadmissible.[22] In the case of CIETAC, this pre-screening extends to the existence and validity of an arbitration agreement and the question of jurisdiction.[23] The Arbitration Court decides whether to dismiss a case for lack of jurisdiction at the pre-screening stage (before an arbitral tribunal is formed).[24] In HKIAC, the Proceedings Committee of the HKIAC Council is responsible for deciding whether an arbitration agreement under the Rules may exist or the arbitration has been properly commenced (before the arbitral tribunal is formed).[25] In ICC Arbitration, the Secretary-General of the Secretariat may refer the decision to the ICC Court of Arbitration on whether, prima facie, an arbitration agreement under the ICC Rules exists.[26] In SIAC, the Registrar has the authority to terminate the arbitration (without prejudice to the claimant) if the Notice of Arbitration does not comply with the specified requirements.[27] The Registrar of SIAC may also refer the matter to the SIAC Court to make a prima facie determination on whether/to what extent the arbitration should proceed.[28] However, the Registrar cannot terminate the arbitration on their own authority.[29] In the SCC, the SCC Board takes the decision on whether the SCC manifestly lacks jurisdiction over the dispute.[30] In SCIA, the Arbitration Court

with Our Editors: China Insights from Dr Li Hu of CIETAC' (*Kluwer Arbitration Blog*, 12 April 2020), www.arbitrationblog.kluwerarbitration.com/2020/04/12/interviews-with-our-editors-china-insights-from-dr-li-hu-of-cietac; CIETAC Arbitration Rules, r 13.4.

[19] HKIAC, 'Tribunal Secretary Service', www.hkiac.org/arbitration/tribunal-secretaries/tribunal-secretary-service; see also HKIAC Arbitration Rules 2024, r 13.4.

[20] Singapore International Arbitration Centre, SIAC Arbitration Rules (2016), r 24.

[21] ICC, '*Guidance Note to Parties and Arbitral Tribunal on the Conduct of Arbitrations under the ICC Rules of Arbitration*' (2021), para 218.

[22] Notable exceptions in this regard are the LCIA and the DIS.

[23] CIETAC Arbitration Rules, art 6.1. However, in practice, it is not unusual for this power to be referred to the tribunal if the jurisdiction is closely linked to the merits; see Wen and Bergmann (n 18) 2.

[24] CIETAC Arbitration Rules, r 6.7.

[25] HKIAC Arbitration Rules, r 19.5; HKIAC, 'Proceedings Committee', www.hkiac.org/about-us/council-members-and-committees/proceedings-committee.

[26] ICC Arbitration Rules, r 6.3. The ICC Court may then deny jurisdiction only if there is prima facie no chance that a valid arbitration agreement exists, although, by default, the tribunal is responsible

[27] SIAC Arbitration Rules, r 6.6.

[28] ibid r 8.2.

[29] ibid r 28.1. Note that the option to defer it to the tribunal is not expressly mentioned.

[30] SCC Arbitration Rules, art 11.

makes the decision on if there is manifestly no arbitration agreement referring to the SCIA rules, or if the claims are made under two or more arbitration agreements that are manifestly incompatible.[31]

Once the institution receives the request for arbitration and the response, the next step is to select the arbitral tribunal – ie, the adjudicators in the dispute. The arbitral tribunal typically consists of one or three arbitrators, though its precise composition varies depending on the applicable arbitration rules and the choice of parties. By default, the selection of an arbitral tribunal is done through party consensus. The procedure in each institution is as follows:

- In CIETAC, the Chairman of CIETAC may act as the appointing authority if the parties so designate or if the parties fail to make their appointments within the specified time limit.[32] The Chairman of CIETAC also has the responsibility to make decisions on challenges to arbitrators.[33] The Secretariat and the CIETAC Arbitration Court are not involved in the appointment process.[34]
- In HKIAC, this power rests with the Appointments Committee of the HKIAC Council, which has the power to decide the number of arbitrators,[35] and appoint the arbitrator(s), if the parties are unable to reach an agreement within the specified time periods.[36] The Proceedings Committee of the HKIAC Council is responsible for deciding challenges to appointment of an arbitrator.[37]
- In the DIS, the Secretariat advises the Arbitration Council on challenges[38] and provides names of possible arbitrators to the parties if requested to do so.[39] The Arbitration Council of the DIS decides on requests by a party that the arbitral tribunal be composed of a sole arbitrator (failing agreement between the parties on the number of arbitrators),[40] as well as any challenges to arbitrators.[41] The Appointing Committee of the DIS acts as the appointing authority if the parties cannot agree on the arbitrators within the specified time limit.[42]
- In the ICC, the Secretariat may be jointly requested by the parties to propose names of potential candidates to serve as arbitrators or non-confidential information on potential arbitrators. The ICC Court has the power to decide that the arbitration shall be undertaken by a sole arbitrator (if the parties are unable to agree on the number

[31] Swiss Rules of International Arbitration, art 5.1. Note that unlike in ICSID, this is only done if one of the parties raises an objection, not *ex officio*.

[32] CIETAC Arbitration Rules, arts 27–29.

[33] ibid arts 32–33.

[34] However, the Secretariat does play an indirect role by pre-screening candidates' qualifications before the responsible committee decides on their appointment to the Panel of Arbitrators maintained by CIETAC, from which arbitrators are to be appointed. See China International Economic and Trade Arbitration Commission, CIETAC Rules on the Conferral of Qualifications of Arbitrators, art 4(1).

[35] HKIAC Arbitration Rules, art 6.1.

[36] ibid arts 6.1, 7.2 and 8.1 (d); see also HKIAC, 'Appointments Committee', www.hkiac.org/about-us/council-members-and-committees/appointments-committee.

[37] ibid art 19.5; see also HKIAC, 'Proceedings Committee', www.hkiac.org/about-us/council-members-and-committees/proceedings-committee.

[38] See DIS Arbitration Rules 2016, Annex I, art 4.5, which reads 'As a basis for any decision of the Case Committees, the Secretariat shall prepare a written statement, which shall advise of any existing practice of other Case Committees in comparable cases and may contain non-binding recommendations.'

[39] ibid art. 9.2 read with Annex 1, art. 2.2.

[40] ibid art 10.2.

[41] ibid art 15.4.

[42] ibid arts 11–12.

of arbitrators),[43] appoint the arbitrator(s) if the parties are unable to agree within the specified time,[44] including the President of the tribunal.[45] The ICC Court decides on the appointment, conformation, challenges and replacement of arbitrators.[46] The parties may also agree that the Court's appointment of the arbitrator will occur in consultation between the parties and the Secretariat. In particular, the parties may agree that any such appointment will occur following a list procedure.[47]

- In the LCIA, the LCIA Court has the power to appoint arbitrators if the parties fail to do so within the specified time,[48] as well as decide on revocation, challenges and replacement.[49] In appointment, LCIA Secretariat assists the LCIA Court by proposing names of potential arbitrators as per the required qualifications.[50]
- In SIAC, the Registrar is given the power to decide the number of arbitrators in the absence of an agreement between the parties.[51] The President of the SIAC Court officially appoints all arbitrators and may appoint an arbitrator whose appointment has been made as per the arbitration agreement.[52] The SIAC Court has the responsibility to decide on the challenges, removal and replacement of arbitrators.[53]
- In SCC, the Board has the authority to decide on the number of arbitrators if the parties have not agreed to a specific number,[54] as well as make appointments of arbitrators where the parties have failed to agree on appointments within the specified time limits.[55] The Board also has the authority to decide on challenges to arbitrators and make appointments for replacement.[56]
- In SCIA, all arbitrator appointments are made by the Court, which has the authority to determine the number of arbitrators[57] as well as make appointments[58] if these have not been agreed between the parties within the specified time limits. The Court also decides on the challenges, removal and replacement of arbitrators.[59]

The role of Dispute Assistants in the process of hearings, deliberations and drafting in commercial arbitration has attracted considerable controversy in commercial arbitrations for a while now[60] and is usually less involved than in its investor-state counterpart.

[43] ICC Rules, r 12.2.
[44] ibid rr 12.3–12.4.
[45] ibid r 12.5.
[46] ibid rr 11.4, 14–15.
[47] Whereby the Secretariat will establish a list of candidates and submit it to the parties (for example, by allowing the parties to strike a limited number of candidates and rank the others by order of preference). See ICC (n 21) 38.
[48] LCIA Rules, arts 5.1 and 7. See also LCIA, 'LCIA Guidance Note to Arbitrator' (2020) art 7.5, which reads: 'The default position under the LCIA Rules is that the LCIA Court will select and formally appoint the arbitrators. Accordingly, any references to "appointments" by parties, or third parties in the Arbitration Agreement or otherwise, will be treated by the LCIA as "nominations" in accordance with Article 7.1.'
[49] ibid arts 10, 12.
[50] LCIA Guidance Note 7.5.
[51] SIAC Rules, r 19.1.
[52] ibid rr 19.2–19.3, 21–23.
[53] ibid rr 27–30.
[54] SCC Rules, art 16.
[55] ibid art 17.
[56] ibid arts 19–20.
[57] SCIA Rules, art 9.
[58] ibid arts 10–11.
[59] ibid arts 13–15.
[60] See, eg, C Partasides, 'The Fourth Arbitrator? The Role of Secretaries to Tribunals in International Arbitration' (2002) 18 *Arbitration International* 151.

The involvement of Institutional Assistants in this phase is uncommon but not entirely unheard of. In CIETAC, it is worth recalling that the administrative secretary who assists in these steps is a part of the Secretariat.[61]

The tribunal secretaries aid arbitrators to differing degrees in these stages. In some instances, the institution may have expressly permitted the involvement of Tribunal Secretaries in a particular stage, while in other cases, there may be prohibitions. In many other instances, the institutions do not have any express prohibition which may be interpreted as permissive. We will examine these further below.

Tribunal Secretaries are likely to attend the hearings in all commercial arbitration institutions.[62]

As for deliberations, the ICC Arbitration,[63] the HKIAC[64] and the CIETAC[65] explicitly allow for their attendance, though data on the actual participation rate are unavailable. As for LCIA, SCAI, SIAC and SCC, the attendance of tribunal secretaries at deliberations is not regulated, although in the absence of an explicit prohibition, it seems likely they will attend.

In the LCIA, although the institution do not endorse any specific tasks, they provide a list of tasks that may be proposed by the arbitral tribunal to the parties for their consent. This list includes 'attend(ing) hearings, meetings, and deliberations; and (t)he extent, if any, to which the Tribunal Secretary carries out substantive tasks, such as summarising submissions, reviewing authorities, and preparing first drafts of awards, or sections of awards, and procedural orders'.[66]

In the case of the tribunal secretaries in the SCAI and the CIETAC, while there is no clear evidence of a permissive institutional practice, their vague regulations and a robust national culture of drafting assistance suggest a strong probability of assistants being involved in operative drafting.[67] In the case of the SIAC, there is no indication of either an institutional practice or a national tradition suggesting the participation of the tribunal secretaries in operative drafting. However, the language of its regulations is vague enough that an arbitrator who is inclined to delegate such duties to their assistant would not face significant hurdles.[68] Notably, the ICC,[69] the HKIAC[70] and the SCC[71] all

[61] *CIETAC Arbitration Rules*, art 13.4.

[62] See, for example, ICC, 'Note to Parties and Arbitral Tribunals on the Conduct of Arbitration under the ICC Rules of Arbitration' (2021) para 224.

[63] ibid para 185.

[64] HKIAC, 'Guidelines on the Use of a Secretary to the Arbitral Tribunal' (2014) art 3.4.

[65] Wen and Bergmann (n 18) 1.

[66] LCIA Guidance Note, para 202.

[67] GK Kohler and A Rigozzi, *International Arbitration: Law and Practice in Switzerland*, 2nd edn (Oxford University Press, 2015) 312; A Eernisse, 'Interviews with Our Editors: China Insights from Dr Li Hu of CIETAC' (*Kluwer Arbitration Blog*, 12 April 2020), www.arbitrationblog.kluwerarbitration.com/2020/04/12/interviews-with-our-editors-china-insights-from-dr-li-hu-of-cietac; Federal Tribunal (Tribunal Fédéral), 21 May 2015, 4A_709/2014, MN 3.2.1–3.2.2.

[68] SIAC, '*Practice Note for Administered Cases – On the Appointment of Administrative Secretaries*' (2015) s 2. However, it must be stressed that this is little more than an educated guess, as there is simply not enough data to support a definitive empirical conclusion.

[69] ICC, 'Note to Parties and Arbitral Tribunals on the Conduct of Arbitration under the ICC Rules of Arbitration' (2021) para 224.

[70] HKIAC, *Guidelines on the Use of a Secretary to the Arbitral Tribunal* (2014) s 3.4(e)–(f). Illustrative examples of non-substantive parts are 'procedural histories and chronologies of events'. In practice, parties seem receptive to this assistance in drafting; see HKIAC, *Report on the Use of HKIAC Tribunal Secretary Service* (3 September 2018), www.hkiac.org/node/2299.

[71] SCC, *Guideline for Arbitrators* (2020) 9.

have detailed descriptions of the permissible tasks of tribunal secretaries, which are limited to non-substantive drafting. Non-substantive drafting includes drafting of the procedural history, facts and summaries of arguments. In these institutions, there is a strong prohibition against delegating any decision-making powers.

The Young ICCA Task Force survey was conducted in 2012 and 2013,[72] and based on this survey, the Young ICCA Guide on Arbitral Secretaries was published in 2014.[73] According to the 2012 survey, 66.8 per cent of the participants supported the secretaries performing legal research for the arbitral tribunal and 60.2 per cent supported them drafting procedural orders. However, only 45.2 per cent of the participants supported the practice that secretaries draft parts of the award, and even fewer (38.7 per cent) supported the secretaries analysing the parties' submissions.[74]

Once an award is drafted, some institutions require the arbitrators to submit the draft to the Secretariat or some other body before the institution renders the award. The same procedure exists in the SIAC, but there it is the Registrar who has to approve the award and make suggestions.[75] The CIETAC rules[76] envisages the same power, although it is unclear which body exercises this. The Secretariat of the DIS can also make suggestions as to form and substance, but in this case, neither is binding upon the arbitrators.[77] In the ICC Arbitration, the ICC Court (with inputs from the Secretariat) has the final authority on questions of form and may also make suggestions as to the substance of a decision. However, the latter are not binding on the tribunal.[78]

III. Observations on the Role of Dispute Assistants

Even though the procedures of commercial arbitration are similar across the institutions, the Secretariat's and tribunal secretaries' involvement may vary significantly. In all of the institutions examined, it is not the Institutional Office, but rather a distinct ('court')-type body that is responsible for decisions with respect to the admissibility of arbitration, appointment of arbitrators, challenges, removal and replacement of arbitrators.

With respect to the tribunal secretaries' role, clear and limiting rules exist in the ICC Arbitration, HKIC and SCC. The LCIA adopts a more permissive approach, allowing the parties to agree on permissible tasks. Notably, the other institutions have somewhat vague rules regulating the use of tribunal secretaries. Vague (or non-existent) rules leave room for interpretation and allow for the use of Dispute Assistants. However, the lack of clarity may have contributed to the controversies that have arisen with respect to the role of Dispute Assistants.

[72] International Council for Commercial Arbitration, *Young ICCA Guide on Arbitral Secretaries, The ICCA Reports No 1* (2014) Annex B, 55–68, and Annex C, 69–86.

[73] ibid.

[74] ibid 2.

[75] *SIAC Arbitration Rules*, r 32.3.

[76] *CIETAC Rules*, art 54.

[77] *DIS Arbitration Rules* 2018, art 39.3 read with German Arbitration Institute (DIS), DIS Arbitration Rules 2016, art 2.2.

[78] *ICC Arbitration Rules*, art 34.

6

The United States–Mexico–Canada Agreement

I. Institutional Overview and Structure

The United States–Mexico–Canada Agreement (USMCA), also known as the Canada–United States–Mexico Agreement (CUSMA) or the Tratado entre México, Estados Unidos y Canadá (T-MEC), includes several modes of dispute settlement concerning different subject matters. This chapter focuses on the state-to-state dispute settlement mechanism under Chapter 31 USMCA, and the role of Dispute Assistants in such disputes.

A. Adjudicators

Disputes under Chapter 31 are adjudicated by a panel. Parties may appoint panellists from a pre-established roster maintained by the Parties;[1] however, appointment from the pre-established roster is not mandatory, and parties have appointed external panellists.[2]

Article 31.8 USMCA sets out the qualifications which roster members and panellists must meet. Each roster member and panellist must meet four requirements:[3]

1. Have expertise or experience in international law, international trade, other matters covered by the USMCA, or the resolution of disputes arising under international trade agreements;
2. Be selected on the basis of objectivity, reliability, and sound judgement;
3. Be independent of, and not affiliated with or take instructions from, a Party; and
4. Comply with the Code of Conduct established by the USMCA Commission.

It is worth mentioning that additional requirements exist for disputes arising under other chapters of the USMCA – for example, Chapter 23 (Labor) and 24 (Environment). In such disputes, the panellists other than the Chair must have expertise or experience in labour law or practice, or environmental law or practice, respectively.[4] In disputes

[1] United States-Mexico-Canada Agreement (USMCA) (signed 30 November 2018, entered into force 1 July 2020), art 31.8.

[2] If panellists are appointed outside the roster, the conditions in art 31.9 USMCA must be followed.

[3] USMCA art 31.8 (2).

[4] ibid art 31.8(3).

arising under other chapters, the disputing parties are to select panellists to 'ensure that the necessary expertise is available on the panel'.[5]

Panels are, by default, composed of five members, but the parties to the dispute may agree to compose a panel of only three members.[6] The parties first endeavour to appoint the panel chair by consensus. If the parties cannot reach a consensus, the panel chair is appointed by one party chosen by lot, in which case the chair may not be a citizen of that party.[7] After the panel chair is chosen, the disputing parties proceed to select the other panellists. If the dispute involves two parties, each will then appoint a panellist (or two). Where the dispute involves three parties, the two complainants appoint one each, and the respondent appoints two.[8] It is worth noting that, rather unusually in international dispute settlements, these panellists must be citizens of the other party to the dispute. The Dispute Assistants do not play a role in the selection of panellists; however, they assist the parties administratively, for example, by contacting the panellists once they are selected, collecting the letters of conflict of interest from the panellists etc.

B. Dispute Assistants

The USMCA Secretariat for Chapter 31 disputes is organised in a decentralised fashion. It consists of three Sections, each maintained by one of the state parties.[9] According to the Rules of Procedure for Chapter 31, only one of the Sections is a 'responsible Section of the Secretariat' for a dispute.[10] The Section of the Secretariat of the responding party in a dispute is tasked with supporting the panel. In practice, however, there may be collaboration with the staff of the other Sections when necessary.[11] At present,[12] the US and Mexican Sections comprise three staff members, while the Canadian Section comprises five staff members.[13] The staff are not necessarily lawyers. The tenure of the staff in each Section varies depending on the Section's internal procedures.[14] The staff of the Secretariat only deal with matters relating to case administration, including

[5] ibid art 31.8(4).

[6] ibid art 31.9(1)(a), 2(a). As of November 2025, in Chapter 31 of the Dispute Settlement, three-person panels have been established and composed in all four two-party disputes (*Canada – Dairy Tariff Rate Quota Allocation Measures*, Panel Report, CDA-USA-2021-31-010 (20 December 2021) (*Canada – Dairy TRQ Allocation Measures I*); *Canada – Dairy Tariff Rate Quota Allocation Measures*, Panel Report, CDA-USA-2023-31-01 (10 November 2023) (*Canada — Dairy TRQ Allocation Measures II*); Panel Report, *United States – Safeguard Measure on Imports of Crystalline Silicon Photovoltaic Products* (*US – Photovoltaic Safeguard Measures*), USA-CDA-2021-10.12-01 (adopted 9 December 2022); Panel Report, *Mexico – Measures Concerning Genetically Engineered Corn* (*Mexico – GE Corn*), MEX-USA-2023-31-01 (circulated 21 December 2023)), while in the one three-party dispute, the panel consisted of five members (*United States – Automotive Rules of Origin, Panel Report*, USA-MEX-CDA-2022-31-01 (14 December 2022) para 19.)

[7] USMCA, arts 31.9 (1)(b), (2)(b).

[8] ibid arts 31.9 (1)(d), (2)(d).

[9] ibid art 30.6.

[10] Rules of Procedure for Chapter 31 of the USMCA (entered into force 1 July 2020) (hereinafter 'Rules of Procedure'), art 2.

[11] This has been the practice in certain cases under the NAFTA.

[12] As on 26 August 2024.

[13] See CUSMA/USMCA/TMEC Secretariat, 'The Secretariat' (Government of Canada, last modified 9 January 2024), www.can-mex-usa-sec.org/secretariat/index.aspx?lang=eng. Note that the US and Mexican Sections are also responsible for handling the administration of other Regional Trade Agreements.

[14] For example, it has been noted that in the US Section, the staff are not hired for a specific fixed term.

arranging meetings and other logistical support for hearings.[15] As will be detailed in section II below, the Sections do not assist the panel in the substantive decision-making functions. These staff of the Sections are Institutional Assistants.

Panellists are allowed to hire one personal 'assistant',[16] defined as 'a person who, under the terms of appointment of a panellist, conducts research for or provides support to a panellist'. Panellists have utilised this provision in practice.[17] However, past practice under the North American Free Trade Agreement (NAFTA) and the Canada–European Union Comprehensive Economic and Trade Agreement (CETA), from the limited number of panel reports available, suggests that panellists use the provision sparingly.[18] These assistants are External Assistants. However, it is pertinent to note that unlike some of the other External Assistants (for example, in the COMESA Court of Justice), the External Assistants to USMCA Arbitrators are not hired by the Secretariats. Further, they are not assigned to the entire bench, but rather work for the individual panellist.

The staff members of the Secretariats and as well as the assistants are bound by Article 9 of the Code of Conduct.[19]

We examine the role of these Dispute Assistants in the dispute resolution process of proceedings under Chapter 31 of the USMCA.

II. The Dispute Resolution Process

The dispute settlement process begins with a complainant party (or two, as in *US – Auto ROOs*) requesting consultations with the respondent party over a trade measure it considers to be in violation of the USMCA.[20] The complainant party sends the consultation request and request for establishment of the panel to the respondent party's Section.[21] If the consultations fail to resolve the matter, the complainant may request the establishment of a panel.[22]

In practice, the Secretariat convenes the panel for a preliminary meeting to introduce themselves, answer any questions and explain other administrative issues (for example, payment processing). In at least one case so far, this first internal meeting served to set the procedural timeline for the proceedings.[23]

[15] Rules of Procedure, art 3.

[16] ibid art 12.

[17] For example: Panel Report, *United States – Automotive Rules of Origin*, USA-MEX-CDA-2022-31-01 (14 December 2022) para 19 (*US – Auto ROOs*); Panel Report, *Canada – Dairy TRQ Allocation Measures*, CDA-USA-2021-31-010 (20 December 2021) para 6; Panel Report, *Canada – Dairy TRQ Allocation Measures*, CDA-USE-2023-31-01 (10 November 2023) para 12. They may be allowed to have more than one assistant at the discretion of the parties.

[18] With respect to the practice under CETA, see K Claussen, 'Old and New Dispute Secretariats' in Symposium on J Pauwelyn and K Pelc, 'Who Guards the Guardians of the System? The Role of the Secretariat in WTO Dispute Settlement'. Claussen notes that only half the panellists in the six panel reports available from the last 10 years have relied on assistants, and only one of the six panel reports makes mention of the functions those assistants served.

[19] Rules of Procedure art 5, read with USMCA, art 31.4.

[20] United States–Mexico–Canada Agreement (signed 30 November 2018, entered into force 1 July 2020) Code of Conduct for Dispute Settlement Proceedings under Chapter 31, art 9.

[21] Rules of Procedure, art 6.1.

[22] ibid art 31.6(4).

[23] Panel Report, *US – Auto ROOs*, 18.

The parties submit their written pleadings to the responsible Section of the Secretariat, which distributes them to the panel and makes them available through the electronic filing system.[24] Assistance at this stage is the main support that the Secretariat provides. This is critical in arbitration proceedings, which are technical and fact-heavy. The panel will then conduct the hearings, at which the Section legal staff and the assistants will be present.[25] The Section staff provide administrative and logistical support in the proceedings.[26]

Once the hearing concludes, the panel will begin drafting the report. As mentioned earlier, the Secretariat staff do not play any role in the substantive aspects of the case and are not involved in deliberations. The drafting is done exclusively by the panellists. If any panellist has an assistant, they may attend the deliberations as their supervisor requires. The assistants do not usually undertake substantive drafting, but may contribute to the generic/descriptive parts of the draft. This is entirely dependent on the working style of the adjudicator.

Separate opinions are possible, and the latest report issued in *Canada – Dairy TRQ Allocation Measures* contains one.[27] Past practice under NAFTA shows a tendency to try to reach a consensus in the final judgment through discussion and debate rather than issuing separate opinions.

III. Observations on the Role of Dispute Assistants

The Institutional Assistants of the Secretariat provide administrative and logistical assistance for the proceedings, but do not provide substantive assistance. However, the Secretariat has information about the practices of past USMCA panels regarding procedural matters, timelines etc. and may share that information with panels when necessary. Even in such cases, it is worth noting that the Secretariat's formal role is still restricted to administrative support.

Additionally, the timelines for the cases under the USMCA, and previously under the NAFTA, are very short. Therefore, the work for the panellists is intense and time-consuming. The panellists undertake the bulk of the substantive work independently, including research, preparation for hearings, and drafting. In some cases, they may choose to hire an External Assistant.[28] The support provided by the assistants usually relates to research on case law and preparation for hearings, and may include other tasks depending on the working style of the adjudicator. The remuneration offered to assistants is minimal and accordingly attracts students without significant prior work experience. This often limits the assistants' role to providing research on case law or making summaries.

[24] Rules of Procedure, art 6.1.
[25] Panel Report, *US – Auto ROOs*, 38.
[26] Rules of Procedure, art 3.
[27] USMCA, art 31.17(5).
[28] As noted above, an assistant has been hired in three out of the five cases so far under Chapter 31 disputes.

7

The East African Court of Justice

I. Institutional Overview and Structure

The East African Court of Justice (EACJ) is the Court of the East African Community, established under Article 9 of the East African Community Treaty. The EACJ is tasked with ensuring adherence to law in the interpretation and application of the East African Community Treaty,[1] and has jurisdiction on disputes concerning the interpretation and application of the Treaty. The EACJ may receive reference from partner states,[2] the Secretary-General of the East African Community[3] or legal/natural persons.[4] Although initially conceived as a court dealing with trade, investment and economic integration,[5] the EACJ also deals with human rights protection in the East African Community.[6]

A. Adjudicators

The EACJ consists of two divisions: the First Instance Division (Trial Court), with original jurisdiction to determine any matter at first instance; and the Appellate Division, with appellate jurisdiction and original jurisdiction with respect to preliminary rulings, advisory opinions and arbitration matters.[7] At present, the First Instance Division has five judges and the Appellate Division also has five judges. The Summit of the Partner States elects the judges for a seven-year term.[8] Judges are selected from 'among persons recommended by the Partner States who are of proven integrity, impartiality and independence and who fulfil the conditions required in their own countries for high judicial office, or who are jurists of recognised competence'.[9]

Dispute Assistants do not play a role in the appointment of the judges of the EACJ.

[1] Treaty Establishing the East African Community (signed 30 November 1999, entered into force 7 July 2000) (hereinafter 'EAC Treaty'), art 23.
[2] ibid art 28.
[3] ibid art 29.
[4] ibid art 30.
[5] J Gathii, 'Mission Creep or a Search for Relevance: The East African Court of Justice's Human Rights Strategy' (2013–14) 24 *Duke Journal of Comparative and International Law* 261.
[6] TP Milej, 'Human Rights Protection by International Courts: What Role for the East African Court of Justice?' (2018) 26(1) *African Journal of International and Comparative Law* 108.
[7] EAC Treaty, arts 32, 34, 35A and 36.
[8] ibid arts 24.2 and 25. 1.
[9] ibid art 24.1.

B. Dispute Assistants

The judges are supported by a Registry, consisting of a registrar, several legal clerks, and a researcher and administrative staff. The Registry is primarily responsible for the custody of all documents filed with the Court.[10] Besides the central registry in Arusha, Tanzania, there are also five sub-registries, each staffed by one clerk, in Dar-es-Salaam, Tanzania; Nairobi, Kenya; Kampala, Uganda; Kigali, Rwanda; and Bujumbura, Burundi.[11] The EAC Council of Ministers appoints the Registrar from 'among citizens of the Partner States qualified to hold such high judicial office in their respective Partner States'.[12] They are Institutional Assistants.

II. The Dispute Resolution Process

A partner state initiating proceedings must first file a reference, which the Registrar will receive and document. Upon the filing of a claim or reference, the Registrar will issue a notification to the respondent requiring the respondent to file a statement of defence or response.[13] Once the parties have submitted their written pleadings, the Court will hold a pre-trial conference where the judges and parties will primarily discuss how to proceed in terms of procedure.[14] At this stage, and at every stage of the proceedings thereafter, the primary responsibility of the Registry is to provide the judges with a complete and up-to-date file of the case. The Registrar will also liaise with the judges to ensure the smooth administration of the matter and will be the point of communication between the Court and the parties.

The Court will then proceed to hold hearings.[15] At least one clerk from the Registry attends the hearings. The clerk performs administrative tasks to ensure the smooth conduct of the hearings and may advise the judges on questions of procedure should it become necessary to do so.

Usually, after the closing of the hearings, the judges deliberate and reach a position on the verdict, and then one of the judges is tasked with drafting a decision for approval by the others. Deliberations include only the judges and are confidential.[16] At the drafting stage, the Registry continues to provide support, especially through the research officer, who may assist with researching specific legal questions and collecting evidence. Given that the caseload of the Court has somewhat exceeded original expectations, it is now not unusual for the Court to direct research requests toward the other officials of the Registry if the research officer is already handling other cases.

[10] Rules of Procedure of the Treaty for the Establishment of the East African Community (entered into force 7 July 2000) (hereinafter 'Rules of Procedure'), r 7.1.

[11] East African Court of Justice, *Court Manual: A Practical Guide to the Law and Practice of the East African Court of Justice* (November 2020) 21.

[12] EAC Treaty, art 45.

[13] Rules of Procedure, rr 25, 28.

[14] ibid r 63.

[15] ibid r 71.

[16] ibid r 78.

The Registry may also support a dissenting judge similarly since dissents are expressly allowed.[17]

Finally, once the judgment is drafted and the judges have agreed to it, it is delivered in open court.[18]

III. Observations on the Role of Dispute Assistants

The EACJ is an example of how the functions of Institutional Assistants can gradually evolve as new developments demand it. While the Registry is formally only intended to file and manage documents for the Court, the increasing caseload has driven the judges to rely on the Registry for assistance in their judicial work. While this assistance is, of course, limited compared to many other dispute settlement mechanisms, the fact that it exists at all shows that such an evolution of functions is a response to specific needs of a Court and aids the Court in successfully fulfilling its mandate.

[17] ibid r 79.3.
[18] ibid r 79.1.

8

The Economic Community of West African States Court of Justice

I. Institutional Overview and Structure

The principal legal organ of the Economic Community of West African States (ECOWAS) is the Court of Justice of ECOWAS (hereinafter 'ECOWAS Court'). From the inception of the integration process, the ECOWAS founding fathers were mindful of the key role an independent judicial organ should play in integrating the Member States. Therefore, Article 11 of the 1975 Treaty Establishing ECOWAS provided for a 'Tribunal of the Community'. The 1991 Protocol on the Court outlined the rules governing the status, constitution and jurisdiction of the regional judicial body, the ECOWAS Court. The 1993 Revised Treaty of ECOWAS confirmed the importance of the Court in Article 15 by establishing the Court of Justice of the Community. The ECOWAS Court is an independent institution with the power to pronounce binding judgments on the Member States, the institutions of the Community and on individuals and corporate bodies. The essential role of the ECOWAS Court is to ensure observance of law and justice in the interpretation and application of the Treaty, as well as other matters identified therein, including adjudicating cases alleging the violation of human rights in any Member State from 2005.[1]

A. Adjudicators

The Court is composed of five judges, appointed by the Authority from nationals of Member States. The Authority consists of heads of state and government of ECOWAS.[2] The judges are persons of high moral character, and possess the qualification required in their respective countries for appointment to the highest judicial office, or are recognised jurists in international law.[3] The Authority appoints the judges for a once-renewable

[1] Protocol Relating to the Community Court of Justice of the Economic Community of West African States (ECOWAS Protocol) (adopted 6 July 1991, entered into force 5 November 1996), art 9; as amended by Amending the Preamble and Articles 1, 2, 9 and 30 of Protocol A/P.1/7/91 Relating to the Community Court of Justice and Article 4(1) of the English Version of the Said Protocol (adopted 19 January 2005) (Supplementary Protocol) A/SP.1/01/05.

[2] Treaty of the Economic Community of West African States (Revised Treaty) (signed 24 July 1993, entered into force 23 August 1995), art 7.

[3] ECOWAS Protocol, art 3.

term of five years.[4] The judges, in turn, elect the President and the Vice-President from amongst their number for a renewable term of three years. The President is responsible for the administration of the Court and presides over the hearings and deliberations.[5]

The Dispute Assistants do not play a role in the appointment of the judges of the ECOWAS Court.

B. Dispute Assistants

The Institutional Office of the Court is headed by the Chief Registrar.[6] In a departure from Rule 9(3) of the Rules of Court, the Chief Registrar is no longer a fixed-term appointment (of six years), but rather a professional civil servant for continuity and institutional memory. The Chief Registrar discharges the following responsibilities:

a) Assisting the Court, the President, and the Judges with their official functions.[7]
b) The acceptance, transmission and custody of documents, and effecting service.[8]
c) Having custody of the seals of the Court and being in charge of the records and publications of the Court.[9]

The Chief Registrar[10] coordinates the interdepartmental activities of the Court. They are assisted by the Deputy Chief Registrar and three Registrars. The Registry Department comprises five divisions: Judicial Process & Case Management; Judicial Certified Translation & Interpretation; Verbatim Reports; Judicial Records, Archives & Publications; and Appeals, Arbitration & Enforcement. Of relevance here is the Judicial Process & Case Management division, which is responsible for the receipt, processing and service of court processes. The role of the Registry is limited to case management, through the receipt of files, and communicating between the relevant actors. Presently, there are 17 lawyers working in the Registry Department, but they do not take part in the judicial work of the judges. They are Institutional Assistants.

In addition to the Registry, the Court has an Administration and Finance Department and a Research and Documentation Department, each headed by a separate Director. The Directors of these two Departments and the Deputy Chief Registrar report to the President of the Court. The President is also responsible for administrative matters like the approval of leave and performance evaluation of the Directors and Chief Registrar. The Chief Registrar is a higher rank than the Directors of these Departments. However, they do not supervise the Directors or even receive their work for review.

The Research and Documentation Department performs the bulk of the judicial assistance work in the Court. The Department presently comprises four non-lawyers

[4] ibid art 4.
[5] ibid art 7.
[6] ibid.
[7] Court of Justice of the Economic Community of West African States, Rules of the Court of Justice of ECOWAS (effective date 2002) (hereinafter 'Rules of Procedure'), art 14(2).
[8] ibid art 14(1).
[9] ibid art 15.
[10] It is equivalent to the Professional and Higher categories as per the International Civil Servant Commission, United Nations Common System of Salaries, Allowances and Benefits (UN Grade scale).

who work in the library and six lawyers, including the Director. The Director allocates work between the legal research team. They are also Institutional Assistants, and staff are not assigned to a specific judge; each staff member may work for multiple judges at a time. The Department also prepares and updates an index of cases, which are categorised based on subject matter, that may be used in their research and drafting. This categorisation function is essential for tracking the jurisprudence of the Court across subject matter.

In addition to the divisions that work for the Court as a whole, the judges also have an Executive Assistant (EA) who works for them individually and form a part of the judge's Chambers. The EAs are lawyers with at least seven years of relevant experience and at a fairly senior level. The judge has complete discretion in selecting their EA. The Court formally hires the EAs upon their selection. The Human Resources division conducts minimal intervention in the selection of the EAs. Any intervention is restricted to verifying that the person chosen by the judge is a qualified lawyer and possesses the minimum experience and qualifications for the role. As the EA is attached to the judge, they assist the judge during their tenure. They are Assigned Assistants.

The next section examines the role of these Dispute Assistants during the course of proceedings before the ECOWAS Court.

II. The Dispute Resolution Process

Cases are brought before the Court by an application addressed to the Court Registry.[11] This application shall set out the subject matter of the dispute and the parties involved, and shall contain a summary of the argument put forward as well as the plea of the plaintiff.[12] The Deputy Chief Registrar ensures that an application made to the Court includes the relevant documents and complies with the requirements of the Rules of Procedure, with support from the legal staff of the Registry Department. In case of a defect, they grant the party 30 days to rectify the error.[13] At this stage, the Registry performs a preliminary review of the application, but exclusively to ensure that the applicant has complied with the Rules of Procedure. If the applicant does not regularise the application within the prescribed deadline, the Court hears the party and takes a decision on the application's admissibility.[14]

Upon receipt of the application, the Chief Registrar of the Court immediately serves notice of the application and all documents on the other party, and the other party files their grounds for defence.[15] The parties also file a reply or counterstatement, rejoinder and any other briefs or documents to support their written submissions.[16] All the documents are addressed to the Chief Registrar of the Court and received by the Registry Department.[17] When the registry receives the case file, they immediately send it out for

[11] ECOWAS Protocol, art 11(1).
[12] ibid.
[13] Rules of Procedure, art 33.
[14] ibid art 33(7).
[15] ECOWAS Protocol, art 11(2).
[16] ibid art 13.
[17] ibid art 13(3).

translations if the judges on the bench are not fluent in the language of the case. This is the primary role fulfilled by the Institutional Office and its Institutional Assistants.

The Court hears cases in three-member benches, which are constituted by the President of the Court. The President also assigns a case to a bench and nominates a Judge Rapporteur for the case.[18] Once the case has been added to the cause list, the Research and Documentation Wing begins working on the case file, with the Director allocating work amongst the lawyers in the team.

The President may fix a date on which the Judge Rapporteur will present their preliminary report to the Court. The Judge Rapporteur also recommends to the bench as to whether preparatory steps (such as a preparatory inquiry) or an oral hearing are appropriate. After considering the Judge Rapporteur's recommendations, the bench decides what actions should be taken. If there are oral proceedings,[19] the Chief Registrar, their Deputy or one of the Registrars attends the sittings of the Court[20] and draws up the minutes of every hearing.[21]

After the proceedings are complete, the Research and Documentation Department shares its draft with the Judge Rapporteur. The Institutional Assistants of the Research and Documentation Department also assists the Judge Rapporteur with research as requested. As mentioned earlier, the judges also have their EAs who undertake research and prepare drafts for them. Once the Judge Rapporteur receives a draft from the Research and Documentation Department, they may compare the draft with the work undertaken by their EA. During this stage, there are usually communications between the Judge Rapporteur and the Research and Documentation Department regarding specific issues in the draft. This shows a balance between the work undertaken by Institutional Assistants and Assigned Assistants in order to produce the best legal outcome. Once the Judge Rapporteur finalises the draft, they share it with the other two members of the bench for deliberation.

Deliberations consist of the judges on the bench and their EAs, although the EAs usually participate only when asked by their judge. There is a practice of the staff and Director of the Research and Documentation Department being asked to join in the deliberations; however, often they do not participate. This may be due to the need to maintain neutrality, as the Research and Documentation Department works for all judges on the bench and cannot appear to take sides in the case of disagreement or diverging opinions on issues. The judges may send specific questions or issues to the Research and Documentation Department to prepare notes or papers relating to the case.

There are no dissenting or separate opinions in the Court, as there is only one decision in each dispute, which is taken by a majority of the members. The Court's deliberations are entirely secret. Judges who disagree with the conclusions reached by the Judge Rapporteur can ask for assistance from the Research and Documentation Department while putting together relevant arguments for the deliberations. The judge

[18] Rules of Procedure Definitions.
[19] ibid art 40.
[20] ibid art 16.
[21] ibid art 49.

may also uses their EA for such research. Thereafter, there are deliberations, and the bench decides by majority vote.

The judgment is drafted in one of the official languages of the Court, depending on the Judge Rapporteur, and thereafter is translated into the other two languages of the Court. In practice, there may be instances where the translated judgment needs corrections, as the translators are not legally trained. Such corrections may necessitate further proofreading by the Research and Documentation Department, the judges or their EAs. However, this has not been possible in every case due to the caseload and the lack of sufficient resources with the Department.

III. Observations on the Role of Dispute Assistants

The ECOWAS Court has a robust institutional structure of Dispute Assistants, with Institutional Assistants as part of the Registry and the Research and Documentation Department, and Assigned Assistants called EAs.

There is a fine balance struck in the ECOWAS Court: on the one hand, the judges receive assistance from the Research and Documentation Department and the Registry, and thus gain from the institutional knowledge of a standing department. At the same time, the judges also have individual assistants (EAs) with whom they can share more private debate and brainstorming sessions.

9

The European Court of Human Rights

I. Institutional Overview and Structure

The European Court of Human Rights (ECtHR), as it stands today,[1] is a permanent regional court which adjudicates on the alleged violations of rights under the European Convention on Human Rights.

A. Adjudicators

The ECtHR presently comprises of 46 judges – that is, the number of judges is equal to the number of contracting parties. There are two phases in the election process: the national phase, where each contracting party nominates three candidates; and the second phase, where the majority of the Parliamentary Assembly of the Council of Europe elects the judge from the three candidates.[2] The plenary Court elects its President and two Vice-Presidents for a three-year term.[3] The President heads the Court and is responsible for directing the work and administration of the Court. The Vice-Presidents of the Court assist the President in their functions. The Dispute Assistants do no play a role in the appointment of the judges of the ECtHR.

The judges of the Court are organised into five administrative Sections.[4] The Court sits in any of the following formations: in a single-judge formation; in Committees of three judges; in Chambers of seven judges; and in a Grand Chamber of 17 judges.[5] It is within the five administrative Sections that the Committees and Chambers are composed.[6] In cases before Chambers, the national judge of the respondent state is required to be part of the Chamber. Therefore, the Court organises the Sections to ensure a balance in the caseload, taking into account the state parties with a high

[1] See Protocol No 11 to the Convention for the Protection of Human Rights and Fundamental Freedoms, Restructuring the Control Machinery established thereby (1994, entered into force 1 November 1998), replacing the former part-time monitoring bodies the European Commission of Human Rights and the European Court of Human Rights.

[2] European Convention on Human Rights (signed 4 November 1950, entered into force 3 September 1953) (ECHR), art 22.

[3] Rules of Court of the European Court of Human Rights (as amended 1 January 2020) (hereinafter 'Rules of the Court'), r 8

[4] ibid r 25.

[5] ECHR, art 26(1).

[6] Rules of the Court, r 27(2).

caseload. When splitting the Court into Sections, the Court also considers the need for an even geographical representation across the Sections to ensure complementarity in legal cultures and language.[7] The composition of the Section is reshuffled every three years to maintain a balance between heavy caseload members, gender ratio, geographical origin of the judges etc. Each Section has its own President and Vice-President.

The Bureau consists of the President, the Vice-President and the Section Presidents, who are tasked with assisting the President in carrying out their function in directing the work and administration of the Court.[8]

B. Dispute Assistants

There are various actors involved in aiding the judges, collectively assisting them in discharging their judicial functions and handling the immense caseload of the Court:

a) *The Registry*: The Registry is the Institutional Office of the Court. The judges of the Court elect a Registrar to head the Registry. The Registrar is elected from candidates of high moral character who possess the legal, managerial and linguistic knowledge and experience necessary to carry out the functions attached to the post.[9] The Registrar has custody of the archives of the Court and is the channel for all communications and notifications made by, or addressed to, the Court in relation to cases brought or to be brought before it.[10] The Registrar is assisted by a Deputy Registrar, who is also elected by the judges of the Court.

The Registry is organised into divisions. It consists of lawyers and administrative staff involved in case processing, and also includes research lawyers, administrative staff, personnel managers, archivists, IT experts, librarians, linguists etc.[11] It also has a language division that deals with translations and ensures that the use of the Court's official languages is of an adequate standard.

The Registry assigns its lawyers (case lawyers) to one of the case-processing divisions based on their knowledge of the languages and legal systems of the countries covered by that division. There are 31 case-processing divisions, under the supervision of a head of division (assisted by an administrative team), who also assigns cases to the case lawyers in their divisions. The case-processing divisions are attached to the Section where the national judge is allocated and follows the judge.

As the Court is organised into Sections, each of the five judicial sections is under the authority of a Section Registrar and assisted by a Deputy Section Registrar.[12] The Section Registrar and Deputy Section Registrar provide legal and administrative services to the Sections. The President of the Court appoints them on a proposal by the Registrar.[13]

The Grand Chamber has its separate registry.

[7] L Bianku and P Kempees, 'The European Court of Human Rights; in F Baetens (ed), *Legitimacy of Unseen Actors in International Adjudication* (Cambridge University Press, 2019) 111.

[8] Rules of the Court, r 9A.

[9] ibid r 15.

[10] ibid.

[11] Bianku and Kempees (n 7) 110.

[12] Rules of the Court, r 18.

[13] ibid.

The Registry and its staff are Institutional Assistants.

b) *Non-judicial Rapporteurs*: When sitting in single-judge formation, the judge is assisted by a Non-judicial Rapporteur, who is part of the Registry. These are usually senior case lawyers who have extensive experience dealing with cases. As will be elaborated further below, they play an influential role in the disposal of cases before single-judge formations. In some cases, the Section Registrars and Deputy Section Registrars are *ex officio* Non-judicial Rapporteurs.[14] Therefore, in such cases, the Institutional Assistants aid individual judges in a particular case.

c) *Filtering Section*: Although not mentioned in the Rules of the Court, a separate Filtering Section assists the Section Registries in reviewing incoming applications. The Filtering Section is headed by its own Registrar.[15] The Filtering Section consists of: (a) case processing lawyers specifically dealing with cases against high case-count countries; and (b) a specialist unit for dealing with requests for interim measures.[16] The case-processing lawyers or the lawyers of the Filtering Section 'filter' incoming cases into those that are to be decided by a single-judge formation and those that require examination by a Committee or a Chamber. In some cases, the applications may also be disposed of administratively by the legal staff of the Registry without judicial involvement.[17] They are Institutional Assistants.

d) *Directorate of the Jurisconsult*: Another key actor assisting the judges is the Jurisconsult, a position created in 2001. The Jurisconsult is officially a member of the Registry and ensures the quality and consistency of its case law by advising on legal issues and precedents.[18] The Jurisconsult helps maintain the integrity and coherence of the Court's jurisprudence. The Directorate of the Jurisconsult includes several divisions, like the case law analysis division, the case law monitoring division, the research division, the standard citations division, the library division and the publications division.[19] The Jurisconsult is chosen by the Bureau of the Court (composed of the President of the Court and the five Section Presidents) and is appointed by the General Secretary of the Council of Europe. They are Institutional Assistants.

The *research and library divisions* carry out legal research at the request of the Judge Rapporteur. They undertake comparative research of past case law and practice across state parties and other jurisdictions. The division typically produces research notes in Grand Chamber cases involving issues of great importance. The Case Law Information Division is in charge of knowledge management both within and outside the court, and maintains the HUDOC database and the Case Law Information Notes available on the Court's website. They are Institutional Assistants.

We will now examine the role of each of these Dispute Assistants in the dispute resolution process of the ECtHR.

[14] It is only when the section president, while communicating a case to the government, already declares part of the application inadmissible, acting as a single judge, that the role of Non-judicial Rapporteur is taken on by the section registrar or deputy registrar.

[15] Bianku and Kempees (n 7) 111.

[16] ibid.

[17] ibid 112.

[18] Rules of the Court, r 18B.

[19] European Court of Human Rights, 'Organisation Chart', www.echr.coe.int/organisation-chart.

II. The Dispute Resolution Process

Once an application is received and registered (ie, that has been considered to meet the formal requirements), the President of the Court decides whether it is prima facie a case to be decided by a single judge or a case to be decided by one of the formations (Chamber or Committee) of the relevant section (ie, the section of which the national judge of the respondent state is a member). In making this decision, the President of the Court can consider the proposal from the Registry's case lawyer. The application is not translated; a legal officer from the Section Registry, who is fluent in the language of the case and the legal system of the respondent state, examines the application. This will be further elaborated below.

A. Single-Judge Formations

Single-judge formations hear a case where the applicant's submitted material is sufficient on its own to disclose that the application is inadmissible or should be struck out of the list.[20] In such cases, the Filtering Section's case lawyers from the relevant country division will prepare a brief note setting out the facts and issues, and the reasons for which the application is inadmissible.[21] The note is subject to the approval of the Non-judicial Rapporteur, who formally makes a proposal before the judge. Thereafter, the judge may decide whether the application is inadmissible or deserves further examination by a Committee or Chamber of Judges. The inadmissibility decisions are akin to reasoned letters in the applicant's language, and do not go into too much detail. At this stage, although the Non-judicial Rapporteurs play an important role (they are explicitly mentioned in Article 24(2) of the Convention), it is the single judge who decides how the application is disposed of. A single judge cannot examine any application against a Member State with respect to which they have been elected.[22]

The single judge may reject the proposal of the Non-judicial Rapporteur and determine that the case deserves to be examined by a Committee or a Chamber of the relevant Section. The respondent state party is informed of the application only if it is transferred for further examination before a Committee or Chamber. Additionally, up to this point, all the communications and submissions are made in the language of the applicant.

B. Committee or Chamber Cases

In cases before a Committee or Chamber, the President of the Section designates a judge as Judge Rapporteur.[23] It is the Judge Rapporteur who examines the application.[24] In many cases, especially for countries that do not have a high caseload, the national judge will act as Judge Rapporteur. The Judge Rapporteur shall decide whether the application is to be considered by a Committee or a Chamber; unless the Section President has directed that a Committee or Chamber should consider the application.[25] A Committee

[20] Rules of the Court, r 49(1).
[21] Bianku and Kempees (n 7) 113.
[22] ECHR, art 26, para 3.
[23] Rules of the Court, r 49(2).
[24] ibid.
[25] ibid r 49(3).

may, by unanimous vote, declare a decision inadmissible or declare it admissible and pronounce judgment on its merits, provided that the substantive legal problem is the subject of well-established case law of the ECtHR.[26] In other cases, the Chamber considers the case.[27] When the Committee does not reach a unanimous decision, the case must be further examined by a Chamber.

After the Registry communicates the application to the respondent state party, it translates the application and accompanying documents into one of the Court's official languages (ie, French or English). The parties then communicate and write further submissions in one of the official languages.[28]

The Judge Rapporteur is responsible for presenting the case before the Committee or the Chamber. The case lawyer of the Section assists the Judge Rapporteur by undertaking all the necessary research and preparing the draft decision or judgment, under explicit instructions from the Judge Rapporteur. The level of instruction and control exercised by the Judge Rapporteur before the first draft depends on the individual judge and other factors like their present caseload. In complicated cases, there may also be a discussion within the Registry regarding the content of the draft. The Section Deputy Registrar reviews the draft for cases before a Committee. In contrast, the Section Registrar reviews the draft in cases before a Chamber. Their 'quality control' involves both jurisprudential review and editorial remarks, as the decisions and judgments have to follow a strict format.

Once the Section Registrar or Deputy Section Registrar clears the draft, they submit it to the Judge Rapporteur, who examines it and takes a position on the case. If the Judge Rapporteur disagrees with points in the draft, they may instruct the case lawyer to rewrite the draft or they may rewrite the draft themself. Once the Judge Rapporteur finalises the draft, the Judge Rapporteur shares their draft with the other judges in the Committee or Chamber. The draft is also sent to the Jurisconsult once the case is on the agenda of a Section meeting for examination by a Chamber. Thereafter, the other judges and the Jurisconsult may provide comments in writing before the judges deliberate on the draft. The judges communicate with the Judge Rapporteur, with the Section Registrar or Deputy Section Registrar in copy, on specific issues with the draft. The role of the Jurisconsult at this stage is further elaborated below.

Before the Chamber's deliberation, the Judge Rapporteur may share amendments to their draft with the judges. This draft is written with the case lawyer's assistance and is reviewed by the Section Registrar or Deputy Section Registrar. At the Section's weekly meeting, the Section's judges discuss the Chamber's drafts. As explained above, within a Section, there are pre-determined compositions of Chambers for each case, with substitute judges, so all the judges of the Section attend the deliberations. In Committee cases, only the three judges in the Committee receive the draft. In principle, the Court follows a written procedure for Committee cases, with no oral deliberations.

At the Chamber's deliberation, the Judge Rapporteur presents the case and the draft. The Section Registrar is present at the deliberations to take account of the votes and discharge other official functions. The case lawyer who had undertaken the drafting is also present at the deliberations to provide assistance or clarifications when the judges

[26] ibid r 53(2), read with ECHR, art 28(1).

[27] ECHR, art 29.

[28] Rules of the Court, r 34. Exceptionally, the President of the Chamber may grant leave for the continued use of the official language of a contracting party.

so request. Neither the Registrar nor the case lawyer participates in the discussions; this is reserved for the judges unless the case lawyer is requested to clarify factual issues. The Jurisconsult is also represented at the deliberations, but is merely there to observe the outcome of the cases. Thereafter, the judges vote to see if there is a majority. If there is no majority, the Chamber adjourns the meeting. In light of the comments made at the deliberations, the case lawyer will revise the draft based on the instructions of the Judge Rapporteur.

If the opinion expressed in the draft is supported by a majority, the judges review the draft paragraph-wise and finalise the judgment. Some written amendments from the Judge Rapporteur may follow in the days after the deliberations, subject to written approval by the judges. Separate opinions are permitted, which the judges undertake to draft themselves. In some cases, they may request the assistance of a case lawyer on some aspects of their opinion.

C. The Grand Chamber

When a chamber of the court relinquishes jurisdiction to a Grand Chamber or the Grand Chamber accepts a request for referral, the Judge Rapporteur designated for the case is in charge. In practice, the case lawyers who draft the judgment for Grand Chamber cases are more experienced. These may be lawyers who are familiar with the language and legal system of the respondent state. They prepare briefing notes and draft judgments on the instructions of the Judge Rapporteur, and under close supervision of a member of the Grand Chamber Registry, who is an experienced senior lawyer.

In most cases before the Grand Chamber, oral hearings are conducted, and the case lawyers are present at these hearings. Immediately after the hearings are completed, the judges convene to have a first deliberation. The Judge Rapporteur presents their report, and then the judge of the respondent state presents a note. Then, the remaining judges take the floor, with the President appearing last. Through this process, a majority position will emerge, and the President chooses a drafting committee composed of the Judge Rapporteur, the national judge of the respondent state and three to four judges who presented the majority opinion or the competing opinions clearly. This drafting committee prepares the draft with the assistance of the Registry. The draft is presented to the Grand Chamber during a second deliberation, discussed paragraph by paragraph and then put to a vote. The staff are present during these deliberations.

As stated before, in the case of both the Grand Chamber and Chamber proceedings, the national judge of the respondent state is required to participate in the proceedings. In a sense, this reduces the dependence of the judges in Chambers and Grand Chambers on the expertise of case lawyers regarding the domestic legal system of a particular case.

D. The Role of the Jurisconsult

The Jurisconsult ensures quality and consistency in the Court's case law.[29] The Jurisconsult receives the draft at the same time as the other judges on the Chamber

[29] Rules of the Court, r 18(B).

or Grand Chamber, reviews the drafts and shares them with the Judge Rapporteur around 10 days before the deliberation of the case by the Chamber or Grand Chamber. For Chamber cases, the aim is to ensure that the approaches followed by the Sections are consistent with the previous case law of the Court, and with similar cases pending before other Sections. The Jurisconsult brings in a horizontal view of all the cases pending and decided by the Court, which may be understandably absent for judges in a specific Section.

The Jurisconsult also has specialised knowledge on the interpretation of case law and would be able to inform the Sections of any inconsistencies. Although the judges are not bound by the Jurisconsult's recommendations, given their experience and specialised institutional knowledge, they would be inclined to accept them in many cases.

III. Observations on the Role of Dispute Assistants

The ECtHR has a complex and sophisticated adjudicatory process. The different formations before which a case may be presented are reflective of the complexity and novel questions raised by a case. Accordingly, the ECtHR also has separate actors that provide assistance at different stages of the proceedings. These are Institutional Assistants who are not assigned to individual judges, but assist all the formation of judges hearing the case or the Court as a whole. As the ECtHR assigns a Judge Rapporteur for each case, the primary responsibility of drafting is undertaken by the Judge Rapporteur, who closely supervises the work undertaken by the case lawyers from the Registry.

10

The Court of Justice of the European Free Trade Association

I. Institutional Overview and Structure

The Court of Justice of the European Free Trade Association (hereinafter 'EFTA Court') is the judicial organ of the European Free Trade Association (EFTA) pillar of the European Economic Area (EEA). The Member States of the EFTA Court are Norway, Iceland and Liechtenstein, but not the fourth Member State of EFTA, Switzerland.[1] The Court is closely modelled after the Court of Justice of the European Union. It is responsible for interpreting the European Economic Area Agreement and settling disputes between the three states and the EFTA Surveillance Authority, which fulfils a similar role to the European Commission.[2]

A. Adjudicators

The Court consists of three judges, one from each Member State. States appoint judges for a six-year renewable term without a term limit.[3] The states choose judges from persons whose independence is beyond doubt and who possess the qualifications required for appointment to the highest judicial offices in their respective countries or who are jurisconsults of recognised competence.[4] The Court is presided over by a President, whom the judges elect for a three-year term.[5] If one judge has to recuse themself from a case, an ad hoc judge replaces them. The other two judges on the Court select the ad hoc judge from a list prepared by the governments.[6]

The Dispute Assistants do not play a role in the appointment of the judges of the EFTA Court.

[1] HH Fredriksen, 'Court of Justice of the European Free Trade Association (EFTA Court)' in HR Fabri (ed), *Max Planck Encyclopedia of International Procedural Law* (Oxford University Press, online edn, June 2018).

[2] Agreement between the EFTA States on the Establishment of a Surveillance Authority and a Court of Justice (signed 2 May 1992, entered into force 1 January 1994) (hereinafter 'Surveillance and Court Agreement'), art 27.

[3] ibid arts 30.1–30.2.

[4] ibid art 30.1.

[5] ibid art 30.3.

[6] ibid art 30.4.

B. Dispute Assistants

The EFTA Court is supported in administrative matters by the Institutional Office, the Registry, headed by a Registrar. The Court appoints the Registrar for a renewable term of three years.[7] The Registry consists of seven staff, mostly assisting in administrative tasks.[8] They are Institutional Assistants.

Similar to the CJEU, the judges of the Court operates in a cabinet system; each judge receives support from two legal secretaries and one personal assistant.[9] Their hiring process is conducted through the cabinet of the judge they work for.[10] They are Assigned Assistants.

We will examine the role of these Dispute Assistants in the dispute resolution process of the EFTA Court below.

II. The Dispute Resolution Process

The Registry of the EFTA Court is responsible for receiving cases and handling all the documents. The Registrar is responsible for maintaining a register of all the pleadings, supporting items and documents, recorded in the order in which they are submitted.[11] The Registrar is also responsible for publishing the relevant details of the case in the EEA Section of the EEA Supplement to the Official Journal of the European Union.

Soon after the document initiating proceedings has been lodged, the President will appoint one of the three judges to act as the Judge Rapporteur.[12] After the parties have filed their written submissions, the Judge Rapporteur, assisted by their legal secretaries, circulates a preliminary report. The report contains proposals regarding procedural steps and timelines.[13] Before the Court hears a case, the Judge Rapporteur, with the help of their cabinet as necessary, prepares a Report for the Hearing. In direct action cases, the Report for the Hearing compiles the arguments from the written submissions.[14] In requests for advisory opinion, the Report for the Hearing compiles the answers proposed by the parties.

The Registrar attends the hearings.[15] Following the hearing, there is a first deliberation, at which the Judge Rapporteur presents the case. The Court asks the Judge Rapporteur to either prepare a draft, if the Court already knows which way it wants to

[7] Rules of Procedure of the EFTA Court (adopted 1994, as amended 2020) (hereinafter 'EFTA Rules of Procedure'), art 11.4

[8] EFTA Court, 'Judges and Staff', www.eftacourt.int/the-court/judges-and-staff. The Registry consists of three Administrative Assistants: one Administrative Assistant/Receptionist, one Senior Administrator, one Financial Officer and one caretaker/driver.

[9] C Baudenbacher, 'The EFTA Court's Working Methods' in *The EEA and the EFTA Court: Decentred Integration* (Hart Publishing, 2014) 243.

[10] See EFTA Court, *Vacancy Announcement No 03/2020* (2020).

[11] EFTA Rules of Procedure, Art 15.

[12] Baudenbacher (n 9) 246.

[13] EFTA Rules of Procedure, art 55.

[14] Fredriksen (n 1) 65. Interestingly, this practice was copied from the CJEU when the EFTA Court was established, but has since been abandoned by the former to expedite its proceedings. For an example, see EFTA Court, *Report for the Hearing in Case E-2/23 by Judge Hreinsson, E-2/23-13 (28 July 2023).*

[15] EFTA Rules of Procedure, art 25.1.

decide, or a pre-draft for a decision.[16] As in the CJEU, the legal secretaries do not attend the first deliberations. The judges continue to discuss the case after these first deliberations, but do so primarily electronically rather than in a dedicated meeting.[17] The Judge Rapporteur and their cabinet will prepare the draft of the decision,[18] and following input and consultations from the other judges, the Court adopts its judgment.

The legal secretaries also undertake research tasks. Following the continental tradition, the EFTA Court does not have dissenting opinions, and deliberations remain strictly secret.[19]

III. Observations on the Role of Dispute Assistants

As the Court operates in a cabinet system with Assigned Assistants for individual judges, the Registry and the Institutional Assistants mainly aid in administrative tasks. The legal secretaries, especially those of the Judge Rapporteur, are intimately involved in the drafting process from the very beginning. Given that they are Assigned Assistants, they operate under the close supervision of their judge and depend on their goodwill, making it easier for the judge to retain control over the draft.[20] In addition, the Judge Rapporteur can devote significant time to each draft, given the light caseload of the Court. Therefore, the concerns on Dispute Assistants overstepping their assigned roles are institutionally and procedurally guarded against. However, as in any court with Assigned Assistants to the judges, this will also depend to some extent on the Judge Rapporteur.

[16] Baudenbacher (n 9) 246.
[17] ibid.
[18] ibid; see also EFTA Court, *Vacancy Announcement No 03/2020* (2020).
[19] EFTA Rules of Procedure, art 26.4; Fredriksen (n 1) 62. As Fredriksen notes, this is a somewhat curious practice given that the legal traditions of the two Nordic Member States are actually very open to the idea of dissenting opinions.
[20] Baudenbacher (n 9) 246.

11

The Inter-American Court of Human Rights

I. Institutional Overview and Structure

The Inter-American Court of Human Rights (IACtHR) is the premier international human rights court in the Americas and is responsible for the application and interpretation of the American Convention on Human Rights.[1]

A. Adjudicators

The IACtHR comprises seven judges who are nationals of the member states of the Organization of American States (OAS), elected by an absolute majority of the state parties at the General Assembly of the OAS from a panel of candidates proposed by the states.[2] Each state may propose up to three candidates. The judges are jurists of the highest moral authority, of recognised competence in the field of human rights, and possess the qualifications required for the exercise of the highest judicial functions in their state of nationality or of the state that nominates them. However, once elected, they serve in their individual capacity. They serve for a term of six years, which is renewable once.[3] They are not employed full-time for budgetary reasons; the judges spend several weeks per year at the Court's seat in San José, Costa Rica.[4]

The Dispute Assistants do not play a role in the appointment of the judges of the IACtHR.

B. Dispute Assistants

The judges of the IACtHR are assisted in their work by the Secretariat, which is led by the Secretary and the Deputy Secretary. The Secretariat comprises several divisions, notably

[1] Statute of the Inter-American Court of Human Rights, OAS Res 448 (adopted October 1979) (hereinafter IACtHR Statute), art 1.

[2] American Convention on Human Rights (signed 22 November 1969, entered into force 18 July 1978) art 52; ibid arts 4.1, 6.1.

[3] IACtHR Statute, art 5.1.

[4] PG Domínguez, 'The Role of the Secretariat in the Inter-American Court of Human Rights: A Comparative Analysis' (2022) 116 *American Journal of International Law: Unbound* 391.

the legal affairs division with around 20 staff lawyers.[5] The members of the Court choose the Secretary for a term of five years and may re-elect the Secretary as often as the Court deems appropriate.[6] They are Institutional Assistants who assist the Court as a whole.

Judges do not have personal assistants who form part of the organisational structure of the Court, although the judges themselves may informally employ them. Such assistants would be External Assistants.

All Secretariat staff are subject to the OAS General Secretariat's administrative standards.[7] We will examine the role of these Dispute Assistants in the dispute resolution process of the IACtHR below.

II. The Dispute Resolution Process

A Member State or the Inter-American Commission on Human Rights can apply to initiate a case before the IACtHR.[8] As a first step, the President will review the application to ensure it meets all formal requirements.[9] The Secretariat will support the President by examining the submission and assigning a legal officer to the case who will aid the Court throughout the rest of the process.[10]

If the preliminary examination finds no issue with the application, the parties will file their written pleadings. The Secretariat checks to ensure that the written pleadings are complete.[11] After the parties' written pleadings, the Court appoints a Judge Rapporteur. The Judge Rapporteur is in charge of the proceedings, particularly the drafting process.[12] The legal officers of the Secretariat assist in the preparation for the oral hearings by circulating a problems paper to the judges highlighting the legal issues arising in the case.

The actual drafting process begins after the oral hearings. The Court may request that the Secretariat researches specific questions of the law, with the Secretariat being particularly proficient at conducting comparative studies on how other human rights bodies deal with an issue.[13] The judges will meet for a first deliberation where they will discuss the direction of the drafting process, and at which the Secretariat staff are present to assist. The legal officer assigned to the case will then prepare a first draft under the direction of the Judge Rapporteur. When the first draft is complete, the legal department receives it and discusses it with the Secretary and the Deputy Secretary.[14] Once the legal officer has amended the draft according to the comments made by the legal department,

[5] ibid.

[6] Rules of Procedure of the Inter-American Court of Human Rights (adopted 1980, as amended 2021) (hereinafter 'Rules of Procedure'), art 7.

[7] IACtHR Statute, art 14.1

[8] ibid art 61.1.

[9] Rules of Procedure, art 38.

[10] PS Alessandri, 'Secretariat: Inter-American Court of Human Rights (IACtHR)' in H Ruiz Fabri (ed), *Max Planck Encyclopedia of International Procedural Law* (Oxford University Press, online edn, November 2021) 29–30.

[11] ibid 37.

[12] Domínguez (n 4) 392.

[13] Alessandri (n 10) 49.

[14] ibid 48.

they will return the draft to the Judge Rapporteur. The Judge Rapporteur retains the final control and has to approve the draft before the remaining judges discuss the draft. The legal officer is present during this discussion. Once approved, the draft is passed to the other judges who review the draft in preparation for the second deliberation.[15]

In the second deliberation, the judges discuss the draft and any changes they may deem necessary. The Secretary, the Deputy Secretary as well as several staff from the legal department, including the director and the lawyer assigned to the case, may be present, but generally do not participate.[16] They participate only at the request and instruction of the Judge Rapporteur. Due to the low caseload of the Court, these discussions can be rather extensive. Once all changes have been implemented and the judges have agreed on a final judgment, the Secretariat will edit and proofread the final text before the Court renders the judgment.[17]

The IACtHR allows for the writing of separate opinions, but whether the Secretariat assists in this is unclear.[18]

III. Observations on the Role of Dispute Assistants

The Secretariat staff who are Institutional Assistants participate extensively in the judgment-drafting process in the IACtHR. The fact that the legal staff approve every draft collectively means that they effectively provide the first draft that the judges discuss.[19] However, any draft is ultimately approved by the Judge Rapporteur and is prepared under their supervision and control. Therefore, although Institutional Assistants play a significant role, they do so under the individual guidance of the Judge Rapporteur.

In terms of institutional safeguards, the fact that the judges appoint the head of the Institutional Office, the Secretary, gives them some control over the Institutional Office. In contrast, the imbalance between the part-time work of the judges and the full-time Secretariat staff may result in expertise accumulating in the Secretariat compared to the bench.[20] However, the limited time that the judges can devote to each case may be precisely why the Secretariat has to take such a central role in the drafting process.

[15] ibid.
[16] Rules of Procedure, art 15.2; Alessandri (n 10) 50.
[17] Alessandri (n 10) 51.
[18] Rules of Procedure, art 65.2.
[19] Domínguez (n 4) 393.
[20] ibid.

12

The International Court of Justice

I. Institutional Overview and Structure

The International Court of Justice (ICJ) is the principal judicial organ of the United Nations, established by the Charter of the United Nations and functioning in accordance with the Statute of the International Court of Justice.[1]

A. Adjudicators

The ICJ is composed of 15 judges, no two of whom are nationals of the same state.[2] They are elected as independent judges from amongst persons of high moral character, who possess the qualifications required in their respective countries for appointment to the highest judicial office, or jurisconsults of recognised competence in international law.[3]

They are elected by the General Assembly and Security Council of the United Nations from a list of persons nominated by the national groups in the Permanent Court of Arbitration and in accordance with the procedure laid out in the ICJ Statute.[4] The judges are elected for a renewable term of nine years.[5] The judges elect a President and Vice-President of the Court for three years; they may be re-elected.[6] In cases where one or both parties do not have a national on the bench, they may choose a judge ad hoc to complement the bench for the case in question.[7] The Dispute Assistants do not play a role in the appointment of the judges of the ICJ.

The judges of the ICJ work full-time[8] and are not permitted to exercise any political or administrative function, or engage in any other occupation of a professional nature other than as members of the court.[9]

[1] Charter of the United Nations (signed 26 June 1945, entered into force 24 October 1945) 1 UNTS XVI, art 92.

[2] Statute of the International Court of Justice (signed 26 June 1945, entered into force 24 October 1945) 33 UNTS 993 (ICJ Statute), art 3.

[3] ibid art 2.

[4] ibid art 4.

[5] ibid arts 4(1), 13(1). Traditionally, each of the Permanent Five was expected to have a judge on the bench. However, this practice was recently departed from when the UN re-elected the Indian judge Justice Dalveer Bhandari over the British candidate Justice Christopher Greenwood in 2017, leaving the UK without a judge on the bench. More recently, the Russian judge Justice Kirill Gevorgian also failed in his bid for re-election, leaving Russia without a judge on the bench as well.

[6] ibid art 21.

[7] ibid art 31(2)–(3).

[8] ibid art 23.

[9] ibid art 16.

B. Dispute Assistants

The judges are assisted by various actors during the course of proceedings before the Court:

a) *The Registry*: The Institutional Office of the ICJ is the Registry. It consists of three departments and seven divisions and is overseen by the Registrar, assisted by a Deputy-Registrar. The Registrar is chosen by the judges for a renewable seven-year term.[10] Furthermore, there is a Special Assistant to the Registrar who is attached to the office of the Registrar. They are Institutional Assistants.

b) *The Department of Legal Matters*: The Department of Legal Matters, which is directly subordinate to the Registrar, is responsible for case management. It consists of the Principal Legal Secretary, who acts as the head of the Department, two first secretaries, five secretaries and an administrative assistant.[11] They are Institutional Assistants.

c) *Associate Legal Officers and Special Assistant to the President*: Formally attached to the Department of Legal Matters are the 15 Associate Legal Officers ('clerks') and the Special Assistant to the President. However, they are assigned to individual judges. They answer to their judges, and it is the judges and the President (or Vice-President in the case of the assistants of the President) who evaluate them. With respect to ad hoc judges, Associate Legal Officers are assigned on a rotational basis. The Registry calls for expressions of interest from the Associate Legal Officers, who take up the position after approval from their assigned judge. In such cases, the Associate Legal Officer would work for two judges simultaneously. They are Assigned Assistants, who are formally part of the Institutional Office.

Associate Legal Officers are contracted for two years (renewable once) and must have at least two years of professional experience. The Special Assistant is required to have five years of experience. However, in practice, the appointments exceed these minimum requirements substantially. The selection process begins with a call for applications, and each judge reviews the applications received from their specific geographical region. From the shortlisted applicants, there is a written examination and an oral interview, conducted by two judges, the Special Adviser to the President and two senior members of the Registry. The judges who sit on the oral interview are on a rotational basis and are not necessarily the judge to whom the Associate Legal Officer is assigned.

d) *Judicial Fellows*: Also assigned to individual judges, but officially attached to the Registry, are 15 Judicial Fellows. The Judicial Fellows are not officials of the Court, but rather interns recommended and sponsored by their respective universities.[12] They serve for 10 months, which can be extended to 12 months.[13] In April 2021, United Nations General Assembly Resolution 75/129 established a trust fund for the Judicial Fellowship

[10] Rules of Court of the International Court of Justice (adopted 1978, as amended 2021) (hereinafter 'Rules of Court'), art 22(1).

[11] International Court of Justice, 'Registry', www.icj-cij.org/registry.

[12] M Hébié, 'Des ombres furtives au Palais de la Paix ? Coup de projecteur sur les assistants juridiques des membres de la Cour internationale de Justice' in JM Thouvenin and JJ Hébart (eds), *La Cour internationale de Justice à 75 ans* (Pedone, 2023) 66.

[13] *ibid 71.*

Programme to grant fellowship awards to nationals of developing countries who recently graduated from a university based in a developing country. The fund aims to improve the geographical and linguistic diversity of the participants in the programme. It is worth noting that the Associate Legal Officers are hired as international civil servants and may serve the judge for up to four years, while the Judicial Fellows are there for a shorter period. Accordingly, there are differences in the level of their involvement with the work of the Court. Similarly, they are Assigned Assistants, even though they are formally part of the Institutional Office.

From the above institutional structure, there are two factors to be kept in mind: the Registry is formally in charge of the Department of Legal Matters and, consequently, also formally in charge of the Associate Legal Officers, the Special Assistant to the President, and the Judicial Fellows. However, the Associate Legal Officers, the Special Assistant to the President, and the Judicial Fellows are attached to individual judges and are under the direction and supervision of their judges. Even for administrative matters like leaves, the approval is first received from the respective judge and thereafter communicated to the Registry. There is also a physical separation. The offices of the Associate Legal Officers, the Special Assistant to the President, and the Judicial Fellows, are situated in the wing of the building for judges. In contrast, the Registry staff operate out of the Peace Palace. Therefore, they are Assigned Assistants under the supervision and control of the individual judges.

The next part will describe the Court's procedure for reaching a judgment and the role of the Dispute Assistants in aiding the judges.

II. The Dispute Resolution Process

A case is initiated by submitting an application or the notification of a special agreement to the Registry, followed by an exchange of parties' written arguments, known as the pleadings.[14] All the judges of the Court hear the case, unless it is submitted to a chamber with the parties' agreement, and includes ad hoc judges for the parties in specific cases. The Registry prepares a summary of arguments, which is an objective summary of the parties' positions and circulates it to all the judges and their Associate Legal Officers.

After the first round of hearings, which the Registrar attends, the President circulates a List of Issues, which brings the attention of the bench to the legal questions considered pertinent for the decision of the case. This List is usually prepared primarily by the Department of Legal Matters and approved by the President.[15] The Department of Legal Matters appends to this List references to the sections of the pleadings and hearings where the parties have raised an issue relating to each of the questions, known as the *précis*.[16] The Associate Legal Officers of each judge also draft a memorandum in preparation for the hearing and revise it as per the oral proceedings.

[14] *Rules of Court*, arts 30(1), 38(1) and 45.

[15] Hébié (n 12) 77.

[16] R Higgins, P Webb, D Akande, A Bianchi and C Brown, *Oppenheim's International Law: United Nations* (Oxford University Press, 2017) para 29.169.

There is a first deliberation immediately after the close of the oral procedure, the so-called 'Article 3 Deliberation', which involves discussing the List of Issues, exchanging initial impressions and giving the judges some guidance for their notes.[17] The Registrar and staff attend this deliberation, but do not participate. The Registry and the Department of Legal Matters prepares an amended List of Issues, which includes references to the second round of oral proceedings and circulates it to the judges after this deliberation.

After this, the judges generally prepare Notes, which lay out their views on how the case should be decided. In producing these Notes, the Associate Legal Officers and Judicial Fellows assist their judges. Assistance may come in the form of, for example, legal research on specific questions, drafting of memoranda for the judge's attention or even drafting part of the Note. The involvement of the assistants very strongly depends on their individual judge and to some extent the legal staff.[18] Notes (like all documents of the Court) may be drafted either in French or English. The Registry's Linguistic Department then translates the Note into the respective other language.[19] The judges only prepare Notes for judgments on merits or advisory proceedings, not for incidental proceedings like preliminary objections.

Once the judges have circulated their Notes, a second deliberation, known as the 'Article 5 Deliberation', takes place. In the second deliberation, the judges discuss the case in further detail and present their Notes. Ad hoc judges speak first, followed by the remaining judges speaking in reverse order of seniority, with the President speaking last. As a result, the ad hoc judges play a significant role, as they must ensure that the deliberations have addressed all points raised by the party that appointed them. Following the second deliberation, the majority view will emerge and the Court will decide on the general direction of the decision.[20]

The judges then form a drafting committee comprising the President and the two members who, in their estimation, most cogently expressed the majority's views. If the President does not concur with the majority, the Vice-President takes their place.[21] If both the President and the Vice-President are not in majority, the most senior judge of the majority presides in the drafting committee instead.[22] Ad hoc judges are normally not chosen for the drafting committee.[23] Throughout the deliberation and the forming of the drafting committee, only the Special Assistant to the President and another assistant of the President are present to take notes. The Registrar also attends and answers any procedural questions that may come up.

After this deliberation, the drafting committee meets. At these meetings, the Associate Legal Officers of the two regular judges and the Special Assistant to the President are present. The Registrar also attends every meeting, accompanied by the Head of the

[17] H Simma and C Ortgies, 'Deliberation and Drafting: International Court of Justice' in *Max Planck Encyclopedia of Procedural Law* (MPEiPro, 2019) MN 43.

[18] Hébié (n 12) 81.

[19] Simma and Ortgies (n 17) 46.

[20] *ibid* 52.

[21] Resolution on Internal Practice of the International Court of Justice (adopted 5 July 1976, as amended) (hereinafter 'Resolution on Internal Practice'), art 6.

[22] ibid.

[23] Simma and Ortgies (n 17) 57.

Department of Legal Matters and two lawyers from the Department.[24] The Registrar actively participates in the discussion and may address any matter (including linguistic matters) and answer any questions relating to jurisprudence, procedure or the previous practice of the Court. The staff from the Registry may also intervene, but only with the permission of their respective judge/Registrar and only exceptionally.

At these meetings, a common practice is to divide the drafting of the judgment between the two judges on the Drafting Committee other than the President. The two judges draft their portions of the judgment before combining them.[25] Judges may rely on all of their assistants to support them, but this is highly dependent on the individual judge. However, it is unheard of for assistants to draft significant parts of the judgment, although they may draft shorter sections on specific topics. The Registry typically drafts the *qualités*, meaning the procedural history of the case, as well as the main facts and the summary of arguments, which is, in principle, prepared and circulated to the Court before the first deliberation and then updated.[26] The Registrar reviews these texts and may discuss them with their Special Assistant. Notably, the first draft of orders for provisional measures is produced by the Department of Legal Matters, reviewed by the Registrar and then approved by the President before circulation to the other judges. The judges thereafter carefully study the drafts and make substantial amendments.[27]

Once the drafting committee has finished the first draft of the judgment, it is circulated to all judges for line-by-line written comments, which the individual assistants may help with. The judges share their comments with the Registry, which prepares a compilation of the comments received from all judges and circulates this compilation to the Drafting Committee.[28] The Drafting Committee revises the draft based on these comments, and the revised draft is then submitted to the plenary for another deliberation, called the First Reading.

During the First Reading, the judges meet physically to debate and comment on the draft. While the Special Assistant to the President, the two Associate Legal Officers of the drafters, the Registrar and some lawyers from the Department of Legal Matters are present here, they are separated physically from the deliberations and do not participate.[29] The Registrar sits with the judges, and their role is similar to their role in Article 3 and Drafting Committee deliberations. After this reading, the Registry incorporates any agreed changes.

This revised draft is then circulated and discussed at the Second Reading, at the end of which the judges vote to produce the final judgment or advisory opinion.[30]

The Statute of the ICJ allows judges to append Declarations and Opinions, and it seems likely that the personal assistants support their judge in drafting them, if required. There may be individual opinions if there is agreement on the outcome but differences in the conclusion, and dissenting opinions if there is disagreement on the outcome

[24] ibid 61.
[25] ibid 62.
[26] M Ollivier and J Hoss, 'Registry: International Court of Justice' in R Wolfrum (ed), *Max Planck Encyclopedia of Public International Law* (Oxford University Press, online edition, 2021) MN 20.
[27] Hébié (n 12) 78.
[28] Simma and Ortgies (n 17) 72–73.
[29] Hébié (n 12) 87.
[30] *Resolution on Internal Practice*, art 8(i).

itself. If there are any separate or dissenting opinions, the judges circulate them after the First Reading. However, it is possible that the majority addresses the issues raised in these opinions through the revised draft, and these opinions might not form a part of the final decision.

III. Observations on the Role of the Dispute Assistants

Both the Institutional Assistants and the Assigned Assistants are involved in various stages of the dispute resolution process before the ICJ. However, several factors temper and constrain these actors in the exercising of their functions.

First, since all judges are full-time and actively involved in all stages of the decision-making process, they retain full control over the work undertaken by their Dispute Assistants. Especially during the drafting process, even judges who are not on the Drafting Committee are closely involved in the decision-making. Therefore, there are institutional and procedural safeguards which guarantee that no judge, let alone their assistants, can exert undue influence over the adjudicative process.[31]

Furthermore, the existence of two separate sets of assistants in the Registry (Institutional Assistants) and the judges' chambers (Assigned Assistants) moderates the influence of any one set of assistants on the decision-making process, since judges do not rely entirely on either for support. The introduction of Judicial Fellowship Programme is also a healthy way to deal with the workload and share expertise and train for the future.

[31] Hébié (n 12) 86.

13

The International Centre for Settlement of Investment Disputes

I. Institutional Overview and Structure

The International Centre for Investment Dispute Settlement (ICSID) is not a court in the traditional sense, but rather an institution that facilitates the work of tribunals in investor-state arbitration cases. ICSID was established by the contracting states to the Convention on the International Settlement of Investment Disputes (hereinafter 'ICSID Convention'). The purpose of ICSID is to provide facilities for the conciliation and arbitration of investment disputes between contracting states and nationals of other contracting states in accordance with the provisions of the ICSID Convention. The institution initially only undertook arbitration and conciliation functions, but now also undertakes mediation and fact-finding functions. This chapter focuses on the ICSID administered arbitration of investment disputes.

ICSID consists of an Administrative Council and a Secretariat, and maintains a Panel of Conciliators and a Panel of Arbitrators. The Administrative Council is composed of one representative of each contracting state,[1] and the President of the World Bank is the *ex officio* Chair of the Administrative Council.[2] The Administrative Council is responsible for a range of functions,[3] notably adopting the rules of procedure for the institution and conduct of conciliation and arbitration proceedings,[4] and the conditions of service of the Secretary-General and Deputy Secretary-General of the Secretariat of ICSID.[5]

A. Adjudicators

As explained in the case of commercial arbitration institutions in Chapter 5 a defining characteristic of international arbitration is that there is no standing court or tribunal which hears disputes, unlike many international tribunals which have a standing

[1] Convention on the Settlement of Investment Disputes between States and Nationals of Other States (adopted 18 March 1965, entered into force 14 October 1966) (hereinafter 'ICSID Convention'), art 4.
[2] ibid art 5.
[3] ibid art 6.
[4] ibid art 6.1(b)–(c).
[5] ibid art 6.1(e).

mechanism or pre-established roster of judges.[6] Individual arbitral tribunals are set up for each case, with the tribunal's exact composition varying according to the parties' agreement and the applicable arbitral rules. In ICSID-administered arbitrations, arbitrators may be appointed from the Panel of Arbitrators maintained by ICSID, or from outside of it, in accordance with the provisions of the ICSID Convention. As this forms an essential step in the dispute resolution process of arbitration, we will cover this in more detail in section II below, including the role played by the Dispute Assistants in the appointment of the arbitrators for ICSID arbitration.

With respect to the Panel of Arbitrators, each contracting state designates up to four persons and the Chair designates 10 persons to serve on the Panel of Arbitrators.[7] They serve on the Panel for a renewable term of six years.[8] The qualifications required for persons to be designated to the Panel of Arbitrators is highly relevant: they must be persons of high moral character and recognised competence in the fields of law, commerce, industry or finance, and who may be relied upon to exercise independent judgement.[9] Specifically, competence in the field of law is important for designation to the Panel of Arbitrators.[10] These qualifications must be met even when the arbitrators are appointed from outside the Panel of Arbitrators. The Chair, when designating persons to serve on Panels, is also responsible for ensuring that due regard is given to ensuring representation on the Panels of the principal legal systems of the world and of the main forms of economic activity.[11] The ICSID Secretariat does provide recommendations to the Chair for making designations to the Panel of Arbitrators, but this list is not disclosed.

We will detail the specific process of appointment of arbitrators below as part of the dispute resolution process.

B. Dispute Assistants

The Secretariat of ICSID is headed by a Secretary-General with assistance from two Deputy Secretaries-General.[12] They are nominated by the Chair and elected by the Administrative Council for renewable terms of six years.[13] The Secretary-General and Deputy Secretaries-General are not permitted to exercise any political functions and are not permitted to hold any other employment or engage in any other occupation without the approval of the Administrative Council.[14] The Secretary-General is the legal representative and the principal officer of ICSID, and is responsible for its administration,

[6] G Born, 'Selection, Challenge and Replacement of Arbitrators in International Arbitration' in *International Commercial Arbitration*, 3rd edn (Wolters Kluwer, 2021) 1764.

[7] ICSID Convention, art 13.

[8] ibid art 15.

[9] ibid art 14.1.

[10] ibid.

[11] ibid art 14.2.

[12] ibid art 9. For an overview, see International Centre for Settlement of Investment Disputes, 'Secretariat – Overview', www.worldbank.org/icsid/secretariat.

[13] ibid art 10.1.

[14] ibid art 10.2.

including the appointment of staff.[15] The Secretary-General also has the power to authenticate arbitral awards rendered pursuant to the ICSID Convention and to certify copies thereof.[16]

The ICSID Secretariat presently has around 70 staff, divided between case management, general administration and financial management, and front office teams.[17] The Secretariat organises its legal staff into five case management teams, each consisting of legal counsel, paralegals and other administrative assistants. They are Institutional Assistants. With respect to arbitration cases, ICSID appoints a tribunal 'secretary' from its staff to administer its cases. This tribunal 'secretary' assists the tribunal in its work and receives support from a paralegal and an administrative assistant.[18] Each legal counsel and senior legal counsel administers around 10 cases at any one time.[19] The assigned secretary and their case team are responsible to the Secretary-General.[20] They are Institutional Assistants.

In addition, with the parties' consent, arbitrators may appoint an assistant of their own as a supplementary case assistant.[21] They are External Assistants.

The Institutional Assistants and the External Assistants are bound by the confidentiality of deliberations and proceedings.[22] Any externally appointed assistants must also sign the same declaration of independence and impartiality as the arbitrators.[23]

In ICSID, the disputing parties do not directly pay the arbitrators. Rather, arbitrators and external assistants must file their claims for fees and reimbursement with the ICSID Secretariat, which will pay them out of the funds it has received from the parties.[24]

II. The Dispute Resolution Process

Any ICSID dispute begins with a request for arbitration addressed to the Secretary-General pursuant to Article 36.1 of the ICSID Convention, which must contain information concerning the issues in dispute, the identity of the parties and their consent to arbitration. As per Article 36.3 of the ICSID Convention, the Secretary-General registers the request unless they find that the dispute is manifestly outside the

[15] ibid art 11.

[16] ibid.

[17] International Centre for Settlement of Investment Disputes, 'Inside the ICSID Secretariat', www.icsid.worldbank.org/inside-icsid-secretariat.

[18] International Centre for Settlement of Investment Disputes, ICSID Administrative and Financial Regulations (hereinafter 'ICSID Administrative Regulations'), reg 28.

[19] International Centre for Settlement of Investment Disputes, 'Inside the ICSID Secretariat: Benjamin Garel, Legal Counsel', www.icsid.worldbank.org/inside-icsid-secretariat-benjamin-garel-legal-counsel.

[20] ICSID Administrative Regulations, reg 12.

[21] B McAsey, 'International Arbitral Institutions' in F Baetens (ed), *Legitimacy of Unseen Actors in International Adjudication* (Cambridge University Press, 2019) 61. Usually, this assistant will be appointed by and work closely with the tribunal president.

[22] International Centre for Settlement of Investment Disputes, ICSID Arbitration Rules (2022), rr 34(1), 66.

[23] International Centre for Settlement of Investment Disputes, 'Tribunal Assistants', www.worldbank.org/icsid/tribunal-assistants.

[24] International Centre for Settlement of Investment Disputes, *Memorandum on Fees and Expenses* (6 July 2005).

jurisdiction of ICSID and, thereafter, notifies the parties.[25] In assisting with this stage, the Secretariat assigns a legal counsel to the case (this is prior to the appointment of a tribunal secretary). The legal counsel examines the request and recommends a course of action to the Secretary-General, who ultimately takes the decision. Given the narrow wording of Article 36.3,[26] it is unsurprising that this procedure is exercised very carefully and only results in non-registration in extremely rare cases.[27]

Next, the arbitral tribunal is constituted pursuant to Articles 37–40 of the ICSID Convention. The tribunal consists of a sole arbitrator or any uneven number of arbitrators as agreed by the parties. In the event that the parties do not agree upon the number of arbitrators and the method of their appointment, the tribunal will consist of three arbitrators, one appointed by each party and the third appointed by agreement of the parties who shall also serve as the president of the tribunal. While the Convention does not explicitly assign the Secretariat a role in this process,[28] it nevertheless works to facilitate the parties' agreement if requested by the parties. The Secretary-General assists the parties by drawing up a ballot/list of possible candidates for them to choose from.[29] Under the ballot procedure, they provide parties with a ballot form containing the names of several candidates, and each party is given a date to return the form indicating which candidates it accepts/rejects.[30] Under the list procedure, ICSID provide the parties with a list of several candidates, and each party can strike a certain number of candidates and rank the remaining candidates.[31] The ICSID Secretariat is not bound by the Panel of Arbitrators when nominating names to the parties.[32] The appointments made pursuant to this process are considered to be appointed by agreement of the parties. The parties may also specifically designate the Secretary-General as the appointing authority[33] or request the assistance of the Secretary-General under Rule 17 of the Arbitration rules.[34] In the event that the tribunal is not constituted within 90 days of notice of registration of the request, or such other period as agreed by the parties, either party may request the Chair of the Administrative Council to appoint the arbitrator(s) not yet appointed.[35]

[25] ICSID Convention, art 36.3.

[26] SD Sutton, 'Emilio Augustin Maffezini v Kingdom of Spain and the ICSID Secretary-General's Screening Power' (2005) 2(1) *Arbitration International* 121–22.

[27] Current numbers on this are hard to find, but as of 2014, it was reported that ICSID had only refused to register a request 18 times in 46 years. See E Obadia and F Nitscheke, 'Institutional Arbitration and the Role of the Secretariat' in *Litigating International Investment Disputes* (Brill, 2014) 93.

[28] Article 38 of the ICSID Convention designates the Chair of the Administrative Council as the default appointing authority.

[29] Obadia and Nitscheke (n 27) 112. This has also been provided on the ICSID website; see International Centre for Settlement of Investment Disputes, 'Selection of the Tribunal (2022)', www.icisd.worldbank.org /procedures/arbitration/convention/selection-tribunal/2022. Since 2009, this informal procedure precedes recourse to the Appointing Authority under art 38(1) of the ICSID Convention. The parties may also specify any other procedure other than the ballot/list procedure; see M Kinnear, Appointment to Arbitral Tribunals at ICSID' (2013) 1(1) *ABA Section of International Law International Arbitration Committee Newsletter* 37. The list may contain five or more names.

[30] International Centre for Settlement of Investment Disputes (n 29).

[31] ibid.

[32] D Caron, 'ICSID in the Twenty-First Century: An Interview with Meg Kinnear' (2010) 104 *American Society of International Law Procedure* 421.

[33] Obadia and Nitscheke (n 27) 113–14. Overall, ICSID appointed 29 per cent of arbitrators in 2022, which includes both appointments by the Chair and the Secretary-General; see International Centre for Settlement of Investment Disputes, *ICSID Annual Report 2022* (2022) 30.

[34] ICSID Arbitration Rules, r 17.

[35] ICSID Convention, art 38; ICSID Arbitration Rules, r 18.

The Chair appoints such arbitrator(s) from the Panel of Arbitrators, and they shall not be nationals of the contracting state party to the dispute or of the contracting state whose national is a party to the dispute.[36] Although not explicitly mentioned, the Secretariat staff also assist in this process; specifically, the ICSID Secretary-General may make recommendations to the Chair regarding potential appointees.[37]

Therefore, in practice, the Dispute Assistants assist the parties or the Chair in appointment of the arbitrators, and the Chair (Appointing Authority) makes such appointment exclusively from the Panel of Arbitrators.[38]

After the tribunal is constituted, there is a first session (within 60 days of the tribunal's constitution) to issue a procedural order. The parties will submit their pleadings, and the hearings will be held as per the schedule decided in the procedural order. At this stage, the assigned tribunal secretary will assist the tribunal administratively, for example, by handling the communication with the parties.[39] At the same time, other Secretariat officials will organise the hearings,[40] administer the finances[41] and register all case-related documents.[42] The tribunal secretary assigned to the case will attend the hearings, and the tribunal assistants appointed externally by the arbitrators may in some instances attend the hearing. The hearings are recorded, and interim decisions are memorialised in awards/orders issued by the tribunal.

The drafting process usually starts once the hearings have been held and the parties have had a chance to advance all their arguments. The tribunal secretary assigned to the case often assists the tribunal at its deliberations by summarising the parties' arguments into a working paper and attending the deliberation.[43]

As in arbitration in general, the exact drafting process and the involvement of any Dispute Assistants will depend on the arbitrators' personal style and preferences, and may vary widely. A common practice is for the presiding arbitrator to prepare the first draft of an award, considering any discussions and deliberations with the wing arbitrators, and then submit it to the wing arbitrators for further comments and discussion. The tribunal secretary assigned to the case may be asked to provide guidance on procedural

[36] ICSID Convention, art 38.

[37] C Schreuer, L Malintoppi, A Reinisch and A Sinclair, 'Article 38: Appointment by Chairman' in *The ICSID Convention: A Commentary*, 2nd edn (Cambridge University Press, 2009) 494. See also M Kinnear, 'Arbitrator Appointment by ICSID', video presentation, www.youtube.com/watch?v=AZNtjwzfN-g, which states (at 3:12) that: 'we probably consider many of the same factors that parties consider, when they make appointments. Most important factors include, first of all, the nationality of the arbitrators, so that we respect the requirements under the ICSID Convention with respect to nationality [ie, that none of the arbitrators appointed by the ICSID Chair may be of the same nationality as either of the parties]. Next, we consider whether there are possible conflicts of interests. We also consider the potential arbitrators knowledge of the relevant laws and their experience in arbitration. Another important factor is language proficiency, depending on the requirements both of the documents and the oral hearings in the case. We also look to the availability of the arbitrator and in particular the manageability of their current caseload, so that we can make sure that we have a timely and expeditious procedure. Finally, we'll look to the cohesiveness of the tribunal and in some cases where a particular expertise is needed, we will try to ensure that there is that kind of expertise on the tribunal'.

[38] The ICSID Chair is also the Appointing Authority under the ICSID Additional Facility Rules, in which case they are not limited to the Panel of Arbitrators for such appointment.

[39] ICSID Administrative Regulations, reg 28(b).

[40] Obadia and Nitscheke (n 27) 125–26.

[41] ICSID Administrative Regulations, reg 15.

[42] ibid reg 29.

[43] ICSID Arbitration Rules, r 34.3.

issues, thus leveraging ICSID's vast institutional memory and expertise.[44] Tribunal secretaries do not engage in comprehensive research for the tribunal, as it is generally expected that the tribunal only incorporates views raised by the parties in their submissions into the final report. The tribunal secretary and the external tribunal assistants may also draft specific paragraphs or sections of an award to allow the president to focus on the more complex questions of a case. For example, it is not uncommon for tribunal secretaries to draft the procedural history, facts and summaries of the parties' submissions, which will then be reviewed and, if necessary, amended by the arbitrators.[45]

Given that the Centre works in English, Spanish and French, the tribunal secretary may have to organise the translation of drafts if a case is administered in more than one language.[46] However, the Centre generally ensures that the arbitrators are capable of working in all languages of the case in order to minimise the time and money spent on interpretation and translation.[47]

The tribunal secretary, and in some cases, external tribunal assistants, will also review the drafts of documents issued by the tribunal, which commonly includes proofreading and editing.[48] Furthermore, the tribunal secretary will try to ensure that the award is internally consistent and that all major points argued by the parties have been addressed, keeping in mind that the final word on any such suggestion lies, of course, with the arbitrators. The same review will be undertaken for any dissenting opinion, if necessary.[49]

III. Observations on the Role of Dispute Assistants

Between providing advice on matters of procedure, assisting in the drafting and reviewing drafts upon request, a tribunal secretary in ICSID plays a significant role in assisting the arbitrators with their decision-making process, even if they are generally not involved in substantive drafting. This is in large part because they are extremely busy, being involved with several disputes at the same time.

The ICSID arbitration tribunal may hire external assistants as supplementary case assistants, with the consent of the parties. The nature and extent of involvement of such assistants are largely dependent on the arbitrator(s), the staff and the needs of the case. It should be kept in mind that ICSID arbitrators are commonly very experienced experts in the field of investment law. They are hand-picked for each case, allowing parties to choose them based on their familiarity with the subject matter of a given case. Consequently, their legal and subject matter expertise may reduce concerns relating to the tribunal secretary or external assistants having an outsized influence.

[44] AR Parra, 'The Role of the ICSID Secretariat in the Administration of Arbitration Proceedings under the ICSID Convention' (1998) 13(1) *ICSID Review – Foreign Investment Law Journal* 97; Obadia and Nitscheke (n 27) 130.

[45] Obadia and Nitscheke (n 27) 130.

[46] ICSID Arbitration Rules, r 7(3).

[47] Parra (n 44) 97.

[48] Obadia and Nitscheke (n 27) 131.

[49] This has not always been without controversy, as the additional opinion of Professor Dalhuisen in the *Vivendi* Case shows; see *Compañía de Aguas del Aconquija SA and Vivendi Universal SA v Argentine Republic (Vivendi)*, Decision on the Argentine Republic's Request for Annulment of the Award rendered on 20 August 2007, 10 August 2010, ARB/97/3, Additional Opinion of Professor JH Dalhuisen, paras 7–8.

14

International Criminal Tribunals

I. Institutional Overview and Structure

In this chapter, we examine three international criminal tribunals: namely, the International Criminal Court (ICC), the Special Tribunal for Lebanon (STL) and the International Criminal Tribunal for the Former Yugoslavia (ICTY).

A. The International Criminal Court

The ICC, established by the Rome Statute,[1] has jurisdiction over the most serious crimes of concern to the international community as a whole, as identified in the Statute. The Court consists of four independent organs:

a) The Presidency, consisting of three judges elected by a majority of their peers as the President and the First and Second Vice-President, which is responsible for the proper administration of the Court.[2]
b) The Chambers, which is responsible for the judicial functions of the Court. It consists of an Appeals Division, composed of the President and four other judges; a Trial Division of no less than six judges; and a Pre-Trial Division of no less than six judges.[3]
c) The Office of the Prosecutor, which is responsible for receiving referrals and any substantiated information on crimes within the jurisdiction of the Court, for examining them, and for conducting investigations and prosecutions before the Court.[4] The Office of the Prosecutor does not fall within the scope of this research project as it is completely independent from the judges.
d) The Registry, which is responsible for the non-judicial aspects of the administration and servicing of the Court.[5]

[1] Rome Statute of the International Criminal Court (adopted 17 July 1998, entered into force 1 July 2002) 2187 UNTS 90, art 1.
[2] ibid art 38.
[3] ibid art 39.
[4] ibid art 42.
[5] ibid art 43.

i. Adjudicators

As per the Rome Statute, the ICC has 18 judges, who are elected as full-time members.[6] The judges must be of high moral character, demonstrate impartiality and integrity, and possess the qualifications required in their respective state for appointment to the highest judicial offices.[7] Further, each such candidate must have either: established competence in criminal law and procedure, and the necessary experience, whether as a judge, prosecutor, advocate or some other similar capacity, in criminal proceedings; or have established competence in relevant areas of international law such as international humanitarian law and the law of human rights, and extensive experience in a professional legal capacity which is of relevance to the judicial work of the Court.[8] Further, the candidates must also have excellent knowledge of and be fluent in at least one of the languages of the Court.

The nominations of candidates for election to the Court are made by the state parties to the Rome Statute and accompanied by a statement detailing how the candidate fulfils the requirements detailed above. Two lists of candidates are made for the election: List A containing the names of candidates with the necessary qualifications in criminal law and procedure; and List B containing the names of candidates with the necessary qualifications in the relevant areas of international law. The elections are organised so as to maintain equivalent proportion of judges qualified on the two lists. The judges are elected by secret ballot at a meeting of the Assembly of State Parties to the Rome Statute. The Dispute Assistants do not play any role in the appointment of the judges of the ICC.

The Presidency serves on a full-time basis and will determine, on the basis of the workload of the Court and in consultation with its members, the extent to which the remaining judges shall be required to serve on a full-time basis.[9]

ii. Dispute Assistants

The Registry is responsible for the non-judicial aspects of the administration and servicing of the Court.[10] The Registrar, head of the Registry, is elected by the judges of the Court through an absolute majority, taking into account any recommendation by the Assembly of States Parties.[11] If the need arises, the judges of the Court elect a Deputy Registrar in the same manner.[12] The Registrar, in turn, appoints the staff members of the Registry on behalf of the Court.[13]

The role of the Registry does not extend to support for the substantive judicial decision-making of the judges of the Chambers. The Registry is responsible for the non-judicial aspects of the administration and servicing of the Court.[14] Given the mandate of the ICC and the nature of criminal trials, the character of the non-judicial

[6] ibid arts 35–36.
[7] ibid art 36(3).
[8] ibid.
[9] ibid art 35(3).
[10] ibid art 43.
[11] ibid art 43(4).
[12] ibid.
[13] ibid art 44(1).
[14] ibid.

functions discharged by the Registry takes on a unique role. The Registry is responsible for three main categories of services: judicial support, external affairs and administrative management.

The administrative functions relate to human resources, budget, finance, procurement, facilities management, travel and transportation. The Registry also ensures a safe and secure environment for those working in or visiting the Court. The judicial support function provides the necessary assistance for judges to conduct the hearings.[15] As a neutral service provider, the Registry supports investigative, prosecutorial and judicial activities through, among other things, court management and eCourt tools, facilitation of victims' participation in proceedings, court interpretation and translation services, information management services, and management of the detention facilities.[16] Finally, the external operations functions include facilitating adequate judicial cooperation with states regarding Chambers' requests; concluding various cooperation agreements with states, such as those on the relocation of witnesses; providing support to and protection of victims and witnesses; informing the general public on judicial and other Court developments; providing outreach activities in the affected communities; and facilitating the Court's operations in the field.[17] Additionally, the Registry has a Legal Office, which is responsible for the legal functions associated with the Registrar's duties. Its primary objective is to ensure the quality and consistency of legal approaches across the various sections of the Registry relating to victim support, case management etc.[18] The staff of the Registry are Institutional Assistants.

The ICC also has another set of Dispute Assistants: Associate Legal Officers, Legal Officers and Legal Advisors to the Chambers (hereinafter collectively referred to as 'Legal Officers in Chambers').[19] The Legal Officers in Chambers are independent of the Registry and work in Chambers. They fall under one of the three divisions: the Pre-Trial, Trial or the Appeals Divisions. The Court further assigns them to specific chambers within the divisions. The history behind the position of Legal Officers is of relevance. Although the they were originally a part of the Registry, they were soon brought into Chambers and considered under the supervision and control of the judges in Chambers. Although administratively the Registrar may retain some control over the Legal Officer's performance review, renewal, periods of leave and the like, the Registrar, in practice, defers to the judges, the legal advisers for the three judicial divisions and, since 2016, to the Head of Chambers on these decisions. Therefore, although they may be formally close to Institutional Assistants, they are not under the substantive supervision and control of the head of the Institutional Office and are functionally Assigned Assistants.

Three positions are relevant here: (i) Legal Officers and Associate Legal Officers; (ii) Legal Advisors; and (iii) Head of Chambers. The Legal Officers, who are grade level P2 (Associate Legal Officer) or P3 (Legal Officer), work within a Chamber's legal team and are under the overall supervision of the Head of Chambers and the direct supervision

[15] International Criminal Court, 'Composition of the Registry', www.icc-cpi.int/about/registry.

[16] Information Criminal Court, 'Information of the Registry', www.icc-cpi.int/about/registry.

[17] Registry of the International Criminal Court, *Comprehensive Report on the Reorganisation of the Registry of the International Criminal Court* (August 2016) 81, www.icc-cpi.int/itemsDocuments/ICC-Registry-CR.pdf.

[18] ibid.

[19] International Criminal Court, 'Judges' Legal Officer', www.icc-cpi.int/get-involved/justice-at-work/story /the-judges-legal-officer.

of the respective Division Legal Advisor. Within the divisions, Legal Advisors assign work to Legal Officers. The Legal Advisors, who are grade level P4, are under the general authority of the President of the Division and the direct supervision of the Head of Chambers.[20] The need to organise the work of the Legal Officers and Associate Legal Officers between the three divisions led to the creation of the Head of Chambers position.

At the beginning of the activities of this Court, the Legal Officers worked for individual judges, with each judge having dedicated Legal Officers working for them. This proved to work against achieving consensus. The current model is one where every chamber has a pool of Legal Officers working for the Chamber as a whole; nonetheless, a Legal Officer may be asked to carry out a specific research or piece of work and this is coordinated via the Legal Advisors, and the Head of Chambers. This model has, in a certain way, also tempered the influence that a single Legal Officer may have on the decision-making process of judges, and this will be elaborated further in section II, where the trial process is detailed.

B. The Special Tribunal for Lebanon

The STL was established in 2005 as an international tribunal for the prosecution of the terrorist attack that took place in Lebanon and related crimes. There are two foundational distinctions between the ICC and STL: the purpose of the STL is to prosecute a specific terrorist act as opposed to crimes as defined by the ICC, and the STL applies the Lebanese Criminal Code to the crimes in question as opposed to international law. Since July 2022, the STL has entered a residual phase to preserve its records and archives, safeguard residual obligations to victims and witnesses, etc. This part elaborates on the institutional structure of the STL when it was operational.

The STL had four independent organs:

a) The Chambers, which is responsible for the judicial functions of the Court.
b) The Prosecutor, which is in charge of the investigation and prosecution of persons responsible for the crimes falling within the jurisdiction of the STL.[21]
c) The Registry, which is responsible for the administration and servicing of the STL.[22] Like the ICC, the Registrar must set up a Victims and Witnesses Unit within the Registry.
d) The Defence Office, which is responsible for protecting the rights of the defence, providing support and assistance to defence counsel and to the persons entitled to Dispute Assistants – including, where appropriate, legal research, collection of evidence and advice –and appearing before the Pre-Trial Judge or a Chamber in respect of specific issues.[23]

[20] International Criminal Court, 'Legal Adviser (P-4)', www.impactpool.org/jobs.
[21] Statute of the Special Tribunal for Lebanon, Annex to UN Security Council Resolution 1757 (2007), UN Doc S/RES/1757 (2007) (10 June 2007), art 11.
[22] ibid art 12.
[23] ibid art 13.

i. Adjudicators

The Chambers of the STL were composed of: one international pre-trial judge, a Trial Chamber comprising three judges (two international and one Lebanese judges), an Appeals Chamber comprising five judges (three international and two Lebanese judges), and two alternate judges (one international and one Lebanese).[24]

The judges of the STL were persons of high moral character, impartiality and integrity, with extensive judicial experience.[25] They were independent in the performance of their functions, without any instructions from any government or other source.[26] The judges were appointed by the Secretary-General of the UN for a three-year period and were eligible for re-appointment by the Secretary-General in consultation with the Government of Lebanon.[27]

The Dispute Assistants did not play any role in the appointment of judges of the STL.

ii. Dispute Assistants

The Registry was the Institutional Office responsible for the administration and servicing of the STL, headed by its Registrar. The Secretary-General appointed the Registrar, who was a staff member of the United Nations (UN).[28] Given the UN's appointment of the Registrar, the Registrar played a crucial role in managing communications between the Court and the UN, and vice versa. The Registry supported to the Chambers, the Prosecutor and the Defence Office. However, this section will focus on the assistance provided to the Chambers. The staff of the Registry are Institutional Assistants.

The functions of the Registry were as follows:

a) The administration of courtrooms and court management duties such as filings,[29] court proceedings, transcripts,[30] preservation of court records[31] and processing of requests for judicial cooperation. The Registry's Judicial Division, managed by the Chief of Judicial Services, provided the necessary support to ensure that hearings ran effectively and efficiently. It included the Court Management and Services Section, the Victims and Witness Unit, the Victims' Participation Unit, the Language Services Section and the Detention Facility.
b) The Registry's Division of Administration handled administrative functions of the STL like human resources, finance, legal advice, information technology, translation and interpretation, preparing the Tribunal's budget, providing security, archiving, and public information and communication.[32]

[24] ibid art 8.
[25] ibid.
[26] ibid art 9.
[27] ibid.
[28] ibid art 12.
[29] Special Tribunal for Lebanon, Rules of Procedure and Evidence (adopted pursuant to art 28 of the STL Statute, 2009, as amended), r 49E.
[30] ibid r 53.
[31] ibid r 54.
[32] Special Tribunal for Lebanon, 'Registry', www.stl-tsl.org/en/about-the-stl/registry.

c) The Registry was also responsible for overseeing the Security and Safety Section and the Public Information and Communications Section.[33]

Like the ICC, the STL also had Legal Officers in Chambers, who assisted the judges substantively in their decision-making and judicial functions. They were, likewise, separate from the Registry. The role and number of Legal Officers varied depending on the Chamber and the individual approaches of the judges. For example, in the Pre-Trial Chamber, four to five Legal Officers were assigned to the Chamber for the single judge. In the Trial and Appeals Chambers, a pool of Legal Officers served the Chamber, not individual judges. These Legal Officers were under the supervision of the judge. However, distinct from the ICC, they were considered part of the Registry. Accordingly, the Registrar was responsible for their appointment, evaluations, appraisals, and other administrative control. Therefore, they were Assigned Assistants who were under the substantive supervision of the judges, but more formally under the administrative control of the Institutional Office.

C. The International Criminal Tribunal for the Former Yugoslavia

The ICTY was a tribunal established through UN Security Council Resolution 827 to deal with war crimes that took place during the conflicts in the Balkans in the 1990s. Like the ICC and the STL, the ICTY had jurisdiction over individual persons. In terms of subject matter, the ICTY was like the ICC in that it covered serious violations of international humanitarian law committed in the former Yugoslavia since 1991.[34] The application of international humanitarian law was in contrast to the STL, which applied the Lebanese Criminal Code. However, unlike the ICC, it was established as a temporary tribunal for the prosecution of a specific set of war crimes.

The Tribunal consisted of the following three organs:[35]

a) the Chambers of the Judges of the ICTY;
b) the Prosecutor, who was responsible for investigating and prosecuting individuals;[36]
c) the Registry, which serviced the Chambers and the Prosecutor;

i. Adjudicators

The ICTY Chambers comprised three Trial Chambers and an Appeals Chamber. Unlike the ICC and the STL, there was no pre-trial Chamber at the ICTY. The Chambers consisted of a maximum of 16 permanent judges and 12 *ad litem* judges.[37] Each Trial

[33] ibid.
[34] Statute of the International Criminal Tribunal for the Former Yugoslavia, Annex to UN Security Council Resolution 827 (1993), UN Doc S/RES/827 (1993) (25 May 1993) (hereinafter 'Statute of the ICTY'), art 1. Articles 2–5 of the Statute identify four different categories of crimes.
[35] ibid art 11.
[36] ibid art 16.
[37] ibid art 12(1).

Chamber consisted of three permanent judges and a maximum of six *ad litem* judges at any given time.[38] After assignment to the Chamber, the permanent judges elected a Presiding Judge from amongst them.[39] The Appeals Chamber consisted of seven permanent judges and two judges appointed from the International Criminal Tribunal for Rwanda.[40] A Chamber composed of five judges would hear each appeal.[41] It also served as the Appeals Chamber for ICTR.

The permanent and *ad litem* judges were persons of high moral character, impartiality and integrity who possessed the qualifications required in their respective countries for appointment to the highest judicial offices. In the overall composition of the Chambers and sections of the Trial Chambers, due account was taken of the experience of the judges in criminal law and international law, including international humanitarian law and human rights law.

ii. Dispute Assistants

The Registry was headed by a Registrar, who was appointed by the UN Secretary-General after consultation with the President of the ICTY, for a renewable term of four years. The staff of the Registry were appointed by the Secretary-General on the Registrar's recommendation. The Registrar's terms and conditions of service were the same as those of an Assistant Secretary-General of the UN.[42] The Registry comprised the Registry Advisory Section, a Judicial Support Division, the Communications Service and the Administration Division. Like the ICC and the STL, the Registry of the ICTY also had a Victims and Witnesses Section.[43]

The ICTY was the first international criminal tribunal to create a role for Legal Officers in Chambers. These Legal Officers assisted the Judges in their decision-making and judicial functions, and were separate from the Registry. In both the Trial and Appeals Chambers, a pool of Legal Officers assisted the Chamber and not individual judges. They were Assigned Assistants.

II. The Trial Process

The adjudication process before the ICC requires a brief elaboration: the trial takes place after the conclusion of the pre-trial phase, where it is determined whether there are substantial grounds to believe the person committed the charges brought by the Prosecutor. The Court issues a decision either confirming or declining to confirm one or more charges.[44] Thereafter, the ICC constitutes a Trial Chamber composed of three judges.[45] Given the criminal nature of the proceedings, various aspects relate to

[38] ibid art 12(2).
[39] ibid art 14(7).
[40] ibid art 14(4).
[41] ibid art 12(3).
[42] ibid art 17(3).
[43] ibid art 22.
[44] Rome Statute, art 61(7).
[45] ibid art 61(11).

evidence, protection of victims and witnesses etc. The Registry and its staff assist the Trial Chamber in these non-judicial aspects of the trial, through a Courtroom officer and other staff for specific disputes.[46] The Registry of the ICC does not provide any judicial assistance to the judges, whether procedural or substantive. The Registry of the STL and the Registry of the ICTY fulfil the same role. Therefore, across the international criminal tribunals, the Institutional Office assists the judges in administrative and non-judicial aspects of the trial only.

The trial includes oral and written submissions by the parties and typically consists of years of trial proceedings. As stated above, every Chamber in the ICC, the STL and the ICTY has a dedicated pool of Legal Officers who assist the judges of the Chamber with the legal and judicial aspects of the trial. The Legal Officers attend the proceedings and assist the judges.

The drafting of the judgment in criminal trials is not a distinct phase that starts after the conclusion of the trial. In 2019, the judges of the ICC announced an update of the *Chambers Practice Manual*, a non-binding document by which judges seek to standardise best practices and provide guidance for the conduct of various aspects of proceedings. They indicated that trial chambers commence the preparation of judgments early on while still appropriately adapting judgments to the needs of specific cases. The practice of the Court has been to assign one or a few Legal Officers at the beginning of the trial to deal exclusively with the drafting of the judgment, and the remaining Legal Officers in the pool to work on the day-to-day trial matters. Even in the STL, the Legal Officers of the Chambers do the drafting. However, this does not imply that the Legal Officers exert control over the judicial decision-making; they undertake the drafting on the instructions of the Judges of the Chamber. Consequently, the influence a Legal Officer can exert is also dependent on the nature of the judge and their command over the proceedings.

In deliberations, the criminal nature of the proceedings necessitates secrecy owing to the need to protect victims and witnesses.[47] In the ICC, the judges, Legal Officers in Chambers – and, at times, the Legal Advisor of the Judicial Division, whether pre-trial, trial or appeals – attend the deliberations. The staff members of the Registry do not participate in the deliberations as they are not even aware of those deliberations. Similarly, in the STL and the ICTY, only the Legal Officers used to attend the deliberations. In practice, the Legal Officers in Chambers, and eventually the legal adviser of the Division, play an active role during the deliberations, engaging in active discussions with the judges. Some deliberations may occur through written exchanges with the Legal Officers and, eventually, the legal advisor marked in copy.

Once the judgment is drafted, some judges may draft separate or dissenting opinions regarding specific issues or charges. Although there is a practice of attempting to achieve unanimity, judges still write separate and dissenting opinions in the ICC. In such cases, the individual judges draft their separate or dissenting opinion with the assistance of one or more Legal Officers, who may themselves have participated in drafting the majority opinion. In practice, ICC judges may request the assistance of a Legal Officer within the Chambers who did not work on the majority opinion. This practice

[46] Registry of the International Criminal Court (n 17) 81.
[47] Rome Statute, art 74(4); International Criminal Court, Rules of Procedure and Evidence (adopted 9 September 2002, entered into force 1 July 2002, as amended), r 141.

allows the ICC judges to ensure there is no conflict of interest in the Legal Officer's drafting of the separate or dissenting opinion.

The last aspect in which judges receive assistance is the issue of language. It has been observed that the Chambers usually comprise judges who are fluent in one of the official languages, ie, French or English. Where some evidence or parts of the proceeding are in a language in which a judge is not fluent, the (associate) Legal Officers often have to explain the evidence and proceedings to the judge. Of course, translators are present to provide French and English translation services in the courtroom.

In the STL, a judge's command of the applicable language was a determining factor in their ability to control a Legal Officer and dictate the direction of the case. Before the STL, the applicable law was Lebanese criminal law, and so the relevant statutes and cases were written in Arabic. Even with translators assisting, the judges relied more on Legal Officers who could provide insights into Lebanon's domestic laws and language.

III. Observations on the Role of Dispute Assistants

Although the registries of the three international criminal tribunals examined do not assist judges in their judicial functions, the criminal nature of the proceedings introduces additional responsibilities that are essential to the functioning of the tribunals. This includes aspects relating to evidence, which is especially important in criminal trials, protection of victims and witnesses etc, where Registry staff provide invaluable assistance to the Chambers.

The role of Legal Officers in Chambers, who assist the judges with their judicial functions, has evolved over time. Such officers used to work directly for individual judges. At present, they answer to a Chamber as a whole. Additionally, there is now a more robust institutional framework for the supervision and control of Legal Officers in Chambers, introduced through Legal Advisers and Head of Legal Officer positions.

15

The International Tribunal for the Law of the Sea

I. Institutional Overview and Structure

The International Tribunal for the Law of the Sea (ITLOS) was established by the 1982 United Nations Convention on the Law of the Sea (UNCLOS). The ITLOS has jurisdiction over any dispute concerning the interpretation or application of UNCLOS and all matters specifically provided for in any other agreement that confers jurisdiction on the Tribunal. Disputes relating to UNCLOS may concern the delimitation of maritime zones, navigation, conservation and management of the living resources of the sea, protection and preservation of the marine environment, and marine scientific research.

A. Adjudicators

The Tribunal consists of 21 judges, who are elected by the state parties of UNCLOS from among persons enjoying the highest reputation for fairness and integrity and of recognised competence in the field of the law of the sea.[1] The Tribunal as a whole also aims for the representation of the principal legal systems of the world and equitable geographical distribution.[2] The state parties to UNCLOS may nominate two persons having the required qualifications, and the judges are elected by secret ballot. They are elected for a renewable term of nine years. The judges are not permitted to exercise any political or administrative function, or associate actively with or be financially interested in any of the operations of any enterprise concerned with the exploration or exploitation of the resources of the sea or the seabed or other commercial use of the sea or seabed.

The judges of the Tribunal elect the President and Vice-President for a renewable term of three years.

The Dispute Assistants do not play a role in the appointment of the judges of the ITLOS.

[1] United Nations Convention on the Law of the Sea (adopted 10 December 1982, entered into force 16 November 1994) 1833 UNTS 3, Annex VI (Statute of the International Tribunal for the Law of the Sea) (UNCLOS), art 2.

[2] ibid.

B. Dispute Assistants

A Registrar heads the Registry of the ITLOS with the support of a Deputy-Registrar. The judges of the Tribunal elect the Registrar and Deputy-Registrar for a renewable period of five years following a competitive selection process.[3] The Registrar is responsible for several matters. First, they deal with terminations and disciplinary measures,[4] and prepare proposals to the Tribunal on appointments and promotions (with the assistance of an appointment and promotion panel).[5] Second, they act as the regular channel of communication between the parties and the Tribunal. Third, the staff of the Registry assists the Tribunal in case administration, for example, by organising the hearing or keeping the case records.[6] The Registrar is, in theory, responsible to the Tribunal as a whole,[7] which in practice means that the Registrar is under the supervision of the President when discharging their duties.[8] In extreme cases, the Registrar may be removed from office by a two-thirds majority of the judges.[9]

The Registry's Legal Office presently consists of the Head of Legal Office (P5), three Legal Officers (two P4, one P3), one Associate Legal Officer (P2) and one Dispute Assistants (G6).[10] A fluctuating number of interns also support the Legal Office.[11] The Registry staff are under the supervision of the Registrar.[12] They are subject to the Staff Regulations and Staff Rules. In particular, they are subject to the same rules of secrecy of the deliberations as the judges.[13]

They are Institutional Assistants, and the judges do not have any Assigned Assistants or External Assistants.

II. The Dispute Resolution Process

The first stage of proceedings following their institution[14] is the written proceedings which consist of the parties' written pleadings enumerated in Article 44.2 of the Rules of the Tribunal. At this early stage, the President prepares the first version of the working paper based on the written pleadings, summarising the parties' submissions, both

[3] International Tribunal for the Law of the Sea, Rules of the Tribunal (adopted 28 October 1997, entered into force 1 November 1997), (hereinafter 'Rules of the Tribunal'), arts 32.1, 33.

[4] International Tribunal for the Law of the Sea, Staff Regulations (adopted 1 October 1997), arts IX and X.

[5] ibid r 4.15.

[6] P Gautier, 'Registry: International Tribunal for the Law of the Sea (ITLOS)' in *Max Planck Encyclopedias of International Procedural Law* (Oxford University Press, last updated June 2018) para 12.

[7] Rules of the Tribunal, art 36.3.

[8] Gautier (n 6) para 15.

[9] Rules of the Tribunal, art 39.2.

[10] International Tribunal for the Law of the Sea, Registry Organigramme (July 2025), www.itlos.org/fileadmin/itlos/documents/registry/Organigram_July_2025.pdf.

[11] See International Tribunal for the Law of the Sea, 'Internship Programme', www.itlos.org/en/main/the-registry/training/internship-programme. There are approximately 20 positions available each year, distributed over four internship periods and four departments.

[12] International Tribunal for the Law of the Sea, *Instructions to the Registry* (adopted on 1 October 1997), art 1.2.

[13] Rules of the Tribunal, art 42.1.

[14] ibid art 54.

on the facts and the law, including the principal contentions of the parties advanced in their written pleadings.[15] The Registry assists in preparing this working paper chiefly by summarising the written pleadings and any new arguments advanced in the hearing for inclusion in a revised working paper.[16] The Registry will also begin its legal research at this early stage. It will compile the existing case law and academic views on the procedural and substantive issues that may be relevant to the case. In this, the staff will be careful to present a balanced account of all existing views rather than analyse them or express opinions on their strength.[17]

The Registrar sits beside the judges on the bench during the hearings, while the Deputy Registrar and Legal Officers are also present.[18] After the close of the oral proceedings, the judges deliberate to determine the majority opinion. The Registrar and some legal officer from the Registry will be present, but generally only intervene in responding to questions from the judges regarding details in the parties' arguments or facts.[19] Like the ICJ, a Drafting Committee will be formed based on these deliberations, which normally consist of five judges, with the President always involved unless they do not share the majority opinion.[20] The working methods of the Drafting Committee depend on its members, particularly the President. However, one constant practice is that the Registrar always attends the Drafting Committee meetings to assist if the judges so require.[21] Despite the Registrar's attendance at the meetings, it is the judges who drive the process.

The Registry only drafts the first part of a judgment containing the procedural history, and the facts of the case, which is referred to as the qualités following the tradition of the ICJ.[22] The Registry staff also take notes on the discussions of the Drafting Committee in case a judge wishes to refer back to them later on.[23]

The Registry may also be called upon to draft individual paragraphs of the reasoning, and it will review the draft to ensure editorial and linguistic consistency within and between the English and French drafts.[24] English and French are the official working languages of the Tribunal, and all judges can draft in at least one of them. The linguistic tasks of the Registry are thus primarily editorial.[25]

After a draft is completed, it is debated in the plenary in first reading, then revised by the Drafting Committee and sent to the plenary again for the second reading.[26] The

[15] International Tribunal for the Law of the Sea, Resolution on the Internal Judicial Practice of the Tribunal (adopted 31 October 1997) (hereinafter 'Judicial Practice Resolution'), art 2.3.

[16] ibid art 5.2; P Gautier, 'The International Tribunal for the Law of the Sea' in F Baetens (ed), *Legitimacy of Unseen Actors in International Adjudication* (Cambridge University Press, 2019) 43–50.

[17] Gautier (n 16) 47.

[18] ibid 45.

[19] Judicial Practice Resolution, art 5. Note that unlike in the ICJ, the judges do not each prepare a detailed note of their views on the case, as art 5.1 shows. The possibility of a process similar to that of the ICJ, foreseen in art 5.7, is not used. See R Wolfrum, 'Deliberation and Drafting: International Tribunal for the Law of the Sea (ITLOS)' in *Max Planck Encyclopedia of International Procedural Law* (Oxford University Press, online edn, January 2021).

[20] Judicial Practice Resolution, Art 6.1–6.2. If the President is in the minority, the Vice-President will sit on the committee instead.

[21] This may occur in particular for procedural questions, as this is where the Registry's main expertise lies.

[22] Gautier (n 6) para 12.

[23] Wolfrum (n 19) para 4.

[24] Gautier (n 16) 48.

[25] Rules of the Tribunal, r 43.

[26] Judicial Practice Resolution, art 8.

duties of the Registry at this stage are likely the same as before the first reading, ie, editorial revisions and further support as requested. The final draft is then voted on by the judges and, if accepted, becomes the judgment.[27]

Dissenting opinions are possible in the ITLOS and the dissent is ultimately the responsibility of the dissenting judge or judges.[28]

III. Observations on the Role of Dispute Assistants

From this overview of the decision-making process, a similar picture to that in the ICJ emerges, albeit with some notable differences. There are several factors which limit the ITLOS Registry's influence on the final judgment. First, like in the ICJ, the ITLOS judges have years of experience and recognised competence in international law of the sea. This expertise allows them to retain firm control over the drafting process. Second, while the Registry assists the judges in their work, it does so only at the judge's request. Third, given the lower caseload and the comparatively large number of judges who are experts in their field, each case receives significant attention from the judges. Finally, unlike the ICJ, judges do not have Assigned Assistants. In practice, the Registry has relatively extensive research duties. However, the Registry's practice is to compile existing case law and academic views rather than analyse them.

[27] ibid art 9.

[28] See, for example, the Joint Dissenting Opinion of Judges Cot, Pawlak, Yanai, Hoffmann, Kolodkin and Lijnzaad and Judge ad hoc Treves, *M/V 'Norstar' (Panama v Italy)* (ITLOS Case No 25).

16

The Iran-US Claims Tribunal

I. Institutional Overview and Structure

The Iran-US Claims Tribunal (hereinafter IUSCT or 'Tribunal') was established as an 'international arbitral tribunal for the purpose of deciding claims of nationals of the United States against Iran and claims of nationals of Iran against the United States', 'official claims of the United States and Iran against each other arising out of contractual arrangements between them for the purchase and sale of goods and services' and certain counterclaims, as specified in the Declaration of the Government of the Democratic and Popular Republic of Algeria Concerning the Settlement of Claims by the Government of the United States of America and the Government of the Islamic Republic of Iran (hereinafter 'Claims Settlement Declaration'), 19 January 1981, as well as disputes between the US and Iran concerning the interpretation or performance of provisions of the Declaration of the Government of the Democratic and Popular Republic of Algeria (hereinafter 'General Declaration'), 19 January 1981.[1]

Before proceeding with the institutional structure and procedure of the IUSCT, it is important to note that the Tribunal's practice has evolved over the years, adapting to the type and volume of cases before it and may evolve in the future. Wherever relevant, the text specifies that a statement refers to present practice.[2]

A. Adjudicators

The IUSCT consists of nine members; the US and Iran appoint three members each, while the remaining members are appointed either by the mutual agreement of the party-appointed members or by an Appointing Authority in the absence of such agreement. Thereafter, the party-appointed members appoint one of the third-country members as President by mutual agreement; in the absence of agreement, the Appointing Authority appoints the President.[3] The President decides, via the issuance of orders, the composition of the Chambers, assignment of cases to the Chambers and relinquishment of a case

[1] Declaration of the Government of the Democratic and Popular Republic of Algeria Concerning the Settlement of Claims by the Government of the United States of America and the Government of the Islamic Republic of Iran (hereinafter 'Claims Settlement Declaration') (19 January 1981), art II.

[2] This Chapter is drafted on the basis of practice followed by the IUSCT in 2023.

[3] Claims Settlement Declaration, art III; Iran–United States Claims Tribunal, Rules of Procedure (adopted 3 May 1983) (Rules of Procedure), arts 6–8. The Appointing Authority is to be agreed upon by the parties. If the parties fail to agree on an Appointing Authority or if the Appointing Authority fails to appoint an

to the Full Tribunal.[4] The Tribunal may either sit in Chambers of three with a Chairman of the Chamber (third-party member) acting as the presiding arbitrator or presiding member,[5] or as a Full Tribunal with nine members and the President of the Tribunal presiding.[6] The Full Tribunal has jurisdiction over the claims and disputes involving the two states.[7] Today, the Tribunal only sits as the Full Tribunal as it has resolved all private claims; only disputes involving the two states remain pending.[8]

The Dispute Assistants do not play a role in the appointment of the members of the IUSCT.

B. Dispute Assistants

The Registry of the Tribunal, as an institution, is presently composed of a Secretary-General, as head of the administration, two co-Registrars (one selected by Iran and the other one by the US), translators (English/Farsi, Farsi/English) and supporting staff. The present practice of the Tribunal is that third parties, such as interpreters and court reporters for hearings, are engaged as needed.[9] The Registry does not provide any legal assistance to the members. Instead, it provides administrative assistance, for example, in relation to the technical aspects of the documents filed by the parties and the organisation of hearings. They are Institutional Assistants.

Members primarily receive legal assistance from the Legal Advisers. The present practice of the Tribunal is that each member is assigned one Legal Adviser, and the President of the Tribunal may be assigned additional Legal Adviser(s).[10] These Legal Advisers are not part of the Registry; the Secretary-General appoints them on the recommendation of their respective member. Accordingly, they are administratively subordinate to the Secretary-General, but work under the supervision and control of their respective member. The exact role played by the Legal Adviser depends on the needs of the member to whom they are assigned. They are Assigned Assistants.

We will examine the role of the Dispute Assistants in the dispute resolution process of the IUSCT below.

II. The Dispute Resolution Process

Each Legal Adviser is assigned to one member of the Tribunal and works for the member individually. However, in practice, there may be collaboration between the

arbitrator within the prescribed time, the Secretary-General of the Permanent Court of Arbitration (PCA) is the default Designating Authority to designate an Appointing Authority.

[4] Claims Settlement Declaration, art III, read with Rules of Procedure, art 5.

[5] Rules of Procedure, definition (j); Iran–United States Claims Tribunal, Presidential Order No 1 (19 October 1981) IUSCTR 1, 95, para 3.

[6] Rules of Procedure, definition (f).

[7] Presidential Order No 1, 2.

[8] C Pinto and B McAsey, 'Iran–United States Claims Tribunal' in R Wolfrum (ed), *Max Planck Encyclopedia of Public International Law* (Oxford University Press online edition, 2012), para 46.

[9] ibid 20.

[10] At present, one of the Legal Advisers of the President is assigned as the Principal Adviser.

Legal Advisers. For example, to the extent that their member may direct, they may coordinate to avoid duplication of tasks between them. Such coordination reportedly takes place between the Legal Advisers of third-country members.

In terms of assistance provided to the members, the Legal Adviser holds various responsibilities under the instruction and guidance of their member. In preparation for hearings, the Legal Adviser assists their respective member as instructed; this may involve preparing a presentation of the key issues arising in a case or summarising the parties' positions. During hearings, the Legal Advisers are present and may assist their respective members, for example, by identifying issues for further inquiry or suggesting draft questions to the parties. Depending on the working relationship between the members and their Legal Advisers, and the individual approach of each member, there may be dialogue between the member and their Legal Adviser, at this stage relating to substantive issues.

After the conclusion of the hearing, the next stage is the deliberations. The deliberations were (and are) to remain secret.[11] Although not explicitly provided for in the rules, the present practice is that the Legal Advisers may be present during the deliberations, if needed. However, they do not participate or intervene directly. They may communicate with their supervisor discreetly, and the member may invite them to provide specific inputs. Some members prepare written memoranda for the deliberations, and the level of contribution of the Legal Advisers to the memoranda varies from member to member. The present practice is that members and Legal Advisers may take notes during the deliberations, as the Tribunal does not keep official minutes of hearings. These notes may become an important reference for subsequent work.

Once completed, the deliberations are followed by the drafting of the award. At present, the practice of the Tribunal is that the President of the Tribunal bears primary responsibility for the drafting process. The President receives assistance from the other members, who may prepare drafts of specific sections of the award or provide comments on drafts written by the President. When the Full Tribunal presently hears the cases before the Tribunal, the third-country members are often invited to prepare a draft award and circulate it to the party-appointed members for their comments. The Legal Advisers to the members play a meaningful role during the drafting process,[12] under the supervision of and in accordance with the instructions given by their respective supervisor. The Legal Advisers may assist their respective supervisors in providing comments on drafts.

III. Observations on the Role of the Dispute Assistants

One instance where the role played by the Legal Adviser before the IUSCT was challenged is worth noting.[13] In August 1991, Iran challenged the Chairman of a Chamber

[11] Rules of Procedure, art 31.

[12] As explained earlier, at present, this is undertaken by the third-party members, and therefore the Legal Advisers of the third-party members fulfil this role.

[13] See generally *LM* Caplan, 'Arbitrator Challenges at the Iran–United States Claims Tribunal' in C Giorgetti (ed), *Challenges and Recusals of Judges and Arbitrators in International Courts and Tribunals* (Brill, 2012) ch 4. Although not directly on the issue, the discussion on challenges by the Iranian government against Judge Krzysztof Skubiszewski on events surrounding an inquiry by the Tribunal's Deputy Secretary-General into the balance of the security account is also worth noting (at 125–26).

of Three Members, Mr Gaetano Arangio-Ruiz, arguing, among other things, that his Legal Advisor (as they were then called) was going beyond their legitimate function and encroaching on Mr Arangio-Ruiz's arbitral functions. By a decision rendered on 24 September 1991, the Appointing Authority rejected the application. In doing so, the Appointing Authority noted the functions of Dispute Assistants, as described by Mr Arangio-Ruiz's Legal Advisor, to include making abstracts of pleadings and other submissions, as well as preparing draft decisions for the arbitrators. However, this did not imply that the decision-making function was delegated to the Legal Advisors. It has been noted that the Advisors draft entirely on the instruction and direction of their members.[14]

Therefore, the challenge clarifies that although the Legal Advisers may draft the award or part thereof, this does not encroach on the arbitrator's mandate. The arbitrator exercises firm control over the decision-making functions, which is not diluted by the assistance provided by the Legal Adviser.

[14] C Partasides, 'The Fourth Arbitrator? The Role of Secretaries to Tribunals in International Arbitration' (2002) 18 *Arbitration International* 147, fn 18, citing *Iran-United States Claims Tribunal Reports* (Cambridge, Grotius Publications Ltd, 1992), vol 27, 291–336.

17

The Dispute Settlement System of the Mercado Común del Sur

I. Institutional Overview and Structure

The Southern Common Market (Mercado Común del Sur or MERCOSUR) has a two-tier dispute settlement system, much like the WTO. It is pertinent to note that the MERCOSUR dispute settlement system has not been used often. Since the entry into force of the Protocol of Olivos in 2004, only two awards have been rendered by an ad hoc tribunal, and only six by the Tribunal Permanente de Revisión (TPR), the latest one being in 2012.[1]

A. Adjudicators

The first stage is an ad hoc tribunal consisting of three members, and this may be followed by the appellate review stage, the TPR, consisting of five arbitrators.[2] Besides appellate review, the TPR is also responsible for emergency measures[3] and examining compliance with its own rulings.[4] It can be called upon as a tribunal of first instance if both parties agree.[5] The Dispute Assistants play a role in the appointment of the arbitrators at the ad hoc tribunal stage, and this is detailed as part of the dispute settlement process in section II below.

B. Dispute Assistants

The TPR receives support from the Secretaría del TPR (ST) in its work. The Consejo del Mercado Común elects a Secretary, who heads the ST, through a public application

[1] Tribunal Permanente de Revisión del MERCOSUR, 'Solicitudes de control de laudos', www.tprmercosur.org/es/sol_contr_laudos.htm. The higher number of TPR decisions is due to the TPR being called upon several times to rule on the implementation of its awards. Prior to the Protocol of Olivos (under the Brasilia protocol), there were 10 awards.

[2] Protocol of Olivos for the Settlement of Disputes in MERCOSUR (adopted 18 February 2002, entered into force 10 May 2004) (hereinafter 'Protocol of Olivos'), arts 17–18.

[3] ibid art 24.

[4] ibid art 30.1.

[5] ibid art 23.

based on merits and qualifications, and based on a proposal of three candidates made by the arbitrators of the TPR for a period of two years, renewable once.[6] Presently, one legal officer, one staff member responsible for library and documentation, one for administrative duties and one for IT services assist the Secretary.[7] The administrative support duties at the first stage of proceedings used to be discharged by the Secretaría del MERCOSUR, the general secretariat of the organisation. Since the entry into force of the Modification Protocol of the Protocol of Olivos in 2018, the ST has taken over these duties as well.[8] All staff are subject to the MERCOSUR Staff Rules.[9] They are Institutional Assistants.

II. The Dispute Resolution Process

Proceedings in front of an ad hoc tribunal are initiated by one Member State notifying the ST, which will then forward the notification to the respondent(s).[10] Each Member State nominates one arbitrator from a list of 48 established in advance by the Member States (each state appoints 12 arbitrators in the list).[11] The parties nominate the presiding arbitrator by agreement or, if necessary, the ST selects one by lot.[12] The ST (ie, the Institutional Assistants) plays a role in the appointment of the arbitrators of the ad hoc tribunal.

During the procedures, the ST is primarily tasked with administrative support, but can be called upon to provide other types of assistance.[13] After receiving the written submissions, the tribunal will hold a hearing, the results of which the ST will record, summarise, distribute to the parties and archive.[14]

The tribunal will then hold deliberations, presided over by the president, and produce the award.[15] Like with other arbitral tribunals, the ST's involvement in advising on drafting or doing research will depend on the preferences of the arbitrators in question, However, given the extremely light caseload, additional assistance is often unnecessary.

The TPR consists of five arbitrators elected by the Member States,[16] but sits in a configuration of three when hearing cases involving only two Member States.[17] The ST

[6] Common Market Group, Resolution on the Secretariat of the Tribunal Permanente de Revisión MERCOSUR/GMC EXT/RES No 66/05 (6 December 2005), art 2.

[7] ibid 3.

[8] Protocol of Olivos, art 5. Note that all subsequently mentioned articles in the Protocol of Olivos have to be read with this in mind.

[9] Consejo del Mercado Común, General Rules for MERCOSUR Staff (Normas Generales para Funcionarios MERCOSUR, MERCOSUR/CMC/DEC No 15/15 (16 July 2015).

[10] Protocol of Olivos, arts 9.1–9.2.

[11] ibid art 10.2(i).

[12] ibid arts 10.3(i)–(ii). Note that the same random selection procedure is applied if one Member State does not nominate its wing arbitrator: art 10.2(ii).

[13] Council of the Common Market, Regulation of the Protocol of Olivos for the Settlement of Disputes in MERCOSUR, MERCOSUR/CMC/DEC No 37/03 (15 August 2003), art 18.2.

[14] See MERCOSUR Arbitral Tribunal, *Uruguay v Argentina, Prohibition of the Importation of Remoulded Tyres*, Award (25 October 2005) para 9.

[15] Council of the Common Market, Model Rules of Procedure for the ad hoc arbitral tribunals of MERCOSUR, MERCOSUR/CMC/DEC No 30/04 (16 December 2004).

[16] Protocol of Olivos, art 18.

[17] Regulation of the Protocol of Olivos for the Settlement of Disputes in MERCOSUR (adopted by the Common Market Council, 2003) (hereinafter 'Regulation of the Protocol of Olivos'), art 20. The third

supports the TPR in research, administrative and judicial matters.[18] It acts as the intermediary for the communication between the parties and the TPR.[19] After holding its hearing on the evidence,[20] the TPR will begin drafting the award. In this context, the assistance of the ST is largely unregulated, but one notable duty the ST has is providing research assistance by compiling relevant precedents and literature for the arbitrators to utilise.[21]

III. Observations on the Role of Dispute Assistants

While the ST can have considerable leeway in assisting its arbitrators, it seems unlikely that this will lead to undue influence, given, inter alia, that the arbitrators have a very low caseload and can therefore focus more of their attention on individual cases.

---

arbitrator is chosen, as in the ad hoc tribunals, by lot by the ST, from among the remaining arbitrator not nationals of either party.

[18] ibid art 35.

[19] Council of the Common Market, *Rules of Procedure of the Tribunal Permanente de Revisión*, MERCOSUR /CMC/DEC No 30/05 (8 December 2005) Art 14.3.

[20] *ibid art* 24.

[21] Regulation of the Protocol of Olivos, art 34.2(f).

18

The Permanent Court of Arbitration

I. Institutional Overview and Structure

The Permanent Court of Arbitration (PCA) is the oldest mechanism for settling disputes between states, originating from the 1899 Hague Convention for the Pacific Settlement of International Disputes.[1] Despite its name, the PCA is not an actual court. Instead, it is an institution that supports tribunals in their work resolving disputes through various dispute settlement procedures, most notably arbitration. It administers disputes under many different arbitration rules, and the cases before it involve various combinations of states, state entities, international organisations and private parties.[2] In explaining the role of the PCA and of its adjudicators and Dispute Assistants, this section will refer to both the UNCITRAL Rules and the PCA Rules. The majority of disputes administered by the PCA fall under the UNCITRAL Rules, so both sets of rules are operating at the same time.[3] According to Bordachar and Doe, this is due to the suitability of the PCA Rules to address various typologies of disputes as well as their similarity in content to the UNCITRAL Rules 2010.[4]

A. Adjudicators

In cases under the UNCITRAL Rules and the PCA Rules, the role of the Dispute Assistants in the appointment of the arbitrators is worth noting. Arbitrators under both these sets of rules are appointed by the parties: in the case of a single arbitrator by consensus; or in the case of a panel of three or five arbitrators – each party appoints one arbitrator, and the two arbitrators then choose the remaining ones.[5] In the case of a three-member tribunal, the third arbitrator acts as the President. In a five-member

[1] Convention for the Pacific Settlement of International Disputes (signed 29 July 1899, entered into force 4 September 1900) 187 CTS 410 (hereinafter 'Pacific Settlement Convention'); see also K Claussen, 'Old and New Dispute Secretariats' (2022) 116 *American Journal of International Law: Unbound* 400–01.

[2] Permanent Court of Arbitration, 'Services', www.pca-cpa.org/en/services.

[3] J Bordachar and M Doe, 'Argentina and the Permanent Court of Arbitration: The Past, Present and Future of Arbitration Involving the State and State Entities on the Río de la Plata' in F Fortese (ed), *Arbitration in Argentina* (Oxford University Press, 2020) 421–22.

[4] Permanent Court of Arbitration, Rules of Procedure (adopted 2012) (Introduction), para 1.

[5] United National Commission on International Trade Law Arbitration Rules (adopted 15 December 1976, revised 2010, with amendments 2013) (hereinafter 'UNCITRAL Rules'), arts 7–8; Permanent Court of Arbitration Rules (adopted 2012) (hereinafter 'PCA Rules'), arts 7–8.

tribunal, the two party-appointed arbitrators select one of the three arbitrators they selected to act as the President. The Hague Convention envisages that the arbitrators, termed 'Members of the Court',[6] were to be chosen from a roster established by the state parties to the Convention.[7] However, parties to PCA cases are not bound to choose arbitrators from that list. While parties sometimes make appointments from that list, they frequently resort to arbitrators outside of it.

In the following instances, the parties may need the assistance of an appointing authority in constituting the tribunal:

a) If the parties have agreed that a sole arbitrator is to be appointed, but have not reached an agreement on the person to be appointed within the specified time period.
b) If the parties have agreed on a three/five-member panel and one of the parties has not notified the choice of arbitrator within the specified time period, or the two party-appointed arbitrators have not agreed on the choice of the remaining/presiding arbitrator.

If the parties have not chosen an appointing authority, either party may request the Secretary-General of the PCA to designate an appointing authority under the UNCITRAL Rules.[8] In practice, the parties may (and frequently do) agree to have the Secretary General of the PCA to act directly as the appointing authority.[9] Appointing Authorities follow a strike-and-rank list procedure when making appointments,[10] where the parties can point to their preferences from a list communicated by the Secretary-General. The default mechanism is different under the PCA Rules, with the Secretary-General of the PCA being the default Appointing Authority.[11]

When the Secretary-General is the Appointing Authority, the International Bureau (detailed below in section I.B) compiles this list based on characteristics communicated by the parties.[12] The Bureau exercises its judgement on the suitability of the candidate if there are conflicting requirements by the parties. Along with the list, they also share the credentials of, and a declaration of conflicts and disclosures[13] from, the candidates. The parties strike off candidates from the list and rank the remaining ones. Thereafter, the Appointing Authority selects the remaining arbitrator(s) or the President most suitable to the parties according to their rankings. Although in theory, parties are free to strike off an unlimited number of candidates, they often agree to restrict the number of strikes to allow the constitution of the tribunal as per the list. If the parties are not able to arrive at any common candidates, the Secretary-General appoints a candidate that

[6] Although this is the official term under the Convention, the note uses the term 'arbitrator' for ease of reference and understanding.

[7] Pacific Settlement Convention (n 1) art 23.

[8] UNCITRAL Rules, art 6.2.

[9] ibid art 6.1.

[10] UNCITRAL Rules, art 8.2; PCA Rules, art 8.2.

[11] PCA Rules, arts 8.1, 9.2, 9.3. This difference is due to the fact that the UNCITRAL Rules were intended to operate in an ad hoc manner, while the PCA Rules recognise the PCA acting as a facilitating entity.

[12] For example, expertise in certain technical issues/laws or language proficiency.

[13] Although there are no binding rules on conflicts, there are soft law guidelines that parties may choose to make applicable – see, for example, International Bar Association, *IBA Guidelines on Conflicts of Interest in International Arbitration* (approved 25 May 2024); UNCITRAL Working Group III, *Draft Code of Conduct for Adjudicators in International Investment Dispute Resolution* (UNCITRAL Working Group III, ISDS Reform).

was reserved from the list and not shared with the parties. Under the PCA Rules, the Secretary-General also decides on any challenges to the arbitrators.[14]

Therefore, the Institutional Assistants of the PCA play an important role in some instances for the appointment of the arbitrators under the UNCITRAL Rules and the PCA Rules.

B. Dispute Assistants

The International Bureau serves as the Institutional office of the PCA. The Administrative Council, consisting of the Member States, elects a Secretary-General to head the International Bureau for a once-renewable term of five years.[15] The International Bureau consists of the Secretary-General and the legal staff of the PCA, including the Deputy Secretaries General, Senior Legal Counsel, Legal Counsel, Assistant Legal Counsel and case managers.[16] The number of legal staff employed is not fixed and may vary depending on the PCA's needs. They are bound by the – somewhat rudimentary – Rules Concerning the Organization and Internal Working of the International Bureau.[17] They are Institutional Assistants.

Where parties to a dispute or a tribunal seek assistance from the PCA, one or more legal counsel from the International Bureau will often serve as the primary assistant, supported by one or more assistant legal counsel and a case manager. At present, the practice is that a Senior Legal Counsel may be assigned as the Tribunal Registrar/Secretary,[18] supported by additional legal staff. This legal team typically supports all members of the tribunal, but, in practice, primarily assists the chair. The Deputy Secretaries-General assign cases to legal counsel and other staff. Assignments are determined by workload and language needs, among other factors.

In some instances,[19] arbitrators may employ their own personal assistants, who work for them individually as tribunal assistants, in addition to PCA staff. They are External Assistants.

The role of Dispute Assistants in the dispute resolution process of the PCA is described below. Before setting out the procedure, it should be recalled that the practices in international arbitration are not uniform and will vary between different arbitrators. This is even more the case in the PCA where different types of disputes and various applicable rules operate together. Therefore, the following procedures may not all feature in all cases. The aim is to detail the role played by the PCA and its Dispute Assistants in the various stages of a case administered under the UNCITRAL Rules and the PCA Rules.

[14] PCA Rules, art 13.4.

[15] Rules of Procedure for the Administrative Council of the Permanent Court of Arbitration (adopted 19 September 1900), art VIII(3).

[16] At present, according to the PCA website, there are 55 legal staff: two Deputy Secretaries-General, five Senior Legal Counsel, 11 Legal Counsel, 20 Assistant Legal Counsel and 17 case managers. See Permanent Court of Arbitration, 'Staff', www.pca-cpa.org/en/about/introduction/staff.

[17] Rules Concerning the Organization and Internal Working of the International Bureau of the Permanent Court of Arbitration (adopted 18 December 1900).

[18] The Tribunal Secretaries in state-to-state disputes are referred to as Tribunal Registrars.

[19] This may be happening is around 20–30 per cent of cases.

II. The Dispute Resolution Process

The proceedings begin when a claimant files a notice of arbitration, which must be sent to the respondent and the International Bureau.[20] After the establishment of the arbitral tribunal, the claimant files a statement of claim, and the respondent files a statement of defence in reaction. Both these documents are sent to the other party, the International Bureau and all arbitrators.[21] All communications must be sent in copy to the International Bureau.[22] Unlike in ICSID, the International Bureau does not conduct a preliminary examination of the file.

In almost all cases, there is a case management conference. Before this case management conference, the members of the International Bureau working on the case assist the tribunal in preparing two documents: the Terms of Appointment/Reference and the Draft Procedural Order No 1. The Terms of Appointment/Reference recounts, inter alia, the procedural steps leading up to the constitution of the tribunal, the procedural rules applicable, any non-binding rules or guidelines that the parties agree to be binding,[23] and the determination of fees and costs and the rates applicable. The International Bureau shares a draft of this Terms of Appointment/Reference with the parties for their approval and comments; the parties subsequently discuss any disagreements during the case management conference. The Procedural Order No 1 provides details and sets out the calendar of procedures.

The Bureau's legal staff assist in the organisation of the hearings; they are present during the hearings, any preliminary meetings and the deliberations. During the hearings, institutional staff assist and provide input only on purely administrative issues. Bureau staff may sometimes be present during tribunal deliberations and may assist by taking notes.

After concluding the hearings, the tribunal will draft the award. The assistance offered by the Bureau staff depends on the case, the parties' agreement and expectations, the applicable rules, and the individual approach of the arbitrators. Owing to their institutional memory and expertise, the tribunal may ask a legal staff to draft the procedural history of a case, or on some specific issues, but, overall, the drafting is the domain of the arbitrators. After the drafting is complete, the Bureau staff support the tribunal through linguistic editing, proofreading and reviewing the drafts.

When it comes to External Assistants, the PCA does not provide any rules regulating the permissible uses of such tribunal secretaries, unlike some other arbitral institutions detailed in Chapter 5. But even in the PCA, in very complex cases, or when the arbitrators have a busy schedule, there may be instances where the External Assistants undertake drafting.[24]

[20] PCA Rules, art 3.

[21] ibid arts 20–21.

[22] ibid art 7.4. This is not the case under the UNCITRAL Rules.

[23] For example, the IBA Rules on the Taking of Evidence in International Arbitration.

[24] See the famous example of the *Veteran Petroleum Limited and Others v Russian Federation (Yukos)*; Gerechtshof Den Haag (Court of Appeal of The Hague), 18 February 2020, ECLI:NLGHDHA:2020:234, paras 6.6.1–6.6.15. Note that this arbitration was conducted under the UNCITRAL Rules, which also do not regulate the use of tribunal secretaries/assistants.

Dissenting opinions are possible in the PCA. The assistance the Bureau staff or the tribunal registrar/secretary provides is limited to proofreading or linguistic checks. However, the External Assistants may assist their members in writing a dissenting opinion.

III. Observations on the Role of Dispute Assistants

PCA legal staff may be involved at every step of a dispute administered by the PCA, and arbitrators in those disputes may call upon them for legal, administrative and logistical assistance, subject to the procedures and rules governing the dispute. In the case of external assistants, it will depend on the individual arbitrator how much control they exercise over the staff.[25]

[25] *ibid para* 6.6.6.

19

The World Trade Organization Dispute Settlement System

I. Institutional Overview and Structure

The Agreement Establishing the World Trade Organization (hereinafter 'WTO Agreement')[1] is a multilateral treaty, with agreements setting out the rights and obligations of WTO members in respect of trade.[2] The Understanding on Rules and Procedures Governing the Settlement of Disputes (DSU)[3] generally guides the dispute resolution processes under the WTO DSS. It consists of several detailed and distinct processes (specifically, 15[4] processes), with Dispute Assistants intervening and assisting adjudicators to differing degrees. We will examine these processes in detail in Part III of this book, specifically Chapters 22 and 23.[5]

Various actors make up the WTO DSS and they each have specific roles and functions under the DSU. For example, the Dispute Settlement Body (DSB), composed of representatives of all WTO members, is responsible for administering and overseeing the entire dispute settlement process – it is the parliament of members discussing various dispute matters. The Director-General (DG) of the WTO convenes the meetings of

[1] Marrakesh Agreement Establishing the World Trade Organization (opened for signature 15 April 1994, entered into force 1 January 1995) 1867 UNTS 3.

[2] World Trade Organization Secretariat, *A Handbook on the WTO Dispute Settlement System*, 2nd edn (Cambridge University Press, 2017) 1.

[3] Understanding on Rules and Procedures Governing the Settlement of Disputes, Marrakesh Agreement Establishing the World Trade Organization, Annex 2, 1869 UNTS 401, 33 ILM 1226 (1994) (DSU).

[4] The 15 processes are: (1) selection of ad hoc panellists by parties in original panel; (2) selection of ad hoc panellists by parties in implementation panels; (3) selection of ad hoc arbitrators by parties in arbitration for the determination of the reasonable period of time for implementation of a ruling; (4) selection of ad hoc arbitrators by parties in arbitration for determination of the level of retaliation; and (5) selection of arbitrators for arbitrations conducted as per art 25 DSU (non-MPIA); (6) selection of ad hoc panellists by DG in original panel; (7) selection of ad hoc panellists by DG in implementation panels; (8) selection of ad hoc arbitrators by DG in arbitration for the determination of the reasonable period of time for implementation of a ruling; (9) selection of ad hoc arbitrators by DG in arbitration for determination of the level of retaliation; (10) original panel proceedings; (11) implementation panel proceedings or compliance panel; (12) arbitration for the determination of the reasonable period of time for implementation of a ruling; (13) arbitration for the determination of level of suspension of concessions; (14) Appellate Body proceedings (not operational); and (15) arbitration under MPIA and DSU art 25 Appeal Arbitrations.

[5] Chapters 22 and 23 in Part III focus on the concerns and recommendations to the WTO DSS, and ch 24 examines the processes and procedures through which these recommendations may be introduced. This chapter aims to provide a general presentation of different WTO dispute processes and its main actors, as background for the in-depth discussion in Part III.

the DSB and has different functions across the stages of a dispute, including the selection of adjudicators in stages when the parties cannot reach an agreement.

In this chapter, for the purposes of the comparative study in Part II, we will focus on the following stages of the dispute resolution process: the original panel stage and the appellate stage. With respect to the appellate stage, the Appellate Body (AB) has not been operational since 2019. In responding to this vacuum, some members created an arbitration appeal mechanism under Article 25 DSU: the Multi-Party Interim Appeal Arbitration Arrangement (MPIA). This Chapter will discuss the previous procedure and practice of the AB when it was operational, as well as the current procedure and practice of the MPIA.

This section provides an overview of the relevant adjudicators (section I.A) in each step, as well as the Dispute Assistants (section I.B) that are involved. Section II explains the dispute resolution process and the functions of these actors in the panel proceedings stage (section II.A) and the appellate proceedings stage (section II.B). For the sake of completeness, we also briefly explain the role of Dispute Assistants in additional processes (section II.C), specifically the arbitration proceedings for determining the reasonable period of time for implementation under Article 21.3 DSU, the proceedings for surveillance of implementation of recommendations/rulings under Article 21.5 DSU (referred to as 'Implementation Panel'), the arbitration proceeding for the determination of the level of suspension of concessions under Article 22.6 DSU, and other arbitrations under Article 25 DSU. As mentioned above, we will return to these additional dispute processes in detail in Part III.

A. Adjudicators

i. The Original Panel Stage

Panels are ad hoc adjudicative bodies established to adjudicate a particular dispute between members.[6] The panel's function is to assist the DSB by making a recommendation or ruling on a dispute that a complainant raises. Accordingly, a panel makes an objective assessment of the factual questions and legal issues referred to it and the conformity of a challenged measure with the covered agreement(s) invoked by the complainant.[7] The panellists are selected for each dispute, and the specific selection process is detailed further along with the dispute resolution process in section II below.

ii. The Appeal Stage

The AB of the WTO was a standing body of seven members, acting as the appellate and final stage of the adjudicatory mechanism.[8] Its mandate was to review the legal aspects of the reports issued by a panel that was appealed. The AB would issue an Appellate Body

[6] WTO Secretariat (n 2) 29.

[7] DSU, art 11.

[8] WTO Secretariat (n 2) 31–32. See also World Trade Organization, 'Decision Establishing the Appellate Body, Recommendations by the Preparatory Committee for the WTO approved by the Dispute Settlement Body', 10 February 1995, WTO Doc WT/DSB/1 (19 June 1995).

Report (hereinafter 'AB Report') that would be adopted by the DSB. The AB became non-operational after the US blocked the launching of a procedure to appoint new AB members to replace those whose terms had expired. We will explain this further below.

iii. The MPIA

In April 2020, a group of WTO members notified the DSB that they had established the MPIA pursuant to Article 25 DSU[9] for resolving appeals in the absence of a functioning AB. There are presently 57 members participating in the MPIA.[10] The appeals are heard by three appeal arbitrators selected from the standing pool of 10 appeal arbitrators (hereinafter 'pool of arbitrators'). We will explain this further below.

B. Dispute Assistants

i. The Original Panel Stage

The DSU states that the WTO Secretariat has the responsibility to assist the panel on 'legal, historical and procedural aspects of the matters dealt with, and of providing secretarial and technical support'.[11] The WTO Secretariat is organised into divisions, headed by a Director who reports to the Deputy Director-Generals (DDG) and to the DG. The Secretariat staff of the Legal Affairs Division (LAD) or of the Rules Division (in the case of trade remedy matters) provide such assistance to panels.[12] Panels are also assisted by staff who are (legal) experts in substantive areas relevant to the dispute (for example, specialists in areas like agriculture, financial services, international standards and economists), sourced from their respective divisions if the need arises.[13] A team assisting a panel typically comprises at least one or more junior legal officers (one of whom is appointed as the 'secretary' to the panel and who assists with communications between the panel and the disputing parties), one legal officer, one senior legal officer and other staff depending on the complexity/requirements of the case.[14] They are *Institutional Assistants*, as they do not work for specific panellists, and instead assist

[9] WTO, *MultiParty Interim Appeal Arbitration Arrangement Pursuant to Article 25 of the DSU*, WTO Doc JOB/DSB/1/Add.12 (30 April 2020) (MPIA).

[10] As of 20 January 2026, the MPIA has the following participants: Australia, Benin, Brazil, Canada, China, Chile, Colombia, Costa Rica, Ecuador, the European Union (with its 27 Member States: Austria, Belgium, Bulgaria, Croatia, Cyprus, Czechia, Denmark, Estonia, Finland, France, Germany, Greece, Hungary, Ireland, Italy, Latvia, Lithuania, Luxembourg, Malta, the Netherlands, Poland, Portugal, Romania, Slovakia, Slovenia, Spain and Sweden), Guatemala, Hong Kong (China), Iceland, Japan, Macao (China), Malaysia, Mexico, Montenegro, New Zealand, Nicaragua, Norway, Pakistan, Paraguay, Peru, the Philippines, Singapore, Switzerland, the UK, Ukraine, Uruguay and Vietnam. See 'MultiParty Interim Appeal Arbitration Arrangement (MPIA)', www.worldtradelaw.net/static.php?type=public&page=mpia.

[11] DSU, art 27.

[12] DA Baker and G Marceau, 'The World Trade Organization' in F Baetens (ed), *Legitimacy of Unseen Actors in International Adjudication* (Cambridge University Press, 2022) 83.

[13] ibid.

[14] JM Wauters, 'The Role of the WTO Secretariat in WTO Dispute: Silent Witness or Ghost Expert?' (2021) 12 *Global Policy* 84.

panels as a whole. There are several other legal staff members from all over the Secretariat who perform legal assistance to negotiations, for implementation, training etc.

The staff working on disputes report to the Director of the LAD/Rules Division, and the DDG in charge of the division. Like all other Secretariat staff, they are appointed by the DG.[15] The panellists do not have direct control over the appointment or appraisal of the staff. However, they provide feedback on the staff assisting them in a dispute, which may become relevant at the time of appraisal.

ii. The Appeal Stage

The DSU envisaged that AB was to be provided with appropriate administrative and legal support as required.[16] When the AB was operational, the AB Secretariat was separate and independent from the WTO Secretariat.[17] It was composed of lawyers and administrative staff, who were appointed by and reported directly to the DG for all administrative matters.[18] Each AB division was assisted by a team of junior staff lawyers led by a senior lawyer, reporting to the director of the AB Secretariat.[19] Previously, in complex disputes, the AB has also sought advice from staff of the Economic Research and Statistics Division. Since the AB became non-operational, there is no longer an AB Secretariat. They were Institutional Assistants, as they were not assigned to a specific AB member/bench.

iii. The MPIA

The MPIA does not (yet) have detailed practice on Dispute Assistants. In principle, the members of the MPIA are assisted by WTO Secretariat staff (so far, two legal staff per appeal arbitration), who are not part of the LAD/Rules Division (as they may have been responsible for and involved in the panel proceedings). When an appeal to the MPIA is confirmed, the arbitrator who acts as the point of contact asks the DG to assign staff for assistance.

II. The Dispute Resolution Process

The WTO DSS covers all disputes arising under agreements listed in Appendix 1 of the DSU (referred to as 'covered agreements').[20] A dispute arises when one or more members (complainant) consider a measure that another WTO member (respondent) has adopted to be inconsistent with the obligations under a covered agreement(s) and challenges that measure in the WTO DSS.

To start with, the DSU envisages bilateral consultations between the parties as the first step towards dispute resolution.[21] A complainant initiates consultations and if the

[15] J Pauwelyn and K Pelc, 'Who Guards the "Guardians of the System"? The Role of the Secretariat in WTO Dispute Settlement' (2022) 116 *American Journal of International Law* 534–37.

[16] DSU, art 17.7.

[17] WTO (n 8).

[18] ibid.

[19] ibid.

[20] DSU, art 1.1. In the DSU, these are referred to as 'covered agreements' and the same terminology has been adopted in this chapter.

[21] ibid art 4.

consultations fail to settle the dispute within the prescribed timeline, they can request the DSB for the establishment of a panel.[22] The panel is (automatically) established by the DSB, by way of the negative consensus rule meaning that a panel is established unless all members present object.[23] As the complainant provides an affirmative vote (which they will in almost all cases) for the establishment of the panel, the negative consensus will not be met and the panel will be established. This framework was designed to provide security and predictability to the rules of the multilateral trading system.[24] The request identifies the specific measures at issue and briefly summarises the legal basis of the complaint. The DSU also provides the standard terms of reference to a panel unless the parties to the dispute agree otherwise.[25]

A. Original Panel Proceedings

i. Selection of Panellists

Once the DSB establishes the panel, the parties must select panel members to make up the panel. As panels are not permanent bodies, there is a specific procedure for their establishment by the DSB in a particular dispute and an additional step to decide the composition of a panel. Panels are normally composed of three members, unless the parties specifically agree to constitute a panel of five members.[26] The ability to choose panellists is the prerogative of the parties to the dispute.[27] However, the DSU has procedural mechanisms to ensure that the dispute settlement process is not stalled due to the unwillingness of the other party (respondent) to appoint panellists.

In terms of nationality, a panel member cannot be a citizen of a member who is a party to the dispute unless the parties agree otherwise.[28] At the same time, panel members serve in their individual capacities and are not representatives of their government or any organisation. In terms of other qualifications, the DSU provides limited guidance. It prescribes that a panel member must be well qualified[29] and independent, with a diverse background and a wide spectrum of experience.[30] There is no formal list of criteria or qualifications for a panel member; rather, the DSU provides an indicative list of examples of who can serve as a panel member without those criteria guaranteeing quality.[31] Unlike some of the other international adjudicatory bodies examined, the DSU does not

[22] ibid.

[23] DSU, art 6.1.The negative consensus rule is applicable at the second DSB meeting on which the request for establish of panel appears on the DSB agenda.

[24] ibid art 3.2.

[25] ibid art 7.1.

[26] ibid art 8.5. So far, only three-member panels have been created.

[27] G Marceau and A Venkataraman, 'Unmasking the Phantom of the Opera', (2022) 116 *American Journal of International Law: Unbound* 396.

[28] DSU, art 8.3.

[29] ibid art 8.1.

[30] ibid art 8.2.

[31] ibid art 8.1. The indicative list of examples on who can serve as a panellist reads: 'persons who have served on or presented a case to a panel, served as a representative of a Member or of a contracting party to GATT 1947 or as a representative to the Council or Committee of any covered agreement or its predecessor agreement, or in the Secretariat, taught or published on international trade law or policy, or served as a senior trade policy official of a Member'.

require panel members to possess a legal or judicial background. However, most WTO panels, particularly in recent years, have included at least one lawyer.[32]

Article 8 DSU on composition of panels envisages specific functions for the Secretariat in assisting the parties for the selection of panellists. The Secretariat maintains an indicative list of candidates who may act as panellists along with their specific areas of expertise (Trade in Goods, Trade in Services or Trade-Related Aspects of Intellectual Property Rights).[33] The DSU does not mandate that the panellists be selected exclusively from the Indicative List,[34] and the Secretariat maintains an additional database with names of past and potential panellists to further assist parties.

The DSU entrusts the Secretariat with the task of proposing the names of potential panellists to the parties.[35] The Secretariat staff meet with the parties to a dispute to hear their preferred 'criteria' for the prospective panellists,[36] and typically propose 'slates' of six names (two potential chairpersons and four panel members) for the parties' consideration.[37] The criteria provided by the parties are often conflicting and the Secretariat staff are tasked with reconciling such contradictions when proposing names. The parties retain the right to reject the nominations proposed by the Secretariat for 'compelling reasons'.[38] The ultimate control for composition of the panel remains with the parties. Additionally, the parties can agree between themselves Assistants have on the panel's composition and exclude the involvement of the Secretariat altogether.[39] Therefore, although Institutional Assistants have an important role in the appointment of panellists, in suggesting possible panellists, the parties can always reject the panellists proposed or choose to exclude their involvement at this stage.

There is a dedicated team in the LAD and the Rules Division (depending on which division has the responsibility for the dispute) assisting the parties at this stage.[40] The Director of the responsible division reviews and approves the work of the dedicated team. Formally, it is not prohibited for the staff of this team to also be assigned to assist panellists in the later stages of the dispute resolution process. However, this may happen rarely since only two or three staff each of the two divisions work on the selection of panellists.

[32] Marceau and Venkataraman (n 27) 395.

[33] DSU art 8.4. To clarify, it is WTO members that propose nominations to the Indicative List, providing relevant information on their knowledge of international trade and the sectors or subject matter of the covered agreements, and the nominations are approved by the DSB.

[34] See 'Count of WTO Panellists, by Appointment Method and Whether on Roster', www.worldtradelaw.net/databases/panellistrosterappointedby.php.

[35] DSU, art 8.6.

[36] This could be relating to the nationality (ie, parties could specifically agree to allow citizens of members whose governments are parties or third parties to the dispute to serve as panellists), expertise, prior experience etc. These meetings are confidential, so no formal minutes exist. However, this has been noted to be the practice anecdotally – see M Pereyra, 'Appointment of WTO Adjudicators: Rules and Evolving Practices' in N Lamp (ed), *Reckoning and Renewal: The World Trade Organization and its Dispute Settlement System at 30. Essays in Honour of Valerie Hughes* (Cambridge University Press, 2023) 47; R Malacrida, 'WTO Panel Composition: Searching Far and Wide for Administrators of World Trade Justice' in G Marceau (ed), *A History of Law and Lawyers in the GATT/WTO: The Development of the Rule of Law in the Multilateral Trading System* (Cambridge University Press, 2015) 314.

[37] However, this may vary depending on the preferences or request of the parties. See Pereyra (n 36) 50.

[38] DSU, art 8.6. Although this is the stated rule, there is no mechanism/threshold to assess what constitutes a 'compelling' reason, and the parties do not necessarily provide the reasons for opposing proposed panellists.

[39] Marceau and Venkataraman (n 27) 396.

[40] Pauwelyn and Pelc (n 15) 539.

If the parties are not able to agree on the composition of the panel within the prescribed timeline, either party (most likely the complainant) may ask the DG to determine the composition of the panel.[41] Prior to making a final determination, the DG is mandated to consult with the parties, which allows them to re-state or refine their preferred criteria.[42] However, the parties are not offered an opportunity to comment on the candidates selected by the DG. Nevertheless, the DG is required to consult with the Chairman of the DSB as well as the Chairman of the Council or Committee that is relevant for the particular dispute.[43] The DG is assisted by the team from the relevant division (the LAD or the Rules Division) that worked on the composition process, who brief the DG on the composition process to date, nominations that have already been turned down by the parties etc.[44] A legal staff from the DG Office often assist the DG with this function.

The DG announces their decision within 10 days from receiving the request to appoint the panel.[45] If prior to requesting the DG to constitute the panel, the parties had agreed on one or two panellists, the DG usually takes the agreement of the parties into account and then appoints only the remaining panellist(s).[46]

ii. The Dispute Resolution Process and Dispute Assistants

After the panel has been composed, the next step is laying down Working Procedures and Timetable of the case. The Secretariat team assigned to the dispute assists the panel in drafting the Working Procedures and the Timetable.[47] The panel approves the Secretariat team's draft and shares it with the parties for their comments. The parties are given an opportunity to present their comments on the draft at an organisational meeting with the panel. At this stage, the staff attend the meeting and take notes. Subsequently, the panel instructs the staff on the necessary revisions to the Working Procedures per the comments received from the parties. The revised Working Procedures are adopted by the panel and become binding.

Thereafter, the parties file their written submissions with the Secretariat Registry.[48] The Secretariat staff play a crucial role at this stage in terms of briefing the panellists on the content of the submissions. They prepare an 'Issues Paper', summarising the arguments put forth by the parties, identifying the legal issues arising and detailing various approaches the panel could take in addressing them. The Issues Paper is a descriptive, analytical and advisory note for briefing the panel. However, naturally, it is not binding on the panel.[49]

[41] DSU, art 8.7.
[42] ibid.
[43] ibid.
[44] G Sacerdoti, A Critical Reaction to Joost Pauwelyn and Krzysztof Pelc's "The WTO Secretariat's 'Open Secret': Unpacking the Controversy" (*EJIL:Talk!*, 5 September 2022), www.ejiltalk.org/a-critical-reaction-to-joost-pauwelyn-and-krzysztof-pelcs-the-wto-secretariats-open-secret-unpacking-the-controversy.
[45] DSU, art 8.7.
[46] Pereyra (n 36) 51.
[47] The template for Working Procedures provided in Appendix 3 of the DSU may be adapted to the needs of the case.
[48] DSU, art 12.6.
[49] G Marceau and DA Baker, 'A Short History of the Rules Division' in Marceau (ed) (n 36) 112–28; V Hughes, 'Working in WTO Dispute Settlement: Pride without Prejudice' in Marceau (ed) (n 36) 405.

Prior to the substantive hearing(s),[50] the panel meets with the Secretariat staff in a closed session to discuss the parties' submissions and the Issues Paper. This provides an opportunity for the panellists to become more conversant with the issues, get a sense of how their fellow panellists see the issues, and request clarifications from the Secretariat staff on research presented in the Issues Paper. The panel also discusses and determines which questions to pose to the parties prior to and during the hearing. In addition to substantive assistance, the Secretariat staff also provide various administrative and logistical support for the hearings at this stage.

During the hearings, the parties present their oral statements to the panel and answer the questions posed by the panel or other parties.[51] The Secretariat staff are also present at the hearings to assist the panel members, but do not participate. They take notes of the proceedings, including on the responses/statements made by the parties.

Thereafter, the panel goes into internal deliberations in order to assess the conformity of the challenged measure with the covered agreement(s) invoked by the complainant. The panel's deliberations are confidential. The Secretariat staff attend and participate in the deliberations, allowing the panellists to benefit from their expertise/experience and request additional research/clarifications on the submissions or jurisprudence as necessary. The role of the Secretariat staff is limited to providing the necessary information. The panel members deliberate and arrive at a decision on the issues raised in the dispute. They inform the Secretariat staff about their findings and reasoning, and, on the basis of such instructions, the staff is tasked with drafting the panel report.

The panel report consists of two main parts: the descriptive part and the findings. The descriptive part is mainly composed of the factual aspects, the claims of the parties, and a summary of the factual and legal arguments of the parties and third parties. The panel first issues a draft of the descriptive part to the parties for written comments.[52] In contrast, the 'findings' set out the panel's reasoning to support its conclusions in upholding or rejecting the complainant's claim.[53] The Secretariat assists the panel in drafting all (or parts of) the report as per their instruction. Individual panellists can express a separate opinion anonymously in the panel report[54] and may seek the Secretariat staff's assistance in producing a separate opinion.

Once a draft report is completed by the staff, the panel meets internally to discuss and finalise the panel report. The report is issued to the parties for review and comments on specific aspects.[55] Subsequently, the panel may adjust the report in light of the parties' comments before issuing the final report that will be translated into the other two official languages before being circulated to the DSB.[56] The panel report must be adopted

[50] There may be two substantive hearings, depending on the working procedure.

[51] The questions are distributed in written form and they provide written responses, but parties have the option to also respond to them orally if they so prefer. After the conclusion of the hearing, the parties are requested to submit written responses to the questions within the prescribed timeframe.

[52] See art 15.1 DSU on issuing of the descriptive part of the report.

[53] ibid art 12.7. This reasoning is a comprehensive discussion of the applicable law in light of the facts established by the panel on the basis of the evidence before it and in light of the arguments submitted by the parties

[54] ibid art 14.3.

[55] There is also an interim review stage as per art 15 DSU, and a review meeting as per art 15.2; however, the specifics of these stages are not directly relevant to the coverage in this chapter.

[56] DSU, art 16.1.

by the DSB within 60 days from its circulation by reversed or negative consensus,[57] unless a party to the dispute formally notifies its decision to appeal.[58] In case of appeal, the panel report will be considered for adoption by the DSB only after the completion of the appeal.

B. Appeal Proceedings

The appeal stage of the WTO was the AB, which is presently not operational. Subsequently, some members set up the MPIA under Article 25 DSU to resolve disputes that are appealed by members in the absence of a functioning AB. In this section, we examine the selection process for the AB members and the MPIA arbitrators, and the dispute resolution process and the role of Dispute Assistants in assisting the AB (while it was operational) and the MPIA.

i. Appointment of AB/MPIA Members

In terms of qualifications, an AB member is required be a person of recognised authority, with demonstrable expertise in law, international trade and the subject matter of the covered agreements generally.[59] The DSU also requires AB members to stay up to date with dispute resolution activities and other relevant activities of the WTO.[60] In terms of nationality, unlike panels, an AB member's nationality does not preclude them from adjudicating a particular appeal. At the same time, the DSU also provides that the AB membership must be representative of the WTO membership. Additionally, an AB member must be unaffiliated with any government.[61] AB members were part-time and were not staff members. They were appointed by consensus of all WTO members for a term of four years, renewable once.[62] A selection committee, presided over by the DG and composed of the Chairs of the DSB, the General Council, the Council for Trade in Goods, the Council for Trade in Services and the TRIPS Council, propose candidates for election.[63] At this stage, the process was run directly by WTO members, with the AB Secretariat providing limited logistical and administrative support. Each appeal was heard by a 'division', composed of three AB members, with a presiding member responsible for conducting the proceedings and coordinating the drafting of the AB Report.[64]

Now, turning to the MPIA, the arbitration procedure is based on the substantive and procedural aspects of Appellate Review pursuant to Article 17 DSU. The qualification provided for pool of arbitrators is identical to that of AB members – ie, they must be persons of recognized authority, with demonstrated expertise in law, international trade

[57] ibid art 16.2.
[58] ibid art 16.4.
[59] ibid art 17.3.
[60] ibid.
[61] ibid.
[62] ibid art 17.2.
[63] WTO (n 8).
[64] ibid.

and the subject matter of the covered agreements generally,[65] and are required to be unaffiliated with any government.[66] Further, the pool of arbitrators is required to stay abreast of WTO dispute settlement activities.[67]

Annex 2 of the MPIA[68] sets out detailed rules for composition of the pool of arbitrators. Each participating WTO member nominates one candidate, who goes through a 'pre-selection process' by a Selection Committee, comprising the same persons as in the case of selection of AB members (ie, the DG, Chairperson of the DSB, GC, and Goods, Services, and TRIPS Councils).

The AB (when it was operational) and the MPIA pool of arbitrators today practised the principle of collegiality. In other words, all the members of the AB and MPIA pool of arbitrators would receive all documents relating to an appeal, not just the specific members/arbitrators sitting in appeal, and they would meet and discuss the elements of each case to ensure 'security and predictability' under the DSU or for the MPAI in order to 'ensure consistency and predictability'.

ii. The Dispute Resolution Process and Dispute Assistants

When the AB was functional, the role of the AB Secretariat was similar to that of the Secretariat staff assisting panels. However, there were certain differences stemming from the structure of the AB. One notable difference was that the AB was a quasi-permanent body and not an ad hoc tribunal. The AB Secretariat staff did not play a role in the composition of the AB or the composition of an AB division for a particular case. Nevertheless, similar to the Secretariat staff at the panel stage, the AB Secretariat assisted the AB members in the work leading up to the issuing of the AB Report. The timeline for the AB report was very short (90 days), so the staff were required to work very quickly. Given that the submissions, proceedings and drafting were often conducted in English, this often placed a burden on non-English-speaking panellists, enhancing their reliance on the AB Secretariat staff for drafting. At present, even though the AB is not functional, parties can file appeals against panel reports. In such cases, parties have been appealing 'into the void', effectively halting the adoption of the panel report indefinitely.

Now, when an appeal to the MPIA is confirmed, the arbitrator who acts as the point of contact (selected by the pool of arbitrators amongst themselves) asks the DG to assign Secretariat staff for assistance in the specific appeal. The staff who assist MPIA arbitrators also have their regular duties and are not exclusively available for the MPIA proceedings. At present, there is no specific information available regarding the functions and assistance offered by the staff. It is an educated guess as to whether the functions discharged would be similar to those of the AB Secretariat staff or in some cases more limited.

[65] MPIA, para 4.
[66] ibid.
[67] ibid.
[68] WTO, *Composition of the Pool of Arbitrators Pursuant to Paragraph 4 of the Communication JOB/DSB/1/Add.12*, WTO Doc JOB/DSB/1/Add.12/Suppl.2 (30 April 2020).

C. Other Dispute Settlement Procedures in the DSU

As mentioned earlier, the WTO DSS has other stages specific to its dispute procedures where staff from the Secretariat may play a role or discharge specific functions. While each of these specific stages will be discussed in further detail in Part III, we will briefly list them here for the sake of completeness.

If a panel report (or, as was the case earlier, AB Report) is adopted by the DSB, the member concerned is required to inform the DSB of their intentions regarding the implementation of the recommendations/rulings of the DSB.[69] In some cases where the member is granted a reasonable period of time to comply with the recommendations, the parties may request an arbitrator to determine what constitutes such a reasonable period of time under Article 21.3(c) proceedings.[70] If the parties have been unable to agree on an arbitrator within 10 days, the DG will make such appointment after consulting with the parties.[71] The AB Secretariat (prior to dissolution) used to assist the parties and DG in this process. The LAD/Rules staff are not involved at this stage, so it is unclear whether the DG is assisted by staff in the selection of Article 21.3 arbitrators now.

When there is disagreement as to the existence/conformity of measures taken to comply with recommendations/rulings of the DSB, the DSU provides recourse for this to be determined by a panel and, wherever possible, the original panel (termed the 'Implementation Panel').[72] If the original panellist(s) are unavailable, the procedure envisaged for the appointment of ad hoc panellists for the original panel will apply, where the parties are assisted by Secretariat staff; failing such agreement between the parties, the DG can be requested to make the appointment. In the Implementation Panel proceedings, the Secretariat staff assist the panellists in arriving at the necessary ruling within the specified time period, discharging similar functions to those performed by them at the original panel stage.

If the concerned member fails to implement the recommendations/rulings within the reasonable period of time, the winning party may request the DSB for authorisation to retaliate through suspension of concessions/other obligations in the covered agreements as per Article 22 DSU.[73] If there is disagreement as to the level of suspension (retaliation), the issue is referred to arbitration. As with the Implementation Panel, the arbitrator in such proceedings consists of the original panel. If the original panellist(s) are unavailable, the Secretariat will assist the parties to find replacement panellists. If parties cannot agree, the DG makes the necessary appointments to constitute the arbitrator.[74] This process operates in the same manner as the selection of ad hoc panellists by the DG for original panels in Article 8.7 (see above). During these retaliation proceedings, the arbitrator is assisted by non-lawyers, in particular economists from the Economics and Statistics Research Division (ERSD). These staff members assist with

[69] DSU, art 21.3. This is undertaken at the DSB meeting held within 30 days from the adopted of the report.

[70] ibid; the specific procedure is provided in art 21.3 on how the reasonable period of time may be determined. Such period either proposed by the member concerned after approval from the DSB or, in the absence of such approval, mutually agreed by the parties to the dispute within the prescribed time period. If the parties cannot reach such agreement, they may request an arbitrator to determine the reasonable period.

[71] ibid fn 12.

[72] ibid art 21.5.

[73] ibid art 22.1.

[74] ibid art 22.6.

calculating the level of nullification/impairment, which in turn determines the level of suspension of concessions or obligation. The Secretariat staff may also assist with other aspects of these proceedings.

Lastly, Article 25 DSU provides an alternative process for dispute settlement through 'expeditious arbitration', which is defined by the disputing parties. The parties agree on the applicable procedures, including on the selection of arbitrators. There has been limited practice of disputes under Article 25.

III. Observations on the Role of Dispute Assistants

The WTO DSS has Dispute Assistants who play a critical role in aiding the adjudicators through the various stages of the dispute resolution process. It is notable that the provisions of the DSU confirm that WTO Members always envisaged assistance to be provided by Secretariat staff. However, controversy has arisen recently in relation to the scope and extent of such assistance. There has been some discussion as to whether the role of the WTO Secretariat and the AB Secretariat has contributed to the AB crisis and its termination.[75] Some of the arguments raised imply that the Secretariat staff assisting panels and the AB exert undue influence over the decision-making process and, in turn, compromise the integrity of the adjudicative dispute settlement process, while others do not agree with this perspective. But this issue is now outdated, given that the AB has not been operational since 2019. The issue that persists is the challenge that these concerns pose to the legitimacy of the WTO DSS (as discussed in Chapter 21 and in Part III) and finding potential solutions to address this.

[75] United States State Committee on Finance, *Hearing before the Committee on Finance, United States Senate*, 104th Congress, S 16 (10 May 1995) 60, www.finance.senate.gov/imo/media/doc/Hrg104-124.pdf; Office of the United States Trade Representative, *Report on the Appellate Body of the World Trade Organization* (February 2020). Although the US does not refer directly to the WTO Secretariat or the AB Secretariat, many of the concerns raised have been linked to the expanded role of the Secretariat. See also Pauwelyn and Pelc (n 15) 561.

PART II

Comparative Study on Dispute Assistants

Part I of this book contained 18 chapters that examined the institutional structures and the role of Dispute Assistants in the dispute resolution process within each identified Dispute Settlement Mechanism (DSM). Part II builds on the descriptive framework and undertakes comparative study. In Chapter 20, we aim to refamiliarise readers with the different terminologies employed by DSMs for Dispute Assistants. We identify categories of Disputes Assistants based on two criteria: formal institutional status, and who they report to. Three categories emerged: (1) Institutional Assistants, who are formally part of the institution and work for the institution as a whole; (2) Assigned Assistants, who are formally part of the institution and work for individual adjudicators/bench of adjudicators; and (3) External Assistants, who are not formally part of the institution and work for individual adjudicators/bench of adjudicators. Thereafter, we map their role and functions across the seven stages of the dispute resolution process, charting the comparative extent of their participation in each stage across identified DSMs. Lastly, we detail the formal and de facto forms of supervision and control exercised over their work. The comparative study establishes the important and widespread nature of the functions discharged by Dispute Assistants. Their expansive functions have raised concerns on the appropriateness of their participation, and whether this encroaches on the mandate granted by the parties to the adjudicators.

Chapter 21 plunges into these concerns and establishes their crucial link with legitimacy of the dispute resolution process. We have identified six common concerns on the role and functions of Dispute Assistants, based on examples that have been raised across the DSMs. While we have categorised these into six separate concerns, it is important to acknowledge the significant overlap between many of them. With respect to each concern, we also identify certain useful practices and procedures that address, mitigate or safeguard against them. Then we turn to the impact of these concerns on three facets of actual and perceived legitimacy of the dispute resolution process: the consent to be bound-by dispute resolution process, the independence and diligence expected of adjudicators, and the expected transparency and procedural fairness of the dispute resolution process. Having detailed the concerns, potential solutions and the need to address these concerns, Part III will examine how these may be operationalised in the complex institutional framework of the WTO dispute settlement system.

20

Situating Dispute Assistants

A Comparative Perspective

In section I, we identify the relevant actors across each of the 20 identified Dispute Settlement Mechanisms (DSMs). We categorise these actors as per the formal structures of control over their work, which provides the starting point for assessing the degree of control adjudicators have over Dispute Assistants. These formal structures include institutional position, hierarchies on reporting and supervision over the work undertaken by Dispute Assistants, as well as administrative control exercised over them – for example, with respect to approval of periods of leave, appraisals or evaluations. Accordingly, Dispute Assistants are grouped into three main categories: Institutional Assistants (section I.A), Assigned Assistants (section I.B) and External Assistants (section I.C).

Section II draws comparisons between the functions discharged by Dispute Assistants in the identified DSMs. We identify seven stages across DSMs where Dispute Assistants play a role. This section is structured based on the general procedural flow of a dispute, starting from the role of Dispute Assistants in the appointment and selection of adjudicators (section II.A), the acceptance of submissions and pre-screening of cases (section II.B), the pre-hearing stage including preparation of notes and research (section II.C), the hearing (section II.D), drafting of the judgment/order/award (section II.E), deliberations on the decision (section II.F) and, finally, the review of the judgment/order/award including translations (section II.G). As we have seen in Chapter 19, the WTO Dispute Settlement System (WTO DSS) has additional stages which shed light on distinct functions of Dispute Assistants,[1] notably non-legal staff such as economists who significantly assist adjudicators in their decision-making functions in some stages. We will return to these stages in Part III of this book.

This comparative exercise runs the risk of blurring distinctions across DSMs. We acknowledge that an important – and arguably the most important – distinction exists between permanent/quasi-permanent and ad hoc dispute resolution process. We remain mindful of the necessary nuances in substance, procedure and practice between DSMs. For each of the seven stages identified, the aim is to showcase the degree and extent of the functions of Dispute Assistants. Through this study, we hope to shed light on the extent of their participation and involvement across DSMs in each stage.

[1] There are additional procedures beyond the panel and Appellate stage, such as the implementation review, arbitration for determining the reasonable period of compliance, and arbitration for determining the level of suspension of concessions. As these stages are unique to the WTO DSS, without comparable stages in other DSMs, we do not include them within the comparative study in this chapter.

Lastly, some of the concerns on the role of Dispute Assistants stem from the alleged lack of supervision and control exercised by adjudicators over their work and, consequently, relating to their influence over the decision-making function. In order to better understand and assess these concerns, Section III details the formal and de facto forms of control that are exercised by adjudicators over Dispute Assistants. The de facto structures and procedures allow adjudicators to exercise control over Dispute Assistants, either directly or indirectly.

I. Identifying the Relevant Actors

In Chapter 1, we briefly explained the broad functional definition of 'Dispute Assistants' adopted by us in this book. The aim of such a definition is to identify all the relevant actors that play a role in the dispute resolution process and contribute to the adjudicative function. To recap, the term 'Dispute Assistant' refers to any person, or group of persons, discharging the following functions in the service of the identified DSM or its adjudicator(s):

a) *Administrative functions* relating to the dispute settlement proceeding without going into the substantive aspects of a case. These are functions of a supportive or logistical nature that aim to expedite and facilitate the adjudicator's work. Examples include arranging travel and accommodation for adjudicators, logistical arrangements for conducting the hearing venues, and communication with the disputing parties.

b) *Assistance in judicial, legal and other dispute-related functions* with respect to specific dispute settlement proceedings or cases. These include the following functions: pre-screening of cases; assistance in the pre-hearing stage through the drafting of notes and/or research; attendance of and participation in hearings; preparation, attendance and participation in deliberations; research and assistance for drafting; drafting of the judgment and/or individual or dissenting opinions; and substantive or formalistic review of the judgments, including translations. Further, in some instances, such assistance also extends to assisting parties with the appointment of adjudicators (for example, in arbitral institutions).[2]

Such an all-encompassing definition allows us to adequately appreciate the multitude of tasks and actors that contribute to the dispute resolution process, irrespective of their level of involvement with the substantive decision-making. These functions may be discharged by legal staff and, in specific instances/disputes, by non-legal staff – for example, in the WTO DSS, economists and other non-legal staff assist panellists, Appellate Body (AB) members and arbitrators, substantively in specific disputes and/or stages of a dispute. In many identified DSMs, non-legal staff like interpreters and translators perform important non-substantive functions in assisting adjudicators during the dispute resolution process. At the same time, we have excluded many administrative

[2] For more on appointing authorities, see P Tzeng, 'Appointing Authorities: Self-Appointment, Party Appointment and Non-appointment' in F Baetens (ed), *Legitimacy of Unseen Actors in International Adjudication* (Cambridge University Press, 2019) 164–88.

and professional actors who perform important work for the DSM, but are not specifically related to the dispute settlement proceeding – for example, the ushers in the WTO (who were previously responsible for printing the relevant documents for a dispute), those working on the budget, in the cafeteria, on the maintenance etc.

Turning to the three categories of Dispute Assistants, we begin our analysis with 'Institutional Assistants', who are often organised in the Institutional Office of the DSM, or in additional institutional departments. We then look at Dispute Assistants who are assigned to adjudicators ('Assigned Assistants') and those externally appointed by individual adjudicators, or by an institutional office for assisting individual adjudicators ('External Assistants').

A. Institutional Assistants

Every DSM has an office assisting adjudicators in the dispute resolution process to differing degrees (which we refer to as the 'Institutional Office'). These offices contain Dispute Assistants who are not personally assigned to a single adjudicator or bench of adjudicators, but rather are 'assigned' to disputes by their institutional supervisor where they assist different adjudicators across different disputes ('Institutional Assistants'). In some cases, Institutional Assistants may be assisting a single adjudicator or a bench of adjudicators for a particular dispute. However, they retain their character as Institutional Assistants as they assist a particular adjudicator/bench only for the duration of an assigned dispute and are usually reassigned after the conclusion of that dispute. Further, they may be assisting more than one adjudicator in different disputes at the same time. Competent adjudicators will be able to monitor the functions discharged by the Institutional Assistants working with them even for a single dispute. The risk or appearance of excessive delegation to Institutional Assistants can be mitigated if adjudicators have the capacity, as well as the obligation, to control the functions of such assistants even when they are not exclusively under the adjudicator's supervision. Such institutional or procedural avenues of control are examined in section III later in this chapter.

The Institutional Assistants may be organised into: (a) the Institutional Office; or (b) additional institutional departments.

i. Institutional Office

In every identified DSM examined in Part I, there is a standing office of Dispute Assistants with institutional designation. They are not ad hoc staff employed for a specific case, but rather enjoy a degree of permanence in the DSM, with a specific supervisor ('head of the Institutional Office') who oversees the work and administrative aspects of the staff. Although the specific names given to these offices vary, we collectively refer to this group as the 'Institutional Office'.

In 13 institutions, the term used for the Institutional Office is the 'Registry'. These are the registries of the International Court of Justice (ICJ), the International Criminal Court (ICC), International Tribunal for the Law of the Sea (ITLOS), the Court of Justice of the European Union (CJEU), the Court of the European Free Trade Association (EFTA Court), the Court of Justice of the Economic Community of West African

States (ECOWAS Court), the Court of Justice of the Common Market for Eastern and Southern Africa (COMESA Court), the East African Court of Justice (EACJ), the European Court of Human Rights (ECtHR), the African Court of Human and Peoples' Rights (ACtHPR), the International Criminal Tribunal for Yugoslavia (ICTY), the Special Tribunal for Lebanon (STL) and the Iran-United States Claims Tribunal (IUSCT). In five institutions, the term used for this Office is the 'Secretariat'. These are the Secretariats of the dispute settlement system of the World Trade Organization (WTO DSS), Mercado Común del Sur (MERCOSUR), the United States- Mexico-Canada Agreement (USMCA), the International Centre for Settlement of Investment Disputes (ICSID) and the Inter-American Court of Human Rights (IACtHR). In the Permanent Court of Arbitration (PCA), the Institutional Office is referred to as the 'International Bureau'. In the commercial arbitration institutions examined in Chapter 5, the nomenclature varies. We detail the specific institutional structure of each Institutional Office below, focusing on the framework of supervision over the Dispute Assistants in the Institutional Office. The list has been ordered according to the size of the legal staff within the institutional office. We examine three arbitration-related institutions (the PCA, ICSID and commercial arbitration institutions) at the very end, owing to the difference in the nature of their functions compared to other institutions:

a) The ECJ and the General Court (collectively referred to as the CJEU) have separate and dedicated registries. A Registrar leads each registry and is assisted by a Deputy Registrar. The ECJ's Registrar acts as the Secretary-General of the CJEU and is therefore responsible for the global administration of the CJEU machinery. The day-to-day functioning of the respective courts falls under the responsibility of the ECJ's Deputy Registrar and the General Court's Registrar and Deputy Registrar. They also keep track of the cases in both courts. The number of staff employed by each Registry differs. Presently, in the ECJ, the Deputy Registrar oversees over 50 staff, while in the General Court, the Registrar and Deputy Registrar have a larger team of over 70 staff. Each Registry employs case administrators and lawyers who handle the procedural aspects of the case, receive the necessary documents, and liaise with national courts and the parties' agents or lawyers depending on the nature of the case. In performing these functions, they work under the supervision of their respective Registry's heads – ie, the Deputy Registrar of the ECJ, the Registrar and Deputy Registrar of the General Court, and, ultimately, the overall supervision of the Registrar of the ECJ. They are not assigned to individual adjudicators or bench of adjudicators, even for the duration of a dispute; rather, they assist the DSM as a whole across cases. As explained in section I.A.ii below, the CJEU also has additional institutional departments with Institutional Assistants – ie, the Research and Documentation Directorate and the Directorate of Multilingualism.

b) The Registry of the ECtHR is headed by a Registrar, who is assisted by a Deputy Registrar. It consists of lawyers and administrative staff involved in case processing and also includes research lawyers, administrative staff, personnel managers, archivists, IT experts, librarians, linguists etc.[3] The Registry also has a language division that deals with translations and ensures that the ECtHR's use of the official languages is of an

[3] F Baetens, 'Unseen Actors in International Courts and Tribunals: Challenging the Legitimacy of International Adjudication' in Baetens (n 2) 1–28.

adequate standard. The Registry comprises several divisions that provide legal and administrative assistance to the judges. There are 31 case-processing divisions, each under the supervision of a head of division (assisted by an administrative team), who assigns cases to the case lawyers in their divisions.[4] The Registry assigns its case lawyers to one of the case-processing divisions based on their knowledge of the languages and legal systems of the countries covered by the division.

The ECtHR organises its judges into five Sections, and the case processing divisions are attached to the sections where the national judge sits and follows the judge. The case processing divisions are attached to each of the five judicial Sections and are under the authority of a Section Registrar who receives assistance from a Deputy Section Registrar.[5] The lawyers of the case processing division assist the judges through various stages of the dispute resolution process and may be assigned to assist the Judge Rapporteur for a particular dispute. They are under the direct supervision of the head of division who assigns the cases and, ultimately, the Section Registrar and Deputy Section Registrar.

c) The Registries of the ICC, the ICTY and the STL are broadly similar in the assistance they provide to judges. A Registrar heads each of the three registries. In the ICC, a Deputy Registrar supports the Registrar. The Registries are responsible for the non-judicial aspects of the administration and servicing of the ICC.[6] Given the mandate of these bodies and the nature of criminal trials, the character of the non-judicial functions their Registry discharges takes on a unique role. In the ICC, the Registry is responsible for three main categories of services: judicial support, external affairs and administrative management. The administrative functions relate to human resources, budget, finance, procurement, facilities management, travel and transportation. The Registry also establishes a safe and secure environment for all those working in or visiting the ICC.[7] The judicial support function provides the necessary assistance for judges to conduct the hearings. As a neutral service provider, the Registry supports investigative, prosecutorial and judicial activities through, among other things, court management and eCourt tools, facilitation of victims' participation in proceedings, court interpretation and translation services, information management services and management of the detention facilities.[8] Finally, the external operations functions include facilitating adequate judicial cooperation with states regarding Chambers' requests; concluding various cooperation agreements with states, such as those on the relocation of witnesses; providing support to and protection of victims and witnesses; informing the general public on judicial and other developments; providing outreach activities in the affected communities; and facilitating the Court's operations in the field.[9] Additionally, the Registry has a Legal Office responsible for the legal functions associated with the Registrar's duties. Its primary objective is to ensure the quality and consistency of legal approaches across

[4] CD Creaner and Z Godzimirska, 'Trust in the Court: The Role of the Registry of the European Court of Human Rights' (2019) 30 *European Journal of International Law* 665, 672.

[5] Rules of the Court European Court of Human Rights (as amended 1 January 2023), r 18.

[6] Rome Statute of the International Criminal Court (Rome, 17 July 1998), art 43(1).

[7] International Criminal Court, 'Registry', www.icc-cpi.int/about/registry.

[8] ibid.

[9] Registry of the International Criminal Court, 'Comprehensive Report on the Reorganisation of the Registry of the International Criminal Court' (August 2016) 81, www.icc-cpi.int/itemsDocuments/ICC-Registry-CR.pdf.

the various sections of the Registry relating to victim support, case management etc.[10] The ICTY and the STL Registries also performed similar functions while they were operational. The Registry staff were not assigned to a single judge or a bench, even for the duration of a dispute; rather, they assisted more generally across cases.

d) The Secretariat of the IACtHR is headed by the Secretary, who is assisted by the Deputy Secretary. The Secretariat has several divisions, most notably the Legal Affairs Division, which presently consists of around 20 staff lawyers. The staff lawyer(s) is assigned to assist the Judge Rapporteur for a particular dispute.[11] They are under the supervision of the Secretary, who assigns the cases to staff lawyers from the Legal Affairs Division. They perform all the functions of the Institutional Office, including receiving case documents and communicating with parties.

e) The Registry of the ECOWAS Court is headed by the Chief Registrar, who coordinates the interdepartmental activities of the Court. A Deputy Chief Registrar and three Registrars assist the Chief Registrar. The Registry Department comprises five divisions: Judicial Process & Case Management; Judicial Certified Translation & Interpretation; Verbatim Reports; Judicial Records, Archives & Publications; and Appeals, Arbitration & Enforcement. Of relevance is the Judicial Process & Case Management division, which is responsible for the receipt, processing and service of court papers. The role of the Registry is limited to case management through the receipt of files and communication between the relevant actors. There are presently over 17 lawyers working in the Registry Department. The legal staff of the Registry are under the supervision of the Deputy Chief Registrar and, ultimately, the Chief Registrar. They are not assigned to judges or a bench, even for the duration of a dispute; rather, they assist the court across cases. As will be explained in section I.A.ii, an additional institutional department, the Research and Documentation Department, does the bulk of the judicial assistance work.

f) The Registry of the ACtHPR is led by a Registrar, who is assisted by a Deputy Registrar. The Registrar assists the ACtHPR in exercising its judicial function and is in charge of the general administration of the ACtHPR's Registry.[12] There are two main divisions under the Registrar: the Legal Division and the Finance Division.[13] A Head of Division leads each division. The Legal Division comprises three Legal Units: the Legal Aid Unit, the Documentation Unit and the Library Unit. The Legal Aid Unit's Legal Officers provide the primary assistance to the judges in their judicial functions. At present, out of the 70 Registry staff, 13 are Legal Officers. The Legal Officers of the Legal Aid Unit are assigned to the Judge Rapporteur for a particular dispute. They are under the supervision of the Head of Legal Division, who assigns cases to specific Legal Officers in the Legal Aid Unit and, ultimately, under the supervision of the Registrar of the ACtHPR.

[10] ibid.

[11] PS Alessandri, 'Secretariat: Inter-American Court of Human Rights (IACtHR)' in H Ruiz Fabri (ed), *Max Planck Encyclopedia of International Procedural Law* (Oxford University Press, online edn November 2021) paras 29–30.

[12] Rules of Court, African Court on Human and Peoples' Rights, r 21.

[13] The Finance and Administration Division consists of the following units: the Finance Unit, the Human Resources Unit, the Procurement Travel and Stores Unit, and the Information Technology Unit. However, as they do not assist the judges with their judicial functions, this is not examined further here.

g) The WTO Secretariat comprises several divisions. Each division is led by a Director, who reports to a Deputy Director-General (DDG) and, ultimately, the Director-General (DG). The Understanding on Rules and Procedures Governing the Settlement of Disputes (DSU) specifies that the Secretariat is responsible for assisting panels, especially on the legal, historical and procedural aspects of the matters dealt with, and for providing secretarial and technical support.[14] Accordingly, staff from the Secretariat's Legal Affairs Division (LAD) and the Rules Division lead the Secretariat assistance to panels. The WTO Secretariat also has a Dispute Settlement Registry, with a Registrar, responsible for, inter alia, administratively supporting LAD and Rules Divisions in their dispute work. The legal staff and non-legal staff from other divisions also assist panels in specific disputes, and adjudicators in specific stages of the dispute[15] (for example, economists from the Economic Research and Statistics Division assist the arbitrator in Article 22.6 proceedings to determine the level of suspension of concessions). Typically, a team assisting a panel comprises at least one or more junior legal officers (one of whom is appointed as the 'secretary' to the panel), one senior legal officer, and other staff, depending on the complexity and requirements of the case.[16] The staff are assigned to the bench of ad hoc panellists for a duration of a dispute. They are under the supervision of the lead lawyer and ultimately under the Director of LAD/Rules Division (depending on which division is responsible for the dispute), who assigns disputes to staff of their division. Although the panellists do not exclusively supervise the staff, they provide feedback on the staff assisting them in a dispute. Such feedback may become relevant during staff appraisals.

Additionally, when the AB was functional, the AB Secretariat was separate and independent from the WTO Secretariat.[17] Prior to December 2019, the AB Secretariat had a Director, seven senior and 10 junior legal advisors, and five support staff. The AB has also sought advice from staff of other operation divisions in complex disputes. The staff of the AB Secretariat were under the supervision of the AB Director, the Chairman of the AB and, ultimately, the DG of the WTO.

After the AB became non-operational, some WTO Members set up the Multi-Party Interim Appeal Arbitration Arrangement (MPIA) under Article 25 DSU to resolve disputes that are appealed by WTO Members in the absence of a functioning AB. In principle, they are assisted by WTO Secretariat staff (so far, two legal staff), who are not part of the LAD/Rules Division (as they may have been responsible for and involved in the prior panel proceedings). We will discuss this further in Part III.

h) The Registry of the ICJ is headed by the Registrar, who is assisted by a Deputy Registrar and a Special Assistant to the Registrar. The Department of Legal Matters,

[14] Understanding on Rules and Procedures Governing the Settlement of Disputes (15 April 1994), Annex 2 to the Marrakesh Agreement Establishing the World Trade Organization (DSU), art 27(1).

[15] DA Baker and G Marceau, 'The World Trade Organization' in Baetens (n 2) 83; DSU, art 27(1).

[16] JM Wauters, 'The Role of the WTO Secretariat in WTO Disputes: Silent Witness or Ghost Expert?' (2021) 12 *Global Policy*, 84.

[17] J Pauwelyn and K Pelc, 'Who Guards the "Guardians of the System"? The Role of the Secretariat in WTO Dispute Settlement' (2015) 19 *European Journal of International Law* 537. As per art 17.7 DSU, the Appellate Body is to be provided with appropriate administrative and legal support as it requires. A 1995 decision of the DSB on the AB states that 'a reasonable level of support in the initial stages of operation of the Appellate Body would be one registrar, three professional assistants with legal training, and sufficient clerical staff'.

which is directly subordinate to the Registrar, assists the ICJ in case management at various stages of the dispute resolution process. It consists of the Principal Legal Secretary, who acts as the head of the department, two first secretaries, five secretaries and an administrative assistant.[18] The staff of the Department of Legal Matters are under the supervision of the Registrar of the ICJ. They may be assigned to assist the bench in a particular dispute by the Principal Legal Secretary, but they are not assigned to individual judges.

i) The Registry of ITLOS is headed by the Registrar, who is assisted by a Deputy Registrar. The Registry's Legal Office consists of the Head of Legal Office, three Legal Officers, an Associate Legal Officer and a Legal Assistant.[19] A fluctuating number of interns also support the Legal Office.[20] The Registry assists ITLOS in case administration, for example, by organising the hearing or keeping the case records, and also more substantively in the dispute resolution process.[21] The staff are under the supervision of the Registrar, who assigns staff to work on specific disputes. However, the staff are not assigned to individual judges. The Registrar also deals with terminations and disciplinary measures[22] and prepares proposals to the ITLOS on appointments and promotions of staff (with the assistance of an appointment and promotion panel).[23]

j) The Registry of the EACJ is headed by a Registrar and includes several court clerks, a researcher and administrative staff. Besides the central registry in Arusha, Tanzania, there are also five sub-registries, each staffed by one clerk, in Dar es Salaam, Tanzania; Nairobi, Kenya; Kampala, Uganda; Kigali, Rwanda; and Bujumbura, Burundi.[24] The Registry assists the judges with administrative aspects of the case. At least one clerk is assigned to the bench for each case. They perform administrative tasks, ensure the smooth conduct of the hearings and advise the judges on matters of procedure if necessary. The recent practice is that the Registry also provides a researcher during the drafting stages to assist the judges. The staff of the Registry, including the researcher, and the clerks of the sub-registries, are assigned to cases by Registrar of the EACJ, and are under the supervision of the Registrar.

k) The Registry of the EFTA Court is headed by a Registrar, with seven staff under their supervision.[25] As the EFTA Court operates in a cabinet system (similar to the CJEU), the Registry does not play a significant role in assisting the judges with their adjudicative functions. However, the Registry supports the EFTA Court in administrative matters. The staff of the Registry are under the supervision of the Registrar of the EFTA Court.

[18] International Court of Justice, 'Registry', www.icj-cij.org/registry.

[19] International Tribunal for the Law of the Sea, *Registry Organigramme* (July 2025), www.itlos.org/fileadmin/itlos/documents/registry/Organigram_July_2025.pdf.

[20] International Tribunal for the Law of the Sea, 'Internship Programme', www.itlos.org/en/internship-programme. There are approximately 20 positions available each year, distributed over four internship periods and four departments.

[21] P Gautier, 'Registry: International Tribunal for the Law of the Sea (ITLOS)' in Ruiz Fabri (n 11) para 12.

[22] International Tribunal for the Law of the Sea, *Staff Regulations* (ITLOS/REG/1/Rev.6, 1 October 2021), arts 9(1) and 10.

[23] International Tribunal for the Law of the Sea, Staff Rules (ITLOS/REG/2/Rev.6, 1 October 2021), r 4.15.

[24] East African Court of Justice, *Court Manual* (2020) 21.

[25] EFTA Court, 'Judges and Staff', www.eftacourt.int/the-court/judges-and-staff.

l) In state-to-state disputes under Chapter 31 of USMCA, the Secretariat is decentralised; it consists of three Sections, each maintained by one of the state parties, and headed by a Secretary.[26] According to the rules, the Section of the Secretariat of the responding party in a dispute supports the panels.[27] However, in practice, there may be collaboration between the staff of other Sections when necessary.[28] At present, the US and Mexican Sections comprise three staff members, while the Canadian Section comprises five staff members.[29] The staff of the Secretariat only deal with matters relating to case administration, including arranging meetings and other logistical support for hearings.[30] The Sections do not assist the panel in the substantively in the dispute. The staff of the Sections are under the supervision of the Secretary of their respective Sections.

m) The Registry of the COMESA Court is headed by a Registrar, who is responsible for the day-to-day administration of the business of the COMESA Court.[31] The staff in the Registry include the Registrar, the Assistant Registrar, administrative and finance staff, a Clerk (providing limited research assistance to judges), an Internal Auditor and IT staff, in addition to the staff from the general service category.[32] Overall, the Registry does not assist the judges substantively in the dispute resolution process and provides administrative support. The staff are under the supervision of the Registrar of the COMESA Court.

n) In the MERCOSUR dispute settlement system, the Secretary heads the Secretaría del TPR (ST), which supports the appellate tribunal, the Tribunal Permanente de Revisión (TPR).[33] The Secretary is assisted by a legal officer, a staff member responsible for library services and documentation, staff for administrative duties, and staff for IT services.[34] The Secretaría del MERCOSUR, the general Secretariat of the broader MERCOSUR organisation, used to discharge the administrative support duties at the first stage of proceedings, the ad hoc tribunal stage. Since the entry into force of the Modification Protocol of the Protocol of Olivos in 2018, the ST performs these duties for both stages of the dispute resolution process.[35] The staff of the ST do not substantively

[26] Agreement between the United States of America, the United Mexican States and Canada (signed on 30 November 2018, entered into force 1 July 2020) (USMCA), art 30.6.

[27] Rules of Procedure for Chapter 31 of the USMCA, art 2.

[28] This has been the practice in certain cases under the NAFTA.

[29] NAFTA Secretariat, 'Home', www.can-mex-usa-sec.org/secretariat/index.aspx?lang=eng. Note that the US and Mexican Sections are also responsible for handling the administration of other Regional Trade Agreements.

[30] Rules of Procedure for Chapter 31 for USMCA, art 3.

[31] Treaty Establishing the Common Market for Eastern and Southern Africa (COMESA Treaty) (signed 5 November 1993, entered into force 8 December 1994) 2314 UNTS 1, art 41.

[32] It should be noted that the COMESA Court consists of the First Instance Division and the Appellate Division, with separate Registries, headed by one Registrar. Although such separate Registries are maintained, the same staff service the judges of both Divisions.

[33] MERCOSUR/GMC/EXT/RES No 66/05, 'Resolution of the Common Market Group on the Secretariat of the TPR' (6 December 2005), art 2.

[34] ibid 3.

[35] Protocolo Modificatorio del Protocolo de Olivos para la Solución de Controversias en el MERCOSUR (adopted 19 January 2007, entered into force 2007), art 5. Note that all subsequently mentioned articles in the Protocolo de Olivos have to be read with this in mind.

assist the adjudicators in the dispute resolution process. The staff of the ST are under the supervision of the Secretary.

o) In the IUSCT, the Secretary-General serves as the head of the administration of the Registry. The Registry consists of two co-Registrars, English–Farsi translators and supporting staff. The Registry does not provide legal assistance to the tribunal members. Instead, it only provides administrative assistance, including assisting with the technical aspects of the filed documents or organising hearings. The registry staff are under the supervision of the Secretary-General of the Registry of the IUSCT.

p) In commercial arbitration institutions, the institutional office is generally headed by a single head with different nomenclatures. A Registrar heads the LCIA[36] and the SIAC,[37] a Secretary-General heads the HKIAC,[38] the SCC,[39] the International Chamber of Commerce Arbitration,[40] the DIS[41] and the CIETAC,[42] and an Executive Director heads the SCAI.[43] They oversee a team of legal officers and administrators, who are often subdivided into smaller case management teams.[44] Arbitrators and tribunals may receive assistance in case management from the institutional office's staff. These staff are commonly referred to as 'tribunal secretaries', though the official designation of these assistants may vary. For example, the HKIAC and the LCIA refer to them as tribunal secretaries, while the International Chamber of Commerce, the SIAC, the SCAI and the SCC call them 'administrative secretaries'. In the International Chamber of Commerce, staff members are not permitted to serve as 'administrative secretaries'.[45] This role could also be filled by an External Assistant (who we have referred to as a 'tribunal assistant').[46]

q) The Institutional Office of the PCA is the International Bureau, which is headed by the Secretary-General of the PCA. The International Bureau also includes the Deputy

[36] London Court of International Arbitration, 'Organisation', www.lcia.org/lcia/organisation.aspx.

[37] Singapore International Arbitration Centre, 'Our Team', www.siac.org.sg/about-us/our-team.

[38] Hong Kong International Arbitration Centre, 'Secretariat', www.hkiac.org/about-us/secretariat.

[39] SCC Arbitration Institute, 'Contact Us', www.sccarbitrationinstitute.se/en/about-scc/contact-us.

[40] International Chamber of Commerce, 'Chairmanship and Secretary General', www.iccwbo.org/governance/chairmanship-and-secretary-general.

[41] German Arbitration Institute (DIS), 'Team', www.disarb.org/en/about-us/team.

[42] Although note that CIETAC actually maintains several Secretariats, one for each seat. See China International Economic and Trade Arbitration Commission (CIETAC), 'Secretariats', www.cietac.org/index.php?m=Page&a=index&id=35&l=en.

[43] Swiss Arbitration Centre, 'Leadership', www.swissarbitration.org/centre/leadership.

[44] In many of the identified DSMs, the administration of the arbitration is undertaken by a 'court' that is assisted by the Institutional Office. The CIETAC has an organ called the arbitration court that oversees case administration. The CIETAC Secretariat is responsible only for the ordinary administrative duties of the Commission. Similarly, the ICC International Court of Arbitration is responsible for the administration of the dispute resolution undertaken by the arbitral tribunals as per the ICC Rules. The ICC Court is assisted by the Secretariat of the Court under the direction of its Secretary General. The LCIA Court is assisted by the Registrar of the LCIA, and the SIAC Court is assisted by the SIAC Secretariat. The Board of the SCC also discharges similar functions, with the assistance of the SCC Secretariat. Arbitrations under the Swiss Rules are administered by the Arbitration Court of the Swiss Arbitration Centre (SCAI Secretariat). In DIS, there is an Arbitration Council and an Appointing Committee distinct from the Secretariat.

[45] International Chamber of Commerce, *ICC Guidance Note to Parties and Arbitral Tribunal on the Conduct of Arbitrations under the ICC Rules of Arbitration* (2021).

[46] As explained in ch 5, the term for these Dispute Assistants varies across the commercial arbitration institutions. We have adopted the term 'tribunal assistants' to refer to Dispute Assistants when they are hired externally, similar to the practice of the PCA and the USMCA.

Secretaries General, Senior Legal Counsel, Legal Counsel, Assistant Legal Counsel and a number of case managers.[47] The number of legal staff employed is not fixed and varies depending on the PCA's needs. Where parties to a dispute or a tribunal seek assistance from the PCA, one or more legal counsel from the International Bureau will often serve as the primary assistant, supported by one or more assistant legal counsel and a case manager. The Deputy Secretaries-General assign cases to legal counsel and other staff. Assignments are determined by workload and language needs, among other factors. At present, the International Bureau's practice is to assign a Senior Legal Counsel as the Tribunal Registrar/Secretary,[48] with the support of additional legal staff. The legal team supports all members of the tribunal, but, in practice, primarily assists the chair. The staff are under the supervision of the Secretary-General of the PCA.

r) The ICSID Secretariat is headed by the Secretary-General, who is assisted by two Deputy Secretaries-General.[49] At present, the staff of the Secretariat comprise around 70 people, divided between case management, general administration and financial management, and front-office teams. The Secretariat further subdivides its legal staff into five case management teams, each consisting of legal counsel, paralegals and legal and administrative assistants. ICSID appoints a legal counsel as 'Secretary to the Tribunal' in each case. The Secretary assists the tribunal in its work with the support of a paralegal and an administrative assistant.[50] Each legal counsel and senior legal counsel handles the administration of around 10 cases at any given time.[51] The Secretary and their case team are under the supervision of the Secretary-General of ICSID, who assigns cases amongst the staff.[52]

From the above review, the staff from the Institutional Office are primarily under the supervision of the head of the Institutional Office (or particular division of the Institutional Office). Even in cases where they are assisting a particular adjudicator (for example, the staff of the ECtHR, the IACtHR and the ACtHPR) or bench (for example, the staff of the WTO DSS, the ICJ, ITLOS, USMCA, the PCA and ISCID) for a particular dispute, they are only working with the adjudicator/bench for the duration of that dispute. The head of the Institutional Office continues to exercise supervision over such staff, although they defer to the decision-making authority of the adjudicators in that particular dispute.

In section I.A.ii below, we will examine some Institutional Assistants who are constituted outside of these Institutional Offices. They may have a different supervisor distinct from or in addition to the head of the Institutional Office. However, they still retain their character as Institutional Assistants.

[47] At present, as per the PCA website, there are 55 legal staff: two Deputy Secretaries-General, five Senior Legal Counsel, 11 Legal Counsel, 20 Assistant Legal Counsel and 17 case managers. See Permanent Court of Arbitration, 'Staff', pca-cpa.org/en/about/introduction/staff.

[48] The tribunal secretaries in state-to-state disputes are referred to as Tribunal Registrars.

[49] For an overview, see International Centre for Settlement of Investment Disputes (ICSID), 'Secretariat – Overview', www.worldbank.org/en/programs/icsid/secretariat-overview.

[50] International Centre for Settlement of Investment Disputes (ICSID), *Administrative and Financial Regulations* (ICSID/15, April 2006), reg 28.

[51] International Centre for Settlement of Investment Disputes (ICSID), 'Inside ICSID Secretariat – Benjamin Garel, Legal Counsel', www.icsid.worldbank.org/inside-icsid-secretariat-benjamin-garel-legal-counsel.

[52] Administrative and Financial Regulations, reg 12.

ii. Additional Institutional Departments

Now, we turn to Institutional Assistants organised in additional departments/divisions distinct from the main Institutional Office. We examine those assistants across three institutions: the CJEU; the ECOWAS Court; and the ECtHR.

a) In addition to the Institutional Office of the CJEU (the Registries of the ECJ and the General Court), two other offices house Dispute Assistants who provide critical assistance to the DSM as a whole: the Research and Documentation Directorate and the Directorate-General of Multilingualism.[53] The Research and Documentation Directorate consists of lawyers. It discharges two main functions. The first is the filtering function, which involves reviewing preliminary ruling applications and some categories of appeals brought before the ECJ. The second function involves conducting comparative research on questions of law and collating jurisprudence across Member States and other jurisdictions. The Research and Documentation Directorate performs the second function less frequently than the first. In both these functions, the staff do not work for individual judges, but work for the CJEU as a whole, and they are under the direct control of the Registrar of the ECJ. The other office is the Directorate-General of Multilingualism, which acts as the language service of the CJEU. The Directorate hires individuals who have completed their education in law and possess the necessary language qualifications.[54] The Dispute Assistants in these Additional Institutional Departments are ultimately under the supervision of the Registrar of the ECJ. The Director-General supervises the day-to-day work of the Directorate-General for Multilingualism.

b) Besides its Registry, the ECOWAS Court has the Research and Documentation Department consisting of non-lawyers and lawyers, who perform the bulk of the judicial assistance work in the ECOWAS Court. The Dispute Assistants in the Additional Institutional Department are not allocated to a particular judge, but rather assist a bench in a dispute. They could be assisting in multiple disputes at a time. A Director heads the department and allocates the work among the legal research team. The Director is supervised by and reports to the President of the Court, including for administrative matters like the Director's leave and performance evaluation. Although the Chief Registrar (of the Institutional Office) is of a higher rank than the Director, they do not supervise or even comment on the Director's work for review.

c) In the ECtHR, the Dispute Assistants in two Additional Institutional Departments are relevant: the Filtering Section and the Directorate of the Jurisconsult, which are distinct from the Institutional Office (the Registry). The Filtering Section assists the Section Registries in reviewing incoming applications.[55] It consists primarily of case processing lawyers who 'filter' incoming cases into those to be decided by a single-judge formation and those that require examination by a Committee or a Chamber, and in some cases, the applications may also be disposed of administratively without judicial involvement.[56] The Filtering Section has its own Registrar who heads the Section and

[53] The CJEU also contains other departments that do not satisfy the definition of Dispute Assistants adopted by us in this book, notably the Directorate-General of Administration and the Directorate-General for the Information, Protocol and Visits Directorate.

[54] Court of Justice of the European Union (CJEU), 'Directorates for Legal Translation', www.curia.europa.eu/jcms/jcms/Jo2_7020/en.

[55] L Bianku and P Kempees, 'The European Court of Human Rights' in Baetens (n 2) 111.

[56] ibid 112.

is formally under the supervision of the Registrar of the ECtHR. Now, turning to the Directorate of the Jurisconsult: although the Jurisconsult is officially a member of the Registry, the staff of the Directorate of the Jurisconsult exercise their functions separately from the Registry. The staff are free from the supervision or control of the Section Registrars, and are under the supervision of the Jurisconsult and, formally, the Registrar of the ECtHR. The Jurisconsult's role is to ensure the quality and consistency of its case law by advising on legal issues and precedents.[57] The Dispute Assistants in both these Additional Institutional Departments are not assigned to individual judges, but rather work for the DSM as a whole.

It is interesting to note that the supervision of the Dispute Assistants in the Additional Institutional Departments of the CJEU and the ECtHR have certain similarities. The staff of the Additional Institutional Department are formally under the supervision of the head of the Institutional Office. In contrast, in the ECOWAS Court, the staff of the Additional Institutional Department have their own supervisor, and this supervisor is in turn under the supervision of the President of the Court rather than the head of the Institutional Office.

While the Institutional Assistants identified above are not entirely under the direct supervision of adjudicators, this does not imply that adjudicators do not exert any supervision or control over their work. In addition to having control over the decision-making process in a particular dispute, there are also de facto forms of control exercised by adjudicators over Institutional Assistants. For example, in the ECOWAS Court, the Director of the Research and Documentation Department is supervised by and reports to the President of the Court, including for administrative matters like the Director's leave and performance evaluation. This indirect control exercised by an adjudicator over the head of the Additional Institutional Department that performs the bulk of judicial assistants can be an essential safeguard against concerns on Dispute Assistants allegedly encroaching over the decision-making domain of adjudicators. We will examine such de facto safeguards across the identified DSMs in section III below.

B. Assigned Assistants

Unlike Institutional Assistants, Dispute Assistants are hired to work entirely under the supervision of individual adjudicators (or benches). In contrast to Institutional Assistants, they do not merely assist an adjudicator/bench of adjudicators for a particular dispute; rather, they follow their respective adjudicator/bench of adjudicators in the disputes that are assigned to them. The following Dispute Assistants are exclusively under the supervision of the adjudicators/bench of adjudicators they are assigned to:

a) Référendaires of the CJEU are legal secretaries to the judges[58] who form part of their cabinets. The judges have complete discretion over the selection of their référendaires, and the general meeting of the Court formally appoints them.[59] At present, the

[57] Rules of Court of the ECtHR, r 18B.
[58] And Advocate Generals. For more information regarding the référendaires of Advocates General, see ch 3.
[59] D Sarmiento, 'Référendaire: Court of Justice of the European Union (CJEU)' in *Max Planck Encyclopedia of International Procedural Law* (Oxford University Press, online edn December 2018) 22. The official appointment is purely a formality, as the general meeting seems to have never rejected a référendaire. However, this

judges of the ECJ have four référendaires and the judges of the General Court have two. Additionally, the General Court has a set of référendaires that are shared between the judges. The President of each Chamber of the General Court[60] is assigned an additional référendaire to assist them with their functions. The other four judges in the Chamber of the General Court share two additional référendaires, with each référendaire working for two judges at a time. Finally, the office of the President has a team of référendaires. These référendaires are available to individual judges for additional assistance when working on a large or complicated case. To reiterate, the référendaires in both the ECJ and the General Court are under the supervision of the adjudicators and are distinct from the Institutional Office (Registry). Therefore, the judges retain full supervision and control over such assistants. The cabinet of the judges also consists of other Dispute Assistants, who are also fully under their supervision and control.

Lecteurs d'arrêts of the CJEU are Dispute Assistants assigned to the Cabinet of the President of the ECJ and the General Court. Their role is distinct from référendaires assigned to the cabinet of the individual judges. Functionally, they do not work for a single judge. However, structurally, the CJEU considers them assigned to an individual judge (the President). They are thus under the supervision of the President of the ECJ or of the General Court. After the judges produce a draft judgment, the Lecteurs d'arrêts provide inputs on its language and ensure its consistency with a judgment's formal requirements. They are senior lawyers who are fluent in French and, because of their experience, may go beyond purely formalistic edits in their role. In practice, it is rare for them to do so.

b) Référendaires of EFTA Court are similar to the référendaires of the CJEU. The EFTA Court also operates on a cabinet system and each judge of the EFTA Court is assigned two référendaires or legal secretaries under their supervision. Therefore, they are under the supervision and full control of their assigned judges. Similarly, the cabinet of the judge conducts the hiring process without any intervention from the Institutional Office (Registry).

c) Legal Advisors of the IUSCT provide legal assistance to their respective tribunal members. The present practice of the IUSCT is that each tribunal member is assigned one Legal Adviser, and the President of the IUSCT may be assigned additional Legal Adviser(s).[61] Legal Advisers are not part of the Registry. The Secretary-General appoints the Legal Advisers on the recommendation of their respective tribunal member. Although they are administratively subordinate to the Secretary-General, they work under the exclusive supervision and control of their respective tribunal member.

d) Legal Officers in Chambers of the ICC and the ICTY are independent of the Registry (Institutional Office) and work 'in Chambers' of the Court. Although the legal officers of the ICC were originally a part of the Registry and assigned to specific judges, the ICC soon placed them in Chambers under the supervision and control of the judges in Chambers as a whole. The Registrar may retain some administrative control over the legal staff performance review, renewal, periods of leave etc. However, in practice,

---

does not imply that every single référendaire proposed by a judge/Advocate General is accepted. The 'rejection' will normally occur informally through the President/Vice-President/President of Chamber warning the proposing judge/Advocate General before the general meeting/plenary conference that the candidate they intend to propose may not be acceptable.

[60] Consisting of five judges.

[61] At present, one of the Legal Advisers of the President is assigned as the Principal Adviser.

the Registrar defers to the judges. The Legal Officers are divided into divisions (for example, in the ICC, the Pre-Trial, Trial and Appeals Divisions) and further assigned to specific chambers of judges within the divisions. Notably, the ICC and the ICTY do not assign the Legal Officers to individual judges, but to a chamber as a whole (ie, a bench of adjudicators). In the ICC, there is a sophisticated framework of actors responsible for supervising the Legal Officers: The Legal Officers are under the overall supervision of the Head of Chambers and the direct supervision of the respective Division Legal Adviser, and within a Chamber's legal team. The Legal Advisors are under the general authority of the President of the Division and the direct supervision of the Head of Chambers. The Head of Chambers was a position that was created to organise the work of the (associate) Legal Officers between the three divisions. Within the three divisions, the Legal Advisors assign work to the Legal Officers. Ultimately, they are all under the supervision and control of judges in the chambers to which they are assigned.

In certain instances, Assigned Assistants may be formally a part of the Institutional Office and/or have the head of such office retaining some level of administrative control over them. This distinction is interesting and understandably impacts the control exercised by the adjudicator over the Dispute Assistant.

a) Associate Legal Officers, Special Assistant to the President and the Judicial Fellows of the ICJ. There are 15 Associate Legal Officers ('clerks') and a Special Assistant to the President, assigned to individual judges. They are hired as international civil servants and are under the supervision of their respective judge, who evaluates them together with the President (or Vice-President in the case of the assistants of the President). The Registry also assigns Associate Legal Officers to ad hoc judges on a rotational basis. Additionally, the Registry assigns every judge a Judicial Fellow. These are not officials of the Court, but rather interns recommended and sponsored by their universities. Although all three categories of Dispute Assistant work directly for the judges, they are officially under the purview of the Department of Legal Matters of the ICJ. The Department of Legal Matters is part of the Registry, the ICJ's Institutional Office. However, the judges retain full control over their Assigned Assistants, even for administrative matters (eg, periods of leave).

b) Executive Assistants of the ECOWAS Court are assigned to every judge of the ECOWAS Court and forms a part of the 'Chambers' of the judge. The judge has complete discretion in selecting their Executive Assistant with legal education and expertise. After a judge selects their Executive Assistant, the Court will formally hire them. The Human Resources division conducts minimal intervention in selecting the Executive Assistants; they only verify that the candidate is a qualified lawyer with the minimum experience and qualifications for the role.

c) Legal Officers of the Special Tribunal for Lebanon (STL). The Legal Officers were organised slightly differently in the STL than in the ICC and the ICTY. Even though the Legal Officers were under the supervision of the Judge in the STL, they were considered part of the Registry, and the Registrar was responsible for their appointment, evaluations, appraisals and other administrative matters.

In all the cases examined above, only the adjudicators supervise the substantive work undertaken by the Assigned Assistants. However, in some cases, such assistants may formally be part of the Institutional Office, with some administrative matters being supervised or controlled by the Institutional Office.

C. External Assistants

Lastly, we examine a category of actors who are not officially part of the DSMs, but rather externally appointed/hired to assist the adjudicators. Therefore, in contrast to Assigned Assistants, they act as 'personal' assistants to their adjudicators. They may be hired by the adjudicators themselves or for them by the DSM for a particular dispute(s). In some DSMs, they are paid privately by the adjudicator, by the parties or even by the Institutional Office:

a) External Researchers in the COMESA Court: In the COMESA Court, External Researchers provide substantive research and assistance to the judges. The COMESA Court recruits these researchers from institutions like the Trade Policy Training Centre in Africa for specific cases; they may be lecturers or students. The scope of their research depends on the complexity of the case, including its substantive aspects. The External Researchers assist a bench as a whole and do not work for specific judges, and they are hired and paid for by the COMESA Court for a particular dispute.

b) Assistants to Panellists of USMCA: Panellists are allowed to hire one personal 'assistant',[62] which is defined as 'a person who, under the terms of appointment of a panellist, conducts research for or provides support to a panellist'. Panellists have utilised this provision in practice.[63] However, from the limited number of panel reports available, past practice under the NAFTA and the CETA suggests that panellists use the provision sparingly.[64] The assistants are bound by Article 9 of the Code of Conduct, as well as being required to submit a 'Declaration of Non-disclosure', along with the staff of the USMCA Secretariat.[65] The names of the assistants are also disclosed to the parties, who have the opportunity to object to their appointment.

c) Assistants to arbitrators in the PCA and ICSID: Like USMCA, the PCA and ICSID allow arbitrators to employ their own External Assistants with the parties' consent.[66] The Institutional Office does not exercise any supervision or control over such assistants. In ICSID, the assistants must also sign the same declaration of independence and impartiality as the arbitrators.[67] This is also the practice for tribunal assistants in the PCA. The IBA

[62] Rules of Procedure for Chapter 31 of USMCA, art 12.

[63] For example *United States – Automotive Rules of Origin*, Panel Report (USMCA Panel, USA-MEX-CDA-2022-31-01, 14 December 2022) para 19 (hereinafter *US – Auto ROOs*); *Canada – Dairy TRQ Allocation Measures*, Panel Report (USMCA Panel, CDA-USA-2021-31-010, 20 December 2021) para 6; *Canada – Dairy TRQ Allocation Measures*, Panel Report (USMCA Panel, CDA-USA-2023-31-01, 10 November 2023) para 12. They may be allowed to have more than one assistant at the discretion of the parties.

[64] With respect to the practice under the CETA, *see* K Claussen, 'Old and New Dispute Secretariats' (2022) 116 *American Journal of International Law: Unbound* 400, 403. Claussen notes that only half the panellists in the six panel reports available from the last 10 years have relied on assistants, and only one of the six panel reports makes mention of the functions those assistants served.

[65] Rules of Procedure for Chapter 31 of the USMCA, art 5, read with Code of Conduct, art 9; Rules of Procedure for Chapter 31 of the USMCA, arts 2–3.

[66] B McAsey, 'International Arbitral Institutions' in Baetens (n 2) 61. Usually, this assistant will be appointed by and work closely with the tribunal president.

[67] International Centre for Settlement of Investment Disputes (ICSID), https://icsid.worldbank.org/resources/content/arbitrators/tribunal-assistants.

Guidelines on Conflicts of Interest in International Arbitration[68] includes within its scope 'arbitral or administrative secretaries and assistants'.[69] We term them 'tribunal assistants'.

d) External Assistants in commercial arbitration institutions: The rules of most commercial arbitration institutions permit arbitrators to employ External Assistants with the parties' consent. However, in CIETAC, the role of tribunal secretary is filled by the Secretariat-appointed case manager, leaving no room for an additional personal assistant.[70] As stated above, the IBA Guidelines on Conflicts of Interest in International Arbitration apply to such External Assistants as well.[71] We term them 'tribunal assistants'.

In all four of the DSMs identified above (USMCA, the PCA, ICSID and commercial arbitration), the adjudicators themselves are selected on an ad hoc basis for specific disputes. Accordingly, their External Assistants are also ad hoc in nature and strictly speaking, are not part of the DSM. They are only guests that support a specific dispute. Consequently, they do not amass institutional expertise. Further, the names of the External Assistants are specifically disclosed to the parties to the dispute.

In this next section, we detail the specific functions discharged by these groups of Dispute Assistants and map the extent of their participation in the dispute resolution process. Thereafter, in section III, we will discuss the formal and de facto frameworks through which adjudicators are able to exert control over these various categories of actors.

II. Dispute Assistants and the Dispute Resolution Process

Each of the seven stages examined below showcase the degree and extent of the functions of all three categories of Dispute Assistants across the identified DSMs. This allows us to understand their contribution to assisting adjudicators in the decision-making function, as well as the implications of institutional control (or lack of) over their functions.

A. The Role of Dispute Assistants in Appointment or Selection of Adjudicators

In some DSMs with ad hoc adjudicators, the Institutional Assistants aid the parties in selection and/or appointment of adjudicators. For example, in the WTO DSS, the DSU tasks the Secretariat (Institutional Assistants) to assist the parties in the selection of

[68] Which have been recognised as a solid soft law instrument reflecting standards expected to apply to conflicts of interests (ie, impartiality and independence), as well as disclosures in specific circumstances

[69] International Bar Association, *IBA Guidelines on Conflicts of Interest in International Arbitration* (approved by the IBA Council, 25 May 2024) pt I, art 5.

[70] D Wen and L Bergmann, 'Comparison between SCC Arbitration and CIETAC Arbitration', www.transnational-dispute-management.com/article.asp?key=1753; see also L Hu, 'Interview with Deputy Secretary General', www.arbitrationblog.kluwerarbitration.com/2020/04/12/interviews-with-our-editors-china-insights-from-dr-li-hu-of-cietac; CIETAC Arbitration Rules, art 13.4.

[71] IBA Guidelines on Conflicts of Interest in International Arbitration, pt I, art 5.

panellists.[72] If the parties are unable to reach an agreement within the specified time period, either party can request the DG of the WTO to establish the panel.[73] While the specific procedures and role of Dispute Assistants are distinct in each identified DSM (as per the pre-established rule/agreement between the parties), we note the critical nature of this function in ensuring timely dispute resolution. In DSMs where the adjudicators are selected on an ad hoc basis, the role of Dispute Assistants ensures that the process is not stalled due to inability of parties to agree on adjudicator(s) and implements a quasi-automaticity/reversed consensus provision. We will examine the practice of five institutions (ie, commercial arbitration institutions, the WTO, the PCA, ICSID and USMCA) below:

a) The practice in commercial arbitration institutions varies according to the institution's rules, as well as the arbitration agreement between the parties. We look at some examples where the parties agree to arbitration under a set of arbitration rules and the related rules of appointment of arbitrators. The Chairman of CIETAC may act as the appointing authority, but the Secretariat and the CIETAC Arbitration Court are not involved in the appointment process.[74] In the International Chamber of Commerce Court of Arbitration, the Secretariat may be jointly requested by the parties to propose names of potential candidates to serve as arbitrators or provide non-confidential information on potential arbitrators. The International Chamber of Commerce Court has the power to decide on the number of arbitrators (if the parties are unable to agree on the number of arbitrators)[75] and appoint the arbitrator(s) if the parties are unable to agree within the specified time,[76] including the President of the tribunal.[77] The International Chamber of Commerce Court decides on the appointment, conformation, challenges and replacement of arbitrators.[78] The parties may also agree that the Chambers' appointment of the arbitrator will occur in consultation between the parties and the Secretariat. In particular, the parties may agree that any such appointment will occur following a list procedure.[79]

b) The Secretariat of the WTO is responsible in assisting the parties with the selection of panellists.[80] The Secretariat is required to maintain an indicative list of qualified

[72] DSU, arts 8.4, 8.6.

[73] ibid art 8.7.

[74] See CIETAC Arbitration Rules, arts 27–29. In CIETAC, the Chairman of CIETAC may act as the appointing authority if the parties so designate, or if the parties fail to make their appointments within the specified time limit. The Chairman of CIETAC also has the responsibility to make decisions on challenges to arbitrators. However, the Secretariat does play an indirect role by pre-screening candidates' qualifications before the responsible committee decides on their appointment to the Panel of Arbitrators maintained by CIETAC, from which arbitrators are to be appointed. See China International Economic and Trade Arbitration Commission (CIETAC), Rules on the Conferral of Qualifications of Arbitrators, art 4.1.

[75] International Chamber of Commerce, ICC Arbitration Rules (2021), r 12.2.

[76] ibid rr 12.3–12.4.

[77] ibid r 12. 5.

[78] ibid r 11.4, 14 and 15.

[79] Whereby the Secretariat will establish a list of candidates and submit it to the parties (for example, by allowing the parties to strike a limited number of candidates and rank the others by order of preference). See International Chamber of Commerce, *Note to Parties and Arbitral Tribunals on the Conduct of the Arbitration under the ICC Rules of Arbitration* (1 January 2019) 38.

[80] Although the Secretariat is tasked with assisting the parties at this stage, the parties are free to bypass this entire process by agreeing inter se on the composition of the panel without assistance from the Secretariat. See GZ Marceau and A Venkataraman, 'Unmasking the Phantom of the Opera: Is There a Hidden Secretariat in the WTO Dispute Settlement System?' (2022) 116 *American Journal of International Law*: Unbound 395–99.

individuals from which panellists may be drawn (hereinafter the 'Indicative List').[81] WTO Members propose nominations to the Indicative List,[82] which are approved by the DSB by positive consensus.[83] The DSU does not require panellists to be selected exclusively from the Indicative List. In order to assist parties in selection of panellists, the Secretariat also maintains an unofficial database with names of past and potential panellists. The DSU entrusts the Secretariat with the task of proposing the names of potential panellists to the parties.[84] They meet with the parties to hear their preferred 'criteria' for the prospective panellists in terms of nationality[85] and expertise.[86] This task is undertaken by dedicated teams within the LAD or the Rules Division (depending on which division has the responsibility for the dispute).[87] The Director of the responsible division reviews and approves the work of the dedicated team. They typically propose 'slates' of six names for the parties' consideration. Although the parties retain the right to reject the nominations made by the Secretariat, the DSU notes that this may only be done for 'compelling reasons'.[88] This process may be repeated several times until the parties reach an agreement on the three panellists.

If the parties cannot agree on three panellists within 20 days after the date of establishment of the panel by the DSB, either party can request the DG to appoint the panellists.[89] The DG is briefed by the Secretariat on the composition process to date, and is informed of the nominations that have already been turned down by the parties.[90] The decision of the DG is final and, unlike during the process when the Secretariat assists the parties with panel selection, parties cannot oppose the DG's nominees even for 'compelling reasons'. We will expand on this, as well as other additional processes unique to the WTO, in Part III.

c) In the PCA, for arbitrations under the UNCITRAL Rules, if the parties have not chosen an appointing authority, either party may request the Secretary-General of the PCA to designate an appointing authority (responsible for selecting an appointing authority). In practice, the parties may, and frequently do, agree to have the

For example, anecdotally it is recalled that such agreement between the parties took place in *United States – Import Prohibition of Certain Shrimp and Shrimp Products – Constitution of the Panel Established at the Requests of Malaysia, Thailand, Pakistan and India*, WT/DS58/9 (10 February 1997).

[81] DSU, art 8.4.

[82] ibid.

[83] ibid art 2.4.

[84] ibid art 8.6. It is WTO Members that can propose individuals for inclusion in the list, which divides the roster panellists into 'governmental' and 'non-governmental'.

[85] For example, as per art 8.3 DSU, parties could specifically agree to allow citizens of WTO Members whose governments are parties or third parties to the dispute to serve as panellists.

[86] These meetings with the parties are confidential and no minutes are published after the composition of the panel. See M Pereyra, 'Appointment of WTO Adjudicators: Rules and Evolving Practices' in N Lamp (ed), *Reckoning and Renewal: The World Trade Organization and its Dispute Settlement System at 30. Essays in Honour of Valerie Hughes* (Cambridge University Press, 2023) 49; R Malacrida, 'WTO Panel Composition: Searching Far and Wide for Administrators of World Trade Justice' in G Marceau (ed), *A History of Law and Lawyers in the GATT/WTO: The Development of the Rule of Law in the Multilateral Trading System* (Cambridge University Press, 2015) 314.

[87] Pauwelyn and Pelc (n 17) 539.

[88] DSU, art 8.6. Although this is the stated rule, there is no mechanism/threshold to assess what constitutes a 'compelling' reason.

[89] ibid art 8.7.

[90] See Pereyra (n 86) 51.

Secretary-General of the PCA act directly as the appointing authority.[91] The mechanism is different under the PCA Rules, with the Secretary-General of the PCA being the default appointing authority.[92] Appointing authorities follow a strike-and-rank list procedure when making appointments,[93] where the parties can point to their preferences from a list communicated by the Secretary-General. When the Secretary-General is the appointing authority, the International Bureau compiles this list based on characteristics communicated by the parties.[94] The Bureau exercises its judgement on the suitability of the candidate if there are conflicting requirements by the parties. The parties strike off candidates from the list and rank the remaining ones. Thereafter, the appointing authority selects the remaining arbitrator(s) or the President most suitable to the parties according to their rankings. If the parties are not able to agree on common candidates, the Secretary-General appoints a candidate that was reserved from the list and not shared with the parties. Under the PCA Rules, the Secretary-General also decides on any challenges to the arbitrators.[95]

c) Similarly, in ICSID, the ICSID Secretariat works to facilitate the parties' agreement if requested by the parties. The Secretary-General assists the parties by drawing up a ballot/list of possible candidates for them to choose from.[96] The ICSID Secretariat is not bound by the Panel of Arbitrators when nominating names to the parties.[97] The parties may also specifically designate the Secretary-General as the appointing authority[98] or request the assistance of the Secretary-General under Rule 17 of the Arbitration Rules.[99] In the event that the tribunal is not constituted within 90 days of notice of registration of the request, or such other period as agreed by the parties, either party may request the Chair of the Administrative Council to appoint the arbitrator(s) not yet appointed.[100] The Secretariat staff also assists in this process; specifically, the ICSID Secretary-General

[91] United Nations Commission on International Trade Law (UNCITRAL), *UNCITRAL Arbitration Rules* art 6.1.

[92] Permanent Court of Arbitration (PCA), PCA Arbitration Rules, arts 8.1 and 9.2–9.3. This difference is due to the fact that the UNCITRAL Rules were intended to operate in an ad hoc manner, while the PCA Rules recognise the PCA acting as a facilitating entity.

[93] UNCITRAL Arbitration Rules, art 8.2; PCA Arbitration Rules, art 8.2.

[94] For example, expertise in certain technical issues/laws and language proficiency.

[95] PCA Arbitration Rules, art 13.4.

[96] E Obadia and F Nitscheke, 'Institutional Arbitration and the Role of the Secretariat' in *Litigating International Investment Disputes* (Brill, 2014) 112; see also International Centre for Settlement of Investment Disputes (ICSID), 'Selection of the Tribunal', www.icsid.worldbank.org/procedures/arbitration/convention/selection-tribunal/2022. Since 2009, this informal procedure precedes recourse to the Appointing Authority under art 38(1) of the ICSID Convention. Under the ballot procedure, ICSID provides parties with a ballot form containing names of several candidates, and each party is given a date to return the form indicating which candidates it accepts/rejects. Under the list procedure, ICSID provide the parties with a list of several candidates, and each party can strike a certain number of candidates and rank the remaining ones. The parties may also specify any other procedure other than the ballot/list procedure.

[97] D Caron, 'ICSID in the Twenty-First Century: An Interview with Meg Kinnear' (2010) 104 *American Society of International Law Proceedings* 421; D Gaukrodger, *Appointing Authorities and the Selection of Arbitrators in Investor-State Dispute Settlement: An Overview* (OECD Consultation Paper, March 2018).

[98] Obadia and Nitscheke (n 96) 113–14. Overall, ICSID appointed 29 per cent of arbitrators in 2022 (including appointments by the Chair and the Secretary-General), see *Annual Report 2022 International Centre for Settlement of Investment Disputes, 30,* https://icsid.worldbank.org/sites/default/files/publications/ICSID_AR.EN.pdf.

[99] International Centre for Settlement of Investment Disputes (ICSID), ICSID Arbitration Rules (2022) r 17.

[100] Convention on the Settlement of Investment Disputes between States and Nationals of Other States (18 March 1965), art 38; ICSID Arbitration Rules (2022), r 18.

may make recommendations to the Chair regarding potential appointees.[101] The Chair must make such an appointment from the Panel of Arbitrators, and such appointees must not be nationals of either party.

d) Although the Secretariat of the USMCA does not play a role in the selection of the panellists, they assist parties in an administrative role. Panels under Chapter 31 disputes of the USMCA are, by default, composed of five members, but the parties to the dispute may agree to compose a panel of only three members.[102] The parties try to appoint the panel chair by consensus, failing which the panel chair is appointed by one party chosen by lot. In such a case, the chair may not be a citizen of that party.[103] After the panel chair is chosen, the disputing parties proceed to select the other panellists. If the dispute involves two parties, each will then appoint a panellist (or two). Where the dispute involves three parties, the two complainants appoint one each, and the respondent appoints two.[104] The 'responsible Section of the Secretariat' (ie, the Secretariat of the responding party)[105] assists the parties administratively by contacting the panellists once they are selected, collecting the letters of conflict of interest from the panellists etc.

The role of Dispute Assistants at this stage has given rise to some concerns as to their potential influence over adjudicators. The Dispute Assistants, who are Institutional Assistants, enjoy a relative degree of standing in the DSM compared to adjudicators who are selected on an ad hoc basis. In the WTO DSS, scholars like Joost Pauwelyn and Krzysztof Pelc have raised concerns over this 'reversal of roles' between the adjudicators and Dispute Assistants. They explain that such a framework might give rise to instances where the adjudicators feel in a position of dependence, and may even raise doubts concerning their influence over the decision-making process. However, there are various circumstances that determine whether these concerns become a reality – for example, the institutional rules on supervision and control over Dispute Assistants, the expertise/experience of the adjudicators and the procedural framework safeguarding against such influence. Further, it also becomes necessary to balance these concerns against the functional importance of the role fulfilled by Dispute Assistants at the stage of appointment and selection of adjudicators – ie, their role in ensuring continuity of the dispute resolution process.[106]

[101] C Schreuer et al, *The ICSID Convention: A Commentary*, 2nd edn (Cambridge University Press, 2009) 494.

[102] USMCA, art 31.9(1)(a) and (2)(a). To date, under Chapter 31 dispute settlement, three-member panels have been constituted in all four two-party disputes (*Canada – Dairy Tariff Rate Quota for Certain Dairy Products I*, Panel Report, USA-CDA-2021-31-01 (20 December 2021); *Canada – Dairy Tariff Rate Quota for Certain Dairy Products II*, Panel Report, USA-CDA-2022-31-01 (21 November 2023); *United States – Safeguard Measure on Imports of Crystalline Silicon Photovoltaic Products*, Panel Report, USA-MEX-2022-31-01 (15 December 2022); and *Mexico – Measures Concerning Genetically Engineered Corn*, Panel Report, USA-MEX-2023-31-01 (17 December 2024). By contrast, in the sole three-party dispute to date, the panel was composed of five members (*United States – Automotive Rules of Origin*, Panel Report, USA-CDA-MEX-2021-31-01 (14 January 2023).

[103] USMCA, art 31.9(1)(b) and (2)(b).

[104] ibid art 31.9(1)(d) and (2)(d). These panellists must be citizens of the other party to the dispute.

[105] Rules of Procedure for Chapter 31 of the USMCA, art 2.

[106] D Gaukrodger, *Appointing Authorities and the Selection of Arbitrators in Investor-State Dispute Settlement: An Overview* (OECD Consultation Paper, March 2018).

B. The Role of Dispute Assistants in Accepting of Submissions and Pre-screening of Cases

In all of the identified DSMs, Institutional Assistants in the Institutional Office and/or other Additional Institutional Departments perform some function in this stage of the dispute resolution process. The degree of their involvement ranges from, at the one end, administrative functions like receiving the documents and communication with the parties, and, at the other end, screening the documents and assessing admissibility of the cases before they are examined by the adjudicator.

The Institutional Assistants of 13 DSMs fall at the beginning of the spectrum, where they receive the submissions and do not further examine the documents for completeness. These Institutional Assistants are part of the Department of Legal Matters of the ICJ, the Registries of the COMESA Court, the EACJ, the EFTA, the ICC, the ICTY, the STL, the ITLOS, the IUSCT and the Secretariat of the MERCOSUR, the PCA, the USMCA and the WTO. In the WTO, as further discussed in Part III, the Institutional Assistants of the Registry receive the submissions, and thereafter pass them along to the Institutional Assistants of the LAD/Rules Division, who undertake more substantive examination.

The Institutional Assistants of the Registry of the ECOWAS Court and the Secretariat of the IACtHR examine the applications received on procedural issues. The Registrar of the ECOWAS Court conducts a preliminary review of the application to ensure that the filing complies with the Rules of Procedure of the Court and provides the applicant sufficient time to rectify the error. The staff of the Secretariat of the IACtHR undertake more functions, assisting the President of the Court in reviewing the submissions to ensure that all formal requirements are met.[107] The staff of the Secretariat assist the President in assessing whether the application provides all the necessary information, including compliance with the stipulated time periods and steps taken to exhaust local remedies. However, the eventual decision-making function rests with the President of the Court. In both cases, the Institutional Office either discharges a very preliminary and procedural review of the documents or assists the adjudicator in examining the documents. No decision-making power rests with the Institutional Office with respect to the dispute.

At the CJEU, the Registries of the ECJ and the General Court also undertake a preliminary review of the application to assess compliance with various procedural requirements. For example, if an individual applicant files an application before the ECJ and if it instead rightfully falls within the jurisdiction of the General Court, the Registry of the ECJ has the power to transfer the case to the General Court.[108] The Institutional Assistants also examine if the file is complete. In preliminary ruling applications and some appeal cases before the ECJ, the Research and Documentation Directorate (Additional Institutional Department) undertakes a more preliminary review, preparing a short report on procedural deficiencies. However, these Institutional Assistants do not make any decisions on the case even when procedural deficiencies exist. The

[107] Rules of Procedure of the Inter-American Court of Human Rights, art 28.

[108] Even where an application is submitted in the form of a letter, the Registry is obliged to respond, explaining why it cannot be registered as a case before the Court. See S Puig and C Brown, 'The Secretary-General's Power to Refuse to Register a Request for Arbitration under the ICSID Convention' (2012) 27(1) *ICSID Review* 172–91.

decision-making power is left to the President of the Court, who makes the decision on the basis of recommendations from the Institutional Assistants. Similarly, in the ECtHR, upon the receipt of an application, the case lawyers of the Filtering Section will prepare a brief note setting out the facts and issues, as well as the reasons for which an application maybe admissible or not.[109] The Non-judicial Rapporteur (which is the Registrar of the Section Registry) approves the note and forwards it to a single judge formation. The judge then decides whether the application is inadmissible or deserves further examination by a 'Committee' or 'Chamber' of judges. At this stage, staff of the Filtering Section (Institutional Assistants) play an essential role in assisting the decision-making by the single judge on how to proceed with the application. Therefore, in both the CJEU and the ECtHR, the Institutional Assistants discharge important functions in assisting adjudicators on how to proceed with a dispute.

In the ICSID Secretariat, a well-defined role is envisaged for the Secretary-General with respect to screening and accepting requests for arbitration. The ICSID Secretariat's involvement is more expansive in scope than the CJEU and the ECtHR, as decision-making power is granted to the head of the Institutional Office – ie, the Secretary-General. As per Article 36.1 of the ICSID Convention, the Secretary-General undertakes screening of requests for arbitrations. At this stage, the case is assigned to a legal counsel who will examine the request and recommend a course of action, with the ultimate decision taken by the Secretary-General. Given the narrow wording of Article 36.3,[110] which refers to the dispute being 'manifestly outside the jurisdiction of the Centre', this discretion is exercised very carefully. It only results in non-registration in extremely rare cases.[111] Therefore, although a more active role is envisaged for the Institutional Assistants and the head of Institutional Office, this is exercised within the confines of the express provision of the ICSID Convention.

The highest level of involvement of Institutional Assistants at this stage is in the ACtHPR. Here, the Head of the Legal Aid Division examines the case to ensure that the criteria for jurisdiction for contentious cases and requests for advisory opinion have been satisfied. If the application fails to satisfy the personal jurisdiction criteria, the Head of the Legal Aid Division instructs a clerk from the Registry to send a letter explaining to the applicant why the case cannot proceed. If the case is found to satisfy the personal jurisdiction criteria, one or more Legal Officers from the Registry are assigned to the case to further examine jurisdiction and admissibility criteria. In contentious cases, various cumulative criteria determine the admissibility of the application. For example, such criteria may include an assessment of whether the evidence used in the complaint is based exclusively on news disseminated through the mass media. It could also be whether the applicants have exhausted local remedies.[112] In a request for an advisory opinion, the Legal Officer examines admissibility based on whether the African

[109] Bianku and Kempees (n 55) 113.

[110] Convention on the Settlement of Investment Disputes between States and Nationals of Other States (opened for signature 18 March 1965, entered into force 14 October 1966) (hereinafter 'ICSID Convention'), art 36(3).

[111] Current figures are difficult to ascertain; however, as of 2014, it was reported that ICSID had refused to register a request only 18 times over a period of 46 years. See E Obadia and F Nitschke, 'Institutional Arbitration and the Role of the Secretariat' in C Giorgetti (ed), *Litigating International Investment Disputes: A Practitioner's Guide* (Brill Nijhoff, 2014) 80–144, at 93.

[112] For a list of criteria for admissibility, see M Wiebusch, 'African Court on Human and Peoples' Rights' in C Binder et al (eds), *Elgar Encyclopedia of Human Rights* (Edward Elgar, 2022) 83.

Commission is already examining the subject matter of the opinion.[113] The Legal Officer thereafter drafts a case note detailing how to proceed with the case. Based on this case note, the Head of the Legal Aid Division makes a recommendation to the Bureau of the Court[114] which cases should be registered on the docket.[115] Although the President makes the final decision, the Legal Officer and Head of the Legal Aid Division play a significant role in making recommendations at this stage.

At the admissibility stage, if Dispute Assistants are granted unguided discretion and decision-making power, this can risk the integrity of the adjudicatory body and encroach upon the domain of the adjudicators. However, our comparative analysis of the identified DSMs reveals a different picture. Amongst the 20 DSMs examined, there are only two where some level of decision-making power is granted to Dispute Assistants. The Head of the Legal Aid Division of the ACtHPR makes the decision on applications that fail to meet the personal jurisdiction criteria, and the Secretary-General of ICSID determines if a request for arbitration is manifestly outside the jurisdiction of the tribunal. Both these actors exercise this decision-making function within the confines of the strict criteria laid down in the governing statute. Further, no Assigned Assistants or External Assistants play a role at this stage of screening or accepting submissions or pre-screening of cases across DSMs.

C. The Role of Dispute Assistants in the Preparation of Notes and Research

Although this is not typically a distinct stage in the dispute resolution process, in this sub-section, we bring together all the research and collating functions discharged by Dispute Assistants. Such assistance may include drafting specific notes summarising the submissions of the parties, the factual and legal issues raised by the parties, research notes on general or specific questions of law, and more general research assistance to adjudicators.

In the following six DSMs, we understand that Dispute Assistants produce specific research documents or notes for the adjudicators:

a) The ICJ: The staff of the Department of Legal Matters of the Registry (Institutional Assistants) review the submissions made by the parties, prepare an objective summary and circulate these to all the judges and their Associate Legal Officers. Further, the staff of the Department of Legal Matters also prepare a 'List of Issues' for each case, which is approved by the President and shared with all the judges. The List of Issues highlights to the judges the legal questions which are pertinent to the case.[116] The Registrar supervises

[113] ibid 85.

[114] Which consists of the President and Vice-President of the Court: Rules of Court of the African Court on Human and Peoples' Rights, r 10.

[115] Although the Bureau, or the President of the Court, is formally free to depart from the recommendation of the Head of the Legal Division on the registration of a case, it remains unclear whether, and how often, this discretion is exercised in practice.

[116] M Hébié, 'Des ombres furtives au Palais de la Paix ? : coup de projecteur sur les assistants juridiques des membres de la Cour internationale de Justice' in J-M Thouvenin and J Joly Hébart (eds), *La Cour internationale de Justice à 75 ans* (Pedone, 2023) 77.

these functions of the Registry staff. The Associate Legal Officers (Assigned Assistants) also prepare a memorandum for their respective judge in preparation for the hearing. The Associate Legal Officers also revise this memorandum in light of the submissions made by the parties during the oral proceedings.

b) The CJEU: The Research and Documentation Directorate (Institutional Assistants) may be requested to conduct comparative research on a question of law and collate the jurisprudence across Member States and even other jurisdictions. The Directorate usually initiates comparative research after the written phase of the case is completed if the Advocate General and/or the Judge Rapporteur find that it is useful to know the practice of Member States on a particular question of law or procedure.

c) ITLOS: The President of ITLOS has the responsibility to prepare a 'working paper' based on the written submissions made by the parties. The working paper summarises the legal and factual submissions made by the parties, and the principal contentions/issues arising in the case.[117] The President is assisted by the staff of the Registry (Institutional Assistants) assigned to the case. The Registry staff summarise the written pleadings made by the parties, and compile relevant research (such as case law and academic views) relating to the substantive and procedural issues in the case.[118] Further, the staff also revise the working paper to include any new arguments raised by the parties during the oral proceedings. The Registrar supervises the work undertaken by the staff. ITLOS does not have Assigned Assistants or External Assistants assisting the judges.

d) The IACtHR: The staff of the Secretariat (Institutional Assistants) assigned to the case will assist the Judge Rapporteur by circulating a 'problems paper'. The problems paper summarises the submissions made by the parties, highlights legal and factual issues arising in the case, and compiles the relevant legal research (including past case law). It is intended to assist the judges in preparing for the oral proceedings. The staff assigned to the case are under the supervision of the Judge Rapporteur, as well as the Secretary and the Deputy Secretary. The IACtHR does not have Assigned Assistants assisting the judges; the judges may have External Assistants, although this is not formally done through the Secretariat.

e) MERCOSUR: The staff of the ST (Institutional Assistants) perform limited functions in assisting the arbitrators. However, one of the notable functions performed by the ST staff is research on and compilation of relevant precedents and literature for the arbitrators to utilise in a dispute.[119] The MERCOSUR does not have Assigned Assistants or External Assistants assisting the arbitrators.

f) The WTO DSS: The Secretariat staff (Institutional Assistants) assigned to the dispute aid panels in case management, legal research and by drafting an 'issues paper'. In the issues paper, the assigned staff summarise the claims of the parties and the facts of the dispute, identify and highlight the legal and factual issues arising in the case, and compile relevant legal research (including the applicability of past case law). The issues

[117] Resolution on the Internal Judicial Practice of the Tribunal (hereinafter 'Judicial Practice Resolution'), art 2.3.
[118] ibid art 5.2; P Gautier, 'The International Tribunal for the Law of the Sea' in F Baetens (ed), *Legitimacy of Unseen Actors in International Adjudication* (Cambridge University Press, 2019) 47–48.
[119] Protocolo Modificatorio del Protocolo de Olivos, art 34.2(f).

paper is drafted prior to the hearings and assists the panellists in preparing for the hearings. The staff are supervised by the lead lawyer assigned to the case and ultimately the Director of the LAD/Rules. The WTO does not have Assigned Assistants or External Assistants. While it was functional, the staff of the AB Secretariat would also draft similar issues papers for the AB members under the supervision of the Director of the AB Secretariat. The (limited) practice with respect to the role of such staff assigned to MPIA arbitrators will be discussed in Part III.

We understand that in the following six DSMs, a Judge Rapporteur, assigned to each case, supervises the work of Dispute Assistants during the dispute: the IACtHR, the ECtHR, the ACtHPR, the ECOWAS Court, the CJEU and the EFTA.

a) In the IACtHR, the Institutional Assistants undertake the preparation of the problems paper under the supervision of the Judge Rapporteur.
b) In the ECtHR, although the case lawyers of the Section Registry (Institutional Assistants) do not prepare a specific document, they support the Judge Rapporteur in all research and drafting functions. They are also supervised by the Section Registrar and the Deputy Section Registrar.
c) Similarly, the Legal Officers of the Registry (Institutional Assistants) of the ACtHPR assigned to the case assist the Judge Rapporteur with research and collation, especially if there is an oral hearing. They are also supervised by the Head of the Legal Aid Unit.
d) In the CJEU and the EFTA Court, the Judge Rapporteur is assisted in research by their référendaire (Assigned Assistants). The référendaire also assists the Judge Rapporteur in the preparation of the 'preliminary report'.
e) In the ECOWAS Court, the staff of the Research and Documentation Department (Institutional Assistants) and Executive Assistants (Assigned Assistants) of Judge Rapporteurs, assist the judge in research. The staff of the Research and Documentation Department are also supervised by their Director. Therefore, there is a mix of Institutional Assistants and Assigned Assistants aiding the Judge Rapporteur.

More generally, in the following 10 DSMs, we understand that Assigned Assistants and External Assistants undertake research, prepare notes and assist their adjudicators in preparing for oral proceedings, as per their specific instructions, requirements and needs. In the IUSCT, the Legal Advisers (Assigned Assistants) assist their respective tribunal member according to their instructions. For example, this may be a presentation of the key issues arising in the case or for an upcoming hearing, summaries of the arguments made by the parties, relevant research on the issues arising in the case etc. As the Legal Advisers in IUSCT are professionals with years of experience, the tribunal members often entrust them with substantive research work. In the ICC, the ICTY and the STL, the Legal Officers in Chamber undertake research as per the requirements of the bench. In the COMESA Court, the external researchers hired for a particular case (External Assistants) assist all/any of judges on a bench with relevant research. Similarly, tribunal assistants in the USMCA, commercial arbitration institutions, the PCA and ICSID (External Assistants) may assist their respective supervisors with the research, as requested by them. In some commercial arbitration institutions, there may be limitations imposed on the extent of research undertaken by External Assistants. For example, the SIAC rules require that tribunal assistants may only provide research assistance with the parties' consent. As mentioned above, in the ECOWAS Court the judges are also supported by their Executive Assistants (Assigned Assistants) in addition to the research provided by the Institutional Office. The Judge Rapporteur may require their Executive Assistant to undertake additional research.

From the above analysis, it is clear that Dispute Assistants undertake a significant role in assisting adjudicators through, inter alia, summarising the submissions made by the parties, compiling the relevant research including case law, and highlighting the legal and factual issues raised. The degree of their participation is highly dependent on the institutional structures as well as the specific requirements of the adjudicators in the dispute. Especially in the case of Assigned Assistants and External Assistants, their research contributions depend on their level of experience and the adjudicator's individual needs and approaches. Institutional Assistants can accumulate a wealth of expertise and experience regarding the procedure and substantive jurisprudence of the institution. However, this research is not undertaken solely under the supervision of the adjudicators in all cases. To ensure that their contributions do not encroach upon the adjudicator's decision-making function, some DSMs have developed safeguards. For example, the Institutional Assistants in the ECtHR, the IACtHR, the ACtHPR and the ECOWAS Court undertake the research under the instructions and supervision of the Judge Rapporteur, which mitigates against such concerns. In another example, the judges of the ICJ and the ECOWAS Court are assisted by Institutional Assistants as well as Assigned Assistants. Such diversification of the sources of research and types of assistance seems to limit the potential influence of any one group of actors over the adjudicators.

D. The Role of the Dispute Assistants during the Hearings

At the hearing stage, the degree of involvement by Dispute Assistants is linked, and in many ways determined, by the role expected of them in the subsequent stages of the dispute resolution process (for example, during the deliberations and the drafting of the decision). At one end of the spectrum, the Dispute Assistant does not attend/participate in the oral proceedings or provides minimal technical support. In some cases, the Dispute Assistants may be instructed to take notes during the oral proceedings that subsequently may be used during the deliberations and drafting. At the other end of the spectrum, Dispute Assistants may actively participate in the oral proceedings, communicating and coordinating with the adjudicators, to suggest questions to the parties or to assist as requested.

In the following 19 DSMs, a member of the Institutional Office may be present at the hearing. In the ACtHPR,[120] the CJEU,[121] COMESA,[122] ECOWAS,[123] the IACtHR,[124] the

[120] The Registrar, the Deputy Registrar and the Legal Officer assigned to the case attend the hearings.

[121] Rules of Procedure of the General Court, art 35(5), OJ L 105/1; Rules of Procedure of the Court of Justice, art 84(1), OJ L 265/1.

[122] COMESA Rules of the Court, r 11(b).

[123] See the case files available at courtecowas.org/decisions-3.

[124] PG Domínguez, 'The Role of the Secretariat in the Inter-American Court of Human Rights: A Comparative Analysis' (2022) 116 *American Journal of International Law: Unbound* 390, 393.

ECtHR, the EFTA,[125] the ICJ[126] and ITLOS,[127] a high-ranking member of the Institutional Office is often present, along with junior staff. In the WTO, the Director of the LAD/ Rules Division can (and does) attend the hearings, and the Secretariat staff assigned to the dispute always attend. In the STL,[128] the ICC[129] and the ICTY, lower-level staff officially represent the Registrar, who does not typically participate. In MERCOSUR,[130] the EACJ,[131] the USMCA,[132] commercial arbitration institutions,[133] the PCA and ICSID, the staff from the Institutional Office are present and generally provide logistical support. Therefore, the attendance of some Institutional Office staff at the hearings appears to be widespread practice. More remarkably, the presence of high-level Institutional staff also appears to be common.

In every DSM with Assigned Assistants, the assistants attend the hearings with their adjudicators. For ease of reference, this refers to the référendaires of the EFTA[134] and the CJEU;[135] the Associate Legal Officers, Special Assistant to the President and the Judicial Fellows of the ICJ; the Legal Officers in Chambers of the ICC,[136] the STL and the ICTY; the Legal Advisers of the IUSCT;[137] and the Executive Assistants of the ECOWAS. With respect to External Assistants in the PCA, ICSID, the USMCA and commercial arbitration institutions, tribunal assistants of individual adjudicators attend hearings if requested to do so by the adjudicator who hired them, with the consent of the parties.[138] We do not have information on whether the external researchers hired in the COMESA Court attend the hearings.

In many cases, the level of involvement of the Dispute Assistants is dependent on the adjudicators. For example, the référendaires of the judges of the CJEU (Assigned Assistants) actively assist their judges during the oral proceedings. The référendaires communicate with their judge, offering clarifications or additional information relevant to the oral submissions. In practice, they communicate either by passing notes through a dedicated staff member or direct messaging on their court laptops. In the WTO, the staff assigned to the dispute are seated with the panellists during the oral proceedings

[125] Rules of Procedure of the EFTA Court, art 14(6).

[126] Rules of Court of the International Court of Justice, art 26.

[127] Rules of the Tribunal of the International Tribunal for the Law of the Sea, art 36(1)(h).

[128] See Judicial Division, Court Management Services Section, www.stl-tsl.org/en/about-the-stl/structure-of-the-stl/registry.

[129] ICC Regulations of the Registry, reg 40.

[130] MERCOSUR, Common Market Group (GMC), Secretaría del Tribunal Permanente de Revisión: Reglamentación del Artículo 35 de la Decisión 37/03, annex I, s 1(2)(e).

[131] Rules of Procedure of the East African Court of Justice, r 75.1.

[132] USMCA Rules of Procedure, art 21.14.

[133] ICC Internal Rules, art 2.4; see also Singapore International Arbitration Centre (SIAC), 'Vacancy for Deputy Counsel', www.siac.org.sg/siac-jobs/deputy-counsel.

[134] Vacancy Notice, www.eftacourt.int/wp-content/uploads/2020/10/Vacancy-announcement-03-2020.pdf.

[135] At the CJEU, it is common for only the référendaire assigned to a case to attend the hearings, with other members of the cabinet joining only where a case is of particular personal interest. See S Kenney, 'Beyond Principals and Agents: Seeing Courts as Organizations by Comparing Référendaires at the European Court of Justice and Law Clerks at the US Supreme Court' (2000) 33(5) *Comparative Political Studies* 593, 610.

[136] International Criminal Court, 'The Judges' Legal Officer', www.icc-cpi.int/get-involved/justice-at-work/story/the-judges-legal-officer.

[137] See Iran-United States Claims Tribunal, *Vacancy Announcement: Legal Adviser at the Iran-United States Claims Tribunal* (The Hague, 2011).

[138] The practice of ICC Arbitration, the HKIAC, the LCIA, the SIAC, the SCAI, the SCC and CIETAC indicates that Secretariat staff attend hearings.

and assist the panellists in preparing questions that may be posed to the parties for their oral and written response.

There is widespread practice of all categories of Dispute Assistants attending hearings and providing important assistance to adjudicators. In all the identified institutions, the Dispute Assistants do not directly pose questions to the parties. Even in the WTO, where the staff assigned to the dispute interact with the parties on many operational issues, they do not directly pose substantive questions to the parties. Therefore, the participation of Dispute Assistants at this stage does not per se impinge on the authority of the adjudicators. An important safeguard at this stage is to ensure that the Dispute Assistants attending the hearings are bound by the same rules of conduct for confidentiality as the adjudicators.

E. The Role of Dispute Assistants in Assisting with Drafting

Dispute Assistants may assist adjudicators by drafting part or all of the decision/judgment/award (and even preliminary or interim awards) that the DSM issues to the parties. In assessing the role of Dispute Assistants at this stage, there are several factors to be kept in mind: (i) whether Dispute Assistants are tasked with drafting the whole or only part of the decision/judgment/award; (ii) which specific sections of the decision/judgment/award are being drafted by the Dispute Assistants; and (iii) which category of Dispute Assistants undertake this drafting, which determines who supervises and controls their functions at this stage. For example, some parts of a decision/judgment/award of a DSM may be non-substantive, such as the procedural background and summaries of submissions made by the parties, or summary of facts. Participation by Dispute Assistants in drafting or assisting in drafting such non-substantive sections does not usually give rise to legitimacy concerns. This may be because these sections do not involve or reflect decision-making that is the domain exclusive to adjudicators and therefore does not raise concerns on potential encroachment on such decision-making. We will be mindful of these distinctions when examining the role of Dispute Assistants below.

We understand that in the following seven DSMs, the Institutional Assistants do not undertake drafting of any part of the decision/judgment/order: the COMESA, the CJEU, the EFTA Court, the EACJ, MERCOSUR, the IUSCT and the USMCA. However, Assigned Assistants in the CJEU, the EFTA and the IUSCT, and External Assistants in the USMCA may assist their adjudicators with drafting. We will discuss this further below.

In the following four DSMs, the involvement of the Institutional Assistants is restricted to certain sections of the decision/judgment/order which may be considered non-substantive. In ICSID, it is not uncommon for the tribunal secretary (Institutional Assistant) to draft the procedural history, facts and summaries of the parties' submissions, which the arbitrators then review and amend as necessary.[139] Allowing the Dispute Assistants to draft these portions of the award enables the arbitrators to focus on the more complex substantive issues in the case. Similarly, in the PCA, the arbitrators may

[139] Obadia and Nitscheke (n 96) 130.

instruct the staff of the International Bureau assigned to the case (Institutional Assistants) to draft the procedural history of a case owing to their institutional memory and expertise, but the substantive drafting is the domain of the arbitrators. With respect to the substantive sections of the draft, the staff of the Bureau may review the language and proofread the draft as per the instructions of the arbitrators. In the ICJ, the staff of the Registry (Institutional Assistants) typically draft the *qualités*, meaning the procedural history, main facts and summary of arguments.[140] They produce the first draft of the *qualités*, which is then reviewed by the Registrar and approved by the President before circulation to the judges, who will carefully study the drafts and make substantial amendments.[141] The Registry may also undertake drafting the first draft of orders for provisional measures in the same manner. Finally, in ITLOS, the Registry only drafts the first part of a judgment containing the *qualités* and the facts of the case.[142] Occasionally the Registry may also draft individual paragraphs of the reasoning, and review the final draft to ensure editorial and linguistic consistency within and between the English and French drafts.[143]

The practice varies considerably in commercial arbitration institutions, but often there is a distinction between parts of the award. In the LCIA, although the institution does not endorse any specific tasks, they provide a list of tasks that may be proposed by the arbitral tribunal to the parties for their consent. This list includes 'attend[ing] hearings, meetings, and deliberations; and [t]he extent, if any, to which the Tribunal Secretary carries out substantive tasks, such as summarising submissions, reviewing authorities, and preparing first drafts of awards, or sections of awards, and procedural orders'.[144] In the case of the SCAI and CIETAC, while there is no clear evidence of a permissive institutional practice, their vague regulations and a robust national culture of drafting assistance suggest a strong probability of assistants being involved in operative drafting.[145] In the case of the SIAC, there is no indication of either an institutional practice or a national tradition suggesting the participation of the tribunal secretaries in operative drafting. However, the language of its regulations is vague enough such that an arbitrator who is inclined to delegate such duties to their assistant would not face significant hurdles.[146] Notably, the International Chamber of Commerce,[147] the HKIAC[148] and

[140] O Corten and H Hoss, 'Registry: International Court of Justice' in *Max Planck Encyclopedia of International Procedural Law* (Oxford University Press, online edn 2021) para 20.

[141] Hébié (n 116) 78.

[142] Gautier (n 21) para 12.

[143] Gautier (n 118)48.

[144] London Court of International Arbitration, *Notes for Arbitrators* (26 October 2017) 202.

[145] For the SCAI, see GK Kohler and A Rigozzi, *International Arbitration: Law and Practice in Switzerland*, 2nd edn (Oxford University Press, 2015) 312; for CIETAC, see A Eernisse, 'Interviews with Our Editors: China Insights from Dr Li Hu of CIETAC' (*Kluwer Arbitration Blog*, 12 April 2020), www.arbitrationblog.kluwerarbitration.com/2020/04/12/interviews-with-our-editors-china-insights-from-dr-li-hu-of-cietac. For the legal limits under Swiss law, see Federal Tribunal (Tribunal fédéral), 21 May 2015, 4A_709/2014, MN 3.2.1–3.2.2.

[146] Singapore International Arbitration Centre (SIAC), *Practice Note for Administered Cases – On the Appointment of Administrative Secretaries* (2015) s 2. However, it must be stressed that this amounts to little more than an informed inference, as there are insufficient publicly available data to support a definitive empirical conclusion.

[147] International Chamber of Commerce, *Note to Parties and Arbitral Tribunals on the Conduct of Arbitration* (2021), para 224.

[148] Hong Kong International Arbitration Centre (HKIAC), *Guidelines on the Use of a Secretary to the Arbitral Tribunal* (2014), s 3.4(e)–(f). Illustrative examples of non-substantive tasks include 'procedural histories and

the SCC[149] all have detailed descriptions of the permissible tasks of tribunal secretaries/assistants, which are limited to non-substantive drafting. Non-substantive drafting includes drafting of the procedural history, facts and summaries of arguments. In these DSMs, there is a strong prohibition against delegating any decision-making powers.

Now, in the following five DSMs, the Institutional Assistants assist the adjudicators with the substantive drafting. In four of these, there is a Judge Rapporteur assigned to the case who is responsible for drafting the final judgment. In the ACtHPR, the ECtHR, the ECOWAS Court and the IACtHR, the Judge Rapporteur is assisted by Institutional Assistants who work under the Judge Rapporteur's individual supervision for a particular case, as well as the review of the head of their Institutional Office. The specific role of the Judge Rapporteur may guard against concerns relating to such Institutional Assistants encroaching upon the decision-making function of the adjudicators. In the ECOWAS Court, an additional safeguard is provided through the Assigned Assistant of the Judge Rapporteur, who may assist with drafting or reviewing the draft of the Institutional Assistants, as per the requirements of their judge. Lastly, in the WTO, the Secretariat staff (Institutional Assistants) assigned to a case will draft as per the instructions of the panellists generally, as well as the supervision of the Director of the LAD/Rules. Similarly, when the AB was operational, the AB Secretariat staff drafted under the instructions of the AB members on the division and the supervision of the AB Director generally. We will discuss the practice of the MPIA in Part III of the book.

We now consider DSMs where the Assigned Assistants assist the adjudicators with the drafting. In the ICJ, the drafting is the responsibility of the judges of the Drafting Committee, who are assisted by their Assigned Assistants. The ICJ has a rigorous deliberation process among the judges of the Drafting Committee where they discuss the draft line by line, which ensures that the decision-making function lies squarely with the judges. As chronologically most of the drafting is undertaken after the deliberation stage in the ICJ, it is detailed in section II.F below. Some of the existing procedural safeguards in the deliberations stage address concerns over Dispute Assistants encroaching upon the adjudicator's decision-making function. When Assigned Assistants are involved in the drafting of substantive parts of the decision, they remain under the overall supervision and control of their adjudicators. Similarly, the Judge Rapporteurs of the CJEU and the EFTA Court are assisted by their référendaires (Assigned Assistants), who are entirely within their supervision and control. We also examine the specific procedure of the CJEU in more detail below in section II.F in order to capture the relationship between the deliberations stage and the drafting stage.

In other DSMs, what we understand from our readings and discussions is that the level of participation by Assigned Assistants in the drafting varies as per the practice of different adjudicators. In the ICC, the ICTY and the STL, the practice has been to assign one or a few Legal Officers at the beginning of the trial to deal exclusively with drafting the judgment. They undertake drafting work according to the instructions of the judges of the Chamber to which they are assigned. Consequently, the involvement of the Legal Officer in drafting depends on the personal working style of the judges and

chronologies of events'. In practice, parties appear receptive to such drafting assistance; see HKIAC, *Report on the Use of HKIAC Tribunal Secretary Service* (3 September 2018), hkiac.org/node/2299.

[149] Stockholm Chamber of Commerce (SCC), *Guidelines for Arbitrators* (2020) 9.

their command over the proceedings. In the IUSCT, the President of the Tribunal bears primary responsibility for the drafting process. Other tribunal members provide input by preparing drafts of parts of the award or providing comments on the draft shared with them. The Legal Advisers of the President and other tribunal members assist them as per their instructions.

Lastly, with respect to External Assistants, the practice varies, depending on the agreement of the parties, the instructions/working style of their adjudicators, the workload of the adjudicators etc. For example, neither ICSID nor the PCA provides rules regulating the permissible use of external assistants, unlike some other commercial arbitral institutions. In complex cases where the arbitrators have a busy schedule, External Assistants may be asked to assist them with the drafting of procedural as well as substantive portions of the award.[150] In the COMESA Court, we were told that the external researchers do not participate in the drafting.

While some concerns have been raised as to the role of Dispute Assistants in drafting, we believe it is important to examine these concerns closely within the institutional and procedural framework of each DSM. Drafting is not deciding. As we have seen in this section, there are various factors that impact the role of Dispute Assistants in drafting, and safeguards that exist to ensure that the decision-making function remains within the control of the adjudicator. One such procedural safeguard is restricting the role of Dispute Assistants (particularly Institutional Assistants) in drafting to non-substantive sections of the decision/judgment/order. Alternatively, the drafting could be undertaken only by Dispute Assistants who are under the supervision and control of the adjudicator, either formally or through de facto frameworks of control (as will be examined in section III below). This could ensure that any drafting is undertaken strictly in accordance with the instructions of the adjudicators.[151] Some DSMs safeguard against such concerns by limiting the role of Dispute Assistants present at the deliberations stage, which is where the decision-making function is primarily fulfilled. Such a limited role in the deliberations ensures that adjudicators are firmly in control of the decision-making process, maintaining the adjudicators' independence without compromising on the assistance from Dispute Assistants.

F. The Role of Dispute Assistants in Deliberations

There is no uniform definition for 'deliberations' as a stage in the dispute resolution process. We use the term 'deliberations' to broadly capture the process through which the adjudicators discuss and arrive at a decision on a particular case/dispute. Dispute Assistants may play several roles at this stage: assisting adjudicators in preparing for deliberations, formally attending the deliberations and/or assisting the adjudicators in the deliberations. In understanding the role of Dispute Assistants at this stage, it

[150] See the well-known *Yukos* litigation: Gerechtshof Den Haag, *Veteran Petroleum Ltd and Others v Russian Federation* (Yukos) (18 February 2020) ECLI:NL:GHDHA:2020:234, 6.6.1–6.6.15. The arbitration was conducted under the UNCITRAL Rules, which likewise do not regulate the use of tribunal assistants.

[151] See World Trade Organization, *Report by HE Mr Petter Ølberg, Chairman of the DSB, and Annex: Consolidated Text Referred to in Mr Molina's Report* (General Council, JOB/GC/385, 16 February 2024) Title VII.

is important to note that in some DSMs, the adjudicators deliberate after a first draft or note has been produced. In other DSMs, the deliberations precede any drafting. As mentioned earlier, in the ICJ the formal drafting is undertaken after deliberations, so we will discuss how the drafting committee operates in this section. Further, with the CJEU as well, we will capture the relevant parts of the drafting of the judgment in this section so as to allow us to discuss the relationship between the deliberation and the drafting stages.

In the following four DSMs, Dispute Assistants play a role in the pre-deliberation stage. The staff of the Registry of the ICJ and the staff of the ICSID Secretariat assigned to the dispute (Institutional Assistants) assist the adjudicators by preparing summaries the parties' arguments and other relevant issues that may arise.[152] The Associate Legal Officers of the ICJ (Assigned Assistants) also assist their judges in preparing for the deliberations. The judges generally prepare notes (for judgments on merits or advisory proceedings, not for incidental proceedings like preliminary objections), which lay out their views on how the case should be decided. In producing these notes, the Associate Legal Officers and Judicial Fellows assist their judges. Assistance may come in the form of, for example, legal research on specific questions, drafting of memoranda for the judge's attention or even drafting part of the note. The involvement of the assistants very strongly depends on their individual judge.[153] In ECOWAS, the judges may send specific questions or issues to the staff of the Research and Documentation Department (Institutional Assistants), who may prepare notes or papers in response. The judges may also call upon their Executive Assistants (Assigned Assistants) to help them prepare for the deliberations. Similarly, the WTO staff assigned to the case interact with the adjudicators and assist them with the relevant research/notes prior to the deliberations.

The Institutional Assistants of seven DSMs attend the deliberations: the ECtHR,[154] the ACtHPR,[155] the IACtHR,[156] ECOWAS,[157] ITLOS,[158] the ICJ[159] and the WTO.[160] The staff in the ECtHR, the ACtHR and the IACtHR may participate as per the instructions/needs of the Judge Rapporteur of the case. In ECOWAS, the staff and Director of the Research and Documentation Department also join the deliberations, though they usually do not participate. This lack of participation may be owing to the need to maintain neutrality as the Department works for all judges on the bench and cannot appear to take sides in disagreements or diverging opinions on issues. In ITLOS, the Registrar and some legal officer from the Registry will be present, but generally only intervene in responding to questions from the judges regarding details in the parties' arguments or facts.[161] The practice of the ICJ is explained below. In the WTO, the staff participate and interact with the panellists during the deliberations.

[152] ICSID Arbitration Rules, r 34.3; for the ICJ, see Hébié (n 116) 77.
[153] Hébié (n 116) 81.
[154] The Registrar of the Section to which the case has been assigned.
[155] The Registry staff assigned to the case.
[156] Secretariat staff assigned to the case.
[157] The Director and staff from the Research and Documentation Department.
[158] The Registrar and some Legal Officer will be present.
[159] The Registrar also attends and answers any procedural questions that may arise.
[160] Secretariat staff assigned to the case.
[161] Judicial Practice Resolution, art 5. Unlike at the ICJ, judges do not each prepare a detailed note setting out their views on the case, as art 5.1 indicates. See R Wolfrum, 'Deliberation and Drafting: International Tribunal

In commercial arbitration institutions, the practice varies. The International Chamber of Commerce Arbitration,[162] the HKIAC[163] and CIETAC[164] explicitly allow for their attendance, though information on the actual participation rates are unavailable. As for the SCAI, the SIAC and the SCC, the attendance of tribunal secretaries at deliberations is not regulated, although in the absence of an explicit prohibition, it seems likely they will attend. As explained above, the LCIA allows parties to consent to list of tasks that may performed by the tribunal secretary, including 'attend[ing] hearings, meetings, and deliberations'.[165]

The Assigned and External Assistants in ECOWAS,[166] the IUSCT,[167] the ICJ,[168] USCMA,[169] the ICC, the STL and the ICTY,[170] the PCA and ICSID[171] attend the deliberations, but only participate when their supervisor so requests. Notably, the référendaires (Assigned Assistants) of the CJEU and the EFTA do not attend the deliberations. In these DSMs, the judges conduct closed-door deliberations. Such closed-door deliberations require the judges to interact face to face and engage in discussions to reach a final decision.

The practice before the CJEU and the ICJ is worth explaining due to the particular procedure and how it influences the drafting of the Judgment.

In the ECJ, after the hearing, if the Opinion of the Advocate General has been requested, the judges will wait until the Advocate General submits their Opinion before commencing deliberations.[172] After the hearings, there is a strict Chinese wall between the Judge Rapporteur and the Advocate General. A référendaire of the Advocate General will draft the Opinion[173] under the instruction and direction of their Advocate General.[174] Once the Advocate General publishes their Opinion, the Judge Rapporteur drafts a memo taking a position on the proposals made in the Opinion; the référendaire of the judge would assist in drafting of this memo. If the Judge Rapporteur disagrees with the Opinion, the President of the Chamber may conduct a 'round table' with the other judges in the Chamber to understand their positions on the issues. In this meeting, only the judges are present, and no Dispute Assistants participate.

for the Law of the Sea (ITLOS)', *Max Planck Encyclopedia of International Procedural Law* (Oxford University Press, online edn, January 2021) para 15.

162 ICC Note to Parties and Arbitral Tribunals on the Conduct of Arbitration, para 185.

163 HKIAC Guidelines on the Use of a Secretary to the Arbitral Tribunal, s 3.4(e).

164 D Wen and L Bergmann, *Comparison between SCC Arbitration and CIETAC Arbitration* (15 April 2011), www.transnational-dispute-management.com/article.asp?key=1753.

165 London Court of International Arbitration, *Notes for Arbitrators* (26 October 2017) 202.

166 Executive Assistant of the judge.

167 Legal Adviser to the member.

168 The Special Assistant to the President and another assistant to the President are present, but only to take notes.

169 Tribunal Assistants to Arbitrator(s).

170 Legal Officers in Chamber.

171 Tribunal Secretaries and External Assistants.

172 Deliberations do not commence earlier because, under art 82(2) of the Rules of Procedure of the Court, the oral part of the procedure is closed only after the Advocate General has delivered an Opinion. In practice, however, and only in very exceptional circumstances such as certain urgent preliminary ruling procedures, judges may engage in informal discussions before the Opinion of the Advocate General is officially published.

173 Only one reféféndaire is assigned to the case.

174 Sarmiento (n 59) 15.

Thereafter, the Judge Rapporteur will charge their référendaire with drafting a *projet de motifs* or a first draft of the judgment, and the *projet* is circulated to the other judges in the chamber after the Judge Rapporteur finalises it. The other judges, with the assistance of their référendaire, will send their comments and notes on the *projet* to the Judge Rapporteur a few days before the deliberations.[175] Thereafter, the Judge Rapporteur will instruct his référendaire to revise the draft into a *projet de motifs modifié*, based on the comments and notes received from the other judges. The judges then hold deliberations in absolute secrecy. Only the judges are allowed to attend. The procedure leading up to the deliberations is designed to develop and promote consensus: judges are allowed to provide their views on the *projet* before deliberations, and the Judge Rapporteur incorporates these views into the final judgment. The face-to-face deliberations conducted exclusively between the judges ensure they retain sufficient control over the final draft. This procedural set-up ensures that no other actor can exert unwarranted influence over the draft.

After the deliberations, the Judge Rapporteur will instruct their référendaire to prepare, based on the *projet de motifs modifié*, a *projet d'arrêt*, incorporating all the final changes decided during the deliberations. It is important to note that although the Assigned Assistants undertake a substantial portion of the drafting, deliberation sessions exclusively amongst adjudicators often ensure that they remain in control and the decision-making function is safeguarded.

In the ICJ, after the judges have all circulated notes detailing their positions, a second deliberation takes place at which the case is discussed in detail. Following the second deliberation, the majority view emerges, and the ICJ will decide on the general direction of the decision.[176] The judges then form a *drafting committee* comprising the President and the two members who, in their estimation, most cogently expressed the majority's views.[177] At the second deliberation, only the Special Assistant to the President and another assistant of the President (Assigned Assistants) are present to take notes. The Registrar also attends and answers any procedural questions that may arise. During the meetings of the drafting committee, the Associate Legal Officers of the two regular judges and the Special Assistant to the President are present. The Registrar also attends every meeting, accompanied by the Head of the Department of Legal Matters and two lawyers from the Department.[178] The Registrar actively participates in the discussion and may address any matter (including linguistic matters) and answer any questions relating to jurisprudence, procedure or the previous practice of the Court. The Assistants and lawyers from the Registry may also intervene, but only with the permission of their respective Judge/Registrar and only in exceptional situations. Thereafter, the drafting of the judgment may be divided between the two judges, who may ask their Assigned Assistants to contribute to the drafting. However, it is unheard of for assistants to draft significant parts of the judgment. The draft is thereafter circulated to all the remaining

[175] ibid; Rules of Procedure of the ECJ, art 32(1)–(2).

[176] Sarmiento (n 59) 52.

[177] Where the President does not concur with the majority, the Vice-President assumes that role. Where neither the President nor the Vice-President forms part of the majority, the most senior judge within the majority instead presides over the drafting committee.

[178] B Simma and C Ortgies, 'Deliberation and Drafting: International Court of Justice' in R Wolfrum (ed), Max Planck Encyclopedia of Public International Law (Oxford University Press, online edn, 2019) para 61.

judges for line-by-line written comments. The judges share their comments with the Registry, which prepares a compilation of the comments received from all judges and circulates this compilation to the Drafting Committee.[179] The Drafting Committee revises the draft based on these comments, and the revised draft is then submitted to the plenary for another deliberation, called the *First Reading*.

During the First Reading, the judges meet physically to debate and comment on the draft. While the Special Assistant to the President, the two Associate Legal Officers of the drafters, the Registrar and some lawyers from the Department of Legal Matters are present here, they are separated physically from the deliberations and do not participate.[180] After this reading, the Registry incorporates any agreed changes and circulates the draft for the Second Reading. At the end of the *Second Reading*, the judges vote to produce the final judgment or advisory opinion.[181]

From the practice of the CJEU and the ICJ discussed above, we see two different types of working procedures that guard against concerns or risk of Dispute Assistants encroaching on the decision-making function of the adjudicators. In the CJEU, this is achieved, inter alia through deliberations exclusively being between the judges, both prior to undertaking the drafting, and subsequently in discussing the draft. Despite the Assigned Assistants of the Judge Rapporteur being tasked with drafting the *projet de motifs* or a first draft, the drafting is undertaken basis the decision and discussions exclusively amongst the judges in the Chamber assigned to the case. Further, the *projet de motifs modifié*, or the second draft modified as per the comments received from other judges, is again discussed and finalised in deliberations exclusively between the judges. These exclusive deliberations between judges preserve the secrecy of deliberations and ensure that Dispute Assistants are not perceived to participate or encroach on the decision-making functions of the adjudicators. Today one wonders whether copying Dispute Assistants on internal deliberation emails could change this view.

In our view, the practice of the ICJ reaffirms that the presence of Dispute Assistants in deliberation does not per se imply encroachment on the decision-making function. Procedures like the formation of the Drafting Committee and the finalisation of the draft through the rigorous First Reading, can introduce safeguards. Dispute Assistants in many DSMs attend deliberations and participate in assisting actively the adjudicators. Institutions where concerns have arisen with respect to the role of Dispute Assistants, specifically on the risk of delegation of the decision-making function and drafting, can explore relevant procedural safeguards.

G. The Role of Dispute Assistants in the Review of the Decision

After the adjudicators deliberate and produce a draft decision, Dispute Assistants may step in and assist in reviewing the draft decision. As with the other functions, the reviewing process of a draft decision takes different forms depending on the DSM's needs. In some DSMs, the Dispute Assistants only proofread the decision. In others, there is a

[179] ibid 72–73.
[180] Hébié (n 116) 87.
[181] Resolution on Internal Practice, art 8(i).

more substantive examination of the draft, including checking the draft's consistency and reasoning. In addition to the above, Dispute Assistants may verify the adjudicators' use of language in multilingual institutions.

In four DSMs – ITLOS, COMESA, the IACtHR and ECOWAS,[182] the Institutional Assistants conduct formal review and proofreading of the adjudicator's final draft, but are not allowed to go beyond this. Similarly, External Assistants (ie, tribunal assistants) in certain commercial arbitration institutions undertake this same function. In ICSID and some commercial arbitration institutions,[183] the Institutional Assistants may go further, checking the logical consistency, conformity with previous case law and other substantive aspects of the draft. Given their vast institutional knowledge and experience of Institutional Assistants, their suggestions are often persuasive. However, the adjudicators retain the final say on any substantive aspect of the decision.

We detail the unique practice of two DSMs, the CJEU and the ECtHR, where separate actors are responsible for review (aspects of) the decision. In the CJEU, this is undertaken by Lecteurs d'arrêts (Assigned Assistants) who, owing to their experience, may sometimes go beyond merely formalistic edits. In the ECtHR, the Directorate of the Jurisconsult (Institutional Assistants) is responsible for ensuring that a judgment is of a certain quality and consistent with the case law of the institution.[184] As explained above, the office of the Jurisconsult reviews the drafts and sends them back to the Judge Rapporteur before the deliberation of the case. This review aims to ensure consistency with prior case law and with cases currently heard by other Sections. Although the recommendations are not binding, the judges may be inclined to accept them given the Jurisconsult's experience and specialised institutional knowledge.

While Dispute Assistants often play some role in reviewing the decisions of the DSM, the final decision-making authority usually remains with the adjudicators. Even in the ECtHR, where the Jurisconsult has specifically been given the authority to substantively review the judgments, the judges are not bound by these recommendations. However, the specialised knowledge and expertise of the Jurisconsult is often considered an asset for the dispute resolution process. Similarly, even in other cases where Institutional Assistants undertake review, the key is to ensure that the decision benefits from their institutional knowledge, while remaining within the intellectual control of the adjudicators.

While it is difficult to generalise in relation to the varied practice amongst the DSMs, the above section reveals the widespread and critical contribution of Dispute Assistants in the dispute resolution process. In order to fully appreciate the impact of their contributions on the decision-making process, it is also necessary examine the ways in which adjudicators exercise control over their functions. The next section examines the formal and de facto frameworks of control over the functions of different categories of Dispute Assistants.

[182] However, this has not been possible in every case, owing to the caseload and the limited resources of the Research and Documentation Department.

[183] At the SIAC, the Registrar must approve the award and may make suggestions. The Secretariat of the DIS may likewise make suggestions as to both form and substance; however, in that case, neither is binding on the arbitrators. In ICC arbitration, the ICC Court acting with input from the Secretariat retains final authority over questions of form and may also make suggestions as to the substance of the decision. However, such substantive suggestions are not binding on the tribunal.

[184] Rules of Court of the European Court of Human Rights, r 18B.

III. Controls over Dispute Assistants: Formal and de Facto Frameworks

A. Institutional Assistants: Potential for de Facto Control and Safeguards

As we have already seen, each DSM has a head of the Institutional Office overseeing the functioning of the Institutional Assistants. In some DSMs, the Institutional Assistants report directly to the head of the Institutional Office. This is seen in the CJEU (the administrators and case lawyers are under the supervision of the Registrar and/or Deputy Registrar); the COMESA Court (the Registry staff are under the supervision of the Registrar); the USMCA (the staff are under the supervision of the Secretary of the Section); the EACJ (the clerks, researcher and administrative staff are under the supervision of the Registrar); the ECOWAS Court (the Judicial Process and Case Management division of the Registry reports to the Registrar and Deputy Registrar); the ECtHR (the case lawyers of the Sections report to the Section Registrar and Deputy Section Registrar, who eventually report to the Registrar of the Court); the EFTA Court (the staff of the Registry report to the Registrar); the IACtHR (the staff lawyers are under the supervision of the Secretary); the ICSID (the case management teams of ICSID report to the Secretary-General and the two Deputy Secretaries-General), the ICC, the ICTY and the STL (the Registry staff report to the Registrar); the IUSCT (the staff of the Registry report to the two co-Registrars); MERCOSUR (the staff report to the Secretary); and the PCA (the legal staff report to the Secretary-General and the Deputy Secretaries-General).

Further, in the following DSMs, a dedicated division within the Institutional Office, with its own supervisor, assists adjudicators across disputes. The supervisors of these divisions tend to report directly to the head of the Institutional Office. In the ACtHPR, the Legal Division, consisting of the Legal Aid Unit, provides primary assistance to judges in their adjudicative functions. A Head of Legal Division supervises the staff of the Legal Aid Unit, who ultimately reports to the Registrar of the Court. Similarly, in the ICJ, the Department of Legal Matters assists the Court's case management work. The ICJ's Department of Legal Matters is directly subordinate to the Registrar. It consists of the Principal Legal Secretary, who acts as the head of the department, under the supervision of the Registrar. In the WTO, the Secretariat staff of the LAD or Rules Division report to the Director of the respective division, and the DDG in charge of the division. Ultimately, the Directors, DDG and the staff all report to the DG of the WTO. Lastly, in ITLOS, the Head of the Legal Office supervises the Registry's Legal Office. The Head of the Legal Office reports to the Registrar. The Registrar is also responsible for dealing with terminations and disciplinary measures. Additionally, although distinct from the Registry, the Research and Documentation Directorate and the Directorate of Multilingualism staff are under the overall supervision of the Registrar of the ECJ.

It follows that one of the metrics to assess the de facto control that adjudicators may have over Institutional Assistants is the control (if any) that the adjudicators could exercise over the head of the Institutional Offices.

In the ACtHPR, this control is prominent; the Registrar, the Deputy Registrar and staff members of the Registry are all appointed by the Court.[185] Further, the Court,

[185] Rules of Court African Court on Human and Peoples' Rights, rr 17.1, 18.1 and 20.

the Bureau (the President and Vice-President) or the President of the Court can issue instructions to the Registry.[186] To a similar but lesser degree, the following heads of Institutional Offices are formally appointed by the relevant adjudicators: the Registrars of the ICJ,[187] the CJEU,[188] the ECOWAS Court,[189] the EFTA Court,[190] the ICC,[191] ITLOS,[192] the ACtHPR,[193] and the Secretary of the ECtHR[194] and the IACtHR.[195]

In contrast, in six DSMs – MERCOSUR, the IUSCT, the COMESA Court, the EACJ, ICSID and the PCA – this power of appointment is not with the adjudicators. Instead, the Member States themselves or their representatives have the power of appointment. Of these seven institutions, only in the MERCOSUR Tribunal Permanente de Revisión (TPR) do the adjudicators play a role in appointing the head of the Institutional Office. The Secretary is elected (through a public application based on merits and qualifications) by the Consejo del Mercado Común based on a proposal of three candidates made by the arbitrators of the TPR.[196] In the remaining six institutions, the adjudicators do not play any formal role in appointing the head of the Institutional Office. The appointment process in these six DSMs works as follows: in the IUSCT, there are two co-registrars, one each selected by the US and Iran. In the COMESA Court, the COMESA Council appoints the Registrar.[197] In the EACJ, the EAC Council of Ministers appoints the Registrar of the central registry.[198] In ICSID and the PCA, the Secretary-General is elected by the Administrative Council, which is composed of representatives from the state parties to the ICSID Convention[199] and the 1899 Hague Convention for the Pacific Settlement of International Disputes, respectively.[200] In the last institution, the USMCA Secretariat for Chapter 31 disputes is decentralised; it consists of three sections, each by one of the state parties and with their individual frameworks for appointment.[201] Amongst these six DSMs where the adjudicators do not play a role, it is important to highlight the somewhat limited role envisaged for the Registry/Secretariat. The Institutional Assistants only perform administrative functions in MERCOSUR, COMESA, USMCA and the IUSCT. In the PCA and ICSID, they perform administrative functions and provide procedural support, but do not often assist the adjudicators in their substantive decision-making functions. In the EACJ, the Registry traditionally

[186] ibid r 16.

[187] Rules of Court of the International Court of Justice, art 22(1).

[188] Rules of Procedure of the General Court, art 32; Rules of Procedure of the Court of Justice of European Union, art 18.

[189] The Chief Registrar is appointed pursuant to r 9 of the Rules of the Community Court of Justice of the Economic Community of West African States.

[190] Rules of Procedure of the EFTA Court, art 11.4.

[191] The Registrar, who heads the Registry, is elected by the judges of the Court by an absolute majority, taking into account the recommendation of the Assembly of States Parties: Rome Statute, art 43(4).

[192] Rules of the Tribunal of the International Tribunal for the Law of the Sea, arts 32.1 and 33.

[193] Rules of Court of the African Court on Human and Peoples' Rights, rr 17.1, 18.1 and 20.

[194] Rules of Court of the European Court of Human Rights, r 15.

[195] Rules of Procedure of the Inter-American Court of Human Rights, art 7.

[196] MERCOSUR, Common Market Group (GMC), Resolution on the Secretariat of the Tribunal Permanente de Revisión (MERCOSUR/GMC/EXT/RES No 66/05, 6 December 2005).

[197] COMESA Treaty, art 41.

[198] Treaty for the Establishment of the East African Community (hereinafter 'EAC Treaty') (signed 30 November 1999, entered into force 7 July 2000) art 45.

[199] Convention on the Settlement of Investment Disputes between States and Nationals of Other States (hereinafter 'ICSID Convention') (18 March 1965) art 10.1.

[200] Rules of Procedure for the Administrative Council of the Permanent Court of Arbitration (19 September 1900) art VIII(3).

[201] USMCA, art 30.6.

performed administrative functions and, more recently, has been taking on substant functions like research assistance owing to the increasing workload.

In two DSMs, the UN Secretary-General appoints the head of the Institutional Office as an external appointing authority. In the ICTY, the UN Secretary-General appointed the Registrar after consultation with the President of the ICTY.[202] In contrast, there was no such consultation in the STL.[203] In both these DSMs, the Institutional Assistants of the Registry do not assist the adjudicators with their judicial functions.

In the ECOWAS Court, the Institutional Assistants who assist the judges with their substantive functions are in the Research and Documentation Department (Additional Institutional Department). They are not under the control of the Institutional Office, but rather the head adjudicator. In the ECOWAS Court, the President of the Court supervises the Director, who in turn supervises and controls the Research and Documentation Department. The Chief Registrar of the ECOWAS Court Registry does not supervise the work of this Department or its Director.

Another avenue of potential de facto control in the case of Institutional Assistants is through the procedure for designation of a Judge Rapporteur to oversee and supervise the functions of staff assigned to a particular case. We understand that in the following four DSMs, a Judge Rapporteur is assigned to each case and supervises the work of Institutional Assistants during the dispute: the IACtHR, the ECtHR, the ACtHPR and the ECOWAS Court.[204] This supervision permeates every stage of the dispute resolution process, most notably the Institutional Assistants' functions relating to research and collation, participation and preparation for the hearing, attendance or participation (if any) in the deliberations, drafting of the judgment/order/award, and the review of the judgment/order/award. The Judge Rapporteur acts as the channel through which the work of the Institutional Assistants is presented to the remaining judges on the bench hearing a case. Even without formal control over the Institutional Assistants, they are able to exert significant de facto control over their participation and contribution to the dispute settlement process.

B. Assigned Assistants and External Assistants: Formal Control and Institutional Safeguards

For Assigned and External Assistants, the position is more straightforward and institutionalised. Both Assigned and External Assistants work for specific adjudicators or a bench of adjudicators and are under their supervision. The DSMs exert varying degrees of control over these assistants in terms of appointment, appraisal or rules of conduct.

[202] Statute of the International Tribunal for the Prosecution of Persons Responsible for Serious Violations of International Humanitarian Law Committed in the Territory of the Former Yugoslavia since 1991 (hereinafter 'ICTY Statute'), annexed to UNSC Res 827 (1993) UN Doc S/RES/827(1993) (25 May 1993) art 17(3).

[203] Statute of the Special Tribunal for Lebanon, attachment to UNSC Res 1757 (2007) UN Doc S/RES /1757(2007) (30 May 2007) (entered into force 10 June 2007) art 12.

[204] The CJEU and the EFTA Court also assign Judge Rapporteurs to each dispute; however, no Institutional Assistants are assigned to work on these cases.

i. Assigned Assistants

The formal control by adjudicators over Assigned Assistants is most significant in the DSMs where the adjudicator selects their own assistant. In the following three DSMs, the adjudicators exercise maximum control over their Assigned and External Assistants:

a) The CJEU's référendaires are selected by their respective superior,[205] who effectively has complete discretion in their selection, although the general meeting of the Court formally appoints the référendaires.[206] However, the référendaires are subject to institutional safeguards as a code of conduct binds them in addition to that generally applicable to the staff of the EU.[207] This code imposes various duties on référendaires – inter alia, duties to abstain in cases when in the past they have been involved or have supported or advised one of the parties.[208] Further, with respect to instances where the référendaires wishes to publicly express their opinions in academic writings and/or public speaking events, they must obtain prior authorisation.[209] Once they have ceased their work, the référendaires are precluded from participating in any way in cases pending if they have participated in these before.[210]

b) Similarly, the référendaires of the EFTA Court and one personal assistant[211] of each judge are hired through the cabinet of the judge they work for.[212] In the ECOWAS Court as well, the judge has complete discretion in selecting their Executive Assistant.

c) The ECOWAS Court then formally hires the Executive Assistant. The Human Resources division of the Registry conducts minimal intervention in their selection, only verifying that the person selected by the judge is a qualified lawyer and possesses the minimum experience and qualifications for the role. In these cases, the adjudicator has direct control over their assistant, and the only institutional supervision is through formal requirements for their appointment.

In other cases, the Institutional Office exercises minimal or formalistic control. In the following five DSMs, the adjudicators retain supervision and control, with some administrative matters being formally undertaken by the Institutional Office:

a) In the IUSCT, the Secretary-General appoints the Legal Advisors of each tribunal member and the Principal Adviser of the President, on the recommendation of their respective tribunal member. Accordingly, they are administratively subordinate to the Secretary-General, but they work under the supervision and control of their respective adjudicators.

[205] As explained, these may be Advocate Generals (in the Court of Justice) or judges (in the General Court and the Court of Justice).

[206] Sarmiento (n 59). The official appointment is purely a formality, as the general meeting appears never to have rejected a référendaire.

[207] Court of Justice of the European Union (CJEU), *Décision du 17 février 2009 portant adoption des règles de bonne conduite des Référendaires.*

[208] Sarmiento (n 59) 11.

[209] ibid.

[210] ibid.

[211] C Baudenbacher, 'The EFTA Court's Working Methods' in R Wolfrum (ed), The EFTA Court and the EEA (Brill Nijhoff, 2018) 243.

[212] See EFTA Court, *Vacancy Notice: Legal Secretary (Référendaire) to Judge Bernd Hammermann* (Luxembourg, 2020)

b) Similarly, in the ICJ, the Associate Legal Officers, the Special Assistant to the President, and the Judicial Fellows are attached to the Department of Legal Matters of the Registry. However, they answer to their judges, who evaluate them together with the President of the ICJ (or Vice-President in the case of the President's assistants). Therefore, while the Registrar is formally in charge, these assistants work under the direction and supervision of their individual judges.
c) In the ICC and the ICTY, the Legal Officers in Chambers are under the supervision and control of the judges. They are distinct from the Registry, although the Registrar may retain some administrative control over their performance review, renewal, leaves etc, although in practice, the Registrar defers to the judges.
d) Likewise, in the STL, the assistants worked under the direction and supervision of their respective Chambers, even though the Registry was formally in charge. While the Registrar was in charge of the administrative matters, the Head of Chambers evaluated the legal officers.

ii. External Assistants

In the case of External Assistants, adjudicators exercise maximum control over their appointment and supervision. In the USMCA, panellists are allowed to have their own assistants,[213] who are not formally part of the Secretariats. They act as tribunal assistants for a particular arbitrator in a specific case and are bound by the same ethical and disclosure obligations on conflicts of interest.[214] Similarly, with the parties' consent, the PCA, ICSID and commercial arbitration institutions allow external assistants for arbitrators, as per the needs of the case. However, the institutions bind the externally appointed assistants by confidentiality commitments, and the assistants must sign the same declaration of independence and impartiality as the arbitrators.[215] The IBA Guidelines on Conflicts of Interest in International Arbitration[216] includes within its scope 'arbitral or administrative secretaries and assistants'.[217] The exception is the COMESA Court, where we are not aware of any formal code of conduct that binds the External Researchers. However, it bears repeating that they are only selected for a particular dispute and retain no institutional memory to exert their own influence in the decision-making process.

[213] Rules of Procedure for Chapter 31 of USCMA, art 12.
[214] ibid art 5, read with Code of Conduct art 9; Appendices 2 and 3 of the Rules of Procedure for Chapter 31. The assistants are bound by art 9 of the Code of Conduct and must submit a 'Declaration of Non-disclosure', alongside the staff of the USMCA Secretariat.
[215] For ICSID Tribunal Assistants, see https://icsid.worldbank.org/resources/content/arbitrators/tribunal-assistants#:~:text=%E2%80%8B%E2%80%8B%E2%80%8B%E2%80%8B%E2%80%8B,Tribunal%20in%20each%20arbitration%20proceeding. See also IBA Guidelines on Conflict of Interest in International Arbitration, approved by the IBA Council, 25 May 2024.
[216] These have been recognised as a robust soft law instrument, reflecting the standards expected regarding conflicts of interest – namely, impartiality and independence – as well as the obligations to make disclosures in specific circumstances.
[217] IBA Guidelines on Conflict of Interest in International Arbitration, approved by the IBA Council, 25 May 2024, pt I, s 5.

IV. Conclusion and Comparative Observations

In this chapter, we have seen the different types of Dispute Assistants that emerge from our study of identified DSMs. They have been categorised into three groups: Institutional Assistants, Assigned Assistants and External Assistants. Within this categorisation, we have tried to understand the extent of their contribution to the dispute resolution process, including through the formal and de facto forms of control that adjudicators exercise over them. The level of control exercised by adjudicators informs our discussion on the boundaries within which Dispute Assistants operate. Further, it is critical in order to understand and address the concerns raised about Dispute Assistants encroaching on the decision-making function of adjudicators. While the highest level of supervision and control are seen in the case of External Assistants and Assigned Assistants, there are other de facto forms of control that exist in some DSMs with respect to Institutional Assistants.

Based on our comparative study, we will make some preliminary observations that form the basis of further discussions on the concerns raised regarding the role of Dispute Assistants in the next chapter.

First, with respect to the appointment of ad hoc adjudicators, Dispute Assistants in some DSMs play a role in assisting the parties in selection and/or appointment of adjudicators. While some scholars have raised concerns with respect to this 'reversal of roles', the consequences of this reversal must be assessed in light of the institutional and procedural frameworks of each institution. For example, in ICSID, the PCA, the USMCA and some commercial arbitration institutions, the role of Institutional Assistants in later stages of the dispute in assisting adjudicators is limited. Further, in assessing these concerns, we must also remain mindful of the functional importance of the role of Dispute Assistants at the stage of appointment and selection of adjudicators in ensuring the timely resolution of disputes.

Second, in all 20 DSMs, Dispute Assistants are involved in receiving submissions/applications and, in some cases, undertake some level of review at this stage. Although in two DSMs (ICSID and the ACtHPR), some limited degree of decision-making power is granted to an Institutional Assistant (the Secretary-General of ICSID and the Head of the Legal Aid Division, respectively), the discretion is narrow and confined to a review of jurisdictional requirements as per the rules agreed by the contracting parties establishing the DSM.

Third, the research/briefing notes and in particular, issues papers prepared by Dispute Assistants are important in assisting adjudicators with their decision-making function. The DSM benefits from the wealth of knowledge and experience that Dispute Assistants provide. Any change should aim to enhance the quality of the information at the disposal of the adjudicators, while limiting any potential influence of the Dispute Assistants' personal views on the adjudicator's final decision. We see examples of such useful practices across DSMs. For example, the Institutional Assistants in the ECtHR, the IACtHR, the ACtHPR and the ECOWAS Court undertake the research under the instructions and supervision of the Judge Rapporteur, which mitigates against such concerns. In another example, the judges of the ICJ and the ECOWAS Court are assisted by Institutional Assistants as well as Assigned Assistants (who are entirely within the supervision and control of the adjudicator). Such diversification of the sources of research and assistance limits the potential influence of any one group of actors over the adjudicators.

Fourth, with respect to hearings, the participation of Dispute Assistants at this stage does not per se give rise to concerns on the legitimacy of the dispute resolution process as Dispute Assistants generally do not interact with the parties directly. An important safeguard at this stage is to ensure that the Dispute Assistants attending the hearings are bound by the same rules of conduct for confidentiality as the adjudicators. This is especially true in the case of External Assistants.

Fifth, the participation of Dispute Assistants in the drafting of judgments is more common than not.[218] Drafting is done by all types of Dispute Assistants (Institutional, Assigned and External). The criticism levelled against the role of Dispute Assistants in drafting per se conflates the task of drafting with the function of decision-making. The solution to such concerns must aim to reinforce that distinction, ensuring that generally decision-making is firmly in the hands of adjudicators. As we have observed, one prominent site to introduce such safeguards to decision-making is through deliberations.

Sixth, deliberations are a critical point in the decision-making process and arguably the stage at which the core decision-making function is discharged. Adjudicators, equipped with their assistants' research/briefing notes, can discuss amongst themselves to arrive at the decision in a dispute. However, the participation of Dispute Assistants itself does not imply that they have distorted the adjudicators' decision-making authority. The Dispute Assistants in many DSMs attend deliberations and in some cases assist adjudicators through participation. DSMs where concerns have arisen with respect to the role of Dispute Assistants – specifically in relation to the risk of delegation of the decision-making function – can explore relevant procedural safeguards. For example, in the ICJ, the formation of the Drafting Committee and finalisation of the draft through the rigorous First Reading ensures the decision-making remains with the adjudicators.

Seventh, the role of Dispute Assistants in reviewing the decision allows the DSM to utilise the knowledge of Dispute Assistants to promote consistency in jurisprudence. The key is to ensure that the decision benefits from their institutional knowledge, while remaining within the intellectual control of the adjudicators.

Keeping the above comparative observations in mind, the next chapter will dive deeper into the concerns that have been raised with respect to the role of Dispute Assistants and identify some useful practices which may mitigate/guard against such concerns.

[218] Of the DSMs examined, only three – MERCOSUR, COMESA and the EACJ – do not involve any Dispute Assistants during the drafting stage.

21

Concerns Regarding the Influence of Dispute Assistants and Useful Practices/Procedures

In writing this book, one of our aims was to explore and explain the actual role and functions of Dispute Assistants widely across various international Dispute Settlement Mechanisms (DSMs). However, the initial catalyst for our interest in the topic stemmed from concerns that were raised with respect to Dispute Assistants and how they impacted the legitimacy of the dispute resolution process. Hence, the subtitle of this book is 'Navigating Legitimacy'. Although we have summarised these concerns in Chapter 1 and referred to them briefly in the previous chapter, we are yet to explore their connection with legitimacy. We use this chapter to dive into these concerns, as well as useful practices from DSMs that may address them. Lastly, we examine their connection with the legitimacy of the dispute resolution process.

Section I recounts examples of concerns across the identified DSMs. In some cases, the concerns have been raised formally through mechanisms available to parties to the dispute and have led to decisions providing some additional guidance on the role of Dispute Assistants. These cases have arisen in the context of certain arbitration institutions, the IUSCT and international criminal tribunals. In other cases, like with the WTO DSS and the CJEU, the concerns have been raised by academics, commentators or Member States. Lastly, in some cases, concerns were identified by us through our discussions with actors from the identified DSMs. Our comparative study has also shown that there is a wealth of practice within DSMs that may address or mitigate against many of these concerns. Accordingly, with respect to each concern, we examine such practices. As Part III of this book is dedicated to the WTO, we have not gone into the details of the varied processes of the WTO in this chapter. Nonetheless, in order to ensure a comprehensive comparison, we make brief references to the WTO wherever relevant.

Section I.A examines concerns on asymmetry between the adjudicator and Dispute Assistants due to institutional frameworks, and some useful procedures and practices on strengthening the relative institutional capacity and subject-matter expertise of the adjudicators. Section I.B examines concerns relating to control over the language of the proceedings and translations, and some useful practices and procedures to mitigate or address them. Section I.C examines concerns relating to the lack of direct supervision and control over the Dispute Assistants, and some useful practices and procedures on diversification of sources of assistance, and checks and balance on the influence of Dispute Assistants. Section I.D reviews concerns on excessive delegation of the decision-making function, and useful practices on enhanced transparency and disclosures. Section I.E zooms in on concerns relating delegation of one specific function to Dispute Assistants – drafting – and the useful practices and procedures that would address them. Lastly, Section I.F examines concerns on independence of adjudicators owing to the functions of Dispute Assistants, and useful procedures on codes of conduct and for challenging role of Dispute Assistants. As will be elaborated below, some of these concerns are applicable to specific types of adjudicators and categories of Dispute Assistants. In other instances, these concerns permeate the very nature of the roles fulfilled by Dispute Assistants across institutions.

Section II returns to the critical question of why this exercise matters to international dispute resolution: legitimacy. We untangle the theoretical basis for these concerns and how each of them affects a facet of legitimacy of the dispute resolution process – specifically, the consent to be bound by dispute resolution process (section II.A), the independence and diligence expected of adjudicators (section II.B), and the expected transparency and procedural fairness of the dispute resolution process (section II.C).

In Section III, we conclude by building on the concerns observed within specific DSMs and distilling the reasoning behind them. In doing so, we hope to abstract the concerns from specific DSMs into principled concerns that may be applicable more generally on the role of Dispute Assistants. Even though the concerns emerge in the context of a specific DSM, they are not exclusively limited to the mechanism from where they emanate. Fundamentally, each of these concerns may impact the legitimacy of dispute resolution undertaken by any DSM, and therefore demands our close attention. At the same time, we also acknowledge that many of the concerns are driven by factors external to Dispute Assistants themselves. The concerns relating to control over language by an adjudicator may be considered inherent to every organisation where international cooperation necessitates adopting a working language. The concerns on excessive delegation of work and drafting may arise in any (international) court that handles a heavy caseload. Our aim in this chapter is not to single out or blame the role of Dispute Assistants in any DSM; rather, we aim to acknowledge the importance of addressing these concerns because they risk the (perceived, even if not demonstrated) legitimacy of the dispute resolution process.

I. Concerns and Useful Practices/Procedures Regarding the Role of Dispute Assistants

The comparative study in the previous chapter established the important and widespread nature of the functions discharged by Dispute Assistants across several stages of the dispute resolution process. The expansive nature of these functions has also raised concerns about the appropriateness of participation of Dispute Assistants, and whether this encroaches upon the mandate granted by the parties to the adjudicators. While we have categorised these into six separate concerns, it is important to acknowledge the significant overlap between many of them. For example, the first concern relates to the asymmetry between the adjudicator and the Dispute Assistant owing to institutional frameworks, ie, the ad hoc or part-time nature of the adjudicator vis-a-vis the more permanent role of the Dispute Assistants. The concern is that the relative expertise and/or capacity of the Dispute Assistants may allow them to exert more control over the decision-making process of the adjudicators. This concern is related, and may lead to, the excessive delegation of specific tasks by the adjudicator to the Dispute Assistant, which again raises doubts as to the decision-making process. While they are not entirely separate, they do raise distinct concerns on legitimacy and deserve to be examined separately.

Similarly, with respect to the useful practices/procedures grouped together with concerns, although we examine them under specific concerns, their utility may not be restricted to that specific concern. In order to avoid repetition, we note when a specific practice/procedure would also contribute to addressing other concerns.

A. Risk of Asymmetry between the Adjudicator and Dispute Assistant Due to Institutional Frameworks

i. Examples of Concerns from the ACtHPR, the IACtHR and the WTO

The role of Institutional Assistants in the ACtHPR and IACtHR may raise concerns relating to the asymmetry between the institutional knowledge of the Registry and Secretariat staff, and the part-time nature of the judges. In the ACtHPR, the judges of the Court perform their functions on a part-time basis during four ordinary sessions annually, each of which lasts at least four weeks. However, the President works on a full-time basis. In the IACtHR, commentators have observed similarly that the part-time work of the judges and the full-time nature of the Secretariat staff's employment have led to more expertise accumulating in the Secretariat than the bench.[1] In these two DSMs, given the limited time that the judges can devote to each case, and the comparatively permanent nature of the Institutional Assistants, judges' reliance on Institutional Assistants may give rise to the impression that the Institutional Assistants exert influence over the decision-making of the adjudicators.

In context of the WTO DSS, scholars have raised concerns as to the role of Dispute Assistants in nominating names of potential panellists to the parties, including the role of the Secretariat as well as the Director-General (DG) in nominating names of panellists outside of the 'Indicative List',[2] and the resulting 'reversal of control' between the Dispute Assistants and the adjudicators.[3] These concerns are all extremely important to

[1] See PG Domínguez, 'The Role of the Secretariat in the Inter-American Court of Human Rights: A Comparative Analysis' (2002) 116 *American Journal of International Law: Unbound* 390, 393.

[2] P Mavroidis, *The WTO Dispute Settlement System: How, Why and Where?* (Cambridge University Press, 2016) 409, 411.

[3] J Pauwelyn and K Pelc, 'Who Guards the "Guardians of the System"? The Role of the Secretariat in WTO Dispute Settlement' (2022) 116 *American Journal of International Law* 534; J Pauwelyn and K Pelc, 'The WTO Secretariat's "Open Secret": Unpacking the Controversy' (*EJIL:Talk!*, 18 August 2022), www.ejiltalk.org/the-wto-secretariats-open-secret-unpacking-the-controversy; see also Prepared Statement by Alan WM Wolff, Hearing before the Committee on Finance, United States Senate, 104th Cong, S 16, 60 (10 May 1995), www.finance.senate.gov/imo/media/doc/Hrg104-124.pdf; B Hoekman and PC Mavroidis, 'To AB or Not to AB? Dispute Settlement in WTO Reform' (2020) 23 *Journal of International Economic Law* 703, European University Institute, Robert Schuman Centre for Advanced Studies, Global Governance Programme Working Paper No RSCAS 2020/34.

address, and other scholars have responded to the subjective merits of many of them.[4] It should be noted that the core concern arises from the institutional design of the WTO DSS, where permanent staff are asked to suggest ad hoc adjudicators to the parties, and in the event that parties cannot agree, the DG is asked to nominate ad hoc panellists. As Part III of this book is dedicated to examining how these concerns have arisen across specific stages of the WTO DSS, we do not go into further details here.

ii. Useful Practices and Procedures on Strengthening the Expertise/Capacity of Adjudicators

In this section, we examine one way to address this concern – by strengthening the relative institutional capacity and subject matter expertise of the available and selected adjudicators. This can be through: (a) re-evaluating the qualifications of adjudicators; (b) strengthening the process of selection of adjudicators; (c) provisions on training; (d) development of expertise through working practices of adjudicators; and (e) systemic changes moving away from the ad hoc nature of adjudicators. At the same time, there are also other procedural changes that can work towards balancing the asymmetry based on diversification of the sources of assistance provided to adjudicators (including Assigned Assistants), procedural checks on the functions of the Dispute Assistants, limiting the role of Dispute Assistants in certain stages, and enhanced transparency and disclosures. We will discuss these other useful practices in sections I.C–I.F below.

a. Qualifications for Adjudicators

As is evident from Part I of this book, each DSM has unique qualifications prescribed for its adjudicators. These qualifications are tailored to the specific demands of the mechanism and its dispute resolution process. While they cannot be directly transposed into another mechanism, they can offer a blueprint on how enhanced qualifications may be included in selecting adjudicators. The examples discussed here go beyond general yet important requirements like 'impartiality', 'independence' and qualifications required for 'holding of high judicial office' in their jurisdictions, and jurists of 'recognised competence'.

Various DSMs require more specific subject-matter expertise for the adjudicators. For example, in ICSID, the qualifications required for persons to be designated to the Panel of Arbitrators is more specific: they must be persons of high moral character and recognised competence in the fields of law, commerce, industry or finance, and who may be relied upon to exercise independent personal judgement.[5] Specifically,

[4] G Marceau and A Venkataraman, 'Unmasking the Phantom of the Opera: Is There a Hidden Secretariat in the WTO Dispute Settlement System?' (2002) 116 *American Journal of International Law: Unbound* 390; JM Wauters, 'The Role of the WTO Secretariat in WTO Disputes: Silent Witness or Ghost Expert?' (2021) 12 *Global Policy* 53; A Steinbach, 'Are the Fingerprints of the WTO Staff on Panel Rulings a Problem? A Reply to Joost Pauwelyn and Krzysztof Pelc' (2022) 33 *European Journal of International Law* 565; G Sacerdoti, 'A Critical Reaction to Joost Pauwelyn and Krzysztof Pelc's "The WTO Secretariat's 'Open Secret': Unpacking the Controversy"' (*EJIL:Talk!*, 5 September 2022), www.ejiltalk.org/a-critical-reaction-to-joost-pauwelyn-and-krzysztof-pelcs-the-wto-secretariats-open-secret-unpacking-the-controversy.

[5] Convention on the Settlement of Investment Disputes between States and Nationals of Other States (ICSID Convention) (18 March 1965) art 14.1.

competence in the field of law is important for designation to the Panel of Arbitrators.[6] These qualifications must be met even when the arbitrators are appointed from outside the Panel of Arbitrators. The Chair, when designating persons to serve on Panels, is also responsible for ensuring that due regard is given to assuring representation on the Panels of the principal legal systems of the world and of the main forms of economic activity.[7]

In the International Criminal Court (ICC), there is an even more robust list of requirements. As per the Rome Statute, in addition to the general requirements,[8] every candidate nominated must have either: established competence in criminal law and procedure, and the necessary experience, whether as a judge, prosecutor, advocate or some other similar capacity, in criminal proceedings; or established competence in relevant areas of international law such as international humanitarian law and the law of human rights, and extensive experience in a professional legal capacity which is of relevance to the judicial work of the ICC.[9] Further, the candidates must also have excellent knowledge of and be fluent in at least one of the languages of the ICC.[10]

Although merely including enhanced or further criteria may not automatically ensure adjudicators with better institutional capacity and/or expertise, it is an important starting point coupled with more rigorous selection procedures.

b. Selection Procedures for Adjudicators

Turning to the manner of selection of the adjudicators, the procedure of the CJEU for the selection of adjudicators is robust. The judges and Advocates-General of the CJEU are appointed by common accord of the governments of the Member States based on the nomination made by a Member State and the recommendations of a Panel of Experts that examines the qualifications of candidates. The panel gives an opinion on candidates' suitability to perform the duties of an adjudicator.[11] The Panel comprises seven persons chosen from among former members of the CJEU, members of national supreme courts and lawyers of recognised competence.[12] The panel uses six criteria to evaluate the suitability of candidates. These are the candidates' legal capabilities; their professional experience; their ability to perform the duties of a judge; their language skills; their ability to work as part of a team in an international environment in which several legal systems are represented; and whether their independence, impartiality, probity and integrity are beyond doubt.[13] Between 2010 and 2022, the panel issued

[6] ICSID Convention, art 14.1.

[7] ibid art 14.2.

[8] Rome Statute of the International Criminal Court (adopted 17 July 1998, entered into force 1 July 2002), art 36(3), which provides that judges must be chosen from among persons of high moral character, impartiality and integrity, possessing the qualifications required in their respective states for appointment to the highest judicial offices.

[9] ibid.

[10] ibid.

[11] Treaty on the Functioning of the European Union (TFEU), art 255.

[12] ibid.

[13] *Seventh Activity Report of the Panel Provided for by Article 255 of the Treaty on the Functioning of the European Union,* www.curia.europa.eu/jcms/upload/docs/application/pdf/2022-07/2022.2597-qcar22002enn_002.pdf, 17, which summarises the panel's work on assessing candidates' suitability to serve as judges and AdvocatesGeneral of the Court of Justice and the General Court. We note that there has been discussion

243 opinions, 27 of which were objections to the selection and nomination of candidates.[14] The panel's assessment of individual candidates is not disclosed to the general public. In order to inform the general public, the panel's activity reports provide detailed information on its working methods and approach to assessment. The panel's opinions have always been followed by the governments of Member States.[15]

The procedure of selection of adjudicators in the CJEU ensures that the qualifications listed in the governing statutes are more than mere formal requirements. Furthermore, it ensures that there is a degree of transparency in how these criteria are assessed by the selection committee, reaffirming the perceived legitimacy of the dispute resolution process. Although it might not be possible to prescribe such procedure for the selection of adjudicators themselves in ad hoc mechanisms, this procedure could instead be used to select the pool or roster of candidates from which ad hoc adjudicators are selected in such DSMs. Furthermore, to enable disputing parties to appoint qualified adjudicators, DSMs can maintain lists of potential candidates that fulfil the criteria and update them periodically.

c. Mechanisms for Training of Adjudicators

To ensure lasting and more continuous capacity building for adjudicators, it may be necessary to move beyond formal criteria, qualifications or selection procedures. In this regard, it is important to explore frameworks that allow adjudicators to keep up with the latest legal developments and case law of the DSMs. This is reminiscent of the 2009 US Proposal on Improvement of Appellate Body[16] with respect to the WTO DSS. One of the three proposals made by the US was for a representative group of WTO Members to coordinate professional development of current and future Appellate Body (AB) members.[17]

However, in the case of ad hoc adjudicators, it becomes more pertinent to ensure that individuals in the pool from which ad hoc adjudicators are selected stay up to date with the latest developments in their area of dispute settlement. The new WTO Multi-Party Interim Appeal Arbitration Arrangement (MPIA) includes provisions requiring the pool of arbitrators to continuously stay abreast of WTO dispute settlement activities.[18] The AB members also had a similar requirement. Previously, while the AB was

among experts recently about the Article 255 Committee, notably its 20-year minimum experience requirement potentially disqualifying competent but young potential candidates; see Symposium on 'The Selection of EU Judges and the 255 Committee' (*EU Law Live*, 21 November 2024). See also JHH Weiler, 'Who Will Judge the Judges Who Judge the Judges? The Curious Case of Gonçalo Manoel de Vilhena de Almeida Ribeiro' (*EU Law Live*, Symposium, 20 September 2024) (discussing the panel's criteria and minimum experience requirements); G Amato, M Cartabia, D Grimm, M Poiares Maduro, RM Moura Ramos and JL da Cruz Vilaça, 'Selecting EU Judges: The Role of the 255 Committee according to the Treaty' (*EU Law Live*, Symposium on 'The Selection of EU Judges and the 255 Committee', 23 September 2024).

[14] *Seventh Activity Report of the Panel Provided for by Article 255 of the Treaty on the Functioning of the European Union* (n 13) 9.

[15] ibid.

[16] *Improvements for the WTO Appellate Body: Proposal by the United States*, Dispute Settlement Body, WT/DSB/W/398 (16 January 2009).

[17] ibid 3.

[18] *Multi-Party Interim Appeal Arbitration Arrangement Pursuant to Article 25 of the DSU* (WTO Document JOB/DSB/1/Add.12, 30 April 2020), para 5.

operational, AB members would meet in 'retreats' annually or semi-annually. The members met and, inter alia, discussed substantive legal issues of recurring importance, current developments and systemic issues of interpretation. At present, although not to the extent of the AB, the members of the pool of arbitrators of the MPIA meet virtually to discuss matters of interpretation, practice and procedure.

Neither of these provisions have been formally detailed with respect to the logistics, specific content of the training, who undertakes the training etc. They were operationalised and developed through the working practices of the DSM. Formalising these practices, with more input and participation from Member States, will be crucial in addressing concerns relating to asymmetry.

d. Development of Expertise through Working Practices of Adjudicators

Besides specific training for adjudicators, certain working practices amongst adjudicators also contribute towards the same goal: development of expertise of adjudicators – for example, in the CJEU, the judges and Advocates General of the ECJ meet for the general meeting, or the 'Réunion Générale',[19] to discuss administrative issues, or proposals in the Preliminary Report of pending cases. This allows judges and Advocates General to interact closely with one another and keep up to date with the relevant issues in pending matters. As we have seen earlier, the Preliminary Report in each case is prepared by the Judge Rapporteur, in consultation with the assigned Advocate General. It recommends, inter alia, the size of the chamber to which the case should be assigned, if there should be an opinion of the Advocate General, if there should be an oral hearing in the case and if there are questions to be clarified before the oral hearing – for example, relating to the relevant national law in the case.[20] In a slightly different practice in the General Court of the CJEU, the Preliminary Report is not sent to all the judges of the General Court. Instead, it is only shared with the Chamber to which the case is assigned, as well as the President and Vice-President of the Court. However, in some types of cases like those involving intellectual property, the Preliminary Report is sent to all the judges for information. Further, every judge receives a summary of every report and there are mechanisms in place for them to obtain the full report if needed. These two procedures allow the judges of the ECJ and the General Court to keep track of the relevant issues in cases before their respective courts.

The 'exchange of views' under the AB Working Procedures, which took place when the AB was operational, also fulfilled the same function.[21] At present, in the MPIA, it is envisaged that the pool of arbitrators will receive all documents relating to appeal arbitration.[22] Further, as we have seen above, the members of the pool of arbitrators are required, to the fullest extent practicable, to discuss matters of interpretation, practice and procedure.[23] This practice is critical, as it allows the adjudicators to strengthen their

[19] Rules of Procedure of the Court of Justice of the European Union, arts 25, 59 and 60.
[20] ibid art 59.
[21] WTO Appellate Body, *Working Procedures for Appellate Review* (WT/AB/WP/1, 15 February 1996), para 4(1).
[22] *Multi-Party Interim Appeal Arbitration Arrangement Pursuant to Article 25 of the DSU* (n 18) para 5.
[23] ibid.

command over procedural and substantive issues, as well as to promote consistency and coherence in decision-making.

f. Moving away from the Ad Hoc/Part-Time Nature of Adjudicators

Lastly, in order to respond to such concerns over the risk of weakness of ad hoc adjudicators, more permanent mechanisms can be envisaged. There have been some attempts to address this imbalance by proposing full-time positions for adjudicators. As it is difficult to examine this practice in the abstract, we will discuss this further in Part III on the WTO DSS. These proposals often require more widespread changes to the institutional frameworks and procedures in place, including increased resources, amended conditions of employment of the adjudicators and enhanced remuneration for increased work.

B. Control over the Language of the Proceedings and Translations

i. Examples of Concerns from the CJEU, the ECOWAS Court and the WTO DSS

As all DSMs must work in a specific language, concerns may arise due to asymmetry in command over the working language between the Dispute Assistants and the adjudicator. As mentioned earlier, such asymmetry between adjudicators and Dispute Assistants, and even amongst different adjudicators working together, is a factor of international cooperation where individuals from different cultures and language traditions work together. Here we specifically try to discuss concerns that may arise when the Dispute Assistants have a stronger command over the working language and, accordingly, their potential to influence the decision of the adjudicator.

French is the working language of the CJEU, and fluency in French is essential to the functioning of the CJEU and the drafting of judgments. In one instance, a scholar raised concerns regarding the quality of judges' work at the CJEU and their ability to work in French as they were not all native French speakers.[24] Given that there is a significant representation of référendaires (Assigned Assistants) who are native French speakers (from France, Belgium etc), the judges may become overly reliant on their référendaires. Further, the preference for native French speakers as référendaires gives Francophones a 'disproportionate influence on shaping EU law'.[25] However, as will be explained below, certain institutional and procedural frameworks of the CJEU provide safeguards against giving undue importance to French language.

With our interactions and interviews with actors from the ECOWAS Court, we have discovered that similar concerns relating to language also arise there.[26] The ECOWAS

[24] AH Zhang, 'The Faceless Court' (2016) 38(1) *University of Pennsylvania Journal of International Law* 71.
[25] ibid 129.
[26] This is what we have understood from our discussions with experts, including members of the Institutional Office.

Court drafts judgments in one of the three official languages of the Court, depending on which judge is appointed as the Judge Rapporteur. The ECOWAS Court's translators then translate the judgment into the other two languages of the Court. However, in practice, the translators do not have legal training or background and there may be instances where there is a need for corrections to be made post-translation. Therefore, the Research and Documentation Department (Institutional Assistants), the judges themselves or their Executive Assistants (Assigned Assistants) conduct further proofreading. However, this has not been possible in every case due to the caseload and the lack of sufficient resources within the Department.

We have gathered that similar concerns relating to language arise in the WTO.[27] When the AB was operational, the quick timeline for producing the AB Report (often in English as the only common language for deliberations) required AB members to rely on the quick drafting skills of AB Secretariat staff who were more proficient in drafting in English. Another dimension of this concern is the fact that the competitive selection process for Secretariat staff may favour candidates who are from certain jurisdictions or legal systems, raising further concerns over the representativeness of the dispute resolution process. For example, given that most common-law jurisdictions are English-speaking, there may be an over-representation of lawyers from common law jurisdictions in the Secretariat. This dimension can also arise in other DSMs with multiple working languages.

ii. Useful Practices/Procedures Relating to Language

Here we examine some useful practices and procedures across DSMs relating to: strengthening the capacity of the adjudicator through specific language requirements at the time of selection, a dedicated department for translations and interpretation, and Assigned Assistants specifically for language related tasks.

In the ICC, it is explicitly provided that candidates must have an excellent knowledge of and be fluent in at least one of the languages of the ICC.[28] Similarly, in the CJEU, the Panel of Experts that examines the qualifications of candidates for judges uses six criteria to evaluate the suitability of candidates. This explicitly includes their language skills.

With respect to the CJEU, there is a dedicated department staffed by experts with adequate legal training and a thorough knowledge of several official languages of the EU.[29] Furthermore, working exclusively in French drives judges to learn the language rather quickly, even if they are not proficient in it when they come to the CJEU.[30] Given the importance of language before the CJEU, the Directorate-General of Multilingualism is the institution's largest service, employing over 1,000 people. While the working language of the CJEU is French, the cases may come in any of the 24 languages of the EU and will then be interpreted/translated at multiple stages. Given that the texts translated

[27] ibid.

[28] Rome Statute of the International Criminal Court, art 36(3).

[29] Rules of Procedure of the Court of Justice, art 42.

[30] D Sarmiento, 'Référendaire: Court of Justice of the European Union (CJEU)' in *Max Planck Encyclopedia of International Procedural Law* (MPIL, December 2018) 3.

are highly technical, the translation service only hires persons who have completed their education in law and possess the necessary language qualifications.[31] Such a dedicated language service reduces the dependence on référendaires for all language related tasks. The CJEU also has another group of Assigned Assistants under the supervision of the President – the Lecteurs d'arrêts. These Assigned Assistants are specifically responsible for examining the compliance of the draft with specific language requirements of the CJEU. This allows judges to remain in control over the decision-making function, while leaving the specific language-related concerns to the domain of this specific set of Assigned Assistants.

In the ACtHPR, given the composition of the judges,[32] the working languages of the Court are English and French, with Arabic judges being provided individual interpreters and making their interventions in French. The translations of the documents and the judgment are done by the Language Unit, employing non-lawyers who may be specialised in legal translations. The Legal Officers of the Legal Aid Unit who are bilingual check the translated drafts of the cases they are assigned, while in other cases another Legal Officer who is fluent in the language of the translation will review the translated draft and assist in taking notes on the translated draft judgment during the deliberations.

With respect to adjudicators from countries where the native language/working language is not one of the prominent working languages of the institution, an essential safeguard could be to provide Assigned Assistants to adjudicators, with dedicated assistance on language. In such cases, in order to guard against excessive reliance on the Dispute Assistants, or incursion on the decision-making function of the adjudicators, procedural safeguards could be instituted. For example, the adjudicator may be allowed to draft in another language, with an Assigned Assistant with expertise in legal translation taking on the responsibility for translation into the working language.

C. Lack of Direct Supervision and Control over the Dispute Assistant

i. Examples of Concerns from the WTO DSS

Pauwelyn and Pelc have raised several concerns on the role of Dispute Assistants in the context of the WTO. One such concern is the lack of formal control exercised by the adjudicators over the staff who assist them. This concern has also been raised by

[31] Court of Justice of the European Union, 'Directorates for Legal Translation', www.curia.europa.eu.

[32] The official languages of the ACtHPR correspond to the official languages of the African Union, and judgments are translated into all these languages. Arabic, English, French and Portuguese serve as the Court's working languages. It is worth noting that Kiswahili and Spanish have recently become African Union working languages; however, the Court's rules have not yet been updated to reflect this change. During the current session, Swahili interpretation has been provided, and some but not all documents have been translated into Swahili. Spanish has occasionally been used for major meetings, both for interpretation and for some meeting documents.

Mavroidis and Hoekman.[33] The Secretariat staff assisting the panel in a dispute are not under the exclusive supervision and control of the panel (ie, the Chairperson of the Panel or individual panellists). Both administratively and with respect to their work, the staff report to the Director of the Legal Affairs Division (LAD) or Rules Division and, ultimately, the Deputy DG (DDG) in charge of their respective division. Within such an institutional framework, there may be situations where the panel or an individual panellist wants a decision in a direction that is different from what is advised by the Director of the LAD/Rules Division.

The concern also goes back to the fear that the Dispute Assistants influence the eventual decision-making function of the adjudicator. As we have seen, there are several DSMs where the Dispute Assistants from the Institutional Office or Additional Institutional Departments are not under the exclusive supervision of the adjudicators. They are also under the supervision and administrative control of the Head of the Institutional Office or some other institutional actor (like the Director of LAD/Rules Division in the WTO Secretariat). In such an organisational framework, this lack of formal supervision and control over the functions of Dispute Assistant could raise concerns relating to the Institutional Assistants exerting influence over the decision-making function.

There may also be concerns on excessive delegation that arise with respect to Assigned Assistants or External Assistants, which will be discussed separately in section I.D below.

ii. Useful Practices/Procedures on Checks on the Functions of Institutional Assistants, and Diversification of Sources of Assistance

A significant safeguard to this concern is through institutional checks that may be introduced over the functions of the Institutional Assistants. In some DSMs, this check is introduced through the procedure of appointing a Judge Rapporteur, who oversees the tasks of the Institutional Assistants closely for each dispute. Such checks could also be introduced through different groups of Dispute Assistants with different mandates in assisting adjudicators. These sets of Dispute Assistant serve to reduce or check the influence that any one set of actors may have over the decision-making function, and balance the overall control exerted by the adjudicator (creating what is termed in constitutional law as 'checks and balances'). With respect to Assigned Assistants/External Assistants, the adjudicator retains full supervision and control over their work. Therefore, introducing such assistants in addition to Institutional Assistants allows for adjudicators to balance any concerns regarding Institutional Assistants exerting undue influence. Further, even in the case of Institutional Assistants, diversifying the sources of assistance amongst different departments, and with distinct administrative heads, will ensure that no single actor exerts undue influence or risks occupying a position of power. This can re-balance the asymmetry even without direct supervision and control over such diverse actors by the adjudicators.

[33] Hoekman and Mavroidis (n 3); see also B Hoekman and PC Mavroidis, *To AB or Not to AB?: Dispute Settlement in WTO Reform* (European University Institute, Robert Schuman Centre for Advanced Studies, Global Governance Programme Working Paper No RSCAS 2020/34, 2020).

a. Judge Rapporteurs and de Facto Control over Institutional Assistants

We have already seen some procedures that ensure de facto control by adjudicators over the work of Institutional Assistants. One prominent example of such de facto control is through the assignment of a Judge Rapporteur, who supervises the work of Institutional Assistants during the dispute. The Secretariat staff of the IACtHR, the Legal Officer of the Registry of the ACtHPR, the staff of the Registry of the ECtHR and the staff of the Research and Documentation Department of the ECOWAS Court (Institutional Assistants) assigned to a dispute specifically work under the supervision of the Judge Rapporteur. Despite being Institutional Assistants, who are under the formal supervision of specific head of the Institutional Office, when they work with the Judge Rapporteur, the adjudicators exercise de facto control over the work of the Institutional Assistants.

b. Checks on the Role of Institutional Assistants, and Diversification in the CJEU

The judges of the General Court and the ECJ have two types of Dispute Assistants: first, the Institutional Assistants, comprising the staff of the Registries of the ECJ and the General Court, the Directorate-General of Multilingualism, the Directorate-General of Multilingualism, and the Research and Documentation Directorate; and, second, the Assigned Assistants who work in the cabinet of the judge, ie, the référendaires, additional assistants who do not work on the substantive aspects of the case and a trainee. Lastly, there are the Lecteurs d'arrêts, who are also Assigned Assistants and report to the President of the respective Court. The Assigned Assistants undertake the substantive assistance, including drafting and research for a case during the dispute resolution process. Such Assigned Assistants work entirely under the supervision and control of their respective judges. The Institutional Assistants, on the other hand, do not participate in the substantive aspects, including drafting of the judgment. However, their participation at important stages with respect to filtering of applications, research and translations ensures complementarity between the different groups of Dispute Assistants. Such varied group of actors act as an informal check on each other's functions, ensuring that the final decision is not, and cannot be, influenced by any single group of actors. Therefore, although the Dispute Assistants undertake substantive functions, they do so within their mandate and without encroaching on the decision-making functions of the judges. They undertake all such functions according to the directions of their judges (in the case of Assigned Assistants) or within the confines of their respective mandates (in the case of Institutional Assistants).

c. Checks on Institutional Assistants and Diversification in the ECOWAS Court

Similarly, the ECOWAS Court also achieves this balance between Institutional Assistants and Assigned Assistants. The Institutional Assistants include the staff of the Registry and the Research and Documentation Department. To recap, the Research and Documentation Department performs the bulk of the judicial assistance work in the Court and is headed by a Director. At the same time, the judges also have individual Assigned Assistants (known as Executive Assistants) who work for them exclusively and form a part of the Chambers of the Judge. The Assigned Assistants are officially hired by the Registry; however, they remain entirely under the supervision and control of the judges. There are two ways in which there are checks on the Institutional Assistants: first, the Director of the Research and Documentation Department reports to the President of the Court, which introduces an element of de facto supervision over the work of the Institutional Assistants by adjudicators; and, second, the judges are not exclusively reliant on the Institutional Assistants, but supplement their work using their Assigned Assistants.

d. Checks on Institutional Assistants and Diversification in the ICJ

Another interesting institutional arrangement of checks on the functions of Institutional Assistants is seen in the ICJ. The judges have two sets of assistants: Institutional Assistants of the Registry and the Department of Legal Matters; and Assigned Assistants – the Associate Legal Officers, the Special Assistant to the President, and Judicial Fellows. The Assigned Assistants are all formally part of the Institutional Office (ie, the Registry and its Department of Legal Matters), but in practice, they are under the supervision and control of their individual judges. Even with respect to administrative matters like periods of leave, their respective judge first gives approval before the request is sent to the Registry. There is even a physical separation between the Assigned Assistants and the Institutional Office. The Associate Legal Officers, the Special Assistant to the President and the Judicial Fellows physically work out of the specific wing assigned to the judges, while the Registry staff operate out of the Peace Palace. The judges are assisted by both sets of Dispute Assistants, ensuring that the judges remain in control of the decision-making process.

e. Other Institutional Practice on Diversification of Assistance

This diversification of sources of assistance between Institutional Assistants and Assigned/External Assistants is achieved to varying degrees across DSMs. In international arbitration, this manifests itself in the distinction between the tribunal secretaries/registrars (Institutional Assistants) and personal assistants (External Assistants). For example, in the PCA, often one or more legal counsel from the International Bureau (Institutional Office) is assigned as the primary assistant for a dispute (tribunal secretary/registrar), with the support of one or more assistant legal counsels and a case manager; and the arbitrators may also have additional personal assistants (External Assistants). In the EFTA, like the CJEU, the same distinction is found between the legal secretaries that the DSM assigns to individual judges and the institutional Registry. In the COMESA Court of Justice, the balance is reflected in the distinction between the Registry staff and the External Assistants that are hired to assist the bench of judges in a particular case.

Maintaining a good balance between the Institutional Assistants and Assigned/External Assistants is an important institutional safeguard to ensure that adjudicators benefit from the expertise of Dispute Assistants, while also retaining control over the decision-making process. In the examples examined above, the adjudicators receive assistance from different sources, facilitating their control over the decision-making process.

D. Risk of Excessive Delegation to the Dispute Assistants

i. *Examples of Concerns from International Arbitration Institutions, the IUSCT and the WTO*

This section looks at concerns that arise with respect to the risk of adjudicators delegating functions to the Dispute Assistants, or allowing Dispute Assistants to participate in certain stages of the dispute resolution process. This could relate to research or collation functions, attendance or participation in the hearing, attendance or participation in the deliberation, drafting (part of) the judgment/award/order and/or review of the judgment/award/order. The concern is that by allowing the Dispute Assistant to participate in these functions, the adjudicator risks failing to satisfy their adjudicative mandate. In other words, the risk is that excessive delegation of some/all of these tasks could risk the Dispute Assistant encroaching upon the decision-making function of the adjudicator. Given the specific concerns raised on delegation of the drafting function to Dispute Assistants (and corresponding useful practices), we will examine these separately in section I.E below.

a. International Arbitration Institutions

DSMs like the PCA, ICSID and commercial arbitration institutions (referred to collectively hereinafter as 'International Arbitration Institutions') have two types of Dispute Assistants: a tribunal secretary, who is an Institutional Assistant assigned from the Institutional Office for a particular case; and the tribunal assistant, who is an External Assistant to individual arbitrators or to tribunal as a whole.[34] The challenges to the role of Dispute Assistants in international arbitration can arise in different ways. The challenge could be argued indirectly as part of a challenge seeking to disqualify an arbitrator or arbitral tribunal, or as part of the challenge to the arbitral award itself.[35] Alternatively, it could arise as a direct challenge to the Dispute.[36] This section examines cases where the challenge arose in the context of excessive delegation of tasks to the tribunal secretary or tribunal assistant.

A useful starting point for this discussion is the seminal 2002 article, 'The Fourth Arbitrator?', by Constantine Partasides. In this article, Partasides highlighted concerns regarding the use (or misuse) of Dispute Assistants in arbitration.[37] The growing

[34] As discussed in ch 20, the specific titles assigned to these Dispute Assistants vary across institutions. For the purposes of this chapter, we use *tribunal secretary* to refer to the Institutional Assistant and *tribunal assistant* to refer to the External Assistant.

[35] See, eg, The Hague Court of Appeal, *Veteran Petroleum Ltd and Others v Russian Federation (Yukos)* (18 February 2020) Case No 200.197.079/01; *P v Q* [2017] EWHC 194 (Comm); Swiss Federal Tribunal, Judgment of 21 May 2015 (2015) 33 *ASA Bulletin* 879; C Partasides, 'The Fourth Arbitrator? The Role of Secretaries to Tribunals in International Arbitration' (2002) 18 *Arbitration International* 147; P Tercier, 'The Role of the Secretary to the Arbitral Tribunal' in LW Newman and RD Hill (eds), *Leading Arbitrators' Guide to International Arbitration*, 3rd edn (Juris, 2014); B Hughes, 'The Problem of Undisclosed Assistance to Arbitral Tribunals' in P Shaughnessy and S Tung (eds), *The Powers and Duties of an Arbitrator: Liber Amicorum Pierre A Karrer* (Kluwer 2017).

[36] JO Jensen, 'Challenge of Secretaries and Arbitrators' in *Tribunal Secretaries in International Arbitration, Oxford International Arbitration Series* (Oxford Law Pro, online edn, 2019).

[37] Partasides (n 35) 147.

perception that tribunal secretaries play an excessive role in arbitrations is what he coins the 'Fourth Arbitrator'. The phrasing is important, as he does not claim that such an excessive role actually existed; rather, he highlights the concerns surrounding the *perception* of the excessive role. He goes on to explain that, irrespective of the justification for such concerns, the concerns adversely affect the legitimacy of the arbitral process and therefore need to be addressed.[38] Although the article brought this issue into mainstream academic debate, challenges to arbitral awards on the grounds of the role of the tribunal secretary pre-date it.[39] We will examine below some notable examples since 2002.

The 2014 International Chamber of Commerce Arbitration between Statoil and the Algerian state oil company Sonatrach is a prominent case of challenge to the arbitral award on the ground, inter alia, that the tribunal secretary had exceeded the scope of their duties.[40] The parties had expressly agreed to the role of the tribunal assistant (referred to as the 'Administrative Assistant' in the International Chamber of Commerce). They specifically agreed that the tribunal assistant would not participate in the decision-making process.[41] Once the award was issued, Sonatrach challenged the award before the England and Wales High Court on the ground, inter alia, that some of the functions discharged by the tribunal assistant were outside the scope of what the parties had consented to.[42] Specifically, they claimed that the tribunal had improperly allowed the tribunal assistant to participate in the deliberations, which was not disclosed to the parties for their agreement. Sonatrach argued that the tribunal assistant had drafted three notes on substantive matters for the tribunal, and the tribunal had declined to disclose these notes to the parties on the grounds of secrecy of deliberations.[43] In other words, Sonatrach claimed that the failure to disclose such notes on the ground of secrecy of deliberations implied that the tribunal assistant had participated in the deliberations. The High Court rejected Sonatrach's claims, noting that the mere drafting of the notes did not imply that the tribunal assistant had participated in the deliberations or decision-making function, even if the notes were part of the deliberations of the tribunal. The ruling of the High Court clarifies what the contours of the decision-making function could be. We reproduce relevant portions of the judgment below:

> 49. Frankly, that should have been an end of the matter and Sonatrach should have accepted the Chairman's word. However, Sonatrach persisted with its complaint in its section 68 application, contending that there was an inconsistency between the Chairman's reference to the secrecy of deliberations, and Ms Noël not exceeding the agreed remit, in other words that she must have participated in the deliberations. I agree with Mr Landau that there is no such inconsistency. The Chairman was not

[38] ibid 147–63.

[39] *Compagnie Honeywell Bull SA v Computacion Bull de Venezuela CA*, Cour d'appel de Paris, 21 June 1990, 1991(1) *Revue de l'Arbitrage* 96 (unofficial translation). One of the earliest recorded challenges to an arbitral award based in part on the conduct of a tribunal secretary appears in this decision, where the appellant alleged interference by the tribunal secretary, but the court upheld the award on the ground that the tribunal was permitted to appoint a secretary and the appellant had not shown how any interference caused prejudice.

[40] *Sonatrach v Statoil* [2014] EWHC 875 (Comm).

[41] ibid 48.

[42] ibid.

[43] ibid.

saying that she had participated in the tribunal's deliberations, just that the notes formed part of the tribunal's deliberations, which are secret. As Fouchard Gaillard Goldman on International Commercial Arbitration state at [1374]: 'Although, again, most laws do not explicitly require deliberations in international commercial arbitration to be secret, such secrecy is generally considered to be the rule.'

Another prominent case involves the challenge to the *Yukos* award brought by the Russian Federation.[44] First, the Russian Federation moved the District Court of The Hague to set aside the US$50 billion award rendered under the aegis of the PCA, as per the UNCITRAL Rules. One of the arguments raised was that the tribunal delegated its adjudicative function (ie, decision-making function) to the Chairman's assistant, Mr Martin Valasek. In this case, Mr Valasek was a tribunal assistant (External Assistant) to the Chairman. Russia made several arguments to support its claim, including that the arbitrators had failed to discharge the mandate entrusted to them. While the District Court set aside the awards on other grounds, the Court of Appeal addressed the claims regarding the role of the tribunal assistant in appeal. The Court of Appeal held that a tribunal has a procedural right to use an assistant or secretary to draft an arbitral award as it sees fit.[45] Such a right was only displaced if there was a contrary agreement by the parties.[46] Although the Court of Appeal noted that the tribunal failed to inform the parties of the nature and extent of Mr Valasek's contribution, this was not considered a major procedural violation so as to support the claim that the tribunal was constituted in violation of statutory rules or rules agreed between the parties.[47] Specifically, the Court noted that in the absence of an explicit agreement between the parties regarding the permitted functions of secretaries/arbitrators, 'it is left to the discretion of the Tribunal to what extent it wishes to use an assistant or secretary for the drafting of the award'.[48]

Now we turn to examples where the role of Dispute Assistant was raised as part of a challenge to the arbitrator. In *P v Q*, the claimant made an application to remove co-arbitrators appointed to an LCIA arbitration tribunal.[49] The claim was made before the England and Wales High Court, alleging that the tribunal had delegated its adjudicative function to the tribunal secretary.[50] The specific LCIA Rules and Notes for Arbitrators at issue are widely permissive with respect to the role of tribunal secretary.[51] In dismissing the claims,

[44] *Yukos Universal Ltd (Isle of Man) v Russia* (UNCITRAL, PCA Case No AA 227, Writ of Summons, 28 January 2015).

[45] *Yukos* (n 35) para 6.6.14.1.

[46] ibid.

[47] ibid paras 6.6.12 and 6.6.14.2.

[48] ibid para 6.6.14.

[49] *P v Q and Others* [2017] EWHC 194 (Comm).

[50] ibid 14: '(1) Ground 1: the Tribunal improperly delegated its role to the Secretary by systematically entrusting the Secretary with a number of tasks beyond what was permissible under the LCIA Rules and the LCIA Policy on the Use of Arbitral Secretaries; (2) Ground 2: the Chairman breached his mandate as an arbitrator and his duty not to delegate by seeking the views of a person who was neither a party to the arbitration nor a member of the tribunal on substantial procedural issues (i.e. the Secretary); (3) Ground 3: the other members of the Tribunal equally breached their mandate as arbitrators and their duty not to delegate by not sufficiently participating in the arbitration proceedings and the decision-making.'

[51] The LCIA Rules provide at art 14.2 that unless otherwise agreed by the parties under art 14.1, the Tribunal shall have the widest discretion to discharge its duties permitted by the applicable law. Further, para 201 of the *Notes for Arbitrators* states: 'The Arbitral Tribunal may not delegate its decision-making function to a Tribunal Secretary. The Arbitral Tribunal is responsible for ensuring that all tasks carried out by the Tribunal Secretary

the Court clarified that the use of a tribunal secretary must not involve any member of the tribunal abrogating or impairing their non-delegable and personal decision-making function. The test to assess whether this function is discharged by the arbitrator is the exercise of independent judgement. However, the fact that the arbitrator receives suggestions or opinions from others, including a tribunal secretary or assistant, would not necessarily mean that the arbitrator failed to exercise their independent judgement.[52]

With respect to direct challenges to the role of tribunal secretaries or tribunal assistants, explicit provisions allowing for such challenges are found in some domestic legislation,[53] arbitration rules, and some international provisions of international tribunals and institutions.[54] This right to challenge tribunal secretaries is derived from an analogous application of the provisions on arbitrator challenges,[55] and includes claims for lack of impartiality and independence.[56] We discuss this in detail below on concerns relating to lack of independence (see section I.F).

Although we have tried to provide examples of different types of challenges to the role of Dispute Assistants in international arbitration, these are by no means exhaustive. The challenges have given rise to various decisions that are specific to the arbitration rules, to domestic arbitration law, to the conduct of the tribunal and the tribunal secretary/assistant in question, and to the parties to the dispute. In deciding on such challenges, courts across different jurisdictions have held that an arbitral tribunal must 'exercise its own discretion'[57] and its 'own judgment',[58] and that an arbitrator must 'make his own decision'.[59] In other words, an arbitrator 'must not substitute the opinion of another for his own'.[60] Therefore, the decision-making function requires arbitrators to bring their own personal and independent judgement to bear on the decision in question and to exercise reasonable diligence in going about discharging that function.[61] The rules of the arbitral institutions (discussed below) have also noted that an arbitral tribunal may not

are performed to the standard required under the LCIA Rules, and tasks performed by the Tribunal Secretary must be carried out under the supervision of the Arbitral Tribunal.'

[52] *P v Q and Others* (n 52) paras 66–67.

[53] Dutch Code of Civil Procedure, art 1035a, read with art 1033(1); Swiss Code of Civil Procedure, arts 365(2), 367–69; Colombian Arbitration Law 2012 (Law No 1563 of 12 July 2012), arts 16(1) and 55.

[54] Arbitration Rules of the Arbitration Institute of the Stockholm Chamber of Commerce 2017, art 24(5) in conjunction with art 19 (hereinafter 'SCC Rules 2017'); Swiss Rules of International Arbitration 2012, art 15(5) in conjunction with arts 9–11 (hereinafter 'Swiss Rules 2012'); LCIA, *Notes for Arbitrators* (26 October 2017), s 80 in conjunction with LCIA Arbitration Rules 2014, art 10 (hereinafter 'LCIA Notes 2017'); HKIAC, Guidelines on the Use of a Secretary to the Arbitral Tribunal (1 June 2014) s 2.7 (hereinafter 'HKIAC Guidelines 2014').

[55] Jensen (n 36).

[56] Dutch Code of Civil Procedure, arts 1033(1), 1035a; Swiss Code of Civil Procedure, arts 365(2), 367(1)(c); SCC Rules 2017, arts 19(1), 24(5); HKIAC Guidelines 2014, s 2.10.

[57] *Sharp v Nowell* (1948) 6 CB 253, 259–60.

[58] *Louis Dreyfus & Co v Arunchala Ayya* (1931) 33 BOMLR 1536, para 50 ('[The arbitrator has not] left to an outsider the burden of deciding any issue in the case instead of exercising his own judgment thereon'); *Total Support Management (Pty) Ltd v Diversified Health Systems (SA) (Pty) Ltd* [2002] ZASCA 14, para 41 ('the arbitrator [must have] exercised his own judgment in deciding the issues'); *cf Giacomo Costa fu Andrea v British Italian Trading Co* [1961] 2 Lloyd's Rep 392, 402.

[59] *Kuala Ibai Development Sdn Bhd v Kumpulan Perunding (1988) Sdn Bhd and Another* [1999] 5 *Malayan Law Journal* 137, 148.

[60] *Whitmore v Smith* (1861) 7 H & N 509, 516; *cf Continental Materials Corp v Gaddis Mining* 306 F 2d 952, 955 (10th Cir 1962).

[61] D Girsberger and N Voser, *International Arbitration: Comparative and Swiss Perspectives*, 3rd edn (Schulthess, 2016) para 733.

delegate 'its decision-making function'[62] and must retain the 'ultimate authority over the decision-making process'.[63] These sources thus focus on the arbitrator's exercise of intellectual control over the decision as the core of what they owe to the parties.

A core distinguishing feature of international arbitration is the parties' freedom to choose a decision-maker they trust.[64] This right is considered a 'cardinal feature' of international arbitration and remains one of the core reasons why parties choose arbitration to resolve their disputes.[65] As a consequence of the parties' expectations when choosing their arbitrator, there is an acceptance that the arbitrator's juridical mandate is *eminently personal*.[66] The challenges raised in arbitration allude to this mandate as preventing the arbitrator from delegating their judicial function to another person. However, as we have seen above, the threshold in order to establish excessive delegation is very high and often does not succeed.

b. The IUSCT

Now we turn to the IUSCT. Early after its establishment, a Member State of the IUSCT raised concerns on the functions of a Legal Adviser when challenging a member of the Tribunal (the adjudicator). As we have explained, Legal Advisers are Assigned Assistants to the members of the Tribunal. The challenge arose in 1991, when Iran wrote to the Claims Tribunal Appointing Authority challenging Mr Gaetano Arangio-Ruiz, the Chairman of Chamber Three, for his alleged failure to perform his arbitral functions.[67] They alleged that he 'failed to act' in terms of Article 13(2) of the UNCITRAL Arbitration Rules 1976. Iran stated that Mr Arangio-Ruiz had been physically present at the Tribunal for 'no more than 40 working days' during the previous 12 months. Furthermore, they noted that he had only spent 14 of those days physically participating in hearings. The claim was made based on the information found in the dissent by the Iranian Member of Chamber Three to a procedural decision rendered by Mr Arangio-Ruiz. According to that dissent, the Iranian member noted:

> In practice, the Parties' detailed briefs, or extended written arguments in support of a given request, are assertedly compressed into short summaries, fit for facsimile transmissions to the Chairman's other places of work. Other Members' memoranda

[62] New York City Bar Association, 'Secretaries to International Arbitration Tribunals: Joint Report of the International Commercial Disputes Committee and the Committee on Arbitration of the New York City Bar Association' (2006) 17 *American Review of International Arbitration* 575, 586.

[63] NG Ziadé, 'Achieving Efficiency in Arbitration: The Role of the Institutions' (2008) 25 *News from ICSID* 3, 5.

[64] G Born, *International Commercial Arbitration*, 3rd edn (Kluwer, 2020) §13.03[A]; GA Bermann, 'International Commercial Arbitration: Present Challenges and Future Prospects' in A Carlevaris et al (eds), *International Arbitration Under Review: Essays in Honour of John Beechey* (ICC, 2015) 63.

[65] C Bühring-Uhle, 'A Survey on Arbitration and Settlement in International Business Disputes: Advantages of Arbitration' in CR Drahozal and RW Naimark (eds), Towards a Science of International Arbitration: Collected Empirical Research (Kluwer 2005) 33; and Queen Mary University and PricewaterhouseCoopers, '2006 International Arbitration Study: Corporate Attitudes and Practices' (2006), www.arbitration.qmul.ac.uk/media/arbitration/docs/IAstudy_2006.pdf, 6.

[66] JMH Hunter and J Paulsson, 'A Code of Ethics for Arbitrators in International Commercial Arbitration' (1985) 13 *International Business Lawyer* 153, 158; FT Schwarz and CW Konrad, *The Vienna Rules: A Commentary on International Arbitration in Austria* (Kluwer, 2009) paras 7–152.

[67] *IranUnited States Claims Tribunal Reports* (Cambridge, Grotius Publications, 1992) vol 27, 291–336.

> or points of view on a given issue are conveyed to him by his legal assistants via telephone contacts. The quality of views which are then expressed in the absence of direct access to the full briefs and to the supporting evidence and exhibits, and in the absence of proper tripartite deliberations, is not difficult to envisage. Awards and other decisions, it goes without saying, are drafted by others.[68]

Iran alleged that it was physically impossible under these circumstances for the Member to have sufficiently studied the documentary record pertaining to the large number of pending cases before him. One of the contentions made in this regard was that, consequently, the Member must have overly relied on his Legal Adviser for tasks that were part of his decision-making mandate. More specifically, Iran claimed that one of the functions discharged by the Legal Adviser was summarising and communicating the parties' pleadings to the Member. Iran alleged that such a function gave the Member a selective understanding of the arguments by parties rather than a complete understanding if he had perused the documents himself. They explained that the subjective assessment of the Legal Adviser on what material was relevant would not necessarily be the same if the assessment was undertaken by the Tribunal member himself. Therefore, Iran claimed that the judgement of the Legal Adviser had substituted the judgement of the member, which in turn, defeated the parties' choice of an arbitrator on the basis of his personal qualifications. Hence, they argued that the arbitrator failed to act as per Rule 13(2) of the UNCITRAL Arbitration Rules 1976.[69]

The Appointing Authority, to whom this challenge was made, considered and dismissed it. The Authority found that the term 'failure to act' in Article 13(2) of the UNCITRAL Arbitration Rules 1976 refers to a situation in which the arbitrator's overall conduct clearly falls below the standard of what may be reasonably expected from an arbitrator.[70] Mr Arangio-Ruiz's conduct was not found to be below such a threshold. The investigations of the Appointing Authority revealed that Mr Arangio-Ruiz had worked on his Claims Tribunal files, even when he was not in The Hague, based on the parties' submissions and the Legal Adviser's summaries of them.[71] It was confirmed that the functions of Legal Advisers include making summaries of pleadings and other submissions, as well as preparing memos and draft decisions for Members.[72] Accordingly, as per the decision of the IUSCT, a tribunal member may use summaries of documents like pleadings and evidence prepared by their Legal Adviser so long as such material is not used to replace their own review and assessment of the factual and legal issues of the dispute.

As we will see in Part III, this concern has also arisen in the context of Secretariat staff and AB Secretariat staff (Institutional Assistants) of the WTO.

[68] *Challenge by Iran to Mr Gaetano ArangioRuiz: Documents Relating to the Challenge: Dissent to Order of 26 July 1991 by Mr Mohsen Aghahosseini* [1992] 27 *IranUnited States Claims Tribunal Reports* 297, 305.

[69] *Challenge by Iran to Mr Gaetano ArangioRuiz, IUSCT, Documents Relating to the Challenge: Letter, The Agent of Iran to the Appointing Authority of 8 August 1991* [1992] 27 *IranUnited States Claims Tribunal Reports* 293, 294.

[70] *Challenge by Iran to Mr Gaetano ArangioRuiz* (Decision of the Appointing Authority, 24 September 1991) [1992] 27 *IranUnited States Claims Tribunal Reports* 328, 332.

[71] ibid 332–33.

[72] Partasides (n 35).

ii. Useful Practices/Procedures on Enhanced Transparency and Disclosures on the Role of Dispute Assistants

a. Transparency, Disclosures and Party Consent in Arbitration Institutions

In this section, we start by discussing the rich practice of arbitration institutions that have aimed to safeguard against excessive delegation of the decision-making function to Dispute Assistants. These practices have been formalised through documents such as guidance documents, notes and rules.

Originally, the trend was that the institutions adopted a restrictive view, discouraging Dispute Assistants from undertaking tasks that are of a legal nature. Such a restrictive view was directly related to preserving the mandate of the arbitrator to perform their decision-making function. For example, the 1996 UNCITRAL Notes on Organizing Arbitral Proceedings[73] noted that administrative services might be secured by engaging a tribunal secretary when the arbitrations are conducted by an institution or by engaging external persons to assist the tribunal. With respect to instances where the tasks of the tribunal secretary or assistant go beyond merely organisational or 'administrative' in nature, it was noted that:

> Differences in views, however, may arise if the tasks include legal research and other professional assistance to the arbitral tribunal (e.g. collecting case law or published commentaries on legal issues defined by the arbitral tribunal, preparing summaries from case law and publications, and sometimes also preparing drafts of procedural decisions or drafts of certain parts of the award, in particular those concerning the facts of the case). Views or expectations may differ especially where a task of the secretary is similar to professional functions of the arbitrators. Such a role of the secretary is in the view of some commentators inappropriate or is appropriate only under certain conditions, such as that the parties agree thereto. However, it is typically recognized that it is important to ensure that the secretary does not perform any decision-making function of the arbitral tribunal.[74]

Similarly, the Note issued by the International Chamber of Commerce Secretariat on 1 October 1995[75] codifying the appointment and role of tribunal secretaries in ICC arbitrations adopted a restrictive approach. They were termed 'administrative secretaries'. The section on 'duties' stated that the duties of the administrative secretary must be strictly limited to administrative tasks.[76] The Note went on to clarify that:

> Such person must not influence in any manner whatsoever the decisions of the arbitral tribunal.
>
> In particular, the administrative secretary must not assume the functions of an arbitrator, notably by becoming involved in the decision-making process of the tribunal or expressing opinions or conclusions with respect to the issues in dispute.[77]

[73] The draft Notes on Organizing Arbitral Tribunals were published as UN Doc A/CN.9/410 (reproduced in *UNCITRAL Yearbook*, vol XXVI: 1995, pt II, III); the revised draft Notes were published as UN Doc A/CN.9/423 (reproduced in *UNCITRAL Yearbook*, vol XXVII: 1996, pt II).

[74] ibid 12, para 27.

[75] Note from the Secretariat of the ICC Court Concerning the Appointment of Administrative Secretaries by Arbitral Tribunals (1 October 1995) 6(2) *ICC International Court of Arbitration Bulletin*.

[76] ibid.

[77] ibid.

Therefore, from the above two Notes issued by UNCITRAL and the International Chamber of Commerce, the practice was initially to limit the tasks of tribunal secretaries/assistants to those of an administrative/non-legal nature. Even now, some arbitral institutions have also adopted a similar restrictive approach in an explicit manner. For example, the Guidelines for Arbitrators of the Stockholm Chamber of Commerce, 2020 states with respect to administrative secretaries that:

> Unless the parties agree otherwise, the secretary's duties are limited to organizational, clerical and administrative functions. The arbitral tribunal may not delegate to the administrative secretary any decision-making or drafting of substantive parts of decisions or awards.[78]

Notwithstanding the above-mentioned examples of the restrictive approach, the realities of the situation are far from simple. Notably, the Young ICCA Task Force survey in 2012 and 2013,[79] based on which the Young ICCA Guide on Arbitral Secretaries was published in 2014,[80] notes this reality. According to the 2012 survey, 66.8 per cent of the participants supported the secretaries performing legal research for the arbitral tribunal and 60.2 per cent supported them drafting procedural orders. However, only 45.2 per cent of the participants supported the practice that secretaries draft parts of the award (45.2 per cent) and even less (38.7 per cent) supported the secretaries analysing the parties' submissions.[81] Based on the responses from these surveys, Article 3 of the Young ICCA Guide reads in part:

> (1) With appropriate direction and supervision by the arbitral tribunal an arbitral secretary's role may legitimately go beyond the purely administrative.
> (2) On this basis, the arbitral secretary's tasks may involve all or some of the following …
>
> (e) Researching questions of law;
> (f) Researching discrete questions relating to factual evidence and witness testimony;
> (g) Drafting procedural orders and similar documents;
> (h) Reviewing the parties' submissions and evidence, and drafting factual chronologies and memoranda summarizing the parties' submissions and evidence;
> (i) Attending the arbitral tribunal's deliberations; and
> (j) Drafting appropriate parts of the award.

The Guide introduces a few new metrics for the assessment of the role of the tribunal secretary/assistant instead of outright restricting them to administrative functions. For example, it states that they may draft appropriate parts of the award, with appropriate direction and supervision by the arbitral tribunal. However, this raises the question of what constitutes 'appropriate' parts of the award.

More recently, institutions have adopted a less restrictive approach, accepting that tribunal secretaries/assistants, allowing their participation beyond purely administrative

[78] Stockholm Chamber of Commerce, '*Guidelines for Arbitrators*' (June 2020) s 2: Administrative Secretaries, www.acerislaw.com/wp-content/uploads/2022/08/scc-guidelines-for-arbitrators.pdf, 8.

[79] International Council for Commercial Arbitration, *Young ICCA Guide on Arbitral Secretaries, The ICCA Reports* No 1 (2014) Annex B, 55–68; Annex C, 69–86.

[80] ibid.

[81] ibid 2.

tasks. For example, breaking away from its earlier position, the UNCITRAL Notes on Organizing Arbitral Proceedings, 2016 accept a broader scope of functions for the secretary to the tribunal:[82]

> 36. Functions and tasks performed by secretaries are broad in range. Secretaries may provide purely organizational support, such as making reservations for hearing and meeting rooms and providing or coordinating administrative services. Some arbitral tribunals wish to have secretaries carry out more substantive functions including legal research and other professional assistance, such as preparing a summary of the facts or the procedural history of the arbitral proceedings, collecting or summarizing case law or published commentaries on legal issues defined by the arbitral tribunal, and preparing draft procedural decisions. However, it is recognized that secretaries are not involved and do not participate in the decision-making of the arbitral tribunal, except in certain rare, specialized types of arbitration (for example, where the specific arbitration rules provide that secretaries are expected to provide legal advice in relation to the decision of the arbitral tribunal if and when the arbitral tribunal is composed only of non-lawyer, subject matter specialists)."[83]

From the above, it is clear that there is no explicit restriction on Dispute Assistants performing substantive tasks like legal research, preparing a summary of the facts or the procedural history of proceedings, collecting/summarising case law or research on legal issues defined by the arbitral tribunal, and preparing draft procedural decisions. However, the Dispute Assistants do not participate in the decision-making function. Another way to read the above permissive provision is that despite undertaking such wide-ranging and substantive functions, the Dispute Assistant does not infringe on the decision-making functions of the arbitral tribunal.

Similarly, the International Chamber of Commerce Note to the Parties and Arbitral Tribunals on the Conduct of the Arbitrations under the International Chamber of Commerce Rules of Arbitration 2021[84] breaks away from the earlier approach of the ICC. Part XX, which deals with 'Administrative Secretaries', specifies that International Chamber of Commerce staff members are not permitted to serve as administrative secretaries. The Note maintains that the administrative secretary shall not perform essential duties of an arbitrator and that it does not release the arbitral tribunal from its duty to personally review the file and/or draft the arbitral decision.[85] However, the Note includes a list of permitted tasks (which are classified as 'organisational and administrative tasks') that may be performed by the administrative secretary.[86] We reproduce this list below:

- "transmitting documents and communications on behalf of the arbitral tribunal;
- organising and maintaining the arbitral tribunal's file and locating documents;

[82] UNCITRAL, Notes on Organizing Arbitral Proceedings (2016), reproduced in *UNCITRAL Yearbook*, vol XXVII: 1996, pt III, annex II, paras 35–37.

[83] ibid para 36.

[84] International Chamber of Commerce, Note to the Parties and Arbitral Tribunals on the Conduct of the Arbitrations under the ICC Rules of Arbitration (2021).

[85] ibid ss XX.A and XX.B.223.

[86] ibid s XX.B.224.

- organising hearings and meetings and liaising with the parties in that respect;
- drafting correspondence to the parties and sending it on behalf of the arbitral tribunal;
- preparing for the arbitral tribunal's review drafts of procedural orders as well as factual portions of an award, such as the summary of the proceedings, the chronology of facts, and the summary of the parties' positions, provided that such procedural orders and portions of the award are subsequently reviewed by the arbitral tribunal itself;
- attending hearings, meetings and deliberations; taking notes or minutes or keeping time;
- conducting legal or similar research; and
- proof-reading and checking citations, dates and cross-references in procedural orders and awards, as well as correcting typographical, grammatical or calculation errors."

It is interesting to note that the above list of permitted tasks includes the drafting of the procedural orders as well as factual portions of an award, so long as such drafts are reviewed by the arbitral tribunal. This is a shift from the earlier Notes issued by the International Chamber of Commerce and is considerably more expansive and permissive in its scope. However, it is worth noting that such tasks are still termed 'organisational and administrative tasks'.

Other examples include the LCIA Guidance Note for Parties and Arbitrators, which notes that the Dispute Assistants may undertake substantive tasks, such as summarising submissions, reviewing authorities and preparing drafts of awards, or sections of awards, and procedural orders.[87] However, all such tasks must be undertaken under the supervision of the arbitral tribunal.[88] Similarly, the HKIAC Guidelines on the Use of a Secretary to the Tribunal 2014 provides a permissive list of substantive tasks that may be performed by the Dispute Assistant, unless the parties agree or the arbitral tribunal directs otherwise.[89] This includes preparing drafts of non-substantive letters for the arbitral tribunal and non-substantive parts of the tribunal's orders, decisions and awards (such as procedural histories and chronologies of events). However, it is explicitly noted that such tasks shall not release the arbitral tribunal from its duty to personally to review the relevant files and materials, and to draft any substantive parts of its orders, decisions and awards.[90]

Article 3 of the Rules of Procedure for Chapter 31 of the USMCA lays out the duties of the staff of the Secretariat (Institutional Assistants). The tasks are limited to administrative functions. Conversely, the functions of External Assistants can be interpreted broadly to include non-administrative tasks. The assistant is defined as a person who, under the terms of appointment of a panellist, conducts research for or provides support to a panellist. Therefore, there is a distinction drawn between the administrative tasks performed by the Institutional Assistants and the more substantive tasks permitted for the External Assistant.

[87] LCIA, *Guidance Note for Parties and Arbitrators,* paras 201–02, www.lcia.org/adr-services/guidance-note.aspx#10.%20%20TRIBUNAL%20SECRETARIES.

[88] ibid para 201.

[89] HKIAC Guidelines 2014, para 3.4.

[90] ibid para 3.6.

A critical reason for preserving the decision-making mandate of the adjudicator relates to the consent for the dispute resolution process which grants the adjudicator this mandate. Parties to the dispute may grant this mandate directly, in the case of arbitration, or indirectly, as in the case of statutory and treaty-based institutions. The majority of the commercial arbitral institution rules provide that a tribunal secretary can only be appointed following consultation with[91] and consent of the parties.[92] For example, the 2015 Practice Note of Singapore International Arbitration Centre (SIAC) and the most recent Arbitration Rules of the SIAC (2025) provide that tribunal secretaries may be appointed after considering the views of the parties.[93] The Swiss Rules of International Arbitration of the Swiss Chambers' Arbitration Institution (SCAI) also provides that the arbitral tribunal may, after consulting with the parties, appoint a secretary.[94] In some institutions, every task performed by the Dispute Assistant must be specifically approved by the parties to the dispute. For example, the LCIA Arbitration Rules 2020, along with the LCIA Guidance Note for Parties and Arbitrators, states that the specific tasks to be performed by the tribunal secretary must be expressly agreed to by the parties.[95] The Stockholm Chamber of Commerce (SCC) Arbitration Rules also has a similar requirement, where the arbitral tribunal must consult the parties regarding the tasks of the administrative secretary.[96]

Therefore, another way to strengthen the legitimacy of the tasks delegated to the Dispute Assistants is through early and proactive engagement with the parties on the scope of their functions. An attractive solution would be for other DSMs to include provisions similar to the LCIA or the SCC to facilitate the parties' consideration on each aspect of the functions discharged by the Dispute Assistant prior to any delegation. The underlying reason for the concern is addressed when the parties themselves determine which tasks can be legitimately undertaken by the Dispute Assistant without diluting the adjudicators' mandate. Additionally, particularly in arbitration, it will be more difficult for a party to mount a challenge against an arbitrator or award based on the involvement of the Dispute Assistant, if such involvement was made transparent throughout the proceedings and if the parties expressly agreed to this involvement.

While such an extensive procedure for requesting consent from the parties may not be feasible in all DSMs, the same outcome may be achieved through institutional procedures. For example, the primary consent of the parties may be obtained with respect to the Dispute Assistant(s) that are working on a specific dispute. Further, a list of prohibited tasks may be agreed upon by the parties and allowing the parties to raise challenges when the scope of delegation exceeds that which is agreed. This will also increase the transparency and accountability of the functions discharged by the Dispute Assistants.

[91] For example, the rules of the Hong Kong International Arbitration Centre (HKIAC), the Singapore International Arbitration Centre (SIAC), the Stockholm Chamber of Commerce (SCC), the London Court of International Arbitration (LCIA), the International Chamber of Commerce (ICC), the Swiss Chambers' Arbitration Institution (SCAI) and the International Centre for Settlement of Investment Disputes (ICSID).

[92] HKIAC Guidelines 2014, Guideline 2.1; SCAI, Guidelines for Arbitrators (2021), Guideline A1.

[93] SIAC, Arbitration Rules of the Singapore International Arbitration Centre (2025) r 24.1, www.siac.org.sg/siac-rules-2025.

[94] Swiss Rules of International Arbitration (2021, Swiss Chambers' Arbitration Institution), art 16(3).

[95] LCIA, Arbitration Rules (October 2020) (hereniafter 'LCIA Rules 2020') arts 14.8, 14.10(i) and 14.11, read with LCIA Guidance Note for Parties and Arbitrators, para 203.

[96] SCC Arbitration Rules (2017), art 24(2); see also SCC Arbitration Rules (2023), art 24(2).

Such list of prohibited tasks can be coupled with the requirement that the adjudicators maintain an adequate record of tasks delegated and discharged by Dispute Assistant. In order to ensure further transparency and accountability, this list of tasks can be specifically excluded from the scope of secrecy of the deliberations in the case of challenge to the role of Dispute Assistants.

b. Transparency and Specific List of Tasks in the ICJ

In the ICJ, the Instructions to the Registry provide a detailed list of duties for each department and division of the Registry. For example, with respect to the Department of Legal Matters, the Instructions to the Registry provide the following list of duties:

> (a) day-to-day management of case files, including drafting diplomatic correspondence, checking that documents submitted by the parties comply with the Statute and the Rules, and preparing documents for distribution to Members of the Court;
> (b) acting as secretariat to the drafting committees and the Rules Committee;
> (c) drafting the qualités and any other part of the Court's draft judgments and advisory opinions requested by drafting committees, preparing drafts of orders of the Court or of the President, and drafting other legal texts;
> (d) preparing for the President drafts of speeches to be given at public hearings of the Court, including for readings of judgments, advisory opinions and orders;
> (e) drafting notes and carrying out research on points of law, giving legal opinions and providing legal support to the Court's other Departments and Divisions, including in regard to the terms of employment of Registry staff;
> (f) preparing minutes of Court meetings and summaries of decisions of the Rules Committee;
> (g) as needed, preparing minutes of other meetings;
> (h) preparing or supervising preparation of the index to the Reports of Judgments, Advisory Opinions and Orders of the Court;
> (i) selecting documents for publication in the series Pleadings, Oral Arguments and Documents;
> (j) keeping the Court's General List of cases;
> (k) preparing for the President draft lists of points for discussion and decision in accordance with Article 3(i) of the Resolution concerning the Internal Judicial Practice of the Court;
> (l) drafting all necessary documents, notes and correspondence concerning relations between the Court and the host State, including questions relating to the privileges and immunities of Members of the Court and Registry staff.[97]

These institutional rules frame and guide with more clarity the mandate and responsibility of Dispute Assistants. They provided a higher degree of legitimacy to the role of Dispute Assistants by formalising the existing practice, increasing transparency on their functions and attempting to bring accountability.

[97] Instructions for the Registry of the International Court of Justice, art 45, www.icj-cij.org/sites/default/files/documents/instructions-for-the-registry-en.pdf.

In the practices examined above, there is an implicit acceptance that Dispute Assistants can (and do) play an important role in aiding the adjudicators reach their eventual decision in a dispute. The safeguards that are observed across some of the identified DSMs allow adjudicators to utilise the skill and expertise of Dispute Assistants, while also maintaining accountability. The crucial element is safeguarding the consent of the parties through enhanced transparency and accountability for the functions discharged by Dispute Assistants.

E. Risk of Excessive Delegation of Decision-Making through Drafting by Dispute Assistants to Dispute Assistants

i. Examples of Concerns from International Arbitration and the WTO DSS

As explained above, the concerns on excessive delegation specifically relating to drafting by Dispute Assistants is examined in this section. This concern is often shaped by the inference that drafting plays a constitutive role in the decision-making process, and the involvement of Dispute Assistants in drafting in particular can raise legitimacy issues.

The set-aside proceedings in the *Yukos* case raised important questions regarding the permissible role of Dispute Assistants (specifically, External Assistants to the arbitrator). One of the grounds raised was that due to the tribunal assistant's involvement in the tribunal's work, the tribunal failed to comply with its mandate, and this constituted impermissible delegation of the arbitrator's personal tasks. Accordingly, Russia claimed that the awards should be set aside. Russia made several arguments to support their claim, including adducing a report from linguistics experts concluding that it was extremely likely that the tribunal assistant had drafted significant portions of several parts of the award.[98] The Hague Court of Appeal rejected the claim, explaining that the linguistic report could only provide evidence on who wrote a certain text, and not whether the author wrote it on their own authority or under the instructions of someone else.[99] Therefore, even assuming that the tribunal assistant had drafted significant portions of the award (including substantive parts), Russia had failed to establish that the tribunal assistant had participated in the actual decision-making process.[100]

Further, the *Yukos* decision also notably rejects the position that delegation of substantive portions of awards to tribunal secretaries or tribunal assistants is per se impermissible. Rather, the Hague Court of Appeal clarified that irrespective of which portion of the award is drafted by the assistant, what is relevant is that the arbitrators check these texts for correctness and completeness.[101]

With respect to the WTO DSS, scholars have raised a prominent concern on the drafting assistance provided to panellists and AB members by the Secretariat staff

[98] The Report suggested (with more than 95 per cent certainty) that he had written at least 60–70 per cent (Chaski's expert opinion) or at least 41 per cent (Daelemans' expert opinion) of Chapters IX (Preliminary Objections), X (Liability) and XII (Quantum) of the Awards. ibid.

[99] *Yukos* (n 35) para 6.6.6.

[100] ibid.

[101] ibid paras 6.6.9–6.6.10.

and the AB Secretariat staff respectively.[102] As will be discussed further in Part III, others have responded that strong and well-informed adjudicators would be able to retain control over the drafting and, more broadly, over the decision-making process. Adjudicators, may further appreciate knowledgeable and competent assistants' contributions to drafting.[103]

ii. Useful Practices and Procedures on Drafting

We explore two kinds of useful practices/procedures: first, on procedural mechanisms that ensure more participation and engagement by the adjudicators in the decision-making process; and, second, mechanisms that restrict the role of the Dispute Assistants in substantive drafting. Although we discuss them with respect to concerns on drafting, they may become relevant even when Dispute Assistants fulfil other important functions without drafting (for example, with respect to research and collating for adjudicators, or participation in deliberations). Some of these practices generally contribute to ensuring that the adjudicators fulfil their mandate and guard against excessive delegation of their decision-making function.

a. Deliberations Exclusively between the Judges in the CJEU

In the CJEU, a clear procedural framework ensures that judges are firmly in charge of the decision-making process, despite the fact that Dispute Assistants undertake most of the drafting. In the ECJ, the Judge Rapporteur must take a position with respect to the Opinion of the Advocate General, and where there is a difference of Opinion, the President of the Chamber may conduct a 'roundtable' discussion with the other judges in the Chamber to understand their positions. This provides the first instance of exclusive face-to-face interactions between the judges, without the presence of Dispute Assistants. It is only after such interactions that the Judge Rapporteur charges their référendaire with drafting a *projet de motifs* or a first draft of the judgment.

Thereafter, once the draft has been modified based on any comments received from other judges, the judges conduct their deliberations in absolute secrecy. Dispute Assistants are not allowed to attend these deliberations. The procedure leading up to the deliberations is designed to develop and promote consensus among judges by allowing the other judges on the Chamber to provide their views on the *projet* and allowing the Judge Rapporteur to incorporate these into the final judgment. Even the deliberation process between the judges is intended to reach a consensus. According to the outcome of the deliberations, the Judge Rapporteur will instruct their référendaire to prepare a *projet d'arrêt*, incorporating all the final changes to the *projet de motifs modifié*. The face-to-face deliberations conducted by the judges ensure that the judges themselves retain sufficient control over the final draft and that no other actor is able to exert unwarranted

[102] See J Pauwelyn and K Pelc, 'WTO Rulings and the Veil of Anonymity' (2022) 33 *European Journal of International Law* 2527; Pauwelyn and Pelc (n 3) 544. They acknowledge that writing the decision is not the same as deciding the case; however, they maintain that even in merely drafting the ruling itself, the Secretariat exerts considerable influence over the way in which legal interpretations and rulings are worded and argued.

[103] Steinbach (n 4) 565; Sacerdoti (n 4).

influence over the draft. There are no dissenting opinions, partly due to the secrecy of deliberations.

Therefore, the exclusive face-to-face interactions of the judges, in two stages, safeguard against claims that the Dispute Assistants encroach upon the decision-making functions, despite undertaking most of the drafting.

b. Judge Rapporteurs and Successive Levels of Review of a Decision in the ECtHR

In the ECtHR, the procedure contains a different form of procedural safeguard: successive levels of review. This is introduced through the Judge Rapporteur and the Committee/Chamber formation of judges, as well as the role of the Jurisconsult, an Institutional Assistant that is separate from the institutional office doing the drafting. Once the draft is finalised, the Judge Rapporteur shares their draft with the other judges in the Committee or Chamber. The draft is also sent to the Jurisconsult. Thereafter, the other judges may provide comments in writing and the Jurisconsult provides their opinion in writing, before the judges deliberate on the draft. The judges exchange communication with the Judge Rapporteur, with the Section Registrar or Deputy Registrar copied in (Institutional Assistants), on specific issues with the draft. As we have already discussed, the Judge Rapporteur is able to exert de facto control on the Institutional Assistants. Additionally, the role of Jurisconsult ensures the quality and consistency of its case law by advising on legal issues and precedents.[104]

The judges discuss the Chamber drafts at the weekly meeting of the Section. At the Chamber deliberations, the Judge Rapporteur presents the case and the draft. The Section Registrar is present at the deliberations to take account of the votes and discharge other official functions. The case lawyer who assists with drafting the judgment is also present at the deliberations. Neither the Registrar nor the case lawyer participates in the discussions. Participation is reserved for judges, unless the judges request specific clarifications for the case lawyer. The Jurisconsult is also represented at the deliberations, but is only there to observe the outcome of the cases. Thereafter, the judges vote to see if they have reached a majority decision. If there is no majority, the meeting is adjourned, and the case lawyer revises the draft on the basis of the instructions of the Judge Rapporteur and in light of the comments made at the deliberations. The Judge Rapporteur maintains full control over the drafting of the judgment.

If there is a majority opinion reached, the judges review each paragraph of the draft and finalise the judgment. The Judge Rapporteur may make some additional written amendments after the deliberations with assistance from the Registry staff, subject to the written approval of the remaining judges.

Similarly, if the case is before the Grand Chamber, the plenary of the Court conducts a hearing. The case lawyer assigned to the case from the Grand Chamber Registry will attend the hearing. Immediately after the hearings close, the judges convene to have a first deliberation. The Judge Rapporteur presents their report and thereafter the judge of

[104] Rules of Court of the European Court of Human Rights (as amended 1 January 2023), r 18B. Although the judges are not bound by the recommendations of the Jurisconsult, given their experience and specialised institutional knowledge, they are inclined in most cases to accept them.

the respondent state presents a note. The remaining judges then take the floor, with the President appearing last. Through this process, a majority position will emerge, and the President chooses a drafting committee composed of the Judge Rapporteur, the national judge of the respondent state, and three to four judges who presented the majority opinion or the competing opinions clearly. This drafting committee prepares the draft with the Grand Chamber Registry's assistance. The committee then presents the draft to the Grand Chamber during a second deliberation, where the draft is discussed paragraph by paragraph and put to a vote.

Such successive rounds of review and discussion between the judges, with the Judge Rapporteur leading the drafting, ensures that the decision making remains within the hands of the judges while also benefiting from the expertise of the Institutional Assistants from the Registry.

c. Deliberations in Specific Formations and the Constitution of the Drafting Committee in the ICJ

The ICJ has introduced procedural safeguards through successive rounds of deliberations in specific formations, as well as restricting the drafting undertaken by certain categories of Dispute Assistant.

With respect to the deliberations, the first deliberation takes place immediately after the close of the oral procedure, termed the 'Article 3 Deliberation'. In this deliberation, the judges discuss the List of Issues (prepared by the Registry), exchange initial impressions and share guidance for their Notes.[105] The Dispute Assistants do not participate in this deliberation. After this, the individual judges generally prepare their Notes, in which they lay out their views on how the case should be decided. They are supported by their Associate Legal Officers and Judicial Fellows (Assigned Assistants), who may, for example, carry out legal research on specific questions, draft memoranda for the judge's attention or even draft part of the Note. The Notes are thereafter circulated amongst the judges, and the second deliberation, termed the 'Article 5 Deliberation', takes place. At this deliberation, the case is discussed in more detail, with each judge presenting their notes. From these deliberations, a majority view emerges and the drafting committee is composed. Throughout the second deliberation and the forming of the drafting committee, only the Special Assistant to the President and another assistant of the President (Assigned Assistants) are present to take notes. The Registrar (Head of the Institutional Office) also attends and answers any procedural questions that may arise.

The drafting committee comprises two members who most cogently expressed the majority's views and the President. At these meetings, the Associate Legal Officers of the two regular judges and the Special Assistant to the President are present (Assigned Assistants). The Registrar also attends every meeting, accompanied by the Head of the Department of Legal Matters and two lawyers from the Department (Institutional Assistants).[106] The Registrar participates in the discussion and may answer any

[105] H Simma and C Ortgies, 'Deliberation and Drafting: International Court of Justice' in *Max Planck Encyclopedia of Procedural Law* (MPEiPro, 2019) para 43.

[106] ibid 61.

questions raised by the judges. The other Institutional Assistants and Assigned Assistants also intervene in exceptional cases, but only with the permission of their respective Judge/Registrar. The two judges who are part of the drafting committee may draft their parts separately, with the help of their Assigned Assistants, depending on the specific practice of the judge.[107] However, it is unheard of for Assigned Assistants to draft significant parts of the judgment, although they may draft shorter sections on specific topics.

Once the first draft is finished, further deliberations take place. The draft is circulated to all judges for line-by-line written comments, which their Assigned Assistants may help with. The Registry compiles the comments received and circulates the same with the Drafting Committee.[108] The Drafting Committee revises the draft and shares the same with the plenary for the next round of deliberations, the First Reading. During these deliberations, the judges physically meet and debate the draft and comment on it. While some Assigned Assistants and Institutional Assistants are present here,[109] they are not seated with the judges and do not participate.[110] Only the head of the Institutional Office, the Registrar, sits with the judges and participates by answering any questions or clarifications requested by them. This is similar to their role in the drafting committee meetings. Thereafter, the Registry incorporates any agreed changes, and the revised draft is then circulated and discussed at the Second Reading. At the end of the Second Reading, the judges vote to produce the final judgment or advisory opinion.[111] A similar procedural safeguard to that of the CJEU emerges, where the Drafting Committee and the remaining judges must justify their positions directly without input from their Dispute Assistants.

Additionally, there is also another safeguard introduced in the ICJ drafting process. The participation of the staff of the Institutional Office (the Registry and the Department of Legal Matters) in drafting is limited to the *qualités,* ie, the procedural history of the case, as well as the main facts and the summary of arguments. The *qualités* is prepared and circulated to the Court before the first deliberation and then updated.[112] The Registry also prepares the first draft of orders for provisional measures, which is then approved by the President before circulation to the judges, who will carefully study the drafts and make substantial amendments.[113] The Institutional Assistants therefore only participate in the drafting of the procedural aspects, which ensures that they do not give the impression of interfering with the substantive decision-making through drafting. This is especially relevant as these Institutional Assistants are not under the direct supervision or control of the judges and, consequently, their participation in drafting might raise additional concerns.

[107] ibid 62.

[108] ibid 72–73.

[109] The Special Assistant to the President, the two Associate Legal Officers assigned as drafters, and the Registrar, together with certain lawyers from the Department of Legal Matters.

[110] M Hébié, 'Des ombres furtives au Palais de la Paix ? : coup de projecteur sur les assistants juridiques des membres de la Cour internationale de Justice' in JM Thouvenin and JJ Hébart (eds), *La Cour internationale de Justice à 75 ans* (Pedone, 2023) 87.

[111] Resolution on Internal Practice, art 8(i).

[112] H Ollivier and C Hoss, 'Registry: International Court of Justice' in *Max Planck Encyclopedia of Procedural Law* (MPEiPro, 2021) para 20.

[113] Hébié (n 110) 78.

F. Risk of the Conduct of the Dispute Assistant Affecting the Impartiality and Independence of the Adjudicator

i. Examples of Concerns on Lack of Independence/Impartiality of the Dispute Assistant from International Criminal Tribunals and Arbitration Institutions

Here we examine some of the relevant case law which addresses concerns raised in relation to the independence of adjudicators in the context of the functions discharged by Dispute Assistants.

The Statutes establishing the ICTY, the ICC and the STL (referred to collectively as 'International Criminal Tribunals') contain specific demands on the impartiality and integrity of the judges of such institutions. Judges are to be persons of high moral character, impartiality and integrity, who possess the necessary qualifications required in their respective countries for appointment to the highest judicial offices.[114] Although there is no equivalent provision for Legal Officers in Chambers, their role remains integral to the functioning of the tribunal.[115] The challenges and concerns relating to the role of those Legal Officers (Assigned Assistants) has arisen primarily from the lack of clarity in the rules on the appropriate scope of the functions of Legal Officers in Chambers.

One of the earliest instances of such a type of challenge in the ICC was the 2006 *Lubanga* case. The challenge related to the role of the Senior Legal Officer assigned to the pre-trial Chamber, who had previously been a part of the prosecution team.[116] The challenge was decided by the plenary of the ICC, which directed that the Senior Legal Officer be removed from the case. However, the ICC declined to provide any further guidance on the implications of such a conflict of interest or lack of independence for the Legal Officer, and its impact on the independence of the judges of the pre-trial Chamber who continued the trial of the accused.[117]

In 2009, the issue arose before the ICTY during the *Florence Hartmann* (former spokesperson for the ICTY Prosecutor) contempt proceedings for disclosing confidential proceedings.[118] The claims relating to the role of the Senior Legal Officer revolved around Rule 15(A) of the ICTY Rules, which disqualified a judge if they have 'any association which might affect his/her impartiality'. The defence claimed that the Senior Legal Officer assigned to the Chamber had also assisted the amicus curiae in the case. Accordingly, this resulted in bias in the chamber and the association with the Senior

[114] ICTY Statute, art 13; ICTR Statute art 12; ICC Statute art 36(3)(a); Statute of the Special Tribunal for Lebanon, art 9(1). Other tribunals contain similar requirements: SCCL Statute art 13(1); ECCC, Agreement between the UN and the Royal Government of Cambodia Concerning Prosecution under Cambodian Law of Crimes Committed during the Period of Democratic Kampuchea (2003), art 3(3); Statute for the Mechanism of International Criminal Tribunals, art 9(1); Kosovo Law on Specialist Chambers and the Specialist Prosecutor's Office, art 27(1).

[115] *Prosecutor v Zejnil Delalić et al*, Case No IT-96-21-A, Appeals Chamber, 22 April 1999, 4.

[116] *Prosecutor v Thomas Lubanga Dyilo*, Case No ICC01/0401/06, PreTrial Chamber I, 26 October 2006, 2, referring to art 41(2) of the ICC Statute and r 4(2) of the ICC Rules.

[117] *Prosecutor v Thomas Lubanga Dyilo*, Case No ICC01/0401/06, PreTrial Chamber I, 26 October 2006.

[118] *Prosecutor v Florence Hartmann*, Report of Decision on Defence Motion for Disqualification of Two Members of the Trial Chamber and of Senior Legal Officer, Case No IT020540R77.5, Panel, 27 March 2009, paras 2, 18–19, 54.

Legal Officer prejudiced the judge's impartiality. The argument rested on the assumption that Rule 15(A) of the ICTY Rules also applied to the Legal Officers. However, the ICTY held that Rule 15(A) applies only to the judges and not to the Legal Officers, and that the rules did not contemplate the disqualification of chamber staff.[119] Importantly, it clarified that the conduct of Legal Officers were not relevant to the assessment of the impartiality of a judge under Rule 15(A). The principle applied here was that the judicial decision-making was entirely within the control of the judges, without any possible undue influence by the Legal Officer. Therefore, any supposed bias on the part of the legal officer would not bring into question the conduct of the judges themselves.

However, in 2009 the International Criminal Tribunal for Rwanda appeals chamber decision in *Bizimungu et al* may have diluted this clear distinction.[120] In the *Bizimungu* case, the defence argued that the Trial Chamber should refrain from engaging a 'legal consultant' who had previously held the position of 'Deputy Registrar' with the tribunal.[121] It should be noted that this challenge was not about Legal Officers in chamber, but rather a legal consultant hired for a particular case, akin to an External Assistant. The defence relied on Rule 15(A) of the Rules of Procedure of Evidence of the International Criminal Tribunal for Rwanda (ICTR), which provides that a judge may not sit in any case in which they have a personal interest or concerning which they have or have had any association which might affect their impartiality. It was argued that this rule applied to the 'legal consultant' and this alleged bias (or appearance of bias) may be imputed to the judges. While the Trial Chamber rejected these claims on the grounds provided by the earlier ruling of ICTY in *Florence Hartmann*,[122] the findings on appeal are insightful. The Appeals Chamber agreed with the Trial Chamber in rejecting the claim. It noted that the defence based these claims on the erroneous notion that Legal Officers (or 'legal consultants') play a central role in the judges' deliberations.[123] The Legal Officers assist judges in legal research and preparation of draft decisions, judgments, opinions and orders, all as per the judges' instructions. They reaffirmed that the judicial decision-making remained solely within the purview of the judges and therefore the Legal Officers were not subject to the same standard or form or type of impartiality as the judges, including because they are not responsible for taking decisions. However, in obiter, the Appeals Chamber went on to say that in some cases, a

[119] *Prosecutor v Florence Hartmann*, Report of Decision on Defence Motion for Disqualification of Two Members of the Trial Chamber and of Senior Legal Officer, Case No IT020540R77.5, Panel, 27 March 2009, para 54.

[120] Although not among the DSMs specifically examined, the ICTR is comparable to the ICTY in terms of its judicial process, use of Dispute Assistants and sharing of institutional resources. The functions and work of both the ICTY and the ICTR are now maintained through the International Residual Mechanism for Criminal Tribunals (IRMCT).

[121] *Prosecutor v Casimir Bizimungu et al*, Decision on the Objections of the Mugiraneza and Bicamumpaka Defence Teams to the Engagement of Mr Everard O'Donnell as a Chamber Consultant, Case No ICTR9950T, Trial Chamber II, 28 August 2009, paras 1, 4, 7, 8, 11–14, 17.

[122] *Prosecutor v Casimir Bizimungu et al*, Decision on the Objections of the Mugiraneza and Bicamumpaka Defence Teams to the Engagement of Mr Everard O'Donnell as a Chamber Consultant, Case No ICTR9950T, Trial Chamber II, 28 August 2009, para 17.

[123] *Prosecutor v Casimir Bizimungu et al*, Decision on Appeals Concerning the Engagement of a Chambers Consultant of Legal Officer, Case No ICTR9950AR73.8, Appeals Chamber, 17 December 2009, paras 1–3, 5, 6, 8, 9, 11, 15–16.

staff's conduct may be so problematic as to impugn the impartiality (or appearance thereof) of the judges or the fundamental guarantees of fair trial.[124] Although the present case did not satisfy such a high threshold, this obiter qualifies the earlier ruling that staff conduct has no bearing on the impartiality of judges. Parties challenging Legal Officers in subsequent cases have relied on this obiter to give strength to their claims, but their challenges have been unsuccessful.[125] The judgments have reaffirmed the position that the conduct of the Legal Officers does not meet the threshold to impugn the impartiality of the judges.

The concern that often arises in the context of International Criminal Tribunals relates to the lack of impartiality/independence of the Legal Officers (Assigned Assistants), and its impact on claims of potential bias or lack of independence by the judges. As we have seen above, case law has reiterated that the decision-making is within the sole purview of the judges, despite the involvement of the Legal Officers through various stages of the trial process, including drafting. Therefore, the position in the International Criminal Tribunals has been that generally a Legal Officer's conduct should have no bearing on a judge's independence, impartiality or fair trial guarantees for the accused. However, as alluded to in *Bizimungu*, there remains the possibility that the conduct of the Legal Officer may be so problematic that they impugn the impartiality or independence of the judges. The solution to these concerns must also account and guard against such an extreme case, where the decision-making may no longer be in the hands of the judges.

Now, turning to arbitration institutions, explicit provisions for the challenge to Dispute Assistants are found in some domestic legislation,[126] arbitration rules, and some international provisions of international tribunals and institutions.[127] The right to challenge tribunal secretaries or assistants is derived from an analogous application of the provisions on arbitrator challenges,[128] and therefore the grounds for challenge to arbitrators apply to tribunal secretaries.[129] This includes the grounds of lack of impartiality and independence of the tribunal secretaries.[130]

[124] ibid 15–16.

[125] *Prosecutor v Pauline Nyiramasuhuko et al*, Judgment and Sentence, Case No ICTR9842T, Trial Chamber II, 24 June 2011, paras 204, 271, 273–74; *Prosecutor v Ratko Mladic*, Decision on Defence Motion for a Fair Trial and the Presumption of Innocence or, in the Alternative, a Mistrial, Case No ICTR0992T, Trial Chamber I, 4 July 2016, paras 1, 2, 5, 18, 24, 26; *Prosecutor v Ratko Mladic*, Decision on Interlocutory Appeal against the Decision on Defence Motion for a Fair Trial and the Presumption of Innocence, Case No IT0992AR73.6, Appeals Chamber, 27 February 2017, para 1.

[126] Dutch Code of Civil Procedure, art 1035 read with art 1033(1); Swiss Code of Civil Procedure, art 365(2) read with arts 367–69; Colombian Arbitration Law 2012 (Law No 1563 of 12 July 2012), arts 16(1), 55.

[127] Arbitration Rules of the Arbitration Institute of the Stockholm Chamber of Commerce (2017), arts 24(5) and 19 (hereinafter 'SCC Rules 2017'); Swiss Rules of International Arbitration (2012), arts 15(5) and 9–11 (hereinafter 'Swiss Rules 2012'); LCIA, Notes for Arbitrators (26 October 2017), s 80 read with LCIA Arbitration Rules (2014), art 10; HKIAC Guidelines 2014, s 2.7.

[128] Either from the relevant domestic law or institutional rules, read together with IBA Guidelines on Conflict of Interest in International Arbitration, approved by the IBA Council, 25 May 2024.

[129] Jensen (n 36).

[130] Dutch Code of Civil Procedure, arts 1033(1), 1035a; Swiss Code of Civil Procedure, arts 365(2), 367(1)(c); SCC Rules (2017), arts 19(1), 24(5); HKIAC Guidelines 2014, s 2.10. See also IBA Guidelines on Conflict of Interest in International Arbitration, approved by the IBA Council, 25 May 2024.

In *Victor Pey Casado and President Allende Foundation v Republic of Chile*, Chile challenged the ICSID secretary assigned to the tribunal. Two grounds were raised: first, that the secretary had carried out an internship with the investor's law firm; and, second, that the secretary's father was currently serving on the law firm's 'scientific council' (with no connection to the specific case).[131] The challenge was accepted and the secretary was replaced with a different staff member.[132] However, it is unclear whether such a decision was motivated by doubts as to the independence of the secretary or, rather, to avoid further procedural delays.[133]

Challenges to Dispute Assistants have also been raised for 'issue conflicts'. They arise from an arbitrator's previous/concurrent engagement with an issue that is central to the dispute[134] – for example, when the arbitrator has previously published/spoken on an open question in the dispute. A similar claim arose in the set-aside proceedings for the *Yukos* case, where the assistant had published an article on calculation of damages in cases of unlawful expropriation (which was a central issue in the case). This was raised as a ground to oppose the enforcement of the awards, claiming that the assistant allegedly 'expressed distinctive views on issues that were squarely before the Tribunal'.[135] However, this claim was not successful.

The WTO Rules of Conduct also allow a party to challenge the independence, impartiality and lack of respect of confidentiality of a WTO legal staff involved in any dispute settlement procedures. Although these proceedings are confidential, William Davey (former Director of the LAD) notes that:

> Two sorts of problems have arisen for the Secretariat. First, because some secretariat staff have served in Member governments in positions dealing with cases that may come before the WTO, the Secretariat ensures that such staff members do not work on those cases . . . Second, there are situations where a Secretariat staff member may be in a relationship with someone outside the WTO who works for a WTO member or a private entity that advises on WTO issues. In such a case, the individuals involved are counseled to be super careful about not talking about such matters with their partners.[136]

Therefore, in some cases, the concerns relating to the impartiality and independence of the Dispute Assistants can have an impact on the independence of the adjudicator or the dispute resolution process. This is especially a concern when there is a lack of formal rules regulating the impartiality and independence of Dispute Assistants, or procedures for accountability of Dispute Assistants.

131 *Victor Pey Casado and President Allende Foundation v Republic of Chile*, ICSID Case No ARB/98/2, Proposal for Disqualification of Two Members of the Arbitral Tribunal, Sir Franklin Berman and Mr VV Veeder (22 November 2016), para 57.

132 *ibid* para 59.

133 Jensen (n 36) 320.

134 W Park, 'Arbitrator Integrity: The Transient and the Permanent' (2009) 46 *San Diego Law Review* 629, 648–50; M Hwang and K Lim, 'Issue Conflict in ICSID Arbitrations' in M Hwang, E Chan and E Lim (eds), *Selected Essays on International Arbitration* (Academy Publishing, 2013) 474.

135 Russian Federation, 'Respondent's Motion to Deny Confirmation of Yukos Awards Pursuant to the New York Convention', US District Court for the District of Columbia (2015) Case No 1:14-cv-01996 (ABJ) 37.

136 WJ Davey, 'Gabrielle Marceau and the WTO Dispute Settlement Rules of Conduct' in *International Trade Law: Past, Present and Future, Tribute to Gabrielle Marceau* (Revue québécoise de droit international, September 2025) 308–21, at 316.

ii. Useful Practices/Procedures on Codes of Conduct with Disclosures and Accountability of Dispute Assistants

In relation to Code of Conducts, there are various examples where general conflict-of-interest and ethical obligations are applicable to Dispute Assistants.

For example, in the ACtHPR, the staff of the registry are international civil servants who are subject to the Staff Regulations and Rules and any other applicable instruments of the African Union. The Staff Regulations of the African Union specify that the staff shall uphold the highest standards of efficiency, competence and integrity, guided by probity, impartiality, confidentiality, fairness, honesty and truthfulness.[137] In the IACtHR, all Secretariat staff are international civil servants subject to the Organization of American States General Secretariat's administrative standards.[138] The administrative standards provide general obligations relating to autonomy in the performance of duties,[139] refraining from any action that may be incompatible with their position as staff members of the OAS,[140] or acting or expressing themselves publicly in any way that might damage or adversely affect the Member State,[141] and confidentiality.[142] There is also a Code of Ethics that generally governs the staff of the OAS, which states in terms of 'conflict of interest' that the staff 'must at all times act in the best interests of the OAS in the performance of their duties. They must observe all OAS policies prohibiting competing personal, financial, or professional interests from interfering in the performance of their duties'.[143] In ICSID, tribunal secretaries and any appointed assistants are bound by the confidentiality of deliberations and proceedings, like the arbitrators.[144] Even externally appointed assistants must also sign the same declaration of independence and impartiality as the arbitrators.[145] Before the PCA, the staff are bound by the Rules Concerning the Organization and Internal Working of the International Bureau,[146] which contains five articles. The only specific obligation is in Article V, which imposes confidentiality obligations stating that the staff of the International Bureau 'are forbidden to communicate to persons outside the Bureau . . . any information concerning the business entrusted to them in the course of their work, or to allow such persons any access to the documents pertaining to the work of the Bureau'.

In this section, we will detail the practices and procedures where specific obligations relating to Dispute Assistants have been introduced.

a. The Code of Conduct of Référendaires of the CJEU

The référendaires (ie, the Assigned Assistants) are bound by a code of conduct,[147] in addition to staff regulations that are generally applicable to the staff of the EU. These

[137] African Union Staff Regulations and Rules (adopted 7 November 2022) r 3.3.
[138] Statute of the InterAmerican Court of Human Rights (IACtHR), art 14.1
[139] Administrative Standards (Organization of American States, OAS), art 29.
[140] ibid art 30.1.
[141] ibid art 30.2.
[142] ibid art 31.
[143] Code of Conduct (OAS), Part V.
[144] ICISD Arbitration Rules, rr 34.1, 66.
[145] ICSID, 'Tribunal Assistants', www.icsid.worldbank.org/procedures/arbitration/convention/for-icsid-tribunal-assistants.
[146] Rules Concerning the Organization and Internal Working of the International Bureau of the Permanent Court of Arbitration (18 December 1900).
[147] CJEU, *Décision du 17 février 2009 portant adoption des règles de bonne conduite des Référendaires* (European Court of Justice).

provisions impose various duties on référendaires, including duties to abstain in cases when in the past they have been involved or have supported or advised one of the parties.[148] Furthermore, in relation to instances where the référendaires wish to publicly express their opinions in academic writings and/or public speaking events, they must obtain prior authorisation to do so.[149] Once they have ceased their work, the référendaires are precluded from participating in any way in cases pending if they have participated in them before.[150] However, the rules do not provide any explicit remedy in the event of a breach of the duties. Commentators have noted that this is probably due to the fact that the référendaires' position depends on a relationship based on trust with their supervisor, the judge or Advocate General. Therefore, any breach of these rules is tantamount to a breach of the relation of trust that serves as the basis of the référendaires' position,[151] and it is the responsibility of their supervisor to take the necessary action.

b. Staff Regulations for the Registry and Instructions for the Registry of the ICJ

The staff of the Registry of the ICJ are bound by the staff regulations for the Registry and the instructions for the Registry, as well as some relevant provisions of the UN Staff Regulations and Staff Rules. All the staff of the ICJ Registry are international civil servants[152] and are prohibited from seeking or accepting instructions from any government or from any other source external to the ICJ.[153] Furthermore, the Registry staff are required to uphold the 'highest standards of efficiency, competence and integrity. The concept of integrity includes, but is not limited to, probity, impartiality, fairness, honesty and truthfulness in all matters affecting their work and status'.[154] They are required to avoid any action and, in particular, any kind of public pronouncement that may adversely reflect on their status, or on the integrity, independence and impartiality that are required by that status.[155]

In terms of conflict of interest, the UN Staff Regulations provide that this occurs when, by act or omission, a staff member's personal interests interferes with the performance of their official duties and responsibilities or with the integrity, independence and impartiality required by the staff member's status as an international civil servant.[156] When an actual or possible conflict of interest does arise, the registry staff have an obligation to disclose the same to the Registrar. The UN Staff Rules elaborate further on certain conduct requirements of the staff, but these are general (for example, prohibition of discrimination or actions with malicious intent, or refusing honours or gifts)[157] and are not specific to dispute settlement. With respect to conflict of interest, the staff rules provide that staff members shall formally recuse themselves from any involvement in a

[148] Sarmiento (n 30) 11.
[149] ibid.
[150] ibid.
[151] ibid.
[152] United Nations Staff Regulations (hereinafter 'UN Staff Regulations'), art I r 1.1(a).
[153] Staff Regulations for the Registry of the International Court of Justice (hereinafter 'ICJ Staff Regulations'), art 2.
[154] ibid art 3.
[155] ibid art 4.
[156] UN Staff Regulations, art I r 1.2(m).
[157] ibid r 1.2(a), (b), (f)–(i), (k), (p), (r)–(u).

matter which might give rise to an actual or possible conflict of interest as per the staff regulation.[158]

The Instructions to the Registry provide a detailed list of duties for each department and division of the Registry. However, there is no mechanism for challenging a staff member for violation of these obligations by the state parties to the ICJ Statute.

c. Staff Rules and Staff Regulations of ITLOS

In ITLOS, the Registry staff are subject to the Staff Regulations and Staff Rules. The Staff Rules provide specific instances of prohibited conduct, including that the 'Staff members shall not seek to influence States Parties *or the Tribunal* in order to obtain a change from a position or decision taken by the Tribunal or the Registrar, or in order to secure support for improving their personal situation or the personal situation of other staff members, or for blocking or reversing unfavourable decisions regarding their status or their colleagues' status'.[159] The specific conflict-of-interest provisions in the Staff Rules relate to instances where the staff member has a 'financial interest'. The staff of the registry are international civil servants[160] and are prohibited from accepting or seeking instructions from any government or authority external to the Tribunal.[161] Furthermore, they are required to refrain from any action and, in particular, any kind of public pronouncement which may adversely reflect on their status or on their integrity, independence and impartiality as international civil servants.[162] They are subject to confidentiality requirements[163] and the same rules of secrecy of the deliberations as the judges[164]

d. The IBA Guidelines on Conflict of Interest in International Arbitration

In international arbitration, arbitrators are required to make disclosures to allow parties to identify and assess potential conflicts of interest, and for institutions and national courts to address challenges properly. The IBA Guidelines on Conflict of Interest in International Arbitration have been recognised as a solid soft law instrument reflecting standards expected to apply to conflicts of interests (ie, impartiality and independence), as well as disclosures in specific circumstances.[165] The Guidelines have General Standards for evaluating a conflict of interest and the obligation to disclose, as well as traffic light-coded illustrative lists ('Red', 'Orange' and 'Green') to assist arbitrators with disclosures, and to assist parties to assess the disclosures. The scope of the Guidelines includes 'arbitral or administrative secretaries and assistants', which reads:

[158] UN Staff Rules, r 1.2(p).
[159] Staff Rules of the International Tribunal for the Law of the Sea (ITLOS), r 1.2(j) (emphasis added).
[160] Staff Regulations, International Tribunal for the Law of the Sea (ITLOS), r 1.1.
[161] ibid art 1.3.
[162] ibid art 1.4.
[163] ibid art 1.5.
[164] Rules of the Tribunal, International Tribunal for the Law of the Sea (ITLOS), art 42.1.
[165] Jensen (n 36) 319; IBA Guidelines on Conflict of Interest in International Arbitration, approved by the IBA Council, 25 May 2024.

> Arbitral or administrative secretaries and assistants, to an individual arbitrator or the Arbitral Tribunal, are bound by the same duty of independence and impartiality as arbitrators, and it is the responsibility of the Arbitral Tribunal to ensure that such duty is respected at all stages of the arbitration.

The standard to assess the conflict of interest is if facts or circumstances exist, or have arisen since the appointment, which from the point of view of a reasonable third person would give rise to justifiable doubts as to the arbitrator's (or, in this case, the tribunal secretary's/assistants') impartiality or independence.[166] The doubts are considered justified if such a reasonable third person would reach the conclusion that there is a likelihood that the arbitrator (or the tribunal secretary/assistant) may be influenced by factors other than the merits of the case in their decision-making process.[167] Part II of the Guidelines contains the Practical Application of the General Standards, with the traffic light-coded lists providing illustrative situations. We briefly describe these below. Although we do not repeat the examples provided in the lists, they are a useful framework for how a specific code of conduct can be framed:

a) The Red List, which has two parts: a 'Non-waivable Red List' and a 'Waivable Red List'. These both describe situations which give rise to justifiable doubts as to the arbitrator's impartiality or independence. The Non-waivable List contains situations which cannot be resolved with acceptance by the parties. The Waivable List covers situations that are not as severe, but are still serious and require the parties to expressly state their willingness to have this person as the arbitrator after becoming aware of the situation. This is an objective standard of conflict of interest. For example, in the Non-waivable Red List, entries include instances where the arbitrator currently or regularly advises a party, or an affiliate of a party, and the arbitrator or the arbitrator's firm or employer derives significant financial income from this.[168] From the Waivable Red List, many entries could have a bearing on the Dispute Assistants. One example is where the arbitrator's law firm or employer had a previous but terminated involvement in the case without the arbitrator being involved themselves.[169] Dispute Assistants in the early stages of their employment may have had internships at many law firms, which increases the risk of such a conflict arising.[170]

b) The Orange List, which contains situations that, depending on the facts of a given case, may, in the eyes of the parties, give rise to doubts as to the arbitrator's impartiality or independence; therefore, the arbitrator has a duty to disclose such situations. In these situations, the parties are deemed to have accepted the arbitrator if, after disclosure, no timely objection is made. This is a subjective conflict-of-interest standard. Examples from this list that would be relevant in the case of Dispute Assistants include where the arbitrator has publicly advocated a position on the case, whether in a published paper or speech, through social media or online professional networking platforms, or

[166] IBA Guidelines on Conflict of Interest in International Arbitration, approved by the IBA Council, 25 May 2024, General Standard 2(b).
[167] ibid.
[168] ibid Part 2, Entry 1.4.
[169] ibid Part 2, Entry 2.3.5.
[170] Jensen (n 36) 320.

otherwise.[171] However, given that this is included within the Orange List, it is not subject to conflict-of-interest concerns per se; rather, as best practice, it would be about making appropriate disclosures to the parties.

c) The Green List, which covers situations where no appearance and no actual conflict of interest can exist either under the subjective or the objective standard; thus, the arbitrator has no duty to disclose situations falling within the Green List. A notable example of an entry in this list is where the arbitrator has previously expressed a legal opinion (such as in a law review article or public lecture) concerning an issue that also arises in the arbitration (but this opinion is not focused on the case).[172] As we have seen previously, this was raised as a concern on the role of the tribunal assistant in the *Yukos* proceedings and was rejected as a valid ground for challenge.

In several commercial arbitration institutions, the Dispute Assistants are explicitly under the same obligations as the arbitrators. For example, under LCIA, the tribunal secretary is also subject to a continuing duty to disclose any circumstances that 'are likely to give rise in the mind of any party to any justifiable doubts as to [their] impartiality or independence'.[173] Such a requirement may be replicated in other DSMs to safeguard against challenges to legitimate cases of delegation. However, even in institutions that are not specifically providing for such coverage in the rules, the IBA Guidelines provide that the Dispute Assistants are within the scope of such independence and impartiality obligations.

e. The WTO Rules of Conduct

Although we will examine this in more detail in Part III, the procedure of the WTO DSS is relevant for other DSMs as well. Specifically, the WTO Rules of Conduct for the Understanding on Rules and Procedures Governing the Settlement of Disputes 1996 (hereinafter 'WTO Rules of Conduct')[174] provide a useful guide for procedures to ensure the accountability of Dispute Assistants. The WTO Rules of Conduct require covered persons to be independent and impartial, to avoid direct or indirect conflicts of interest and to maintain confidentiality.[175] The covered persons in these rules include the adjudicators, as well as the Secretariat Staff and the AB Secretariat Staff.[176]

[171] IBA Guidelines on Conflict of Interest in International Arbitration, *approved* by the IBA Council, 25 May 2024, General Standard 2(c), Part 2, Entry 3.4.2.

[172] ibid Part 2, Entry 4.1.1.

[173] LCIA Rules 2020, art 14.14.

[174] Davey (n 136) 316.

[175] WTO Rules of Conduct for the Understanding on Rules and Procedures Governing the Settlement of Disputes (1996), arts II, IV (covered persons).

[176] In several AB proceedings involving requests for additional procedures to protect confidential information, the AB has confirmed that Secretariat staff and experts advising panels are subject to the confidentiality requirements in the Rules of Conduct: Appellate Body Report, *Canada – Measures Affecting the Export of Civilian Aircraft*, WT/DS70/AB/R (2 August 1999) para 146; Appellate Body Report, *Brazil – Export Financing Programme for Aircraft*, WT/DS46/AB/R (2 August 1999) para 124; Appellate Body Report, *European Communities and Certain Member States – Measures Affecting Trade in Large Civil Aircraft*, WT/DS316/AB/R (18 May 2011) Annex III, para 17; Appellate Body Report, *United States/Canada – Continued Suspension of Obligations in the EC – Hormones Dispute*, WT/DS320/AB/R (16 October 2008) paras 435, 442. Panels have made similar statements in respect of panellists, Secretariat staff, and experts advising panels: Panel Report, *Australia – Measures Affecting Importation of Salmon (Article 21.5 – Canada)*, WT/DS18/RW (18 February

The WTO Rules of Conduct provide a comprehensive procedure to challenge and possibly disqualify a covered person where there is evidence of a material violation of the obligations contained in the Rules of Conduct that may impair the integrity and impartiality of the dispute settlement mechanism.[177] Specific procedure is provided for each category of covered persons:

- In the case of Secretariat staff, a complaint is lodged with the WTO DG. The evidence of a material violation of the Rules of Conduct is to be lodged only with the DG, who shall provide it to the staff member; consult with the staff member who is challenged and with the panel; if necessary, take appropriate disciplinary action in accordance with the Staff regulations; and inform the parties to the dispute, the panel and the Chairperson of the DSB.
- In the case of the AB Secretariat staff, a complaint was to be lodged with the AB, which would take the final decision. The evidence of a material violation of the Rules of Conduct was to be provided to the other disputing party and thereafter to the AB and the person concerned, and a decision was taken by the AB. The persons concerned and the parties would be heard, and the decision would be reported to the parties and the Chair of the DSB, with relevant supporting information. The same procedure is followed for the MPIA today.

Therefore, under these rules, a disputing party could challenge the role of the Institutional Assistants on the specific grounds provided.[178]

II. The Theoretical Basis for Concerns and Their Relationship with Legitimacy

Now we turn to the theoretical foundations that underpin the concerns identified above and examine their relationship with legitimacy of the dispute resolution process. We begin with a brief discussion of the concept of 'legitimacy' employed by us here.

The concept of legitimacy travels through different disciplines, picking up various traits and features along the way. While several scholars have examined this important and evolving concept in more general terms,[179] we restrict our discussion here to legitimacy as it applies to international dispute resolution mechanisms and the role of Dispute Assistants. Our analysis builds on the critical work undertaken by Freya Baetens and other authors in *Legitimacy of Unseen Actors in International Adjudication*.[180] We

2000) para 7.7; Panel Report, *European Communities – Export Subsidies on Sugar (Australia)*, WT/DS265/R (15 October 2004) paras 2.13, 2.18 fn 8; Panel Report, *Australia – Measures Affecting the Importation of Apples from New Zealand*, WT/DS367/R (9 August 2010) para 7.24.

[177] WTO Rules of Conduct for the Understanding on Rules and Procedures Governing the Settlement of Disputes (1996), art VIII.

[178] However, these proceedings would be confidential, and consequently no publicly available instances of such challenges exist.

[179] TM Franck, *Fairness in International Law and Institutions* (Oxford University Press, 1998) 7, 22, 25–26; R Wolfrum and V Röben (eds), *Legitimacy in International Law* (Springer, 2008); N Grossman, HG Cohen, A Føllesdal and G Ulfstein (eds), *Legitimacy and International Courts* (Cambridge University Press, 2018).

[180] F Baetens (ed), *Legitimacy of Unseen Actors in International Adjudication* (Cambridge University Press, 2019).

have tried to expand this study by assessing the concerns that arise across 20 DSMs and undertaking a comparative analytical study across this wider set of mechanisms, actors and practice.

We understand legitimacy as the justification of authority, which, in the case of international courts and tribunals, is the justification of authority to resolve disputes or decide cases.[181] Scholars have identified two distinct yet related facets of legitimacy: a normative dimension, and a sociological dimension.[182] Normative legitimacy is about the authority per se of an international court or tribunal.[183] On the other hand, sociological legitimacy is about the *perception* of authority. If the parties to an international court or tribunal consider its judgment/order/decision to have authority, then it has sociological legitimacy.[184] The parties may disagree with a specific judgment/order/decision without questioning its overall authority to render judgments/orders/decisions.[185] Although the normative and sociological facets are distinct, they are by no means disconnected.

The aim of this section is not to undertake a comprehensive overview of all elements of legitimacy of international courts and tribunals. Rather, we tap into three elements that impact normative and sociological legitimacy: consent; independence and diligence of adjudicators; and procedural fairness and transparency. While there may other elements within the multidimensional concept of legitimacy, we limit ourselves here to these three elements in our efforts to understand its relationship with the concerns on the role of Dispute Assistants identified in this book

First, international courts and tribunals are created on the basis of state *consent*.[186] Both normative and sociological elements of legitimacy are closely tied to the 'consent' of states and other parties to submit to the jurisdiction of such institutions.[187] In section II.A, we discuss how the concerns on the role of Dispute Assistants may impact this foundational consent, and consequently, the legitimacy of the dispute resolution process of the DSMs.

Second, an important facet of the authority of international courts and tribunals is the *independence and diligence of its adjudicators*.[188] In section II.B, we discuss how the concerns on the role of Dispute Assistants may adversely impact the independence and diligence expected from adjudicators and, consequently, the legitimacy of DSMs.

Lastly, the procedural legitimacy (ie, the manner of decision-making) also has an impact on the sociological and normative legitimacy of international courts

[181] D Bodansky, 'The Legitimacy of International Governance: A Coming Challenge for International Environmental Law?' (1999) 93 *American Journal of International Law* 596, 601.

[182] N Grossman, 'Legitimacy and International Adjudicative Bodies' (2009) 41 *George Washington International Law Review* 107. For a list of such scholars, see F Baetens, 'Unseen Actors in International Courts and Tribunals: Challenging the Legitimacy of International Adjudication' in Baetens (n 180) fn 12.

[183] HG Cohen, A Føllesdal, N Grossman and G Ulfstein, 'Legitimacy and International Courts: A Framework' in Grossman et al (n 179) 1–40.

[184] ibid.

[185] RO Keohane and A Buchanan, 'The Legitimacy of Global Governance Institutions' (2006) 20(4) *Ethics & International Affairs* 405, 410; E Voeten, 'Public Opinion and the Legitimacy of International Courts' (2013) 14 *Theoretical Inquiries in Law* 411, 415.

[186] M Kumm, 'The Legitimacy of International Law: A Constitutionalist Framework of Analysis' (2004) 15 *European Journal of International Law* 907, 907–08.

[187] Y McDermott and W Elmaalul, 'Legitimacy' in WA Schabas and S Murphy (eds), *Research Handbook on International Courts and Tribunals* (Edward Elgar, 2017) 229–31.

[188] EA Posner and JC Yoo, 'Judicial Independence in International Tribunals' (2005) 93 *California Law Review* 3.

and tribunals.[189] In section II.C, we discuss how the concerns on the role of Dispute Assistants may adversely impact transparency and procedural fairness, and, consequently, the legitimacy of DSMs.

A. The Effect of Concerns on the Consent of the Parties

International adjudication, in contrast to domestic adjudication, owes its creation and mandate to party consent.[190] Various legal and political scholars have debated whether such state consent is in and of itself sufficient to establish legitimacy.[191] While we do not claim that state consent is the exclusive basis for legitimacy, it still remains an important facet of it. Therefore, in this section, we examine how the concerns over the role of Dispute Assistants impact state consent.

To recount our discussions in Part I, the consent to international adjudication is established in different ways across the DSMs examined:

- In some cases, the DSM is established through a treaty amongst states, which specifies, inter alia, its functions, a standing body of adjudicators, designates the law it may apply and mandates specific procedures. These are the ACtHPR, the CJEU, the COMESA Court of Justice, the EACJ, the ECOWAS Court of Justice, the ECtHR, the EFTA Court, the IACtHR, the ICJ, the ICC,[192] ITLOS, and the AB of the WTO DSS (when it was operational) and today, the MPIA. Similarly, the ICTY was established by the Security Council (SC) and functioned in accordance with the ISCTY Statute, and the STL was established by an agreement between the UN and the Lebanese Republic and functioned in accordance with the Statute of the STL (SC Resolution 1757 (2007)).[193] The specific consent to submit a dispute may require additional steps like a *compromis* or subsequent treaty designating a particular forum.
- In some other cases, the DSM is established by states through a treaty to facilitate the resolution of a disputes, of a specific subject matter/set of disputes, with ad hoc adjudicators appointed by the parties in a specific dispute (in some cases from a pre-established roster). The treaties capture the consent of the parties to be bound by the decision of such bodies, as well as the mandate of the adjudicators. This includes

[189] Wolfrum and Röben (n 179) 6–7; S Treves, 'Aspects of Legitimacy', 171–73; A Cassese, 'The Legitimacy of International Criminal Tribunals', 493; Cohen et al (n 183) 1–40.

[190] Bodansky (n 181) 605: 'Legal legitimacy is what connects an institution's continuing authority to its original basis in state consent. The authority of the International Court of Justice, for example, derives from its Statute to which UN Member States consented. And the Court's continuing authority depends on its acting in accordance with the Statute. If it went outside or against the Statute, then its actions would lack legitimacy.'

[191] A Buchanan, *Justice, Legitimacy, and Self-Determination: Moral Foundation for International Law* (Oxford University Press, 2004) 303; A Osiander, 'Sovereignty, International Relations and the Westphalian Myth' (2001) 55 *International Organization* 251; WJ Magnuson, 'The Responsibility to Protect and the Decline of Sovereignty: Free Speech Protection under International Law' (2010) 43 *Vanderbilt Journal of Transnational Law* 255.

[192] D Akande, 'The Jurisdiction of the International Criminal Court over Nationals of Nonparties: Legal Basis and Limits' (2003) 1 *Journal of International Criminal Justice* 618. Given that nationals of non-party states can be tried under certain circumstances, and crimes committed on the territory of non-party states can be prosecuted following a United Nations Security Council referral of the situation to the prosecutor, there are concerns as to whether the sufficient standard of state consent is met.

[193] Similar to the ICC, concerns may arise that such a resolution is insufficient to establish consent, as it does not include the state whose nationals are subject to trial.

ICSID, the IUSCT, the PCA (in some cases), the USMCA, MERCOSUR and the WTO DSS.

- Lastly, with respect to commercial arbitration institutions, individual ad hoc arbitral tribunals are set up for each case, with the tribunal's exact composition varying according to the parties' agreement and the applicable arbitral rules.[194] The institution assists the parties to varying degrees, as we have seen in detail in Chapter 5. The consent of the parties to such arbitration, and the rules of the commercial arbitration institution, is established through the arbitration agreement.

From the above, we can see that although the 'consent' is manifested through different instruments, the adjudicative process across the DSMs receives its authority from the consent of the parties. This clearly forms a part of the normative legitimacy of the institution.

Now, turning to how the specific concerns impact the consent of the parties, we start with concerns that arise with respect to asymmetry between the adjudicator and the Dispute Assistant. When Dispute Assistants are more permanent than the adjudicators, there is a risk that the Dispute Assistants may unduly influence the decision-making process of the adjudicators. The consent of the parties, through whichever form it is manifested, was provided for the decision-making *by the adjudicators*, not the Assistants. At the same time, in most institutions, the existence of Dispute Assistants is acknowledged in the founding documents or implicitly by the parties. However, this is not sufficient, because those concerns arise from the *perception* of legitimacy. The *perception* that the mandate has been exceeded is what puts the legitimacy of the DSM at risk.

Concerns on excessive delegation of tasks, including drafting, to the Dispute Assistants raises the concern that the adjudicators did not actually fulfil their mandate as provided by the consent of the states. This goes beyond perception and raises normative concerns on the legitimacy of the adjudicative process, and whether the parties consented to such delegation. These concerns have arisen most prominently in the context of arbitration, as the arbitrator has a duty to apply their mind personally to the dispute which is linked to the *intuitu personae* nature of their appointment.[195] For example, the International Chamber of Commerce Rules require the arbitrator to 'establish the facts of the case'[196] and to make a reasoned[197] and enforceable award.[198] The LCIA Rules require the arbitrator to impose a form of social order by deciding the parties' dispute[199] and producing a written reasoned award.[200] However, as we have seen, the arbitration agreement is merely one form through which the consent of the parties is manifested. Although not of a similar personal nature, the appointments of adjudicators in other DSMs also carry with them the same responsibility to apply their mind and decide the dispute. This goes directly to the normative legitimacy of the dispute resolution process.

[194] G Born, *International Commercial Arbitration*, 3rd edn (Wolters Kluwer, 2021) 1764.
[195] C Sim, 'The Essence of Adjudication: The Legitimacy of Case Managers in International Arbitration' in Baetens (n 180).
[196] ICC, Arbitration Rules (2017), r 25(1).
[197] ibid r 32.
[198] ibid r 35.
[199] LCIA, Arbitration Rules (2014), rr 22.3, 26.5.
[200] ibid r 26.2.

B. The Effect of Concerns on the Independence and Diligence of Adjudicators

An important element of procedural fairness and legitimacy is the independence and diligence of the adjudicator. In consenting to an adjudicative process, states seek to ensure that their disputes will be decided by fair and unbiased adjudicators. If adjudicators lack independence and impartiality, then the dispute settlement mechanism may be seen as lacking justified authority.

Concerns have arisen such that the independence or impartiality of the Dispute Assistant could in turn impact the independence of the adjudicator. As a caveat, we admit that it is difficult and almost impossible to develop global ethical standards across DSMs on what constitutes 'independence'.[201] Our aim is not to reach such a standard, but rather to show that each DSM expects certain ethical standards of independence from its adjudicators, and how the role of Dispute Assistants can impact them.

We start by examining the relevant provisions across the DSMs that impose ethical standards on adjudicators. For the sake of clarity, we start with mechanisms with permanent adjudicators and then discuss mechanisms for ad hoc adjudicators. From these provisions, it is clear that even with differing language across institutions, there is a minimum expectation of independence, impartiality and some form of diligence in performance of their duties:

- The ACtHPR: The judges are elected in their individual capacity from among jurists of high moral character and recognised practical, judicial or academic competence and experience in the field of human and peoples' rights.[202] They take an oath to discharge their duties, 'honourably, faithfully, independently, impartially and conscientiously'.[203] In terms of independence, it is specified that this shall be ensured in accordance with 'international law'.[204] Further, the rules of the court note that no judge shall hear the case if they have previously acted as an advocate etc for one of the parties, have a personal interest in the case, have a personal or professional relationship with any of the parties, have expressed opinions publicly that may affect their impartiality, or any other reason that may call into doubt their impartiality or independence.[205]
- The CJEU: The judges of the CJEU take an oath to perform their duties impartially and conscientiously and to preserve the secrecy of the deliberations of the CJEU.[206] The judges may not hold any political or administrative office or engage in any occupation (unless specifically exempted). Furthermore, they are subject to certain restriction on appointments after their term of office.[207] They may not take part in any case in which they have previously taken part for one of the parties, or as a

[201] Y Shany, 'Squaring the Circle? Independence and Impartiality of Party-Appointed Adjudicators in International Legal Proceedings' (2008) 30 *Loyola of Los Angeles International and Comparative Law Review* 473.

[202] Protocol on the Establishment of the African Court of Human and Peoples' Rights, art 11.

[203] ibid art 16. See also Rules of the Court, ACtHPR, r 3.

[204] Protocol on the Establishment of the African Court of Human and Peoples' Rights, art 17. See also Rules of the Court, ACtHPR, r 5.

[205] African Court on Human and Peoples' Rights (ACtHPR) Rules of the Court, r 9.

[206] Protocol on the Statute of the Court of Justice of the European Union, art 2.

[207] ibid art 4.

member of a court or tribunal, or in any other capacity.[208] They are also governed by a Code of Conduct for members and former members of the CJEU, which provides that they shall devote themselves fully to the performance of their duties and shall perform their duties with complete independence, integrity, dignity and impartiality, and with loyalty and discretion.[209] They are also required to provide a declaration of interest on taking office and in each triennial partial renewal of the Court.[210]

- The COMESA Court of Justice: The judges must be persons of impartiality and independence who fulfil the conditions required for the holding of high judicial office in their respective countries of domicile or who are jurists of recognised competence.[211] In the case of direct or indirect interest in a case before the Court, the judge is required to report the same to the President. The judges are required to take an oath/affirmation prior to taking up their duties, which states that they will 'well and truly serve the Common Market for Eastern and Southern Africa (COMESA) as a Judge . . . [and] will perform duties impartially and conscientiously and . . . preserve the secrecy of the deliberations of the Court'.[212]
- The EACJ: The judges must be persons of proven integrity, impartiality and independence, who fulfil the conditions for holding high judicial office or who are jurists of recognised competence.
- The ECOWAS Court: The Protocol on the Community Court of Justice specifies that the judges of the ECOWAS Court shall be independent, of high moral character and possess the qualifications for appointment to the highest judicial offices or be jurisconsults of recognised competence in international law, particularly in areas of Community law or regional law, and with a minimum of 20 years of professional experience.[213] Before taking office, each judge is required to take oath stating that they will perform their duties 'honourably, impartially, and conscientiously'.[214]
- The ECtHR: The oath taken by judges when taking office states that they will discharge their functions honourably, independently and impartially, and will keep all deliberations secret.[215] The specific obligations relating to integrity, independence, impartiality, diligence and competence, discretion and confidentiality, expression and contacts, additional activity, favours and advantages, decorations and honours are elaborated in the Resolution on Judicial Ethics adopted in 2021.
- The EFTA Court: Prior to taking office, the judges of the EFTA Court are required to take an oath to perform their duties 'impartially and conscientiously' and preserve the secrecy of deliberations.[216] Judges are prohibited from holding any political or administrative office and may not engage in any occupation (unless specifically exempted by the EFTA States acting by common accord).[217] Furthermore, they

[208] ibid art 18.
[209] Code of Conduct for Members and Former Members of the Court of Justice of the European Union (2021/C 397/01).
[210] ibid art 5.
[211] Treaty Establishing the Common Market for Eastern and Southern Africa (COMESA Treaty), art 20.
[212] COMESA Court (2016) Rules of the Court, Form A of sch III.
[213] Protocol Establishing the Community Court of Justice (ECOWAS), art 3.
[214] ibid art 6. See also Rules of Procedure of the ECOWAS Court, art 3,
[215] European Court of Human Rights (ECtHR) Rules of the Court, r 3.
[216] Statute of the EFTA Court, art 2, Protocol 5.
[217] ibid art 4.

provide a declaration stating that both during and after their term of office, they will respect the obligations arising therefrom, particularly with respect to the acceptance of certain appointments or benefits after their term has ended.[218]

- The IACtHR: The judges of the IACtHR are elected in their individual capacity from among jurists of highest moral authority and of recognised competence in the field of human rights, who possess the qualifications for the exercise of the highest judicial office.[219] Upon assuming office, the judges take an oath to exercise their functions 'honourably, independently, and impartially', and maintain the secrecy of deliberations.[220] Article 18 of the Statute of the Court provides a list of activities and positions that are incompatible with the position of the judge. Further, judges may not participate in deciding any case in which they (or their family) have a direct interest or in which they have previously taken part.[221] There is also an additional responsibility on all judges and staff to conduct themselves in a manner that is in line with 'international judicial function'.[222]
- The ICJ: The judges of the ICJ are independent persons of high moral character, who possess the qualifications required for appointment to the highest judicial offices or are jurisconsults of recognised competence in international law.[223] Judges are not permitted to exercise any political or administrative function, or engage in any occupation of a professional nature.[224] The ICJ has further compiled decisions adopted by the Court concerning the permissible external activities of its members, with the general rule that the judges must give absolute priority to their judicial functions over external activities.[225] Further, they are not permitted to act as an agent/counsel/advocate in any case, or participate in any case in which they had previously participated.[226] Prior to taking office, judges are required to make a solemn declaration that they will exercise their powers 'honourably, faithfully, impartially and conscientiously'.[227]
- International criminal tribunals: In the ICC, the judges must be persons of high moral character, impartiality and integrity who possess the qualifications required for appointment to the highest judicial offices.[228] Prior to taking office, judges are required to take an oath to discharge their functions 'impartially and conscientiously'.[229] Furthermore, the judges must be independent in the performance of their functions and must not engage in any activity which is likely to interfere with their function or affect confidence in their independence.[230] The Rules of Procedure and Evidence contain detailed rules on the disqualification of a judge, including for having a personal interest in the case, involvement in any legal proceeding in which

[218] ibid. See also Rules of Procedure of the EFTA Court art 5.
[219] Statute of the InterAmerican Court of Human Rights (IACtHR), art 4.
[220] ibid art 11.
[221] ibid, art 19.1.
[222] ibid, art 20.1.
[223] Statute of the International Court of Justice (ICJ), art 2.
[224] ibid, art 16.
[225] International Court of Justice, '*Compilation of Decisions Relating to Practice Directions and Other Texts*', www.icjcij.org/othertexts/compilationdecisions#footnote_2.
[226] ibid, art 17.
[227] ibid, art 20. See also Rules of the Court, ICJ, art 4.
[228] Rome Statute of the International Criminal Court, art 35(3).
[229] ibid art 44.
[230] ibid art 40.

the person being prosecuted was/is an opposing party, performance of functions prior to taking office which could adversely affect their impartiality, or expression of opinions that could adversely affect their impartiality. In the STL, the judges were persons of high moral character, impartiality and integrity, with extensive judicial experience, who were independent in the performance of their duties.[231]

- ITLOS: The judges are to be independent persons with the highest reputation for fairness and integrity and of recognised competence in the field of the law of the sea.[232] Prior to taking office, they make a solemn declaration to exercise their powers 'honourably, faithfully, impartially and conscientiously'.[233] They are not permitted to exercise any political or administrative function, or associate actively with or be financially interested in any enterprise concerned with the exploration/exploitation of the sea or the seabed etc, or act as an agent/counsel/advocate in any case.[234] Furthermore, they may not participate in any case in which they had previously taken part for one of the parties, or as a member of a national/international court or tribunal, or any other capacity.[235]
- The WTO AB: The AB, while it was operational, comprised persons of recognised authority, with demonstrated expertise in law, international trade and the subject matter of the covered agreements more generally.[236] They served in their individual capacity and did not participate in any disputes that would create a direct or indirect conflict of interest.[237] The Rules of Conduct for the DSU provide more detailed obligations on covered persons, including AB members. They were to be independent and impartial, avoiding any direct or indirect conflicts of interest, and respecting the confidentiality of proceedings, with the observance of requisite standards of conduct the integrity and impartiality.[238] The rules elaborated on the self-disclosure requirements of covered persons through an illustrative list which includes financial interests, professional interests, other active interests, statements of personal opinion, and employment or family interests.[239] The same rules apply to the MPIA.
- With respect to ad hoc adjudicators, there are similar requirements. When there is a specific pool or roster from which such adjudicators are selected, the requirements may be for inclusion within such a pool.[240] For example, in the WTO DSS, the DSU provides that panellists should be selected with a view to ensuring the independence of the members, a sufficiently diverse background and a wide spectrum of experience. The Rules of Conduct, including the disclosures, are applicable to all panellists, arbitrators, experts and staff. In other cases, the appointing authority has been tasked with taking such considerations into account. For example, the IUSCT Rules of Procedure provide that the appointing authority shall take into account

[231] Statute of the Special Tribunal for Lebanon (STL), art 9.
[232] *Statute of the International Tribunal for the Law of the Sea* (ITLOS), art 2.
[233] ibid art 11.
[234] ibid art 7.
[235] ibid art 8. See also Rules of the Court, ITLOS, art 5.
[236] Understanding on Rules and Procedures Governing the Settlement of Disputes (DSU), art 17.1.
[237] ibid art 17.3
[238] Governing Principle, Rules of Conduct of the Understanding on Rules and Procedures Governing the Settlement of Disputes (DSU, WTO), r II.
[239] ibid Annex 2.
[240] ICSID Convention, art 14; USMCA, art 31.8.

considerations of independence and impartiality when making such appointment.[241] Further, disclosure requirements are applicable to any prospective arbitrator/arbitrator on circumstances that will give rise to justifiable doubts as to their impartiality or independence.[242]

Independence can be understood as exercising their duties free from external influence or interference.[243] Impartiality, although closely related to independence, is concerned with the internal predispositions of the adjudicator: the subject matter of the dispute, the parties, the parties' positions etc.[244] It forbids any bias, personal prejudice etc. With respect to the concerns over the role of Dispute Assistants, the lack of independence and impartiality of the Dispute Assistants can impact the *perception* of independence of the adjudicators. The risk that adjudicators have delegated their decision-making function to Dispute Assistants without sufficient monitoring and supervision compounds such a perception. This risk is exacerbated in DSMs where there are no specific obligations or disclosures imposed on Dispute Assistants themselves or procedures to challenge their role. Furthermore, there is an obligation on adjudicators to exercise 'diligence' in some form in the fulfilment of their duties.[245] This is directly impacted by concerns on the excessive delegation of decision-making functions to Dispute Assistants.

C. Effect on Expected Procedural Fairness of the Dispute Resolution Process

The procedural fairness of the adjudicative process has been argued to be linked to the acceptance of the outcome by its intended audience.[246] As with the general notion of legitimacy itself, the specific scope of what constitutes procedural legitimacy is ambiguous. Different scholars have argued for different elements, including the independence and impartiality of judges, equal access to the court, consistency and the right to be heard.[247] The main issue seems to be the opacity or lack of transparency surrounding

[241] Rules of Procedure (International United States Claims Tribunal, IUSCT), r 6.

[242] Rules of Procedure (International United States Claims Tribunal, IUSCT) art 9; Arbitration Rules (Permanent Court of Arbitration, PCA), Art 11.

[243] S Shetreet, 'Independence and Accountability of the Judiciary: Comparative Analysis of the Theories and the Realities with Lessons for the Asia-Pacific' in HP Lee and M Pittard (eds), *Asia-Pacific Judiciaries: Independence, Impartiality and Integrity* (Cambridge University Press, 2017) 9–34; A Seibert-Fohr, 'International Judicial Ethics' in CPR Romano, KJ Alter and Y Shany (eds), *The Oxford Handbook of International Adjudication* (2013; online edn, Oxford Academic, 2014); Burgh House Principles on the Independence of the International Judiciary.

[244] A Seibert-Fohr, 'International Judicial Ethics' in Romano, Alter and Shany (n 243); *Legal Consequences of the Construction of a Wall in the Occupied Palestinian Territory*, Order of 30 January 2004, ICJ Rep 2004, 3; *Mauritius v United Kingdom*, Reasoned Decision on Challenge (30 November 2011) paras 45, 67, 165, 167.

[245] C Brown, 'The Evolution and Application of Rules Concerning Independence of the International Judiciary' (2003) 2 *Law and Practice of International Courts and Tribunals* 63, 92–93.

[246] Y McDermott and W Elmaalul, 'Legitimacy' in WA Schabas and S Murphy (eds), *Research Handbook on International Courts and Tribunals* (Edward Elgar, 2017) 235–56; TR Tyler, 'The Role of Perceived Injustice in Defendants' Evaluations of Their Courtroom Experience' (1984) 18 *Law and Society Review* 51, 51–74; EA Lind and TR Tyler, *The Social Psychology of Procedural Justice* (Plenum, 1988); KF Röhl, 'Procedural Justice: Introduction and Overview' in KF Röhl and S Machura (eds), *Procedural Justice* (Ashgate, 1997) 1.

[247] N Vidmar, 'Procedural Justice and Alternative Dispute Resolution' in KF Röhl and S Machura (eds), *Procedural Justice* (Ashgate, 1997) 121, 128.

the specific roles the dispute resolution process. Their precise role is not disclosed to the parties or the public, which gives rise to the *perception* of a lack of procedural fairness.[248]

At the same time, this need for transparency and procedural fairness must be balanced with the confidentiality of deliberations that is applicable across all institutions. The breach of such confidentiality could risk the ability of the court or tribunal to render its judgment and may even risk of exposing adjudicators to claims of lack of impartiality.

As Freya Beatens notes, there is a need for international courts and tribunals to be viewed as legitimate in the eyes of their intended beneficiaries. Legitimacy influences the overall effectiveness of international dispute settlement and compliance with the decisions of a DSM. The legitimacy of international courts and tribunals is even more relevant today than in the past. Many of the DSMs we have examined are also part of larger international organisations, and the legitimacy of the dispute resolution organ can, in turn, impact the legitimacy of the larger organisation, and vice versa.[249] Therefore, concerns over the role of Dispute Assistants that impact the legitimacy of international courts and tribunals must be addressed in order for the reputation of the organisation to which they are tied to be preserved.

III. Distilling Concerns Regarding the Role of Dispute Assistants

This chapter has recounted examples of concerns that have arisen in the context of specific DSMs, and related useful practices/procedures that may address these concerns. We have identified the following six broad concerns on the roles of Dispute Assistants, the functions they discharge and the alleged influence they may have over adjudicators:

a) A recurring concern relates to the asymmetry in institutional and subject-matter expertise of adjudicators vis-a-vis Dispute Assistants. These concerns have arisen with respect to Institutional Assistants (inter-alia Secretariat staff of the WTO, Registry staff of the ACtHPR and Secretariat staff of the IACtHR), with adjudicators who are *either* ad hoc or part-time in comparison to the staff. As a consequence of this asymmetry, further concerns may arise with respect to the excessive delegation of the decision-making function, as observed above. Similar concerns were raised in other DSMs with a combination of Institutional Assistants and ad hoc/part-time adjudicators.

b) Another element of the asymmetry relates to command over the language of the DSM, with Institutional Assistants (Registry staff of the CJEU, Registry and Research and Documentation Department staff of the ECOWAS, and Secretariat staff of the WTO) and Assigned Assistants (référendaires and Lecteurs d'arrets of the CJEU, and Executive Assistants of the ECOWAS Court). However, such concerns are far from exclusive to these DSMs and are perhaps more pronounced in the case of mechanisms without dedicated language units. Further, as we have already noted, these concerns are to a certain extent intrinsic to every organisation that brings together individuals from different cultures and language traditions for international cooperation.

[248] E Voeten, 'Public Opinion and the Legitimacy of International Courts' (2013) 14 *Theoretical Inquiries in Law* 411, 414.

[249] ibid.

c) Another concern relates to the lack of formal supervision exercised by adjudicators over the Dispute Assistants. This concern has specifically arisen in the context of the WTO with respect to Institutional Assistants (Secretariat staff) and ad hoc panellists/part-time AB members. We have clarified that in reality, the situation is more balanced and that there is no complete lack of supervision over the work of the Dispute Assistants. Nonetheless, the potential of such supervisory framework to threaten the decision-making authority of the adjudicators creates the appearance of illegitimacy and should be addressed. The principled concern relating to the supervision and control of Dispute Assistants is applicable across many of the DSMs examined.

d) The concerns over the excessive delegation of decision-making functions to the Dispute Assistant have been raised in international arbitration, the IUSCT and the WTO. Such concerns have arisen with respect to all three categories of Dispute Assistants: Institutional Assistants (tribunal secretaries, or Secretariat staff of the WTO), Assigned Assistants (Legal Advisers of the IUSCT) and External Assistants (tribunal assistants). The principled reason behind such concerns is the personal nature of the arbitrator's mandate, which requires them to fulfil their mandate of exercising decision-making in the dispute. In the case of arbitration institutions, the mandate comes from the consent of the parties to arbitration. In other institutions, the mandate is from a statute or treaty that establishes the mechanism for dispute resolution, to which the Member States have consented. The corollary of such concerns is that the Dispute Assistant cannot exceed the permissible mandate consented to by the disputing parties. A prominent facet of this concern relates to parties' consent to the functions of Dispute Assistants, which is relevant across all of the DSMs examined.

e) The risk of excessive delegation is more specifically manifested with respect to some functions, notably the drafting or assisting in the drafting of the decision. These concerns have arisen in International Arbitration institutions, and the WTO, with respect to all three categories of Dispute Assistants: Institutional Assistants (tribunal secretaries and staff of the WTO Secretariat), Assigned Assistants (Legal Advisers of the IUSCT) and External Assistants (tribunal assistants). However, as we have seen, Dispute Assistants across various DSMs participate in the drafting process to varying degrees. Therefore, concerns relating to the excessive delegation of the drafting function are principled, which is relevant across all of the DSMs examined.

f) In international criminal courts, concern have been raised over the risk to the independence of judges owing to the conduct of Legal Officers in Chambers (Assigned Assistants). The reason behind such concerns relates to the lack of any specific procedure or standard of impartiality or independence that is applicable to Legal Officers themselves (as reinforced through the case law). The lack of a specific procedure to challenge Dispute Assistants and a standard of conduct applicable to such actors is relevant across DSMs, with very few mechanisms providing active guidance in this respect.

In Part III of this book, we will examine the above concerns more deeply within the context of the different stages of the WTO DSS. We will also explore the ways in which the useful practices/procedures identified in this chapter can be implemented or transposed into the WTO system.

PART III

Dispute Assistants and the WTO DSS

This book seeks, inter alia, to clarify the role and functions of Dispute Assistants in international dispute settlement processes across various identified Dispute Settlement Mechanisms (DSMs). While Part I focused on explaining the current practice with respect to Dispute Assistants, Part II drew comparisons between their institutional structures, procedures and practices, detailed the concerns that have arisen with respect to the involvement of Dispute Assistants and its potential impact on legitimacy, and identified useful practices that can address, mitigate and/or safeguard against such concerns. In Part III, in Chapters 22, 23 and 24, we will expand on these issues using the complex and multifaceted framework of the WTO Dispute Settlement System (WTO DSS).

The role of Dispute Assistants in the WTO DSS is unique. The historical background, established practice and the explicit treaty provisions (including internal regulations and staff rules) confirm the acknowledgement and acceptance by WTO Members[1] of the participation and involvement of legal staff in dispute settlement proceedings. The history of dispute settlement under GATT reveals the reasons for the prominent role of Dispute Assistants in the WTO DSS today. Indeed, Robert Hudec recounts a series of controversial or 'failed'[2] panel decisions in the late 1970s and early 1980s,[3] where the panels did not receive assistance from lawyers.[4] This led to a deliberate acceptance by Members of the need to provide panelists with formal legal assistance and for a more legalistic approach to disputes generally.[5] The establishment of the Office of Legal

[1] In this part (chs 22, 23 and 24), we shall henceforth refer to 'WTO Member(s)' as 'Member(s)'

[2] A Porges, 'The Legal Affairs Division and Law in the GATT and the Uruguay Round' in G Marceau (ed), *A History of Law and Lawyers in the GATT/WTO: The Development of the Rule of Law in the Multilateral Trading System* (Cambridge University Press, 2015) 225.

[3] GATT Panel Report, *United States – Tax Legislation (DISC)*, L/4422 (adopted 7 December 1981) BISD 23S 98 (see also L/5271, BISD 28S 114); GATT Panel Report, EEC – *Programme of Minimum Import Prices, Licences and Surety Deposits for Certain Processed Fruits and Vegetables* (adopted 18 October 1978) BISD 25S 68; GATT Panel Report, *European Communities – Refunds on Exports of Sugar (Australia)*, L/4833 (adopted 6 November 1979) BISD 26S 290; GATT Panel Report, *European Communities – Refunds on Exports of Sugar – Complaint by Brazil*, L/5011 (adopted 10 November 1980) BISD 27S 69;GATT Panel Report, *Spain – Measures Concerning Domestic Sale of Soyabean Oil – Recourse to Article XXIII:2 by the United States*, L/5142 (17 June 1981) (unadopted).

[4] RE Hudec, 'The Role of the GATT Secretariat in the Evolution of the WTO Dispute Settlement Procedure' in J Bhagwati and M Hirsch (eds), *The Uruguay Round and Beyond: Essays in Honour of Arthur Dunkel* (Springer, 1998) 112.

[5] G Marceau and DA Baker, 'A Short History of the Rules Division' in Marceau (n 2) 112–28. They also note other factors as contributing to this shift, such as negotiation of new, more complex rules on non-tariff barriers, and the newly binding character of art II GATT after the end of developed country exchange rate restrictions.

Affairs in the early 1980s,[6] which later became the LAD, the explicit codification of Secretariat assistance in Article 27.1 DSU, and the inclusion of (panel) Secretariat and AB Secretariat staff within the scope of the Rules of Conduct[7] were deliberate decisions on the part of the Members, recognising the need for Dispute Assistants to assist with the dispute settlement process, as a formal part of the Uruguay Round package.

Nonetheless, concerns have been raised about the WTO DSS in relation to the role of adjudicators and the functions discharged by Dispute Assistants. Even if they have not been demonstrated, these claims adversely impact the legitimacy of the WTO DSS. Therefore, they deserve closer attention, examination and discussion regarding possible ways of addressing these. Part III of this book is dedicated to that endeavour.

In Chapter 21, we identified six broad concerns relating to the role of Dispute Assistants and examined how they impact the legitimacy of the dispute resolution process. To recap, these are three risks arising out of potential asymmetry between adjudicators and Dispute Assistants owing to: institutional capacity/legal or sectoral expertise, lack of direct supervision/control over the functions of Dispute Assistants, and language requirements. Three additional concerns raised are the risk of excessive delegation of tasks to the Dispute Assistant, including different decision-making matters, the risk of excessive delegation of the drafting function to the Dispute Assistant and, finally, concerns over the independence of the adjudicator from the Dispute Assistants in some circumstances. Although one or more of these concerns may have arisen in specific DSMs, the risk of such concerns is not limited to the mechanism from which they emanate. Specifically, many of these concerns have been raised with respect to Dispute Assistants in the WTO DSS.

We acknowledge that to a certain extent, a strict separation of concerns into six categories may be artificial, as many of the concerns overlap. For example, the potential asymmetry between the adjudicator and Dispute Assistant due to institutional capacity/legal or sectoral expertise has an impact on the subsequent delegation of tasks to the Dispute Assistant. Such asymmetry may also explain the enhanced role played by Dispute Assistants at different stages of the dispute resolution process, such as during deliberations or drafting the ruling. However, we acknowledge these concerns separately in order to discuss their distinct impact on legitimacy. For instance, the potential asymmetry between the adjudicator and the Dispute Assistant poses a risk to legitimacy of the decision-making function, even without excessive delegation of tasks by the adjudicator to the Dispute Assistant. Even in the WTO DSS, where the participation of Secretariat staff is explicitly accepted by Members (ie, Article 27 DSU), the (potential) asymmetry between adjudicators and staff assisting the dispute process poses a risk to the legitimacy of the dispute resolution process as it raises the *potential* of delegation exceeding that granted by the parties. In other words, parties may have accepted that Dispute Assistants perform some functions to assist the arbitrator, but they have not accepted delegation of decision-making. Similarly, the *actual* delegation of tasks to the Dispute Assistant that encroaches on the decision-making function of the adjudicator adversely impacts legitimacy, even in the absence of any actual asymmetry between the

[6] See generally Å Lindén, 'The First Years of the GATT Legal Service' in Marceau (n 2) 135–40.

[7] Rules of Conduct for the Understanding on Rules and Procedures Governing the Settlement of Disputes, WTO Doc WT/DSB/RC/1 (11 December 1996).

actors. This becomes relevant in understanding the structure of the chapters in Part III, which is detailed below.

The Structure of Part III

With respect to the structure of Part III, as mentioned before, there are 15 processes that are part of the WTO DSS.[8] We have broadly grouped them into two categories: Chapter 22, which deals with the role of Dispute Assistants in assisting parties/the Director-General (DG) in the selection of ad hoc adjudicators; and Chapter 23, which deals with the role of Dispute Assistants in assisting the adjudicators with the dispute settlement process. Each of these chapters details the concerns relating to legitimacy arising from the functions discharged by Dispute Assistants, the relevant procedures and practices associated with these concerns, and possible suggestions to address them, inspired by and drawing from the useful practices of the identified DSMs as well as existing proposals for reform.

In mapping these concerns across these two broad stages identified in Chapters 22 and 23, we have grouped concerns according to the specific stage at which they arise, given the functions discharged by the Dispute Assistants, irrespective of the stage at which suggested solutions to address those concerns may be implemented. For example, the concern relating to the asymmetry between the adjudicator and Dispute Assistant due to control over the working language arises owing to the functions discharged in assisting adjudicators with the dispute resolution process covered in Chapter 23.[9] However, a potential solution for such concern could be introduced at the stage of selection of adjudicators (thematically covered in Chapter 22) as well as rules on panels' working languages. In order to avoid confusion and repetition, we group these solutions in the chapter where the specific concern arises – ie, in this case, during the adjudication process discussed in Chapter 23, even if the solution would be implemented at the stage of selection (discussed in this book in Chapter 22).

[8] The 15 processes are: (1) selection of ad hoc panellists by parties in original panel; (2) selection of ad hoc panellists by parties in implementation panels; (3) selection of ad hoc arbitrators by parties in arbitration for the determination of the reasonable period of time for implementation of a ruling; (4) selection of ad hoc arbitrators by parties in arbitration for the determination of the level of retaliation; and (5) selection of arbitrators – art 25 DSU (non-MPIA); (6) selection of ad hoc panellists by the DG in the original panel; (7) selection of ad hoc panellists by DG in the implementation panels; (8) selection of ad hoc arbitrators by the DG in arbitration for the determination of the reasonable period of time for the implementation of a ruling; (9) selection of ad hoc arbitrators by DG in arbitration for the determination of the level of retaliation; (10) original panel proceedings; (11) implementation of panel proceedings; (12) arbitration for the determination of the reasonable period of time for the implementation of a ruling; (13) arbitration for the determination of level of suspension of concessions; (14) Appellate Body proceedings (not operational); and (15) the MPIA and the Understanding on Rules and Procedures Governing the Settlement of Disputes, Marrakesh Agreement Establishing the World Trade Organization, Annex 2 (adopted 15 April 1994) art 25.

[9] We note that there have been instances where parties have selected an entirely Spanish-speaking panel; however, the proceedings continued to take place in English as the Rules Division did not have the requisite language capacity to conduct the proceedings in Spanish. See WTO Panel Report, *Mexico – Anti-Dumping Duties on Steel Pipes and Tubes from Guatemala*, WT/DS331/R (8 June 2007). As we will explain further below, the panel report was drafted in Spanish in at least 11 different disputes in the WTO.

Further, there may be overlaps between solutions for different concerns within a specific stage of the dispute process. For example, the introduction of enhanced selection criteria for adjudicators is a useful practice that addresses two concerns: the asymmetry between adjudicators and Dispute Assistants as well as potential excessive delegation of duties to the Dispute Assistant. This manner of grouping the solutions with the concerns results in fewer instances of repetition.

The last chapter, Chapter 24, tackles a practical question relating to the implementation of the suggestions for reform. We examine various routes through which these suggestions may be introduced into the WTO DSS based on internal procedures/mechanisms, guidance documents, 'soft' law voluntary standards and other informal instruments. The aim is to show the paths of normative possibilities existing in the WTO for reform relating to Dispute Assistants that do not necessarily rely on the formal amendment procedure.

22

Dispute Assistants and Selection Processes of Ad Hoc Adjudicators

I. Introduction

This chapter focuses on the functions of Dispute Assistants of the WTO, ie, staff of the Secretariat, in procedures for selecting ad hoc adjudicators. We trace these functions across five specific procedures in the WTO Dispute Settlement System (DSS): the selection of ad hoc panellists in two types of panels – *first*, original panels (Article 8 DSU) and, *second*, compliance/implementation panels (Article 21.5 DSU);[1] and the selections of arbitrators across three types of procedures – *first*, arbitration for the determination of the reasonable period of time for implementation (Article 21.3 (c) DSU), *second*, arbitration for the determination of the level of suspension of concessions (Article 22.6 DSU) and, *third*, arbitrations by mutual agreement of the parties under Article 25 DSU.[2] In each of these procedures, the staff of the Secretariat participate to differing degrees in facilitating the parties to reach an agreement on the selection of the adjudicators. Except for procedures for arbitration under Article 25 DSU (which are specifically based on agreement between the parties), if the parties are unable to reach such an agreement, the Director-General of the WTO (DG) is given the authority to select the adjudicators if so requested by one of the parties.[3] Such decision-making power is granted to the DG precisely to ensure that dispute procedures are not halted or unduly delayed by the unwillingness of one of the parties, furthering the security and predictability of the multilateral trading system.[4] In exercising this decision-making function, the DG is often assisted by Secretariat staff. With respect to arbitrations under Article 25, the disputing parties agree on the applicable procedures including for the selection

[1] By 'compliance/implementation review panel', we mean a panel selected to determine whether measures taken to comply with recommendations/rulings of the Dispute Settlement Body (DSB) (relating to a panel report or, in earlier cases, an Appellate Body (AB) report) are consistent with WTO obligations. See Understanding on Rules and Procedures Governing the Settlement of Disputes, Marrakesh Agreement Establishing the World Trade Organization, Annex 2, 1869 UNTS 401, 33 ILM 1226 (1994) (hereinafter 'DSU'), art 21.5. We will now use the term 'compliance panels'.

[2] As we will elaborate further below, the role of Dispute Assistants for the selection of arbitrators under art 25 is limited.

[3] It should be noted that unless the original panellists become unavailable, they are expected to serve as members of a possible compliance panel established pursuant to art 21.5 DSU or as members of the arbitrator tasked with the determination of the level of suspension of concessions (ie, the level of nullification or impairment of benefits) pursuant to art 22.6 DSU. See DSU, arts 21.5 and 22.6.

[4] DSU, art 3.2.

of arbitrators, often limiting the role of Secretariat staff at this stage. The Multi-Party Interim Appeal Arbitration Arrangement (MPIA)[5] is an appeal arbitration arrangement under Article 25; however, it follows a distinct process. Given that the MPIA is not ad hoc and has a specific process for the composition of the pool of arbitrators, it will be examined in the next chapter.

We begin this chapter with the procedure for the composition of original and compliance panels (section II), detailing the functions discharged by the Secretariat staff and the DG (section II.A), the specific concerns raised on these functions (section II.B), the relevant WTO provisions, practice and existing proposals for reform on these concerns (section II.C), and, lastly, proposing certain suggestions for reform to address these concerns (section II.D). Next, we turn to the role of Secretariat staff and the DG in the selection of arbitrators (section III), in arbitration for the determination of the reasonable period of time for implementation (section III.A), and in arbitration for the determination of the level of suspension of concessions (section III.B). The functions of Secretariat staff and the DG for the selection of arbitrators are conceptually similar to their functions at the stage of selection of panellists, so the same suggestions for reform are applicable here as well. Lastly, we turn to the (very limited) practice of Secretariat staff and the DG in the appointment of arbitrators under Article 25 arbitrations (section IV). To reiterate, this is limited to arbitrations under Article 25 that are not part of the MPIA.

II. Dispute Assistants in the Composition of Original (and Compliance) Panels

The WTO DSS covers all disputes arising under agreements listed in Appendix 1 of the DSU (referred to as 'covered agreements').[6] A dispute arises when one or more WTO Members[7] consider a measure adopted by another Member to be inconsistent with the obligations under a covered agreement(s) and they challenge that measure in the WTO DSS. In order to ensure that the dispute process is not stalled due to the unwillingness of the other party (the respondent) to appoint adjudicators (panellists), the establishment of the panel for original and compliance review panel proceedings is effected through the DSB decision-making rule of negative/reverse consensus (which achieves 'quasi-automaticity' for the decision).[8] As panels are ad hoc bodies established for each dispute, the parties must thereafter agree on the composition of the panel by selecting three (or exceptionally five) panellists.[9]

[5] *Multi-Party Interim Appeal Arbitration Arrangement pursuant to Article 25 of the DSU*, WTO Doc JOB/DSB/1/Add.12 (30 April 2020).

[6] DSU, art 1.1. In the DSU, these are referred to as 'covered agreements' and the same terminology has been adopted in this chapter.

[7] In this part, ie, chs 22, 23 and 24, we shall henceforth refer to 'WTO Member(s)' as 'Members'.

[8] ibid art 6.1. The negative consensus rule means that a panel is established unless all Members present object. As the complainant provides an affirmative vote (which they will, in almost all cases) for the establishment of the panel, the panel will be established.

[9] ibid art 8.5. So far, all panels established in the WTO era have been composed of three panellists.

A. Facilitating Agreement of the Parties and Assisting the DG

As noted by Maria Pereyra, the procedure for composition of panels has evolved over the years, with relevant actors developing practices that effectively complement the rules of the DSU.[10] This is especially true with respect to the functions discharged by Secretariat staff in the selection of ad hoc panellists for original and compliance panels. At the same time, there is a degree of opacity around the actual practice, with limited literature and anecdotal accounts by insiders. This section aims to bring further clarity to this issue, before discussing the specific concerns that have been raised.

i. Agreement by the Parties on Selection of Panellists

Article 8 DSU provides that panels shall be composed of well-qualified governmental and/or non-governmental individuals[11] and includes a range of illustrative and alternative qualifications for panellists. Panellists may be persons who have 'served on or presented a case to a panel, served as a representative of a Member or of a contracting party to the General Agreement on Trade and Tariffs (GATT) 1947 or as a representative to the Council or Committee of any covered agreement or its predecessor agreement, or in the Secretariat, taught or published on international trade law or policy, or served as a senior trade policy official of a Member'.[12] These criteria are not mandatory, but rather illustrative. In terms of selection of panellists, the DSU prescribes that the independence of the members should be ensured as well as the selection of members with a sufficiently diverse background and a wide spectrum of experience.[13] Further, citizens of WTO Members whose governments are parties to the dispute or third parties to the dispute are not allowed to serve as panellists, unless the parties to the dispute specifically agree otherwise.[14]

Article 8 DSU requires the Secretariat to assist the parties at the stage of selection of ad hoc panellists in two main ways: through the maintenance of an 'Indicative List'; and by proposing nominations of potential panellists to the parties. We will examine each of these below.

The Secretariat is required to maintain an Indicative List of qualified individuals from which panellists may be drawn.[15] For each of the individuals, the List indicates their specific areas of expertise (trade in goods, trade in services, or trade-related aspects of intellectual property rights). Members propose nominations to the Indicative List, providing relevant information on their knowledge of international trade and the

[10] M Pereyra, 'Appointment of WTO Adjudicators: Rules and Evolving Practices' in N Lamp (ed), *Reckoning and Renewal: The World Trade Organization and Its Dispute Settlement System at 30. Essays in Honour of Valerie Hughes* (Cambridge University Press, 2023) 47.

[11] J Pauwelyn, 'The Rule of Law without the Rule of Lawyers? Why Investment Arbitrators are from Mars, Trade Adjudicators from Venus' (2015) 109 *American Journal of International Law* 761, 772–73.

[12] DSU, art 8.1; G Marceau, C Quinn and JPM Hoyos. 'Judging from Venus: A Response to Joost Pauwelyn' (2015) 109 *American Journal of International Law: Unbound* 204.

[13] DSU, art 8.2; WTO Panel Report, *Mexico – Measures Affecting Telecommunications Services,* WT/DS204 /R (2 April 2004) para 7.2.

[14] DSU, art 8.3; WTO Panel Report, *United States – Measure Affecting Imports of Woven Wool Shirts and Blouses from India* WT/DS33/R (25 January 1997) para 7.19.

[15] DSU, art 8.4.

sectors or subject matter of the covered agreements.[16] The nominations are approved by the DSB by positive consensus.[17] Approval by the DSB is mostly a formality, with almost every name proposed being approved without debate.[18] It should be noted that in practice, the Indicative List has not been updated by regular and revised proposals by Members, as it should have been.[19] Therefore, in order to further assist parties, the Secretariat also maintains an unofficial 'database' with names of past and potential panellists. Unlike the Indicative List, this database is not publicly available or accessible to the disputing parties. Rather, as will be explained below, the Secretariat considers and makes use of the Indicative List as well as the database in making proposals for potential panellists to the parties.

The DSU entrusts the Secretariat with the task of proposing the names of potential panellists to the parties.[20] The practice is that prior to proposing nominations for a panel, the Secretariat meets with the disputing parties to hear their preferred 'criteria' for panellists in terms of nationality[21] and expertise.[22] The criteria provided by the parties may often be conflicting, requiring the Secretariat staff to suggest names after seeking to reconcile such contradictions. Although the Indicative List is utilised, the Secretariat often suggests names outside of it (either from the database or from institutional contacts) in order to meet the criteria of the parties.[23] The DSU does not require that panellists be selected exclusively from the Indicative List. Petros Mavroidis has shown that majority of individuals who served on panels since 1995 were not part of the list.[24] For example, the Secretariat can proposes 'slates' of six names (two potential Chairpersons and four potential panellists) for the parties' consideration.[25] At this stage, the parties retain the right to reject the nominations proposed by the Secretariat.

[16] ibid. The Members may suggest 'governmental' or 'non-governmental' individuals for inclusion.

[17] ibid art 2.4.

[18] Maria Pereyra notes that anecdotally, she recalls only one instance where the DSB rejected the proposal for addition to the indicative list, where Saudi Arabia opposed the nomination made by Qatar. See WTO Dispute Settlement Body, 'Minutes of the Meeting' (30 September 2019) WTO Doc WT/DSB/M/434, paras 9.1–9.3. Given that this was during the diplomatic tensions between Qatar and Saudi Arabia, the blocking of this nomination was likely due to political reasons rather than the qualifications of the candidate; see Pereyra (n 10) 48.

[19] Although it was originally envisaged that individuals included in the Individual List could only serve as panellists for two years from the date of inclusion, this was subsequently revised. With WTO Doc WT/DSB/44 (12 December 2007), inclusion became permanent unless Members removed names from the list.

[20] DSU, art 8.6.

[21] For example, as per art 8.3 DSU, parties could specifically agree to allow citizens of Members whose governments are parties or third parties to the dispute to serve as panellists.

[22] These meetings with the parties are confidential and no minutes are published after the composition of the panel. See Pereyra (n 10) 49; R Malacrida, 'WTO Panel Composition: Searching Far and Wide for Administrators of World Trade Justice' in G Marceau (ed), *A History of Law and Lawyers in the GATT/WTO: The Development of the Rule of Law in the Multilateral Trading System* (Cambridge University Press, 2015) 314.

[23] While the specific reasons for the limited use of the Indicative List is beyond the scope of this book, we note that one of the prominent recommendations made in the Molina Report on DS reform is on the need to rapidly revise and build up an effective Indicative List and to periodically update it. See WTO, 'Report by the Convenor of the Informal DS Reform Discussions – Mr Marco Molina, Special Meeting of the General Council, Report by H.E. Mr Petter Olberg, Chairman of the DSB', WTO Doc JOB/GC/386 (16 February 2024) (hereinafter 'Molina Report').

[24] PC Mavroidis, *The WTO Dispute Settlement System: How, Why and Where?* (Edward Elgar, 2022) 420. He shows how out of 313 panels composed and 939 panellists selected, 650 panellists were selected outside the Indicative List, while 289 panellists were from the Indicative List. See also Pereyra (n 10) 47; WorldTradeLaw.net, 'Count of WTO Panellists, by Appointment Method and Whether on Roster', www.worldtradelaw.net/databases/panelistrosterappointedby.php.

[25] However, this may vary depending on the preferences or request of the parties. See Pereyra (n 10) 50.

However, the DSU notes that this may be done only for 'compelling reasons'.[26] In practice the parties do not necessarily provide reasons for opposing proposed panellists and it is not considered to be the role of the Secretariat to inquire or determine whether the reasons provided are 'compelling'.

The parties might agree on the full composition of a panel after receiving the first slate of names, although this is not the usual outcome. It may be that parties agree on one or perhaps two names, but not the third. In such circumstances, the parties can request the Secretariat to propose more names, and this process may be repeated several times.[27] Although it is the responsibility of the Secretariat to assist parties at this stage, the parties are also free to bypass this entire process by agreeing inter se on the composition of the panel (without assistance from the Secretariat).[28]

There are dedicated teams within Legal Affairs Division (LAD) or the Rules Division (depending on which division has the responsibility for the dispute) that discharge the functions listed above.[29] The Director of the division responsible for dispute reviews and approves the work of the dedicated team, while the staff of this dedicated team participate in the meetings with the parties. Formally, it is not prohibited for staff who assist parties during the selection process to also be assigned to assist panellists in later stages of the dispute resolution process, of the same dispute or in other disputes. However, this happens rarely, since these teams consist of only two to three staff from each of the two divisions. However, as we will see below, this has attracted criticism.

ii. *Request to the DG to Compose the Panel*

If the parties are unable to agree on three panellists within 20 days after the date of establishment of the panel by the DSB, either party can request the DG to compose the panel.[30] The DG is briefed by the Secretariat staff on the composition process to date and is informed of the nominations that have already been turned down by the parties.[31] In a substantial number of cases that advance to the DG stage, there may be partial agreement between the parties on the panel composition (ie, sometimes one or two panellists may have been agreed on by the parties).[32] In such cases, the DG typically takes the agreement of the parties into account and then appoints only the remaining panellist(s).[33]

[26] DSU, art 8.6. There is no mechanism/threshold to assess what constitutes a 'compelling' reason.

[27] ibid.

[28] G Marceau and A Venkataraman, 'Unmasking the Phantom of the Opera: Is There a Hidden Secretariat in the WTO Dispute Settlement System?' (2022) 116 *American Journal of International Law: Unbound* 395. For example, anecdotally it is recalled that such agreement between the parties took place in WTO Panel Report, *United States – Import Prohibition of Certain Shrimp and Shrimp Products – Constitution of the Panel Established at the Requests of Malaysia, Thailand, Pakistan and India*, WT/DS58/R (15 May 1998). However, it is worth mentioning that this not a common practice.

[29] J Pauwelyn and K Pelc, 'Who Guards the 'Guardians of the System'? The Role of the Secretariat in WTO Dispute Settlement' (2022) 116 *American Journal of International Law:* Unbound 535, 539.

[30] DSU, art 8.7.

[31] Pereyra (n 10) 51.

[32] Malacrida (n 22) 316.

[33] ibid. As noted by Maria Pereyra, the Panel Constitution Note does not indicate which of the panellists were agreed by the parties and which were selected by the DG. However, she observed that the Constitution Note for the recent dispute, WTO Panel Report, *China – Measures Concerning Trade in Goods (Complaint by*

Prior to making a final determination, the DG is required to consult with the parties, which allows them to re-state or refine their preferred criteria.[34] However, this is not intended to offer the parties the opportunity to comment on the candidates selected by the DG. Further, the DG also consults with the Chairman of the DSB as well as the Chairman of the Council or Committee that is relevant for the particular dispute.[35] The obligation on the DG is only to *consult* and does not require the DG to obtain the agreement of any other actor when fulfilling this mandate.[36] The decision of the DG is final and, in contrast to the prior process on parties' agreement facilitated by the Secretariat, the parties cannot oppose the DG's nominees, even for 'compelling reasons'.

In discharging this function, the DG is assisted by the team from the relevant division (the LAD or the Rules Division) that worked on the selection of panellists in the prior stage. They brief the DG on the processes and nominations made during the previous stage, and assist them with making the selection. The DG must announce their decision within 10 days of receiving the request to appoint the panel. Although the DG is often requested to compose panels, parties will try to agree on composition in order to avoid the risk of the DG appointing panellists who are not known by or considered advantageous to the parties. It is difficult to ascertain the specific number of panellists appointed by the DG,[37] but the annual reports of the DSB reports that the DG was involved in the composition of 70 per cent of the panels.[38]

An exceptional situation arose in two recent disputes: *India – Tariffs on ICT Goods (EU)* (DS582) and *India – Tariffs on ICT Goods (Chinese Taipei)* (DS588). As recounted by India before the DSB, the complainants (EU and Chinese Taipei) in the disputes refused to initiate the process under Article 8.6, ie, providing 'criteria' to the Secretariat and receiving the slate of nominations of potential panellists.[39] India noted that the complainants did not request the Secretariat for nominations, and the Secretariat declined to provide the slate of potential panellists unless both parties requested it.[40] However, given that 20 days had passed since the establishment of the panel, the complainants requested the DG to proceed with the composition of the panel in both disputes.[41] The DG proceeded to select the same panellists for both the disputes.

the European Union), WT/DS610/R (27 February 2023), states that the parties agreed on two names, but could not agree on a third one, which was then chosen by the DG.

[34] DSU, art 8.7.

[35] ibid.

[36] PC Mavroidis and L Johannesson, 'Black Cat, White Cat: The Identity of the WTO *Judges' (2015) 49 Journal of World Trade* 685.

[37] The WTO document on composition of the panel does not specify which panellist(s) were agreed between the parties, and which panellist(s) were selected by the DG. Rather, even if the parties had agreed to two panellists (out of the three) and the DG appoints the one remaining panellist, it is considered as a panel constituted by the DG.

[38] Mavroidis (n 24) 421. Out of the 313 panels composed, he notes that there was DG involvement in 219 of them. Additionally, he also shows that, over time, the DG has been appointing panellists more often. Dividing the disputes into two sets (DS 1–300 and DS 301–595), the second set has higher number of instances where the DG was involved in the composition of the panel (131 out of 164, as opposed to 88 out of 149).

[39] WTO Dispute Settlement Body, 'Minutes of the Meeting, Held in the Centre William Rappard on 28 August 2020', WT/DSB/M/44 (2 November 2020) para 9.1.

[40] ibid para 9.2.

[41] WTO Secretariat, *India – Tariff Treatment on Certain Goods in the Information and Communications Technology Sector – Constitution of the Panel Established at the Request of the European Union,* WT/DS582/10 (1 September 2020); WTO Secretariat, *India – Tariff Treatment on Certain Goods in the Information and Communications Technology Sector – Constitution of the Panel Established at the Request of the Chinese Taipei,* WT/DS588/8 (1 September 2020).

iii. Compliance Panels

Where a panel (or as was the case earlier, the AB) concludes that a challenged measure is inconsistent with a covered agreement, it recommends that the concerned Member bring the measure into conformity with that agreement, and may also suggest the ways in which these recommendations may be implemented.[42] The panel report is adopted by the DSB through the negative consensus rule, unless a party notifies its decision to appeal.[43] While the AB was operational, the AB report was final and unconditionally accepted by the disputing parties, and adopted by the DSB by way of the negative consensus rule.[44] In both cases, the concerned Member is required to comply with the recommendations or rulings of the DSB. If there is disagreement as to the existence or consistency of measures taken to comply with such recommendations or rulings, the DSU envisages that this should be determined through recourse to a panel (ie, the compliance panel) and, wherever possible, recourse to the original panel.[45]

When recourse to the original panel is not possible (due to unavailability or disagreement between the parties), the procedure detailed above with respect to the composition of original panels is followed. Therefore, the parties agree on three panellists to compose the compliance panel, with the facilitative role discharged by the Secretariat as detailed above. If the parties are unable to reach an agreement on three panellists within 20 days, either party may request the DG to compose the panel, in the same manner as detailed above.

B. Concerns Raised on the Role of Dispute Assistants

The role of Dispute Assistants in assisting parties and the DG in the composition of panels has invited criticism from Joost Pauwelyn and Krzysztof Pelc, as well as Petros Mavroidis. We recount their criticism here without engaging with the substance of their claims.

Pauwelyn and Pelc contend that by providing names of potential panellists, this effectively reverses the 'control' that adjudicators are expected to exert over Dispute Assistants.[46] They argue that the panellists owe their appointment, at least in part, to the staff who subsequently assist them through the course of the dispute.[47] Additionally, they explain that there is a certain degree of financial control exerted by the staff over the panellists, as the staff assisting on a dispute approves the accounts submitted by panellists which specifies the number of days worked and, thereby, the reimbursement due to panellists.[48] In practice, the Director of the LAD/Rules Division is responsible for approving the financial claim form submitted by the panellists.[49] Accordingly, Pauwelyn and Pelc raise the concern that panellists will be inclined to show loyalty and agree with

[42] DSU, art 19.1.
[43] ibid art 16.4.
[44] ibid art 17.4.
[45] ibid.
[46] Pauwleyn and Pelc (n 29) 540.
[47] ibid.
[48] ibid.
[49] Malacrida (n 22) 311–33.

the position taken by the Secretariat if they wish to seek re-appointment or to ensure compensation for all days worked.

Pauwelyn and Pelc maintain that if the same actors are tasked with appointment and approval of financial reimbursement, as well as assisting the panellists through the dispute process, there is a risk of a conflict of interest on the part of Dispute Assistants/Secretariat staff concerned, as they could unduly influence the decision-making function of the panellists.[50] This, in turn, they argue, adversely impacts the legitimacy of the dispute resolution process. In other words, through this 'reversal of roles', there is a risk that the Dispute Assistants would influence the adjudicative function. As discussed in Chapter 21, this adversely impacts one of the core elements of legitimacy of the dispute resolution process demanding the *independence of adjudicators.*

Mavroidis raises a different issue, particularly with respect to the role of the Secretariat in proposing nominations of potential panellists to the parties under Article 8.6.[51] He notes that the existence of a 'non-roster list' (ie, the unofficial database of potential panellists maintained by the Secretariat) is in and of itself problematic, as it lacks statutory justification.[52] He argues that when nominating potential panellists to the parties, the Secretariat should be constrained to the Indicative List established by Members under Article 8.6 DSU. This concern is further compounded by the lack of transparency regarding the criteria used by the Secretariat for the inclusion of individuals in the unofficial database or their nomination to the parties,[53] as well as a lack of clear statutory language requiring the independence of panellists from the Secretariat.[54] In other words, for Mavroidis, when the Secretariat proposes names of potential panellists beyond the Indicative List, it is acting beyond the scope of the mandate granted to it under Article 8.6. This adversely impacts another core element of legitimacy discussed in Chapter 21 regarding the *consent of the parties* to jurisdiction. This concern is important precisely because this discretion is exercised in relation to the selection of adjudicators. Accordingly, legitimacy demands that the discretion is exercised closely in line with the mandate granted by the parties.

With respect to the composition of panels by the DG, Mavroidis notes that when appointments are made from outside the Indicative List, the membership does not have the opportunity to endorse or approve of the DG's selection. Given that the DG is assisted by staff from the Secretariat, Mavroidis raises the concern that the parties have to essentially 'live by the choice of the Secretariat',[55] raising the same legitimacy concerns as discussed above. He explains that the role of the DG in panel selection has been 'scrutinized, and on occasion chastised'.[56] He recounts the issue that arose with the establishment of the compliance panel in *US – Upland Cotton* dispute, where Brazil

[50] As we will explain further in ch 23, this is related to the concern on the potential influence that the staff are able to exert over adjudicators during the panel proceedings.

[51] Mavroidis (n 24) 409.

[52] He recounts the legislative history of art 8, as well as the practice of its evolution under GATT, to argue that the right to propose named for inclusion within a roster is exclusively with the membership. See generally Mavroidis (n 24).

[53] ibid 410.

[54] ibid 556–59.

[55] Mavroidis (n 24) 410, 421.

[56] ibid 441.

requested the DG to determine the composition of the Panel.[57] The US had objected to the nomination of two of the three original panellists as they were nationals of the third parties to the dispute (which the US objected to for these proceedings). Subsequently, Brazil requested the DG to appoint the original three panellists as all three were available. The DG only nominated one of the three original panellists and selected two new panellists. Brazil raised this issue before the DSB, noting that the appointment by the DG goes against the letter and spirit of Article 21.5 of the DSU (which states that a compliance dispute shall be decided wherever possible by resort to the original panel). The European Community (EC), one of the third parties to the dispute, also unsuccessfully raised this argument before the compliance panel.[58] A similar issue was also raised in *Guatemala-Cement II*, where the panel stated that they would be unable to rule or make a finding on the substance of the panel composition process (which involved the selection of the panel by the DG under Article 8.7).[59] In *US – Zeroing (Article 21.5 – EC)*, the panel held that:

> The European Communities has failed to point to any provision of the DSU, and we know of none, that would give us authority to make a finding or ruling with respect to the application, by the Director-General of the WTO, of the provisions of the DSU regarding panel composition contained in Article 8.7.
>
> Article 8.7 is clear that whenever there is no agreement between the parties, the ultimate power to compose the panel rests with the Director-General of the WTO. Consequently, we refrain from ruling on the substance of the EC claim with respect to the composition of this panel by the Director-General.[60]

At appeal, while agreeing with the above finding of the panel, the AB noted that:

> In our view, Article 8.7 confers on the Director-General the discretion to compose panels, which was properly exercised in this case. We therefore find that the Panel did not err in refraining, in paragraphs 8.17 and 9.1(a) of the Panel Report, from making a finding on whether it was improperly composed.

The above ruling may be interpreted as leaving a small window of opportunity open to challenge the discretion of the DG under Article 8.7 if such discretion is not 'properly exercised'. While panels may not have the jurisdiction to review their composition, this leaves it open for the AB (or, rather, any potential appeal stage), to revisit this issue.

The main concern raised by the parties is that the DG may end up selecting panellists they have never heard of, or whom they would have opposed had they known. In assessing this concern, it is important to recall that the DG usually accepts the panellists who have already been agreed to by the parties, so they will often select only one or

[57] ibid.

[58] WTO Panel Report, *United States – Subsidies on Upland Cotton (Article 21.5 – Brazil)*, WT/DS267/RW (18 December 2007) para 8.28.

[59] ibid; WTO Panel Report, *Guatemala – Anti-Dumping Investigation Regarding Portland Cement from Mexico (Guatemala – Cement II)*, WT/DS156/RW (17 July 2000) para 8.11.

[60] WTO Panel Report, *United States – Measures Relating to Zeroing and Sunset Reviews (EC) (Article 21.5 – EC)*, WT/DS322/RW (19 December 2008) paras 8.16–8.17.

two panellists for a dispute. Moreover, the DG practice is not to nominate candidates rejected by a party in the previous stage of the selection process.[61] It should be noted that the DG selects panellists who have *not* been suggested to the parties in the earlier stage and who are sometimes not known by the parties. Indeed, DGs have introduced new and occasionally less known experts with a view to expanding the pool of experienced panellists. This issue has been addressed in the Report by the Convenor of the Informal DS Reform Discussions – Mr Marco Molina (hereinafter 'Molina Report'), which we will discuss in the next section.

Further, some concerns have been informally raised that if the same staff who were involved in nominating names of parties also assist the DG in the panel selection process, this may fail to offer the parties a completely new attempt at reaching a consensus.[62] It has also been reported informally that some names of potential panellists (either from the unofficial database or otherwise) are kept in the 'Secretariat's pocket' in order to reserve them for the stage of DG panellist selection should the parties not be able to reach an agreement. At the same time, such practice was developed in order to ensure the quality of panellists appointed at the DG stage, reinforcing the security and predictability of the WTO DSS.

C. Relevant WTO Provisions, Practice and Proposals

In order to better understand the concerns raised above, it is useful to examine the specific rules that exist with respect to the role of Dispute Assistants at the stage of selection of ad hoc panellists, as well as proposals made on reform relating to this stage.

i. Relevant Provisions and Practice of the WTO

This section examines the provisions of the Marrakesh Agreement Establishing the World Trade Organization (hereinafter 'Marrakesh Agreement'), the DSU, the WTO Rules of Conduct for the Understanding on Rules and Procedures Governing the Settlement of Disputes (hereinafter 'WTO Rules of Conduct') and the WTO Staff Regulations which apply to Dispute Assistants.

a. The Marrakesh Agreement

The Marrakesh Agreement includes important guidance on the nature of the mandate of the DG and the Secretariat staff. Article VI notes that the responsibilities of the DG and the Secretariat staff shall be exclusively international in character.[63] Accordingly, they are to discharge their duties independently of any instructions from any

[61] Malacrida (n 22) 312.

[62] However, the aim of art 8.7 is more about offering the parties a quick and expeditious step to resolve their disagreement by the DG appointing the panellists directly.

[63] Marrakesh Agreement Establishing the World Trade Organization, 15 April 1994, 1867 UNTS 3, art VI(4).

government or any authority outside the WTO.[64] The direction that '[t]hey shall refrain from any action which might adversely reflect on their position as international officials' necessarily includes responsibilities explicitly mentioned in Articles 8 and 27 DSU. The WTO Members have a corresponding duty to respect the international character of the responsibilities of the DG and the Secretariat staff, and they must not seek to influence them in the discharge of their duties.[65]

The DG and the Secretariat staff are required to discharge all their responsibilities, including those with respect to selection of panellists in Article 8 DSU, with the standards of impartiality and independence expected of international civil servants. Although the Marrakesh Agreement imposes standards of independence and impartiality in all their official functions including when assisting parties and the DG in the selection of panellists and arbitrators, the responsibility is framed in general terms and does not detail the specific duties of or prohibitions on the staff involved.

b. The DSU

Article 8 DSU explicitly recognises a role for the Secretariat staff in assisting the parties in selection of panellists. Although not mandated by the DSU, staff members are guided during this stage by the preferences, criteria or qualifications for panellists conveyed by disputing parties, which may often be contradictory.[66] While it is conceptually possible for staff to favour certain panellists during this stage, there are relevant ethical obligations in place that may guide the functions discharged by the staff.

Along with the explicit prescription in Article 8, Article 27.1 DSU states that the Secretariat shall have the responsibility of assisting panels, 'especially on the legal, historical and procedural aspects of the matters dealt with' and of providing secretarial and technical support.[67] This is fairly broad in scope and does not appear to exclude any specific involvement in the disputed matter. The wording of this provision becomes important for the scope and application of the WTO Rules of Conduct (see below).[68]

c. The WTO Rules of Conduct

The WTO Rules of Conduct were adopted by the WTO Members in 1996.[69] As per Article IV of the WTO Rules of Conduct, the rules apply to members of the Secretariat 'called upon to assist the panel in accordance with Article 27.1 of the DSU'.[70] With respect to Secretariat staff assisting the parties under Article 8.6, the question is whether 'the panel'

[64] ibid.

[65] ibid.

[66] Pereyra (n 10) 49.

[67] DSU, art 27.1.

[68] *Rules of Conduct for the Understanding on Rules and Procedures Governing the Settlement of Disputes*, WTO Doc WT/DSB/RC/1 (11 December 1996).

[69] *ibid*; *see also* V Hughes, 'A Tribute to Gabrielle Marceau: An Invaluable Contribution' in *International Trade Law: Past, Present and Future – Tribute to Gabrielle Marceau* (Revue québécoise de droit international, September 2025) 533–34; WJ Davey, 'Gabrielle Marceau and the WTO Dispute Settlement Rules of Conduct' in *International Trade Law: Past, Present and Future – Tribute to Gabrielle Marceau* (Revue québécoise de droit international, September 2025) 308–21.

[70] Rules of Conduct, r IV.1.

in the above rule also includes 'parties'. Further, given that at the stage of composition of the panel in Article 8.6, the panel is yet to be constituted, it is not explicitly clear whether the WTO Rules of Conduct apply to staff who assist the parties and/or the DG at this stage. However, the accepted practice has been to consider the Rules of Conduct applicable to such staff, and Secretariat staff recount that this has always been the case. It is generally considered that the DG is not a covered person under Article IV of the WTO Rules of Conduct.

Pursuant to the Governing Principle of the WTO Rules of Conduct, each covered person shall be independent and impartial, and shall maintain confidentiality.[71] Further, the panellists as well as Secretariat staff covered by the WTO Rules of Conduct are required to consider only issues raised in, and necessary to fulfil, their responsibilities within the dispute settlement proceeding. They are also prohibited from delegating this responsibility to any other person.[72]

The WTO Rules of Conduct set out specific duties for each 'covered person'. For example, prior to confirmation of their appointment, panellists are required to complete the disclosure form as per Annex 3 of the WTO Rules of Conduct.[73] They have a continuing duty[74] to disclose any information likely to affect their independence or impartiality, or which could give rise to justifiable doubts as to the integrity and impartiality of the dispute settlement mechanism.[75] Annex 2 of the WTO Rules of Conduct provides an illustrative list of information that is required to be disclosed, which includes information on their financial,[76] business, and property interests relevant to the dispute, professional interests,[77] other active interests,[78] statements of personal opinion,[79] on issues relevant to the dispute, and employment or family interests.[80] The information provided is disclosed to the Chair of the DSB for consideration by the parties to the dispute. Secretariat staff assigned to assist in a dispute must make the same disclosure to the DG.[81] The DG is explicitly given the power to determine whether a legal staff member is to be removed from a dispute for fear of inconsistency with the WTO Rules of Conduct.[82] However, the information relating to the names of staff assisting in a dispute is not required to be shared with the Members or the DSB. The DG decides, including in light of 'available Secretariat resources', if the potential conflict of interest is sufficiently material to warrant non-assignment of a particular Secretariat staff to the

[71] ibid r II.

[72] ibid r III.2.

[73] ibid r VI.

[74] This continuing duty exists while participating in the dispute settlement mechanism, and until such time as the DSB makes a decision on adoption of a report relating to the proceeding or notes its settlement.

[75] Rules of Conduct, Annex 3.

[76] For example, investments, loans, shares, interests and other debts. See ibid Annex 2(a).

[77] For example, a past or present relationship with private clients, or any interests the person may have in domestic or international proceedings, and their implications, where these involve issues similar to those addressed in the dispute in question, See ibid Annex 2(b).

[78] For example, active participation in public interest groups or other organisations which may have a declared agenda relevant to the dispute in question, See ibid Annex 2(c).

[79] For example, publications, public statements. See ibid Annex 2(d).

[80] For example, the possibility of any indirect advantage or any likelihood of pressure which could arise from their employer, business associates or immediate family members. See ibid Annex 2(e).

[81] We discuss this further in section III relating to Dispute Assistants in panel proceedings.

[82] The practice is that typically, the Secretariat errs on the side of caution. If there is any known issue that may give rise to a conflict of interest, staff members typically excuse themselves (or are asked to do so by the Director).

dispute.[83] This reference to 'available Secretariat resources' provides additional evidence that the Members were aware of the direct involvement of the Secretariat staff in the WTO DSS.[84] The disclosures made by the panellists and the Secretariat staff are not disclosed to the public, including the instances where any conflict is declared.[85]

d. The WTO Staff Regulations

The WTO Staff Regulations, which were adopted pursuant to the above-mentioned Article VI of the Marrakesh Agreement, provide the fundamental conditions of employment and the rights, duties and obligations of the WTO and its staff members.[86] Specifically, Regulation 1.5 states that staff members shall conduct themselves in an appropriate manner and avoid any activity which may adversely reflect on their status as international civil servants, or on the integrity, independence and impartiality required by that status.[87]

More specifically, Regulation 1.8 requires staff members to make prior disclosures relating to information concerning their interest in any matter within the purview of the WTO that may affect the appropriateness of assigning functions to them. [88] Specifically with respect to dispute settlement matters, the obligation to disclose includes continuous disclosure obligations detailed in Annex B of the Staff Regulations.[89] Annex B, which is entitled 'Standards of Conduct in the World Trade Organization', clarifies the basic principles and standards of conduct required of the staff of the WTO. Four basic and fundamental considerations are elaborated, namely: integrity,[90] international outlook based on loyalty to the WTO,[91] independence[92] and impartiality.[93] With respect to participation of staff members in the dispute settlement process, paragraph 34 of Annex B corresponds to the text of footnote 2 to the WTO Rules of Conduct. It reiterates that when a staff member is considered to assist in a dispute, they have an obligation to disclose to the DG the information required to be disclosed by Rule VI:2 of the WTO Rules of Conduct, including participation in earlier formal consideration of the specific measure at issue in a dispute under any provision of the WTO Agreement. Such participation may be through formal legal advice under Article 27.2 DSU[94] or through any

[83] *Rule of Conduct.* See also the WTO General Council, Staff Regulations of the World Trade Organization, WTO Doc WT/L/510 (7 July 2004) Annex B, para 34.

[84] Additionally, as we have already seen in ch 19, art 27.1 DSU explicitly states that the Secretariat has the responsibility to assist panels, 'especially on the legal, historical and procedural aspects of the matters dealt with, and of providing secretarial and technical support'.

[85] The US had raised an allegation against the last standing AB member, Hong Zhao from China, on her alleged ties to the Chinese government. However, these allegations were not made at the time of her appointment. *See* 'US Takes Appellate Body Fight to a New Level' (*Politico*, 6 March 2020), www.politico.com /newsletters/morning-trade/2020/03/06/us-takes-appellate-body-fight-to-a-new-level-785913; and Mavroidis (n 24) 406.

[86] *WTO Staff Regulations,* Annex 2.

[87] ibid reg 1.5.

[88] ibid reg 1.8.

[89] ibid

[90] ibid para 2, Annex B.

[91] ibid para 3.

[92] ibid para 4.

[93] ibid para 5.

[94] Article 27.2 notes that the Secretariat may provide assistance to Members in DS on their request and may also need to provide additional legal advice and assistance to developing country Members. With respect to such developing country Members, the Secretariat provides an expert from the WTO technical cooperation services.

involvement with the dispute as an official of a Member or otherwise professionally before having joined the Secretariat. The DG considers all such disclosures in deciding on the assignment of staff to a dispute and may decide that a potential conflict of interest of not sufficiently material to warrant non-assignment of the staff member to a particular dispute. As with the WTO Rules of Conduct, it is unclear whether the requirement under paragraph 34 applies to staff who assist in the panel selection process.

e. Procedures on Remuneration, Reimbursement etc

The DSU includes minimal provisions with respect to the remuneration of panellists. Article 8.11 DSU provides that the panellists' expenses, including travel and subsistence allowance, shall be met from the WTO budget.[95] It further states that the expenses shall be in accordance with criteria to be adopted by the General Council, based on the recommendations of the Committee on Budget, Finance and Administration.

Although the decisions by the General Council are public, there is a perception of lack of information on the remuneration provided to panellists. For example, in their 2015 article, Petros Mavroidis and Louise Johannesson note the lack of transparency with respect to the remuneration of panellists.[96] We clarify the following based on the latest publicly available decision of the General Council and gleaned from the writings of scholars with experience working in the WTO DSS:[97]

- Until 2015, panellists employed by a government did not any receive any fee for panel work.[98] At the end of 2015, the WTO General Council decided to allow governmental panellists to claim CHF 300 for each full day of panel work,[99] although some panellists are prohibited from receiving fees for panel work by rules governing their employment.
- Until 2015, non-governmental panellists received in fees 600 CHF/day for panel work.[100] At the end of 2015, the WTO General Council decided to increase the daily fees of non-governmental panellists to CHF 900 (as of 1 January 2016).[101]
- Under the GATT and today, the WTO will cover the costs of flights, hotel rooms, other travel expenses and per diem for days worked in accordance with United Nations standard rates.[102]

It has been noted that panellists often claim fees for a number of days of work significantly less than the actual time devoted to panel work.[103] This may be because they are well aware of the

[95] DSU, art 8.11.
[96] Mavroidis and Johannesson (n 36).
[97] Marceau, Quinn and Hoyos (n 12) 288.
[98] As noted by Mavroidis and Johannesson, this was following an unofficial 'memorandum' dating back to 1992. See Mavroidis and Johannesson (n 36) 3.
[99] WTO General Council, 'Minutes of the Meeting Held on 30 November and 7 December 2015', WTO Doc WT/GC/M/160 (23 February 2016), read with WTO Committee on Budget, Finance and Administration, 'Report of the Meeting Held on 23 and 30 October and 6 and 16 November 2015', WTO Doc WT/BFA/151 (20 November 2015).
[100] As noted by Mavroidis and Johannesson, this was following an unofficial 'memorandum' dating back to 1992; see Mavroidis and Johannesson (n 36) 3. This understanding is also confirmed in Hughes (n 69) fn 9.
[101] WTO General Council (n 99).
[102] Marceau, Quinn and Hoyos (n 12) 290.
[103] Mavroidis and Johannesson (n 36) 3.

budgetary limitations. Mavroidis and Johannesson warn that panellists may hence devote less time on the dispute and may instead rely on the assistance of the Secretariat staff.[104]

Although the DSU does not specify the scope of the Secretariat's involvement in respect of panellists' remuneration (except that DS costs are covered by the WTO regular budget), their assistance in the administrative tasks, calculation of hours worked, choice of hotel and flights etc are extremely standardised.[105] The Directors of the LAD/Rules Division have final sign-off on all panellists' accounts. Further, the total remuneration per day for panellists was approved by the Members as per the General Council's decision,[106] and the overall expenditure on panellists' fees is approved on an annual basis. Any manipulation of such remuneration by the Secretariat staff would constitute bad faith actions in violation of their obligations of independence under the Marrakesh Agreement, the WTO Rules of Conduct, and the Staff Regulations.

ii. Proposals for Reform

The following proposals are examined here: the EU proposals on a permanent roster, the proposal on a Permanent Roster of Panel Chairs by Thailand, the proposal on an Indicative List by Canada, and the proposals made in the Report by the Convenor of the Informal DS Reform Discussions, Mr Marco Molina. There are also other proposals from the GATT era that reveal the legislative history and context of the present provisions; however, we do not examine them here.[107] Given that a significant aspect of the concerns raised relates to the alleged control exercised by Secretariat staff over ad hoc panellists, the proposals examined here are aimed at safeguarding against such risk by, inter alia, moving away from the ad hoc nature of the panellists, increasing the participation/control of parties through specific procedures and/or providing further guidance on the functions/discretion of the Secretariat at this stage.

a. Proposals on a Permanent Roster from the EU

Three of the proposals made by the EC[108] as part of its efforts to improve procedures in the DSU are examined here. The first proposal, the Contribution of the European Communities and its Member States to the Improvement of the WTO Dispute Settlement Understanding (hereinafter 'First EU Proposal on Panel Reform'),[109] proposes an array of amendments aimed at facilitating the earliest possible resolution of disputes and

[104] ibid 8–9.

[105] In practice, panellists are provided with a time sheet to use to track their hours. We tried obtaining these timesheets, but they are not publicly available.

[106] WTO General Council (n 99).

[107] For a discussion on these proposals relating to selection of adjudicators and the history of 'panels', see Mavroidis (n 24) 406. See also G Marceau and A Comont, 'Le Canada dans le développement du mécanisme de règlement des différends du GATT et de l'OMC : l'engagement historique d'un acteur essentiel' (2025) *Canadian Yearbook of International Law/Annuaire canadien de droit international* 1.

[108] It should be noted that since 1 December 2009, 'European Union' has been the official name in the WTO as well as in the outside world. Before that, 'European Communities' was the official name in WTO business for legal reasons, and that name continues to appear in older material. We use 'EC' when referring to the specific proposals, but retain 'EU' in our short form of the proposals

[109] WTO, 'European Communities and its Member States, Contribution to the Improvement of the WTO Dispute Settlement Understanding', WTO Doc TN/DS/W/1 (13 March 2002).

effective trade compensation – specifically, moving from ad hoc panellists to more permanent panellists. They reasoned[110] that changing the way in which panellists are selected and providing them with a more permanent basis for their work would likely to lead to faster procedures and increase the quality of the panel reports.[111] Accordingly, they proposed amending Article 8 DSU to establish a roster of panellists.[112] Members would make nominations to include qualified[113] individuals on the roster to be established by the DSB. Similar to the practice of the AB, the panellists for each dispute would be appointed through random selection, with no party involvement.[114] The proposed amendments to Article 8 remove the role of the Secretariat as well as the DG in the appointment process. However, the proposal notes that the panellists would be provided with 'administrative and legal support' during the dispute as required.

The subsequent proposal from the EC, the Contribution of the European Communities and its Member States to the Improvement of the WTO Dispute Settlement Understanding, (hereinafter 'Second EU Proposal on Panel Reform'),[115] allows parties the flexibility to agree on having up to two panellists from outside the roster of panellists with particular expertise in the subject matter of the dispute.[116] However, the Chairman of the panel must always be selected from the roster and appointed by the DG on a random basis within five days of the establishment of the panel.[117] For individuals outside the roster, the parties may agree on the panellists or request the DG, in consultation with the Chairman, to nominate the panellists.[118] If the parties are unable to reach an agreement on such panellists within 10 days of the establishment of the panel, either party can request the DG to appoint those remaining panellists from the roster on a random basis.[119] This proposal envisages a role for the DG in the selection of panellists from outside the roster, albeit in limited circumstances when the parties explicitly agree and request the DG to do so.

[110] They detail four arguments in favour of moving away from ad hoc panellists. First, there are delays in selection of ad hoc panellists due to increased demand and insufficient supply. Second, the increased complexity in the substantive and procedural aspects of the cases has led to an increased workload for the panellists. Moving to a system of permanent panellists would most likely result in fewer reversals of panel reports, reducing the total time frame of the procedure. Third, it would enhance the credibility and legitimacy of the panel process, as the possibility of conflict of interests would be eliminated. Lastly, it would increase the involvement of developing countries in the panel process. ibid 2–3. See also WTO, 'India's Questions to the European Communities and its Member States on Their Proposal Relating to the Improvements of the DSU Communication from India', WTO Doc TN/DS/W/5, 7 May 2002.

[111] ibid 2.

[112] The number to be decided from time to time by the General Council (not less than 20); ibid.

[113] We will discuss the specific qualifications required for permanent panellists in section III. The first EU Proposal provides that they shall be persons of recognised authority, with demonstrated expertise in international trade law, the economy or policy and the subject matter of the covered agreements generally, and/or past experience as a GATT/WTO panellist. The panellists included in the roster would perform their tasks on a full-time basis and would stay abreast of dispute settlement activities and other relevant activities of the WTO. Further, the roster should be broadly representative of the membership of the WTO.

[114] ibid 3. In case of a direct or indirect conflict of interest, the panellist is required to disqualify themselves, and a new drawing would be made for the particular case.

[115] EC Contribution to DSU Reform TN/DS/W/1.

[116] ibid 3; DSU art 8.2.

[117] EC Contribution to DSU Reform TN/DS/W/1.

[118] ibid.

[119] ibid.

The subsequent proposals made by the EC are confidential and hence not publicly available.[120] We recount the information available on the Third EU Proposal,[121] as it was later discussed in the Report by the Chairman, Ambassador Ronald Saborio Sotto, in the Special Session of the DSB.[122] This proposal gave further guidance on how the functions would be discharged by the Secretariat under Article 8 DSU. It was proposed that after asking the parties for their criteria, the Secretariat would present a single list of persons meeting at least one of the requested criteria (to the greatest extent possible). The list could typically comprise between 12 and 20 names, and the parties were given the right to veto one to three persons depending on the size of the list.[123] Thereafter, the parties would rank the remaining nominations in their order of preference, and the Secretariat would determine which nomination received the highest preference by adding the results of the ranking of the respondent and the complainant. The Secretariat would thereafter verify the parties' agreement on the resulting panel composition and check whether those persons are available to serve on the panel. A second list of nominations may be presented in exceptional circumstances and on a combined request by both parties. If the DG is requested to appoint panellist(s), the DG is required to do so from persons in the list of nominations proposed by the Secretariat and not vetoed by parties, who the DG considers most appropriate.

Although the reasons for the proposal made by the EU do not directly relate to concerns on the role of the Secretariat in the selection process of panellists, these three proposals nevertheless address such concerns by providing further guidance on the specific functions of the Secretariat and DG in discharging their duties under Article 8 DSU.

b. Proposals on a Permanent Roster of Panel Chairs: Panel System, Communication from Thailand

Building on the First EU Proposal for Panel Reform, Thailand proposed a system that would retain the existing practice (ie, mutual agreement on complete panel composition based on nominations proposed by the Secretariat, or panel composition by the DG at the request of either party), along with the option to allow either party to request that the panel Chair be appointed by 'lot', or through random selection from a 'Roster of Panel Chairs'.[124] Such a roster would be established by the DSB, based on an indicative list of candidates prepared by the DG with particular qualifications, experience and expertise, along with prior experience as a panellist and willingness/availability to serve

[120] See WTO Dispute Settlement Body, Special Session, 'Minutes of the Meeting Held on 15 July 2005', WTO Doc TN/DS/M/27 (29 July 2005), referring to WTO Doc JOB(05)/144, where the discussions on the proposal were done in 'informal mode'. See also JOB(05)/48, referred to in WTO Dispute Settlement Body, Special Session, 'Minutes of the Meeting Held on 5 April 2005' WTO Doc TN/DS/M/24 (26 May 2005).

[121] WTO, 'Draft Consolidated Text of the Chairman', WTO Doc JOB(05)/144/Rev.1 (2005).

[122] WTO, 'Report by the Chairman, Ambassador Ronald Sabario Soto to the Trade Negotiations Committee, Special Session of the Dispute Settlement Body', WTO Doc TN/DS/25 (21 April 2011).

[123] That is, each party could reject one of those nominations where the list comprises no more than 10 persons, two where it comprises between 11 and 20 persons, and three where it comprises more than 20 persons. The parties may otherwise object to the list only in the event of a conflict of interest as referred to in the Rules of Conduct.

[124] WTO, 'Contribution to Improve the Dispute Settlement Understanding: Panel System, Communication from Thailand', WTO Doc TN/DS/W/31 (22 January 2003) para 4.

as Chair upon request.[125] Under Article 8.7 DSU, if there is no agreement between the parties on the composition of the panel within 20 days after its establishment, either party may request the DG to determine the composition of the panel. They proposed that at this stage, either party should be given the option to request the DG to appoint the Chair of the panel from the Roster of Panel Chairs through a draw of lots.[126] In the event that concurrent requests are received from the parties, the DG would have the discretion to decide how best to proceed, in consultation with the parties.[127]

Thailand noted that no changes would be required to the existing Article 8 DSU provisions to accommodate their proposal. Thus, they retained the role of the Secretariat to assist the parties in the appointment of panellists, while also providing the parties with an additional procedural option of selecting panel chairs from a permanent Roster of Panel Chairs.

c. Proposals on Indicative List: Proposal from Canada

The Canadian proposal on the improvement of the WTO Dispute Settlement Understanding tackles a range of issues,[128] including the establishment of a new panel roster to replace the existing Indicative List.[129] Canada proposed that each WTO Member may nominate one individual to the Panel Roster; the nomination would include a statement of qualifications of the nominee's capabilities and capacity to serve as a panellist.[130] The Roster would be submitted to the General Council for approval. Each person would remain on the roster for five years and could be re-appointed for a further period of five years by the General Council. The Panel Roster would be maintained by the Secretariat, including the qualification statements, and this information would be made available to Members.[131]

They proposed that in nominating names to the parties under Article 8.6 DSU, the Secretariat should be bound by the panel roster.[132] However, the parties retain the right to propose names of individuals outside the roster as panellists.[133] Further, with respect to the DG appointment, they propose that such panellists should be drawn from the Roster, unless the DG determines that insufficient expertise is available from the roster for a particular dispute.[134] If that is the case, the DG may appoint panellist(s) from outside the panel roster.[135]

The Canadian proposal envisages a continuing role for the Secretariat and the DG in the appointment process; however, it limits their discretion to candidates on the panel roster (unless exceptionally determined by the DG).

[125] ibid para 6.
[126] ibid para 9(b).
[127] ibid para 10.
[128] WTO, 'Contribution of Canada to the Improvement of the WTO Dispute Settlement Understanding, Communication from Canada', WTO Doc TN/DS/W/41 (24 January 2003).
[129] ibid 4.
[130] ibid.
[131] ibid 15, para 4.
[132] ibid 16, para 6.
[133] ibid.
[134] ibid 16, para 7.
[135] ibid.

d. The Molina Report

The Molina Report[136] was the result of the informal dispute settlement reform process following a solution-oriented, interest-based and bottom-up approach to negotiations and was circulated by the Chairperson of the General Council.[137] The draft Consolidated Text, which is Annex I to the Molina Report, is an impressive effort by Members to implement solutions for reform of the dispute settlement process. It consists of a total of nine titles, each dedicated to one aspect of the WTO DSS. Even if the Molina Report is not formally binding, it remains evidence of the work and views of a great number of Members interested and active in dispute settlement reform. Even if it was formally set aside due to a lack of consensus, some of the concepts, approaches, mechanisms and provisions developed in Molina's report are worth reviewing because they carry some weight in influencing the potential and actual practice of Members. Such DS practices may also expand into preferential agreements. In this section, the reform proposals in Title II with respect to 'Panel Proceedings' are discussed.

Starting with the responsibilities of the Secretariat to maintain an Indicative List, the Molina Report makes impressive efforts to improve this list. There are enhanced qualification criteria,[138] including high ethical standards introduced for inclusion within the List. We will discuss the specific qualification criteria in Chapter 23, along with its role in addressing concerns that arise on the asymmetry between Dispute Assistants and adjudicators. For the purposes of this chapter, what is more relevant is *how* this Indicative List is intended to be utilised rather than *what* qualifications for inclusion have been suggested.

Each Members is encouraged to nominate up to three citizens for inclusion on the Indicative List and may also nominate one person who is not a citizen of that Members.[139] The list is recomposed every four years in order to ensure that it remains up to date.[140] The Secretariat is envisaged to support the Members by compiling a database of interested and eligible individuals seeking to be nominated by a Member to the Indicative List.[141] Additionally, the Members may request assistance from the Chairperson of the DSB in composing and recomposing the Indicative List.[142] Once the Indicative List has been adopted by the DSB, it is to be made available online for Members to access, along with relevant information relating to the qualifications of each person on the list.[143]

Thereafter, the Secretariat is encouraged to use this Indicative List in proposing nominations to the parties for potential panellists under Article 8.6 DSU.[144] However, they are not bound by this List. Turning to the DG selection process under Article 8.7 DSU, each party is required to submit to the DG a list comprising at least 30 individuals[145] from the Indicative List.[146] Thereafter, the DG is required to consult with the parties

[136] Molina Report (n 23) Title VII.
[137] ibid para 1.12.
[138] ibid Title II, ch II.II(3), (4), (5) and (6).
[139] ibid Title II, ch II.II(1).
[140] ibid Title II, Ch II.II(9).
[141] ibid Title II, Ch II.II(12).
[142] ibid Title II, Appendix I. For a more detailed discussion on the role of the DSB Chairperson at this stage, see ch 23, section II.B.
[143] ibid Title II, Ch II.II(13).
[144] ibid Title II, Ch II.II(15).
[145] Or such other number as agreed between the parties
[146] Molina Report (n 23) Title II, Ch II.III(1).

to obtain their panel composition criteria, examine the lists submitted by each party to determine whether there is any overlap between the lists, and determine the composition of the panel by appointing the panellists from the overlap, taking into account the parties' panel composition criteria.[147] If the overlap between the lists provided by the parties provides less than three potential panellists, the DG would complete the panel composition and may consider other individuals on the lists provided by the parties.[148] Although not explicitly mentioned, the DG is not restricted to the lists provided by the parties or the Indicative List maintained by the Secretariat in completing the panel composition.[149] The only guiding factor is that the DG is requested to consider 'ensuring a sufficiently diverse background and a wide spectrum of experience'.[150]

The Molina Report does not restrict Secretariat discretion in nominating potential panellists (although they are generally bound by the Indicative List). If parties ask the DG to compose the panel, there are additional steps introduced before the exercise of discretion by the DG. However, there is no guidance on Secretariat support to the DG in the composition of the panel. The text focuses on enhancing the participation of Members in the formulation of the Indicative List, and parties' participation during the DG panel composition process.

D. Suggestions on the Role of Dispute Assistants in the Composition of Original and Compliance Panels

We have looked at the concerns, the relevant provisions of the WTO, and proposals for reform relating to the role of Dispute Assistants in the appointment of ad hoc panellists. These concerns impact the legitimacy of the dispute resolution process in two ways. *First*, they raise doubts as to whether the consent of the Members captured in Article 8 DSU is respected in situations where the Secretariat/DG exercises discretion in a manner contrary to that envisaged in the DSU. For example, Mavroidis would argue that the proposal of names of potential panellists outside the Indicative List is beyond the mandate granted to the Secretariat under Article 8.6 DSU. *Second*, the 'reversal of roles' between the adjudicator and Dispute Assistants raises doubts as to the independence of the adjudicators in exercising their adjudicative function. For example, Pauwelyn and Pelc argue that the control exercised by Secretariat staff over adjudicators through nominations/procedures for remuneration raise legitimacy concerns. The suggestions discussed below aim to address, minimise or safeguard against these concerns and, accordingly, strengthen the legitimacy of the WTO DSS.

Given that the DSU explicitly acknowledges and mandates the Secretariat staff and the DG in assisting parties with selection of panellists, the concern is not so much with their involvement per se. With respect to the Secretariat staff, it is about ensuring that their functions are exercised within the mandate given to them by the WTO Members, ie, to *assist* the disputing parties in the selection process,[151] as well as that it does not compromise the independence of the adjudicative functions. With respect to the DG

[147] ibid Title II, Ch II.III(2)
[148] ibid.
[149] ibid Title II, Ch II.III(2) and (3).
[150] ibid Title II, Ch II.III(3).
[151] Malacrida (n 22) 311–33.

selection process, it is about ensuring that the consent of the parties reflected in Article 8.7 is respected. To that end, the following suggestions for reform are examined: (i) transparency regarding the Dispute Assistants involved in the process; (ii) rules on the accountability of Dispute Assistants participating in the composition of panels; (iii) prohibition on Dispute Assistants who participate in composition to assist panellists in the dispute resolution process (iv) rules on the role of Dispute Assistants and DG in panel composition; and (v) creation of a permanent roster of panellists or limiting ad hoc panellists.

i. Transparency Regarding the Dispute Assistants Involved in the Process

The first step in addressing the legitimacy concerns that arise with respect to Dispute Assistants is ensuring that there is information symmetry between the parties and the Secretariat. Accordingly, rules must ensure transparency regarding the names of staff involved during the selection process of panellists. Specifically, the names of the staff who assist in nominating potential panellists to the parties, those advising the DG in composing the panel, the Assistant to the DG, and the staff who eventually assist the panellists during the panel proceedings must be continuously disclosed to the parties and, eventually, to the public at large. This was the earlier practice in the early stages of the WTO DSS, where the Note by the Secretariat on the Constitution of the Panel would specifically list the names of staff who were assigned to the dispute.[152] However, it was discontinued by the Secretariat in order to retain the flexibility to change the staff working on the dispute at a later stage of the proceedings (especially given the increasing workload on disputes).

This practice should be re-introduced and the parties should be informed of the names of the staff involved in process of selection of the panellists. Additionally, the names should also eventually be disclosed to the public and other Members through the panel composition note. Furthermore, this should be a continuous process of transparency, updating these disclosures of any changes to the composition of the staff who assist the parties (Article 8.6 DSU), the DG (Article 8.7 DSU) and the panellists (Article 27.1 DSU). Such disclosures would enhance transparency and legitimacy of the dispute resolution process, and reinforce the consent of the parties reflected in Article 8 and 27 DSU. This also allows parties to raise objections, if any, to the participation of any particular staff (see the suggestion in section II.D.ii below) and strengthens the overall accountability of the selection process.

ii. Rules on Accountability for Dispute Assistants Involved in the Process

While the WTO has a robust system on accountability of staff through its WTO Rules of Conduct, and Staff Regulation, a concern that arises at this stage is that these rules are not explicitly applicable to staff who assist at the stage of *selection of panellists*.[153] As discussed above, these rules are explicitly made applicable to staff who assist panellists

[152] WTO Secretariat, *United States – Standards for Reformulated and Conventional Gasoline, Constitution of the Panel Established at the Request of Venezuela*, WTO Doc WT/DS2/3 (3 May 1995); see also WTO Secretariat, *Japan – Taxes on Alcoholic Beverages, Constitution of the Panel Established at the Requests of the EC, Canada and the United States*, WT/DS8/6, WT/DS10/6, WT/DS11/3 (6 November 1995).

[153] However, as we have noted in section II.C, the standards of independence and impartiality continue to apply to all staff irrespective of the stage of the dispute.

in the dispute process under Article 27.1 DSU. Therefore, it may be useful to extend (clearly) the application of these rules to include staff who assist parties in the selection of panellists, either by proposing names of potential panellists under Article 8.6 DSU or in assisting the DG with selection of panellists under Article 8.7 DSU.

In order to further expand on these rules, inspiration may be drawn from other adjudicatory bodies, notably the IBA Guidelines on Conflict of Interest in International Arbitration (hereinafter 'IBA Guidelines').[154] Like the WTO Rules of Conduct, the IBA Guidelines have a General Standard for evaluating conflict of interest and an obligation to disclose.[155] In contrast, however, the illustrative list in the IBA Guidelines is more nuanced and detailed than that found in Annex 2 of the WTO Rules of Conduct (Illustrative List of Information to Be Disclosed). Part II of the IBA Guidelines contains the Practical Application of the General Standards, with traffic light-coded lists (Red, Orange and Green) providing illustrative situations of potential conflict of interest. It should be noted that the IBA Guidelines apply equally to arbitrators and Dispute Assistants (termed 'tribunal assistants').[156] Rather than drawing on the specifics of the content of these lists, here we focus on the structure of the three types of lists on conflict of interest:

a) The Red List, which has two parts, a 'Non-waivable Red List' and a 'Waivable Red List'. These both describe situations that give rise to justifiable doubts as to the arbitrator's impartiality or independence. The Non-waivable List contains situations that cannot be resolved by acceptance by the parties. The Waivable List covers situations that are not as severe but are nevertheless serious; they require the parties to expressly state their willingness to have this person as the arbitrator after becoming aware of the situation.

b) The Orange List: this covers situations which, depending on the facts of a given case, may, in the eyes of the parties, give rise to doubts as to the arbitrator's impartiality or independence and, therefore, the arbitrator has a duty to disclose such situations. In these situations, the parties are deemed to have accepted the arbitrator if, after disclosure, no timely objection is made. This is a subjective standard of conflict of interest, which requires making appropriate disclosures to the parties. The parties may thereafter object if such disclosures give rise to justifiable doubts in relation to impartiality or independence.

c) The Green List: this contains situations where no appearance and no actual conflict of interest can exist either under the subjective or the objective standard. Thus, the arbitrator has no duty to disclose situations falling within the Green List.

Building on this model, specific items suited to the WTO DSS could be integrated into disclosures under Red, Orange and Green Lists. Taking one example relevant to the case of Dispute Assistants in the stage of selection of ad hoc adjudicators: if the parties are concerned about Dispute Assistants recommending adjudicators who hold a certain position aligned with that of the Secretariat, it may be possible to include

[154] International Bar Association, Guidelines on Conflict of Interest in International Arbitration (approved by the IBA Council 25 May 2024) General Standard Part I.
[155] ibid.
[156] ibid.

in the Orange List the requirement to disclose a list of all cases in which the Dispute Assistant has previously assisted. While it is often specific staff who are responsible for assisting parties at this stage, it is possible that such staff may have previously held a different role in assisting the panellists during the dispute. Such disclosure would allow parties to consider whether their previous involvement in cases raises concerns in the present dispute and, if so, they could object to their participation in the *selection process* at issue. However, the DG could retain the power to decide that a potential conflict of interest is not sufficiently material to warrant non-assignment of the staff, including due to available Secretariat resources.[157] Although many Members may already (informally) be aware of who the staff involved in the selection process are, the explicit disclosure requirements formalise the practice and increase accountability.

At present, the WTO Rules of Conduct require similar disclosures to be made by Secretariat staff to the DG with respect to their participation in an earlier formal consideration of the specific measure at issue in a dispute under any provision of the WTO Agreement, including through formal legal advice under Article 27.2 DSU.[158] Through an internal memo, the DG mandated that the Directors of the LAD and the Rules Division would receive the disclosures of staff in their respective division. The Dispute Assistants are also asked to confirm their compliance with the WTO Rules of Conduct in an email to the Registry. However, these disclosures only take place at a later stage, when deciding staffing for the dispute, after the composition of the panel. The requirement for disclosures should be made explicitly applicable to Secretariat staff assisting in the selection of the panel, allowing parties to object to the participation of the particular Dispute Assistant in proposing potential panellists under Article 8.6 or in assisting the DG in selecting the panellists under Article 8.7 DSU. Parties may want to take into account the prior panel participation of any legal staff who would be subsequently involved in a selection process of the panellists. Nonetheless, the DG should retain the power to decide that, despite such a conflict of interest, the staff ought to continue assisting the parties with the selection process, taking into account the available resources of the Secretariat.[159]

iii. Prohibition on Dispute Assistants Who Participate in Composition to Assist Panellists in the Dispute Resolution Process

One of the concerns raised above argues that panellists would be beholden to the Dispute Assistants involved in the nomination of panellists if they are interested in being re-appointed.[160] This gives rise to the risk that the same Dispute Assistants, who would thereafter assist the panellists during the panel proceedings or implementation stage, would be able to exert undue influence over their decision-making function. This naturally raises concerns as to the independence of the adjudicator and, consequently, impacts the legitimacy of the dispute resolution process. In other words, the risk is that the panellists, rather than using their own decision-making mandate, would defer to

[157] Rules of Conduct, fn 2.
[158] ibid; WTO Staff Regulations, Annex B, para 34.
[159] Rules of Conduct, fn 2.
[160] Pauwelyn and Pelc (n 29).

the decisions made by the Dispute Assistants. Therefore, in safeguarding against this risk, a possible solution would be to separate these functions entirely. In other words, the team of Secretariat staff who are responsible for proposing names of potential panellists to the parties (Article 8.6) should be distinct from the staff assisting the DG in the composition of the panel (Article 8.7), and the staff who are responsible for assisting panellists subsequently during the course of the dispute resolution process. Although this will not eliminate such risk entirely (as non-confidential information could still be shared between the two groups of staff), it creates a safeguard against concerns that compromise the legitimacy of the WTO DSS. If the DG is requested to compose the panel (Article 8.7), a specific and independent legal assistant should be designated to assist the DG with this process, who is distinct from the team from the LAD or the Rules Division that assisted the parties in composition (Article 8.6). To ensure that the DG is informed of the relevant nominations that were put to the parties (and rejected by them), sufficient briefing and written record of the slate of panellists offered to the parties can be maintained and supplied to the DG.

With respect to Directors, in order to retain their functions at the stage of proposing names of potential panellists to the parties and even with respect to assisting the DG in the composition of the panel, it may be possible to restrict their role in the later stages of the dispute in assisting panellists. This would avoid any appearance of potential dependence of panellists on Secretariat staff. The concern with the continued role of the Directors is due to the position of power occupied by them as senior staff who supervise and control the work of all Dispute Assistants in assisting panellists during the dispute. At the same time, the Directors' institutional memory (if they stay in place long enough) and experience are assets in identifying suitable candidates with the necessary expertise and other qualifications requested by the parties. Therefore, their role could be retained at the panel composition stage and restricted in later stages of the dispute. Alternatively, as will be elaborated further in Chapter 23, the Directors may also choose to continue to play a supervisory substantive role during the panel proceedings. This would mean that their role during the panel composition stage should be restricted or done away with, unless parties and Members accept the situation. If so, their supervisory role at the stage of panel composition could be fulfilled by staff who exclusively work in this stage and do not thereafter assist the panellists/other adjudicators in the dispute themselves or supervise any staff who assist the panellists/other adjudicators. Of course, such changes would also have to be reflected explicitly in the job description and mandate of the Director. This is necessary to protect Director(s) from being held responsible for work that they did not supervise, as well as to ensure transparency and accountability in the system.

iv. Rules on Role of Dispute Assistants and the DG at the Panel Composition Stage

The concern that has arisen relates to the scope of the discretion afforded to the Secretariat and the DG in nominating potential panellists beyond the scope of the Indicative List (which is constituted by WTO Members).[161] However, in limiting or restricting the discre-

[161] Mavroidis specifically raises this concern on the role of Secretariat staff in nominating names of potential panellists beyond the Indicative List.

tion of the Secretariat or the DG at this stage, other considerations and related reforms must be kept in mind. The first and foremost is that the Indicative List has not been updated regularly by the Members, and accordingly, is utilised relatively rarely. Further, limiting the discretion of Dispute Assistants should not come at the cost of compromising the expertise and experience of the panellists who are selected. Therefore, any such suggestion for reform must also be accompanied by corollary proposals on revising and updating the Indicative List by Members. At the same time, even with strengthened requirements on the Indicative List, the risk of compromising the expertise and experience of panellists may persist if Members do not strictly comply with enhanced qualification criteria and their duty to duly update the Indicative List.[162] Indeed the Molina Report, which proposes a strengthened Indicative List, only encourages the Secretariat to rely on this List in proposing potential panellists to parties.[163] Implicitly acknowledging this possible risk, the Molina Report does not limit the discretion of the Secretariat to this List.

A middle ground is revealed in Thailand's proposal on allowing either party to request that the panel Chair be appointed by 'lot' (ie, through random selection) from a 'Roster of Panel Chairs' established by the DSB.[164] Inclusion within the roster would be dependent on specific qualifications, expertise, experience (including prior experience as a panellist) and willingness/availability to serve as Chair upon request and subsequently approved by the DSB.[165] Rather than mandating that the panel Chair *must* come from the roster, either party has the right to exercise the option to request the DG to appoint the Chair of the panel by drawing lots from the Roster of Panel Chairs.[166] Such a middle ground could ensure that the consent of the parties is reinforced, while also leaving sufficient room to explore suitable candidates with expertise and experience outside of it. The discretion remains with the disputing parties.

Similarly, at the DG selection stage, given the lack of opportunity afforded to parties to reject selections made by the DG, the general rule should be that the selection of panellists must be from a 'roster' or revised 'Indicative List'. Of course, the parties may agree to forgo this requirement, given the specific demands of the case. Two possible options exist that would limit and guide the discretion of the DG. *First*, as suggested by Thailand and later by the Third EU Proposal, if the DG selects the Chair of the panel, such selection must be from the 'roster' or Indicative List. The DG would have the discretion to deviate from the roster or list only in the case of the remaining panellists. *Second*, the general rule is that all selections are made from the roster or list, with exceptional power granted to the DG to select individuals from outside of it. Drawing inspiration from the Canadian proposal, the DG could in principle be required to nominate names from the roster or list, unless the DG determines that insufficient expertise is available from the roster for a particular dispute.[167] The residual discretion in both options is retained to account for exceptional

[162] We will examine in detail what the scope of such criteria could be in ch 23, along with other proposals on strengthening the experience and expertise of adjudicators to address concerns relating to asymmetry between adjudicators and Dispute Assistants.

[163] Molina Report, Title II, Ch II.II(15).

[164] WTO, 'Contribution to Improve the Dispute Settlement Understanding: Panel System, Communication from Thailand', WTO Doc TN/DS/W/31 (22 January 2003), para 4.

[165] ibid para 6.

[166] ibid para 9(b).

[167] WTO, 'Contribution of Canada to the Improvement of the WTO Dispute Settlement Understanding, Communication from Canada', WTO Doc TN/DS/W/41 (24 January 2003) 16, para 7.

situations where, for example, all the potential panellists with the relevant experience/ expertise in a dispute have already been suggested and exhausted at the Secretariat stage or are simply unavailable. Even if the Indicative List is modified and updated regularly, such situations can still arise. Therefore, allowing some guided discretion to the DG to nominate panellists beyond the Indicative List accounts for such scenarios.

v. Creation of a Permanent Roster of Panellists or Limiting Ad Hoc Panellists

A more far-reaching suggestion that has arisen in some of the proposals examined earlier with systemic implications on the WTO DSS. This is drawn from the First EU Proposal and the Second EU Proposal on Panel Reform,[168] which move away from a fully ad hoc system of panellists. These proposals were motivated by delays arising from selecting qualified and uncontested panellists. The First EU Proposal suggested the creation of a standing body, or fixed roster, of a minimum of 20 professionals, who would serve as full-time panellists.[169] This proposal argued that such a pre-established roster would reduce delays and ensure higher-quality and more consistent jurisprudence, as panellists would commit more time to and gain familiarity with WTO law and procedures.[170]

Mavroidis also proposes a similar framework, with a return to one-instance adjudication staffed by competent judges or a 'WTO Court'.[171] Our discussion here is restricted to one aspect of his proposal: permanent judges (as opposed to ad hoc panellists), where the role of the Secretariat and the DG in the selection of panellists is restricted.[172] The move towards permanent judges could enhance the independence of the adjudicators from the Secretariat. The aim is to separate the judicial function of the WTO from the legislative (and executive) functions of the organisation. This includes giving the adjudicators the right to appoint their own clerks, who would be independent of the WTO Secretariat.[173]

Such a framework naturally addresses the concerns raised on the role of the Dispute Assistants in the panel composition process as it would fundamentally change the ad hoc nature of the panel. However, at the same time, a standing panel would also limit the flexibility afforded to parties to change and even do away with some panellists for any reason, whether compelling or not (as in the present system). It would also restrict the ability to appoint experts with specialised knowledge relevant to certain disputes.[174] Further, this may also lead to relatively inexperienced panellists chosen for political and geographical diversity reasons, thus compromising the overall quality of the WTO DSS. Finally, a permanent body would be much more expensive and would likely increase WTO budget requirements and WTO Members' contribution. These factors have

[168] For a discussion on the establishment of a permanent panel body, see WJ Davey, 'The Case for a WTO Permanent Panel Body' (2003) 6(1) *Journal of International Economic Law* 177; T Cottier, 'The WTO Permanent Panel Body: A Bridge Too Far?' (2003) 6(1) *Journal of International Economic Law* 187; and JHJ Bourgeois, 'Comment on a WTO Permanent Panel Body' (2003) 6(1) *Journal of International Economic Law* 211; see also EU Petersmann, 'WTO Negotiators Meet Academics: The Negotiations on Improvements of the WTO Dispute Settlement System' (2003) 6(1) *Journal of International Economic Law* 237.

[169] WTO, 'Contribution of the European Communities and its Member States to the Improvement of the WTO Dispute Settlement Understanding', WTO Doc TN/DS/W/1 (13 March 2002).

[170] ibid 2.

[171] Mavroidis (n 24) 529.

[172] ibid 543. We will discuss other aspects in ch 23.

[173] ibid 559.

[174] Bourgeois (n 168) 211.

prompted the EU to modify its own proposals to suggest that the Chairs of panels come from a pre-agreed roster, appointed by the DG through lot, while the other two panellists could be selected on an ad hoc basis by the parties for each dispute (Second EU Proposal).[175] This remains a controversial position with limited consensus or support among other WTO Members, most notably the US.

III. The Role of Dispute Assistants in the Appointment of Arbitrators

A. Appointment of Arbitrators for Proceedings to Determine the Reasonable Time Period of Implementation under Article 21.3 DSU

As per Article 21.3 DSU, at a DSB meeting held within 30 days after the date of adoption of the panel or AB Report, the Member concerned is required to inform the DSB of their intentions with respect to the implementation of the recommendations and rulings of the DSB.[176] If it is impracticable to comply immediately, the losing Member is granted a reasonable period of time to comply.[177] The reasonable period of time is either proposed by the Member concerned after approval from the DSB[178] or, in the absence of such approval, mutually agreed by the parties to the dispute within the prescribed time period.[179] If the parties cannot reach such mutual agreement, the parties may request an arbitrator to determine the reasonable period.[180] If the parties cannot agree on an arbitrator within 10 days of referring the matter to arbitration, the DG appoints the arbitrator within 10 days after consulting the parties.[181]

The AB Secretariat used to assist with the selection of arbitrators under Article 21.3.[182] However, since the dissolution of the AB Secretariat, the LAD staff (or Rules Staff) who assist with the composition of panels have not been involved or asked by the parties to assist in the selection of arbitrators. The parties ask the DG directly to appoint an Article 21.3 arbitrator.[183] As noted by Pereyra, all Article 21.3(c) arbitrators were chosen from among current or former AB members or experienced panellists.[184]

[175] WTO, 'Contribution of the European Communities and its Member States to the Improvement of the WTO Dispute Settlement Understanding', WTO Doc TN/DS/W/38 (23 January 2003)

[176] DSU, art 21.3.

[177] ibid. See also M Qian, '"Reasonable Period of Time" in the WTO Dispute Settlement System' (2012) 15(1) *Journal of International Economic Law* 257; and PC Mavroidis et al, 'Ask for the Moon, Settle for the Stars: What is a Reasonable Period to Comply with WTO Awards?' (2017) 16(2) *World Trade Review* 395.

[178] DSU, art 21.3(a).

[179] ibid art 21.3(b).

[180] ibid art 21.3(c).

[181] ibid fn 12.

[182] Interestingly, the relevant WTO page for information relating to 'Arbitrations under Article 21.3(c) of the DSU' is filed under 'Appellate Body': WTO, 'Arbitrations under Article 21.3(c) of the DSU', www.wto.org/english/tratop_e/dispu_e/arbitrations_e.htm

[183] WTO Secretariat, *Ukraine – AntiDumping Measures on Ammonium Nitrate, Appointment of the Arbitrator by the DirectorGeneral under Article 21.3(c) of the DSU, Note by the Secretariat*, WTO Doc WT/DS493/12 (18 December 2019); and WTO Award of the Arbitrator, *United States – Certain Methodologies and their Application to AntiDumping Proceedings Involving China*, WT/DS471/RPT (19 January 2018) para 1.4.

[184] Pereyra (n 10) 59.

The selection process by the DG functions in a similar way to other selection processes for ad hoc adjudicators under Article 8. Therefore, the following suggestions for reform relating to Dispute Assistants and the DG at the stage of composition of panels also applies to this stage as well: (i) transparency regarding the Dispute Assistants involved in the process, specifically advisors to the DG; (ii) rules on the accountability of Dispute Assistants participating in assisting the DG with the selection of arbitrators; (iii) prohibition on Dispute Assistants who participate in composition to assist panellists in the dispute resolution process; and (d) rules on the role of DG in the selection of arbitrators.

B. Appointment of Arbitrators for Proceedings to Determine the Level of Suspension of Concessions under Article 22.6 DSU

In a WTO dispute, if the losing party fails to bring the challenged measure into conformity with the relevant WTO provision or otherwise comply with the recommendations and rulings within the reasonable period of time, the winning party may request authorisation from the DSB to retaliate in the form of suspension of concessions or other obligations under the covered agreements.[185] If the losing party objects to the level of suspension of concessions (which ought to be equivalent to the level of nullification of benefits), they can refer the matter to arbitration.[186] Such arbitration is generally performed by the original panel, if panellists are available, or by an arbitrator appointed by the DG.[187] Panellists of the original panel (which also make up the compliance review panel) therefore become the 'Arbitrator'[188] and are requested to evaluate the effects of the violation which is usually not a component of the determination by the panel and the AB.[189]

Although the 'Arbitrator' in such cases is supposed to be composed of the same panellists as the original panels, sometimes it may become necessary to find one or more new panellists to constitute the arbitration panel.[190] In such cases, the DG process would function similarly to the process for composition of panels under Article 8.7.

[185] DSU, art 22.1; PC Mavroidis, 'Suspension of Concessions (Retaliation)' in *The WTO Dispute Settlement System* (Edward Elgar, 2022) 298.

[186] DSU, art 22.6. See generally K Kim, 'The 'Equivalent' Standard in WTO Arbitrations of Trade Remedy Disputes' (2021) 55(6) *Journal of World Trade* 991; WTO, *WTO Analytical Index: Guide to WTO Law and Practice*, 3rd edn (Cambridge University Press, 2012) 1843.

[187] DSU, art 22.6.

[188] ibid.

[189] In some agreements, like the Comprehensive and Progressive Agreement for Trans-Pacific Partnership (CPTPP), the dispute settlement procedure provides that the panel will determine the violation if any and the level of nullification.

[190] As of 31 December 2021, all arbitrations under art 22.6 DSU have been referred to the original panel, except WTO Arbitration, *United States – Anti-Dumping Act of 1916 (European Communities) (Article 22.6 – United States)*, WT/DS136/ARB (24 February 2004) and WTO Arbitration, *United States – Measures Concerning the Importation, Marketing and Sale of Tuna and Tuna Products (Mexico) (Article 22.6 – United States)*, WT/DS381/ARB (25 April 2017). In these cases, the Chairman of the original panel was no longer available. However, the other two arbitrators were members of the original panel.

Therefore, the suggestions for reform given in the list at the end of section II.A above relating to the role of Dispute Assistants and the DG apply here as well.

IV. The Role of Dispute Assistants in the Appointment of Arbitrators under Article 25 (Non-MPIA) Procedures

Lastly, Article 25 DSU allows for 'expeditious arbitration' as an alternative means of dispute settlement for disputes, or parts of disputes, based on the clear agreement of both parties. The parties are also required to accordingly agree to the applicable procedures, including the procedure for appointment of the adjudicators (ie, arbitrators). The MPIA is an arrangement concluded using Article 25 DSU and the Statement on a mechanism for developing, documenting and sharing practices and procedures in the conduct of WTO disputes (WTO Doc JOB/DSB/1). There has been limited practice of disputes under Article 25: a total of 14 disputes where procedures under Article 25 were agreed by the parties. Of these 14, the arbitrator was constituted in six cases (including MPIA arbitration) and the award was circulated in three cases.[191] This section explains the four cases (non-MPIA) where the arbitrator was constituted. The cases on retaliation mandated to arbitrators under the MPIA will be discussed in Chapter 23:[192]

- With respect to the first arbitration under Article 25, *US – Section 110(5) Copyright Act*, the parties agreed to Article 25 arbitration proceedings to determine the level of nullification or impairment of benefits to the EU from the inconsistent measure.[193] The parties had agreed that the members of the original panel should serve as arbitrators; however, the Chairperson of the original panel and one member were no longer available. In accordance with the agreed procedures, the DG appointed two arbitrators to replace them.[194]
- In the reciprocal disputes, *US – Steel and Aluminium Products (EU)* and *EU – Additional Duties (US)*, the same individuals who served as panellists were also the arbitrators.[195] The DG did not play a role in the appointment. The parties had informed the WTO Members that the arbitration would be immediately suspended for an indefinite period of time upon the selection of the arbitrators.

[191] *See WTO*, 'Dispute Settlement Information Tables', *WTO Analytical Index*, 79–80, www.wto.org/english/res_e/publications_e/ai17_e/tableofcases_e.pdf. This list was updated as of December 2024, and since then, there has been one more dispute: *China – Enforcement of Intellectual Property Rights (Complaint by the European Union)*, WTO Doc WT/DS611/13 (Constitution of the Arbitrator, 2023).

[192] It should be recalled that under the MPIA, arbitrators are not ad hoc, but are selected generally for a period of 3 years, renewable once.

[193] WTO, *United States – Section 110(5) of the US Copyright Act, Recourse to Article 25 of the DSU – Agreed Procedures*, WTO Doc WT/DS160/15 (3 August 2001).

[194] WTO Secretariat, *United States – Section 110(5) of the US Copyright Act, Recourse to Article 25 of the DSU, Constitution of the Arbitrator – Note by the Secretariat*, WTO Doc WT/DS160/16 (13 August 2001).

[195] WTO, *United States – Certain Measures on Steel and Aluminium Products (Complaint by the European Union)*, WTO Doc WT/DS548/19 (Agreed Procedures, 2022); WTO, *European Union – Additional Duties on Certain Products from the United States (Complaint by the United States)*, WTO Doc WT/DS559/7 (Agreed Procedures, 2022); WTO, *United States – Certain Measures on Steel and Aluminium Products (Complaint by the European Union)*, WTO Doc WT/DS548/22 (Constitution of the Arbitrator, 2022).

- In *Turkey – Pharmaceutical Products*, the EU (member of the MPIA) and Turkey (not a member of the MPIA) agreed on procedures for appeal arbitrations between them.[196] As per the agreed procedures, the arbitrator was composed of one former AB member, one MPIA appeal arbitrator and another individual randomly selected from the combined list.[197] However, the constitution note does not specify how the random selection was conducted.[198]

In all these cases, the parties agree on specific procedures for the appointment of arbitrators, including any potential role of the Secretariat and the DG. While it is entirely at the discretion of the parties to determine the extent of the functions discharged by the Secretariat and the DG, if such functions are agreed to and included, then the corollary duties given in the list at the end of section II.A above could also be explored.

V. Conclusion

In this chapter, we have recounted the specific functions discharged by Dispute Assistants in the selection of adjudicators across five stages of the WTO DSS and related ethical concerns: specifically, the selection of ad hoc panellists in original panels (Article 8 DSU) and compliance panels (Article 21.5 DSU), the selection of arbitrators in arbitration for the determination of the reasonable period of time for implementation (Article 21.3 (c) DSU), arbitrations for the determination of the level of suspension of concessions (Article 22.6 DSU), and arbitrations by mutual agreement of the parties under Article 25 DSU. We have examined the existing procedure, practice and proposals relating to these concerns. Our suggestions build on this analysis and are specifically geared towards enhancing the legitimacy of the role of Dispute Assistants. Broadly, the suggestions for reform aim to increase *transparency* regarding the specific actors involved, *accountability* regarding the scope/participation of these actors, limiting the *potential influence* of such actors over the adjudicative function, and guiding the *discretion* exercised by these actors in the adjudicator selection stage. These suggestions, both individually and collectively, contribute to strengthening the consent of the Members to the functions of Dispute Assistants reflected in various provisions of the DSU, while enhancing the legitimacy of the dispute resolution system.

[196] *WTO, Turkey – Pharmaceutical Products, Agreed Procedures*, WTO Doc *WT/DS583/10 (25 March 2022). Agreed procedures were also communicated for the EU – Safeguard Measures on Steel* dispute, but the case was not appealed and no arbitrator was constituted. See Pereyra (n 10) 58–59.

[197] WTO, *Turkey – Certain Measures Concerning the Production, Importation and Marketing of Pharmaceutical Products (Complaint by the European Union)*, WTO Doc WT/DS583/10 (Agreed Procedures for Arbitration, 2022) para 7; WTO, *Turkey – Certain Measures Concerning the Production, Importation and Marketing of Pharmaceutical Products (Complaint by the European Union)*, WTO Doc WT/DS583/13 (Constitution of the Arbitrator, 2022).

[198] As can be gathered from the names selected, one former AB member (Mr Seung Wha Chang) and two MPIA roster members (Mr Mateo Diego-Fernandez Andrade and Mr Guohua Yang) were selected. See WTO, *Turkey – Certain Measures Concerning the Production, Importation and Marketing of Pharmaceutical Products (Complaint by the European Union)*, WTO Doc WT/DS583/13 (Constitution of the Arbitrator, 2022).

23

Dispute Assistants and the WTO Adjudicative Process

I. Introduction

This chapter explores the functions discharged by Dispute Assistants across adjudicative processes in the WTO DSS and the concerns raised in those contexts. We have grouped these processes into three categories, which broadly capture the specific functions and roles discharged by Dispute Assistants and adjudicators.

First, in section II, we examine Dispute Assistants assisting adjudicators in original and implementation/compliance review panel ('compliance review panel') processes. Although the legal and procedural issues in the processes differ, they involve similar types of functions discharged by Secretariat staff in assisting panellists. In some cases, the same Dispute Assistants may be assigned on the original panel and the compliance panel, but this is not necessarily the case. We detail the concerns that have arisen with respect to Dispute Assistants in panel stages (section II.A), the relevant WTO provisions, practice and proposals for reform relating to these concerns (section II.B), and, lastly, we discuss our suggestions for reform (section II.C).

Second, in section III, we examine Dispute Assistants in arbitration processes, across three distinct procedures: for the determination of the reasonable period of time for implementation of a recommendation/ruling (Article 21.3 DSU); in arbitrations under Article 25 (excluding the appeal procedures agreed under Multi-Party Interim Appeal Arbitration Arrangement (MPIA), which are examined separately below); and arbitrations for the determination of level of suspension of concessions and obligations (Article 22.6 DSU). While briefly explaining the former two, our focus is on the latter proceedings relating to the determination of the level of suspension of concessions and obligation (in the context of legitimate retaliation). The main characteristic of this stage is the assistance provided by non-legal staff, in addition to the legal staff, specifically economists from the Economics and Statistics Research Division (ERSD). We also discuss assistance, including advice, from non-legal staff from other (operational) divisions dealing with WTO rules on matters such as agriculture, international standards, services and intellectual property. In these Article 22.6–7 DSU proceedings, the Dispute Assistants aid the arbitrator in determining the level of nullification or impairment of benefits resulting from the breach of the WTO obligation as determined in the panel or AB ruling, which in turn determines the level of suspension of concession or obligation. More broadly, we examine the concerns that have arisen with respect to assistance to adjudicators by economists and other non-legal staff (section III.A), the relevant WTO provisions and proposals for reform relating to these concerns (section III.B) and our suggestions for reform (section III.C).

Third, in section IV, we examine Dispute Assistants in appeal stage(s) process. As already explained in Chapters 19 and 22, the appellate stage of the WTO consisted of the AB, but it is presently not operational. When the AB stopped operating, some Members set up the MPIA under Article 25 DSU to resolve disputes that are appealed from a panel report.[1] This section examines the (limited) functions of Dispute Assistants at the stage of selection of appeal adjudicators, as well as their functions in assisting adjudicators in the dispute resolution process of the AB, the MPIA and any other potential appeal stage. We detail the concerns on the role of Dispute Assistants that assisted AB members, and the way in which these concerns presently play out in the case of staff assisting MPIA arbitrators (section IV.A), the relevant WTO provisions, practice and proposals for reform relating to these concerns (section IV.B), and our suggestions for improving the current MPIA and any potential future appeal stage (section IV.C).

The next Chapter 24 will examine how some of our suggestions for improving these processes can be implemented in the WTO DSS. They might best be introduced at specific stages of the dispute settlement process or may serve as broader structural changes that impact more than one stage of the dispute settlement process.

II. Dispute Assistants in the Original and Compliance Panel Proceedings

As explained in Chapter 22, panels are ad hoc adjudicative bodies established to determine the consistency of measures implemented by a Member when challenged by one or more Members and alleged to be inconsistent with obligations under covered agreement(s) (referred to as 'original panel proceedings'). The concerned (losing) Member is required to comply with the recommendations and rulings of the panel report (and the AB Report when it existed) as adopted by the DSB. If there is disagreement as to the existence or consistency of measures taken to comply with such recommendations or rulings, a compliance review panel is established to make this determination (compliance review panel proceedings).[2] The adjudicators in original and compliance review panels (ie, panellists) are traditionally diplomats and governmental officials, some of whom possess a legal background. Specifically in the case of disputes relating to trade remedies, panellists tend to be practitioners and officials of national investigating authorities or other governmental authorities.

[1] WTO, '*MultiParty Interim Appeal Arbitration Arrangement Pursuant to Article 25 of the DSU*', WTO Doc JOB/DSB/1/Add.12 (2020) (MPIA).

[2] *Understanding on Rules and Procedures Governing the Settlement of Disputes*, Marrakesh Agreement Establishing the World Trade Organization, Annex 2 (adopted 15 April 1994), art 21.5. The DSU envisages that wherever possible, the compliance panel should be composed of the original panellists.

The panellists are assisted by Secretariat staff of the Legal Affairs Division (LAD),[3] along with (legal and non-legal) staff from other substantive areas relevant to the dispute (for example, from divisions on agriculture, market access, services, intellectual property (IP), specialists or economists), depending on the claims raised or staff of the Rules Division (for trade remedy matters like industrial subsidies, safeguard measures and anti-dumping disputes).[4] A team assisting a panel typically comprises one or more junior staff (one of whom is appointed as the 'secretary' to the panel and who assists with communications between the panel and the disputing parties), one legal officer and/or one senior legal officer, and other staff depending on the complexity/size/requirements of the case.[5]

After the panel is composed, the Secretariat team assigned to the dispute assists the panel in drafting the Working Procedures and timetable for the dispute and during the related 'organisation meeting'.[6] Usually, after the parties file their first written submissions,[7] the Dispute Assistants draft the first Issues Paper, which summarises the facts and the arguments put forward by the parties, identifies the legal issues that arise and details the various approaches the panel could take in addressing the factual and legal issues.[8] In closed session discussions with the panellists, the Dispute Assistants also suggest questions that may be sent out to the parties before the hearing. The Dispute Assistants typically participate in all meetings of the panellists, with or without the parties. At the end of each internal panel meeting, the panel Chair and panellists give a series of instructions to the Secretariat staff relating to subsequent questions to the parties, future research and notes needed, drafts to be initiated etc. The panel's deliberations are confidential, and the Dispute Assistants attend and participate in the deliberations. Even legal interns may contribute to research for notes and other drafts and may sometimes attend the deliberations without participating. The panellists decide on the specific points raised in Issues Papers and, with the assistance of the Secretariat staff, work on the panel reasoning and findings. The Dispute Assistants thereafter produce a first draft panel report which is reviewed, line by line, with all panellists in meetings conducted across a few days – multiple drafts may be exchanged by assistants and panellists.

In their daily work for a panel, the Secretariat staff report to their administrative superior (ie, the Director of the LAD or Rules Division). Although the Director is ultimately responsible for conducting the annual performance evaluation of such staff (with the primary responsibility on the supervisor), the panellist's degree of satisfaction with the work of Dispute Assistants is still relevant to these evaluations. So, it is expected that Dispute Assistants will follow the instructions of the panellists, even while under

[3] DA Baker and G Marceau, 'The World Trade Organization' in F Baetens (ed), *Legitimacy of Unseen Actors in International Adjudication* (Cambridge University Press, 2019) 83.

[4] ibid.

[5] JM Wauters, 'The Role of the WTO Secretariat in WTO Disputes: Silent Witness or Ghost Expert?' (2021) 12 *Global Policy* 3, 84.

[6] The template for Working Procedures provided in Appendix 3 of the DSU may be adapted to the needs of the case.

[7] DSU, art 12.6.

[8] The Issues Paper is a descriptive, analytical and advisory note for briefing the panel which is not binding upon the panel. See Baker and Marceau (n 3); V Hughes, 'Working in WTO Dispute Settlement: Pride without Prejudice' in G Marceau (ed), *A History of Law and Lawyers in the GATT/WTO: The Development of the Rule of Law in the Multilateral Trading System* (Cambridge University Press, 2015) 400.

the supervision of the Director.[9] However, as will be discussed later, tensions may arise when the instructions differ.

A. Concerns Raised over the Role of Dispute Assistants

Many of the concerns that have been raised in the recent years in relation to the WTO DSS have focused on the AB, specifically interpretations and conclusions put forward in AB reports. The concerns relating to Secretariat support for panellists have received comparatively less attention. This section recounts concerns raised relating to: (i) the risk of asymmetry between the capacity/expertise of panellists (ad hoc) and the Secretariat staff (permanent); (ii) the risk of asymmetry between the panellists and Secretariat staff due to command over the working language; (iii) the lack of direct supervision or control over the Secretariat staff by the panellists; and (iv) the risk of excessive delegation of tasks, including decision-making and drafting, to the Dispute Assistants. The core of these concerns relates to the alleged undue influence that Dispute Assistants may exert over the decision-making function of the panellists. This raises the risk that the adjudicators are failing to fulfil their adjudicative function as per the consent of the Members to the WTO DSS, and Dispute Assistants go beyond assisting the panellists. As we have seen in detail in Chapter 21, this adversely impacts the core facets of legitimacy of the dispute resolution process. It is important to note that these concerns are not strict categories and they naturally overlap.

i. Risk of Asymmetry between the Capacity/Expertise of Panellists (Ad Hoc) and the Secretariat Staff (Permanent)

We start with concerns arising from the ad hoc nature of the adjudicators, where panellists are selected to deal with individual disputes, while Secretariat staff often hold long-term positions within the Secretariat (as Institutional Assistants). This leads to the risk of asymmetry between the capacity and expertise of the adjudicators, and the Secretariat staff who assist them. At the same time, it is important to recall that the role of Dispute Assistants in the WTO DSS was a conscious decision on the part of Members. The series of controversial or 'failed'[10] panel decisions in the late 1970s and early 1980s,[11] where

[9] Panel chairpersons traditionally write a letter to the Director of the LAD and the Rules Division, expressing gratitude for the support received. More granular feedback is also certainly shared informally from the senior staff lawyers who supervised the junior lawyers. This forms the fundamental basis for their performance evaluations.

[10] A Porges, 'The Legal Affairs Division and law in the GATT and the Uruguay Round' in Marceau (n 8) 225.

[11] GATT Panel Report, *United States – Tax Legislation (DISC)* (US – DISC), L/4422 (adopted 7 December 1981) BISD 23S 98 (see also L/5271, BISD 28S 114); GATT Panel Report, *EEC – Programme of Minimum Import Prices, Licences and Surety Deposits for Certain Processed Fruits and Vegetables* (EEC – Minimum Import Prices) (adopted 18 October 1978) BISD 25S 68; GATT Panel Report, *European Communities – Refunds on Exports of Sugar (Australia)* (EC – Sugar Exports (Australia)), L/4833 (adopted 6 November 1979) BISD 26S 290; GATT Panel Report, *European Communities – Refunds on Exports of Sugar – Complaint by Brazil* (EC – Sugar Exports (Brazil)), L/5011 (adopted 10 November 1980) BISD 27S 69; GATT Panel Report, *Spain – Measures Concerning Domestic Sale of Soyabean Oil – Recourse to Article XXIII:2 by the United States* (Spain – Soyabean Oil), L/5142 (17 June 1981) (unadopted).

the panels did not receive assistance from lawyers,[12] led to a deliberate decision by the Members to provide panellists (sometimes without legal background) with credible legal assistance under the Understanding on Rules and Procedures Governing the Settlement of Disputes (DSU), and for a more legalistic approach to disputes generally.[13] Therefore, this explicit consent of Members to the role of Dispute Assistants must be kept in mind when assessing the impact of this concern over the legitimacy of the WTO DSS.

The first record of such concerns was made by Alan Wolff,[14] in a statement before the Committee on Finance of the US Senate in 1995.[15] He expressed concerns that in cases where the Secretariat staff are permanent and the adjudicators (panellists) are selected ad hoc for a particular dispute,[16] the former may be in a position to exert 'substantial influence' on decision of the adjudicators. We reproduce the relevant part of his statement below:

> *Powerful, ensconced staff.* Another troubling procedural aspect of the system is the effective authority of the WTO secretariat. The secretariat advisors may remain the same from year to year while the panellists serve only infrequently. The secretariat, therefore, is in a position where it may exert a substantial influence on the panel decisions. With ad hoc panellists and very limited time, the authority of the secretariat – unelected officials appointed without effective review by WTO member representatives – is likely to grow. The impact of this type of influence on the WTO Appellate Body is also unknown.[17]

Over the years, various scholars have reframed and furthered this concern.[18] Robert Hudec recounted some criticisms of the role played by the Secretariat, specifically that the staff have no mandate to participate in the decision-making function[19] and have no visible responsibility for what is decided.[20] However, Hudec added that such concerns are misdirected at the staff of the Secretariat. Rather, he explains, the real concern is the legal expertise (or lack thereof) of the adjudicators – ie, the panellists.[21]

[12] RE Hudec, 'The Role of the GATT Secretariat in the Evolution of the WTO Dispute Settlement Procedure' in J Bhagwati and M Hirsch (eds), *The Uruguay Round and Beyond: Essays in Honour of Arthur Dunkel* (Springer, 1998) 112.

[13] G Marceau and DA Baker, 'A Short History of the Rules Division' in Marceau (n 8) 112. They also note other factors as contributing to this shift, such as the negotiation of new, more complex rules on non-tariff barriers, and the newly binding character of art II GATT after the end of developed country exchange rate restrictions.

[14] Alan Wolff later became a Deputy Director-General of the WTO in 2015–21.

[15] AW Wolff, '*Prepared Statement*', Hearing before the Committee on Finance, United States Senate, 104th Cong, S 16, 60 (10 May 1995), www.finance.senate.gov/imo/media/doc/Hrg104-124.pdf.

[16] Although he does not attach this criticism to the AB Secretariat, he mentions the impact of this type of influence on the AB is unknown (at the time, as the AB had only been functional for over a year).

[17] Wolff (n 15).

[18] H Nordström, 'The WTO Secretariat in a Changing World' (2005) 39 *Journal of World Trade* 819; JD Greenwald, 'A Comparison of WTO and CIT/AFC Jurisprudence in Review of US Commerce Department Decisions in Antidumping and Countervailing Duty Proceedings' (2013) 21 *Tulane Journal of International and Comparative Law* 261; EU Petersmann 'The establishment of a GATT Office of Legal Affairs and the limits of "public reason"' in Marceau (n 8) 182–207.

[19] R Hudec, 'The New WTO Dispute Settlement Procedure: An Overview of the First Three Years' (1999) 8 *Minnesota Journal of Global Trade* 34–35.

[20] ibid.

[21] ibid.

More recently, Pauwelyn and Pelc have examined the role of the WTO Secretariat and AB staff, and have raised several concerns regarding their functions.[22] As we understand it, their primary concern goes back to the one raised by DDG Wolff in 1995: the institutional design of the WTO DSS where the staff are permanent, while the adjudicators are ad hoc or part-time. Given this institutional design, they argue that the enhanced role played by the staff at various stages of the dispute resolution process allows them to exercise control over the decision-making function that is beyond their mandate and within the purview of the adjudicators.[23]

Mavroidis re-frames this issue in line with what Hudec has explained above. He notes that the real concern is related to the (lack of) expertise of some panellists. The involvement of the staff per se is not a concern for him, but rather the question is the extent and the nature of their involvement. He notes:

> It is, of course, one thing for the Secretariat to interact with Bob Hudec or Bill Davey, whenever these two reputed experts have acted as panellists. In this case, they would not have much to add, if anything, to the expertise of panellists. But Hudec and Davey represent less than 0.5% of all appointments. As we are moving along the spectrum of relative knowledge of the GATT across panellists, it is, as per Long's admission and experience, to be expected that the involvement of the Secretariat increases. This is no stricture against the Secretariat. Its involvement has statutory underpinnings. It is by statutory fiat that the Secretariat has an active role to play in the preparation of panel reports. The question is where to draw the line between involvement in line with the statutory mandate, and beyond it. This is definitely a line in the sand, a moving target.[24]

Another dimension of the asymmetry of expertise/capacity between permanent Dispute Assistants and ad hoc panellists arises in the case of non-legal staff who also assist in some panel proceedings. This concern arises most significantly in the context of economists that assist adjudicators at the stage of arbitration for determining the level of suspension of concessions or obligations. Therefore, we will return to this concern and possible solutions in section III below.

The concern on asymmetry is not about the actual existence of asymmetry between the adjudicators and the Dispute Assistants (which would be extremely onerous to establish or prove); rather, it relates to the decision-making mandate of adjudicators based on the consent of Members, which is a key facet of the legitimacy of the dispute resolution process. In the WTO, the Members specifically set up a dispute settlement framework with a panel stage consisting of ad hoc adjudicators, and Secretariat staff with the responsibility to assist panels, 'especially on the legal, historical and procedural aspects of the matters dealt with, and to provide secretarial and technical support'.[25] While such

[22] J Pauwelyn and K Pelc, 'Who Guards the "Guardians of the System"? The Role of the Secretariat in WTO Dispute Settlement' (2022) 116 *American Journal of International Law* 534; J Pauwelyn and K Pelc, 'The WTO Secretariat's "Open Secret": Unpacking the Controversy' (*EJIL:Talk!*, 18 August 2022), www.ejiltalk.org/the-wto-secretariats-open-secret-unpacking-the-controversy.

[23] Pauwelyn and Pelc, 'Who Guards the "Guardians of the System"?' (n 22) .

[24] PC Mavroidis, *The WTO Dispute Settlement System: How, Why and Where?* (Edward Elgar, 2022) 423.

[25] DSU, art 27.1.

asymmetry per se seems to have been consented to by the Members in the DSU, the concern arises with the impression that Dispute Assistants are not 'assisting', but are rather deciding or contributing to the decision-making, beyond what was consented to by the Members. Over the years, this asymmetry has grown as Secretariat staff have gained institutional knowledge on past jurisprudence owing to their relatively more permanent role, as opposed to panellists who are selected ad hoc. This in turn raises the risk of Secretariat staff undertaking functions beyond what was originally envisaged by the Members, and the potential risk of encroaching on the decision-making function of the panellists. Therefore, in devising solutions to address such concerns, the aim is to ensure that the impression of asymmetry does not raise doubts as to the (legality of) decision-making process and adversely impact the legitimacy of the WTO DSS.[26]

ii. Risk of Asymmetry between Panellists and Staff Due to Command over Working Language

In the WTO, the panel reports must be circulated in English, French and Spanish. The translation division carries out the translation, but with some assistance and review by legal staff who have worked on the dispute with the panellists. Translators are not required to have a legal background; however, the reviewers and most translators who work on DS matters have a legal background.

The WTO DSS proceedings are usually undertaken in English, sometimes in Spanish[27] and rarely in French.[28] In practice, most of the dispute work is undertaken in English. A concern that arises in this context is a bias against panellists from countries/jurisdictions where the native language/working language is not one of the working languages of the Dispute Settlement Mechanism (in practical terms, English). Similarly, the extremely competitive hiring process for staff in the Secretariat may also favour candidates with a good command of English. This may limit the diversity of the adjudicators and staff of the Secretariat by favouring candidates with a common law (and English-speaking) background as opposed to a civil law (and non-English-speaking) background.

Further, panellists who are not native speakers of English can sometimes feel dependent on the Secretariat staff assigned to the dispute, particularly if rapid drafting

[26] There are also scholars and practitioners who believe this dissatisfaction is not present or sufficient enough to warrant changes to the present system. The aim in this section is to capture the concerns and think of ways of improving the legitimacy.

[27] For example, the panel reports in the following disputes were initially drafted in Spanish: WTO Panel Report, *Dominican Republic – Safeguard Measures on Imports of Polypropylene Bags and Tubular Fabric*, WT/DS415/R (31 January 2012); WTO Panel Report, *Dominican Republic – Safeguard Measures on Imports of Polypropylene Bags and Tubular Fabric*, WT/DS416/R, WT/DS417/R, WT/DS418/R (31 January 2012); WTO Panel Report, *Mexico – Anti-Dumping Duties on Steel Pipes and Tubes from Guatemala*, WT/DS331/R (8 June 2007); WTO Panel Report, *Argentina – Measures Relating to Trade in Goods and Services*, WT/DS453/R (30 September 2015); WTO Panel Report, *Peru – Additional Duty on Imports of Certain Agricultural Products*, WT/DS457/R (27 November 2014); WTO Panel Report, *Colombia – Measures Relating to the Importation of Textiles, Apparel and Footwear*, WT/DS461/R (27 November 2015); WTO Panel Report, *Costa Rica – Measures Concerning the Importation of Fresh Avocados from Mexico*, WT/DS524/R (24 April 2018); WTO Panel Report, *Panama – Measures Concerning the Importation of Certain Products from Costa Rica*, WT/DS599/R (2 December 2022); WTO Panel Report, *Dominican Republic – Anti-Dumping Measures on Corrugated Steel Bars*, WT/DS605/R (28 April 2023).

[28] For example, the proceedings in WTO Panel Report, *European Communities – Measures Affecting Asbestos and Products Containing Asbestos*, WT/DS135/R (18 September 2000) were conducted in French.

is necessary. This imbalance also extends to other associated tasks like understanding the submissions of the parties, research notes on specific issues, oral submissions and answers to questions. In such cases, command over the working language would no longer be a technical issue of translations, but rather would control the substantive information made available to panellists. The concern that then arises is the potential influence exerted by Secretariat staff over the adjudicative function of the panellists, beyond the assistance consented to by WTO Members. As already explained, the appearance of such concerns also adversely impacts the legitimacy of the WTO DSS.

Of course, many of these concerns are inherent to all international organisations, where a single working language must be adopted to facilitate the process. The aim in listing this concern is also to examine ways in which it may be mitigated within the confines of the WTO DSS.

iii. Lack of Direct Supervision and Control over Secretariat Staff

A concern raised by Pauwelyn and Pelc[29] is the lack of formal control exercised by the adjudicators over the staff who assist them. They explain that the staff do not report directly to the adjudicators and are assigned to disputes by their respective staff Director, who is ultimately responsible for the good functioning of the DSS. This may lead to concerns if the Directors and panellists have differing or conflicting views on the substantive aspects of a dispute. In such cases, the Secretariat staff assisting the panellists may be forced to choose between their loyalty to their direct and institutional supervisor (ie, Director), and the instructions from panellists who are selected ad hoc for a particular dispute. As the Secretariat staff are the primary (and singular) source of 'legal historical and procedural' assistance to panellists, there must be a great deal of trust between them. Such There may be instances where the flow of information to panellists is influenced by the Directors. Such risk of divided loyalties for the Secretariat staff raises the concern that the outcome of a dispute may not reflect the decision-making authority of the panellists. This, in turn, adversely impacts the legitimacy of the WTO DSS.

iv. Risk of Excessive Delegations of Adjudicatory Functions Including Drafting

Given the institutional design of the WTO, Pauwelyn and Pelc argue that the enhanced role played by the staff at various stages of the dispute resolution process allows them to exercise control over the decision-making function that is beyond their mandate and within the purview of the adjudicators.[30] In other words, there may be a risk that the ad hoc panellist may delegate tasks to Secretariat staff beyond what was originally envisaged by the Members and the parties, and, in turn, fail to fulfil their mandate. In our understanding, this concern can also be traced back to that raised by Alan Wolff in 1995: the institutional design of the WTO DSS where the staff are permanent while the adjudicators are ad hoc or part-time. Such concern is compounded by the fact that the

[29] Pauwelyn and Pelc, 'Who Guards the "Guardians of the System"?' (n 22) 549.
[30] ibid 546; Pauwelyn and Pelc, 'The WTO Secretariat's "Open Secret"' (n 22).

WTO DSS has become more complex over the years, with robust jurisprudence developed through cases. Such excessive delegation would adversely impact the core facet of legitimacy regarding the consent of the Members to the WTO DSS.

Pauwelyn and Pelc specifically take issue with the drafting undertaken by the Secretariat staff.[31] They acknowledge that writing the decision is not the same as deciding the case. However, they maintain that with drafting the panel/AB report ruling, the Secretariat exerts considerable influence over the way in which legal interpretations and rulings are worded and argued.[32] They explain that in the WTO DSS, which operates with a form of de facto precedent, the exact words and reasoning used in reaching a conclusion matter as much as the ruling itself.[33] In a more detailed piece, using two distinct text analysis approaches, they demonstrate that the Dispute Assistants of the WTO 'hold the pen' for the adjudicators. However, in our view, strong and well-informed adjudicators will nonetheless be able to retain control over the decision-making process, and may further appreciate knowledgeable and competent assistants' contributions to drafting. The important point is that adjudicators understand fully the matter and make the decision and instruct the drafters on the content of the decision.[34]

Petros Mavroidis and Bernhard Hoekman have also raised a similar point in the context of dispute settlement reform at the WTO.[35] Mavroidis has built on this concern, specifically relating to the lack of institutional firewall between Secretariat staff assisting panels and those advising on legal issues outside the context of disputes in committees/negotiations.[36] He notes that this problem is compounded when the Secretariat staff are involved in drafting of the reports, coupled with the lack of transparency over the precise scope and functions of the Secretariat in assisting panellists.[37] The main issue, he argues, is whether the panellists have sufficient expertise to discharge their own decision-making function and can control the work of the Dispute Assistants.[38] He also mentions the theoretical possibility that the Secretariat may be complicit in this system, through the selection process where they assist the parties and advise the DG.[39]

[31] J Pauwelyn and K Pelc, 'WTO Rulings and the Veil of Anonymity' (2022) 33 *European Journal of International Law* 2 527.

[32] Pauwelyn and Pelc, 'Who Guards the "Guardians of the System"?' (n 22) 544.

[33] ibid 545.

[34] A Steinbach, 'Are the Fingerprints of the WTO Staff on Panel Rulings a Problem? A Reply to Joost Pauwelyn and Krzysztof Pelc' (2022) 33 *European Journal of International Law* 2 565; G Sacerdoti, 'A Critical Reaction to Joost Pauwelyn and Krzysztof Pelc's "The WTO Secretariat's 'Open Secret': Unpacking the Controversy"' (*EJIL:Talk!*, 5 September 2022), www.ejiltalk.org/a-critical-reaction-to-joost-pauwelyn-and-krzysztof-pelcs-the-wto-secretariats-open-secret-unpacking-the-controversy.

[35] B Hoekman and PC Mavroidis, 'To AB or Not to AB? Dispute Settlement in WTO Reform' (2020) 23 *Journal of International Economic Law* 703.

[36] Mavroidis (n 24) 424.

[37] ibid.

[38] ibid 426.

[39] ibid. He states: 'The difference is this: while nomination at the bench for Appellate Body members depends exclusively on the will of WTO members, this is, on occasion, not the case for panellists. And of course, the Secretariat, if operating strategically, could advance nominations knowing, ex ante, that they are unacceptable to one of the disputing parties, and push complainants to request that the DG intervenes to compose the panel. There is, of course, no tangible proof that the Secretariat has de facto behaved this way, but it is a theoretical possibility that the membership should entertain when thinking about a do-over of the current DSU and start contemplating a DSU 2.0.'

This concern can impact all three facets of legitimacy that were identified in Chapter 21. Starting with the consent of Members to be bound by the WTO DSS, the excessive delegation (or the risk of delegation) of functions may lead to Secretariat staff exceeding their mandate as consented to by the Members in the DSU. Further, such concern creates a perception that the panellists have failed to diligently fulfil their decision-making mandate and exercise independent judgement in arriving at the decision. Lastly, the lack of information and transparency on the precise role and functions discharged by the staff also adversely impacts the procedural fairness of the dispute resolution process.

As we have seen, each of these concerns, whether individually and collectively, demands our attention because these allegation affect the legitimacy of the WTO DSS as a whole. Before turning to potential suggestion to mitigate them, we briefly detail the relevant provisions, practice and proposals in the WTO that relate to these concerns.

B. Relevant Provisions, Practices and Proposals

i. *Relevant Provisions and Practices of the WTO*

a. The DSU

Article 27.1 DSU explicitly states that the Secretariat is responsible for 'assisting panels, especially on the legal, historical and procedural aspects of the matters dealt with, and of providing secretarial and technical support'.[40] Further, the Secretariat is also responsible for conducting special training courses for interested Members on dispute settlement procedures and practices so as to enable their experts to be better informed.[41]

It should be recalled that the DSU envisages the appointment of ad hoc panellists for specific disputes and requires the Secretariat to support parties in selecting such panellists (as explained in Chapter 22). Therefore, a certain asymmetry in terms of institutional permanence between the panellists (ad hoc) and the Secretariat staff (permanent)[42] who assist them has been written into the provisions of the DSU and accepted by the Members of the WTO. However, this does not mean that the asymmetry on *expertise/capacity* is not relevant in the WTO DSS. Rather, when such asymmetry encroaches upon the decision-making function of the panellists, the panellists would be failing to fulfil their mandate and the Secretariat staff would be acting beyond their mandate in Article 27.1.

b. The WTO Rules of Conduct

During the initial years of the WTO when the WTO Rules of Conduct were being negotiated, the US insisted that the Dispute Assistants should also be bound by the same standards as those applicable to the panellists, AB members and experts in any WTO

[40] DSU, art 27.1.

[41] ibid art 27.3.

[42] While we generally say the Secretariat is 'permanent', we do not imply that all its staff are employed as permanent staff. There have been periods where some of the staff in LAD/Rules Divisions were hired on contract basis when the Secretariat was faced with a large number of disputes.

adjudication process. These actors, termed 'covered persons', are required to be independent and impartial so as to avoid direct or indirect conflicts of interest and to maintain confidentiality.[43] While these rules are very relevant to assessing allegations of conflict of interest of Secretariat staff, their inclusion also reveals something more fundamental. It confirms that WTO Members were aware that the Secretariat staff would be closely involved in assisting panellists with the dispute process and would discharge crucial tasks as part of the dispute resolution process. This is in line with the practice under GATT, where staff from operation divisions[44] were already assisting panels (including drafting panel reports). Subsequently, staff from LAD started assisting all panels. The Members were aware of this history when negotiating the WTO Rules of Conduct.[45]

The obligations under the WTO Rules of Conduct draw on the Marrakesh Agreement and the DSU.[46] To ensure that these obligations are respected, each covered person is expected to: (1) adhere strictly to the provisions of the DSU; (2) disclose the existence or development of any interest, relationship of matter that is likely to affect or give rise to justifiable doubts as to their independence or impartiality; (3) take due care to avoid any direct or indirect conflicts of interest in respect of the subject matter of the proceedings; (4) consider only issues raised in and necessary to fulfil their responsibilities within the dispute settlement proceeding and not delegate this responsibility to any other person; and (5) not incur any obligation or accept any benefit that could (interfere with or) give rise to justifiable doubts as to proper performance.[47]

With respect to Secretariat staff assisting panels, the relevant disclosures are to be made to the DG,[48] who thereafter decides on the assignment of staff to assist in a dispute.[49] The DG also has the discretion to decide that the potential conflict of interest is not sufficiently material to warrant non-assignment of a particular staff to assist in the dispute.[50] Further, these rules do not impede the Secretariat's responsibility to respond to Members' requests for assistance and information.[51]

The provisions of the WTO Rules of Conduct are an additional confirmation of the consent of WTO Members on staff participation in the panel proceedings. However, despite such acknowledgement, some of the academic literature discussed earlier raise concerns over the excessive delegation and undue influence exerted by staff when these staff activities go beyond their mandate under the DSU and the Rules of the Code of Conduct.

[43] WTO, *Rules of Conduct for the Understanding on Rules and Procedures Governing the Settlement of Disputes*, WTO Doc WT/DSB/RC/1 (11 December 1996), art II read with art IV ('covered persons').

[44] Before 1988, the LAD did not exist. The assistance to panellists was the responsibility of the staff of the operational divisions, including the Rules Division. See generally Marceau and Baker (n 13) 112.

[45] ibid.

[46] As per art VI:4 of the WTO Agreement, the Secretariat staff shall not seek to accept instructions from any government or other authority external to the WTO in the discharge of their duties. Further, they are required to refrain from any action which might adversely reflect on their position as international officials. Article 27.2 DSU refers explicitly to the 'continued impartiality of the Secretariat' when it states that a WTO legal expert 'shall assist developing country Members in a manner ensuring the continued impartiality of the Secretariat'.

[47] WTO Rules of Conduct, art III; see also G Marceau, 'Rules on Ethics for the New WTO Dispute Settlement Mechanism' (1998) 32 *Journal of World Trade* 57.

[48] WTO Rules of Conduct, r VI(4)(c).

[49] ibid fn 2.

[50] ibid.

[51] ibid r IV(2).

c. The WTO Staff Regulations

We have already explained the relevant provisions of the staff regulations applicable in the case of Secretariat staff assigned to assist in a dispute in Chapter 22.[52] To reiterate, Regulation 1.8[53] and para 34 of Annex B[54] are especially relevant for staff assisting in dispute settlement, and additional prescriptions, obligations and duties can be introduced therein.

d. Supervision of Secretariat Staff Assisting Panels

The Secretariat staff assisting the panel, both administratively and in terms of their work, report to the Director of the LAD or Rules Division and the DDG in charge of their respective division. They are not under the direct supervision of the panellists who they are tasked with assisting. In such cases, it is relevant to remember that although the panellists do not directly supervise the work of the staff, they do play a role in their appraisal and evaluation.

However, there may be situations where a panel or an individual panellist disagrees with a position that is advised by the Secretariat staff or the Directors. There have also been instances of disagreements between the Rules Division and the LAD on legal interpretation.[55] In such cases, it is important to ensure that the decision-making function is retained by the panellist, while benefiting from the institutional memory and expertise of the Secretariat staff and the Director. Reform proposals must aim to reinforce the capacity of panellists to retain full control of the decision-making function and the overall dispute-resolution process.

ii. Proposals for Reform

a. Proposal on Permanent Panellists: The First EU Proposal

In Chapter 22, we saw three proposals made by the EC on reform of the ad hoc panel system. The first proposal, the Contribution of the European Communities and its Member States to the Improvement of the WTO Dispute Settlement Understanding (hereinafter 'First EU Proposal on Panel Reform'),[56] and the subsequent proposal from

[52] Section 22.2.3(A)(iv), ch 22.

[53] WTO, *Staff Regulations of the World Trade Organization*, adopted by the General Council, WTO Doc WT/L/510 (7 July 2004) reg 1.8 requires staff members to make prior disclosures relating to information concerning their interest in any matter within the purview of the WTO, which may affect the appropriateness of assignment of certain functions to them

[54] ibid para 34, Annex B reiterates that when a staff member is considered to assist in a dispute, they have an obligation to disclose to the DG the information required to be disclosed by r VI:2 of the Rules of Conduct, including their participation in earlier formal consideration of the specific measure at issue in a dispute under any provisions of the WTO Agreement. Such participation may be through formal legal advice under art 27.2 DSU as well as any involvement with the dispute, as an official of a WTO Member government or otherwise professionally, before having joined the Secretariat. The DG considers all such disclosures in deciding on the assignment of staff to a dispute and may decide that a potential conflict of interest is not sufficiently material to warrant non-assignment of staff to a particular dispute.

[55] G Marceau, A Porges and DA Baker, 'Introduction and Overview' in Marceau (n 8) 1.

[56] WTO, 'European Communities and its Member States, Contribution to the Improvement of the WTO Dispute Settlement Understanding', WTO Doc TN/DS/W/1 (13 March 2002).

EC, the Contribution of the European Communities and its Member States to the Improvement of the WTO Dispute Settlement Understanding (hereinafter 'Second EU Proposal on Panel Reform'),[57] aimed to establish a roster of permanent panellists and move away from a completely ad hoc system of panellists. This section will detail the proposed criteria for inclusion in the roster and how it raises the qualifications over those in Article 8 DSU at present.

In terms of qualifications for inclusion in the roster, the First EU Proposal required that they be 'persons of recognized authority, with demonstrated expertise in international trade law, economy or policy and the subject matter of the covered agreements generally, and/or past experience as a GATT/WTO panellist'. Additionally, they shall be unaffiliated with any government.[58] This is similar to the qualifications for AB members and significantly more detailed than the illustrative requirements in Article 8.1 at present. Further, persons on the roster would perform their functions on a full-time basis and have the responsibility to 'stay abreast of dispute settlement activities and other relevant activities of the WTO' and be broadly representative of membership in the WTO.

The Second EU Proposal modified one aspect in terms of the qualification: it removes the requirement that the panellists on the roster be 'unaffiliated with any government'. However, it retains that they serve in their individual capacities and not as government representatives, nor as representatives of any organisation.

b. Proposal on Improved Panel Roster: The Canadian Proposal

The Canadian Proposal on Improvement of the WTO Dispute Settlement Understanding suggests the establishment of a new panel roster to replace the existing Indicative List.[59] They proposed transforming the current Indicative List (under Article 8.4 DSU) into a streamlined panel roster with more detailed selection criteria.[60] The proposal notes that the lack of reliance of the current Indicative List may be partly owing to the absence of appropriate criteria for candidates. They draw inspiration from the selection criteria for AB members and propose the inclusion of the following language (underlined) in Article 8.1:

> Panels shall be composed of well-qualified governmental and/or non-governmental individuals <u>with demonstrated expertise in law, international trade and the subject matter of the covered agreements generally,</u> including persons who have served . . .[61]

Each WTO Member would nominate one individual (who may or may not be a national) for inclusion within the revised panel roster, along with the statement of qualifications that identifies their capabilities and capacity to serve as a panellist in reference

[57] WTO, 'European Communities and its Member States, Contribution to the Improvement of the WTO Dispute Settlement Understanding', WTO Doc TN/DS/W/38 (23 January 2003).

[58] Panellists shall serve in their individual capacities and not as government representatives, nor as representatives of any organisation.

[59] WTO, 'Contribution of Canada to the Improvement of the WTO Dispute Settlement Understanding, Communication from Canada', WTO Doc TN/DS/W/41 (24 January 2003) 4.

[60] ibid.

[61] ibid 15, para 1.

to the above included qualifications.[62] The nominations and accompanying qualification would thereafter be transmitted to a committee which will verify whether the nominees meet the requisite level of expertise to serve as a panellist.[63] The committee is intended to be the same as the selection committee for appointments to the AB (ie, the Chairs of the five main Councils of the WTO: Goods, Services, Trade-Related Aspects of Intellectual Property Rights (TRIPS), the DSB and the General Council).[64] Thereafter, once the committee approves the panel roster, it would be approved by the General Council. Individuals are eligible for a once-renewable term of five years, on approval by the General Council.[65] The selection process for AB members (which shares similarities with elements of the Canadian proposal) has itself been the subject of criticism for being a largely political process, with concerns on its ability to ensure the requisite expertise for AB members. However, these proposals show that Members have taken the initiative in improving the qualification criteria as well as the selection process for panellists.

To recap, the proposal required that the Secretariat nominates names of potential panellists exclusively from the revised panel roster, while parties retain the right to agree on potential panellists from outside of it.[66] At the stage of DG nomination, the DG would in principle be required to nominate names from the roster, unless the DG determines that insufficient expertise is available from the roster for a particular dispute.[67]

c. Proposal on Specific Expertise: The Proposal from Chile and the US

As part of their proposal on flexibility and Member control in the WTO DSS, Chile and the US made an array of proposals on the DSU.[68] On the qualifications of panellists, they proposed that Article 8.2 DSU be amended to include the following language (underlined):

> Panel members should be selected with a view to ensuring the independence of the members, <u>expertise to examine the kind of matter at issue in the dispute</u>, a sufficiently diverse background and a wide spectrum of experience.[69]

In section IV below, we examine the proposal made by Alan Wolff for a reconstituted AB, with a proportionate number of adjudicators to the number of disputes per sector. For example, he suggests that 'the number of AB members serving at any time with in-depth knowledge of the conduct of domestic trade remedies proceedings shall be commensurate with the share of cases on that subject'.[70] While this proposal is

[62] ibid para 4.
[63] ibid.
[64] ibid.
[65] ibid.
[66] ibid 16, para 6.
[67] ibid para 7.
[68] WTO, '*Flexibility and Member Control, Revised Textual Proposal by Chile and United States, Communication from Chile and United States*', *WTO Doc* TN/DS/W/89 (31 May 2007).
[69] ibid 4.
[70] AW Wolff, WTO 2025: Restoring Binding Dispute Settlement (PIIE Working Paper No 22-5, Peterson Institute for International Economics, April 2022) 27, www.piie.com/sites/default/files/documents/wp22-5.pdf.

specifically on the appeal stage, the underlying principle is relevant in the case of panellists as well.

d. Proposals on Transparency with Respect to Secretariat Support: The LDC Group, Joint Proposal by Cuba, Honduras, India etc

In 2002, the LDC Group made an array of proposals on reform of the DSU.[71] With respect to Secretariat support, they acknowledged the broad scope of support envisaged under Article 27.1 of the DSU. They stated that: 'Often, such support is pernicious and impacts heavily on the outcome of the case, especially when it takes the form of legal research and other internal commentary on matters of procedure.'[72] Accordingly, they proposed that such assistance, particularly the legal research undertaken by the Secretariat and other commentary prepared in the course of and for use in the case, should be shared with the parties. They reasoned that this becomes important in 'completing the picture' as to how exactly a decision was reached.

Similarly, the proposal made jointly by Cuba, Honduras, India etc highlighted that the Secretariat has an obligation to remain neutral when assisting the panels.[73] The proposal took issue with instances where the Secretariat has provided panels with negotiating history, which does not have the approval of Members.[74] Accordingly, they proposed that all the documents, notes, information etc made available by the Secretariat to the panels be given promptly to the parties to the dispute.[75] This would enable parties to submit their views on the documents, which may be used by the panel in resolving the dispute. They proposed the inclusion of language within the Working Procedure (Appendix 3 of the DSU) to reflect such requirement.[76] Jordan submitted a proposal agreeing with this amendment and adding that such information should also be shared with 'third parties'.[77]

The implementation of these proposals could raise concerns over the confidentiality of the deliberation process. However, as will be discussed in the next section, procedural steps can be instituted to safeguard against this concern, while allowing some parts of the work to be shared with the parties.

e. Mavroidis' Proposal on a 'WTO Court'

Mavroidis also suggested a return to one-instance adjudication staffed by competent judges, ie, a 'WTO Court'.[78] He recommended a pool of 15 judges, divided into

[71] WTO, 'Negotiations on the Dispute Settlement Understanding, Proposal by the LDC Group, Communication from the LDC Group', *WTO Doc* TN/DS/W/17 (9 October 2002).

[72] ibid 5, para 20.

[73] WTO, '*Negotiations on the Dispute Settlement Understanding, Proposal on DSU by Cuba, Honduras, India, Malaysia, Pakistan, Sri Lanka, Tanzania, and Zimbabwe, Communication from Cuba, Honduras, India, Malaysia, Pakistan, Sri Lanka, Tanzania, and Zimbabwe*', WTO Doc TN/DS/W/18 (7 October 2002).

[74] ibid 5.

[75] ibid.

[76] ibid 5–6.

[77] WTO, '*Jordan's Contributions towards the Improvement and Clarification of the WTO Dispute Settlement Understanding, Communication from Jordan*', *WTO Doc* TN/DS/W/43 (28 January 2003).

[78] Mavroidis (n 24) 529.

Chambers of three and five members, adjudicating disputes according to the value of the disputes.[79] These Chambers would be competent to decide a dispute finally and not just submit a report to the DSB to be adopted by consensus.[80] Further, he proposed that the plenum would act like the AB for all the Chamber decisions In terms of qualifications, the threshold criteria is 'proven technical expertise' in WTO issues. He proposed that two to four members should have demonstrable expertise in GATS and TRIPS. The members may be trade economists and/or experts in international trade policy (not necessarily lawyers), detailing a selection process for these permanent judges inspired by the CJEU.[81] The Article 253 CJEU procedure sets up a panel (comprised of former judges) to evaluate candidates who meet the specified threshold criterion. Accordingly, with respect to the WTO, he suggested a panel comprising 'the most experienced panellists, (some) former AB members, former heads of the WTO legal affairs divisions, could be asked to scrutinize those who meet the threshold criteria, and select the WTO judges accordingly'.[82] Further, in terms of support, Mavroidis recommends that such judges should be assisted by their own clerks independently of the WTO Secretariat.

f. The Molina Report

Three aspects of the Molina Report are relevant in addressing the concerns raised in the panel proceedings stage: (a) qualification of individuals to be included in the Indicative List; (b) guidance on Secretariat support; and (c) transparency with respect to Rules of Conduct and Staff Regulations.

Qualification of Individuals to Be Included in the Indicative List

The Molina Report introduces several changes with respect to the selection and composition of panels. Notably, it introduces extensive criteria for the inclusion of individuals within the Indicative List maintained by the Secretariat staff under Article 8.4 DSU.[83] Such individuals are required to have:

- 'significant relevant experience', which consists of at least 10 years of: (a) experience as a legal practitioner principally dealing with international economic and trade law matters – for example, experience as a legal practitioner in international dispute settlement on international trade law matters, as a panellist, arbitrator or counsel to the parties, or senior legal support to an arbitration tribunal or panel; or (b) experience relating to the subject matter of the covered agreements – for example, experience as a government official, conciliator, mediator, negotiator or diplomat directly relating to the subject matter of the covered agreements; experience in the conduct of, or participation in, domestic trade remedies proceedings; or experience within domestic authorities or the private sector, the activity of which directly relates to the subject matter of the covered agreements (such as customs authorities);[84]

[79] ibid 533.
[80] ibid 529. His proposal includes various other elements that we do not recount here.
[81] ibid 555.
[82] ibid.
[83] WTO, 'Report by H.E. Mr Petter Ølberg, Chairman of the DSB, and Annex: Consolidated Text Referred to in Mr Molina's Report' (General Council, JOB/GC/385, 16 February 2024).
[84] ibid Title II, ch II.II (3)–(4).

- Academic experience may also be taken into account to satisfy 'significant relevant experience', provided that the nominated person also possesses at least four years of the practical experience set out above.[85]
- High ethical standards.[86]
- The ability to effectively communicate orally and in writing in one or more of the official working languages of the WTO.[87]

Finally, in making nominations to the Indicative List, Members must strive to promote gender balance and geographical representation, as per Article 8.2 DSU.[88]

The Molina Report also envisages the procedure for the Chairperson of the DSB to assist Members in composing and re-composing the Indicative List. The Chairperson, with support from Secretariat staff, is given the responsibility to check whether the nominations made by Members meet the qualification requirements stated above,[89] and to consult with the nominating Member in order to make such determination.[90] Following such consultation, the Chairperson may also recommend against such a relevant individual from being nominated, however, the nominating Member retains the right to proceed with the specific nomination.[91] In order to enhance transparency, the Chairperson is required to inform the membership (without specifying the nominating Member or relevant individual) if any such recommendation against a nomination was made and the nominating Members nevertheless decided to proceed with the same nomination.[92] Procedure is also envisaged whereby any other Member could request confidential consultations with the Chairperson to understand specific details on such disclosure relating to the nominating Member and their nomination(s).[93]

Guidance on Secretariat Support

Title VII of the draft Consolidated Text to the Molina Report lists the provisions with respect to 'Secretariat Support'. Notably, at the very beginning, it is acknowledged that high-quality support by the Secretariat is envisaged by the DSU.[94] Rather than considering a strong Secretariat as threatening the legitimacy of the WTO DSS, the text reflects the merits of enhancing the expertise of the staff assisting the panellists.[95] A counter-argument may be raised that such enhanced expertise on the part of the staff may increase the concerns over asymmetry between staff and panellists. However, the Molina Report accounts for such counter-arguments by correspondingly enhancing the qualification criteria for panellists for inclusion in the Indicative List.

With respect to the responsibilities of panellists and scope of support provided by the staff, it is explicitly stated that the adjudicators will have full responsibility for the decision-making.[96] With respect to drafting, the panellists are required to draft the

[85] ibid Title II, ch II.II (5).
[86] ibid Title II, ch II.II (6)(a).
[87] ibid Title II, ch II.II (6)(b).
[88] ibid Title II, ch II.II (2)
[89] ibid Title II, Appendix I, (2).
[90] ibid Title II, Appendix I, (3).
[91] ibid Title II, Appendix I, (4).
[92] ibid Title II, Appendix I, (5).
[93] ibid.
[94] ibid Title VII, ch I(1).
[95] ibid.
[96] ibid Title VII, ch II(1)(a)

conclusions section of the report.[97] The Secretariat staff can assist the panellists with drafting any part of the report other than the 'conclusions' section, but only on the basis of written instructions provided by the adjudicators.[98] Further, to ensure that the support provided is responsive to the submissions of the parties, the Secretariat staff are prohibited from providing 'Issues Papers' before the first written submissions have been provided by the parties, including with preliminary ruling matters.[99]

Transparency with Respect to the WTO Rules of Conduct and Staff Regulations
Lastly, to enhance the independence, impartiality and integrity of the WTO DSS, the Molina Report suggests that the Secretariat be required to share the WTO Rules of Conduct and the Staff Regulations with the parties, third parties and members of the panel.[100] Such proactive measures to ensure the transparency of the possible avenues of challenging the Secretariat staff strengthen the legitimacy of the support functions fulfilled by the staff.

C. Suggestions on the Role of Dispute Assistants in Original and Compliance Panel Proceedings

We have looked at the concerns, the relevant provisions of the WTO, practices and existing proposals for reform relating to the role of Dispute Assistants in panel proceedings (including compliance review panels). We will now discuss some of our suggestions that may address, minimise or safeguard against these concerns. Again, given that the DSU explicitly acknowledges the role of the Secretariat in assisting panels, the issue is not so much with their involvement per se but how (italicised) they assist.

The first group of suggestions reflects the need to *enhance the expertise of both panellists and legal staff*. Accordingly, we examine suggestions for relating to: (i) detailed criteria for eligibility as panellists; (ii) transparency on meeting criteria for inclusion in the Indicative List; (iii) assignment of (at least one) panellist with prior expertise; and (iv) training of (potential) panellists as well as staff. These suggestions are probably the best way to eliminate or undue any potential asymmetry of knowledge and expertise between panellists and Dispute Assistants, ensuring that panellists are authentic experts who continue to develop their expertise. These must be read along with the suggestions on enhancing the Indicative List and improving the selection of panellists discussed in Chapter 22.

The second group of suggestions relate to *how the panellists work together with the secretariat staff, and/or amongst themselves*. This includes: (v) listing of duties, restrictions and obligations of Dispute Assistants and panellists; (vi) providing External Assistants to panellists; (vii) diversification of sources of assistance, including advice; (viii) requiring that Dispute Assistants only undertake drafting under instructions from the panellists; and (ix) requiring that some panel deliberations take place exclusively among panellists.

[97] ibid Title VII, ch II(1)(c).
[98] ibid Title VII, ch II(2)(b).
[99] ibid Title VII, ch II(3).
[100] ibid Title VII, ch II(4).

Finally, suggestions on *increased transparency and accountability are crucial to the procedural legitimacy of the WTO DSS*. Accordingly, we examine: (x) transparency on the role of Dispute Assistants; and (xi) accountability through record on delegation.

i. Detailed Criteria for Eligibility as Panellists

Several proposals discussed above suggest revised eligibility criteria for panellists. The Molina Report also includes extensive criteria for individuals to be included as part of the Indicative List[101] and requires that such a list be made available online for Members to access, along with relevant information relating to the qualification requirements of each person on the list.[102]

The International Criminal Court (ICC) also has an extensive list of qualifications required for an individual to be nominated as a judge. As per the Rome Statute, in addition to the general requirements,[103] every candidate nominated must have either: established competence in criminal law and procedure, and the necessary experience, whether as a judge, prosecutor, advocate or some other similar capacity, in criminal proceedings; or have established competence in relevant areas of international law such as international humanitarian law and the law of human rights, and extensive experience in a professional legal capacity which is of relevance to the judicial work of the ICC.[104] This is principally similar to the practical experience required in the Molina Report.[105] Another similarity between the Molina Report and the ICC requirements is that the candidates must also have excellent knowledge of and be fluent in at least one of the languages of the ICC.[106]

Therefore, an enhanced set of criteria for inclusion within the Indicative List (and eventually as panellists) is recommended. This could include more nuanced requirements relating to established competence in international economic and trade law matters, or the subject matter of covered agreements, through practice (of a significant number of years – for example, 10 years, as in the Molina Report), or through practice and academic experience (with minimum number of years in practice – for example, four years, as in the Molina Report). Additionally, explicit requirements relating to language, with the ability to effectively communicate orally and in writing in at least one of the official languages of the WTO could be included. Further qualifications and/or experience criteria may be included as 'valuable assets' guiding the selection process – for example, a certain number of years of experience with treaty negotiations, experience as an adjudicator in areas relating to international economic law or international/domestic trade law; or experience in writing in one of the official languages (through publications or other professional tasks).

[101] Maintained by the Secretariat under art 8.4 DSU.

[102] Molina Report Title II, ch II.II(13).

[103] *Rome Statute of the International Criminal Court* (adopted 17 July 1998, entered into force 1 July 2002) 2187 UNTS 3, art 36(3), which states that the judges must be chosen from among persons of high moral character, impartiality and integrity, who possess the qualifications required in their respective states for appointment to the highest judicial offices.

[104] ibid.

[105] Molina Report, Title II, ch II.II (3)–(4).

[106] Rome Statute, art 36(3); Molina Report, Title II, ch II.II 6(b).

ii. Transparency on Meeting Criteria for Inclusion in the Indicative List

The Molina Report envisages that the Secretariat will support the Members in making nominations to the Indicative List by compiling a database of interested and eligible individuals seeking to be nominated by a Member to the Indicative List.[107] In doing so, the Secretariat could be tasked with launching a call for expressions of interest from qualified individuals and providing them with an opportunity, in a standard electronic form, to outline how those individuals meet the necessary qualifications identified. Such a database could be made available to Member. Once the Indicative List is adopted by the DSB, it is also made available to Member along with relevant information relating to the qualification requirements of each person on the list.[108] This mechanism would be useful in ensuring 'expert' panellists.

The practice of the CJEU in the appointment of judges is also relevant here. The CJEU's Panel of Experts examines the qualifications of candidates and makes recommendations to Member States.[109] The Panel of Experts gives an opinion on candidates' suitability to perform the duties of an adjudicator.[110] The Panel of Experts uses six criteria to evaluate the suitability of candidates: their legal capabilities; their professional experience; their ability to perform the duties of a judge; their language skills; their ability to work as part of a team in an international environment in which several legal systems are represented; and whether their independence, impartiality, probity and integrity are beyond doubt.[111] The opinions issued by the Panel have always followed by the governments of Member States,[112] and furthers transparency on the qualifications of those nominated. As part of their recommendations relating to reform of the WTO DSS, Mavroidis and Hoekman also recommend borrowing from the practice of the Panel of Experts of the CJEU for panel members and AB members.[113] As detailed above, Mavroidis suggests that such that a panel could comprise (most) experienced panellists, (some) former AB members and former heads of the WTO LAD. The selection panel would scrutinise the threshold criteria for nominees and select the WTO judges accordingly.[114] The Molina Report also envisages a role for the Chairperson of the DSB to assess whether the nominations made by WTO Members meet the qualification criteria for inclusion within the Indicative List.[115]

[107] Molina Report, Title II, ch.II.II(12).

[108] ibid Title II, ch II.II(13).

[109] Consolidated Version of the Treaty on the Functioning of the European Union [2016] OJ C202/47, art 255 (TFEU).The Panel comprises seven persons chosen from among former members of the CJEU, members of national supreme courts and lawyers of recognised competence.

[110] ibid.

[111] European Commission, *Seventh Activity Report of the Panel Provided for by Article 255 of the Treaty on the Functioning of the European Union* (2022) 17, www.curia.europa.eu/jcms/upload/docs/application/pdf/2022-07/2022.2597-qcar22002enn_002.pdf.

[112] ibid.

[113] PC Mavroidis and B Hoekman, *WTO Dispute Settlement and the Appellate Body Crisis: Back to the Future* (Working Paper, 18 March 2020); JHH Weiler, 'Who Will Judge the Judges Who Judge the Judges? The Curious Case of Gonçalo Manoel de Vilhena de Almeida Ribeiro' (*EU Law Live, Symposium*); G Amato, M Cartabia, D Grimm, MP Maduro, RMM Ramos and JL Vilaça, 'Selecting EU Judges: The Role of the 255 Committee According to the Treaty' (EU Law Live, Op-Ed).

[114] ibid.

[115] Molina Report, Title II, Appendix I.

Similarly, in making nominations to the Indicative List, Members must state how their candidates meet the criteria listed. Such a framework for transparency ensures that the formal criteria for selection of panellists follow through in practice. These disclosures must be made public so as to allow the wider membership to demand accountability. For inclusion within the Indicative List, a Committee/Commission of Experts (decided through a consensus of WTO Members) may be tasked with screening nominations for inclusion within the Indicative List. The Committee could be required to circulate to the membership relevant information about the qualifications of individuals proposed for inclusion in the Indicative List in non-restricted documents. This could act as a safeguard against turning nominations for the Indicative List into a purely political exercise and compromising the quality/expertise of potential panellists in the process. Finally, in our view, the Secretariat should continue to maintain a database of potential candidates with their qualifications, but should make it accessible to the Members.

iii. Assignment of Panellists with Prior Expertise

Along with increased transparency with respect to the specific qualifications, experience and expertise of panellists in the Indicative List, it is possible to include subject-matter expertise for a certain proportion of individuals included within the Indicative List. Further, for specific disputes, the Chair of the panel could be required to be selected from such individuals with specific expertise. The Chile and US proposal examined earlier includes potential language suggesting that the panellists must be selected with a view to ensure expertise to examine the kind of matter at issue in the dispute.[116] However, the requirement of expertise should not be used as a proxy to limit the representativeness of panels. For example, with respect to trade remedy disputes, experience should not be restricted to expertise in investigation authorities in importing countries; it must also include expertise from exporting countries. Limiting such a requirement to panel chairs therefore ensures that there is a balance struck.

iv. Training of Potential Panellists and Secretariat Staff

There is some previous practice with AB members on their training and development. These were referred to as 'retreats' which took place annually or semi-annually, where the AB members met and, inter alia, discussed substantive legal issues of recurring importance, current developments and systemic issues of interpretation. The MPIA does not conduct such retreats. However, the chosen pool of arbitrators are required to continuously stay abreast of WTO dispute settlement activities.[117] Although this not the same as the retreats of AB members, the pool of arbitrators presently meet virtually to discuss matters of interpretation, practice and procedure, but for specific disputes only, in line with the AB 'exchange of views' in the Working Procedures of the AB. Building on such practice, given that physical meetings may be less feasible due to budget constraints, virtual meetings and trainings could be formalised.

[116] WTO, '*Flexibility and Member Control, Revised Textual Proposal by Chile and United States, Communication from Chile and United States*', *WTO Doc* TN/DS/W/89 (31 May 2007).

[117] MPIA, para 5.

While such reform may be difficult in the case of ad hoc panellists, it is possible to require candidates in the Indicative List to attend such virtual sessions conducted on an annual/semi-annual basis. This could be expanded to include instruction on the obligations under the Rules of Conduct as well as the list of duties, restrictions and obligations, applicable to panellists (discussed below in section II.C.v). Completion of such training can also be further introduced as criteria for their re-nomination in any future revised Indicative List. If training of all individuals on the Indicative List is not feasible, such training could also be made mandatory for individuals who wish to serve as the Chair of a panel, coupled with limiting the discretion of the DG to making appointments of the Chair only amongst such individuals.

The Molina Report makes an important observation on the need to develop the expertise of the legal support staff to ensure the relevant subject-matter expertise.[118] The Secretariat staff may also be required to undergo relevant training, in particular to ensure awareness and development of expertise in new areas of international (economic) law. This could include the obligations under the WTO Rules of Conduct as well as the list of duties, restrictions and obligations applicable to the staff (discussed below in section II.C.v). The specific extent and form of the training would depend on the budgetary allocation available. There is already-existing practice where the team that assisted panellists in a dispute provides an overview of the findings and conclusions to the other staff. Presently, this is undertaken informally, and it is not compulsory for all staff to attend. This practice could be formalised and take place monthly, requiring attendance by all Dispute Assistants. It can be expanded to include information sharing on international trade law jurisprudence outside the WTO DSS as well.

v. Listing of Duties, Restrictions and Obligations of Panellists and Secretariat Staff

With respect to listing the specific duties, restrictions and obligations of panellists and Dispute Assistants, the practice of arbitration institutions provides some suggestions for reform. For example, the UNCITRAL Notes on Organizing Arbitral Proceedings 2016 accept a broader scope of functions for the secretary to the tribunal, including substantive functions like legal research, and other professional assistance such as preparing a summary of the facts or the procedural history of the arbitral proceedings, collecting or summarising case law, general research on legal issues defined by the arbitral tribunal and preparing draft procedural decisions.[119] However, secretaries should not be involved or participate in the decision-making of the arbitral tribunal.[120] Several other arbitral institutions include a permissive list of tasks that may be performed by Dispute Assistants – for example, the International Chamber of Commerce Note to the Parties and Arbitral Tribunals on the Conduct of the Arbitrations under the International

[118] Molina Report, Title VII, ch I(1).
[119] UNCITRAL, '*Notes on Organizing Arbitral Proceedings*', *2016* UNCITRAL Yearbook, vol XXVII (1996) III Annex II, paras 35–37.
[120] ibid para 36.

Chamber of Commerce Rules of Arbitration, 2021,[121] the LCIA Guidance Note for Parties and Arbitrators,[122] and the HKIAC Guidelines on the Use of a Secretary to the Tribunal 2014.[123]

A similar approach may be adopted, with Working Procedures for panels providing an explicit list of duties that may be performed by the Secretariat staff as part of their duties under Article 27.1 DSU. Below we reproduce the list in the International Chamber of Commerce Note to the Parties and Arbitral Tribunals on the Conduct of the Arbitrations for guidance:

- transmitting documents and communications on behalf of the arbitral tribunal;
- organising and maintaining the arbitral tribunal's file and locating documents;
- organising hearings and meetings and liaising with the parties in that respect;
- drafting correspondence to the parties and sending it on behalf of the arbitral tribunal;
- preparing for the arbitral tribunal's review drafts of procedural orders as well as factual portions of an award, such as the summary of the proceedings, the chronology of facts, and the summary of the parties' positions, provided that such procedural orders and portions of the award are subsequently reviewed by the arbitral tribunal itself;
- attending hearings, meetings and deliberations; taking notes or minutes or keeping time;
- conducting legal or similar research; and
- proof-reading and checking citations, dates and cross-references in procedural orders and awards, as well as correcting typographical, grammatical or calculation errors.

Concurrently, such a list should be supplemented by a list of duties of panellists, including tasks that cannot be delegated to the Secretariat staff. In ICSID and the PCA, the tribunal secretary (Institutional Assistant) plays a limited role during drafting. In ICSID, the secretary and the other staff may draft the procedural history, facts and summaries of the parties' submissions.[124] This division between substantive drafting left to the adjudicators, with procedural and case history undertaken by the Institutional Assistants, is considered a good tool to ensure engagement by the adjudicators in the decision-making process, while restricting the role of the Dispute Assistants in substantive drafting. With respect to commercial arbitration institutions, the Guidelines for Arbitrators of the Stockholm Chamber of Commerce 2020 explicitly provide that the arbitral tribunal may not delegate any decision-making or drafting of substantive parts of decisions or awards to the secretary, unless this is agreed by the parties.[125]

[121] International Chamber of Commerce, '*Note to the Parties and Arbitral Tribunals on the Conduct of the Arbitrations under the ICC Rules of Arbitration*' (2021).

[122] London Court of International Arbitration (LCIA), '*Guidance Note for Parties and Arbitrators*', www.lcia.org/adr-services/guidance-note.aspx#10.%20%20TRIBUNAL%20SECRETARIES, paras 201–02.

[123] Hong Kong International Arbitration Centre (HKIAC), '*Guidelines on the Use of a Secretary to the Arbitral Tribunal*' (1 June 2014) para 3.4.

[124] E Obadia and F Nitschke, 'Institutional Arbitration and the Role of the Secretariat' in C Giorgetti (ed), Litigating International Investment Disputes: A Practitioner's Guide (Brill Nijhoff, 2014) 130.

[125] Stockholm Chamber of Commerce (SCC), *Guidelines for Arbitrators* (June 2020), s 2, 'Administrative Secretaries' 8, www.acerislaw.com/wp-content/uploads/2022/08/scc-guidelines-for-arbitrators.pdf.

This approach is reflected in the Molina Report, which provides in Title VII, Chapter II the 'Responsibilities of Adjudicators and Scope of Support Provided by Secretariat Staff' and ascribes the responsibility to draft the conclusion section of panel reports to the adjudicators themselves (without Secretariat support). The Molina Report does not provide further guidance on what is specifically included within the 'conclusions'. With respect to panel reports, the section entitled 'Conclusion' is presently limited to the specific findings of the panel on each of the claims raised by the complainant. This may be expanded to include certain aspects of the reasoning for the finding as well. The supervisor of the staff (the Director or DS Registrar, as will be discussed below in section II.C.vii) could have an additional duty to ensure that the staff under their supervision and control do not undertake such prohibited tasks.

Further, to ensure that the support provided is responsive to the submissions of the parties, the Secretariat staff may be required to work on any research or Issues Papers for the panellists only after the first written submissions have been provided by the parties, including in the case of preliminary ruling requests.[126]

Similarly, the role of the legal staff in specific stages of the dispute could be limited or regulated. As will be discussed further below, the participation in deliberation meetings could be regulated and include a space where adjudicators discuss their first views on the dispute exclusively between themselves. The assistance during deliberations should generally be limited to participation or interventions by staff only as and when requested by the panellists. The list of duties should restrict the staff from leading or taking charge of the deliberations and should require the panellists to raise specific questions/areas where the staff may provide input.

While including such specific duties, restrictions and obligations on the panellists and staff in the panel Working Procedures, such rules must also find a place in the WTO Rules of Conduct, allowing parties recourse in the event of a violation of these requirements. The challenge could be raised against the panellist or the staff by any party to a dispute, in the same manner as is envisaged at present under Article VIII of the WTO Rules of Conduct.[127] Currently, with respect to panellists, the party making such a challenge is required to submit evidence of such a violation to the Chair of the DSB.[128] Thereafter, the Chair provides the panellist concerned with the evidence and, if the matter is not resolved, shares all the relevant information with the parties to the dispute.[129] The Chair of the DSB, along with the DG and a specific number of Chairs of Councils, decide whether a material violation has taken place, after providing the panellist and the parties a reasonable opportunity to be heard.[130] If a material violation is found, the challenged panellist is disqualified and the Chair of the DSB would revoke their appointment.[131] With respect to Secretariat staff, the party making such a challenge provides the evidence to the DG, who shares the evidence with the concerned staff, and

[126] ibid Title VII, ch II(3).
[127] WTO Rules of Conduct, art VIII.
[128] ibid arts VIII:1 and 5.
[129] ibid arts VIII:6 and 7.
[130] ibid art VIII:8.
[131] ibid art VIII:9; W Davey, 'Gabrielle Marceau and the WTO Dispute Settlement Rules of Conduct' in *Le droit du commerce international: passé, présent, future – Hommage à Gabrielle Marceau* (Bruylant, 2020) 315–16, where he lists instances where Rules of Conduct issues have arisen regarding panellists.

informs the other party (or parties) and the panel.[132] The DG is responsible for taking appropriate action in accordance with the Staff Regulations (disciplinary action) and informs the parties, the panel and the Chair of the DSB of the decision.[133] The specific violations of the obligations under the list of duties, restrictions and obligations could follow this same procedure. As will be discussed further in Chapter 24, additional provisions to that effect could be added to the current Rules of Conduct

vi. Hiring of External Assistants to Panellists

In order to reduce or counterbalance the asymmetry between the panellists who are ad hoc and the Secretariat staff who are permanent (Institutional Assistants), a possible avenue is to introduce Dispute Assistants who are within the direct control and supervision of the adjudicators. Several DSMs follow such a pattern:

a) In the CJEU, the judges of the General Court and the ECJ have two types of Dispute Assistants: first, the Institutional Assistants, who comprise the staff of the Registries of the ECJ and the General Court, the Directorate-General of Multilingualism and the Research and Documentation Directorate; and, second, the Assigned Assistants who work in the cabinet of the judge, ie, the référendaires, additional assistants who do not work on the substantive aspects of the case, and a trainee. Lastly, there are the Lecteurs d'arrêts, who are also Assigned Assistants and report to the President of the respective court.

b) In the ICJ, the judges have two sets of assistants: Institutional Assistants of the Registry and the Department of Legal Matters; and Assigned Assistants (Associate Legal Officers, the Special Assistant to the President and Judicial Fellows). The Assigned Assistants are all formally part of the Institutional Office (ie, the Registry and its Department of Legal Matters); however, they are functionally under the supervision and control of their individual judges. Even for administrative matters like periods of leave, the approval is first received from the respective judge and thereafter communicated to the Registry.[134]

c) In the ECOWAS Court of Justice, the judges have Institutional Assistants, which include the staff of the Registry and the Research and Documentation Department (they perform the bulk of the judicial assistance work in the Court and are headed by a Director). To keep such a department distinct from the Registry, the Director is under the supervision of the President of the Court rather than the Registrar. At the same time, the judges also have individual Assigned Assistants (known as Executive Assistants) who work for them exclusively and form a part of the Chambers of the judge. The Assigned Assistants are officially hired by the Registry; however, they remain entirely under the supervision and control of the judges.

[132] *Rules of Conduct,* art VIII:11.

[133] ibid art VIII:12 and 13. See Davey (n 131) 316–17, where he examines the types of issues that arise with respect to Secretariat staff.

[134] There is also a physical separation. The Associate Legal Officers, the Special Assistant to the President and the Judicial Fellows work out of the wing for judges. In contrast, the Registry staff operate out of the Peace Palace. Therefore, they are Assigned Assistants under the supervision and control of the individual judges.

d) In the COMESA Court of Justice, there is a distinction between the Registry staff (Institutional Assistants) and the external assistants who are hired by the Registry to assist the judges in a particular case (External Assistants).

However, adjudicators in these DSMs are not ad hoc and therefore are conceptually different from the ad hoc panellists of the WTO.[135] The practice of Institutional Assistants and External Assistants may be more suited in the case of ad hoc panellists. Such an equilibrium is struck in the PCA, where one or more legal counsel from the International Bureau (Institutional Office) serves as the primary assistant (tribunal secretary/registrar) with the support of one or more assistant legal counsels and a case manager; the arbitrators may also have additional personal assistants (External Assistants).

Therefore, either panellists could be provided a certain budget to hire their own External Assistants, as in the case of the PCA, or the Secretariat facilitates hiring individual External Assistants for the panellists. There are various ways in which such External Assistants can be selected – for example, in the ECOWAS Court of Justice, the judge has complete discretion in selecting their Executive Assistants, who are then formally hired by the Court. The ECOWAS Registry conducts minimal intervention, which is often restricted to verifying that the person chosen by the judge is a qualified lawyer and possesses the minimum experience and qualifications for the role.[136] On the other hand, in the COMESA Court of Justice, the external researchers are hired by the Registry with minimal involvement from the judges of the Court.[137] The specific qualifications and expertise required may be determined as per the discretion of the panellist and the needs of each dispute. Such a system would allow the panellist to retain full supervision and control over their assistants, who would report to them directly. In all cases, the panellist would have full supervision and control over such assistants, including in their selection. Of course, hiring such external assistants would incur additional expenditure.

A possible counter-argument to this proposal could be that it might allow/enable panellists to more easily delegate their tasks to their personal Assigned/External Assistants. This contrasts with the present system, where the staff of the Secretariat assist the adjudicators, but are also under the supervision and control of the Secretariat Director. In any case, such External Assistants must be bound by the same WTO Rules of Conduct (including the proposed duties, restrictions and prohibitions discussed above) as the Secretariat staff in discharging their functions. The list of duties, restrictions and obligations on panellists and Dispute Assistant remains equally important, as panellists may be inclined to delegate tasks to their External Assistant beyond the mandate consented to by the Members. Suitable amendments can be introduced to accommodate the differences between the Institutional Assistants and the External Assistants. For example, unlike the Secretariat staff, the DG would not have the authority to hear challenges against the External Assistants; rather, this should be heard by the respective adjudicator. While they would be bound by the same ethical rules as the staff, they

[135] The proposal made by Mavroidis for a 'WTO Court' recommends such a model with permanent judges and individual clerks for each judge.

[136] For further discussion, see ch 8.

[137] For further discussion, see ch 4.

would not be officially a part of the Secretariat and accordingly would not have benefits accruing to the staff: access to the WTO insurance, pension contributions etc.

vii. Diversification of Sources of Assistance, Including Advice

Diversifying the source of assistance, including advice, can be very useful in limiting the powers of any single Dispute Assistant and ensuring a better balance between panellists and Dispute Assistants. This also addresses the concerns on lack of direct supervision over the Dispute Assistants by adjudicators by providing them with Assigned or External Assistants. The practices of the ICJ and the ECOWAS Court detailed above point to instances of such diversification.

The WTO already practises some degree of diversification of advice from different Dispute Assistants, where the panels are assisted by staff from the LAD and/or Rules Divisions, as well as staff from other relevant operational divisions that may be relevant to the dispute. In practice, legal advice to the adjudicators comes (exclusively) from the LAD and the Rules Division and staff from operational divisions are responsible for the more factual or expert aspects of the dispute. A potential avenue in the WTO DSS for further diversification could be through enhancing the role the Dispute Settlement Registry (hereinafter 'DS Registry') where (new) legal staff (including qualified lawyers) could be asked to provide procedural advice.

The DS Registry of the WTO was created in 2001 by the then Director of the LAD, Pieter Jan Kuijper.[138] The functions of the DS Registry have greatly evolved over the 20 years since its establishment, including the qualifications and functions of its Registrar (DS Registrar). At present, the Registrar has been described as the 'central contact point that is the face of the WTO dispute settlement system for delegates and panellists'.[139] The DS Registrar also coordinates with other Secretariat support services assisting panels (like translators, conference services, security and archives)[140] and manages the e-filing application. Given the evolution of the DS Registry since its establishment, it is conceivable that the Registry could evolve further to undertake a more active role in assisting panellists. If the post of Registrar was more senior, such legal staff could undertake some of the functions previously performed by the Director. For example, like in the ICJ, the DS Registrar could be made administratively in charge of the staff assisting the panellists if the Director participates in the selection of panellists.

Therefore, drawing from the varied practice of other DSMs, there could be three categories of Dispute Assistants involved directly in panel proceedings.

The *first* category consists of the Registrar and the Dispute Assistants in the Registry (Institutional Assistants). They would be tasked with providing administrative and procedural assistance to the panellists, allowing panellists to benefit from their institutional memory. The tasks performed by the Registry staff could be similar to those of

[138] PJ Kuijper, 'From Seattle to Doha: From the Surreal to the Unreal – A Personal Account' in Marceau (n 8) 374–88.

[139] M Goldstein and L Medrano, 'Bringing WTO Dispute Settlement into the TwentyFirst Century: Modernizing the Administration of Dispute to Better Serve Members' in N Lamp (ed), *Reckoning and Renewal: The World Trade Organization and its Dispute Settlement System at 30: Essays in Honour of Valerie Hughes* (Hart Publishing, 2024) 81–85.

[140] ibid.

the Research and Documentation Directorate of the CJEU, who undertake comparative research on a question of law and collate the jurisprudence across Member States and even other jurisdictions.[141] In the WTO DSS, the Registry staff could similarly be tasked with preparing research notes on specific procedural or institutional issues relevant to the dispute. The research would be agnostic of the arguments of the parties in dispute and restricted to general questions of law and/or summarising the facts of the case.[142] This would also allow such research work to be used in other disputes, without breaching the confidentiality of the DSS. The Registry staff could be responsible for maintaining the DeskBook/One Note, the Analytical Index and Basic Instruments and Selected Documents (BISD), and ensuring their development. In other DSMs, like ICSID,[143] the PCA[144] and the USMCA,[145] tribunal secretaries (from the Institutional Office) are often tasked with drafting the procedural history, facts and summaries of the parties' submissions, which will then be reviewed and, if necessary, amended by the arbitrators.[146] Similar tasks could also be undertaken by the DS Registry staff. Some of these functions could be performed by paralegals, who could assist in drafting the procedural history of the dispute or summarising parties' submissions. Lastly, the Registry could also have language experts who would remain available for assisting individual panellists with specific aspects of the dispute, including on questions of drafting. More generally, and beyond disputes, Registry staff could also be responsible for treaty functions and related work performed by WTO lawyers, with disputes taking priority.

The *second* category would be the staff of the LAD/Rules Divisions (and other divisions) who today assist panellists with more substantive aspects of the dispute proceedings. Such staff, especially the senior staff, would continue to provide specific advice for a dispute, as per the needs of the panellists. They would have more substantive involvement than the assistance provided by the Registry. The concerns that may arise with respect to the role of Directors supervising the work of such legal staff can be addressed in two ways. In Chapter 22, we examined how this could be done if Directors choose to be involved in the panel selection stage, allowing the system to benefit from their years of experience and networks. In such cases, they would no longer be involved in assisting the panellists directly or in supervision the staff who assist the panellists. The administrative supervision of the staff could then be taken over by the DS Registrar, similar to the situation in the ICJ, while the adjudicators would control the substantive aspects of the dispute. Alternatively, where the Director continues to assist panellists in the dispute, they would no longer participate in the panel selection stage. They could substantively review the work of the staff assisting panellists, as well

[141] For further discussion, see chs 3 and 21.

[142] As we will see further in section IV.B below, there may be some similarities between the role of the Registry suggested by us and the 'Office of Legal Counsel' (OLC) proposed by Alan Wolff. However, Wolff's proposal does not envisage the OLC assisting adjudicators, but rather as an independent organ advising the DG/Secretariat on legal questions of interpretation of the WTO Agreement. It would file amicus curiae briefs in cases, with the power to refer the matter to the DSB and investigate suspected deviations from the WTO Rules. This is fundamentally different from conducting legal research and drafting notes upon request from adjudicators. Therefore, the staff of the DS Registry remain 'Dispute Assistants' even with such expanded scope of functions. For further details on the OLC, see Wolff (n 70) 31.

[143] For further discussion, see ch 13.

[144] For further discussion, see ch 18.

[145] For further discussion, see ch 6.

[146] For further discussion on other DSMs where such tasks are performed, see ch 21.

as their administrative control. In this case, procedural safeguards could be introduced that limit the exclusive power of the Director who would often have develop a unique expertise over the years, with a risk of intensive asymmetry. For example, a specific term limit could be placed on the role of the Director (for example, rotation to a different role after five years) to guard against concentration of power in the position.

The *third* and last category of Dispute Assistants could be externally appointed for each panellist for the duration of a specific dispute (as explained in section II.C.vi above) or for the duration of the mandate of the adjudicator or for other shorter durations. If hiring such External Assistants for each dispute is not feasible, the possibility of Assigned Assistants (from the Secretariat) from the disputes divisions, or other relevant division, could be explored. Such Assigned Assistants would counterbalance the exclusive reliance on the institutional legal staff, and such assistance would last only for the duration of the dispute. This is like the system in ECOWAS, where the judges have Executive Assistants under their supervision and control, and receive assistance from the Research and Documentation Department

Even if all three categories of Dispute Assistants are not useful for every dispute, some degree of diversification would ensure that the risk of potential over influence of any single group of Dispute Assistants will necessarily be moderated. The aim of this suggestion is to create checks and balances through the sources of assistance offered to the adjudicators. At the moment, when the staff from the operations divisions participate, they can challenge the advice provided by the lead lawyers (eg, from the LAD).[147] However, dispute settlement matters mainly fall under the responsibility of the Rules/LAD Divisions and directors. To ensure that such diversification does not interfere with the mobility of the staff, these categories need not be strictly permanent, but rather implemented as per the needs of a dispute, allowing staff to undertake other tasks as well. This diversified structure of assistance would allow staff to focus on a narrower set of tasks, while allowing adjudicators to retain control over the decision-making functions.

Further, the list of duties, restrictions and obligations (explained above in section II.C.v) must be mindful of the working relationship between the three categories of Dispute Assistants so as to ensure a smooth operation of the dispute resolution process. Finally, this suggestion would require increased budgetary allocation.

viii. Drafting under Instructions from Panellists

The Molina Report explicitly suggests that the adjudicators will have full responsibility for the decision-making.[148] To ensure this, the Secretariat staff would only assist the panellists with drafting parts of the report other than the conclusions section and only on the basis of written instructions provided by the adjudicators.[149] However, the Report does not go into the specifics of what such instructions would entail. We will try to build on this aspect here.

[147] Panels by the Rules Division rarely involve staff from other divisions, except for the mixed cases under the joint responsibility of the LAD/Rules Division.

[148] Molina Report, Title VII, ch II(1)(a).

[149] ibid Title VII, ch II(2)(b).

In specifying the level of detail required from such instructions, a balance must be struck between accountability and efficiency. If very detailed instructions are required, given the strict timelines, adjudicators may not have the time to draft instructions themselves. For example, there may be instances where they orally instruct the Dispute Assistants to draft these instructions as well and then sign it. Even in such situations, there remains a level of accountability with the written record in terms of how the delegation and drafting was undertaken by the Dispute Assistants. Instructions that do not provide sufficient guidance on the reasoning would fail to safeguard against concerns over delegation of the decision-making function. Therefore, keeping these factors in mind, the instructions could specify the section heading(s) of the report to be drafted and, in cases where substantive drafting is requested, state the general reasoning and the legal finding clearly. As the drafting and thinking of the adjudicators evolve in a dispute, the instructions for drafting will often have to be supplemented with further details and guidance. Therefore, there may be several sets of instructions for drafting provided to the Dispute Assistants.

When the panellists collectively are assisted by a team of Dispute Assistants (Institutional Assistants, as is currently the case), the instructions for drafting should be given collectively to the team of Dispute Assistants. Alternatively, if panellists were to be assisted by one Dispute Assistant working with the Institutional Assistants, the mandate should be given more specifically, forcing panellists in practice to agree on how they would divide up the work. Thus, instructions must be more specific. In such cases, once the decision in principle has been reached by the panel, the instructions for drafting should be shared with the Institutional Assistants collectively and Assigned Assistants more specifically. The panellists could also instruct their External Assistants to draft any specific sections of the award (as an alternative that could be used in deliberations over a drafts by other Dispute Assistants) and/or assist them in reviewing the draft shared by the Institutional Assistants and other parts of the panel report.

In the event of a challenge or otherwise, the specific instructions would also become relevant in assessing compliance with the list of duties, restrictions and obligations (discussed above in section II.C.v). These written instructions could be disclosed to the Chair of the DSB and other relevant parties if a challenge is raised and proceeds against the panellist.

ix. Specific Deliberations Exclusively between Panellists

The procedural framework of the CJEU provides a useful indicator on how adjudicators can remain firmly in charge of the decision-making, even though Dispute Assistants undertake substantial drafting. This happens through two stages of face-to-face deliberations exclusively amongst the adjudicators. In the ECJ, when there is a difference of opinion between the Judge Rapporteur and the Advocate General, the President of the Chamber may conduct a 'roundtable' discussion with the other judges in the Chamber to understand their positions, without any Dispute Assistants being present. It is only after such interactions that the Judge Rapporteur charges their référendaire with drafting a *projet de motifs* or a first draft of the judgment. Thereafter, once the draft has been modified based on any comments received from other judges, the judges conduct their deliberations in absolute secrecy without any Dispute Assistants being in attendance.

This procedure allows the other judges on the Chamber to provide their views on the *projet* to the Judge Rapporteur for incorporation into the final judgment. Therefore, such face-to-face deliberations both at the beginning and at the end of the dispute process ensure that the judges themselves retain sufficient control over the final draft.

The ICJ has another unique practice with successive levels of deliberations amongst judges to ensure sufficient opportunity for each adjudicator to present their views. The first deliberation takes place immediately after the close of the oral procedure and is termed the 'Article 3 Deliberation'. In this deliberation, the judges discuss the List of Issues (prepared by the Registry), exchange initial impressions and share guidance for their Notes.[150] The Dispute Assistants do not participate in this deliberation. Thereafter, the individual judges generally prepare Notes in which they lay out their views on how the case should be decided, assisted by their Assigned Assistants. The Notes are then circulated amongst the judges, and the second deliberation, termed the 'Article 5 Deliberation', takes place. At this deliberation, the case is discussed in more detail, with each judge presenting their notes. From these deliberations, a majority view emerges and the drafting committee is composed. Throughout the second deliberation and the forming of the drafting committee, only the Special Assistant to the President and another assistant of the President (Assigned Assistants) are present to take notes. The Registrar (Head of the Institutional Office) also attends and answers any procedural questions that may arise. These two deliberations ensure that the judges meet face to face, without the participation of their Dispute Assistants, to decide on the direction of the decision prior to drafting.

Even during the First Reading of the draft circulated by the Drafting Committee, the judges physically meet to debate the draft and comment on it. While some Assigned Assistants and Institutional Assistants are present here,[151] they are not seated with the judges and do not participate.[152] Only the head of the Institutional Office, the Registrar sits with the judges and participates by answering any questions or clarifications requested by the judges (similar to their role in the drafting committee meetings). A similar procedural safeguard to that of the CJEU emerges, where the judges must justify their positions in successive deliberations directly without input from their Dispute Assistants.

Similarly, in the WTO, a period of the deliberations could be conducted without the Secretariat staff, both before the drafting begins and after in order for adjudicators to discuss the draft in detail amongst themselves. This could start being established within the current rules. This would oblige panellists to immerse themselves in the issues from the beginning and would reassure the parties that the decision-making remains firmly within the intellectual control of the panellists.

[150] B Simma and A Ortgies, 'Deliberation and Drafting: International Court of Justice' in R Wolfrum (ed), *Max Planck Encyclopedia of Public International Law (MPEiPro)* (Oxford University Press, 2019) para 43.

[151] *The Special Assistant to the President, as well as the two Associate Legal Officers of the drafters, and the Registrar and some lawyers from the Department of Legal Matters.*

[152] M Hébié, 'Des ombres furtives au Palais de la Paix ?: coup de projecteur sur les assistants juridiques des membres de la Cour internationale de Justice' in JM Thouvenin and JJ Hébart (eds), *La Cour internationale de Justice à 75 ans* (Pedone, 2023) 87.

x. *Transparency on the Role of Dispute Assistants*

In Chapter 22, we suggested that the names of all Secretariat staff involved in a specific dispute should be mentioned in the composition note of the panel, as was done in earlier WTO panels.[153] Further, the parties, as well as the public more generally, should remain informed and notified about any changes to the Dispute Assistants assigned to or assisting in the dispute. At the same time, the parties as well as the membership should strictly respect their obligations under the WTO Agreement[154] and not act in any manner that would threaten, intimidate or influence the staff working on the dispute or who have worked on a dispute.

Further, the Members' proposals examined earlier recommend that the research notes produced by the Secretariat for panellists could also be shared with the parties to ensure that they receive the complete picture of information driving the decision-making process of the panellist.[155] However, the demands for transparency need to be balanced with the confidentiality of deliberations that is crucial to the WTO DSS. Two options exist, which can be implemented individually or in combination with each other. The first option is to share with the disputing parties any notes prepared by the Secretariat staff before they receive instructions from panellists with prior approval of the panellists. These documents would be outside the scope of the confidentiality of deliberations and would reduce concerns on the undue influence exerted by the Secretariat without instructions from the panellists. The second option is for panellists to specifically review and share certain procedural/factual research notes with the parties to the dispute, but without asking for the parties' approval as this would lead to undue delays – for example, notes prepared by the Registry on issues unrelated to the specific facts of the dispute, the procedural history of the dispute or the summary of parties' submissions. These options would have to be supplemented with additional rules (perhaps included in the Rules of Conduct) on what specific aspects would be outside the scope of confidentiality of deliberations. Importantly, this should not be considered an avenue for parties to raise concerns with every aspect of these notes and delay the proceedings.

Another aspect that could be shared with the parties is a draft 'statement of facts', similar to the descriptive sections of the panel report at present, the goal of which would be to facilitate an 'agreed statement of facts'.

In summary, even if WTO Members consented to the assistance provided by the Secretariat in the DSS, adding further transparency on the actions and activities of

[153] For example, see WTO Secretariat, *United States – Standards for Reformulated and Conventional Gasoline – Constitution of the Panel Established at the Request of Venezuela – Note by the Secretariat*, WTO Doc WT/DS2/3 (3 May 1995); see also WTO Secretariat, *Japan – Taxes on Alcoholic Beverages – Constitution of the Panel Established at the Requests of the European Communities, Canada and the United States – Note by the Secretariat*, WTO Docs WT/DS8/6, WT/DS10/6, WT/DS11/3 (6 November 1995).

[154] For example, art VI:4 of the Marrakesh Agreement specifies that: 'The Members of the WTO shall respect the international character of the responsibilities of the Director-General and of the staff of the Secretariat and shall not seek to influence them in the discharge of their duties.'

[155] See WTO, '*Negotiations on the Dispute Settlement Understanding, Proposal on DSU by Cuba, Honduras, India, Malaysia, Pakistan, Sri Lanka, Tanzania, and Zimbabwe, Communication from Cuba, Honduras, India, Malaysia, Pakistan, Sri Lanka, Tanzania, and Zimbabwe*', *WTO Doc* TN/DS/W/18 (7 October 2002); WTO, '*Negotiations on the Dispute Settlement Understanding, Proposal by the LDC Group, Communication from the LDC Group*', WTO Doc TN/DS/W/17 (9 October 2002).

Dispute Assistants could enhance understanding of the dispute system and its actors, and promote trust in the WTO DSS.

xi. Accountability through Records on Delegation

To strengthen accountability on the specific tasks delegated to the Secretariat, adjudicators could maintain adequate records setting out the tasks assigned to and performed by the staff. In the event of a challenge to the tasks performed by the Dispute Assistant or the delegation of tasks by the adjudicator, this record of the list of tasks could assist in determining the veracity of the challenges. The record of such tasks furthers accountability in terms of how delegation will be undertaken and supplements the list of duties, obligations and prohibitions on the Dispute Assistants and adjudicators stated above.

III. Dispute Assistants in Arbitrations

As we have already seen in Chapter 22, the WTO DSS envisages recourse to arbitration for the determination for the reasonable period of time for the implementation of recommendations and rulings of the DSB (Article 21.3 DSU) and for the determination of the level of suspension of concessions (Article 22.6 DSU). After briefly discussing arbitrations under Articles 21.3 and 25 DSU, we turn to arbitrations under Article 22.6 DSU, which will be the main focus of this section – specifically, the concerns; provisions, practice and proposals, and suggestions on the role of non-legal staff in assisting adjudicators (arbitrators as well as panellists). Members may also through mutual agreement resort to expeditious arbitration as an alternative to any of the procedures in the WTO DSS (Article 25), ie, original/compliance proceedings, arbitration for the determination of a reasonable period of time, arbitration for the determination of the level of suspension of concessions, and appeal stage proceedings. The MPIA (see section IV below) is one such arrangement specifically for appeal proceedings.

A. Arbitrations for the Determination of a Reasonable Period of Time (Article 21.3 DSU)

The functions discharged by Dispute Assistants in assisting the arbitrator[156] in determining the reasonable period of time shares similarities with the functions discharged in the original and panel proceedings detailed above. In some cases, the same individuals may work on both stages of the same dispute; however, this is not necessarily the case. To recall, at the original and compliance review panel stages, we made suggestions

[156] Although the DSU envisages that it can be an individual or a group, all arbitrations for the determination of reasonable period of time have been conducted by one arbitrator. See 'Count on WTO Arbitrators/Panellists by Appointment Method and Whether on Roster', www.worldtradelaw.net/databases/rptawards.php.

relating to enhancing the expertise of both panellists and legal staff;[157] how the panellists work together with the secretariat staff and/or amongst themselves;[158] and increased transparency and accountability.[159] Many of these suggestions for reform can be transposed to arbitrations for the reasonable period of time, but must be adapted to suit the specificities of these arbitrations. For example, the arbitrator in these proceedings would have mostly been sitting or former AB members, or other experts.[160] Therefore, the concerns over asymmetry would not be significant at this stage. Further, the award of the arbitrator should be produced within a relatively short timeline,[161] limiting some of the procedural suggestions made with respect to the panel stage.

B. Arbitrations under Article 25 (Non-MPIA)

The procedure under Article 25 DSU is considered an alternative to the dispute resolution procedures envisaged in the WTO DSS, where the parties agree on specific procedures that are applicable for a particular stage/stages of their dispute.[162] In Chapter 22, examples of these specific procedures for selection of arbitrators agreed under Article 25 were examined.[163] Article 25 does not specify the functions of Dispute Assistants (if any) in aiding adjudicators. In contrast, the MPIA procedures specifically envisage the role of Secretariat staff in assisting appeal arbitrators. Similar

[157] See section II.C: (i) detailed criteria for eligibility as panellists; (ii) transparency on meeting criteria for inclusion in the Indicative List; (iii) assignment of panellists with prior expertise; and (iv) training of potential panellists as well as staff on new issues.

[158] See section II.C: (v) listing of duties, restrictions and obligations of Dispute Assistants and panellists; (vi) External Assistants to panellists; (vii) Diversification of sources of assistance; (viii) drafting by Dispute Assistants under express instructions from the panellists; (ix) specific panel deliberations exclusively among panellists.

[159] See section II.C: (x) transparency on the role of Dispute Assistants; (xi) accountability through record on delegation.

[160] Mavroidis notes that there are only three cases in which the arbitrator was not a sitting or former AB member. In two cases (WTO , United States – Anti-Dumping and Countervailing Measures on Certain Products from Viet Nam – Recourse to Article 21.3(c) of the DSU – Award of the Arbitrator, WT/DS429/13 (17 July 2012) and WTO, United States – Certain Methodologies and Their Application to Anti-Dumping Proceedings Involving China – Recourse to Article 21.3(c) of the DSU – Award of the Arbitrator, WT/DS471/12 (15 January 2018), the arbitrator was Simon Farbenbloom, who was a member of the original panels; and in one case (WTO Arbitrator's Award, United States – Anti-Dumping and Countervailing Measures on Large Residential Washers from Korea – Recourse to Arbitration under Article 21.3(c) of the DSU, WT/DS464/15 (4 April 2017), the arbitrator was Claudia Orozco, an international trade law consultant. See Mavroidis (n 24) 321–22.

[161] Article 21.3 DSU provides that the award should be within 90 days of the date of adoption of the recommendations and rulings.

[162] In some cases, the recourse to art 25 may also be hinted at in the sequencing agreements entered between parties. For example, in United States – Anti-Dumping Measures on Certain Oil Country Tubular Goods from Korea, the *Understanding between the Republic of Korea and the United States Regarding Procedures under Article 21 and 22 of the DSU*, WTO Doc WT/DS488/16, it was envisaged that if the parties agree to procedures under art 25 for review of the compliance panel report (under art 21.5 DSU), they will amend the agreement accordingly.

[163] See also, WTO Panel Report, United States – Section 110(5) of the US Copyright Act, WT/DS160/R (15 June 2000), the US and the EU agreed to procedures under art 25 to determine the level of suspension of concessions. With respect to selection of arbitrators, they agreed that if the original panellists were not available and the parties could not agree on a replacement, 'the parties shall request the Director-General of the WTO to appoint a replacement within one week of the request'. See, *United States – Section 110(5) of the US Copyright Act*, Recourse to Article 25 of the DSU, WT/D160/15 (3 August 2001).

provisions may be provided within other Article 25 processes to increase the transparency and accountability of staff who assist such arbitrators.[164] The names of staff involved in the arbitration process should be mentioned in the composition note of those proceedings.

C. Arbitrations for the Determination of the Level of Suspension of Concessions (Article 22.6 DSU)

If the losing party fails to comply with the recommendations and rulings of the DSB within a reasonable period of time, the winning party may request authorisation from the DSB to retaliate in the form of suspension of concessions or other obligations under the covered agreements.[165] These countermeasures are considered a temporary remedy to be applied until the losing party brings its measure into compliance with recommendations and rulings, or the parties otherwise reach an agreement.[166] The party imposing such measures must ensure that the suspension of concessions or obligations are substantially equivalent to the damage suffered (referred to as the level of nullification or impairment of benefits)[167] and they must also respect the discipline in Article 22.3 DSU requiring that the concessions must normally be suspended in respect of the same sector(s) where the violation occurred.[168] If the losing party does not object, the DSB grants authorisation to impose countermeasures as proposed. However, if the losing party argues that the proposed level of suspension exceeds the level of nullification/impairment of benefits and/or that they failed to respect the discipline in Article 22.3, the matter is referred to arbitration.[169] Generally, such arbitration is performed by the original panel if the members are available, or by an arbitrator appointed by the DG.[170]

This arbitration process stands in contrast to the panel proceedings, as well as the appeal stage proceedings (including appeal arbitrations under Article 25), where the complainant is not required to demonstrate effects of the measure or to quantify the nullification of benefits they provoke. In the panel and appeal stage proceedings, a violation of the measure per se is rebuttably presumed to bring nullification of benefits, pursuant to Article 3.8 DSU. In contrast, in Article 22.6 proceedings, the 'arbitrator'[171] is tasked with determining the permissible level of suspension of concessions, which

[164] The situation regarding art 25 DSU of MPIA is discussed in section IV below.

[165] DSU, art 22. Alternatively, or additionally, the parties could also reach an agreement on compensation due to the winning party. However, parties have agreed to compensation only once since the advent of the WTO (in the aftermath of the dispute *US – Section 110(5) Copyright Act*).

[166] Article 22.1 DSU clarifies that neither compensation nor the suspension of concessions or other obligations are to be preferred to the full implementation of the adopted panel or AB Report.

[167] ibid art 22.4.

[168] ibid art 22.3.

[169] ibid art 22.6

[170] ibid.

[171] The expression 'arbitrator' refers to either to an individual or a group. Such arbitration is generally performed by the original panel, if members are available, or by an arbitrator appointed by the DG. As we have seen in ch 22, section III.B, sometimes it may become necessary to find one or more new panellists to constitute the 'arbitrator'.

must be equivalent to the level of nullification or impairment of benefits. Given the nature of the determinations to be made at this stage, the Secretariat staff who assist the arbitrator are usually economists. Legal staff from the Secretariat are also involved and contribute with respect to the working procedures, assisting with the meeting of parties and in drafting the decision of the arbitrator.[172] Our focus in this section will be on the functions discharged by non-legal staff.

Turning now to the procedure, the party wishing to impose countermeasures presents a quantification of nullification or impairment of benefits as well as the methodology used to arrive at that level, and the other party may present their own calculations and methodology. Typically, the burden of proof is on the party opposing the countermeasures to show how and why the level of nullification or impairment calculated by the winning WTO Member is incorrect.[173] The task of the arbitrator is to determine what the correct level of nullification or impairment (and thus the correct level of retaliation) is, using whichever methodology they deem appropriate.[174] They make this determination in light of the advice provided by staff economists of the Secretariat assigned to the dispute. Additionally, the arbitrator may also be required to determine if the discipline in Article 22.3 has been violated, ie, that retaliation is in the same sector, unless certain circumstances apply allowing for cross-retaliation.

The quantitative determination of the permissible level of suspension – ie, the level of nullification or impairment of benefits – is typically made by considering the amount of trade lost by the requesting Member as a result of the continued application of the inconsistent measures once the reasonable period of time for implementation has expired.[175] The calculation involves using a counterfactual – ie, what the trade flow would have been had the losing party brought its measures into compliance within the set deadline.[176] This calculation necessarily involves theoretical and quantitative economic analysis. To this end, the staff economists from the Economics Research and Statistics Division (ERSD) or other divisions of the Secretariat assist the arbitrator by running data simulations, validating methodologies used by the parties to demonstrate their allegations, commenting on parties' expert reports and testing assumptions raised in parties' submissions (for example, demand responsiveness, substitution possibilities and exchange rate impacts) on their calculation and methodology.[177] Further, in quantifying the appropriate level of nullification or impairment, staff economists play a central role in assessing trade losses, market access restrictions or adverse effects arising from

[172] C Cantore and P Mavroidis, 'Arbitration on the Level of Retaliation: Dispute Settlement System of the World Trade Organization (WTO)' in R Wolfrum (ed), *Max Planck Encyclopedia of International Procedural Law (MPEiPro)* (Oxford University Press, 2019).

[173] WTO Arbitrators' Decision, European Communities – Measures Concerning Meat and Meat Products (Hormones) – Recourse to Arbitration by the European Communities under Article 22.6 of the DSU (Canada), WT/DS48/ARB (12 July 1999) para 9. However, there have been instances where the contrary view was also taken.

[174] They are only bound by the requirement that the level of nullification cannot be higher than that originally proposed by the winning party wishing to impose countermeasures.

[175] WTO Arbitrators' Decision, United States – Measures Affecting the Cross-Border Supply of Gambling and Betting Services – Recourse to Arbitration under Article 22.6 of the DSU by the United States, WT/DS285/ARB (21 December 2007) para 3.12.

[176] CP Bown, 'The WTO Secretariat and the Role of Economics in DSU Panels and Arbitrations' in Marceau (n 8) 343–66.

[177] Cantore and Mavroidis (n 172) para 26.

a measure found to be inconsistent with WTO rules.[178] They develop the counterfactual scenarios using tools like trade flow analysis (before/after measure), econometric modelling (elasticities, demand substitution), partial equilibrium or general equilibrium models,[179] and price and cost comparisons. Some of these methodologies are also relevant in panel proceedings stage.[180]

The role of staff economists is even more essential in the case of cross-retaliation.[181] Article 22.3 of DSU prescribes a certain discipline on how countermeasures may be used. Generally, the retaliation should occur in respect of the same sector (goods for goods, services for services, IP for IP).[182] If it is not 'practicable or effective' to suspend concessions in respect of the same sector, countermeasures can be in respect of other sectors covered under the same agreement. When retaliation in the same agreement is not 'practical or effective' and if the circumstances are 'serious enough', the aggrieved party may seek to suspend concessions or other obligations under another WTO Agreement.[183] Economists contribute in terms of assessing whether sectoral retaliation is sufficient in restoring balance and in considering the economic equivalence of retaliation when moving across sectors (eg, suspending rights in another sector or another agreement).

In summary, the economic analysis forms the very basis for the determination required to be made by the arbitrator in proceedings to determine the level of suspension of concessions. The contribution by the economists in these proceedings ensures that retaliation authorisations are grounded in rigorous economic analysis, even if the process ultimately remains a legal one. Although the specific tasks do not involve legal skills, the Dispute Assistants aid adjudicators in making binding legal determinations on the level of what will become the DSB authorised retaliation.

D. Concerns Regarding Assistance Provided by Non-legal Staff

As explained above, the nature of arbitration proceedings for determining the level of suspension necessarily requires the arbitrator to make the determination based on economic and econometric analysis. Further economic and econometric arguments and evidence is presented by the parties during the proceedings.[184] The role of

[178] ibid paras 23–30.

[179] EJ Balistreri, PC Mavroidis and TJ Prusa, 'What If? Tinkering with the Counterfactual: A Comment on US – Washing Machines (Article 22.6 – US)' (2021) 20(4) *World Trade Review* 421.

[180] Wauters (n 5) 83–91.

[181] CP Bown and J Pauwelyn, 'Introduction: Trade Retaliation in WTO Dispute Settlement: A MultiDisciplinary Analysis' in CP Bown and J Pauwelyn (eds), *The Law, Economics and Politics of Retaliation in WTO Dispute Settlement* (Cambridge University Press, 2010) 1–20; W Zdouc, 'Crossretaliation and Suspension under the GATS and TRIPS Agreements' in CP Bown and J Pauwelyn (eds), *The Law, Economics and Politics of Retaliation in WTO Dispute Settlement* (Cambridge University Press, 2010) 515–35.

[182] Zdouc (n 181) 518, 520.

[183] ibid 522.

[184] WTO Appellate Body Report, *Japan – Taxes on Alcoholic Beverages*, WT/DS8/AB/R, WT/DS10/AB/R, WT/DS11/AB/R (4 October 1996); WTO Appellate Body Report, *Korea – Taxes on Alcoholic Beverages*, WT/DS75/AB/R, WT/DS84/AB/R (18 January 1999); WTO Appellate Body Report, *Chile – Taxes on Alcoholic Beverages*, WT/DS87/AB/R, WT/DS110/AB/R (13 December 1999); WTO Appellate Body Report, *United States – Subsidies on Upland Cotton*, WT/DS267/AB/R (3 March 2005).

Secretariat staff economists in assisting with such proceedings[185] has attracted criticism from scholars due to (a) being outside the mandate of the DSU and (b) contrary to due process considerations in the WTO DSS. With respect to the role of non-legal staff more generally, concerns also arise in relation to (c) the increasing asymmetry between the capacity/expertise of the adjudicator vis-a-vis the Dispute Assistant.

i. No Specific Mandate for Secretariat Staff Economists

Jasper Wauters argues that, on a fundamental level, the text of Article 27.1 DSU limits the role of the WTO Secretariat to assistance on 'legal, historical and procedural aspects of the matters dealt with, and of providing secretarial and technical support'.[186] He argues that economic and econometric assistance is beyond the scope of this mandate. This is a very narrow interpretation of this provision. Article 27.1 DSU uses the word 'especially' prior to 'legal, historical and procedural aspects of the matters dealt with, and of providing secretarial and technical support', implying an indicative rather than an exhaustive list of assistance to be provided by the Secretariat.

Like the legitimacy concerns examined in the previous section, this concern about the mandate raises the risk that the Secretariat staff are acting beyond their mandate and that adjudicators are not fulfilling their decision-making mandate. This may be argued impacting the consent of the parties to the dispute resolution process and compromising the actual and perceived legitimacy of the WTO DSS.

ii. Due Process Concerns on Assistance by Secretariat Staff Economists

Wauters notes that the due process obligations of the WTO DSS are: a fundamental obligation to provide opportunity to parties to respond to claims, arguments or evidence relied on by the Panel;[187] to test the evidence with the parties;[188] and to appoint independent experts.[189] Therefore, he argues that these due process obligations are not adhered to when Secretariat staff assist the panellists in providing economic and econometric analysis.

Wauters explains that the due process concerns arise because there is a lack of transparency in respect of the non-legal staff working on the dispute, as well as regarding the work/advice provided by them to the arbitrator. For example, the parties are not given the opportunity to comment on or counter the advice provided by these staff members

[185] As we have explained at the beginning of this chapter, such non-legal staff are considered 'Dispute Assistants' when providing such assistance to adjudicators, as per the functional definition adopted by us in this book.

[186] Wauters (n 5) 86.

[187] He refers to arts 12.6 and 15.1 DSU, which provide that written submissions shall be provided to the panel; Appendix 3 of the DSU, which provides for the panel to conduct two substantive meetings with the parties where they present their case orally; and art 15.1 DSU, which provides that, following the consideration of rebuttal submissions and oral arguments, the panel shall issue the descriptive (factual and argument) sections of its draft report to the parties to the dispute, so that parties can comment.

[188] WTO Appellate body Report, *United States – Continued Existence and Application of Zeroing Methodology, WT/DS350/AB/R (4 February 2009)* para 347.

[189] WTO Appellate Body Report, United States – Continued Suspension of Obligations in the EC – Hormones Dispute, WT/DS320/AB/R; WTO Appellate Body Report, Canada – Continued Suspension of Obligations in the EC – Hormones Dispute, WT/DS321/AB/R (16 October 2008) paras 433–36, 482.

(unless specifically shared by the arbitrator).[190] Nor do parties have any way of knowing what level of expertise the staff members have or whether there is any conflict of interest or appearance thereof.[191]

Mavroidis also raises the issue of lack of transparency with respect to the calculation of the level of suspension of concessions. He explains that: 'The inconsistencies observed regarding the choice of counterfactual, the lack of explanation regarding important choices (why is payment of interest unwarranted?), the "let the sleeping dogs lie" attitude towards important issues, such as how to allocate retaliation rights when dealing with GVCs, all call for a retooling of the process using more transparent and expertise-loaded process.'[192]

The due process concerns alleged go to the heart of the procedural legitimacy of the WTO DSS, impacting both actual and perceived legitimacy.

iii. The Increasing Asymmetry between the Capacity/Expertise of Adjudicators vis-a-vis Their Dispute Assistant

In section II.A above, the concerns relating to asymmetry between, on the one hand, the capacity and expertise of panellists (ad hoc) and, on the other hand, Secretariat staff (permanent) were examined. The risk of asymmetry may also arise at the panel proceedings stage where adjudicators often do not possess sufficient economic expertise and complex economic/economic evidence and/or arguments are raised by the parties. Wauters has noted that panels are regularly required to address complex economic arguments and evidence when resolving disputes, as WTO law is more than just a matter of legal interpretation.[193] Accordingly, the parties make arguments that are economically complex and submit evidence based on economic or econometric models. In cases where panels have engaged with such arguments and evidence,[194] the concern arises as to whether the panellists possessed the necessary qualifications and/or expertise to make such assessments. Bown has observed that most panellists lack the qualifications

[190] Wauters (n 5) 88. He notes that the DSU does not discuss 'evidence' and does not, for example, provide for the involvement of experts that may be cross-examined by the parties, which is in contrast to the ICJ with well-defined procedures to have recourse to outside sources of expertise (art 50 of the ICJ Statute read with art 67 of the Rules of the Court). Further, he notes that parties are certainly not given the opportunity to 'cross-examine' support staff such as members of the ERSD or others.

[191] ibid.

[192] Mavroidis (n 24) 371.

[193] Wauters (n 5) 83–91. He notes several instances where legal determinations under WTO Agreements require assessment of economic arguments: questions about the cross-price elasticity of products in the context of a likeness analysis; questions relating to 'injury' to the domestic industry and whether it is caused by dumped or subsidised imports or was the result of a sudden increase in imports in trade remedy disputes; the determination of the benefit from a financial contribution and its alleged adverse effects such as price suppression or displacement in the context of subsidies etc.

[194] Notably, WTO Appellate Body Report, Brazil – Measures Affecting Imports of Retreaded Tyres, WT/DS332/AB/R (3 December 2007) required environmental or regulatory economic expertise and experience with constructing cost-benefit analyses. In WTO Appellate Body Report, United States – Certain Country of Origin Labelling (COOL) Requirements, WT/DS384/AB/R, WT/DS386/AB/R (29 June 2012), both Canada and the US submitted an econometric study to assess the impact of the US's 'Country of Origin Labelling' measure on the imports of Canadian cattle as a share of US feed or slaughter placements and on the price difference between imported Canadian and US livestock.

necessary to fully engage with complex economic questions.[195] It should be noted that the DSU does not impose specific qualifications for panellists when dealing with disputes with complex economic questions. Economist staff from the ERSD[196] have assisted panellists in understanding and assessing economic arguments and evidence submitted by the parties. Such factors may compound and increase the existing perception of asymmetry between the adjudicator and the Dispute Assistants.

With respect to arbitration for the determination of the level of suspension of concessions, this risk is more pronounced. In 2010, Bown examined the economic 'expertise' of 23 arbitrators across 10 DSU disputes that proceeded to the stage of arbitration for determining the level of suspension,[197] using information on the arbitrators' professional position (at the time of the arbitration) as well as the highest university degrees received. He concluded that only one of the arbitrators examined possessed the expertise at the level necessary to interpret technical economic evidence or to construct the economic counterfactuals that are critical to arbitration proceedings.[198] In such proceedings, an economist from the ERSD is assigned to the dispute from the beginning of the arbitration proceedings.[199] As explained earlier, economic evidence and analysis plays a central role in assessing evidence, as well as decision-making in arbitrations for the determination of the level of suspension of concessions. If the arbitrator does not possess sufficient economic expertise in making such determinations, there may be a perception that they are excessively reliant on the economic staff who assist them at this stage even in the decision-making process. Again, this can raise concerns over the asymmetry between the adjudicator and the Dispute Assistants.

E. Relevant WTO Provisions, Practice and Proposals

i. Relevant Provisions and Practice

We have already discussed the general provisions of the WTO Rules of Conduct and Staff Regulations that impose obligations on Secretariat staff assisting panellists, AB members and other adjudicators in the WTO DSS. The crux of those provisions mainly related to 'legal' assistance. However, Secretariat staff other than lawyers also assist adjudicators across various stages of the WTO DSS and such provisions are equally applicable to them. In the case of arbitrations for the determination of the level of suspension of concessions, it is most prominently economists who assist the arbitrator. The role of economists at the panel stage is often more limited – for example, economists are usually not staffed on disputes involving the Rules Division and rarely so

[195] C Bown, *The WTO Secretariat and the Role of Economics in DSU Panels and Arbitrations* (Peterson Institute for International Economics and CEPR, Working Paper, 1 August 2008) 45, www. papers.ssrn.com /sol3/papers.cfm?abstract_id=1263982; see also CA Thomas, 'Of Facts and Phantoms: Economics, Epistemic Legitimacy, and WTO Dispute Settlement' (2011) 14(2) *Journal of International Economic Law* 16.

[196] ibid 17. Bown notes that the LAD is entirely made up of lawyers, and the Rules Division contains a mix of lawyers and other professionals, with very few of them possessing the necessary qualifications to assist the panels with complex economic and econometric questions.

[197] ibid 405–09.

[198] ibid 405.

[199] ibid 412.

with LAD-assisted panels. This is in part due to the fact that traditionally the 'effects' of a measure (except for trade remedies) are presumed when there is a violation of a provision of the covered agreements (Article 3.8 DSU). When the AB was operational, economists were sometimes requested to assist in some appeal proceedings along with the AB Secretariat staff – for example, to assist with the understanding of effects of different types of subsidies. More generally, non-legal staff assist adjudicators when a dispute involves elements relevant to the work of their respective operation division. For example, especially in the context of disputes involving technically complex agreements (like the Agreement on the Application of Sanitary and Phytosanitary Measures (SPS) or the Agreement on Technical Barriers to Trade (TBT)) or sectors (like financial services), the staff from these operational divisions play an important role in assisting and advising adjudicators in relevant stages. This following section examines the provisions and practice regulating the functions of such non-legal staff, in particular the economists.

a. Article 27 DSU

Article 27.1 DSU provides that: 'The Secretariat shall have the responsibility of assisting panels, especially on the legal, historical and procedural aspects of the matters dealt with, and of providing secretarial and technical support.' Bown argues that the 'technical' support referred to in this provision includes the responsibility to provide 'technical economic support' to panellists.[200]

Other scholars like Wauters, Gros and Thomas argue that the 'technical support' in Article 27 more likely refers to incidental administrative matters.[201] They rely on the construction of Article 27.1, where the first part of the sentence referring to 'legal, historical, and procedural' relates to the 'matters dealt with', while the second part referring to 'technical support' is grouped with 'secretarial'.[202] Therefore, they believe that such non-legal staff are beyond the scope of the support envisaged in Article 27.

b. Article 13 DSU

In considering the due process concerns that arise with respect to non-legal staff, it is useful to refer to Article 13 DSU. This provides that the panel has the right to seek information and technical advice from any individual or body.[203] The AB explained that the rationale for the right to consult with experts is that such authority is 'indispensably necessary to enable a panel to discharge its duty imposed by Article 11 of the

[200] ibid 405.

[201] Wauters (n 5) 86; G Gros, 'Unseen Actors as Unseen Experts: Ghosts in International Adjudication' in F Baetens (ed), *Legitimacy of Unseen Actors in International Adjudication* (Cambridge University Press, 2019) 353, referring to Y Fukunaga, 'Experts in WTO and Investment Litigation' in JA HuertaGoldman, A Romanetti and FX Stirnimann (eds), *WTO Litigation, Investment Arbitration, and Commercial Arbitration* (Kluwer Law International, 2014) 165; CA Thomas, 'Of Facts and Phantoms: Economics, Epistemic Legitimacy, and WTO Dispute Settlement' (2011) 14(2) *Journal of International Economic Law* 295.

[202] Wauters notes that this reading is confirmed by the WTO Secretariat, *A Handbook on the WTO Dispute Settlement System*, 2nd edn (Cambridge University Press, 2017) 18.

[203] G Marceau and JK Hawkins, 'Experts in WTO Dispute Settlement' (2012) 3(3) *Journal of International Dispute Settlement* 493.

DSU'.[204] Panels may seek such advice from Expert Review groups (as per Article 13.2 and Appendix 4 of the DSU) or individual experts. Panels have wide discretion when deciding when and how to consult with experts,[205] and, specifically, Appendix 4 (setting out rules and procedures applicable to Expert Review Groups) need not apply per se to situations where a panel chooses to consult with individual experts.[206] However, before a panel seeks such information or advice from any individual or body within the jurisdiction of a Member, it is required to inform the authorities of that Member.[207]

Panels have utilised the option to consult individual experts in several cases, specifically under the SPS Agreement and the TBT Agreement, which contain explicit provisions addressing when panels may seek advice from experts.[208] The benefit of relying on such expert advice has been recognised in WTO jurisprudence.[209] Outside the WTO, ICJ Judges Al-Khasawneh and Simma, in a joint dissenting opinion, also point to the importance of recourse to outside expertise in ensuring transparency, openness and procedural fairness.[210] Notably, they commended the 'best practice' developed in the WTO DSS to readily consult outside sources in order to better evaluate the evidence submitted.[211]

The systematic resort to outside experts by WTO panels (under Article 13 DSU) is widely established and recognised. Therefore, although there is no obligation on panels to seek the advice of experts under the DSU, there is a right and an established practice of doing so. Certain procedures have also developed over time that govern how panels operate when consulting experts (for example, presenting a list of questions agreed by the parties to which the experts respond, or defining the scope of the mandate of the expert, which is limited to assisting with understanding the evidence submitted and arguments made, but does not include decision-making).[212] Further, the WTO Rules of Conduct extend to 'experts' covered under Article 13.1 and 13.2 DSU.[213]

Article 13 could be used not only for consulting economists from outside the Secretariat but also for consulting staff from the Secretariat. More generally, wide

[204] WTO, *Appellate Body Report, United States – Import Prohibition of Certain Shrimp and Shrimp Products (US – Shrimp)* WT/DS58/AB/R (6 November 1998) para 106.

[205] Specific rules may be applicable under specialised agreements – for example, *Agreement on Technical Barriers to Trade (TBT Agreement)*, art 14(2), 14(3); *Agreement on the Application of Sanitary and Phytosanitary Measures (SPS Agreement)*, art 11(2); *Agreement on Subsidies and Countervailing Measures (SCM Agreement)*, art 24(3).

[206] WTO *Appellate Body Report, European Communities – Measures Concerning Meat and Meat Products (EC – Hormones)* WT/DS26/AB/R, WT/DS48/AB/R (16 January 1998) para 148.

[207] DSU, art 13.1.

[208] SPS Agreement, art 11.2; TBT Agreement, art 14(2), 14(3). This in itself raises some questions about what is considered 'scientific' under the WTO DSS and if econometrics is included.

[209] WTO *Appellate Body Report, Japan – Measures Affecting Agricultural Products (Japan – Agricultural Products II)* WT/DS76/AB/R (22 February 1999) paras 127–30; WTO *Panel Report, Australia – Measures Affecting Importation of Salmon (Article 21.5 – Canada)* WT/DS18/RW (20 March 2000) para 6.2; WTO *Panel Report, European Communities – Measures Affecting the Approval and Marketing of Biotech Products* WT/DS291/R, WT/DS292/R, WT/DS293/R (21 November 2006) paras 4.1006–4.1010.

[210] *Pulp Mills on the River Uruguay (Argentina v Uruguay)* (Judgment of 20 April 2010) Joint Dissenting Opinion of Judges Simma and AlKhasawneh [2010] ICJ Rep 103–04, paras 13–14.

[211] ibid para 16.

[212] Marceau and Hawkins (n 203) 502.

[213] WTO *Rules of Conduct*, r IV. See also, WTO *Appellate Body Report, Canada – Continued Suspension of Obligations in the EC – Hormones*, WT/DS321/AB/R (16 October 2008) para 481.

discretion has been afforded to panels under Article 13.[214] Further, Article VI of the WTO Agreement and Regulation 1.4 of the Staff Regulations affirm that Secretariat staff are international civil servants who shall not seek or accept instructions from any government or any other authority external to the WTO in the discharge of their duties.[215] Secretariat staff are not within the jurisdiction of any Member and, accordingly, permission does not need to be sought from the Member before requesting information or advice from them under Article 13.1 DSU.

ii. *Proposals for Reform*

a. Increasing the Economic Capacity of Adjudicators and the Secretariat

Based on his extensive analysis, Bown makes a series of policy recommendations to improve the economic analysis in WTO dispute settlement proceedings.[216] Although these recommendations are not restricted to concerns about the role of economists that serve as Dispute Assistants, they are nevertheless important policy options to address concerns about asymmetry. Starting with the qualifications of panellists, he recommends that in each dispute, at least one of the three panellists/arbitrators should have formal graduate training in economics.[217]

Further, with respect to Secretariat staff economists, Bown recommends that each dispute be staffed with an economist (with sufficient expertise) from the relevant division, along with LAD/Rules Division staff.[218] Additionally, he proposes that a second economist from the division should be cleared to work on the case, so that the lead economist has the opportunity to collaborate and discuss the issues when necessary. This approach implies a need to expand the Secretariat staff to include those with the necessary expertise and skill in economics.[219] However, we recall that not all disputes involve economic arguments/assessments, and an assessment of trade effects is generally not required to establish an infringement of an obligation of a covered agreement (as per Article 3.8 DSU), except in trade remedies disputes.[220] Further, there have been relatively few disputes that have proceeded to the stage of arbitration for the determination of the level of suspension of concession/obligation where this explicit determination of level of nullification of benefits is undertaken.[221] Additionally, some trade remedies and subsidies disputes involve an assessment of 'injury'[222] and they could benefit from economic assessments.

[214] WTO *Appellate Body Report, Canada – Measures Affecting the Export of Civilian Aircraft (Canada – Aircraft)* WT/DS70/AB/R (20 August 1999) para 185; WTO *Appellate Body Report, European Communities – Measures Concerning Meat and Meat Products (EC – Hormones)* WT/DS26/AB/R, WT/DS48/AB/R (16 January 1998) para 148.

[215] *Staff Regulations*, reg 1.4.

[216] Bown (n 195) 391–445.

[217] ibid 430.

[218] ibid 412.

[219] ibid 431.

[220] Article 3.8 DSU provides that where there is an infringement of the obligations under a covered agreement, the action is considered prima facie to constitute a case of nullification or impairment. Therefore, there is a presumption that a breach has an adverse impact on other Members.

[221] There have been 28 arbitrations under art 22.6 DSU; see WorldTradeLaw.net, 'Suspension Awards', www.worldtradelaw.net/databases/suspensionawards.php.

[222] See, for example, art 5 of the SCM Agreement; arts 3 and 4 of the Anti-Dumping Agreement.

b. Utilising the Power under Article 13 DSU

In concluding his article on the role of non-legal Secretariat staff assisting panellists, Wauters recommends that instead of relying on internal experts from the Secretariat, panels should utilise the power under Article 13 in a transparent manner and they should seek outside expert opinion for economic or econometric analysis, which is particularly relevant for arbitrations in determining the level of retaliation.[223] It should be recalled that engaging such experts would incur additional costs.

c. Proposals on Transparency

Although not specifically relating to the proceedings on level of suspension of concessions, we recall some of the proposals on increased transparency in respect of the role of the Secretariat that would also address due process concerns. The 2002 LDC Group proposal[224] and the joint proposal by Cuba, Honduras, India etc[225] examined in section II.B propose that any assistance undertaken by the Secretariat during and for use in a dispute should be shared with the parties. As explained above, this includes legal research undertaken by the Secretariat and other commentary prepared during and for use in the case. This proposal is also relevant in the case of assistance provided by Secretariat staff economists, both at the panel stage and the arbitration stage.

F. Suggestions on the Role of Non-legal Staff in Assisting Adjudicators

Economic and econometric analysis plays a crucial role in the determination of the level of suspension of concessions. Although nullification of benefits is presumed in WTO law, the expertise of economists to assess the effect of measures and market-related issues could be expanded. Understanding the economic effects of certain WTO choices can improve decision-making. More generally, the expertise of non-legal staff can become relevant across different stages of the WTO DSS. Article 27 DSU, the GATT and WTO practices including budgetary decisions seem to confirm that Members want the staff to be involved to facilitate the dispute settlement process. Therefore, any solution to the concerns raised should allow adjudicators to benefit from the expertise of non-legal staff without compromising the legitimacy or due process of the proceedings. We examine three suggestions: (i) assignment of non-legal staff for each dispute; (ii) resort to external experts under Article 13 DSU; and (iii) enhancing transparency on the functions of non-legal staff.

[223] Wauters (n 5) 87..

[224] WTO, '*Negotiations on the Dispute Settlement Understanding, Proposal by the LDC Group*', *WTO Doc* TN/DS/W/17 (9 October 2002).

[225] WTO, '*Negotiations on the Dispute Settlement Understanding, Proposal on DSU by Cuba, Honduras, India, Malaysia, Pakistan, Sri Lanka, Tanzania and Zimbabwe*', *WTO Doc* TN/DS/W/18 (7 October 2002); WTO, '*Jordan's Contributions towards the Improvement and Clarification of the WTO Dispute Settlement Understanding, Communication from Jordan*', WTO Doc TN/DS/W/43 (28 January 2003).

i. Assignment of Non-legal Staff for Each Dispute

In practice, the WTO DSS often involves non-legal staff who join the team to assist panellists in disputes. The number of staff assigned at each stage, their specific duties and the extent of work expected from them varies depending on the complexity and needs of the dispute.

The proposal of Bown examined above suggests that economists should be included in every dispute from the beginning of the dispute process, along with expanding the number of economists in the Secretariat who have sufficient expertise and capacity to assist in disputes involving econometric and economic analysis.[226] This implies that even in cases where economic staff do not provide extensive assistance or provides minimal assistance (ie, an opinion on a very limited question of economics/econometrics), a staff economist could be assigned to more panel proceedings. While it would be useful to have continuity in staff in order to ensure the development of their expertise necessary to assist the arbitration on the level of suspension, this proposal may not be feasible or advisable in the current context of the WTO financial limitations.

With respect to the possibility of using Article 13 DSU to hear the views of specific staff economists – this would be radically different from the present practice where adjudicators request the DG to assign one or two staff economists to assist in the dispute. In that context, Article 13 should not be utilised to detract from this staffing prerogative of the staff management and allocation by the DG and seek assistance from staff other than those assigned by the DG, through the route of 'expert opinion'. This could raise conflicts or clashes in relation to the management of staff.

Today, the ERSD has fewer than 10 economists available to respond to the needs of the DSS. They are allocated to specific disputes on an ad hoc basis based on specific expertise and seniority determined by the Director of the ERSD. There were periods where the Division was overburdened by disputes, which add to their everyday tasks in applied and econometric research and writings. There are also several economists in the different divisions of the Secretariat who participate in panels as expert staff from the operations division (for example, economists with expertise in agriculture or in services).

Increase assistance with respect to economics/econometrics could be institutionalised through *distinct economic office for disputes*, separate from LAD/Rules Divisions. The main work of economists from that the new office would be to assist (all) disputes. If all disputes are to involve economists, many more economists would be needed. In terms of assistance offered to adjudicators, this would not be significantly different from the current situation where individual economists from the ERSD are assigned to assist. However, this would encourage a more systemic consideration of economics assessment. Of course, setting up such an office would involve considerable budget commitments as well as a decision on how the staff of such an expert office are to be selected. If the number of disputes increase, more economists would be needed. This is where one may consider dividing up those who work on disputes and those who do research and write reports etc. Having a permanent office with economists working only on disputes may today be a waste of resources; the current system offers more flexibility

[226] Bown (n 195) 412, 431.

where the Director of the ERSD assigns an economist to disputes when the early evaluation of the matters seems to call for it or when adjudicators so request. The ERSD Director allocates economist staff based on needs, capacity, expertise and ethics, while taking into account the (significant) workload of the division.

Nonetheless, the appreciation of the effects of any measure and of any violation can improve the understanding and inform decision-making. Further, the participation of economists can enhance the accountability and the reputation of the DSS. In all cases, since economists can play such an important role in the DSS, more transparency of the criteria for staff involvement in a dispute would enhance accountability (see further below).

ii. Resort to External Experts under Article 13 DSU

In the case of economic expertise for panel proceedings or arbitration for the determination of the level of suspension of concessions, Article 13 DSU allows for resort to external experts (either individuals or an expert review group).[227] This would be similar to scientific experts who provide technical information and opinions in disputes under the SPS Agreement.[228] Such experts would not be under the supervision/control of adjudicators; rather, they would provide information and/or opinions as requested by the panel. The role of dedicated non-legal staff examined above is different from these external experts under Article 13. The external experts are independent of the adjudicators, while the non-legal staff of the Secretariat interact and support the adjudicators as per their needs on an active basis. It would be difficult to substitute the level of assistance offered by staff economists through external experts. Further, selecting external experts for each dispute could lead to delays and increase the timeline for proceedings.[229]

As these external experts would not fall within the scope of 'Dispute Assistants', we will not discuss them further here. We note that in order to guarantee procedural legitimacy, some of the disclosure requirements under the Rules of Conduct should also be made applicable if panellists/arbitrators seek information from external experts. But encouraging adjudicators to consult outside economists via Article 13 DSU, as is done with other outside experts, may enhance the transparency of the economic advice, allow parties to ask questions and challenge economic assessments that can inform the adjudicators. This would certainly enhance accountability.

[227] See generally C Valles, 'Different Forms of Expert Involvement in WTO Dispute Settlement Proceedings' (2018) 9 *Journal of International Dispute Settlement* 367.

[228] Article 11.2 of the SPS Agreement. Even under art 14.2 of the TBT Agreement, the panel has the right to establish a technical expert group to assist in questions of a technical nature, although this has not been utilised.

[229] J Pauwelyn, 'The Use of Experts in WTO Dispute Settlement' (2002) 51 *International and Comparative Law Quarterly* 325.

iii. Transparency on Non-legal Staff and Their Assistance

With respect to non-legal staff more generally, the selection of such expert staff from operational divisions to work with the team assisting the adjudicators is generally left to the Directors of the relevant divisions (the Trade and Environment Division, TBT, SPS, Agriculture, ERSD etc.). Given that the type and amount of expertise required for each dispute varies significantly, the present system where each dispute is staffed with lawyers from the LAD/Rules Division working together with lawyers and others from relevant operation divisions may be best suited for the flexibility it offers.

While the present system of allocation of non-legal staff has its benefits, it also creates a layer of opacity around the staff who assist adjudicators. The first step in ensuring the transparency of non-legal staff is disclosing their names to the parties. In line with the suggestion on including the names of Dispute Assistants assisting panellists within the panel composition note,[230] this should also include the names of non-legal staff assisting panellists and arbitrators.

To increase accountability, the WTO Rules of Conduct must explicitly be made applicable to such non-legal staff. We have already discussed how a traffic light-coded illustrative list of disclosures structured on the IBA Guidelines could be introduced to strengthen the conflict of interest and disclosure obligations of such non-legal staff as well. The concerns or objections would be raised with the DG, as envisaged in the WTO Rules of Conduct, who will thereafter take the appropriate action.[231] The DG retains the discretion to decide, including in light of the available Secretariat resources, that a potential conflict of interest is not sufficiently material to warrant non-assignment of a particular non-legal staff to assist in a dispute.[232]

Lastly, there could be procedural rules that allow for disclosure of some aspects of the assistance provided by the non-legal staff to the parties. For example, part of the opinion/research notes/written assistance provided by the economists to the panellists/arbitrator could be specifically approved by the panellist/adjudicator and disclosed to the parties, allowing the parties to engage with such material in their written submissions. However, this should be done within a very strict timeline so as to ensure that the time limit for the final report/award is respected. In this way, both the staff advice and the parties' comments on these notes can be taken into account in the decision-making process. Within the existing timeline, this will be difficult to achieve.

As always, the best way to ensure accountability and legitimacy is transparency in the selection of adjudicators and of staff working on a dispute, ensuring that the consent of Members to the DSS is respected and enforced.

[230] This practice existed in earlier panel disputes; see, for example, WTO Secretariat, *United States – Standards for Reformulated and Conventional Gasoline – Constitution of the Panel Established at the Request of Venezuela – Note by the Secretariat*, WTO Doc WT/DS2/3 (3 May 1995); WTO Secretariat, *Japan – Taxes on Alcoholic Beverages – Constitution of the Panel Established at the Requests of the European Communities, Canada and the United States – Note by the Secretariat*, WTO Docs WT/DS8/6, WT/DS10/6, WT/DS11/3 (6 November 1995).

[231] WTO Rules of Conduct, art VIII:12.

[232] ibid fn 2.

IV. Dispute Assistants in the Appeal Stages

As already seen in Chapter 19, the AB of the WTO was a standing body of seven members acting as the appellate and final stage of the adjudicatory mechanism.[233] However, since 2019, the AB has been non-operational. In April 2020, the MPIA was established under Article 25 DSU[234] for resolving appeals in the absence of a functioning AB. There are currently 57 Members participating in the MPIA.[235] This section examines the functions discharged by Dispute Assistants when the AB was operational and the current practice of the MPIA.

A. The Appellate Body (When it was Operational)

The mandate of the AB was to review the legal aspects of the reports issued by a panel that had been appealed.[236] The AB issued an AB Report that was adopted by the DSB by reverse consensus. We briefly reiterate here the key actors and their functions as they stood when the AB was operational.

In terms of qualifications, the DSU provides that an AB member must be a person of recognised authority, with demonstrable expertise in law, international trade and the subject matter of the covered agreements generally.[237] The DSU also requires that AB members stay up to date with dispute resolution and other relevant activities of the WTO.[238] AB members were nominated for four years, but they worked part-time on disputes they were assigned to and in exchanges of views for all disputes. They were provided with a monthly retainer[239] to ensure that they were available as needed and otherwise were paid on an appeal-by-appeal basis.[240] This included a fully adequate daily

[233] DSU, art 17. See also Decision Establishing the Appellate Body, Recommendations by the Preparatory Committee for the WTO approved by the Dispute Settlement Body on 10 February 1995, WT/DSB/1, dated 19 June 1995.

[234] MPIA (n 1).

[235] As of 20 January 2026, the MPIA has the following participants: Australia; Benin; Brazil; Canada; China; Chile; Colombia; Costa Rica; Ecuador; the EU (with its 27 Member States: Austria, Belgium, Bulgaria, Croatia, Cyprus, Czechia, Denmark, Estonia, Finland, France, Germany, Greece, Hungary, Ireland, Italy, Latvia, Lithuania, Luxembourg, Malta, the Netherlands, Poland, Portugal, Romania, Slovakia, Slovenia, Spain and Sweden); Guatemala; Hong Kong, China; Iceland; Japan; Macao, China; Malaysia; Mexico; Montenegro; New Zealand; Nicaragua; Norway; Pakistan; Paraguay; Peru; the Philippines; Singapore; Switzerland; Ukraine; the UK; Uruguay; and Vietnam. See 'MultiParty Interim Appeal Arbitration Arrangement (MPIA)', www.worldtradelaw.net/static.php?type=public&page=mpia.

[236] DP Steger, 'The Appellate Body and its Contribution to WTO Dispute Settlement' in DLM Kennedy and JD Southwick (eds), *The Political Economy of International Trade Law: Essays in Honor of Robert E Hudec* (Cambridge University Press, 2002) 483.

[237] DSU, art 17.3.

[238] ibid; WTO, 'Working Procedures for Appellate Review', WTO Docs WT/AB/WP/6, para 4.

[239] See WTO, 'Decision Establishing the Appellate Body, Recommendations by the Preparatory Committee for the WTO Approved by the Dispute Settlement Body on 10 February 1995', WTO Doc WT/DSB/1 (19 June 1995) para 12, which reads at the relevant part 'the compensation should be high enough to provide an incentive for a member not to take on work which might create a conflict of interest. Accordingly, it would appear that the retainer should be set at a minimum of SF 7,000 per month, plus a fully-adequate daily fee, travel expenses and a per diem'.

[240] DP Steger, 'The Founding of the Appellate Body' in G Marceau (ed), *A History of Law and Lawyers in the GATT/WTO: The Development of the Rule of Law in the Multilateral Trading System* (Cambridge University Press, 2015) 449.

fee, travel expenses and a per diem.[241] AB members were appointed by consensus of all WTO Members for a once-renewable term of four years.[242] A selection committee, composed of committee chairs and the DG, proposed candidates for election.[243] At this stage, the process was run directly by WTO Members, with the AB Secretariat, including providing limited logistical and administrative support. However, the DG[244] presided over the selection committee with the Chairs of the DSB, the General Council, the Council for Trade in Goods, the Council for Trade in Services and the TRIPS Council.

Each appeal was heard by a 'division' composed of three AB members, with a presiding member responsible for conducting the proceedings and coordinating the drafting of the AB Report.[245] The AB Chairman was elected by the AB members and was responsible for the overall internal functioning of the AB.[246] Article 17.1 provides that AB members serve on appeals 'on rotation', as per the Working Procedures for Appellate Review. Paragraph 6 of the Working Procedures for Appellate Review adds that the following principles shall be taken into account when constituting a division: random selection, unpredictability and the opportunity for all members to serve regardless of their national origin.[247]

When the AB was functional, the AB Secretariat provided legal assistance to the AB members on appeals.[248] The AB and the AB Secretariat staff were intended to be legally independent from the WTO Secretariat that served panels.[249] The AB Secretariat was composed mainly of legal professionals and administrative staff who were appointed by and reported directly to the DG for all administrative matters.[250] Each AB division was assisted by a team composed of one or more junior legal staff and a lead senior legal staff. Although the staff reported to the Director of the AB Secretariat, operationally AB staff were 'answerable to the Appellate Body.'[251] Unlike panellists who serve on an ad hoc basis, AB members used to work part-time and spent several weeks in Geneva

[241] See also L Johannesson and PC Mavroidis, '*Black Cat, White Cat: The Identity of WTO Judges*' European University Institute, Robert Schuman Centre for Advanced Studies, *Global Governance Programme Policy Paper No RSCAS 2015/17* (Columbia Public Law Research Paper No 14463, 2015) 6.

[242] DSU, art 17.2.

[243] WTO, '*Decision Establishing the Appellate Body, Recommendations by the Preparatory Committee for the WTO Approved by the Dispute Settlement Body on 10 February 1995*', *WTO Doc* WT/DSB/1 (19 June 1995). However, the requirement of consensus implies that any single WTO Member can block the appointment of an AB member by casting a negative vote. Consequently, the AB became non-operational after the US blocked the launching of a procedure to appoint new AB members to replace those whose terms had expired.

[244] The DG is the head of the Institutional Office of the WTO, with specific functions envisaged under the DSU for assisting disputing parties with appointment of adjudicators as well as specific role to receive disclosures and assess conflicts of Secretariat staff under the Rules of Conduct. However, the DG is not themselves bound by the disclosure or conflict of rules provisions of the Rules of Conduct.

[245] DSU, art 17.1; WTO (n 238) paras 6–7.

[246] WTO (n 238) para 5.

[247] ibid para 6.

[248] WTO, '*Decision Establishing the Appellate Body, Recommendations by the Preparatory Committee for the WTO approved by the Dispute Settlement Body on 10 February 1995*', WTO Doc WT/DSB/1 (19 June 1995).

[249] ibid.

[250] ibid. However, the DG is not involved substantively in the dispute and did not assist the AB members in the decision-making process.

[251] See WTO, '*Recommendations by the Preparatory Committee to the WTO, SubCommittee on Institutional, Procedural and Legal Matters, Establishment of the Appellate Body*', PC/IPL/13 (approved 6 December 1994), and agreed to by the DSB in '*Minutes of Meeting, Held in the Centre William Rappard on 10 February 1995*' WTO Doc WT/DSB/M/1 (28 February 1995) para 17.

interacting with the AB Secretariat staff. The AB members and the AB Secretariat formed part of a close-knit collective (due in large measure to the relative isolation from the WTO Secretariat in keeping with the requirement to maintain confidentiality between the panel and appellate stages of a dispute, despite being housed in the same building). The AB Chairperson worked on a regular basis with the Director of the AB Secretariat, including on administrative matters. The AB staff assisted the AB members in, inter alia, setting the timetables and adjusting the working procedures, when necessary;[252] drafting the Issues Paper;[253] attending hearings and suggesting questions that may be posed to the parties; attending and participating in the deliberations; and assisting in drafting of the AB Report upon instruction from AB members.

Writing on her experience as the first AB Director, Debra Steger recounts the evolution of the role of the AB Secretariat and the working practices of the AB.[254] She details the origin of the 'Issues Paper', which was a background paper consisting of a summary of the parties' arguments, a list of the claims, and the arguments on appeal. Initially, the staff did not offer any of their own analyses or opinions on the merits of the case. However, upon the request and instructions of the AB members themselves, the staff were tasked with cautiously providing options rather than offering an assertive view.[255] Notably, she discusses the unique deliberation process which allowed the AB members to develop and refine their own views regarding the issues.[256] The AB members on a division came to Geneva before the oral hearing to discuss the case and prepare questions for the hearing, and they stayed for the hearing, the exchange of views with AB members who were not on the division, the deliberations and the entire drafting process of the report, up until it was signed and sent to translation. This allowed the AB members to develop their own opinions during deliberations. Further, this aimed to ensure that the division was firmly in control of the process of drafting the ruling.

B. The MPIA

The legal basis for the MPIA arbitration is Article 25 DSU and the process of this appeal stage is based on the substantive and procedural aspects of old appellate review that became defunct in 2019. The appeals are heard by three appeal arbitrators selected from the standing pool of 10 appeal arbitrators (hereinafter 'pool of arbitrators'). The qualifications requested from the pool of arbitrators are identical to that of AB members – ie, they must be persons of recognised authority, with demonstrated expertise in law, international trade and the subject matter of the covered agreements generally.[257] Further,

[252] WTO (n 238). These procedures were decided by the AB, with some case-specific adjustments that the AB Secretariat staff help in making.

[253] Steger (n 240) 454.

[254] ibid.

[255] ibid 453. Recounting her experience as the first AB Director, she notes: '*In the first issues papers, the Secretariat did not offer any of its own analyses or opinions on the merits of the case. The Appellate Body members, however, very soon asked us to provide them with our legal analyses and views on the merits of the issues appealed. Even then, I counselled my lawyers to be prudent and to provide the Appellate Body members with options rather than to be too assertive in promoting one point of view.*'

[256] ibid 455.

[257] MPIA, para 4.

the pool of arbitrators is required to stay abreast of WTO dispute settlement activities.[258] Like the principle of collegiality in the AB, although an appeal is decided by three appeal arbitrators, all 10 members of the pool of arbitrators receive all documents relating to the appeal arbitration proceedings and all arbitrators discuss matters of interpretation, practice and procedure to the greatest extent practicable. In practice, these discussions may not be as detailed as the discussions undertaken by the AB members in their exchange of views. The pool of arbitrators has identical requirements to AB members in respect of being unaffiliated with any government and regarding conflicts of interest.[259]

Annex 2 of the MPIA[260] contains detailed rules on original composition of the pool of arbitrators. Within 30 days of the establishment of the MPIA, each participating WTO Member nominated one candidate. The nominated candidates went through a 'pre-selection process' to ensure they met the required qualifications, which was carried out by a committee composed of the DG, the Chairpersons of the DSB, the GC and Goods Council, the Services Council and the TRIPS Council. The committee recommended candidates to participating Members, who then composed the first pool of arbitrators by consensus. The first pool of arbitrators was constituted in July 2020.[261] The MPIA provides for the re-composition of the pool in the same manner, two years after its composition. In July 2022, MPIA participating Members informed the DSB that the composition of the pool would remain unchanged.[262] In May 2025, a (partial) re-composition was finalised.[263]

With respect to the appointment of appeal arbitrators from the pool of arbitrators for a specific appeal, the same procedure as prescribed in the Working Procedures for Appellate Review is applicable (ie, random, unpredictable selection, and rotation).[264] So far, two cases have been adjudicated under the MPIA: *Colombia – Frozen Fries265* and *China – IPRs Enforcement (EU)*.[266] With respect to the appointment of arbitrators from the pool of arbitrators, the constitution notes of the disputes do not reveal any further details regarding the random selection.

The MPIA does not (yet) have detailed practice on Dispute Assistants. In principle, they are assisted by WTO Secretariat staff (so far, two legal staff), who are not part of the LAD/Rules Division (ie, no one who may have been responsible for and involved

[258] ibid.

[259] ibid.

[260] WTO, '*Composition of the Pool of Arbitrators pursuant to paragraph 4 of Communication*', *WTO Docs JOB/DSB/1/Add.12* (2020).

[261] WTO, '*MultiParty Interim Appeal Arbitration Arrangement Pursuant to Article 25 of the DSU (Supplement 5)*', WTO Doc JOB/DSB/1/Add.12/Suppl.5 (2020).

[262] WTO, '*MultiParty Interim Appeal Arbitration Arrangement Pursuant to Article 25 of the DSU (Supplement 8)*', WTO Doc JOB/DSB/1/Add.12/Suppl.8 (2022).

[263] WTO, '*MultiParty Interim Appeal Arbitration Arrangement Pursuant to Article 25 of the DSU (Supplement 14)*', WTO Doc JOB/DSB/1/Add.12/Suppl.14 (2025), introducing four new arbitrators: Mr Ichiro Araki (Japan), Ms Ana T Caetano (Brazil), Mr Esteban B Conejos Jr (the Philippines) and Mr Paul Richard O'Connor (Australia).

[264] WTO, *MultiParty Interim Appeal Arbitration Arrangement Pursuant to Article 25 of the DSU*, WTO Doc JOB/DSB/1/Add.12 (2020) para 6.

[265] MPIA Award, *Colombia – AntiDumping Duties on Frozen Fries from Belgium, Germany and the Netherlands, Arbitration under Article 25 of the DSU, Award of the Arbitrators*, WTO Doc WT/DS591/ARB25 (21 December 2022).

[266] MPIA Award, *China – Enforcement of Intellectual Property Rights, Arbitration under Article 25 of the DSU, Award of the Arbitrators*, WTO Doc WT/DS611/ARB25 (21 July 2025).

in panel proceedings). When an appeal to the MPIA is confirmed, the arbitrator who acts as the 'point of contact' requests the DG to assign legal staff for assistance; so far, two legal staff have been assigned for MPIA proceedings. It is worth noting that the staff who assist MPIA arbitrators also have their regular duties and are not exclusively available for the MPIA proceedings. Although there is no specific information available regarding the functions and assistance offered by the staff, it is safe to assume that the functions discharged would be similar to those of the AB Secretariat staff or, in some cases, more limited.

C. Concerns over the Role of Dispute Assistants in the Old AB and the MPIA

The following concerns were raised regarding the AB and the AB Secretariat while it was operational. We recount them here (without attesting to their accuracy) to understand how they might continue today or in a potential future appeal stage. The MPIA does not have an institutional Secretariat; Secretariat staff are assigned on a case-by-case basis by the DG following a request by the Members of the MPIA. Some of the concerns raised about the AB have been (partly) addressed with this MPIA framework, while some persist. These concerns, irrespective of their accuracy, have an impact on the legitimacy of the appeal stage concerned and the WTO DSS in general. As was already explored in Chapter 21, the (perception of) risks brought by these concerns also adversely impacts the (perceived) legitimacy of the dispute resolution process, even if the concerns themselves do not manifest in every dispute or situation.

i. Risk of Asymmetry between AB Members and the AB Secretariat Staff

Concerns over asymmetry have been raised differently in respect of the AB. When the AB was operational, the adjudicators were not ad hoc. Most served two terms totalling eight years. However, in comparison to the permanent staff of the AB Secretariat, the AB members generally worked part-time as and when appeals arose. As noted earlier, Wolff raised this concern with respect to Secretariat staff, but at that point the AB had not been operational long enough know the impact of such concerns. His concern was as follows:

> *Powerful, ensconced staff.* Another troubling procedural aspect of the system is the effective authority of the WTO secretariat. The secretariat advisors may remain the same from year to year while the panellists serve only infrequently. The secretariat, therefore, is in a position where it may exert a substantial influence on the panel decisions. With ad hoc panellists and very limited time, the authority of the secretariat- unelected officials appointed without effective review by WTO member representatives- is likely to grow. *The impact of this type of influence on the WTO Appellate Body is also unknown.*[267]

[267] Wolff (n 15) (emphasis added).

Decades later, Paul Blustein raised this concern directly. In discussing the AB crisis, he pointed to the role of the AB Secretariat and its Director at the time.[268] He reported on what he called the controlling role of the AB Secretariat and, more specifically, of the Director of the AB Secretariat in various stages of the dispute resolution process, including drafting the ruling.[269] He argued that the US considered the AB Secretariat responsible for the adherence of the AB to precedent and suggested that the Secretariat staff itself should implement an informal form forms of stare decisis or precedent.[270] The underlying assumption is that the staff exerted control over the adjudicators in their decision-making functions, owing to the Secretariat's legal knowledge, institutional expertise, standing, availability and drafting expertise.[271]

There have also been concerns with respect to the asymmetry between the AB members and the staff due to language issues. The AB members relied on AB Secretariat staff for a variety of tasks, including drafting AB reports, which had to be carried out within the relatively short timeframe prescribed for AB reports (90 days from the filing of the appeal). The short timeframe tends to favour those who can write quickly and who have experience writing in English. In some cases, the AB members could have been excessively reliant on the AB Secretariat staff.

Some of the above concerns, like the alleged asymmetry of knowledge, expertise and experience or language proficiency, seem to have been addressed with the MPIA. The pool of MPIA arbitrators established in 2020 includes several experts who have previously served as panellists in WTO disputes. One possible reason for this shift could also be that unlike the AB, the MPIA pool of arbitrators is considered more of an expert body than a politically nominated judicial body. For instance, Professor Thomas Cottier, at the time of his appointment to the pool of arbitrators, was the Chairperson of an ongoing dispute in which the three complainants and certain third parties were also MPIA participants.[272]

However, this does not necessarily imply that concerns on asymmetry have been done away with. Most notably, this is because expertise in one sector does not imply or ensure expertise in the subject matter of a specific dispute. These concerns may have re-surfaced in the context of the most recent MPIA dispute in *China – Enforcement of Intellectual Property Right*s on China's practice of Standard Essential Patent and Anti-Suit Injunction covering technology critical for implementing an industry standard, like Wi-Fi or 5G, requiring their owners to license them on fair, reasonable and non-discriminatory (FRAND) terms for product compatibility, balancing innovation incentives with broad access for manufacturers. This was a very technical area of trade

[268] P Blustein, China Inc. in the WTO Dock: Tales from a System under Fire (Centre for International Governance Innovation, 2017) 11.

[269] Blustein admits that this is not uncommon, and judges elsewhere also depend on clerks for assistance with their functions, including research and drafting.

[270] Specifically, the US argued that the AB's rulings on trade remedies deviated from the wording of the Agreements and that the AB failed to rectify this through subsequent proceedings.

[271] Blustein notes that this position is not undisputed – the power and control alleged may be overstated, and AB members who are well-versed with their cases have no difficulty in disagreeing with the staff or the Director.

[272] Professor Cottier informed the parties to the dispute about his appointment to the MPIA pool of arbitrators, inviting them to raise concerns, if any. None of the parties raised objections regarding the effect of the appointment to the MPIA pool of arbitrators on Cottier's ability to discharge his functions in the dispute 'independently and impartially'.

relating to IP rights. The panellists and legal staff who worked on the dispute at the panel stage were recognised experts in this field. They rejected some of the claims made by the EU.[273] The EU appealed the panel report before the MPIA. The MPIA reversed some restrictive aspects of the panel report on provisions of the TRIPS.[274] The MPIA award has raised concerns (informally) on whether the MPIA arbitrators for the dispute held the necessary expertise. While they are renowned experts in international trade law, their expertise and experience with respect to such a complex area of IPR has raised concerns. The past tensions on the reversal of panel rulings by the AB on zeroing are being recalled. Of course, some dissatisfaction with the arbitrators is natural in disputes where there is a winning and a losing party. Without going into the veracity of these recent claims, our point is rather the specific vulnerability that this situation reveals. It is principally important to ensure the technical expertise and experience of adjudicators in WTO disputes where complex technicalities are involved.

ii. Lack of Direct Supervision and Control

Like the concerns raised in the context of panels, Pauwelyn and Pelc contended that the AB members did not have direct supervision or control over the AB staff, who reported to their Director. They also claimed that the Director in turn controlled the flow of documentation and advice that was presented (or not presented) by the staff to the AB members for use at AB meetings. As noted above, although they reported to the Director of the AB Secretariat in practice, officially the AB staff were 'answerable to the Appellate Body'.[275] Blustein also highlights the controlling role of the AB Secretariat and, more specifically, of the Director of the AB Secretariat in various stages of the dispute resolution process, including drafting the ruling.[276] He explains the extensive level of supervision exercised by the AB Secretariat Director, including in discussions with AB members, which has led to some dissatisfaction amongst WTO Members.[277] At the same time, he also acknowledges that competent AB members would be able to push back against such Dispute Assistants.[278] As in the case of panel proceedings, these concerns (whether real or not) adversely impact the legitimacy of the WTO DSS by creating the perception that the staff are exceeding the mandate agreed by Members, and that AB members were not completing their mandate.

[273] WTO Panel Report, China – Enforcement of Intellectual Property Rights (European Union), WT/DS611/R (21 February 2024). See also Freshfields Bruckhaus Deringer, 'WTO Dispute Settlement Update – Frozen Fries Put the MPIA to the Test' (Risk & Compliance *Blog*), https://riskandcompliance.freshfields.com/post/102idx0/wto-dispute-settlement-update-frozen-fries-put-the-mpia-to-the-test; S Pahis, 'Appeals after the Appellate Body' (2024) 23 World Trade Review 296.

[274] Notably, see MPIA Award, *China – Enforcement of Intellectual Property Rights*, paras 4.84 and 4.86. For a discussion of the award, see E Bonadio, M Kansara and V Tayal, 'Litigating Patented Standards: The EU-China WTO Dispute on Anti-Suit Injunctions' (*European Intellectual Property Review*, forthcoming).

[275] WTO, '*Recommendations by the Preparatory Committee to the WTO, SubCommittee on Institutional, Procedural and Legal Matters, Establishment of the Appellate Body*', *WTO Doc* PC/IPL/13 (approved 6 December 1994), agreed to by the DSB in '*Minutes of Meeting, Held in the Centre William Rappard on 10 February 1995*', WTO Doc WT/DSB/M/1 (28 February 1995) para 17.

[276] Blustein (n 268) 11.

[277] ibid.

[278] ibid.

With the MPIA, as there is no distinct Secretariat assisting the arbitrators and there is also no distinct Director supervising or controlling the work undertaken by the staff. The MPIA Arbitrators directly supervise the functions discharged by the staff assisting in an appeal arbitration. The staff are assigned on an ad hoc basis for each dispute and are 'answerable, regarding the substance of their work, only to appeal [A]rbitrators'.[279] However, as they are not dedicated staff, they also have additional responsibilities (outside of disputes) which might affect the time available to them to devote to the dispute. The staff would be reporting to their divisional Directors with respect to their other responsibilities. It will take more time (and disputes) to reveal if and how such an arrangement would result in similar concerns over lack of supervision and control.

iii. Excessive Delegation of Tasks Including Drafting

Like concerns that were raised at the stage of panel proceedings, the risk of asymmetry between the appeal stage adjudicators and the Dispute Assistants raises concerns over excessive delegation of their adjudicative function. Further, many pointed to the necessity of AB members to rely on Secretariat expertise and experience to be able to draft very quickly in light of the relatively short timeframe for producing the AB reports. And this raised concerns that AB members delegated too much of their drafting function.

In addressing this concern, it is important to recall the distinction between decision-making and drafting. The specific mandate of the AB member is to fulfil their decision-making obligations. This has not specifically, or implicitly, been argued to include an obligation to draft the AB report. On the contrary, the DSU requires the AB to be assisted in administrative and *legal* matters by a distinct Secretariat.[280] Further, the WTO Rules of Conduct are equally applicable to AB members and staff of the AB Secretariat. This is an explicit acknowledgement of the substantive assistance provided by such staff. So, drafting alone need not be problematic if it is only to implement decisions made by AB members.

iv. Risk of Financial Control by Secretariat over Adjudicators

Pauwelyn and Pelc noted that while the AB staff did not play a formal role in the selection of AB members, they exercised some control over the members as they 'hold the strings' over the AB members' payment and reimbursement requests.[281] AB members received a relatively small monthly retainer. In addition, actual days worked and related expenses were claimed and approved by the Director of the AB Secretariat.[282] They argue that this

[279] WTO, 'Decision Establishing the Appellate Body – Recommendations by the Preparatory Committee for the WTO, approved by the Dispute Settlement Body on 10 February 1995', WTO Doc WT/DSB/1 (19 June 1995) para 7. See also J Pauwelyn, '*The WTO's Multi-Party Interim Appeal Arbitration Arrangement (MPIA): What's New?*' (2023) 22 *World Trade Review* 693.

[280] DSU, art 17.7, read with WTO, 'Establishment of the Appellate Body', WTO Doc WT/DSB/1 1995, paras 15–17.

[281] Pauwelyn and Pelc, 'Who Guards the "Guardians of the System"?' (n 22) 540.

[282] ibid; Johannesson and Mavroidis (n 241) 6.

was also relevant at the stage of setting timetables:[283] '[a]s adjudicators work and get paid part-time, setting hearing dates and oversight over the number of days allocated to each case also ends up determining the number of days that adjudicators devote to each dispute, and thus how much they get paid'.[284] For these authors, this concern raises doubts as to the independence of the adjudicators and, accordingly, adversely impacts the perception of legitimacy of the WTO DSS. However, as with panellists, the amounts involved are so minimal that it is very doubtful whether AB members would follow Secretariat advice in order to receive such amounts.

The MPIA arbitrators hearing appeals are also paid out of the regular WTO dispute settlement budget, with amounts corresponding to panellists' remuneration (as they are like panellists under Article 25 DSU) distinct from the way in which AB members used to be paid. It is unclear if such concerns arise in the context of the MPIA. In contrast, the staff of the AB Secretariat (when it was operational) and the staff assigned to MPIA arbitrations are paid a fixed annual salary, with no oversight by adjudicators as to their remuneration.[285]

D. Relevant WTO Provisions, Practice and Proposals

i. Relevant Provisions and Practice

a. The Rules of Conduct

The DSU required AB members to be 'unaffiliated with any government' and to 'not participate in the consideration of any disputes that would create a direct or indirect conflict of interest'.[286] The WTO Rules of Conduct, which were adopted to promote impartiality and independence by establishing mechanisms for addressing potential conflicts of interest, apply to AB members and AB Secretariat staff.[287]

The WTO Rules of Conduct also apply to the MPIA pool of arbitrators and staff assisting them.[288]

b. Working Procedures of the Old AB

An important aspect of the Working Procedures of the AB was the principle of collegiality '[to] ensure consistency and coherence in decision-making'.[289] The Working Procedures explicitly provide that the AB members shall convene on a regular basis to discuss matters of policy, practice and procedure.[290] Further, both the DSU and the Working Procedures require that they 'shall stay abreast of dispute settlement activities and other relevant activities of the WTO'[291] and that 'each member shall receive all

[283] Pauwelyn and Pelc, 'Who Guards the "Guardians of the System"?' (n 22) 541.
[284] ibid.
[285] In terms of their work, the staff reported to the Director of the AB Secretariat in practice and were officially 'answerable to the Appellate Body'.
[286] DSU, art 17.3.
[287] WTO Rules of Conduct, r IV.
[288] MPIA para 11.
[289] *Working Procedures for Appellate Review*, para 4(1).
[290] ibid.
[291] ibid para 4(2); DSU, art 17.3.

documents filed in an appeal'.[292] Accordingly, the division responsible for deciding each appeal was required to exchange views with the other members before finalising the AB Report.[293] In practice, all seven members would come to Geneva for an exchange of views in respect of every appeal in order to encourage consistency and coherence of decisions.

Debra Steger has explained the process as follows:

> All Appellate Body members receive copies of all the pleadings in every appeal as well as copies of the issues paper, the oral statements, the division's questions and the transcripts of the oral hearing. The other four Appellate Body members come to Geneva immediately after the oral hearing for the exchange of views, during which all seven members will discuss the procedural and substantive issues in the case. An exchange of views can take as long as the members choose, but all seven members do not have to come to a consensus on all issues because the division is responsible for taking the decision in the appeal. On matters of procedure and practice that are likely to arise in other cases, however, the Appellate Body members will do their best to arrive at a consensus view. In most of the early cases, on issues such as burden of proof, standing, representation by private counsel, standard of review and amicus curiae submissions, they deliberated until all seven members agreed on the result. On the substantive issues in a particular appeal, the other members will give their views but will leave it to the division to decide the case and work out the drafting details.[294]

As explained above, the principle of collegiality[295] and the requirement to stay abreast of dispute settlement activities and other relevant activities of the WTO are also applicable to the MPIA pool of arbitrators. In practice, MPIA arbitrators exchange views virtually rather than in person in Geneva. It should also be noted that only the three appeal arbitrators who decide the appeal receive payment for their work on the appeal, as panellists. The other seven arbitrators are not paid for their work during the exchange of views. Unlike AB members, the members of the pool of arbitrators do not receive a monthly retainer.

c. The MPIA Secretariat Support

As explained above, unlike the AB, the MPIA does not have a permanent secretariat. Rather, the DG is responsible for ensuring that the appeal arbitrators are provided with 'appropriate administrative and legal support'.[296] The support is intended to be entirely separate from the WTO Secretariat staff supporting the panels – ie, the staff of the LAD/ Rules Division. The two staff assigned to assist appeal arbitrators are under their supervision and control with respect to the appeal work.

[292] *Working Procedures for Appellate Review*, para 4(1).
[293] ibid para 4(3).
[294] Steger (n 240) 457.
[295] As we have noted before, the pool of arbitrators of the MPIA meet virtually instead of physically meeting in Geneva like the AB members.
[296] Decision Establishing the Appellate Body, para 7.

ii. *Proposals for Reform*

a. 2009 US Proposal

In 2009, the US proposal on the improvement of the AB[297] made three significant suggestions:

- *Part-time to full-time work*: The US notes that the part-time nature of the AB members should be reconsidered, with corresponding changes to their conditions of service.[298]
- *Training of AB members*: One of the three proposals made by the US was for a representative group of WTO Members to coordinate professional development of current and future AB members.[299] The proposal envisaged the training to include intensive and comprehensive review of WTO-related issues, including past case law, the structure of the WTO system, and the process for conducting WTO negotiations and drafting covered agreements.[300] Further, as WTO covered agreements span a significant breadth of issues, disciplines and approaches, the proposal also envisaged opportunities for AB members to become familiar with the broad range of legal systems and traditions of the WTO Members and provisions of the covered agreements.[301]
- *Assigned Assistants*: Lastly, the US specifically acknowledged the benefit of having assigned assistants for each AB member.[302] It proposed, inter alia, that AB members should be provided with a law clerk (ie, an Assigned Assistant) in addition to the AB Secretariat staff (ie, Institutional Assistant). The US argued that such an arrangement would allow AB members to be confident that they have assistance in conducting the research and any other tasks that may be relevant in expressing their views and discharging their functions.[303]

b. 2018 Proposal from the EU, China, India etc

In 2018, a proposal was made by the EU, China, India and others relating to the WTO DSS.[304] They proposed, inter alia, that the WTO should employ the AB members on a full-time basis, with AB work being their exclusive occupation.[305] Further, in order to increase the efficiency and capacity of the AB to deliver within the time limits, they proposed to increase the number of AB members from seven to nine. The proposal acknowledged that such change should be coupled with appropriate changes to the conditions of employment of the AB members, such as enhanced remuneration. They

[297] WTO, '*Improvements for the WTO Appellate Body, Proposal by the United States, Dispute Settlement Body*', WTO Doc WT/DSB/W/398 (16 January 2009).
[298] ibid 1–2.
[299] ibid 3.
[300] ibid.
[301] ibid.
[302] ibid.
[303] ibid 2.
[304] WTO, '*Communication from European Union, China, India and Montenegro, Revision*', WTO Doc WT/GC/W/753/Rev.1 (11 December 2018); and WTO, '*Communication from European Union, China, Canada, India, Norway, New Zealand, Switzerland, Australia, Republic of Korea, Iceland, Singapore and Mexico to the General Council*', WTO Doc WT/GC/W/752 (26 November 2018).
[305] WTO, '*Communication from European Union, China, India and Montenegro, Revision*', WTO Doc WT/GC/W/753/Rev.1 (11 December 2018) 2.

also proposed to provide one single but longer (six to eight years) term for AB members, which would enhance the independence of the AB and its members.[306]

This proposal acknowledges the important role of the AB and, in turn, recommends an expansion of the resources of the AB Secretariat providing AB members with the necessary administrative and legal support. Further, it reiterates that the objective should be to attract and retain staff with the highest standards of efficiency, competence and integrity, while ensuring the broadest possible diversification.[307]

c. USTR Report on the Appellate Body of the WTO 2020

The US had raised a series of concerns with respect to the content of several reports.[308] The USTR Report does not directly address concerns relating to the asymmetry between the AB Secretariat and AB members. However, one specific paragraph is worth mentioning. In comparing the competence of panellists vis-a-vis AB members, and WTO Secretariat staff vis-a-vis AB Secretariat staff, it notes:

> Further, there is no basis to assume that individuals appointed to the Appellate Body will be more qualified than those serving on panels. Indeed, individuals appointed to panels often have had more experience in the WTO system, including with disputes, and with the types of issues involved in disputes, than those appointed to the Appellate Body. *And the WTO Secretariat supporting the work of the panellists generally is deeply engaged in the activities of the WTO, including the work in WTO Committees monitoring WTO Members' trade regimes and the negotiations for new WTO rules*, whereas the Appellate Body Secretariat does not engage in those functions and has more limited experience. As a result, the WTO dispute settlement system has been weakened [in the AB DS process]. Disputes are taking longer, WTO rights and obligations are not respected, and there is diminished confidence in the results of a dispute.[309]

While the above paragraph seems to suggest that having staff with practical experience in committees and negotiations is a strength, many would argue that adjudicators should not receive assistance from staff involved in related negotiations, which could compromise their independence.[310] This position of the US is therefore a contrary view on the concern on asymmetry between the Secretariat and the adjudicators, one that considers expertise and negotiation awareness amongst the Secretariat staff involved in assisting disputes an advantage instead of a concern. This is somewhat like the logic of the earlier proposal by the EU, China, India and others, which also recognises the importance of having a competent and efficient AB Secretariat assisting AB members.

306 ibid 1.

307 ibid 2.

308 Office of the United States Trade Representative, *Report on the Appellate Body of the World Trade Organization* (February 2020).

309 ibid 120 (emphasis added).

310 Mavroidis (n 24) 424, who notes that: 'The absence of an institutional firewall between the Secretariat members assisting panels, and those entrusted with providing advice on legal issues outside the context of disputes, is problematic.' However, it should be noted that most Dispute Assistants in the LAD do not work in Committees or in negotiation contrary to Dispute Assistants from the Rules Division, who often accumulate expertise in disputes and in committees and operational work.

d. Restoring Binding Dispute Settlement: Paper from Alan Wolff

The recent working paper from Alan Wolff is an ambitious set of proposals to restore an appellate stage in the WTO DSS.[311] While he does not deal with the role of the AB Secretariat, his proposals on the qualifications and requirements from adjudicators at the appellate stage are relevant to the concerns raised above. He proposes that the qualifications of AB members should include demonstrated expertise in law, international trade and the subject matter of the covered agreements generally. Further, AB members should combine the skills of being a lawyer and a trade negotiator. Notably, he recognises the importance of having AB members with real trade expertise, particularly in trade remedies.[312]

In a similar vein to the 2018 proposal made by EU, China, India and others,[313] Wolff also recommends expanding the number of AB members from seven to 25 in order to address the concerns with respect to overwork. More significantly, he notes that it would also allow for specialisation amongst AB members – especially for trade remedies. Jennifer Hillman also made a similar suggestion to create a special AB exclusively to hear appeals of trade remedy decisions. This specialised body could be made up of members chosen with a strong background in trade remedy law.[314]

In a bold move, Wolff also makes a far-reaching systemic suggestion to establish the Office of Legal Counsel (OLC). The power of the OLC would include, inter alia, filing amicus curiae briefs on key points of legal interpretation, limited to providing information on the negotiating history to discern the intention of the parties to the agreement. He also envisages the OLC to have the power to review the panel/AB report and examine if they have resolved a question that was otherwise not covered by the rules, as negotiated, and thereafter refer the matter to the DSB. This is a significantly different role from what is presently envisaged for the WTO/AB Secretariat and ventures outside the scope of 'Dispute Assistants'.

This most closely resembles the role of the Advocates General of the ECJ. As we have seen, Advocates General present to the Court their view on a case in the form of an 'Opinion'.[315] They are not representatives of either party; instead, they assist the Court (although they do not present an Opinion in every case). Candidates for Advocate General of the ECJ, like the judges, are expected to be persons whose independence is beyond doubt and who possess the qualifications required for appointment to the highest judicial offices in their respective countries or who are jurisconsults of recognised competence.[316] The Advocate General's Opinion draws legitimacy from the fact that the EU Member States themselves appoint the Advocates General for a term of six years.[317]

[311] Wolff (n 15).

[312] ibid 27, Table 1.

[313] WTO, '*Communication from European Union, China, India and Montenegro Revision*', WTO Doc WT/GC/W/753/Rev.1; and WTO, '*Communication to the General Council*', WTO Doc WT/GC/W/752.

[314] J Hillman, '*Three Approaches to Fixing the World Trade Organization: The Good, the Bad and the Ugly?*' (*Institute of International Economic Law*, 10 December 2018), www.law.georgetown.edu/wp-content/uploads/2018/12/Hillman-Good-Bad-Ugly-Fix-to-WTO-AB.pdf.

[315] TFEU, art 252(2).

[316] ibid art 253(1).

[317] ibid. Of the 11 Advocates General, five come from the most populated Member States (France, Germany, Italy, Poland and Spain), while the rest are appointed from the remaining Member States on a rotational

In the case of a distinct expert office in the WTO Secretariat, while such an extensive process might not be practical, legitimacy could still be ensured through the increased participation of WTO Members in setting up this expert office. Although many of the oversight functions of the OLC are beyond the scope of this book, the proposal with respect to filing amicus curie briefs can inspire specific research tasks that can be fulfilled by the DS Registry.

E. Suggestions on the Role of Dispute Assistants in the MPIA or Any Potential Future Appeal Stage

Before discussing our suggestions for reform, we highlight the overlap between the concerns that arise at the appeal stage with those that arise with respect to the WTO Secretariat assisting panellists. Accordingly, several solutions proposed in section II.C with respect to panel proceedings would be equally relevant in the case of the old AB, today's MPIA or any potential future appeal stage. At the same time, there are notable differences that arise depending on the organisational framework of any potential future appeal stage. For example, the AB was a standing body, where the adjudicators were not ad hoc, allowing for more institutional practices to evolve. The MPIA, although not entirely ad hoc, comprises a pool of arbitrators that may be reconstituted (at least in part) every two years. The MPIA does not have access to any permanent Secretariat, so the asymmetry of knowledge is different. A completely de-institutionalised appeal stage, like ad hoc panellists, can also be envisaged and introduced in the future. The specific institutional nature of the appeal stage and the type of assistants, if any, would determine which reforms could be usefully implemented. Keeping that factor in mind, we will now examine three categories of proposals for any appeal stage.

The first category of proposals relates to the enhancement of expertise of adjudicators and Dispute Assistants through qualifications and training. The second category relates to working practices and rules for adjudicators and Dispute Assistants, and increased transparency and accountability. The third and last category relates to systemic changes that may be introduced by removing the part-time nature of adjudicators, increasing the number of adjudicators and 'de-institutionalising' any appellate stage.

i. The Enhancement of Expertise of Adjudicators/Dispute Assistants

In section II.C, we examined suggestions for reform on enhancing the expertise of panellists and Dispute Assistants through detailed qualification criteria for adjudicators, transparency on meeting criteria for selection as adjudicators, assignment of adjudicators with prior expertise, and training of potential adjudicators and dispute assistants. These suggestions present a crucial path to dealing with concerns on asymmetry of expertise between adjudicators and Dispute Assistants by ensuring that adjudicators are authentic experts who continue to develop their expertise. Further, scholars have noted that enhanced qualifications for adjudicators would reduce the risk of delegation

basis: R Manko, European Parliament Research Service, *Role of Advocates General at the CJEU*, October 2019, www.europarl.europa.eu/thinktank/en/document/EPRS_BRI(2019)642237.

of substantive tasks to Dispute Assistants.[318] We do not repeat the details of these suggestions here, but instead focus on some limitations of these suggestions with respect to appeal adjudicators.

The need for specific subject-matter expertise must be accounted for within the AB members. There were recurring allegations that some AB members did not always have the appropriate expertise in trade remedies and thus could not properly consider such matters when they arose on appeal. Irrespective of whether these claims are correct, the allegations themselves weaken the legitimacy of the AB process. The MPIA adopts the same qualifications prescribed for previous AB members, with a distinct selection process.[319] Although the expertise of MPIA members is obvious in many areas of international trade, appropriate reform should aim to enhance specific subject-matter expertise across differing areas of the WTO DSS. The additional expertise required should not be limited to trade remedies, but could be expanded to include other specific subject matter areas like IP rights, agriculture and services. However, the number of permanent AB members (when the AB was operational) or MPIA members is too small to ensure sufficient diversity in subject-matter expertise amongst the adjudicators. Even with respect to the assignment of adjudicators for an appeal, the present framework of the MPIA (based on the practice of the AB) is through a formula, but is limited to 10 members from the pool of arbitrators. This does not allow for possible subject-matter expertise within a certain bench. In this regard, the systemic changes explored below in sections IV.E.iii, IV.E.iv and IV.E.v address these gaps.

ii. Working Practices for Adjudicators and Dispute Assistants, Rules on Transparency and Accountability

In section II.C, we explored suggestions relating to working practices for adjudicators and Dispute Assistants through the listing of duties, restrictions and obligations of adjudicators as well as Dispute Assistants; external assistants for adjudicators; the diversification of sources of assistance; drafting by Dispute Assistants under express instructions from the adjudicators; and specific deliberations exclusively amongst adjudicators. Further, we also explored suggestions on transparency regarding the role of dispute assistants and accountability through a record of delegations. These suggestions for reform are equally relevant in the case of an appeal stage that resembles the earlier AB. Without repeating the details of those suggestions, we here examine four aspects that are unique to Dispute Assistants in the appeal stage:

The first relates to specific duties, restrictions and obligations applicable to Dispute Assistants at the appeal stage. As in the panel proceedings stage, it is necessary to ensure that the support provided is responsive to the submissions of the parties. The Molina Report recommends that the Secretariat staff be prohibited from providing Issues Papers before the first written submissions have been provided by the parties, including with preliminary ruling requests.[320] In a similar vein, at the appeal stage, the Dispute

[318] Hudec (n 19) 34–35; Sacerdoti (n 34); Hoekman and Mavroidis (n 35).

[319] As noted earlier, there is a pre-selection committee consisting of the DG, the Chairperson of the DSB and the Chairpersons of the Goods, Services, TRIPS and General Councils that recommend candidates (amongst those nominated by Members) who meet the qualification criteria.

[320] Molina Report, Title VII, ch II(3).

Assistants could be directed to work on an appeal only after the appeal has been filed and therefore be limited to the legal issues raised. This is notably different from the practice before the AB, where AB Secretariat staff would begin working on a potential appeal from when the panel report is issued, even before its translation and circulation. Such practice did allow the AB to extensively and thoroughly deal with all possible questions of law within the short time limit for AB reports. However, it may also encourage extensive analytical exercises on questions not strictly raised by the parties in their appeal. In a potential future appeal stage, directing Dispute Assistants to commence work on an appeal subsequent to such an appeal being filed may make it harder to meet a short time limit like 90 days, but it also provides an opportunity to ensure that the appellate stage focuses only on the specific issues raised in appeal as intended by the parties.

The second suggestion relates to procedures for parties to raise challenges with respect to adjudicators and Dispute Assistants for a violation of new duties, restrictions, and obligations. In contrast to the panel stage, such a challenge would have to be raised in the same manner as was envisaged with respect AB members/AB Secretariat staff under Article VIII of the WTO Rules of Conduct.[321] When the AB was operational, the party making such a challenge was required to submit evidence of such a violation to the other party and thereafter to the standing AB.[322] The standing AB would then take appropriate action after providing the person concerned and the parties to the dispute with a reasonable opportunity to be heard.[323] They would thereafter inform the parties to the dispute and the Chair of the DSB of their decision, together with the relevant supporting information.[324] If a violation is found, the challenged AB member or the concerned legal staff would automatically be replaced. These provisions are applicable with respect to MPIA arbitrators as well.[325] For any potential appeal stage, this specific procedure and the consequences of the challenge would have to be established accordingly, but the duties, obligations and responsibilities of adjudicators and Dispute Assistants would be further defined, monitoring their respect would be easier.

Third, with respect to more permanent appeal stage adjudicators, it is possible to envisage Assigned Assistants who are attached to each adjudicator for their term (as opposed to External Assistants hired on an ad hoc basis for panel proceedings stage). Similar to the practice of the CJEU, the adjudicators would have full discretion in selecting their Assigned Assistants, including in prescribing their qualifications and expertise, and conducting their selection. As in the ECOWAS Court,[326] the Secretariat may formally hire the Assigned Assistant with minimal interventions (for example, they could verify that they possess the necessary qualifications stated by the candidate). As they are hired by the Secretariat, they would be staff who are international civil servants, but they would report exclusively to the appeal adjudicator. The adjudicator would be

[321] Rules of Conduct, art VIII.
[322] ibid arts VIII:1, 14.
[323] ibid art VIII:16.
[324] ibid art VIII:17.
[325] MPIA, Annex I, para 11.
[326] Every judge of the ECOWAS Court has an Executive Assistant, who forms a part of the 'Chambers' of the judge. The judge has complete discretion in selecting their Executive Assistant. After a judge selects their Executive Assistant, the Court will formally hire them. The Human Resources division conducts minimal intervention in selecting the Executive Assistants; they only verify that the candidate is a qualified lawyer with the minimum experience and qualifications for the role.

responsible for the supervision and control of the Assigned Assistant, including administrative aspects of supervision (periods of leave, appraisal and performance evaluation etc). The Assigned Assistants would be hired only for the term of the adjudicator, like the référendaires of the CJEU. They would be bound by the WTO Rules of Conduct, just as the AB Secretariat staff were, in discharging their functions with necessary adaptations. In the case of the référendaires of the CJEU, their respective adjudicators were responsible for assessing the conflicts and disclosures made by their Assigned Assistants, who work at their discretion. A similar framework could be envisaged for Assigned Assistants, where the evidence of an alleged violation can be raised with the respective adjudicator. The decision-making on the alleged violation could be undertaken by the respective adjudicator or by all the appeal adjudicators as a whole (as was the case previously with respect to the AB and the AB Secretariat, and currently with the MPIA). Assigned Assistants may also be hired by each adjudicator; even if not civil servants, they would need to comply with all Staff Rules and Regulations, Rules of Conduct and treaty rules applicable to staff and adjudicators.

It is also possible to envisage that the appeal stage adjudicators would work with both their Assigned Assistants and Institutional Assistants. This would oblige the adjudicators to monitor the work of their respective Assistants and the work of Institutional Assistants.

Fourth, the introduction of Assigned Assistants may also ensure that the position of Director does not become a position of power that exerts control over the decision-making function. In the case of Assigned Assistants, the Director would not exercise any supervision or control over these actors who remain under the direct supervision of the adjudicator. The Registry of the appeal stage could provide necessary administrative support to the adjudicators with respect to the hiring, payment etc of the Assigned Assistants.

iii. Removing the Part-Time Nature of Adjudicators

An important systemic change that could increase the efficiency of the work undertaken by the AB members and re-balance the asymmetry between them and the staff would be moving away from the part-time nature of the AB members. This is in line with the 2009 proposal from the US[327] as well as the 2018 proposal from EU, China, India and others[328] examined earlier. This systemic change could address some concerns by reducing the asymmetry between adjudicators and Dispute Assistants. However, this proposal is unrealistic in the current context, except if a system like the MPIA was made with more permanent adjudicators. Further, this would naturally have budgetary implications where the salaries and terms of employment of the appeal adjudicators would have to be revised to reflect the full-time nature of the position as well as the tasks expected of them.

[327] WTO, '*Improvements for the WTO Appellate Body, Proposal by the United States, Dispute Settlement Body*', WTO Doc WT/DSB/W/398 (16 January 2009).

[328] WTO, '*Communication from European Union, China, India and Montenegro, Revision*', WTO Doc WT/GC/W/753/Rev.1; and WTO, '*Communication from European Union, China, Canada, India, Norway, New Zealand, Switzerland, Australia, Republic of Korea, Iceland, Singapore and Mexico to the General Council*', WTO Doc WT/GC/W/752. .

iv. Increasing the Number of Adjudicators

To ensure sufficient and diverse expertise amongst adjudicators, it might also become necessary to increase the number of appeal adjudicators. This would also allow each division/member to devote the necessary time for each appeal and respond to the call for ensuring that the adjudicators hearing an appeal during the appeal stage process always have the necessary expertise and experience. Various proposals have included this suggestion, including the EU proposal (nine AB members), Mavroidis (a WTO Court of 15 judges) and Alan Wolff's suggestion (25 AB members). The MPIA, which has 57 participants, has a pool of 10 arbitrators.[329] Such an increase could allow for a certain number of appeal adjudicators to be devoted to specific areas of expertise. As will be discussed below, in order to be truly representative of the need for expertise, the number of adjudicators would need to increase. We will explore below how to calculate the number of adjudicators necessary to cover the minimum areas of WTO expertise.

v. De-institutionalising the Appeal Stage

This suggestion for reform moves away from a permanent court-like framework of the AB and even a semi-standing mechanism supported by an institutional secretariat (like the MPIA). It transforms the role of the Secretariat to administrative and logistic support, similar to Secretariats of institutions like the USMCA. There could be a roster of appeal adjudicators maintained by the WTO DG or the DS Registry who have the requisite qualifications in terms of expertise, experience and language. Here we examine three elements of this suggestion: (a) the subject-matter expertise of appeal adjudicators; (b) the manner of inclusion within the roster and selection for appeals; and (c) Dispute Assistants for such appeal adjudicators.

a. Subject-Matter Expertise

In terms of subject-matter expertise, the roster of appeal adjudicators could expand on the existing three categories in the Indicative List. Currently, the Indicative List provides the sectoral experience of candidates from each Member for Trade in Goods, Trade in Services and/or TRIPS. Each of these can be further subdivided as follows:

- Trade in Goods: for example, general, agriculture (including subsidies), SPS, TBT and the Agreement on Trade-Related Investment Measures.
- Trade Remedies: for example, anti-dumping, subsidies and countervailing measures, safeguards and balance of payments.
- Trade in services: for example, general, financial services, domestic regulation of services, and digital services. Additionally, the diversification could also include subject-matter expertise in some relevant sectoral classifications of services.
- Trade in Intellectual Property: for example, general, copyright, trademarks, geographical indications, industrial designs, patents and anti-competitive practices.

[329] For the present list of pool of arbitrators, see WTO, 'Statement on Mechanism for Developing, Documenting and Sharing Procedures in the Conduct of WTO Disputes', WTO Doc JOB/DSB/1/Add.12/Suppl.14. However, in terms of remuneration, only the three who decide an appeal are paid.

This suggestion draws inspiration from the proposal for reform made by Wolff, who specifically discussed the need to ensure that appeal adjudicators with in-depth knowledge of domestic trade remedies proceedings is commensurate with the share of cases on that subject. He proposed having a specific proportion of the roster reserved for persons with expertise (he refers to 'hands-on national administrative experience') in anti-dumping, subsidisation, countervailing duties, safeguards and balance of payments measures. While we draw inspiration from this proposal, we expand on it in two ways. First, as detailed above, this need for expertise for adjudicators is not limited to disputes relating to trade remedies. Accordingly, the roster for appeal adjudicators should be expanded to cover the broad subject matter diversity of the WTO DSS. Second, especially with respect to trade remedies, it is important that the expanded roster is geographically representative and not limited to candidates from importing countries who initiate national investigations. Candidates from exporting countries with expertise/experience should also be included.

b. Inclusion within the Roster and Selection for Appeals

In terms of inclusion within the roster, various types of de-institutionalisations can be explored. In the first option, similar to the MPIA, the WTO Members could nominate names for each category of the roster. These nominations would be examined by a Panel of Experts/Committee, which would recommend a certain number of candidates for inclusion within each category. This could be coupled with transparency and disclosure requires similar to those in the CJEU Panel of Experts for the selection of judges,[330] for example, on the qualifications of those nominees proposed to the DSB for consideration. The second option would be further de-institutionalisation, with no role for a Panel of Experts in the pre-selection stage. As in the case of the Indicative List at the panel stage, the Members could decide by consensus on the composition of the roster of appeal adjudicators, with a specific number of adjudicators in each category, depending on the proportion of cases in light of the statistics of the past years. Rules should be agreed to determine the specific categories of expertise in the roster, the number of nominations to be made by each Members for each category, etc. For example, if there are 10 categories of expertise, it may be necessary to have at least two experts per category and some categories (like trade remedies) with many more panellists (maybe up to 50 per cent of the total number of adjudicators), leading to a higher number of adjudicators. Agreement would need to be reached for a selection procedure, the duration of the potential mandate and arguably a rotation mechanism to revise the list.

Next, turning to the manner of the selection of appeal adjudicators from the roster for a specific appeal, there are again different options, each with its own merits and drawbacks. If the selection is done in the way it was in the AB (through the formula), the formula would need to be changed to include a variable on subject-matter expertise. For instance, the selection may a priori take place only among adjudicators who hold expertise in the area of the dispute. Another approach would be to require that at least the Chair of the Appeal stage (or even the panel stage) be selected from the specific lists

[330] TFEU, art 255. The Panel of Experts comprises seven persons chosen from among former members of the CJEU, members of national supreme courts and lawyers of recognised competence.

of candidates in the roster with the relevant subject-matter expertise. This would ensure that other adjudicators on the roster (even if they do not hold the special expertise of the dispute), or from outside the roster if parties agree, can gain experience in what would for them be a new area, while ensuring the requisite expertise amongst the adjudicators. If the selection process is completely de-institutionalised, the parties may agree to select the necessary appeal adjudicators freely between themselves, from the roster or not, with the option to ask the DG to make appointments from the roster if the parties are unable to agree on appeal adjudicators.

c. Dispute Assistants

The Dispute Assistants for such appeal adjudicators could also be de-institutionalised, with support from External Assistants who could be hired through the Secretariat, on a case-by-case basis or directly by the adjudicator. This would be similar to how External Assistants are appointed in the COMESA Court of Justice. Alternatively, the adjudicator could be provided with a specific budget to hire the necessary External Assistant, without any support from the Secretariat. The specific qualifications and expertise required may be specified as per the discretion of the adjudicator and the needs of each dispute. Such a system would allow the adjudicator to retain full supervision and control over their assistants, who would report to them directly. This contrasts with the present system, where the staff of the Secretariat assist the adjudicators, but are also under the supervision and control of the Director. Like the Assigned Assistants discussed in section IV.E.ii above, the adjudicator would retain full discretion in the hiring, performance and administrative aspects (performance evaluation, periods of leave etc) of their External Assistants during the course of the dispute. No one but the adjudicator would have any role in the supervision of or control over such External Assistants' work. In this organisational framework, the budgetary implications would have to account for External Assistants to specifically be in Geneva during (part of) the course of the dispute.

While such Dispute Assistants would be bound by the (improved) Rules of Conduct, they would not be officially a part of the WTO Secretariat and, accordingly, would not receive the benefits accruing to the staff, like access to the WTO insurance and pension contributions. The WTO Rules of Conduct would have to reflect these differences as applied to External Assistants. In section IV.E.ii above, we looked at the practice of the CJEU, with the respective adjudicator being responsible for assessing the conflicts and disclosures of their référendaires. A similar framework could be envisaged for External Assistants, where the evidence of an alleged violation can be raised with the respective adjudicator.

V. Conclusion

In this chapter, we have recounted the specific functions discharged by Dispute Assistants in assisting adjudicators through the various stages of the dispute resolution process of the WTO DSS. We have grouped the various procedures into three analytical categories: Dispute Assistants in panel proceedings, Dispute Assistants in arbitration proceedings and Dispute Assistants in appeal proceedings. The unique and complex procedures of the WTO DSS have established the critical role of Dispute Assistants, while also giving rise to concerns over the legitimacy of these functions. To address these concerns, we have examined the existing provisions, practice and proposals for reform, and have drawn on the comparative study of the practice of other DSMs conducted in Part II of this book. Our suggestions for reform build on this framework, and broadly on these concerns through the enhancement of qualifications and training of adjudicators and Dispute Assistants; detailed working practices for adjudicators and Dispute Assistants that guard against excessive delegation; and increased transparency and accountability, and certain systemic changes.

While some readers may wonder if these concerns warrant such careful attention and reform, we believe they demand attention precisely because of the critical role fulfilled by Dispute Assistants across all stages of the WTO DSS. The system has functioned partly owing to the functions and support provided by the Dispute Assistants, and the solution cannot do away with their role. These suggestions for reforms, both individually and collectively, aim to contribute to strengthening the consent of the Members to the WTO DSS, increasing procedural legitimacy of the WTO DSS, as well as reinforcing the independence and diligence of the adjudicators.

24

How Can Possible Reform Be Implemented in the WTO DSS?

I. Introduction and Caveats

This chapter is devoted to examining potential ways in which the suggestions identified in the previous chapters to respond to ethical concerns raised against Dispute Assistants can be implemented as part of the WTO Dispute Settlement System (DSS). The Members' proposals for reform we have examined also touch upon different aspects of the WTO DSS. Some of our suggestions are principles, while others are more specific provisions, like duties, restrictions and obligations, on the functions discharged by Dispute Assistants and, correspondingly, the adjudicators, including disclosures or ethical obligations. Other suggestions are more in the form of processes or procedural changes that may be introduced in the dispute resolution process. Further, some possible changes are systemic in nature changing institutional aspects of the WTO DSS, for example, moving away from the ad hoc panel system. Different instruments can be used to implement these changes, collectively, individually or in different permutations and combinations, at different speeds.

Before detailing these instruments, we begin with a few important caveats.

First, the decision-making framework of the WTO consists of formal provisions within the WTO Agreement and covered agreements,[1] which are further supplemented by decisions, other instruments, and evolving practice of its Members.[2] The general rule in Article IX:1 of the WTO Agreement refers to the continuation of the GATT consensus practice.[3] Despite voting being an option when consensus is not possible,

[1] J Tijmes-Lhl, 'Consensus and Majority Voting in the WTO' (2009) 8 World Trade Review 417, 435; JH Jackson, Sovereignty, the WTO and Changing Fundamentals of International Law (Cambridge University Press, 2006) 108; ME Footer, 'The Role of Consensus in GATT/WTO Decision-Making' (1997) 17 Northwestern Journal of International Law & Business 653. For more recent discussion, see G Marceau, R Walker and N Koumadoraki, 'Silence in WTO' (2022) 56(2) Journal of World Trade 187.

[2] For example, see the discussion in A Peres, 'Transience of (In)Formality: The Role of Joint Initiatives in Reforming the WTO Negotiations' (2024) 23 World Trade Review 385; G Marceau and A Nandakumar, 'How Can the JSI on E-commerce Become Part of the WTO Framework?' (2025) 20(5) Global Trade and Customs Journal 309.

[3] Footnote 1 explains that: 'The [decision- making] body concerned shall be deemed to have decided by consensus . . . if no Member, present at the meeting when the decision is taken, formally objects to the proposed decision.' In practice, the decision-making for amendments requires a consensus, i.e. the absence of opposition by a Member of the Ministerial Conference present. Marrakesh Agreement Establishing the World Trade Organization (15 April 1994) (hereinafter 'Marrakesh Agreement') arts IX:1 and X, X:3-4 read with art X:2, 5 and 6 and X:8. See generally, G Marceau and R Walker, 'WTO Members' Silence and WTO Decision-Making' in D Azaria (ed), State Silence across International Law (Oxford University Press, 2025) 182. For a

the practice of the Members reaffirms the requirement of consensus for decision-making.[4] With respect to amendments, there is a sophisticated mechanism in Article X,[5] with different thresholds for voting and for formal instruments of acceptance (ie, ratification) by Members.[6] Notably, with respect to amendments to the provisions of the DSU (Annex 2 of the WTO Agreement), amendments can only be made by strict consensus of the Ministerial Conference and take effect for all Members upon approval by the Ministerial Conference.[7] As we will discuss in this chapter 24, amendments to the WTO Agreement or the DSU are by no means the only instruments through which the suggestions discussed in the previous Chapters can be implemented in the WTO DSS.

Second, beyond the formal provisions for decision-making in the WTO, the Members have developed a rich practice for how changes and reform can be implemented.[8] As the WTO Agreement does not offer an exhaustive list of tools or negotiating arrangements for reform,[9] Members have adopted several decisions on different matters to respond to the need of its membership and the global economy.[10] Further, with respect to the DSS, there are various examples of developments that were not the result of formal decisions or organisational arrangements, but rather informal changes in response to the needs of Members who accepted and approved the changes. This includes the evolution

history of the consensus rule and its scope, see JH Jackson, 'Designing and Implementing Effective Dispute Settlement Procedures: WTO Dispute Settlement, Appraisal and Prospects' in AO Krueger (ed), The WTO as an International Organization (University of Chicago Press, 1988) 161–80.

[4] Although the text of art IX acknowledges that the matter may be put to voting when reaching a consensus is not possible, the practice of Members has been that voting is not resorted to even when they cannot reach a consensus. The only time the membership voted on an issue was back in 1995 regarding draft decisions on the accession of Ecuador and certain waivers. However, even on that occasion, when 'the General Council held votes by postal ballot . . . this came only after reaching consensus on each matter'. Thereafter, the General Council adopted a decision (in the form of a Chairman's statement, which we will discuss further below) that accessions and waivers would henceforth be decided by consensus. See Decision-Making Procedures under Articles IX and XII of the WTO Agreement, Statement by the Chair, WTO Doc WT/L/93 (24 November 1995); C Grasstek, The History and Future of the World Trade Organization (World Trade Organization, 2013) 312; and 'Minutes of Meeting Held in the Centre William Rappard on 15 November 1995', WTO Doc WT/GC/M/8 (13 December 1995) 6. Further, the selection procedures for the DG provides that, in the event that a consensus cannot be reached on a single candidate, 'recourse to a vote for the appointment of a Director-General shall be understood to be an exceptional departure from the customary practice of decision-making by consensus, and shall not establish any precedent for such recourse in respect of any future decisions in the WTO'. See 'Procedures for the Appointment of Directors-General, Adopted by the General Council on 10 December 2002', WTO Doc WT/L/509 (20 January 2003).

[5] ibid art X.

[6] ibid art X:3–4, read with art X:2, 5 and 6.

[7] ibid art X:8. See also Grasstek (n 4) 66.

[8] T Cottier, 'A Two-Tier Approach to WTO Decision-Making' in DP Steger (ed), Redesigning the World *Trade Organization for the Twenty-First Century* (CIGI and Wilfrid Laurier University Press, 2010) 60 (noting the 'process of continuous evolution').

[9] R Adlung and H Mamdouh, 'Plurilateral Trade Agreements: An Escape Route for the WTO?', WTO Working Paper ERSD-2017-03 (2017) 1, 7.

[10] For example, see the discussion in A Venkataraman, 'Taking Initiatives in the WTO: The Role of an Executive Head in Steering Change' in G Marceau and H Gött (eds), *International Organization Initiatives: How and Why Organizations Adapt and Change* (Oxford University Press, 2025), including notably the discussions on initiatives in response to the COVID-19 crisis like the taskforce of experts from within the Secretariat to monitor the impact of COVID-19 on trade flows and the overall global economy, and the Trilateral COVID-19 Technical Assistance Platform between the WTO, the WHO and WIPO.

of the appointment procedure for panellists and arbitrators,[11] the creation of the DS Registry[12] (and subsequently the Appellate Body (AB) Registry), the working arrangement between the Legal Affairs Division (LAD) and the Rules Division in assisting panels,[13] the arrangements for translations of DS work in the LAD, the Rules Division and the AB Secretariat, the transparency mechanisms agreed upon by Canada and other Members in JOB/DSB/1/Add. 1–10, etc., Therefore, while formal instruments remain important, it is equally important to appreciate and recognise the informal practices[14] through which WTO reform has historically taken place.

Third, the form of the action, as well as the specific content of the changes, will influence the success of achieving consensus for decision-making.[15] For example, an amendment to the DSU which affects the rights of Members may require many rounds of negotiations to arrive at a text that is agreeable to all Members (often resulting in watered-down, lowest common denominator outcomes).[16] In that context, in decisions relating to technical aspects on the duties, obligations and prohibitions on Secretariat staff that do not result in amendments to the DSU, it may be easier to agree upon. Guidelines are a good example of such soft law instruments for which consensus may be easier to achieve. Indeed, while an amendment to the DSU may be considered the 'royal route' to introduce changes to the WTO DSS, other forms of action may be able to move the needle towards the necessary changes. For example, as we will discuss below, decisions by the General Council or the Dispute Settlement Body (DSB) that are in form of guidelines (soft law) can provide the impetus for further negotiations, while providing the necessary structure for practice to evolve. These instruments are not intended to be standalone actions, but rather envisaged in combination and interaction with each other.

Fourth, a sub-group of Members can adopt certain practices[17] that will be implemented by interested Members. A prominent example is the 'Statement on a Mechanism

[11] M Pereyra, 'Appointment of WTO Adjudicators: Rules and Evolving Practices' in N Lamp (ed), Reckoning and Renewal: The World Trade Organization and its Dispute Settlement System at 30: Essays in Honour of Valerie Hughes (Hart Publishing, 2024) 47.

[12] M Goldstein and L Medrano, 'Bringing WTO Dispute Settlement into the Twenty-First Century: Modernising the Administration of Disputes to Better Serve Members' in Lamp (n 12) 81–85; PJ Kuijper, 'From Seattle to Doha: From the Surreal to the Unreal – a Personal Account' in G Marceau (ed), A History of Law and Lawyers in the GATT/WTO: The Development of the Rule of Law in the Multilateral Trading System (Cambridge University Press, 2015) 388.

[13] G Marceau, A Porges and DA Baker, 'Introduction and Overview' in Marceau (n 13) 1–59; and G Marceau and D Baker, 'A Short History of the Rules Division' in Marceau (n 13) 113.

[14] A Peres (n 2) 385–407.

[15] See generally M Elsig and T Cottier, 'Reforming the WTO: The Decision-Making Triangle Revised' in T Cottier and M Elsig (eds), Governing the World Trade Organization: Past, Present and Beyond Doha (Cambridge University Press, 2011) 289–312.

[16] AB Zampetti, P Low and PC Mavroidis, 'Consensus Decision-Making and Legislative Inertia at the WTO: Can International Law Help?' (2022) 56 Journal of World Trade 1, 2.

[17] See also the Agreement Establishing the Advisory Centre on WTO Law (ACWL) (30 October 2001), which was established by some Members to create 'a source of legal training, expertise and advice on WTO law readily accessible to developing countries, in particular the least developed among them, and countries with economies in transition'. In terms of membership, developed countries are members of the ACWL, but are not entitled to its services; 39 developing countries are members of the ACWL; and 43 Least Developed Countries that are Members of the WTO or in the process of acceding to the WTO are entitled to the services of the ACWL without having to become ACWL members.

for Developing, Documenting and Sharing Practices and Procedures in the Conduct of WTO Disputes' of 2016,[18] which provided the legal basis for the MPIA.

Lastly, the aim of this chapter is not to undertake an in-depth analysis of all the possible tools that are available in the WTO in order to implement dispute settlement reform. Various scholars have already discussed the possible reform of the consensus-based decision-making process at the WTO.[19] We do not seek to re-litigate these issues but rather propose new ways of working forward, within the existing WTO framework. The forms of action discussed below can be implemented cumulatively, or sometimes alternatively, coupled with ongoing discussions for future reform and evolving practices from Members.

With those important considerations in mind, we discuss the following instruments for reform: amendments and interpretations of the WTO Agreement (section II); other consensus- based decisions (section III) with DSB/General Council Decisions, Guidelines, DSB Practices and Chairman's statements; decisions or practices by sub-group of Members (section IV); and Decisions by the DG and other Secretariat Practices (section V)

II. Amendments and Authoritative Interpretations of WTO Agreements

To introduce changes to the DSS the most formal process is the amendment. As noted earlier, the WTO Agreement has different process for amending different provisions as well as specific detailed procedures for each amendment to take effect for Members.[20] For example, amendments to certain provisions (for example, the Most Favoured Nation principle in Article I of GATT) requires acceptance by all Members to take effect (as distinct from consensus).[21] The amendment procedure has been utilised successfully four times, and each of these is in force for all the Members.[22] While the provisions of the WTO Agreement regulate the conduct of the Secretariat staff in general terms,[23]

[18] 'Statement on a Mechanism for Developing, Documenting and Sharing Practices and Procedures in the Conduct of WTO Disputes', WTO Doc JOB/DSB/1 (11 July 2016).

[19] J Kelsey, 'The Illegitimacy of Joint Statement Initiatives and Their Systemic Implications for the WTO' (2022) 25(2) Journal of International Economic Law; M Elsig, 'Different Facets of Power in Decision-Making in the WTO', NCCR Trade Regulation Working Paper No 2006/23 (2006) 13; P Low, WTO Decision-Making for the Future, Staff Working Paper ERSD-2011-05 (2 May 2011); Elsig and Cottier (n 17); Zampetti, Low and Mavroidis (n 18); QXM Liao, 'The WTO of the Future: Keeping the WTO Digitally Relevant through the JSI on E-Commerce' (2024) 25(5–6) Journal of World Investment & Trade 623; Marceau and Walker (n 3).

[20] Marrakesh Agreement, art X.

[21] Marrakesh Agreement, art X:2.

[22] Amendment of the TRIPS Agreement (General Council, Amendment of the TRIPS Agreement, WT/L/641 (8 December 2005)); Agreement on Government Procurement (Committee on Government Procurement, Adoption of the Results of the Negotiations under art XXIV:7 of the Agreement on Government Procurement, GPA/113 (2 April 2012)); incorporation of the Trade Facilitation Agreement (Protocol Amending the Marrakesh Agreement Establishing the World Trade Organization – Agreement on Trade Facilitation, WTO Treaty Series No 47, WT/LET/1030, WT/L/940 (27 November 2014), entered into force 22 February 2017); and Agreement on Fisheries Subsidies (Ministerial Decision of 17 June 2022, WT/MIN(22)/33, WT/L/1144 (22 June 2022).

[23] Marrakesh Agreement, art VI.

these are foundational provisions that would not require changes for the implementation of the suggestions we put forward.[24]

Amendments to any provisions of the DSU are made by consensus of the DSB Ministerial Conference (or the General Council) and shall take effect upon that decision.[25] We have examined the proposals from EU, Canada and Thailand that could be implemented via amendment. The formal provisions for amendments include detailed steps but have not been fully used. All decisions, including for amendments, have been consensus without any vote. With the WTO, the GATT practice of consensus has continued to grow.

We believe that several aspects of our suggestions can be implemented without amending the provisions of the DSU. For example, aspects of putting in place a roster of panellists may also be implemented via softer instruments, and for a certain period, and in certain circumstances, in a softer trial manner with a view to facilitating the reform. Details on qualifications and process for inclusion within the roster may be agreed through means other than consensus-based decisions like decisions/practices by a sub-group of Members, or via (ad hoc) voluntary schemes of Members, and even initiatives by the Secretariat's proposals. The listing of more specific duties and obligations of Secretariat staff could be part of an Administrative Note with Guidelines based on the basic neutrality obligation of staff. These additional more detailed provisions do not alter or amend the provisions of the DSU, they rather add to further clarify them.

Turning to authoritative interpretations of the provisions of the WTO Agreement, Article IX:2 provides that the Ministerial Conference and the General Council have the authority to adopt interpretations, if approved by three-quarters of the Members.[26] Article IX:1 makes it clear that interpretations should not be used in a manner that undermines amendment provisions, but the distinction between the two remains unclear. In *EC – Bananas III (Article 21.5 – Ecuador II)/EC – Bananas III (Article 21.5 – US)*, the AB noted that interpretations under Article IX:2 are only meant to clarify the meaning of existing obligations and not to modify their content.[27] Although the legal value of such an interpretation has been noted to be that of a 'subsequent agreement' under the Vienna Convention on the Law of Treaties,[28] Article IX:2 has yet to be used in the WTO framework.

[24] Although more clarity could be achieved by listing specific functions, including dispute settlement, amending the Marrakesh Agreement would require consensus by the GC or the Ministerial Conference and the domestic ratification of two-thirds of Members. It would be an extremely sensitive issue and may lead to requests for other changes to the Marrakesh Agreement.

[25] Marrakesh Agreement, art X:8.

[26] With respect to the Agreements listed in Annex I, the interpretation can only be made on the basis of a recommendation by the Council overseeing that Agreement. See, for example, WTO Appellate Body Report, United States – Measures Affecting the Production and Sale of Clove Cigarettes, WT/DS406/AB/R (24 April 2012) paras 250–54 on interpretative value of para 5.2 of the Doha Ministerial Decision on Implementation-Related Issues and Concerns.

[27] WTO Appellate Body Reports, European Communities – Regime for the Importation, Sale and Distribution of Bananas (Article 21.5 – Ecuador II)/European Communities – Regime for the Importation, Sale and Distribution of Bananas (Article 21.5 – United States), WT/DS27/AB/RW2/ECU and WT/DS27/AB/RW2/USA (11 April 2005) para 393.

[28] ibid. See also WTO Panel Report, US – Clove Cigarettes, WT/DS406/R (24 April 2012) paras 7.569–7.576.

Some of our suggestions, like listing of the duties, obligations and prohibitions on the role of the Secretariat (and panellists) in dispute settlement proceedings, could be part of an authoritative interpretation of Articles 27 and 11 of the DSU. However, given that this has never been utilised, with a burdensome decision-making process (that is similar to the amendment process), and as alternatives are available, we will explore other instruments that can achieve or contribute to this reform.

There is one more form of decision-making envisaged in the WTO Agreement that is not directly relevant for the suggestions examined in the previous chapters: waivers (Article IX:3 and 4).[29] Waivers under Article IX:3 are also adopted by consensus since the 1995 WT/L/93 decision that provides that Members will first explore consensus, before using the specific voting rules envisaged in Article IX and XII.

III. Other Forms of Consensus-Based Decision-Making

In this section we explore three other examples of consensus-based actions: decisions by the General Council or the DSB (III:A); Guidelines (III.B); and DSB practices (III.C). Finally, we also discuss Chairman's Statements (III:D) even when such statements are issued in the personal/institutional capacity of the Chairman (in contrast to a Members' decision). We consider these instruments in this section as it can qualify the consensus given to a Members' decision.

Consensus may be easier to reach with these instruments if the language used is of soft law, and when they 'add to', rather than amend/alter Members' rights and obligations. For example, a DSB decision to amend the Rules of Conduct would require consensus; however, if the decision relates to the duties of Secretariat staff and does not amend/alter the obligations of Members, consensus to add to Rules of Conduct may be achieved more readily. Similarly, a decision that offers policy space at the implementation stage on what can constitute a conflict of interest or what should be disclosed, for example through Guidelines, could also provide the impetus of initial consensus. We will explore these options below.

A. DSB or General Council Decisions

The DSB, or the General Council convening as the DSB, is responsible for administering the provisions of the DSU and is the primary avenue for negotiating, discussing and adopting reform relating to aspects of the dispute settlement system.[30] Given that several of our suggestions relate to providing more clarity on existing rules of the DSU, DSB decisions could expand on these specific provisions. For example, with respect to Article 8 of the DSU, a DSB decision could suggest more precise selection procedure for the

[29] See also Decision-Making Procedures under Articles IX and XII of the WTO Agreement, Statement by the Chairman, as agreed by the General Council on 15 November 1995, WT/L/93 (24 November 1995).

[30] Understanding on Rules and Procedures Governing the Settlement of Disputes, Marrakesh Agreement Establishing the World Trade Organization, Annex 2, 1869 UNTS 401, 33 ILM 1226 (1994) (hereinafter 'DSU'), art 1.

appointment of adjudicators, their selection criteria, the manner of reforming the existing Indicative List, and the responsibilities of the Secretariat staff and Director-General (DG) in assisting the parties in this process. This is in part what the Molina Report suggested. With respect to Article 27 of the DSU, a DSB decision could accordingly detail the specific scope of assistance provided by Dispute Assistants to adjudicators, including their duties, obligations, and prohibitions. The decision could also provide the related duties, obligations and prohibitions of adjudicators, in terms of receiving assistance from Dispute Assistants.

Another example of a DSB consensus decision is that of the Rules of Conduct for the DSU adopted in 1995.[31] We have already examined several provisions of the Rules of Conduct and changes that may be introduced to address concerns on the role of Dispute Assistants. For example, with respect to staff who assist the parties in appointment of panellists, we suggest that the adjudicators' selection process be expressly included within the scope of the Rules of Conduct and that staff involved in the panel selection process be considered a 'covered person' against whom challenges can be raised. Further, at present, Annex 2 of the Rules of Conduct, which provides an illustrative list of information to be disclosed by covered persons, consists of only five entries. The IBA Guidelines on Conflict of Interest provides a framework to amend Annex 2, with traffic-light colour-coded disclosures that may be introduced for different covered persons. Amending the Rules of Conduct would have to be through a consensus decision of the DSB, if it is to be applicable to all DSB Members. However, given that our suggested changes do not amend the obligations of Members, consensus on such issues may be (slightly) less burdensome to achieve and Members may see their benefits.

The provisions of the Staff Regulations, adopted by the General Council in 1998,[32] that deal with the duties, obligations and privileges of the Secretariat staff, including their standards of conduct with respect to the WTO DSS, with a cross-reference to the Rules of Conduct, could be amended.[33] This provision may be suitably changed in line with amendments to the Rules of Conduct, and further provisions may be introduced. Similarly, such amendments to the duties, obligations and privileges of the staff would have to be adopted by a consensus of the General Council.[34] However, as they do not amend the obligations of Members, consensus on such issues may be (slightly) less burdensome to achieve.

B. Guidelines

In the WTO, guidelines can be adopted by Members in councils, committees and other bodies etc through consensus. The content of guidelines is of soft law: they help

[31] 'Rules of Conduct for the Understanding on Rules and Procedures Governing the Settlement of Disputes', WTO Doc WT/DSB/RC/1 (11 December 1996).

[32] Conditions of Service Applicable to the Staff of the WTO Secretariat, Annex 2, Decision Adopted by the General Council and the ICITO Executive Committee on 16 October 1998, WTO Doc WT/L/282 (21 October 1998).

[33] ibid Annex B, para 34.

[34] ibid reg 13.1.

standardise procedures,[35] practices,[36] reporting[37] or even norms in particular areas.[38] A example of guidelines are the 'Guidelines for the Appointment of Officers to WTO Bodies' adopted by the General Council in 2002.[39] These lay down the qualifications and procedures for appointment of Chairpersons, the level of representation and their term of office.[40]

The legal significance of the guidelines in the WTO agreements depends on the specific language used in the context of issuance of the guidelines, and the text used within the guidelines themselves.[41] For example, in *US – Gambling*, the AB discussed the interpretative value of the 1993 Scheduling Guidelines and concluded that they constitute supplementary means of interpretation under Article 32 VCLT.[42] Importantly, the AB resorted to these Guidelines to interpret the scope of the US Schedule of Commitments entry on 'Other recreational services (except sporting)', as the ordinary meaning was not clear and given the importance of the Scheduling Guidelines during the negotiations of the Schedule of Commitments.[43] Although, by definition, guidelines do not require mandatory actions from Members, they are an important decision-making instruments that can guide Members' actions. With respect to our suggestions discussed in the previous chapters, guidelines can introduce inter alia, improvements to the selection process, the Indicative List, including criteria for inclusion, and a series of DSM working practices for the Secretariat staff, the DG, panelists, parties and Members. Our suggestions on specific duties, obligations and prohibitions on Secretariat staff can also be provided in such guidelines. Guidelines are consensus-based tools, which grant them legitimacy but at the same time, they benefit from the flexibility of being 'soft' law instruments that facilitate implementation and responses to matters - and they can eventually become 'hard' law.[44]

[35] For example, WTO General Council, 'Procedures for the Circulation and Derestriction of WTO Documents', WTO Doc WT/L/452 (16 May 2002).

[36] For example, WTO General Council, 'Guidelines for Arrangements on Relations with Non-governmental Organisations', WTO Doc WT/L/162 (23 July 1996).

[37] For example, WTO Committee on Agriculture, 'Notification Requirements and Formats', G/AG/2 (30 June 1995). See further Committee on Agriculture, 'Notification Requirements and Formats – TRQ Administration –Table MA:1', WTO Doc G/AG/2/Add.3 (25 March 2023).

[38] For example, WTO Committee on Technical Barriers to Trade, 'Guidelines on Conformity Assessment Procedures: Non-prescriptive Practical Guidelines to Support Regulators in the Choice and Design of Appropriate and Proportionate Conformity Assessment Procedures', WTO Doc G/TBT/54 (19 March 2024); WTO Committee on Technical Barriers to Trade, 'Notification Guidelines', WTO Doc G/TBT/52 (15 November 2023).

[39] WTO General Council, 'Guidelines for the Appointment of Officers to WTO Bodies', WTO Doc WT/L/510 (21 January 2003).

[40] ibid.

[41] For example, see WTO Panel Report, EC – Export Subsidies on Sugar, WT/DS265/R (15 October 2004) para 7.176, where the Panel referred to the same Agriculture Committee notification guidelines (G/AG/2 and Add.1) regarding how Members should notify export subsidy commitments.

[42] WTO Appellate Body Report, US – Measures Affecting the Cross-Border Supply of Gambling and Betting Services, WT/DS285/AB/R (7 April 2005) para 196, referencing the Scheduling of Initial Commitments in Trade in Services: Explanatory Note, MTN.GNS/W/164, 3 September 1993.

[43] ibid paras 196–208.

[44] See generally, ME Footer "The (Re)Turn to "Soft Law" in Reconciling the Antinomies in WTO Law" (2010) 11(2) Melbourne Journal of International Law 11:2 241.

C. DSB 'Practices' under the DSU

WTO Members have agreed on 'practices' to address certain procedural concerns or to facilitate the implementation of other obligations/procedures.[45] A practice could be set aside by a Member if it is no longer deemed appropriate. In 1996, the DSB agreed on the 'Working Practices Concerning Dispute Settlement Procedures' relating to four procedural issues: date of circulation in the DSU, communications under the DSU, time periods under the DSU and other covered agreements, and notifications of requests for consultations.[46] These Working Practices have been important for the smooth functioning and the automaticity of the DSS. For example, the clarification relating to 'date of circulation', 'issuance to all Members' or 'issuance to the Members' specifies which date counts for the relevant deadlines and timeframes in the automatic/reversed consensus process of the WTO DSS.[47] With respect to time periods, the practice clarifies that when a time period within which certain action must be taken expires on a non-working day, such action can be lodged on the first working day following the day on which such a time period would normally expire.[48] This instrument was agreed by Members' consensus at the DSB and was made public from the beginning. With respect to the specific suggestions discussed in the previous chapters, some of the clarifications relating to the manner in which Members can utilise the Indicative List, or the assessment of criteria for inclusion within the Indicative List, could be introduced via a DSB (soft) practice (and with Chairman's statement, discussed below).

D. Chairman's Statements

Although this form of action is not consensus-based decision-making by Members, we examine Chairman's statements here for their ability to build consensus for other instruments examined above and sometimes to qualify a more formal prior agreement.[49] In GATT and WTO tradition, a Chairman's statement is usually intended to provide clarification of or further elaboration to a decision or action taken or suggested to be taken by a WTO body, issued by the Chair of a negotiating body – ie, the Ministerial Conference, General Council DSB or a specialised committee.[50]

[45] For a discussion and examples, see G Marceau and C Marquet, 'Practices and Ways of Doing Things in the World Trade Organization (WTO) Law' in HR Fabri and DB Hess (eds), International Law and Litigation: A Look into Procedure (Nomos Verlagsgesellschaft, Baden-Baden 2019) 513-550

[46] WTO DSB, 'Working Practices Concerning Dispute Settlement Procedures', WTO Doc WT/DSB/6, 6 June 1996.

[47] The practice specifies that the date is the 'date printed on the WTO document to be circulated with the assurance of the Secretariat that the date printed on the document is the date on which this document is effectively put in the pigeonholes of delegations in all three working languages'.

[48] 'Guidelines for the Appointment of Officers to WTO Bodies', WTO Doc WT/L/510, 2. See also WTO, 'Illustrative List of DSU Provisions Referring to Time-Periods', WT/DSB/W/10/Add.1.

[49] J Odell, 'Chairing a WTO Negotiation' in EU Petersmann and J Harrison (eds), Reforming the World Trading System (Cambridge University Press, 2005) 473.

[50] HMG Ruse-Khan, 'The Role of Chairman's Statements in the WTO' (2007) 41(3) Journal of World Trade 475, 489.

There are various examples of Chairman's statements[51] and here we will examine one particular case to clarify certain features of those instruments and their role in working with consensus decisions. We refer to the chair statement made with respect to the temporary waiver of Article 31(f) TRIPS,[52] and the subsequent TRIPS amendment inserting Article 31 *bis* and an Annex into Annex 1(c) of the WTO Agreement.[53] The proposal for temporary waiver was extremely controversial. The Chairman's statement was able to address concerns of the US and the pharmaceutical industry that worried about circumvention of imports of waiver-medicine that could be too easily re-exported to EU or other rich markets.[54] The temporary waiver decision[55] and subsequently, the TRIPS Amendment, were adopted by the General Council 'in light of the chairman's statement'.[56]

The Panel Report in *US – FSC* considered the legal value of the Chairman's statement to the 1981 Understanding, to the interpretation of the SCM Agreement. The panel concluded that the statement was an 'integral part of the overall package agreed among the contracting parties' and thus plays a critical role in assessing the legal value of the 1981 understanding.[57] The Panel also gave weight to the interventions made by some GATT contracting parties relating to the statement.[58] Therefore, the legal significance of a specific Chairman's statement will depend on the content/phrasing of such statement, and Members' reactions at the time of adoption.

For our suggestions based on consensus, a statement from the Chair could also be used to add specific explanations and examples with respect to the duties, obligations and prohibitions on the role of the Secretariat, as well as the corresponding duties of the panellists. The Chairman Statement could relate, for example, to the Rules of Conduct or the DSU, or be autonomous, and could include inter alia precisions and clarifications of existing rules and principles.

[51] For example, in the Agreement on Textiles and Clothing (ATC, 1995), the Chairman's statement at the adoption of the ATC clarified certain transitional arrangements. In China's WTO accession (2001), the Chairman's statement on transitional review mechanisms helped record Members' shared understanding. In the Russia Accession Protocol, the Chairman's statement clarified that English was only the binding language for the schedules. There are a few DSB practices explained in Chairman's statements, like the process for third-party participation or notifications to committees and deadlines falling on Saturdays. Further, WTO General Council, 'Minutes of the Meeting of 15 November 1995', WTO Doc WT/GC/M/8 (13 December 1995) 6 explains the Chair Statement addressing the relation between the general consensus principle under art IX:1 and specific options for voting under art IX:3 and XII:2 of the WTO Agreement.

[52] General Council, Decision of 30 August 2003, WTO Doc WT/L/540 and Corr 1 (1 September 2003).

[53] General Council, Decision of 6 December 2005, WTO Doc WT/L/641 (8 December 2005).

[54] General Council, 'Minutes of the Meeting of 25, 26 and 30 August 2003', WTO Doc WT/GC/M/82 (13 November 2003) para 29 and Annex I.

[55] ibid para 30.

[56] WTO General Council, 'Minutes of the Meeting of 1, 2 and 6 December 2005', WTO Doc WT/GC/M/100 (27 March 2006) paras 29–33.

[57] WTO Panel Report, United States – Tax Treatment for 'Foreign Sales Corporations', WT/DS108/R (20 March 2000) para 7.69.

[58] ibid para 7.71.

IV. Decisions or Practices by Sub-group(s) of Members

In an attempt to overcome the limitations of consensus decision-making,[59] Members are expanding the use of sub-groups' actions and agreements. In the area of dispute settlement, Canada proposed the 'Statement on a Mechanism for Developing, Documenting and Sharing Practices and Procedures in the Conduct of WTO Disputes' in 2016 to facilitate reform.[60] Members that endorse this mechanism participate in developing, documenting and sharing practices and procedures in the conduct of disputes. They are invited to circulate, either individually or in collaboration with other Members, documents that set out agreed, proposed or model practices and procedures to reform the conduct of WTO disputes. Even Members that do not endorse the Statement are also allowed and encouraged to participate. As listed in paragraph 6, the proposals circulated via this mechanism could relate to the following:

a. Documents that indicate their intention to follow, either unilaterally or on a reciprocal basis with other Members, certain practices and procedures in their future disputes;
b. Documents that set out procedural agreements between parties in specific disputes that might serve as models for other disputes and/or for other disputing parties;
c. Documents, developed by one or more Members, that contain sample, model or proposed practices and procedures; or,
d. Any other document, developed by one or more Members, that sets out practices and procedures that aim to improve dispute settlement.

So far, there have been 12 notifications under this mechanism[61] including the MPIA. They cover shared practices on written notifications (Add.2), transparency and open hearings (Add.3), third-party participation (Add.4, Add.9), streamlining proceedings (Add.5), panel composition (Add.7), electronic filing (Add.8), publication of timetables and procedural rulings (Add.10), and interim appeal arbitration (bilateral Add.11, multi-party Add.12/MPIA). Accordingly, the duties, obligations and prohibitions on

[59] For example, Zampetti, Low and Mavroidis (n 18).

[60] WTO, 'Statement on a Mechanism for Developing, Documenting and Sharing Practices and Procedures in the Conduct of WTO Disputes', WTO Doc JOB/DSB/1 (11 July 2016).

[61] WTO DSB, 'Statement on a Mechanism for Developing, Documenting and Sharing Practices and Procedures in the Conduct of WTO Disputes', WTO Doc JOB/DSB/1 (11 July 2016); 'Endorsements of the Mechanism for Developing, Documenting and Sharing Practices and Procedures in the Conduct of WTO Disputes and of Circulated Practice Documents', WTO Doc JOB/DSB/1/Add.1, JOB/DSB/1/Add.1 /Rev.1 and JOB/DSB/1/Add.1/Rev.2; Dispute Settlement Body, 'Statement on a Mechanism for Developing, Documenting and Sharing Practices and Procedures in the Conduct of WTO Disputes – Addendum: Written Notifications', WTO Doc JOB/DSB/1/Add.2; 'Additional Practices and Procedures in the Conduct of WTO Disputes – Transparency of Dispute Proceedings', WTO Doc JOB/DSB/1/Add.3; 'Participation of Third Parties in Dispute Proceedings', JOB/DSB/1/Add.4; 'Improving and Streamlining Dispute Proceedings', WTO Doc JOB/DSB/1/Add.5; 'Annotated Sequencing Agreement', WTO Doc JOB/DSB/1/Add.6; 'Panel Composition', WTO Doc JOB/DSB/1/Add.7; 'Electronic Filing', WTO Doc JOB/DSB/1/Add.8; 'Responses to Third-Party Requests to Participate in Consultations', WTO Doc JOB/DSB/1/Add.9; 'Publication of Working Procedures, Timetables, Working Schedules, and Preliminary or Procedural Rulings', WTO Doc JOB/DSB/1/Add.10; 'Interim Appeal Arbitration Pursuant to Art 25 of the DSU', WTO Doc JOB/DSB/1/Add.11; 'Multi-Party Interim Appeal Arbitration Arrangement Pursuant to Art 25 of the DSU', WTO Doc JOB/DSB/1/Add.12, together with supplements for participating Members, WTO Doc JOB/DSB/1/Add.12/Suppl.1–Suppl.15.

Secretariat staff can be shared through this mechanism, their specific roles in certain stages of the dispute process (some deliberations, drafting the conclusion etc). These provisions can include model clauses and best practices.

These new mechanisms do not amend the DSU, but they improve its implementation. The mechanism records practices and procedures that can informally lead to concurrent voluntary practices (and reforms) by interested Members. These new practices and procedures may eventually form the basis of consensus-based formal decisions, including a new plurilateral agreement, or other agreements like Free Trade Agreements (FTAs) and thus develop relevant state practice. They form building blocks and steps in the road to membership-wide reform, while allowing all Members in the meantime to participate in, and benefit from, evolving beneficial practices.

Almost all of our suggestions can be introduced, initially, through this mechanism for a sub-group of Members. Participation in such mechanism would remain open, while developing relevant state practices for growing number of participants.[62] However, one important caveat to note is that any proposals that require budgetary changes would also require a consensus of Members at the Budget Committee.

V. Decisions by the DG and Secretariat Practices

The WTO Agreement grants the DG the power to appoint staff members of the Secretariat to their dispute settlement related duties and conditions of service in accordance with regulations adopted by the Ministerial Conference.[63] We have already seen the provisions of the Staff Regulations in this regard. The Staff Regulations, the Staff Rules, as well as the Rules of Conduct provide the DG with rights to make decisions on staffing and resources for assisting panellists, even in difficult situations. Notably, footnote 4 of the Rules of Conduct provides that the DG must consider the relevant disclosures made by Secretariat staff (like all covered persons) in deciding on the assignment of members of the Secretariat to assist in a dispute.[64] The DG retains the power to determine that a potential conflict of interest is not sufficiently material to warrant non-assignment of a particular member of the Secretariat to assist in a dispute, particularly in light of available Secretariat resources.

Further, under the MPIA, the DG has the responsibility to ensure that a pool of arbitrators is provided with appropriate administrative and legal support, with specific WTO Secretariat staff assigned to assist arbitrators in these appeal arbitrations.[65]

From the above provisions, it is clear that the Members have granted the DG with sufficient powers to make decisions related to staffing of DS processes, including ensuring competence and ethical compliance by staff. The specific instruments through which such decisions could be implemented, in addition to staff regulations, are the Staff Rules

[62] For a discussion of development of practices at the WTO, see Marceau and Marquet (n 46) 513–50.

[63] Marrakesh Agreement, art VI:3.

[64] Rules of Conduct, fn 2, r IV.

[65] 'Multi-Party Interim Appeal Arbitration Arrangement Pursuant to Art 25 of the DSU, JOB/DSB/1/Add.12 (30 April 2020), Annex 1 (Agreed Procedures for Arbitration under Art 25 of the DSU in the Dispute DS X) para 7.

(which may be amended by the DG and does not require Members' approval) and the Administrative Memoranda (which may be issued by the DG). Rule 115.2 of the Staff Rules states that amendments may be made by the DG and subsequently informed to the General Council. However, amendments that carry financial implications or creating new rights for staff require approval from the General Council prior to their entry into force.[66]

Our specific suggestion on the organisation of the work in the Secretariat, including listing more specific duties, obligations and prohibitions on staff in the decision-making process can be implemented through Staff Rules and Secretariat working practices issued as Administrative Memoranda by the DG. Staff Rules contain many provisions through which some of our suggestions may be implemented. For example, Rule 104.5 relates to 'Notification by staff members and obligation to provide information', which includes the rule that staff members may at any time be required by the DG to provide information concerning facts prior to their appointment and relevant to their suitability for employment, or concerning facts relevant to their integrity, conduct and service as staff members. This provision could be changed to include specific obligations with respect to transparency. Further, rules relating to career development include provisions on 'training', in which specific training and development for Secretariat staff assisting in dispute settlement can be envisaged. Similarly, Administrative Memoranda may be issued by the DG relating to procedural aspects of the assistance granted by Dispute Assistants to the adjudicators. Currently, the Directors of LAD, Rules Division and the AB Secretariat also play an important part in the assignment of specific Dispute Assistants to specific DSS tasks and for how long. A DG Administrative Memoranda can guide those staffing decisions in this regard, provide safeguards and enhance legitimacy.

Finally, turning to our suggestions that can be accommodated through informal practices, the WTO DSS has used informal mechanisms to respond to new needs such as: the evolution of the appointment procedure for panellists and arbitrators,[67] the creation of the DS Registry[68] (and subsequently the AB Registry), and the working arrangement between the LAD and the Rules Division in assisting panels.[69] LAD Registry was set up in 2001 by the then LAD Director, Peter Jan Kuijper, prompted by the need to systematise the large amount of dispute settlement-related paperwork and to keep track of communications with the parties, as well as the complications in record keeping that arose from the increasing dispute settlement workload. Kuijper undertook discussions with Secretariat staff, the Director of the Rules Division, Jan Woznoski, his DDG Andrew Stoler, in order to ascertain their views on the creation of such a DS Registry. Given that this proposal related to a manner of organisation of the Secretariat (which was within its mandate), it was (fairly) uncontroversial for the DG to obtain funding for setting up the DS Registry. Thereafter, the LAD hired a person with great experience in electronic archiving who worked for the UN Compensation Commission

[66] Conditions of Service Applicable to the Staff of the WTO Secretariat, Annex 2, Decision Adopted by the General Council and the ICITO Executive Committee on 16 October 1998, WTO Doc WT/L/282 (21 October 1998), regulation 13.2.

[67] Pereyra (n 12) 47.

[68] Goldstein and Medrano (n 13) 38.

[69] Marceau, Porges and Baker (n 14) 1–59; Marceau and Baker (n 14) 113. From these articles, it is evident that the Rules Division existed prior to the LAD, and the LAD was created specifically to assist panels with the dispute settlement process. However, due to political concerns raised by Members, the LAD did not deal with trade remedies disputes, and assistance to panellists for such disputes was provided by the Rules Division.

for Iraq and Kuwait, and he was tasked with setting up a well-ordered electronic registry for all cases entering the dispute settlement system.[70] As we have already noted, the DS Registry has evolved significantly over the years, now undertaking digital function to facilitate the dispute settlement process.[71] In the same manner, the Registry could expand to include other functions as suggested in this book including more involvement in procedural matters of disputes

These internal Secretariat decisions on staff practices or 'ways of working' can also be used to introduce some diversification of legal assistance, the creation of a standing office for legal research or the inclusion of economists' assistance more generally in the DSS, and from the beginning of the dispute process. However, as we have seen from the example of the DS Registry given above, such changes would require the support of the DG as well as DDGs and no opposition from Members. Further, any budgetary implications will require the participation of Members, and the Committee on Budget Finance and Administration decides by consensus.

We have discussed several types of changes at different stages of the WTO DSS that could help in responding to ethical concerns raised against Dispute Assistant. These suggestions for reform aim to improve the legitimacy of the WTO DSS. Through this chapter, we have shown the various routes available in the WTO framework to implement these changes using hard, medium and soft law norms.

[70] Kuijper (n 13) 387.
[71] Goldstein and Medrano (n 13) 81–85.

25

Conclusion

The conclusion we reach today is different from the one we thought we would be writing when we started working on this book.

The starting point for our research was the increasing attention paid to legitimacy of the WTO Dispute Settlement System (WTO DSS), specifically on the competence of its adjudicators and the functions discharged by Secretariat staff assisting them. These conversations unfolded against the background of dissatisfaction of some WTO Members on the outcome of certain WTO disputes and the interpretations of the law in these reports. However, in writing this book, our intention was not to review these disputes: we did not examine substantive aspects of WTO law, its interpretation by adjudicatory bodies, or whether this may be traced back to the functions discharged by Secretariat staff in assisting adjudicators in their decision-making function. Rather, our aim was to take a step back from the WTO, looking towards the procedures and practices of other international adjudicatory bodies to compare the scope and breadth of actions by actors similar to WTO Secretariat staff assisting adjudicators in other dispute settlement systems We termed them 'Dispute Assistants'.

In Part I, upon reviewing the practice and procedures of 20 identified 'Dispute Settlement Mechanisms' (DSMs), it became clear that several categories of Dispute Assistants provide important assistance to adjudicators at various stages of the dispute resolution process. We grouped these actors based on two criteria: formal institutional status; and who they reported to. Three categories of Dispute Assistants emerged: (1) Institutional Assistants, who are formally part of the institution and work for the Secretariat of the institution (ie, Institutional Office) as a whole; (2) Assigned Assistants, who are formally part of the institution and work for individual adjudicators/bench of adjudicators; and (3) External Assistants, who are not formally part of the institution and work for individual adjudicators/bench of adjudicators.

Chapter 20 in Part II detailed the functions discharged by Dispute Assistants in seven distinct stages of the dispute resolution process and the formal and de facto controls exercised over different categories of Dispute Assistants. On the basis of that analysis, we were able to chart a comparative view situating the relevant actors across these 20 DSMs. While the administrative and logistical functions discharged by such actors remained uncontroversial, their role and contribution to the decision-making process warranted closer attention. Through our interactions with adjudicators, Dispute Assistants and other relevant actors in these institutions, we came to realise that many of the concerns that were raised in the WTO DSS were also present in other DSMs. At the same time, several institutional frameworks, procedures and practices confronted and mitigated these concerns at their root. This complex web of legitimacy concerns and potential solutions, spanning various DSMs and categories of Dispute Assistants, prompted the comparative analytical exercise undertaken in Chapter 21 of this book.

Six risks have been raised with respect to Dispute Assistants: (1) asymmetries of knowledge and experience between adjudicators and Dispute Assistants due to institutional frameworks; (2) asymmetries in command over the working language; (3) lack of direct supervision and control by adjudicators over Dispute Assistants; (4) excessive delegation of functions to Dispute Assistants; (5) excessive delegation (specifically of drafting) by Dispute Assistants; and (6) the conduct of Dispute Assistants affecting the independence and impartiality of adjudicators. These concerns all impact different facets of legitimacy of the international dispute resolution process. Starting with the constitutive consent of states/parties to any dispute settlement procedure, whether in the form of an agreement, a treaty or a comprimissory clause in a treaty, this consent specifically hinges on the dispute resolution function being discharged by the specific adjudicators. These concerns raise the question of whether such consent has been disregarded, with the decision-making function having been encroached upon by Dispute Assistants. Further, even beyond the consent of parties, these concerns also impact other aspects of legitimacy. These risks also threaten the actual and perceived independence and diligence expected from adjudicators, as well as the procedural fairness expected from the international dispute resolution process. Chapter 21 examined each of these three facets of legitimacy in detail.

At the same time, the practice and procedure of DSMs also provide several avenues to respond to these concerns. Such useful mechanisms and practices preserve the mandate of adjudicators, while also enabling them to benefit from the knowledge, expertise and experience of Dispute Assistants. They are aimed at ensuring and reassuring the consent of the parties to the dispute resolution process, strengthening the procedural fairness of the DSMs, and the independence and diligence expected from adjudicators. We briefly recount six of our findings below.

First, we consider the risk of asymmetry between adjudicators and Dispute Assistants due to institutional frameworks. This concern may arise in DSMs where adjudicators are selected on an ad hoc basis or discharge their functions on a part-time basis, while the Institutional Assistants enjoy more relative permanence. The Institutional Assistants, as full-time staff, accumulate greater institutional expertise and capacity. This structural asymmetry raises a *perception*, whether justified or not, of greater expertise and capacity on the part of the Dispute Assistants in comparison to the adjudicators. The risk is the potential for Dispute Assistants to exert significant influence over the decision-making function of adjudicators, which increases with the complexity of disputes, heavy caseloads and the limited availability of adjudicators.

These asymmetries can primarily be addressed through strengthening the expertise and capacity of adjudicators. For example, *enhanced qualification criteria* will enable the selection of adjudicators who are not reliant on the expertise of Institutional Assistants. The ICSID mandates individuals designated as arbitrators to have competence in law, commerce, industry or finance, and the ability to exercise independent personal judgement. The ICC qualification criteria for judges combine subject-matter expertise, extensive experience and proficiency in working language. Rigorous *selection procedures* ensure transparency and adherence with these qualification criteria. The selection procedure of judges of the CJEU is based on nominations of a Panel of Experts assessing the suitability of candidates on: their legal capabilities; their professional experience; their ability to perform the duties of a judge; their language skills; their ability to work as part of a team in an international environment in which several legal systems are represented; and whether their independence, impartiality, probity and integrity are beyond doubt. Some DSMs also have *working practices and procedures* that enable adjudicators to develop subject matter expertise and institutional expertise. For example, the European Court of Justice of the CJEU conducts periodic meetings termed the 'Réunion Générale', where judges (and Advocates General) meet to discuss administrative issues and pending cases, allowing them to keep up to date with the relevant issues in pending matters. The WTO AB Working Procedures also provided for an 'exchange of views' where all AB members received documents relating to appeal and discussed matters of interpretation, practice and procedure. Such procedure was aimed at ensuring consistency and coherence in decision-making, and at drawing on the individual and collective expertise of the adjudicators. Although to a lesser extent, presently the MPIA pool of arbitrators also receives all documents relating to appeal arbitration proceedings and discuss them as practicable. Some DSMs include practices like the *training of adjudicators* to enhance their institutional knowledge; for example, the WTO AB, while it was operational, conducted annual/semi-annual 'retreats' for AB members to discuss substantive legal issues of recurring importance, current developments, systemic issues of interpretation etc.

Second, concerns may arise when the Dispute Assistants have a stronger command over the working language of the DSM and, accordingly, raising the risk of influencing the decision of the adjudicator. For example, French is the sole working language of the CJEU. Most référendaires (Assigned Assistants) are native Francophones, whereas not all judges are. This has raised concerns over the potential for such Assigned Assistants to exert a disproportionate influence in shaping the law, especially given their role in the drafting process. Similarly, in the WTO DSS, English is the main working language. As the drafts have to be produced within strict timelines, the competitive hiring process for Secretariat staff (Institutional Assistants) often favour lawyers who are fluent English speakers (mostly from common law jurisdictions). This raises additional concerns about the potential of certain jurisdictions and legal systems to disproportionately influence the decision-making process. The ECOWAS Court also faces challenges owing to limited legal training for translators. The staff of the Research and Documentation Department (Institutional Assistants) often undertake corrections in the drafts post-translation to ensure legal accuracy.

Various safeguards exist to address these language concerns. Some DSMs like the ICC and the CJEU introduce stringent language proficiency requirements at the stage of selection of adjudicators to balance this asymmetry. The CJEU also has a dedicated department staffed with experts with adequate legal training and a thorough knowledge of several official languages of the EU. Further, the Lecteurs d'arrêts are a distinct group of Assigned Assistants who are under the supervision of the President of the Court and are specifically responsible for examining the compliance of the draft with specific language requirements of the CJEU. This allows adjudicators to retain control over the decision-making function.

Third, concerns arise in DSMs where adjudicators exercise limited formal control over the functions of the Dispute Assistants. For example, in the WTO, the Secretariat staff who assist panellists (Institutional Assistants) are under the supervision of the Directors of their Division (specifically, the Legal Affairs Division (LAD) or the Rules Division). In situations where the adjudicators take a different legal position than that held by the Directors of LAD or the Rules Division, the Institutional Assistants may be in a position of conflict of loyalty. Such a supervisory framework raises the risk that the Institutional Assistants may not be able to follow the instructions given by adjudicators and thus may end up encroaching upon the decision-making authority of the adjudicators.

To safeguard against this risk, some DSMs have developed certain checks and de facto forms of control over the functions of Institutional Assistants. A prominent means of de facto control is through the 'Judge Rapporteur', who oversees the functions of the Institutional Assistants closely for each dispute. For example, Secretariat staff of the IACtHR, the Legal Officer(s) of the Registry of the ACtHPR, staff of the Registry of the ECtHR and the staff of the Research and Documentation Department of the ECOWAS Court (Institutional Assistants) assigned to a case specifically work under the supervision of the Judge Rapporteur for a particular dispute. Checks over the functions of Institutional Assistants can also be introduced through the introduction of other types of Dispute Assistants under the supervision and control of adjudicators. For example, in the CJEU, the Institutional Assistants of the Registries of the ECJ and the General Court, the Directorate-General of Multilingualism, and the Research and Documentation Directorate assist all the judges across cases. At the same time, judges also have Assigned Assistants who work in their cabinets (ie, the référendaires), additional assistants who do not work on the substantive aspects of the case, and a trainee. Further, another group of Assigned Assistants, the Lecteurs d'arrêts, report to the presidents of the respective courts and conduct linguistic reviews of the drafts produced. Similar checks are present to varying degrees through diversification of assistance in the ECOWAS Court, the ICJ, the COMESA Court and the PCA. Diversifying the sources of assistance amongst different departments and language services, with distinct administrative heads; and Assigned/External Assistants, ensures that no single actor exerts undue influence or risks occupying a position of power. Such checks operate together to check the power of Dispute Assistants, while balancing the overall decision-making power of adjudicators.

Fourth, a prominent concern is adjudicators excessively delegating functions to Dispute Assistants or allowing Dispute Assistants to participate too actively in certain stages of the dispute resolution process, risking encroaching upon the adjudicator's decision-making process. In some situations, such delegation may imply that adjudicators have failed to satisfy their adjudicative mandate. International arbitration has long confronted allegations that Dispute Assistants act as a 'Fourth Arbitrator'. Such challenges have been raised indirectly as part of challenges to disqualify arbitrator(s) or arbitral tribunal, as part of the challenge to arbitral award itself or, in some cases, even as a direct challenge to the Dispute Assistant. The standard boils down to assessing whether arbitrators retain actual decision-making and intellectual control over the outcome, irrespective of what tasks are performed by the Dispute Assistants. In a challenge to one of the members (the institution's term for adjudicators) of the IUSCT, it was confirmed that the Legal Advisers (Assigned Assistants) could provide support to the adjudicators by preparing summaries of pleadings and other submissions, preparing memos and even drafting decisions. Such functions were permitted as long as they do not replace the adjudicator's decision-making, review and assessment of the factual and legal issues of the dispute. From the cases, it becomes clear that the threshold for proving such excessive delegation is extremely high. Nonetheless, concerns, even when not proven, pose a threat to the perceived legitimacy of the dispute resolution, which is intrinsically tied to parties' consent to specific adjudicators.

The safeguards must accordingly mitigate against the apprehension that decision-making is undertaken by actors other than the adjudicators. There is rich practice in various commercial arbitration institutions and the ICJ on enhancing transparency on the role of Dispute Assistants by providing a general list of tasks performed by them. Further, commercial arbitration institutions couple general disclosures with more case-specific disclosures and enhancing explicit party consent to the functions discharged by Dispute Assistants. For example, many commercial arbitral institution rules provide that a Dispute Assistant can only be appointed following consultation with, and the consent of, the parties. Some institutions even go so far as to require party consent to every task performed by Dispute Assistants (the LCIA Arbitration Rules 2020 along with the LCIA Guidance Note for Parties and Arbitrators).

Fifth, there are legitimacy concerns that are raised in relation to Dispute Assistants participating in the drafting of judgments/orders/awards or DS reports. This concern is rooted in the understanding that drafting plays a constitutive role in the decision-making process. However, in the context of arbitration, the equation of drafting with decision-making has been rejected. For example, the Court of Appeal of The Hague in the *Yukos* proceedings held that the delegation of substantive portions of awards to Dispute Assistants does not per se imply that they participated in decision-making functions; rather, the important consideration is whether the arbitrators check these texts for correctness and completeness. However, as stated above, these concerns still adversely affect the perception of legitimacy of the perception of legitimacy of the dispute resolution process. Similar concerns have been raised in the WTO DSS, where Secretariat lawyers prepare large portions of panel and AB drafts. In the WTO, where WTO Members have explicitly placed the responsibility on the Secretariat staff to *assist* the selected adjudicators, this distinction between decision-making and drafting becomes crucial.

Various practices have allowed institutions to reassure parties that adjudicators retain intellectual control over decisions, even in cases where Dispute Assistants participate in and contribute to substantial portions of the draft. For example, in the CJEU, the drafting is undertaken and assisted by référendaires (Assigned Assistants) who are strictly under the supervision and control of their respective adjudicators. This strong judicial control is supplemented through working practices where judges interact exclusively amongst themselves in deliberations, without the presence of Dispute Assistants. There are two sets of such deliberations: first, in a roundtable to discuss their views on the direction of the decision before drafting; and, second, final deliberations on the draft. These face-to-face discussions, the iterative project drafting process and the absolute secrecy of deliberations ensure that assistants do not encroach or intrude upon decision-making. Similar procedures are also present in the ECtHR and the ICJ, ensuring that the judges retain full intellectual ownership and control over drafts, despite the significant contributions made by Dispute Assistants.

Sixth, and lastly, there is the risk that the conduct of Dispute Assistants may affect the independence or impartiality of the adjudicator. For example, in international criminal tribunals, challenges have been raised as to whether alleged bias on the part of Legal

Officers (Assigned Assistants) results in bias by the judges by association. The case law has generally clarified that judicial decision-making was entirely within the control of the judges, without any possible undue influence by the Legal Officer. Therefore, any supposed bias on the part of the Legal Officer would not (generally) bring into question the conduct of the judges themselves and would not (usually) compromise the impartiality/independence of the judges in discharging this function or fair trial guarantees for the accused. At the same time, the possibility is acknowledged that the conduct of Dispute Assistants in some cases may be so problematic as to impugn the impartiality/independence of the judges. Independence of adjudicators is a key facet of legitimacy, and solutions must guard against such an extreme case.

Some DSMs have reassured parties as to the independence of adjudicators by imposing some form of ethical obligations on Dispute Assistants. Many institutions rely on general staff regulations and codes of conduct to ensure impartiality, confidentiality and independence, although specific provisions relating to Dispute Assistants are limited. Some notable examples provide avenues to strengthen this aspect of legitimacy. For example, in the CJEU, there is a dedicated code of conduct on référendaires requiring abstention in matters where they have prior involvement, prior authorisation for public academic activities and post-employment restrictions on participation in cases. While breaches of obligations under this code are treated as breaches of trust in the judge–assistant relationship, there is no official mechanism for parties or other actors to challenge référendaires. In that regard, both arbitration institutions and the WTO DSS offer useful practices. In the WTO DSS, specific Rules of Conduct allow disputing parties to challenge Secretariat staff on grounds such as conflicts of interest, lack of independence and impartiality. The International Bar Association (IBA) Guidelines on Conflict of Interest in International Arbitration include a detailed list of disclosures applicable to arbitrators as well as Dispute Assistants.

Having undertaken this comparative exercise, mapping concerns and solutions across various DSMs, we realised that concerns over the role and activities of Dispute Assistants are by no means limited to the WTO DSS; rather, these concerns are generalisable and are found beyond the institutions where they arise. Further, the WTO system also offers important potential solutions. Lastly, the rich practice of Dispute Assistants and unique procedures of the WTO DSS provide fertile terrain to examine how some of these solutions can be operationalised and implemented in responding to the concerns. This brought us to Part III of this book.

The situation of Dispute Assistants in the WTO DSS is different from other institutions for a number of reasons. *First*, their role is explicitly consented to by WTO Members through provisions like Articles 8 and 27 of the Understanding on Rules and Procedures Governing the Settlement of Disputes (DSU). Additionally, the WTO Rules of Conduct and Staff Regulations impose independence, impartiality, conflict-of-interest obligations and disclosure duties on the staff assisting adjudicators, similar to the obligations imposed on the adjudicators themselves, acknowledging the important role of Dispute Assistants in the dispute resolution process. *Second*, the history of dispute settlement under GATT reveals the reasons for the prominent role of Dispute Assistants today. A series of controversial panel decisions in the late 1970s and early 1980s led to a deliberate acceptance by WTO Members of the need to provide panellists with credible legal assistance, enabling a more legalistic approach to disputes. This was reinforced through the establishment of the AB (with automatic right of appeal) to maintain rule of law and public international law principles of treaty interpretation. Since it was accepted that not all adjudicators would have a legal background, legal assistance became necessary. *Third*, beyond legal assistance, the Dispute Assistants often include staff who are experts in other substantive areas of the WTO covered agreements – for example, agricultural trade, international standards, tariffs and market access, services, environment and intellectual property. Notably, economists from the Economic Research and Statistics Division (ERSD) play a critical role in panel, appeal and arbitration proceedings where economic and econometric evidence and arguments are advanced. It confirms that WTO Members consent to and acknowledge the critical functions discharged by the Secretariat staff in ensuring the continued functioning of the system. The focus, then, is on drawing boundaries between aspects that contribute to legitimacy and those that detract from it.

We see that many of the institutional frameworks that make Dispute Assistants indispensable to the WTO DSS also inadvertently raise concerns relating to their legitimacy. This is evidenced at the selection stage of ad hoc adjudicators, as well as in providing assistance to adjudicators in the dispute resolution process. At the selection stage of ad hoc adjudicators, the Secretariat staff ensure the continuity and automaticity of the dispute resolution process by assisting parties in composition of the panel. They do so, inter alia, by proposing names to disputing parties on potential panellists. Further, the WTO Director-General (DG), with assistance from Secretariat staff, can be the appointing authority in cases where disputing parties are unable to agree on such panellists within the prescribed timeframe. This ensures that neither party is able to indefinitely delay the dispute resolution process. While these are undoubtedly important functions, concerns relate to whether the staff exceed their mandate in proposing names to parties/DG outside the indicative list of panellists, and whether they subsequently exert some inappropriate control over the decision-making function of panellists they may subsequently be assisting. This is especially true in cases where there is no separation between staff who assist in appointment of adjudicators and staff who assist them, creating a *perception* that the staff may adversely impact the independence of the adjudicators.

At the stage of assisting adjudicators, with respect to ad hoc panellists and arbitrators, the Dispute Assistants often provide the necessary normative institutional expertise and experience. The Secretariat staff are repositories of knowledge with continuous exposure to the jurisprudence, procedural evolution and working practices. This allows them to assist ad hoc adjudicators who are sometimes (understandably) less conversant with the intricacies of the WTO DSS. Further, even with respect to more permanent adjudicators, like the AB members (when the AB was operational) or the MPIA pool of arbitrators, they serve on a part-time basis and often reside in different countries. This leaves a gap in terms of the day-to-day management of the disputes – for example, in terms of coordinating communications with parties, drafting procedural decisions and preparing research notes/summaries. The Secretariat staff, working out of Geneva, attentively fill this gap, ensuring the smooth functioning of the dispute resolution process. At the same time, such a framework embeds a certain degree of asymmetry into the system. Secretariat staff can interact more closely with the dispute, often leading to earlier, faster and more holistic understanding. The adjudicators also rely on the expertise of the Secretariat staff for substantive inputs, for example, through an 'Issues Paper' which summarises the relevant legal issues, puts forward options for legal reasoning, assessments of prior case law etc. Dispute Assistants from operational divisions (whether legal or non-legal staff) also provide unique technical expertise in various trade-related areas. This is especially important today with vast accumulated jurisprudence and the increasing complexity of submissions/issues in disputes. The work of the Secretariat staff allows adjudicators to focus their attention on the novel and normative questions that arise. However, the concern remains whether such assistance crosses over to decision-making territory, within the mandate of adjudicators. Irrespective of whether such asymmetry is proven (which would be an onerous and impossible burden), apprehensions on its very existence itself raise concerns over the perceived legitimacy of the WTO DSS.

These concerns are compounded through differing commands over working language, the institutional framework for the supervision and control of Dispute Assistants, as well as a lack of transparency over the role of Dispute Assistants. As most of the dispute resolution work is undertaken in English, adjudicators who lack specific proficiency in the working language may become dependent on the Secretariat staff who assist them. This is not merely the techno-legal operation of translations or interpretations, but permeates the very conceptual aspects of the dispute. For example, the WTO DSS imposes strict timelines within which several decisions are to be produced. The Secretariat staff with greater proficiency in English are often tasked with preparing the first drafts, which frame the conceptual basis on which the eventual decision is presented. While this does not imply that the staff are making the decision, it does increase their influence over the decision-making authority of the adjudicators. This, at the very least, adversely impacts the appearance of independence and, at worst, compromises the independence of the adjudicators. With respect to supervision and control, we have seen how the role of Directors (who supervise the work of Secretariat staff) may become positions of power that influence the decision-making functions of the adjudicators. Lastly, the lack of transparency relating to the staff who are assisting panellists, the 'informal' list of potential panellists maintained by the Secretariat and the scope of the actual functions discharged by the Secretariat, including non-legal staff, compounds the concerns over procedural legitimacy.

Any attempts to address these concerns must consider the explicit treaty provisions on the responsibility of the Secretariat staff in assisting with the selection of adjudicators (Article 8 DSU) and assisting the adjudicators (Article 27 DSU). Their role significantly contributes to the institutional stability, memory and continuity of a dispute settlement system built around ad hoc and part-time adjudicators. At the same time, their functions also reveal vulnerabilities that must be recognised and addressed. They are not always a product of improper behaviour, but are often a consequence of institutional design. Therefore, the solution to these concerns does not lie in diminishing the essential role of Dispute Assistants; rather, it must strengthen the capacity and expertise of adjudicators, introduce diversification in the sources of assistance offered to adjudicators, create certainty as the role of adjudicators and Dispute Assistants, and instil further transparency and accountability in the functions discharged by Dispute Assistants. This ensures a Secretariat that is assisting rather than leading, visible rather than opaque, and accountable rather than above reproach. This is the conceptual foundation for the reform suggestions examined in Chapters 22 and 23. Our suggestions span across five broad themes.

The *first* theme relates to *strengthening the capacity and expertise of adjudicators*. This is driven by the understanding that we cannot isolate the concerns over the role of Secretariat staff from the role, expertise and experience of the adjudicators they are assisting. While enhancing the qualification and selection procedure of adjudicators can formally account for asymmetry, it is also incumbent upon WTO Members to translate this prescription into practice. Proposals on establishing a roster of panellists encounter difficulties precisely because WTO Members may nominate candidates for political or geographical reasons, in turn limiting the expertise and experience of adjudicators. Therefore, such qualifications must also be supplemented with continuous training and development of ad hoc and permanent adjudicators (as well as Dispute Assistants) to further the quality of decisions overall. Even beyond such formal mechanisms, the working procedures also provide avenues to enhance the expertise of adjudicators. For example, we propose that adjudicators conduct some deliberations exclusively between themselves; this will ensure their intellectual control over the decision-making function.

The *second* theme, *diversification of sources of assistance*, supplements the capacity and expertise of adjudicators, while also acting as a check and limitation on the functions of Dispute Assistants. For example, incorporating Assigned/External Assistants into the dispute resolution process who are exclusively under the supervision and control of individual adjudicators limits the reliance on Institutional Assistants (ie, the Secretariat staff). It allows the WTO DSS to continue with ad hoc/part-time adjudicators, without compromising the legitimacy of the dispute resolution process. This also creates checks on the role of Institutional Assistants, ensuring that they do not exceed their formal mandate. Through clear demarcations of tasks between different categories of Dispute Assistants, it avoids the perception that any one category of assistants exerts undue influence over adjudicators. For example, the DS Registry could evolve to fulfil certain procedural tasks, including factual research functions. The core drafting functions could be exclusively undertaken by the Assigned/External Assistants, with functional support from Institutional Assistants of the Secretariat. This would naturally limit the possibility of supervisory positions (for example, Directors) accumulating disproportionate influence over time.

The *third* theme requires *clarity* on the functions of Dispute Assistants as well as adjudicators. These set of reforms must grapple with the reality that the influence of Dispute Assistants is a product of a system that has placed them in a position where their functions are indispensable. Therefore, clarity must begin with the recognition that they perform functions that go beyond administrative tasks. There must be internal clarity on the boundaries between support and influence, articulated and formalised, reducing the risk of functional overreach. In the WTO, where adjudicators serve temporarily, this clarity is critical. It requires that adjudicators engage with substantive legal issues that define their mandate, while assistants focus on supporting, rather than leading, adjudicatory functions. This also benefits the Dispute Assistants, with fewer pressures to assume decision-making responsibilities and increased protection from being criticised for exceeding their role. Various suggestions for reform across different stages of the WTO DSS are made in this regard. For example, our suggest for reform that Dispute Assistants participating in the selection of ad hoc adjudicators must be restricted from assisting panellists in the later stages of the dispute resolution process. Further, the discretion afforded to Dispute Assistants and DG at the panel composition stage should be guided/limited to a reformed and updated Indicative List approved by the WTO Members, with deviations being exceptional. At the stage of assisting adjudicators, for example, we propose that WTO Members should agree on a list of duties, restrictions and obligations of adjudicators and Dispute Assistants (also supplementing the transparency and accountability themes explored below). Further, Dispute Assistants should only undertake drafting based on clear written instructions from adjudicators, including reasons for a particular finding. Lastly, rules must also prevent the concentration of power in certain positions (for example, Directors), which risks exceeding the formal remit of Secretariat support. Term limits for supervisory positions could be implemented to limit such roles accumulating power over time. Therefore, clarifying which tasks may be performed by Dispute Assistants and which must remain the exclusive responsibility of adjudicators becomes essential to preserving the integrity of the adjudicatory process.

The *fourth* theme, closely tied to but distinct from reforms on clarity, is *transparency.* While clarity relates to the internal dimension of legitimacy, transparency relates to its external dimension. It acknowledges the right of all stakeholders (disputing parties, other adjudicators, WTO Members and the public at large) to be aware of the relevant actors and the extent of their involvement. Unlike adjudicators, who are formally appointed and publicly identified, there is a level of opacity around Secretariat staff. Despite undertaking significant tasks, their names are not disclosed and their involvement in specific disputes as well as their general duties remain unclear. While such invisibility may have been instituted to guarantee neutrality, it has now become a source of suspicion. Our suggestions include the disclosure of names of staff who assist panels, including regarding changes to staffing during the course of a dispute, and sharing certain aspects of research undertaken by staff to the disputing parties. In the context of the latter reform, it is necessary to balance the need for transparency with the secrecy of deliberations. Accordingly, we have explored procedural options to ensure this balance – for example, sharing with the parties such research and notes prepared by the Secretariat without receiving instructions or requests from the adjudicators, or when work is performed by staff before the start of the formal work of adjudicators. Additionally, certain procedural/factual research notes by the DS Registry could be shared with the parties after being specifically reviewed by the panellists.

These suggestions for reforms are not merely about disclosures in a specific dispute, but rather critically impact how the legitimacy of the entire WTO DSS is *perceived* and how its outcomes are *received*. The invisibility of key actors erodes the trust of WTO Members and the general public in the dispute resolution system, especially in the context of highly sensitive international trade relations. The procedural legitimacy of the WTO DSS is not merely about the substantive accuracy of its outcomes; it also depends on the shared perception amongst WTO Members that these outcomes are produced by fair and transparent processes. Coupled with the reforms relating to clarity, transparency strengthens adjudicatory autonomy by clearly delineating and declaring the boundaries of staff involvement. This maintains accountability of staff and allows adjudicators to better discharge their supervisory role.

Building on this, the last theme of reforms relates to *accountability*. The present framework of accountability is built around general disclosures applicable equally to adjudicators and Dispute Assistants. This framework fails to capture the complete realities of contributions made by Dispute Assistants. In a system where Dispute Assistants frame issues, participate in discussions and draft substantial portions of reports, failing to engage with these functions obscures the true dynamics of adjudication. Drawing inspiration from instruments such as the IBA Guidelines, a more nuanced and useful framework for raising challenges and conflicts can be implemented. Such a framework would enable adjudicators and parties to understand when a staff member's involvement might be inappropriate, while simultaneously protecting Dispute Assistants from unfair or speculative challenges. The reforms under the themes of clarity and transparency necessarily operate together to enable accountability if such challenges are raised, allowing for evidence-backed decisions on the existence of conflicts.

The themes of reforms identified above do not require a complete institutional overhaul or a consensus-based treaty amendment. They are both pragmatic and principled. They are pragmatic as they tap into less controversial forms of consensus-based decision-making like DSB/General Council decisions on the rules of conduct, Guidelines, DSB practices, or Chairman's statements on the list of duties, restrictions and obligations for Dispute Assistants and adjudicators. The provisions of the Rules of Conduct can be modified in this manner to enhance ethical obligations and controls. Some of these reforms could also be explored by a sub-group of WTO Members, or even as part of the Working Procedures in a single dispute, and can eventually be adopted by larger membership incrementally. Some aspects could also be implemented within existing frameworks through administrative decisions by the DG or informal Secretariat practices. At the same time, these reforms are built around principled themes that materially contribute to the actual and perceived legitimacy of the WTO DSS.

We also acknowledge that the WTO DSS, and the WTO more generally, is an institution at a crossroads. The role of its Dispute Assistants is tied to larger conversations on dispute settlement reform: on standards of review, rules of interpretation and administration of evidence, and tied to changes to substantive norms relating to agriculture, e-commerce, the environment, subsidies, local content, economic security etc. Any suggestions exclusively on the practice of Dispute Assistants will remain artificial if separated from this larger context, and most importantly, from reforms to the role of adjudicators. The provisions of the draft Consolidated Text of the Report by the Convenor of the Informal DS Reform Discussions – Mr Marco Molina (hereinafter 'Molina Report') show this interconnection. The provisions on Secretariat support (Title VII) are situated along with broader reforms like guidelines for adjudicators on treaty interpretation (Title V), procedures to discuss dispute settlement reports in relevant WTO bodies (Title VI, Chapter I) and the establishment of an Advisory Working Group to 'discuss, build consensus, and provide guidance' on legal interpretations developed by adjudicators (Title VI, Chapter II). Similarly, we believe the debate about Dispute Assistants is also a debate about who are the WTO adjudicators and, ultimately, a debate about the kind of adjudicatory institution that the WTO wishes to be.

The concerns surrounding Dispute Assistants are not merely operational difficulties, but are symptomatic of deeper institutional vulnerabilities. The aim of this book is not to point fingers or unduly criticise the functioning of any single mechanism; rather, we hope we have highlighted the risks posed by such concerns if these are left unaddressed. The mere appearance of such concerns itself poses a risk to legitimacy, irrespective of whether they are proven or demonstrated. In a geopolitical environment where the very legitimacy of international institutions is itself being called into question, the dispute resolution mechanisms must strive to protect themselves from such concerns. The comparative procedure and practice of DSMs provide ample potential solutions to address them. The study of the WTO DSS reveals that it does not require institutional overhaul, but can provide important safeguards in the face of greater legitimacy challenges. Lastly, we reiterate that the reform suggestions made in this book are safeguards rather than neat or clear solutions to problems arising with respect to Dispute Assistants. All dispute settlement processes are operated by human beings, and even the best processes and procedural rules cannot eliminate the concerns and the risks altogether. The aim, then, is to establish guardrails and provide avenues of action towards a more legitimate system.

BIBLIOGRAPHY

Books

Buchanan A, *Justice, Legitimacy and Self-Determination: Moral Foundation for International Law* (Oxford University Press, 2004)
Franck, TM, *Fairness in International Law and Institutions* (Oxford University Press, 1998)
Girsberger D and Voser N, *International Arbitration: Comparative and Swiss Perspectives*, 3rd edn (Schulthess, 2016)
Grossman N, Cohen HG, Føllesdal A and Ulfstein G (eds), *Legitimacy and International Courts* (Cambridge University Press, 2018)
Higgins R, Webb P, Akande D, Bianchi A and Brown C, *Oppenheim's International Law: United Nations* (Oxford University Press, 2017)
Jackson JH, *Sovereignty, the WTO and Changing Fundamentals of International Law* (Cambridge University Press, 2006)
Mavroidis PC, *The WTO Dispute Settlement System: How, Why and Where?* (Cambridge University Press, 2022)
Schreuer C et al, *The ICSID Convention: A Commentary*, 2nd edn (Cambridge University Press, 2009)
Schwarz FT and Konrad CW, *The Vienna Rules: A Commentary on International Arbitration in Austria* (Kluwer, 2009)
Wolfrum R and Röben V (eds), *Legitimacy in International Law* (Springer, 2008)
World Trade Organization Secretariat, *A Handbook on the WTO Dispute Settlement System*, 2nd edn (Cambridge University Press, 2017)

Book Chapters

Alessandri PS, 'Secretariat: Inter-American Court of Human Rights (IACtHR)' in H Ruiz Fabri (ed), *Max Planck Encyclopedia of International Procedural Law* (Oxford University Press, 2021)
Baetens F, 'Unseen Actors in International Courts and Tribunals: Challenging the Legitimacy of International Adjudication' in Baetens F (ed), *Legitimacy of Unseen Actors in International Adjudication, Studies on International Courts and Tribunals* (Cambridge University Press, 2019)
Baker DA and Marceau G, 'The World Trade Organization' in Baetens F (ed), *Legitimacy of Unseen Actors in International Adjudication* (Cambridge University Press, 2019)
Baudenbacher C, 'The EFTA Court's Working Methods' in International Tribunal for the Law of the Sea (ed), *The Contribution of the International Tribunal for the Law of the Sea to the Rule of Law: 1996–2016* (Brill Nijhoff, 2018)
Bianku L and Kempees P, 'The European Court of Human Rights' in Baetens F (ed), *Legitimacy of Unseen Actors in International Adjudication* (Cambridge University Press, 2019)
Bordachar J and Doe M, 'Argentina and the Permanent Court of Arbitration: The Past, Present and Future of Arbitration Involving the State and State Entities on the Río de la Plata' in Fortese F (ed), *Arbitration in Argentina* (Oxford University Press, 2020)
Born G, 'Selection, Challenge and Replacement of Arbitrators in International Arbitration' in *International Commercial Arbitration*, 3rd edn (Wolters Kluwer, 2021)

Bown CP, 'The WTO Secretariat and the Role of Economics in DSU Panels and Arbitrations' in Marceau G (ed), *A History of Law and Lawyers in the GATT/WTO: The Development of the Rule of Law in the Multilateral Trading System* (Cambridge University Press, 2015)

Bown CP and Pauwelyn J, 'Introduction: Trade Retaliation in WTO Dispute Settlement: A Multi-Disciplinary Analysis' in Bown CP and Pauwelyn J (eds), *The Law, Economics and Politics of Retaliation in WTO Dispute Settlement* (Cambridge University Press, 2010)

Cantore C and Mavroidis P, 'Arbitration on the Level of Retaliation: Dispute Settlement System of the World Trade Organization (WTO)' in Wolfrum R (ed), *Max Planck Encyclopedia of International Procedural Law (MPEiPro)* (Oxford University Press, 2019)

Caplan LM, 'Arbitrator Challenges at the Iran–United States Claims Tribunal' in Giorgetti C (ed), *Challenges and Recusals of Judges and Arbitrators in International Courts and Tribunals* (Brill, 2012)

Clarke KM, Jalloh CC and Nmehielle VO, 'Introduction: Origins and Issues of the African Court of Justice and Human Peoples' Rights' in Jalloh CC, Clarke KM and Nmehielle VO (eds), *The African Court of Justice and Human Peoples' Rights in Context: Development and Challenges* (Cambridge University Press, 2019)

Cohen HG, Føllesdal A, Grossman N and Ulfstein G, 'Legitimacy and International Courts – A Framework' in N Grossman, HG Cohen, A Føllesdal and G Ulfstein (eds), *Legitimacy and International Courts: Studies on International Courts and Tribunals* (Cambridge University Press, 2017)

Corten C and Hoss H, 'Registry: International Court of Justice' in Wolfrum R (ed), *Max Planck Encyclopedia of International Procedural Law* (Oxford University Press, 2021)

Cottier T, 'A Two-Tier Approach to WTO Decision-Making' in Steger DP (ed), *Redesigning the World Trade Organization for the Twenty-First Century* (Waterloo, CIGI and Wilfrid Laurier University Press, 2010)

Elsig M and Cottier T, 'Reforming the WTO: The Decision-Making Triangle Revised' in Cottier T and Elsig M (eds), *Governing the World Trade Organization: Past, Present and Beyond Doha* (Cambridge University Press, 2011)

Fredriksen HH, 'Court of Justice of the European Free Trade Association (EFTA Court)' in Fabri HR (ed), *Max Planck Encyclopedia of International Procedural Law* (Oxford University Press, online edn, 2018)

Fukunaga Y, 'Experts in WTO and Investment Litigation' in JA Huerta-Goldman, A Romanetti and FX Stirnimann (eds), *WTO Litigation, Investment Arbitration and Commercial Arbitration* (Kluwer Law International, 2014)

Gathii J, 'The COMESA Court of Justice' in Howse R, Fabri HR, Ulfstein G and Zang M (eds), *The Legitimacy of International Trade Courts and Tribunals* (Cambridge University Press, 2018)

Gautier P, 'The International Tribunal for the Law of the Sea' in Baetens F (ed), *Legitimacy of Unseen Actors in International Adjudication* (Cambridge University Press, 2019)

Gautier P, 'Registry: International Tribunal for the Law of the Sea (ITLOS)' in Wolfrum R (ed), *Max Planck Encyclopedia of International Procedural Law* (Oxford University Press, 2018)

Goldstein M and Medrano L, 'Bringing WTO Dispute Settlement into the Twenty-First Century: Modernizing the Administration of Dispute to Better Serve Members' in N Lamp (ed), *Reckoning and Renewal: The World Trade Organization and its Dispute Settlement System at 30: Essays in Honour of Valerie Hughes* (Hart Publishing, 2024)

Heeren F, 'The Court of Justice of the European Union' in Baetens F (ed), *Legitimacy of Unseen Actors* (Cambridge University Press, 2019)

Hudec RE, 'The Role of the GATT Secretariat in the Evolution of the WTO Dispute Settlement Procedure' in J Bhagwati and M Hirsch (eds), *The Uruguay Round and Beyond: Essays in Honour of Arthur Dunkel* (Springer, 1998)

Hughes B, 'The Problem of Undisclosed Assistance to Arbitral Tribunals' in Shaughnessy P and Tung S (eds), *The Powers and Duties of an Arbitrator: Liber Amicorum Pierre A Karrer* (Kluwer, 2017)

Hughes B, 'Working in WTO Dispute Settlement: Pride without Prejudice' in Marceau G (ed), *A History of Law and Lawyers in the GATT/WTO: The Development of the Rule of Law in the Multilateral Trading System* (Cambridge University Press, 2015)

Hwang, M and Lim, K, 'Issue Conflict in ICSID Arbitrations' in Hwang, M, Chan, E and Lim, E (eds), *Selected Essays on International Arbitration* (Academy Publishing, 2013)

Jackson JH, 'Designing and Implementing Effective Dispute Settlement Procedures: WTO Dispute Settlement, Appraisal and Prospects' in Krueger AO (ed), *The WTO as an International Organization* (University of Chicago Press, 1988)

Jensen JO, 'Challenge of Secretaries and Arbitrators' in *Tribunal Secretaries in International Arbitration*, Oxford International Arbitration Series (2019; online edn, Oxford Law Pro)

Kuijper PJ, 'From Seattle to Doha: From the Surreal to the Unreal – a Personal Account' in Marceau G (ed), *A History of Law and Lawyers in the GATT/WTO: The Development of the Rule of Law in the Multilateral Trading System* (Cambridge University Press, 2015)

Lindén Å, 'The First Years of the GATT Legal Service' in Marceau G (ed), *A History of Law and Lawyers in the GATT/WTO: The Development of the Rule of Law in the Multilateral Trading System* (Cambridge University Press, 2015)

Malacrida R, 'WTO Panel Composition: Searching Far and Wide for Administrators of World Trade Justice' in G Marceau (ed), *A History of Law and Lawyers in the GATT/WTO: The Development of the Rule of Law in the Multilateral Trading System* (Cambridge University Press, 2015)

Marceau G, `Consultations and the Panel Process in the WTO Dispute Settlement System` in Yerxa R and Wilson B (eds), *Key Issues in WTO Dispute Settlement: The First Ten Years* (Cambridge University Press, 2005)

Marceau G and Baker DA, 'A Short History of the Rules Division' in Marceau G (ed), *A History of Law and Lawyers in the GATT/WTO: The Development of the Rule of Law in the Multilateral Trading System* (Cambridge University Press, 2015)

Marceau G and George M, `The Role of the Secretariat in WTO Dispute Settlement: Lessons from Other Adjudicatory Bodies' in Lamp N (ed), *Reckoning and Renewal: The World Trade Organization and Its Dispute Settlement System at 30, Essays in Honour of Valerie Hughes* (University of Toronto Press, 2025)

Marceau G and Walker R, 'WTO Members' Silence and WTO Decision-Making' in Azaria D (ed), *State Silence across International Law* (Oxford University Press, 2025)

Marceau G, Porges A and Baker DA, 'Introduction and Overview' in Marceau G (ed), *A History of Law and Lawyers in the GATT/WTO: The Development of the Rule of Law in the Multilateral Trading System* (Cambridge University Press, 2015)

Mavroidis PC, 'Suspension of Concessions (Retaliation)' in *The WTO Dispute Settlement System* (Edward Elgar, 2022) 298

McAsey B, 'International Arbitral Institutions' in Baetens F (ed), *Legitimacy of Unseen Actors in International Adjudication* (Cambridge University Press, 2019)

McDermott Y and Elmaalul W, 'Legitimacy' in Schabas WA and Murphy S (eds), *Research Handbook on International Courts and Tribunals* (Edward Elgar, 2017)

Mwenda KK, 'Court of Justice of the Common Market for Eastern and Southern Africa (COMESA)' in *Max Planck Encyclopaedias of International Law* (Oxford University Press, online edition, 2019)

Obadia E and Nitschke F, 'Institutional Arbitration and the Role of the Secretariat' in Giorgetti C (ed), *Litigating International Investment Disputes: A Practitioner's Guide* (Brill Nijhoff, 2014)

Odell J, 'Chairing a WTO Negotiation' in Petersmann EU and Harrison J (eds), *Reforming the World Trading System* (Cambridge University Press, 2005)

Ollivier M and Hoss J, 'Registry: International Court of Justice' in Wolfrum R (ed), *Max Planck Encyclopedia of Public International Law* (Oxford University Press, online edition, 2021)

Pereyra M, 'Appointment of WTO Adjudicators: Rules and Evolving Practices' in Lamp N (ed), *Reckoning and Renewal: The World Trade Organization and Its Dispute Settlement System at 30: Essays in Honour of Valerie Hughes* (Toronto University Press, 2024)

Petersmann EU 'The establishment of a GATT Office of Legal Affairs and the limits of "public reason"' in G Marceau (ed), *A History of Law and Lawyers in the GATT/WTO: The Development of the Rule of Law in the Multilateral Trading System* (Cambridge University Press, 2015)

Pinto C and McAsey B, 'Iran–United States Claims Tribunal' in Wolfrum R (ed), *Max Planck Encyclopedia of Public International Law* (Oxford University Press, online edition, 2012)

Porges A, 'The Legal Affairs Division and Law in the GATT and the Uruguay Round' in Marceau G (ed), *A History of Law and Lawyers in the GATT/WTO: The Development of the Rule of Law in the Multilateral Trading System* (Cambridge University Press, 2015)

Röhl KF, 'Procedural Justice: Introduction and Overview' in Röhl KF and Machura S (eds), *Procedural Justice* (Ashgate, 1997)

Saavedra Alessandri P, 'Secretariat: Inter-American Court of Human Rights (IACtHR)' in Ruiz Fabri H (ed), *Max Planck Encyclopedia of International Procedural Law* (Oxford University Press, 2021)

Sarmiento D, 'Référendaire: Court of Justice of the European Union (CJEU)' in *Max Planck Encyclopedia of International Procedural Law* (Oxford University Press, online edn, 2018)

Schreuer C, Malintoppi L, Reinisch A and Sinclair A, 'Article 38 – Appointment by Chairman' in *The ICSID Convention: A Commentary*, 2nd edn (Cambridge University Press, 2009)

Seibert-Fohr A, 'International Judicial Ethics' in Romano CPR, Alter KJ and Shany Y (eds), *The Oxford Handbook of International Adjudication* (2013; online edn, Oxford Academic, 2014)
Shetreet S, 'Independence and Accountability of the Judiciary: Comparative Analysis of the Theories and the Realities with Lessons for the Asia-Pacific' in Lee HP and Pittard M (eds), *Asia-Pacific Judiciaries: Independence, Impartiality and Integrity* (Cambridge University Press, 2017)
Sim C, 'The Essence of Adjudication: The Legitimacy of Case Managers in International Arbitration' in Baetens F (ed), *Legitimacy of Unseen Actors in International Adjudication* (Cambridge University Press, 2019)
Simma B and Ortgies A, 'Deliberation and Drafting: International Court of Justice' in Wolfrum R (ed), *Max Planck Encyclopedia of Public International Law (MPEiPro)* (Oxford University Press, 2019)
Steger DP, 'The Appellate Body and its Contribution to WTO Dispute Settlement' in Kennedy DLM and Southwick JD (eds), *The Political Economy of International Trade Law: Essays in Honor of Robert E Hudec* (Cambridge University Press, 2002)
Tercier P, 'The Role of the Secretary to the Arbitral Tribunal' in Newman LW and Hill RD (eds), *Leading Arbitrators' Guide to International Arbitration* (Juris, 2014)
Tzeng P, 'Appointing Authorities: Self-Appointment, Party Appointment and Non-Appointment' in Baetens F (ed), *Legitimacy of Unseen Actors in International Adjudication, Studies on International Courts and Tribunals* (Cambridge University Press, 2019)
Uhle CB, 'A Survey on Arbitration and Settlement in International Business Disputes: Advantages of Arbitration' in Drahozal CR and Naimark RW (eds), *Towards a Science of International Arbitration: Collected Empirical Research* (Kluwer, 2005)
Venkataraman A, 'Taking Initiatives in the WTO: The Role of an Executive Head in Steering Change' in Marceau G and Gött H (eds), *International Organization Initiatives: How and Why Organizations Adapt and Change* (Oxford University Press, 2025)
Vidigal G, 'Sequencing: Dispute Settlement System of the World Trade Organization (WTO)' in *Max Planck Encyclopedias of International Law* (Oxford University Press, online edn, 2020)
Wiebusch M, 'African Court on Human and Peoples' Rights' in Binder C, Kaltenbach F and Sadoff S (eds), *Elgar Encyclopedia of Human Rights* (Edward Elgar, 2022)
Wolfrum R, 'Deliberation and Drafting: International Tribunal for the Law of the Sea (ITLOS)' in *Max Planck Encyclopedia of International Procedural Law* (Oxford University Press, 2021)
Zdouc W, 'Cross-Retaliation and Suspension under the GATS and TRIPS Agreements' in Bown CP and Pauwelyn J (eds), *The Law, Economics and Politics of Retaliation in WTO Dispute Settlement* (Cambridge University Press, 2010)

Journal Articles

Akande, D, 'The Jurisdiction of the International Criminal Court over Nationals of Non-parties: Legal Basis and Limits' (2003) 1 *Journal of International Criminal Justice* 618
Akingube, 'The Role of the Registry and Legal Division of the African Court on Human and Peoples' Rights in Dispute Settlement' (2022) 116 *American Journal of International Law: Unbound* 385
Balistreri, EJ, Mavroidis, PC and Prusa, TJ, 'What If? Tinkering with the Counterfactual: A Comment on US – Washing Machines (Article 226 – US)' (2021) 20(4) *World Trade Review* 1
Bodansky, D, 'The Legitimacy of International Governance: A Coming Challenge for International Environmental Law?' (1999) 93 *American Journal of International Law* 596
Bonadio, E, Kansara, M and Tayal, V, 'Litigating Patented Standards: The EU-China WTO Dispute on Anti-Suit Injunctions' *European Intellectual Property Review* (forthcoming)
Bourgeois, JHJ, 'Comment on a WTO Permanent Panel Body' (2003) 6(1) *Journal of International Economic Law* 211
Claussen, V, 'Old and New Dispute Secretariats' (2022) 116 *American Journal of International Law: Unbound* 400
Cottier, T, 'The WTO Permanent Panel Body: A Bridge Too Far?' (2003) 6(1) *Journal of International Economic Law* 187

Creaner, CD and Godzimirska, Z, 'Trust in the Court: The Role of the Registry of the European Court of Human Rights' (2019) 30 *European Journal of International Law* 665
Davey, WJ, 'The Case for a WTO Permanent Panel Body' (2003) 6(1) *Journal of International Economic Law* 177
Domínguez, PG, 'The Role of the Secretariat in the InterAmerican Court of Human Rights: A Comparative Analysis' (2022) 116 *American Journal of International Law: Unbound* 391
Footer, ME, 'The Role of Consensus in GATT/WTO Decision-Making' (1997) 17 *Northwestern Journal of International Law & Business* 653
Gathii, J, 'Mission Creep or a Search for Relevance: The East African Court of Justice's Human Rights Strategy' (2013–14) 24 *Duke Journal of Comparative and International Law* 261
Greenwald, JD, 'A Comparison of WTO and CIT/AFC Jurisprudence in Review of US Commerce Department Decisions in Antidumping and Countervailing Duty Proceedings' (2013) 21 *Tulane Journal of International and Comparative Law* 261
Grosse Ruse-Khan, HM, 'The Role of Chairman's Statements in the WTO' (2007) 41(3) *Journal of World Trade* 475
Grossman, N, 'Legitimacy and International Adjudicative Bodies' (2009) 41 *George Washington International Law Review* 107
Hoekman, B and Mavroidis, PC, 'To AB or Not to AB? Dispute Settlement in WTO Reform' (2020) 23 *Journal of International Economic Law* 703
Hudec, R, 'The New WTO Dispute Settlement Procedure: An Overview of the First Three Years' (1999) 8 *Minnesota Journal of Global Trade* 34
Kelsey, J, 'The Illegitimacy of Joint Statement Initiatives and Their Systemic Implications for the WTO' (2022) 25(2) *Journal of International Economic Law* 2
Kim, K, 'The "Equivalent" Standard in WTO Arbitrations of Trade Remedy Disputes' (2021) 55(6) *Journal of World Trade* 991
Kumm, M, 'The Legitimacy of International Law: A Constitutionalist Framework of Analysis' (2004) 15 *European Journal of International Law* 907
Liao, QXM, 'The WTO of the Future: Keeping the WTO Digitally Relevant through the JSI on E-Commerce' (2024) 25(5–6) *Journal of World Investment & Trade* 623
Magnuson, WJ, 'The Responsibility to Protect and the Decline of Sovereignty: Free Speech Protection under International Law' (2010) 43 *Vanderbilt Journal of Transnational Law* 255
Marceau, G, 'Rules on Ethics for the New WTO Dispute Settlement Mechanism' (1998) 32 *Journal of World Trade* 57
Marceau, G and Hawkins, JK, 'Experts in WTO Dispute Settlement' (2012) 3(3) *Journal of International Dispute Settlement* 493
Marceau, G and Nandakumar, A, 'How Can the JSI on E-commerce Become Part of the WTO Framework?' (2025) 20(5) *Global Trade and Customs Journal* 309
Marceau, G and Venkataraman, A, 'Unmasking the Phantom of the Opera' (2022) 116 *American Journal of International Law: Unbound* 396
Marceau, G, Quinn, C and Hoyos, JPM, 'Judging from Venus: A Response to Joost Pauwelyn' (2015) 109 *American Journal of International Law: Unbound* 204
Marceau, G, Walker, R and Koumadoraki, N, 'Silence in WTO' (2022) 56(2) *Journal of World Trade* 187
Mavroidis, PC and Johannesson, L, 'Black Cat, White Cat: The Identity of the WTO Judges' (2015) 49 *Journal of World Trade* 685
Mavroidis, PC, Meagher, N, Prusa, TJ and Yanguas, T, 'Ask for the Moon, Settle for the Stars: What is a Reasonable Period to Comply with WTO Awards?' (2017) 16(2) *World Trade Review* 395
Milej, TP, 'Human Rights Protection by International Courts: What Role for the East African Court of Justice?' (2018) 26(1) *African Journal of International and Comparative Law* 108
New York City Bar Association, 'Secretaries to International Arbitration Tribunals: Joint Report of the International Commercial Disputes Committee and the Committee on Arbitration of the New York City Bar Association' (2006) 17 *American Review of International Arbitration* 575
Nordström, H, 'The WTO Secretariat in a Changing World' (2005) 39 *Journal of World Trade* 819
Osiander, A, 'Sovereignty, International Relations and the Westphalian Myth' (2001) 55 *International Organization* 251
Pahis, S, 'Appeals after the Appellate Body' (2024) 23 *World Trade Review* 296
Park, W, 'Arbitrator Integrity: The Transient and the Permanent' (2009) 46 *San Diego Law Review* 629

Parra, AR, 'The Role of the ICSID Secretariat in the Administration of Arbitration Proceedings under the ICSID Convention' (1998) 13(1) *ICSID Review – Foreign Investment Law Journal* 97
Partasides, C, 'The Fourth Arbitrator? The Role of Secretaries to Tribunals in International Arbitration' (2002) 18 *Arbitration International* 147
Pauwelyn, J, 'The Rule of Law without the Rule of Lawyers? Why Investment Arbitrators are from Mars, Trade Adjudicators from Venus' (2015) 109 *American Journal of International Law* 761
Pauwelyn, J, 'The WTO's Multi-Party Interim Appeal Arbitration Arrangement (MPIA): What's New?' (2023) 22 *World Trade Review* 693
Pauwelyn, J and Pelc, K, 'Who Guards the "Guardians of the System"? The Role of the Secretariat in WTO Dispute Settlement' (2015) 19 *European Journal of International Law* 537
Pauwelyn, J and Pelc, K, 'WTO Rulings and the Veil of Anonymity' (2022) 33 *European Journal of International Law* 2
Peres, A, 'Transience of (In)Formality: The Role of Joint Initiatives in Reforming the WTO Negotiations' (2024) 23 *World Trade Review* 385
Petersmann, EU, 'WTO Negotiators Meet Academics: The Negotiations on Improvements of the WTO Dispute Settlement System' (2003) 6(1) *Journal of International Economic Law* 237
Posner, EA and Yoo, JC, 'Judicial Independence in International Tribunals' (2005) 93 *California Law Review* 3
Puig, S and Brown, C, 'The Secretary-General's Power to Refuse to Register a Request for Arbitration under the ICSID Convention' (2012) 27(1) *ICSID Review* 172
Qian, M, '"Reasonable Period of Time" in the WTO Dispute Settlement System' (2012) 15(1) *Journal of International Economic Law* 257
Sennekamp, A and Damme, IV, 'A Practical Perspective on Treaty Interpretation: The Court of Justice of the European Union and the WTO Dispute Settlement System' (2014) 3(2) *Cambridge Journal of International and Comparative Law* 1
Shany, Y, 'Squaring the Circle? Independence and Impartiality of Party-Appointed Adjudicators in International Legal Proceedings' (2008) 30 *Loyola of Los Angeles International and Comparative Law Review* 473
Sutton, SD, 'Emilio Augustin Maffezini v Kingdom of Spain and the ICSID Secretary-General's Screening Power' (2005) 2(1) *Arbitration International* 121
Tijmes-Lhl, J, 'Consensus and Majority Voting in the WTO' (2009) 8 *World Trade Review* 417
Tyler, TR, 'The Role of Perceived Injustice in Defendants' Evaluations of Their Courtroom Experience' (1984) 18 *Law and Society Review* 51
Valles, C, 'Different Forms of Expert Involvement in WTO Dispute Settlement Proceedings' (2018) 9(3) *Journal of International Dispute Settlement* 367
Wauters, JM, 'The Role of the WTO Secretariat in WTO Disputes: Silent Witness or Ghost Expert?' (2021) 12 *Global Policy* 83
Zampetti, AB, Low, P and Mavroidis, PC, 'Consensus Decision-Making and Legislative Inertia at the WTO: Can International Law Help?' (2022) 56 *Journal of World Trade* 1
Zhang, AH, 'The Faceless Court' (2016) 38(1) *University of Pennsylvania Journal of International Law* 71

Reports, Notes, Working Papers and Others

Adlung, R and Mamdouh, H, 'Plurilateral Trade Agreements: An Escape Route for the WTO?' (WTO Working Paper ERSD-2017-03, 2017)
Bown, C, *The WTO Secretariat and the Role of Economics in DSU Panels and Arbitrations* (Peterson Institute for International Economics and CEPR, Working Paper, 1 August 2008) 45, wwwpaperssrncom/sol3 /paperscfm?abstract_id=1263982
COMESA Council of Ministers, 'Seventeenth Meeting Report' (4–5 June 2004, Nile International Conference Centre, Kampala, Uganda)
Elsig, M, 'Different Facets of Power in Decision-Making in the WTO' NCCR Trade Regulation Working Paper No 2006/23 (2006) 13
HKIAC, *Guidelines on the Use of a Secretary to the Arbitral Tribunal* (2014)

HKIAC, *Report on the Use of HKIAC Tribunal Secretary Service* (3 September 2018)
ICC, 'Guidance Note to Parties and Arbitral Tribunal on the Conduct of Arbitrations under the ICC Rules of Arbitration' (2021)
ICC, *Guidance Note to Parties and Arbitral Tribunal on the Conduct of Arbitrations under the ICC Rules of Arbitration* (2021)
ICSID, *Annual Report 2022* (2022)
ICSID, *Memorandum on Fees and Expenses* (6 July 2005)
International Chamber of Commerce, *ICC Guidance Note to Parties and Arbitral Tribunal on the Conduct of Arbitrations under the ICC Rules of Arbitration* (2021)
LCIA, 'LCIA Guidance Note to Arbitrator' (2020)
Low, P, WTO Decision-Making for the Future Staff Working Paper ERSD-2011-05 (2 May 2011)
Mavroidis, PC and Hoekman, B, *WTO Dispute Settlement and the Appellate Body Crisis: Back to the Future* (Working Paper, 18 March 2020)
Office of the United States Trade Representative, *Report on the Appellate Body of the World Trade Organization* (February 2020)
Van Grasstek, C, *The History and Future of the World Trade Organization* (World Trade Organization, 2013)
Wolff, AW, *WTO 2025: Restoring Binding Dispute Settlement* (PIIE Working Paper No 22-5, Peterson Institute for International Economics, April 2022)
WTO, 'Recommendations by the Preparatory Committee to the WTO, Sub-Committee on Institutional, Procedural and Legal Matters', WTO Docs PC/IPL/13 (approved 6 December 1994)
WTO, 'Report by the Chairman, Ambassador Ronald Sabario Soto to the Trade Negotiations Committee, Special Session of the Dispute Settlement Body', WTO Doc TN/DS/25 (21 April 2011)
WTO, 'Report by the Convenor of the Informal DS Reform Discussions – Mr Marco Molina, Special Meeting of the General Council, Report by HE Mr Petter Olberg, Chairman of the DSB', WTO Doc JOB/GC/386 (16 February 2024)
WTO, *Conditions of Service Applicable to the Staff of the WTO Secretariat, Annex 2*, Decision Adopted by the General Council and the ICITO Executive Committee on 16 October 1998, WT/L/282 (21 October 1998)
WTO, *Report by HE Mr Petter Ølberg, Chairman of the DSB, and Annex: Consolidated Text Referred to in Mr Molina's Report* (General Council, JOB/GC/385, 16 February 2024)
WTO Committee on Budget, Finance and Administration, 'Report of the Meeting Held on 23 and 30 October and 6 and 16 November 2015', WTO Doc WT/BFA/151 (20 November 2015)
WTO Dispute Settlement Body, 'Minutes of the Meeting' (30 September 2019) WT/DSB/M/4343
WTO Dispute Settlement Body, 'Minutes of the Meeting, Held in the Centre William Rappard on 28 August 2020', WT/DSB/M/44 (2 November 2020)
WTO Dispute Settlement Body, Special Session, 'Minutes of the Meeting Held on 5 April 2005', WTO Doc TN/DS/M/24 (26 May 2005)
WTO Dispute Settlement Body, Special Session, 'Minutes of the Meeting Held on 15 July 2005', WTO Doc TN/DS/M/27 (29 July 2005)
WTO General Council, 'Minutes of the Meeting Held on 30 November and 7 December 2015', WTO Doc WT/GC/M/160 (23 February 2016)
WTO General Council, Decision of 30 August 2003, WT/L/540 and Corr 1 (1 September 2003)
WTO General Council, Decision of 6 December 2005, WT/L/641 (8 December 2005)
WTO General Council, 'Minutes of the Meeting of 1, 2 and 6 December 2005', WT/GC/M/100 (27 March 2006)
WTO General Council, 'Minutes of the Meeting of 15 November 1995', WT/GC/M/8 (13 December 1995)
WTO General Council, 'Minutes of the Meeting of 25, 26 and 30 August 2003', WT/GC/M/82 (13 November 2003)
WTO Secretariat, 'European Union – Additional Duties on Certain Products from the United States (Complaint by the United States)', WTO Doc WT/DS559/7 (Agreed Procedures, 2022)
WTO Secretariat, 'India – Tariff Treatment on Certain Goods in the Information and Communications Technology Sector – Constitution of the Panel Established at the Request of the European Union', WTO Doc WT/DS582/10 (1 September 2020)
WTO Secretariat, 'Japan – Taxes on Alcoholic Beverages, Constitution of the Panel Established at the Requests of the EC, Canada and the United States', WTO Doc WT/DS8/6, WT/DS10/6, WT/DS11/3 (6 November 1995)

WTO Secretariat, 'Turkey – Certain Measures Concerning the Production, Importation and Marketing of Pharmaceutical Products (Complaint by the European Union)', WTO Doc WT/DS583/13 (Constitution of the Arbitrator, 2022)
WTO Secretariat, 'Turkey – Certain Measures Concerning the Production, Importation and Marketing of Pharmaceutical Products (Complaint by the European Union)', WTO Doc WT/DS583/10 (Agreed Procedures for Arbitration, 2022)
WTO Secretariat, 'Turkey – Certain Measures Concerning the Production, Importation and Marketing of Pharmaceutical Products (Complaint by the European Union)', WTO Doc WT/DS583/13 (Constitution of the Arbitrator, 2022)
WTO Secretariat, 'Ukraine – Anti-Dumping Measures on Ammonium Nitrate, Appointment of the Arbitrator by the Director-General under Article 213(c) of the DSU, Note by the Secretariat', WTO Doc WT/DS493/12 (18 December 2019)
WTO Secretariat, 'United States – Section 110(5) of the US Copyright Act, Recourse to Article 25 of the DSU – Agreed Procedures', WTO Doc WT/DS160/15 (3 August 2001)
WTO Secretariat, 'United States – Standards for Reformulated and Conventional Gasoline, Constitution of the Panel Established at the Request of Venezuela', WTO Doc WT/DS2/3 (3 May 1995)
WTO Secretariat, 'United States – Certain Measures on Steel and Aluminium Products (Complaint by the European Union)', WTO Doc WT/DS548/22 (Constitution of the Arbitrator, 2022)
WTO Secretariat, 'United States – Certain Measures on Steel and Aluminium Products (Complaint by the European Union)', WTO Doc WT/DS548/19 (Agreed Procedures, 2022)
WTO Secretariat, *China – Enforcement of Intellectual Property Rights (Complaint by the European Union)*, WTO Doc WT/DS611/13 (Constitution of the Arbitrator, 2023)
WTO Secretariat, *United States – Import Prohibition of Certain Shrimp and Shrimp Products – Constitution of the Panel Established at the Requests of Malaysia, Thailand, Pakistan and India*, WTO Docs WT/DS58/R (15 May 1998)

Websites and Online Sources

Amato, G et al, 'Selecting EU Judges: The Role of the 255 Committee According to the Treaty' (EU Law Live, Symposium on the Selection of EU Judges and the 255 Committee, 23 September 2024), https://eulawlive.com/op-ed-selecting-eu-judges-the-role-of-the-255-committee-according-to-the-treaty
Blog Droit Européen, 'Découvrez la fonction de lecteurs d'arrêt à la CJUE, interview Anne Schneider part 1' (20 January 2017), https://blogdroiteuropeen.com/2017/01/20/decouvrez-la-fonction-de-lecteur-darret-a-la-cjue-interview-anne-schneider-part-1
China International Economic and Trade Arbitration Commission, 'Secretariats', www.cietac.org/index.php?m=Page&a=index&id=35&l=en
COMESA Court of Justice, 'Staff Members', www.comesacourt.org/comesa-court-of-justice-staff-members
Court of Justice of the European Union, 'Annual Reports', www.curia.europa.eu/jcms/jcms/Jo2_10744
Court of Justice of the European Union, 'Directorates for Legal Translation', www.curia.europa.eu/jcms/jcms/Jo2_7020/en
Court of Justice of the European Union, 'Research and Documentation Directorate', www.curia.europa.eu/jcms/jcms/Jo2_7024
CUSMA/USMCA/TMEC Secretariat, 'The Secretariat' (Government of Canada, last modified 9 January 2024), www.can-mex-usa-sec.org/secretariat/index.aspx?lang=eng
Eernisse A, 'Interviews with Our Editors: China Insights from Dr Li Hu of CIETAC' (*Kluwer Arbitration Blog*, 12 April 2020), www.arbitrationblog.kluwerarbitration.com/2020/04/12/interviews-with-our-editors-china-insights-from-dr-li-hu-of-cietac
EFTA Court, 'Judges and Staff', www.eftacourt.int/the-court/judges-and-staff
EFTA Court, 'Vacancy Notice', www.eftacourt.int/wp-content/uploads/2020/10/Vacancy-announcement-03-2020.pdf

European Commission, *Seventh Activity Report of the Panel Provided for by Article 255 of the Treaty on the Functioning of the European Union* (2022), www.curia.europa.eu/jcms/upload/docs/application/pdf/2022-07/2022.2597-qcar22002enn_002.pdf
European Court of Human Rights, 'Organisation Chart', www.echr.coe.int/organisation-chart accessed 6 January 2026
Freshfields Bruckhaus Deringer, 'WTO Dispute Settlement Update – Frozen Fries Put the MPIA to the Test' (*Risk & Compliance Blog*), www.riskandcompliance.freshfields.com/post/102idx0/wto-dispute-settlement-update-frozen-fries-put-the-mpia-to-the-test
General Court, 'Criteria for the Assignment of Cases to Chambers' [2023] OJ C286/2, https://eur-lex.europa.eu/legal-content/EN/TXT/PDF/?uri=CELEX:C2023/286/02
German Arbitration Institute (DIS), 'Team', www.disarb.org/en/about-us/team
Hillman J, 'Three Approaches to Fixing the World Trade Organization: The Good, the Bad and the Ugly?' (*Institute of International Economic Law*, 10 December 2018), wwwlawgeorgetownedu/wp-content/uploads/2018/12/Hillman-Good-Bad-Ugly-Fix-to-WTO-ABpdf
Hong Kong International Arbitration Centre, 'Appointments Committee', www.hkiac.org/about-us/council-members-and-committees/appointments-committee
Hong Kong International Arbitration Centre, 'Proceedings Committee', www.hkiac.org/about-us/council-members-and-committees/proceedings-committee
Hong Kong International Arbitration Centre, 'Secretariat', wwwhkiacorg/about-us/secretariat
Hong Kong International Arbitration Centre, 'Tribunal Secretary Service', www.hkiac.org/arbitration/tribunal-secretaries/tribunal-secretary-service
Hong Kong International Arbitration Centre, 'Report on the Use of HKIAC Tribunal Secretary Service' (3 September 2018), www.hkiac.org/node/2299
ICSID, 'Inside the ICSID Secretariat: Benjamin Garel, Legal Counsel', www.icsid.worldbank.org/inside-icsid-secretariat-benjamin-garel-legal-counsel
ICSID, 'Selection of the Tribunal', www.icsid.worldbank.org/procedures/arbitration/convention/selection-tribunal/2022
ICSID, 'Secretariat – Overview', www.worldbank.org/en/programs/icsid/secretariat-overview
ICSID, 'Tribunal Assistants', www.worldbank.org/icsid/tribunal-assistants
Instructions for the Registry of the International Court of Justice, International Court of Justice, https://www.icj-cij.org/sites/default/files/documents/instructions-for-the-registry-en.pdf, wwwicj-cijorg/sites/default/files/documents/instructions-for-the-registry-enpdf
International Chamber of Commerce, 'Chairmanship and Secretary General', www.iccwbo.org/governance/chairmanship-and-secretary-general
International Chamber of Commerce, 'Counsel Swiss Italian Team, ICC Dispute Resolution Services, Paris', www.iccwbo.org/careers/job-opportunities/counsel-swiss-italian-teamicc-dispute-resolution-services-paris
International Court of Justice, 'Compilation of Decisions Relating to Practice Directions and Other Texts', www.icj-cij.org/other-texts/compilation-decisions#footnote_2
International Court of Justice, 'Registry', www.icj-cij.org/registry
International Criminal Court, 'Composition of the Registry', www.icc-cpi.int/about/registry
International Criminal Court, 'Information of the Registry', www.icc-cpi.int/about/registry
International Criminal Court, 'Judges' Legal Officer', www.icc-cpi.int/get-involved/justice-at-work/story/the-judges-legal-officer
International Criminal Court, 'Legal Adviser (P-4)',, w www.impactpool.org
International Criminal Court, 'Registry', www.icc-cpi.int/about/registry
International Tribunal for the Law of the Sea, 'Internship Programme', www.itlos.org/internship-programme
International Tribunal for the Law of the Sea, 'Registry Organigramme' (July 2025), https://www.itlos.org/fileadmin/itlos/documents/registry/Organigram_July_2025.pdf
International Tribunal for the Law of the Sea, 'Registry Organigramme' (July 2025), www.itlos.org/fileadmin/itlos/documents/registry/Organigram_July_2025.pdf
Judicial Division, Court Management Services Section, wwwstl-tslorg/en/about-the-stl/structure-of-the-stl/registry

London Court of International Arbitration, 'Guidance Note for Parties and Arbitrators', www.lcia.org/adr-services/guidance-note.aspx#10.%20%20TRIBUNAL%20SECRETARIES
London Court of International Arbitration, 'Organisation', www.lcia.org/lcia/organisation.aspx
Permanent Court of Arbitration, 'Services', www.pca-cpa.org/en/services
Permanent Court of Arbitration, 'Staff', www.pca-cpa.org/en/about/introduction/staff
Queen Mary University and PricewaterhouseCoopers, '2006 International Arbitration Study: Corporate Attitudes and Practices' (2006), www.arbitration.qmul.ac.uk/media/arbitration/docs/IAstudy_2006.pdf
Registry of the International Criminal Court, 'Comprehensive Report on the Reorganisation of the Registry of the International Criminal Court' (August 2016), www.icc-cpi.int/itemsDocuments/ICC-Registry-CR.pdf
Sacerdoti G, 'A Critical Reaction to Joost Pauwelyn and Krzysztof Pelc's "The WTO Secretariat's 'Open Secret': Unpacking the Controversy"' (*EJIL:Talk!*, 5 September 2022), www.ejiltalk.org/a-critical-reaction-to-joost-pauwelyn-and-krzysztof-pelcs-the-wto-secretariats-open-secret-unpacking-the-controversy
Singapore International Arbitration Centre, 'Arbitration Rules of the Singapore International Arbitration Centre' (2025), www.siac.org.sg/siac-rules-2025
Singapore International Arbitration Centre, 'Our Team', www.siac.org.sg/about-us/our-team
Singapore International Arbitration Centre, 'Vacancy for Deputy Counsel', www.siac.org.sg/siac-jobs/deputy-counsel
Special Tribunal for Lebanon, 'Registry', www.stl-tsl.org/en/about-the-stl/registry
Stockholm Chamber of Commerce Arbitration Institute, 'Contact Us', www.sccarbitrationinstitute.se/en/about-scc/contact-us
Stockholm Chamber of Commerce, Guidelines for Arbitrators, 'Administrative Secretaries' (June 2020), www.acerislaw.com/wp-content/uploads/2022/08/scc-guidelines-for-arbitrators.pdf
Swiss Arbitration Centre, 'Leadership', www.swissarbitration.org/centre/leadership
Tribunal Permanente de Revisión del MERCOSUR, 'Solicitudes de control de laudos', www.tprmercosur.org/es/sol_contr_laudos.htm
United States State Committee on Finance, *Hearing Before the Committee on Finance, United States Senate, 104th Congress, S 16* (10 May 1995),
www.finance.senate.gov/imo/media/doc/Hrg104-124.pdf
'US Takes Appellate Body Fight to a New Level' (*Politico*, 6 March 2020), www.politico.com/newsletters/morning-trade/2020/03/06/us-takes-appellate-body-fight-to-a-new-level-785913
Weiler, JHH, 'Who Will Judge the Judges Who Judge the Judges? The Curious Case of Gonçalo Manoel de Vilhena de Almeida Ribeiro' (EU Law Live, Symposium, 20 September 2024), https://eulawlive.com/who-will-judge-the-judges-who-judge-the-judges-the-curious-case-of-goncalo-manoel-de-vilhena-de-almeida-ribeiro-by-joseph-h-h-weiler/
Wen D and Bergmann L, 'Comparison between SCC Arbitration and CIETAC Arbitration' (15 April 2011), www.biicl.org/files/5712_bergman_15-04-11_biicl.pdf 1
Wolff WA, Prepared Statement, Hearing Before the Committee on Finance, United States Senate, 104th Cong, S 16, 60 (10 May 1995), www.finance.senate.gov/imo/media/doc/Hrg104-124.pdf
WorldTradeLaw, 'Multi-Party Interim Appeal Arbitration Arrangement (MPIA)', wwwworldtradelawnet/staticphp?type=public&page=mpia
WTO, 'Arbitrations under Art 213(c) of the DSU', wwwwtoorg/english/tratop_e/dispu_e/arbitrations_ehtm
WTO, Dispute Settlement Information Tables, WTO Analytical Index 79–80, wwwwtoorg/english/res_e/publications_e/ai17_e/tableofcases_epdf

INDEX

www.ingramcontent.com/pod-product-compliance
Ingram Content Group UK Ltd.
Pitfield, Milton Keynes, MK11 3LW, UK
UKHW021854220926
475869UK00003B/189